Cryptocurrency

A Guide to Navigating the World of Digital Assets

Richard Skiba

AFTER MIDNIGHT
PUBLISHING

Skiba, Richard (author)

Cryptocurrency: A Guide to Navigating the World of Digital Assets

ISBN 978-1-7636112-8-3 (paperback) 978-1-7636112-9-0 (eBook)

Non-fiction

Contents

Chapter One
Introduction to Cryptocurrency

What is Cryptocurrency?

Cryptocurrencies are digital or virtual forms of currency secured by cryptography, operating independently of central authorities and utilizing decentralized technologies like blockchain [1]. This decentralization eliminates the need for intermediaries like banks, enabling global accessibility and transactions without geographical boundaries [2]. The security of cryptocurrencies is ensured through cryptographic techniques that safeguard transactions and control the creation of new units, making them resistant to fraud and counterfeiting [3]. While transactions are recorded on a public ledger, the identities of parties involved are often pseudonymous, offering a degree of anonymity [4].

Cryptocurrency, often referred to as crypto, is a digital or virtual form of currency that relies on cryptography for security. Unlike traditional currencies issued and regulated by governments, cryptocurrencies operate on decentralized networks, typically based on blockchain technology. Cryptocurrencies function by [5]:

- **Digital and Decentralized Nature**: Cryptocurrencies exist purely in digital form and do not have a physical counterpart like coins or banknotes. They operate on decentralized networks, which means there is no central authority or institution controlling them. Instead, transactions and the issuance of new units are managed collectively by the network of users.

- **Peer-to-Peer Transactions**: Cryptocurrencies enable direct peer-to-peer transactions without the need for intermediaries like banks. Transactions are verified and recorded in a public ledger called the blockchain, which is maintained by participants in the network.
- **Security through Cryptography**: Cryptography plays a crucial role in ensuring the security of cryptocurrency transactions. It involves advanced mathematical techniques for encrypting data, which secures the transfer of funds and the integrity of the transaction records.
- **Public Ledger (Blockchain)**: The blockchain is a decentralized and distributed ledger that records all transactions across the network. Each transaction is verified by network nodes through cryptographic algorithms and added to the blockchain in a chronological order. This transparency and immutability make blockchain a trusted system for recording transactions.
- **Mining and Creation of Cryptocurrency**: New units of cryptocurrencies are typically created through a process called mining. Mining involves solving complex mathematical puzzles using computational power. Miners compete to validate transactions and are rewarded with newly minted coins. This process also helps to secure the network and verify transactions.
- **Cryptocurrency Wallets**: Cryptocurrencies are stored in digital wallets, which can be software applications, hardware devices, or even paper copies that store public and private keys. These keys are essential for accessing and managing cryptocurrency holdings securely.
- **Speculation and Investment**: Cryptocurrencies have gained popularity not only for their potential as a medium of exchange but also as speculative assets. Price volatility and speculative trading have contributed to their appeal as investment vehicles.
- **Future Applications**: Beyond financial transactions, blockchain technology, which underpins cryptocurrencies, has the potential to revolutionize various industries. It could be used for trading financial assets like bonds and stocks, supply chain management, voting systems, and more, leveraging its transparency, security, and efficiency.

Figure 1: Bitcoin (₿) is a cryptocurrency invented in 2008 by an unknown person or group of people using the name Satoshi Nakamoto and started in 2009, when its implementation was released as open-source software. Jorge Franganillo, CC BY 2.0, via Wikimedia Commons.

Cryptocurrencies have diversified significantly since the introduction of Bitcoin in 2009 [5]. Here's a detailed exploration of some prominent examples [5]:

- **Bitcoin**:
  - **Introduction**: Bitcoin, launched in 2009 by an anonymous entity known as Satoshi Nakamoto, marked the beginning of cryptocurrencies. It operates on a decentralized peer-to-peer network, using blockchain technology to secure transactions.
  - **Key Features**: Bitcoin is known for its limited supply (capped at 21 million coins), its role as a store of value, and its widespread acceptance as a digital currency. It remains the most widely recognized and traded cryptocurrency globally.
- **Ethereum**:
  - **Introduction**: Created in 2015 by Vitalik Buterin, Ethereum is not just a cryptocurrency but a decentralized platform that enables developers to build and deploy smart contracts and decentralized applications (DApps).

- **Key Features**: Ethereum's cryptocurrency is called Ether (ETH). It differs from Bitcoin in that it facilitates more complex transactions beyond simple peer-to-peer payments. Ethereum's blockchain supports programmable contracts and has become a foundation for various blockchain-based innovations.

- **Litecoin**:
  - **Introduction**: Introduced in 2011 by Charlie Lee, Litecoin is often referred to as the "silver to Bitcoin's gold." It was designed to provide faster transaction confirmation times and a different hashing algorithm (Scrypt) compared to Bitcoin's SHA-256.
  - **Key Features**: Litecoin aims to be a more efficient cryptocurrency for smaller transactions and day-to-day use. It shares many technological similarities with Bitcoin but has implemented certain improvements to enhance usability and transaction speed.
- **Ripple (XRP)**:
  - **Introduction**: Ripple was launched in 2012 by Ripple Labs Inc. as both a payment protocol and a digital currency (XRP). Unlike Bitcoin and Ethereum, Ripple focuses on facilitating fast and low-cost cross-border payments and settlements.
  - **Key Features**: Ripple's consensus ledger, known as the XRP Ledger, does not require mining like Bitcoin and uses a consensus protocol to validate transactions. It has gained attention for its partnerships with financial institutions and its potential to disrupt traditional banking systems.
- **Altcoins**:
  - **Definition**: Altcoins refer to all cryptocurrencies other than Bitcoin. They encompass a vast array of digital currencies, each with its own unique features and purposes.
  - **Diversity**: Altcoins include thousands of cryptocurrencies, each designed with specific goals in mind, such as enhancing privacy (e.g., Monero), facil-

itating smart contracts (e.g., Cardano), or serving niche communities.

- **General Characteristics**:
  - **Decentralization**: Most cryptocurrencies operate on decentralized networks, reducing reliance on central authorities.
  - **Cryptographic Security**: All cryptocurrencies use cryptography to secure transactions and control the creation of new units.
  - **Global Accessibility**: Cryptocurrencies enable global transactions without the need for intermediaries, offering financial inclusion to unbanked populations.

Cryptocurrency's utility as a medium of exchange has evolved since Bitcoin's inception, though its widespread adoption for everyday transactions remains a work in progress. Here's a detailed exploration of what you can currently buy with cryptocurrency and how its use has expanded [5]:

- **Technology and E-commerce Sites**:
  - **Newegg.com, AT&T, Microsoft**: These tech giants accept cryptocurrency payments on their websites, allowing customers to purchase a variety of tech products and services using Bitcoin and sometimes other cryptocurrencies.
  - **Overstock, Shopify, Rakuten, Home Depot**: Overstock was one of the pioneers in accepting Bitcoin for online purchases. Shopify and Rakuten have also integrated cryptocurrency payments, while Home Depot has explored similar avenues, broadening the scope of goods available for purchase with crypto.
- **Luxury Goods**:
  - **Bitdials**: This online luxury retailer specializes in high-end watches like Rolex and Patek Philippe, offering them in exchange for Bitcoin. Luxury goods are increasingly becoming accessible to crypto holders looking to diversify their portfolios or make extravagant purchases.
- **Cars**:

   - **Car Dealers**: From mainstream automotive brands to high-end luxury dealerships, some car dealerships have embraced cryptocurrency as a payment option. This includes both new and used cars, reflecting a growing trend in the automotive sector towards digital payments.

- **Insurance**:

   - **AXA**: In April 2021, Swiss insurer AXA announced its acceptance of Bitcoin for insurance premium payments across various insurance lines, except for life insurance due to regulatory constraints. This move underscores cryptocurrency's potential utility in sectors traditionally reliant on fiat currencies.

   - **Premier Shield Insurance**: This US-based insurer allows policyholders to pay for home and auto insurance using Bitcoin, providing flexibility and convenience for crypto holders seeking insurance coverage.

- **Cryptocurrency Debit Cards**:

   - **BitPay**: For consumers looking to spend cryptocurrency at retailers that do not directly accept digital currencies, cryptocurrency debit cards like BitPay offer a solution. These cards convert cryptocurrency holdings into fiat currency at the point of sale, enabling seamless transactions at millions of merchants worldwide.

While the adoption of cryptocurrency for everyday purchases has seen significant strides, challenges remain, including price volatility, regulatory uncertainties, and integration complexities for merchants. Despite these hurdles, the expanding list of industries and companies accepting cryptocurrency illustrates its growing acceptance and integration into global commerce. As technology advances and consumer demand evolves, the future of cryptocurrency as a viable alternative to traditional payment methods continues to unfold.

Figure 2: A Bitcoin ATM or bitcoin teller machine (BTM) currently found in Ave. BU-5, Santa Juanita, Bayamón, Puerto Rico 00960, inside Puma Gas Station. PuertoCrypto, CC0, via Wikimedia Commons.

A Bitcoin ATM or bitcoin teller machine (BTM) currently found in Ave. BU-5, Santa Juanita, Bayamón, Puerto Rico 00960, inside Puma Gas Station. PuertoCrypto, CC0, via Wikimedia Commons.

Buying cryptocurrency involves several steps to ensure safety and efficiency. Here's a detailed explanation of how to buy cryptocurrency [5]:

Step 1: Choosing a Platform

The first step is selecting a platform where you can buy and trade cryptocurrencies. You typically have two main options:

- **Traditional Brokers**: These online brokers offer a range of financial assets, including cryptocurrencies, alongside stocks, bonds, and ETFs. They often have lower trading costs but may provide fewer crypto-specific features.

- **Cryptocurrency Exchanges**: These platforms specialize in buying, selling, and trading cryptocurrencies. They offer a wide variety of digital assets, wallet storage solutions, interest-bearing accounts, and more. However, they may charge higher fees compared to traditional brokers.

When choosing a platform, consider the following factors [5]:

- **Cryptocurrency Selection**: Check which cryptocurrencies are available for trading.
- **Fees**: Compare trading fees, deposit and withdrawal fees, and any other charges associated with the platform.
- **Security**: Look for platforms with robust security measures, such as two-factor authentication (2FA) and cold storage options for funds.
- **Payment Methods**: Evaluate accepted payment methods, such as debit/credit cards, ACH transfers, and wire transfers.
- **User Interface**: Assess the platform's usability, including its web and mobile interfaces.
- **Regulatory Compliance**: Ensure the platform operates within regulatory frameworks to protect your investments.

Step 2: Funding Your Account

Once you've chosen a platform, the next step is to fund your account to start trading cryptocurrencies. Methods for funding your account typically include:

- **Debit/Credit Cards**: Many exchanges allow you to purchase cryptocurrencies directly using fiat currencies (e.g., USD, EUR, GBP) via debit or credit cards. Note that some credit card companies may restrict cryptocurrency transactions due to their volatility.
- **ACH Transfers**: Some platforms support ACH transfers for depositing funds from your bank account.
- **Wire Transfers**: Direct wire transfers are another common method for funding accounts, especially for larger amounts.

Each funding method may have different processing times and associated fees, so it's essential to review these details carefully before proceeding.

Step 3: Placing an Order

Once your account is funded, you can place an order to buy cryptocurrency:

- **Order Placement**: Navigate to the trading section of your chosen platform (web or mobile), select the cryptocurrency you wish to purchase, and specify the amount.

- **Order Types**: Choose from different order types such as market orders (executed immediately at the current market price) or limit orders (executed only when the price reaches a specified level).

- **Confirmation**: Review your order details, including fees and total cost, before confirming the purchase.

Alternative Investment Vehicles

Beyond direct purchases on exchanges, there are alternative ways to invest in cryptocurrencies:

- **Payment Services**: Platforms like PayPal, Cash App, and Venmo allow users to buy, sell, or hold cryptocurrencies within their apps.

- **Bitcoin Trusts and ETFs**: These investment vehicles enable indirect exposure to cryptocurrencies through traditional brokerage accounts, offering shares tied to the value of Bitcoin or other digital assets.

- **Blockchain Stocks or ETFs**: Invest indirectly in cryptocurrencies by purchasing stocks or ETFs of companies involved in blockchain technology development or cryptocurrency transactions.

Choosing the best investment approach depends on your financial goals, risk tolerance, and preferred method of investment. Whether you opt for direct crypto exchanges or indirect investments through traditional financial products, understanding the risks and benefits is crucial for making informed decisions in the evolving cryptocurrency market.

Storing cryptocurrency securely is crucial to protect your digital assets from hacks and theft. Here's a detailed explanation of how to store cryptocurrency [5]:

Cryptocurrency wallets are digital tools that store your private keys, which are essential for accessing and managing your cryptocurrencies. Private keys are unique cryptographic keys that allow you to authorize transactions on the blockchain network associated with each cryptocurrency.

Types of Cryptocurrency Wallets

- **Hot Wallets**:
  - **Definition**: Hot wallets are software-based wallets that store your private keys online, typically provided by cryptocurrency exchanges or accessed through online platforms.
  - **Accessibility**: Convenient for frequent trading and transactions due to immediate access via the internet.
  - **Security**: Vulnerable to hacking and cyberattacks since they are connected to the internet.
  - **Examples**: Wallets provided by exchanges like Coinbase, Binance, or software wallets such as Electrum or MyEtherWallet.
- **Cold Wallets** (Hardware Wallets):
  - **Definition**: Cold wallets are physical devices designed to store private keys offline, providing a higher level of security.
  - **Security**: Offers protection against online threats such as hacking because private keys are stored offline.
  - **Usage**: Ideal for long-term storage of significant amounts of cryptocurrency that you don't plan to trade frequently.
  - **Examples**: Ledger Nano S, Ledger Nano X, Trezor Model T.

Steps to Store Cryptocurrency Safely

- **Choose a Wallet Provider**:

  - Research and select a reputable wallet provider that offers the type of storage (hot or cold) that suits your needs.
  - Consider factors such as security features, user interface, supported cryptocurrencies, and customer support.
- **Set Up Your Wallet**:
  - Follow the provider's instructions to create and set up your wallet account.
  - Generate and securely store your recovery seed phrase. This phrase is crucial for recovering access to your wallet if you forget your password or lose access.
- **Transfer Your Cryptocurrency**:
  - If your cryptocurrency is currently stored on an exchange or another wallet, initiate a transfer to your newly set up wallet.
  - Ensure you enter the correct wallet address and verify the transaction details before confirming.
- **Security Best Practices**:
  - **Enable Two-Factor Authentication (2FA)**: Add an extra layer of security to your wallet account by enabling 2FA wherever possible.
  - **Keep Software Updated**: Regularly update your wallet software to protect against vulnerabilities and security threats.
  - **Use Strong Passwords**: Create strong, unique passwords for your wallet accounts and avoid using easily guessable information.
- **Regular Backups**:
  - Backup your wallet regularly, especially if it's a software wallet. Store backups securely in multiple locations (e.g., encrypted USB drives, offline storage) to prevent data loss.
- **Monitor Your Accounts**:

- Regularly monitor your wallet accounts and transactions for any unauthorized activity.
- Stay informed about security best practices and updates from your wallet provider.

Cryptocurrency fraud and scams have unfortunately become prevalent as the popularity of digital currencies has risen. Here's a detailed explanation of the types of cryptocurrency fraud and scams, as well as safety measures and tips for investing safely [5]:

Types of Cryptocurrency Scams

- **Fake Websites**:
  - **Description**: Fraudulent websites mimic legitimate cryptocurrency exchanges or investment platforms. They use fake testimonials and promises of guaranteed high returns to lure unsuspecting investors.
  - **Risk**: Investors who deposit funds into these fake platforms often lose their money entirely, as the scammers disappear once they've collected enough funds.
- **Virtual Ponzi Schemes**:
  - **Description**: Similar to traditional Ponzi schemes, cryptocurrency Ponzi schemes promise high returns to investors. New investor funds are used to pay returns to earlier investors, creating a cycle of apparent profitability until the scheme collapses.
  - **Example**: BitClub Network, which defrauded investors of over $700 million before its operators were apprehended in 2019.
- **Celebrity Endorsements and Rumours**:
  - **Description**: Scammers impersonate celebrities or influential figures online, claiming endorsement of a particular cryptocurrency. They create false hype to inflate the price, allowing them to sell off their holdings at a profit before the scheme is exposed.

  - **Risk**: Investors who buy into these rumours often suffer losses when the price crashes after the scam is revealed.

- **Romance Scams**:

  - **Description**: Scammers build relationships with victims on dating apps or social media platforms, then persuade them to invest in cryptocurrencies. The victims transfer funds to the scammer's account, believing they are investing, but end up losing their money.

  - **Statistics**: The FBI received over 1,800 reports of crypto-focused romance scams in the first seven months of 2021, resulting in $133 million in losses.

- **Fake Exchanges and Traders**:

  - **Description**: Fraudsters set up fake cryptocurrency exchanges or pose as legitimate traders offering unrealistic returns on investments.

  - **Risk**: Investors who deposit funds or trade with these fraudulent entities risk losing their investments entirely, as these operations are designed solely to defraud.

- **Cryptocurrency Hacking**:

  - **Description**: Hackers target cryptocurrency exchanges and wallets to steal digital assets. They exploit vulnerabilities in security systems or use phishing attacks to gain access to private keys.

  - **Examples**: Notable hacks include Coincheck losing $534 million and BitGrail losing $195 million in 2018.

Safety Measures and Tips for Investing in Cryptocurrency

- **Choose Reputable Exchanges**:

  - Research and select well-established cryptocurrency exchanges with strong security measures and a good reputation. Read reviews and consider recommendations from experienced investors.

- **Use Secure Wallets**:
    - Preferably use hardware wallets (cold wallets) to store large amounts of cryptocurrency securely offline. Alternatively, use reputable software wallets (hot wallets) with strong security features.
- **Educate Yourself**:
    - Understand the basics of blockchain technology, how cryptocurrencies work, and the risks involved in investing.
    - Stay informed about common scams and fraud tactics to recognize warning signs.
- **Diversify Your Investments**:
    - Spread your investments across different cryptocurrencies to mitigate risk. Avoid putting all your funds into one asset, such as Bitcoin, despite its popularity.
- **Prepare for Volatility**:
    - Cryptocurrency prices can be highly volatile, leading to substantial gains or losses. Only invest funds that you can afford to lose without affecting your financial stability.
- **Be Cautious of Unrealistic Promises**:
    - Avoid investments promising guaranteed high returns or endorsed by celebrities without thorough verification.
    - Verify information independently and avoid succumbing to FOMO (Fear of Missing Out) induced by social media hype.
- **Security Practices**:
    - Enable two-factor authentication (2FA) on all accounts associated with cryptocurrency transactions.
    - Use strong, unique passwords and keep them secure. Regularly update

software and firmware on wallets and devices.

One of the key features of cryptocurrencies is their limited supply, with many having a capped maximum number of coins or tokens that can ever be created, enforced through embedded protocols in the cryptocurrency's code [6]. Beyond simple transactions, cryptocurrencies serve various purposes such as facilitating smart contracts, decentralized applications (DApps), and tokenization of assets [7]. Bitcoin, introduced in 2009 as the first decentralized cryptocurrency by an anonymous entity known as Satoshi Nakamoto, remains the most well-known in the market [8]. Since then, thousands of other cryptocurrencies, often referred to as altcoins, have been created, each with unique features and applications [9].

The integration of cryptocurrencies, particularly Bitcoin, into retirement savings plans has gained significant attention, highlighting the growing acceptance and adoption of digital assets in traditional financial systems [10]. Cryptocurrencies operate on decentralized networks, typically utilizing blockchain technology to ensure transparency, security, and immutability of transactions [11]. The emergence of cryptocurrencies has challenged conventional banking systems and monetary policies, offering advantages to overcome limitations in traditional financial systems [12]. Despite the advantages, debates exist around the security of cryptocurrencies due to the lack of authoritative control, raising concerns about their safety and reliability [13].

The high volatility and inherent risk associated with cryptocurrency investments have prompted studies to analyse the determinants of value perception and factors influencing individuals' intentions regarding cryptocurrency adoption and investment decisions [14]. Cryptocurrencies have been identified as a new form of digital asset that functions through blockchain technology, aiming to serve as an instrument of exchange [15]. The global nature of cryptocurrencies allows for potentially more secure and lower-cost transfers accessible to individuals in remote regions through smartphones [16]. Blockchain technology, fundamental to the popularity of cryptocurrencies, has also been recognized for its potential in enhancing supply chain performance and logistics management [17].

Research has shown that cryptocurrencies like Bitcoin have impacted the current financial legal landscape, emphasizing the increasing importance of regulating these digital assets [18]. The rise of cryptocurrency adoption in various regions, including Pakistan, has been facilitated by the establishment of crypto exchanges, educational initiatives, and supporting infrastructure [19]. The impact of monetary systems on income inequality and wealth distribution has been explored, suggesting that utilizing cryptocurrency systems could promote economic equality by providing equal access to finance and investment opportunities [20]. Additionally, studies have quantified the sustainability of Bitcoin and blockchain technologies, highlighting the need to assess the environmental impact and long-term viability of these digital assets [21].

Cryptocurrencies represent a transformative force in the global financial landscape, offering decentralized, secure, and efficient means of transactions and asset management. The adoption and acceptance of cryptocurrencies continue to grow, challenging traditional financial systems and prompting regulatory considerations to ensure their sustainable integration into the economy. As the market evolves and technologies advance, further research and analysis will be crucial in understanding the implications, risks, and opportunities presented by cryptocurrencies in the modern financial ecosystem.

Cryptocurrency's classification as 'money' is a topic of debate, often assessed against the key characteristics that define traditional forms of money [22]:

1. **Widely Accepted Means of Payment**: Money is typically recognized and accepted universally within a nation's economy for transactions. While cryptocurrencies can be used for buying and selling goods and services, their acceptance remains limited compared to national currencies. Surveys indicate that only a small percentage of cryptocurrency holders regularly use them for daily transactions, indicating a lack of widespread acceptance.

2. **Store of Value**: Money should retain its purchasing power over time, allowing it to serve as a reliable store of value. Cryptocurrencies, however, are known for their price volatility. Significant fluctuations in value can occur rapidly, making it challenging for cryptocurrencies to maintain stable purchasing power. This volatility undermines their effectiveness as a store of value compared to more stable forms of money.

3. **Unit of Account**: Money serves as a standard measure for pricing goods and services within an economy. In many countries, prices are quoted and transactions conducted in the national currency (e.g., Australian dollars). While some businesses accept cryptocurrencies as payment, they are not commonly used as a unit of account. This means cryptocurrencies are not widely adopted for everyday price comparisons or financial reporting.

Given these criteria, cryptocurrencies currently do not fully meet the standards typically associated with traditional money. They can function as a means of payment in certain contexts but lack broad acceptance, price stability, and widespread use as a unit of account [22].

It's worth noting that central banks are exploring the concept of digital currencies issued by themselves, often referred to as central bank digital currencies (CBDCs). Unlike cryptocurrencies, CBDCs would be issued and regulated by a central authority, potentially offering characteristics more aligned with traditional money, such as stability and official recognition within the financial system. Therefore, while cryptocurrencies have characteristics of money to some extent, they do not meet all the criteria required for broader recognition as a mainstream form of money [22].

A Central Bank Digital Currency (CBDC) represents a digital form of sovereign currency issued and regulated by a country's central bank. Unlike cryptocurrencies, which are decentralized and operate independently of any central authority, CBDCs are backed by the full faith and credit of the issuing government. They are designed to function similarly to physical cash but in a digital form, providing a secure and regulated means of conducting transactions within an economy [22].

One of the fundamental aspects distinguishing CBDCs from cryptocurrencies is their legal tender status. As an official form of currency, CBDCs would be universally accepted as a means of payment, just like physical cash or electronic bank deposits. This acceptance ensures that CBDCs can be used for various transactions, from everyday purchases to large-scale financial settlements, across the entire economy [22].

Another critical difference lies in the stability and reliability of CBDCs as a store of value. Unlike many cryptocurrencies, which are notorious for their price volatility driven by market speculation and demand, CBDCs would be designed to maintain stable purchasing power. This stability is crucial for fostering confidence among users and businesses, supporting financial planning, and facilitating economic transactions without the risk of significant value fluctuations [22].

Furthermore, CBDCs would serve as a standard unit of account within their respective economies. For example, a CBDC issued by the Reserve Bank would be denominated in Australian dollars, allowing it to serve as a consistent measure for pricing goods and services. This characteristic enhances the efficiency of economic transactions, simplifies accounting and financial reporting, and promotes price transparency across sectors [22].

Cryptocurrency Transactions

Cryptocurrency transactions operate through electronic messages within a decentralized network, employing blockchain technology for confirmation and security. The process begins when Alice initiates a transaction by sending a message containing the recipient's electronic address (public key), the amount of cryptocurrency to be transferred, and a timestamp indicating the transaction's initiation [22].

Once initiated, Alice's transaction is broadcasted across all nodes participating in the cryptocurrency network. Each node maintains a complete ledger of all transactions ever conducted, known as the blockchain. Transactions, including Alice's, enter a transaction pool (mempool), awaiting validation and inclusion in a new block [22].

Miners, specialized participants with powerful computers, compete to solve a complex cryptographic puzzle based on pending transactions. The first miner to solve the puzzle creates a new block, incorporating Alice's transaction along with others from the mempool.

Upon solving the puzzle, the miner broadcasts the newly created block to the network. Other nodes verify the block's validity, ensuring all transactions within it are legitimate and that the cryptographic proof of work provided by the miner is accurate. Consensus among nodes is crucial, achieved through mechanisms like Proof of Work (PoW), confirming the block's authenticity [22].

Once validated and accepted by the network, the new block is appended to the end of the blockchain. This blockchain serves as a decentralized and immutable ledger, sequentially recording all transactions conducted within the cryptocurrency network. Alice's transaction is now confirmed and permanently added to the blockchain record.

Confirmation of a transaction like Alice's occurs relatively quickly upon inclusion in a block. However, for enhanced security and irreversibility, it is common practice in blockchain networks, such as Bitcoin, to wait for multiple subsequent blocks to be added on top of the block containing Alice's transaction. This process, often requiring six additional blocks, ensures that the transaction is deeply buried within the blockchain, making it computationally impractical and highly secure to reverse. Thus, ensuring finality and trust in cryptocurrency transactions [22].

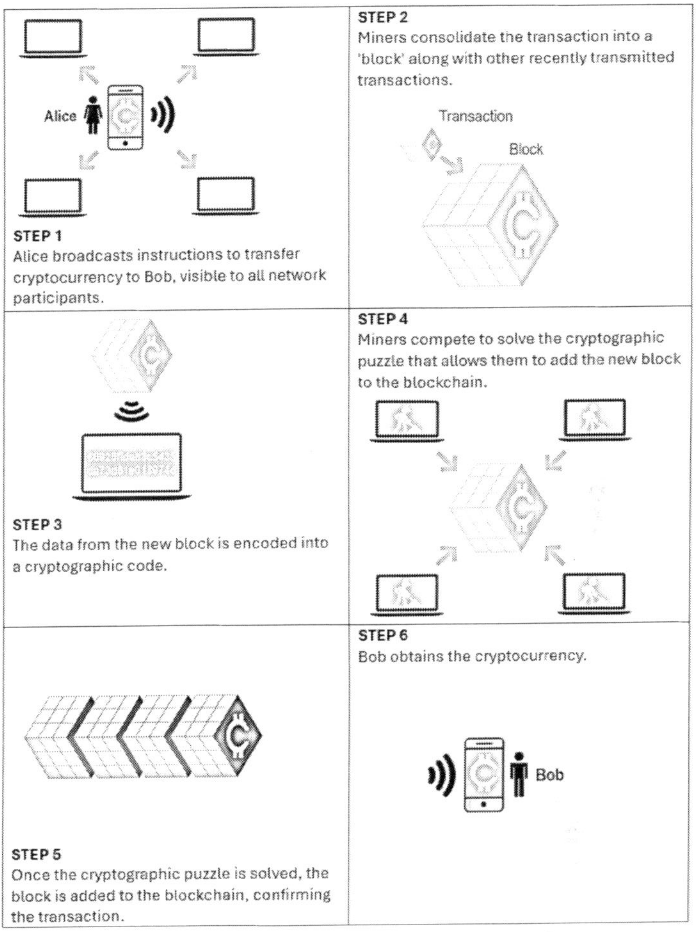

Figure 3: Cryptocurrency transactions [22].

History of Digital Currency

The history of digital currency traces back several decades, characterized by transformative technological advancements and paradigm shifts in finance. Here's a detailed chronological overview of its key milestones.

In the 1980s and early 1990s, a significant period in the development of digital cash systems and cryptographic protocols occurred before the widespread use of the Internet. David , an American cryptographer, made notable contributions during this era by introducing innovative concepts related to anonymous digital cash and cryptographic protocols [23]. 's work was foundational in establishing secure digital transactions, envisioning a future where financial privacy and security could be greatly enhanced through digital means. Companies like DigiCash and CyberCash emerged as pioneers in electronic money during the 1990s, with DigiCash, founded by , creating eCash, one of the earliest forms of digital currency backed by real-world currencies [23].

Chaum's extensive work on unconditionally anonymous protocols aimed to create the digital equivalent of cash, ensuring anonymity and security in transactions [23]. His vision of security without identification in transaction systems provided a practical solution to privacy concerns, aiming to render concepts like "Big Brother" obsolete [24]. The development of digital cash schemes involved cryptographic protocols for withdrawal, transfer, deposit, and division, meeting the security and anonymity needs of all participants [25]. These schemes were designed to prevent undetected reuse or forgery, offering assurance of authenticity for customers and banks [25].

The concept of digital cash and cryptographic protocols is closely linked to the idea of usage-based pricing and digital transactions, as explored by Mackie-Mason and Varian [26]. The emergence of digital cash systems necessitated innovative cryptographic tools and methodologies [27]. Their research focused on methodologies for off-line digital cash using general cryptographic tools, underscoring the importance of robust cryptographic foundations in ensuring the security and integrity of digital transactions [27].

Moreover, witness hiding proofs and applications, such as those discussed by Chen [28], significantly enhanced the security of electronic cash systems. Witness hiding proofs were crucial for applications like electronic cash and digital signatures, ensuring the confidentiality and integrity of transactions [28]. The integration of digital cash into multiparty protocols, enabled by verifiable signature sharing as discussed Franklin & Reiter [29], facilitated secure distributed auctions and cash escrow services, further enhancing the utility and security of digital cash systems.

In the field of cryptography, the RSA algorithm, utilized in applied cryptography protocols [30], played a vital role in securing digital transactions. Robust cryptographic algorithms like RSA were essential for safeguarding the confidentiality and integrity of digital cash systems [30]. Additionally, the development of privacy-protecting off-line electronic cash systems challenged the notion that such systems must be based on blind signature issuing protocols, as highlighted by Brands [31]. This research debunked the popular belief, emphasizing the importance of diverse cryptographic approaches in ensuring the privacy and security of electronic cash systems [31].

Overall, the Pre-Internet Era of the 1980s and early 1990s witnessed a transformative period in the development of digital cash systems and cryptographic protocols. Visionaries like David Chaum and pioneering companies such as DigiCash laid the groundwork for secure and anonymous digital transactions, shaping the future of financial privacy and security in the digital age.

The 1990s and early 2000s saw the emergence of pioneering digital currency initiatives like DigiCash and CyberCash, which faced challenges leading to their closure. These early ventures highlighted the significant hurdles in integrating digital currencies into traditional financial systems and gaining widespread consumer acceptance. Regulatory uncertainties, technological constraints, and market reception were significant obstacles during this period [32].

The concept of digital money predates Bitcoin, with its origins dating back to the 1980s and 1990s, exemplified by projects such as David Chaum's DigiCash and Wei Dai's b-money [32]. These early experiments laid the foundation for the development of digital currencies and emphasized the complexities involved in establishing these innovative forms of financial transactions within existing frameworks.

As digital currencies evolved, research explored their features, functions, and potential impacts on the financial landscape. Studies have compared digital currencies with traditional fiat currencies, highlighting the advantages and disadvantages inherent in these new forms of monetary exchange [33]. Understanding these differences is crucial for policymakers, financial institutions, and consumers navigating the changing landscape of digital finance.

The development of digital currencies has not been without challenges. Issues such as data security and vulnerabilities to cyber-attacks have been scrutinized, underscoring the importance of protecting digital assets in an increasingly interconnected financial ecosystem [34]. Addressing these security concerns is essential for building trust and confidence in digital currency systems.

Furthermore, the rise of digital currencies has sparked discussions on their implications for economic sanctions and regulatory frameworks. The decentralized nature of cryptocurrencies has raised concerns about potential risks of sanction evasion, leading to diverse regulatory approaches globally [35]. Balancing innovation with regulatory oversight is a critical consideration in the ongoing evolution of digital currencies.

At the core of discussions on digital currencies is the role of central banks and their potential issuance of digital currencies. The introduction of central bank digital currencies (CBDCs) has initiated debates on their impact on existing cryptocurrencies and the broader financial landscape [36]. Understanding the dynamics between CBDCs and private digital currencies is crucial for anticipating potential shifts in the monetary system.

The adoption of digital currencies has been studied in various regions, providing insights into the different drivers, challenges, and success stories across different contexts. Research has examined digital currency adoption in Africa, offering unique perspectives on the global landscape of digital finance [37]. These analyses offer valuable insights into the diverse paths of digital currency integration worldwide.

Moreover, the intersection of digital currencies with financial inclusion has been a key focus of research. Scholars have explored how central bank digital currencies could enhance financial access for underserved populations [36]. By investigating the connection between digital currencies and financial inclusion, researchers aim to identify ways to leverage these technologies to bridge economic disparities.

In the context of the evolving monetary system, the emergence of digital currencies has prompted reflections on their impact on traditional banking sectors. Studies have analysed how digital currencies influence banking operations in Europe, highlighting the transformative potential of these technologies [38]. Understanding the implications of digital currencies on banking institutions is crucial for navigating the changing financial landscape.

As digital currencies gain momentum, discussions on their legal governance and regulatory frameworks have become increasingly relevant. Scholars have stressed the importance of establishing clear legal frameworks for digital currencies to mitigate risks such as money laundering and data breaches [39]. Developing robust regulatory mechanisms is essential for creating a secure and stable environment for digital financial transactions.

The period from the 1990s to the early 2000s witnessed the early stages of digital currency development, characterized by innovation and challenges. The experiences of pioneering ventures like DigiCash and CyberCash laid the groundwork for subsequent advancements in digital finance. As researchers delve into the intricacies of digital currencies, addressing issues related to regulation, security, and adoption will be crucial in shaping the future trajectory of financial systems.

The emergence of Bitcoin in 2008 marked a significant milestone in the realm of digital currencies and blockchain technology. Satoshi Nakamoto introduced Bitcoin through a whitepaper that outlined a decentralized digital currency system [40]. This system leveraged blockchain technology to enable peer-to-peer transactions without the need for intermediaries like banks [41]. The release of this whitepaper was a pivotal moment, setting the stage for the first Bitcoin transaction in January 2009, which initiated the Bitcoin blockchain and the issuance of bitcoins as its native cryptocurrency [42].

Nakamoto's whitepaper described Bitcoin as a peer-to-peer cash system where a network of nodes verified transactions to prevent double-spending, laying the foundation for the decentralized and trustless nature of Bitcoin transactions [41]. This innovative concept of a decentralized, distributed, and cryptographically secured ledger formed the basis of Bitcoin and subsequent blockchain-based systems [40]. The whitepaper introduced a protocol with robust cryptographic security, emphasizing the birth of Bitcoin as a groundbreaking digital currency [40].

The impact of Nakamoto's whitepaper extended beyond the creation of Bitcoin, influencing the broader adoption of blockchain technology in various sectors. The whitepaper not only introduced Bitcoin but also catalysed the development of blockchain technology, which has since found applications in fields like agriculture, finance, and supply chain management [43]. The success of Bitcoin as the first application of blockchain technology sparked debates in banking and finance sectors, with some considering it a potential successor to traditional fiat currency systems [44].

The whitepaper's release in 2008 paved the way for the development of blockchain technology, which has evolved into a widely adopted innovation in modern society [45]. Blockchain's architectural design, characterized by distributed and encrypted data storage, has enabled secure and transparent transactions across various industries [42]. The decentralized nature of blockchain technology has led to the creation of diverse applications beyond cryptocurrencies, including smart contracts, decentralized finance, and supply chain management systems [46].

Furthermore, the whitepaper's emphasis on decentralization, trustlessness, and cryptographic security laid the groundwork for the emergence of new blockchain-based systems and cryptocurrencies [40]. The principles outlined in Nakamoto's whitepaper have influenced the governance and control mechanisms of blockchain technology, shaping its applications in sectors like healthcare, energy, and e-commerce [47]. The whitepaper's innovative concepts have driven the evolution of blockchain technology, enabling enhanced decentralization and security in Web 3.0 applications [48].

The release of the Bitcoin whitepaper in 2008 by Satoshi Nakamoto was a seminal moment that introduced the world to a decentralized digital currency system powered by blockchain technology. This event not only led to the creation of Bitcoin but also catalysed the widespread adoption of blockchain technology across diverse industries, revolutionizing the way transactions are conducted and data is secured. Nakamoto's whitepaper laid the foundation for a new era of decentralized, trustless, and transparent systems that continue to shape the digital landscape today.

The 2010s marked a significant period in the cryptocurrency world with the emergence of alternative cryptocurrencies, commonly known as altcoins, following the success of Bitcoin. These altcoins, such as Litecoin, Ripple, and Ethereum, brought about various innovations aimed at improving upon the limitations of Bitcoin. For instance, Ethereum, introduced in 2015, revolutionized the landscape by introducing smart contracts, which are self-executing contracts with the terms of the agreement directly written into code. This innovation paved the way for decentralized applications (dApps) and the tokenization of assets, expanding the utility of blockchain technology beyond just being a digital currency [49].

Ethereum, in particular, played a pivotal role in advancing the capabilities of blockchain technology by offering a Turing-complete programming language called Solidity for developing smart contracts. This language enabled developers to create complex agreements and applications that could be automatically executed on the blockchain, enhancing the efficiency and security of transactions [49]. The introduction of smart contracts on the Ethereum platform represented a significant leap forward in the evolution of cryptocurrencies, allowing for a wide range of decentralized applications to be built on its network.

Smart contracts, as implemented on platforms like Ethereum, are essentially self-executing contracts with the terms of the agreement directly written into lines of code. These contracts automatically enforce and execute the terms of the agreement when predefined conditions are met, eliminating the need for intermediaries and enhancing the security and transparency of transactions [50]. The decentralized nature of smart contracts ensures that transaction and contract information is open, transparent, and tamper-proof, contributing to a more trustless and efficient system [51].

The rise of Ethereum and its smart contract capabilities led to a surge in research and development focused on analysing and enhancing the security and functionality of these contracts. Various studies have been conducted to evaluate the vulnerabilities and risks associated with smart contracts, aiming to improve their resilience to attacks and exploits [52]. Additionally, tools like SolidityCheck have been developed to quickly detect potential issues in smart contracts through regular expressions, highlighting the importance of ensuring the robustness of these automated agreements [53].

Furthermore, the economic implications of smart contracts, particularly in the context of Ethereum, have been a subject of interest. The execution of smart contracts on the Ethereum blockchain incurs costs in the form of gas, a unit used to measure the computational effort required to process transactions. Understanding the economics behind smart contracts is crucial for optimizing their efficiency and ensuring cost-effective utilization of blockchain resources [54].

In the realm of security, the integrity and protection of smart contracts have been a focal point of research. Tools like ContractGuard have been developed to defend Ethereum smart contracts by embedding intrusion detection mechanisms, safeguarding them against potential threats and vulnerabilities [55]. Ensuring the security of smart contracts is paramount to maintaining the trust and reliability of blockchain-based applications and transactions.

Moreover, the performance and scalability of blockchain platforms supporting smart contracts, such as Ethereum, have been subjects of investigation. Studies have been conducted to analyse the efficiency of blockchain-based smart grids and to compare implementations on platforms like Ethereum and Hyperledger, aiming to enhance the functionality and usability of smart contract applications [56]. Improving the performance of blockchain networks is essential for enabling the widespread adoption of decentralized applications and ensuring seamless user experiences.

The expansion of alternative cryptocurrencies and the introduction of smart contracts in the 2010s have significantly transformed the landscape of blockchain technology. Platforms like Ethereum have spearheaded innovations that go beyond traditional digital currencies, enabling the development of decentralized applications and automated agreements that enhance security, transparency, and efficiency in transactions. The research and development efforts focused on smart contracts underscore the importance of continuously improving their security, performance, and economic viability to unlock the full potential of blockchain technology in the years to come.

The period from 2017 to the present has indeed seen a surge in mainstream attention towards cryptocurrencies, resulting in significant market growth and the introduction of numerous new digital assets through initial coin offerings (ICOs) [57]. This increased interest has not only led to substantial global investments but has also spurred governments and financial regulators worldwide to develop regulatory frameworks to oversee the expanding crypto market [57]. Regulators face the challenge of balancing innovation in the cryptocurrency space with concerns regarding consumer protection, financial stability, and the prevention of illicit activities [57].

Academic research has predominantly concentrated on regulatory aspects and ICOs, while industry articles have placed more emphasis on exchanges and cryptocurrencies themselves [57]. The rise of cryptocurrencies has raised worries about potential illicit activities, particularly money laundering, resulting in varied regulatory responses from outright bans to more inclusive approaches that integrate cryptocurrencies into existing financial regulatory frameworks [58]. The necessity for a comprehensive regulatory framework for cryptocurrencies, including popular options like Bitcoin and Ethereum, has become increasingly evident [59].

Regulatory frameworks play a critical role in shaping the adoption and use of cryptocurrencies by providing clarity on how transactions should adhere to the legal boundaries governing traditional fiat currencies [60]. Inconsistencies in regulations can create uncertainty among users and impede the widespread adoption of cryptocurrencies [14]. Despite the decentralized nature of cryptocurrencies, governments and regulators are actively participating in discussions to establish appropriate frameworks that ensure compliance and mitigate risks associated with digital assets [61].

The regulatory landscape concerning cryptocurrencies varies significantly across different jurisdictions, with some countries advocating for stringent regulations to combat money laundering and terrorist financing, while others are exploring more flexible approaches to accommodate the evolving crypto market [62]. The dynamic nature and high volatility of the cryptocurrency market underscore the importance of regulatory interventions to protect investors and maintain market stability [63]. Additionally, the emergence of new digital assets like Ethereum, Litecoin, and Dogecoin has further emphasized the need for regulatory clarity and oversight [63].

As the cryptocurrency market evolves, there is a growing recognition of the necessity for regulatory frameworks that not only address the unique characteristics of digital assets but also align with existing legal frameworks related to fraud and insider trading [64]. The development of ethical frameworks for responsible AI and machine learning applications in cryptocurrency trading reflects a broader effort to ensure the integrity and transparency of digital asset transactions [64]. By synthesizing existing literature and insights from regulatory experts, policymakers can strive to establish robust regulatory frameworks that promote innovation while safeguarding investors and maintaining market integrity [65].

The increased mainstream attention and regulation of cryptocurrencies from 2017 to the present have marked a significant transformation in the financial landscape, prompting governments, regulators, and researchers to engage in discussions on how to effectively manage the challenges and opportunities presented by digital assets. The establishment of clear and comprehensive regulatory frameworks is crucial to ensure the sustainable growth and integrity of the cryptocurrency market while addressing concerns related to consumer protection, financial stability, and illicit activities.

Central Bank Digital Currencies (CBDCs) have gained significant attention globally, particularly with the rise in popularity of cryptocurrencies. These digital representations of sovereign currencies are being explored by central banks worldwide to leverage blockchain technology for improving payment systems and updating financial infrastructures while ensuring regulatory oversight and stability [66]. While many countries are still in the pilot and research phases of CBDC implementation, some high-income nations have begun cautiously integrating these digital currencies into their economies [67].

Research confirms that CBDCs are essentially digital versions of domestic currencies issued by central banks, with a unit of account equivalent to the respective national currency [68]. The primary objective behind CBDC development is to address potential threats posed by private sector digital currency issuances to monetary policy and financial market stability. Central banks are investigating CBDCs as a means to uphold financial market stability, maintain monetary policy effectiveness, and counter risks [69]. These digital currencies are considered central bank liabilities that can facilitate payments, offering benefits such as reducing financial instability sources, enhancing payment system efficiency and safety, and deterring tax evasion and illicit activities [70].

The exploration of CBDCs is a global trend, with central banks worldwide contemplating the issuance of these digital currencies. The potential advantages of CBDCs include enhancing money demand, optimizing payment systems, expanding the money multiplier effect, and directly influencing monetary policy effectiveness [71]. Additionally, the introduction of CBDCs is viewed as an inevitable progression in the digital finance realm, necessitated by increasing digitalization [72].

A crucial aspect associated with CBDCs is their impact on financial inclusion. Studies suggest that interest-bearing CBDCs could decrease cash demand, promote financial inclusion, and enable holding central bank digital currency without requiring a traditional bank account [73]. Furthermore, CBDCs have the potential to offer improved payment options for financial transactions in the circular economy, fostering greater financial inclusion for unbanked individuals and supporting distressed businesses in the circular economy [74].

While CBDCs offer promise in enhancing financial systems and inclusivity, challenges and considerations exist. Risks associated with CBDC implementation include governance issues, regulatory challenges, interoperability concerns for cross-border payments, and potential impacts on monetary regulation [75]. Central banks are responsible for establishing governance frameworks for CBDCs to ensure effective regulation and mitigate associated risks [76].

The exploration and development of Central Bank Digital Currencies (CBDCs) signify a significant shift in the global financial landscape. These digital representations of sovereign currencies have the potential to transform payment systems, enhance financial inclusion, and modernize monetary policy frameworks. However, the integration of CBDCs into national economies necessitates careful consideration of regulatory, governance, and interoperability aspects to ensure successful implementation and risk mitigation.

Cryptocurrencies are continuously evolving, driven by technological advancements such as decentralized finance (DeFi) applications, stablecoins pegged to traditional currencies, and enhanced scalability solutions [77]. The entry of institutional investors, financial institutions, and technology giants into the crypto space is contributing capital, credibility, and infrastructure that could propel broader adoption and market maturation [77]. Despite these advancements, challenges persist, including regulatory uncertainties, cybersecurity risks, and environmental concerns related to energy-intensive mining practices [77]. However, the promise of digital currencies lies in their potential for financial inclusion, facilitating cross-border payments, and fostering transformative innovations in global finance [77].

The development and adoption of Layer-two solutions are identified as a significant trend aimed at enhancing the scalability and efficiency of blockchain networks [78]. These solutions play a crucial role in addressing the scalability challenges faced by blockchain technologies, making them more viable for widespread use [78]. Additionally, the growing interest in sustainable blockchain solutions and the potential impact of central bank digital currencies are expected to further shape the future of the cryptocurrency ecosystem [77].

Blockchain technology, the foundation of cryptocurrencies like Bitcoin, operates on decentralized principles and cryptographic concepts to provide secure and reliable decentralized solutions [79]. The decentralized nature of blockchain, maintained through proofs-of-work, not only ensures transaction integrity but also serves to generate the monetary supply in cryptocurrencies [79]. Recent advances in blockchain technology have shown significant promise in improving various sectors, including patient care and information management in healthcare [80].

The rise of digital currencies and the underlying blockchain technology has garnered significant attention across various sectors, indicating a growing interest in the potential applications and benefits of these innovations [81]. Blockchain-based decentralized cryptocurrencies have become a focal point of interest and deployment in recent years, reflecting the increasing relevance and adoption of this technology [82]. Decentralized Applications (DApps) built on blockchains provide distributed trusted applications that leverage the security and transparency of blockchain technology [83].

Cryptography forms the fundamental basis of blockchain technology, ensuring the security and integrity of decentralized systems [84]. Innovations such as Zk-SNARKs-based anonymous payment channels aim to enhance transaction speeds in cryptocurrencies, enabling high-frequency transactions on a global scale [85] The integration of cryptography in blockchain systems is essential for ensuring the privacy and security of transactions, especially in scenarios like secure e-voting systems [86].

Efforts to address scalability issues in blockchain systems have led to the exploration of solutions like sharding, cooperative mining systems, and demand-aware payment channel networks [87-89]. These approaches aim to improve the scalability and efficiency of blockchain networks, making them more capable of handling increased transaction volumes and diverse application domains [87-89]. Additionally, research on blockchain storage, scalability, and availability underscores the importance of these aspects in ensuring the robustness and sustainability of blockchain systems [90].

As the adoption of cryptocurrencies continues to grow, the scalability of blockchain technologies has become increasingly crucial for their widespread acceptance and utility [91]. The scalability challenges faced by blockchain systems are being addressed through various mechanisms, including off-chain transactions, payment channel networks, and sharding techniques [91-93]. These solutions aim to enhance the performance and scalability of blockchain networks, making them more efficient and adaptable to evolving demands [91-93].

The potential applications of blockchain technology extend beyond cryptocurrencies to areas like supply chain management, genomics, and Internet of Things (IoT) integration [94-96]. Blockchain's role in enhancing traceability, security, and transparency in supply chains has positioned it as a transformative technology for modern supply chain operations [94]. Moreover, the integration of blockchain in genomics and IoT systems highlights its versatility and potential to revolutionize diverse industries [95, 96].

The current trends in cryptocurrencies and blockchain technology reflect a dynamic landscape characterized by ongoing innovations, increased institutional involvement, and a focus on scalability and efficiency improvements. While challenges such as regulatory uncertainties and cybersecurity risks persist, the transformative potential of digital currencies in fostering financial inclusion and driving global financial innovations remains promising. The future outlook for cryptocurrencies and blockchain technology hinges on continued advancements in scalability solutions, sustainable blockchain practices, and the exploration of new applications across various sectors.

Chapter Two
Decentralization, Blockchain, and Cryptography

Decentralization

Decentralization in the context of cryptocurrency refers to the fundamental principle that underpins many cryptocurrencies, including Bitcoin and Ethereum. It encompasses several key aspects that differentiate these digital currencies from traditional centralized financial systems:

Key Aspects of Decentralization in Cryptocurrency:

- **Decentralized Ledger (Blockchain):** Cryptocurrencies operate on decentralized ledgers, typically known as blockchains. A blockchain is a distributed database maintained by a network of computers (nodes) spread across the globe. Each node stores a copy of the entire blockchain, and all nodes work together to validate and record transactions in blocks.

- **Peer-to-Peer Transactions:** Cryptocurrencies enable direct peer-to-peer transactions without intermediaries like banks. Users can transfer funds directly to each other across the network without relying on a central authority to facilitate or verify transactions. This decentralization reduces transaction costs and eliminates the need for traditional financial institutions.

- **Consensus Mechanisms:** Decentralized consensus mechanisms ensure agreement among network participants regarding the validity of transactions and the state of the ledger. Bitcoin, for example, uses Proof of Work (PoW), where miners compete to solve complex mathematical puzzles to add new blocks to the blockchain. Ethereum is transitioning to Proof of Stake (PoS), where validators are chosen to create new blocks based on the number of coins they hold.

- **Immutable and Transparent Transactions:** Transactions recorded on a blockchain are immutable, meaning they cannot be altered or deleted once confirmed. This transparency ensures that all transaction history is publicly verifiable, enhancing trust among participants and reducing the risk of fraud or manipulation.

- **Censorship Resistance:** Decentralized cryptocurrencies are resistant to censorship and control by any single entity or government. This feature is particularly valuable in regions with unstable financial systems or limited access to traditional banking services, where cryptocurrencies can provide financial freedom and inclusion.

Decentralization in cryptocurrency signifies a significant departure from traditional financial systems by distributing control and authority across a network of participants rather than consolidating power in a central entity. This transformative concept is exemplified by cryptocurrencies like Bitcoin and Ethereum, which operate on decentralized ledgers known as blockchains. These blockchains are distributed databases maintained globally by nodes, with each node storing a complete copy of the ledger, ensuring transparency and resilience [97]. Transactions within these cryptocurrencies are grouped into blocks, validated through consensus mechanisms, and added to the chain chronologically, eliminating the need for a central authority to manage transaction records and ensuring data integrity and security through cryptographic techniques [97].

A pivotal aspect of decentralization in cryptocurrency is the facilitation of peer-to-peer transactions, enabling users to engage in direct transactions without intermediaries such as banks. This direct interaction through cryptographic keys allows for seamless and efficient fund transfers globally, bypassing the traditional banking infrastructure and re-

Validators are chosen to create new blocks and confirm transactions, which is more energy-efficient than PoW.

- **Delegated Proof of Stake (DPoS):** An adaptation of PoS, DPoS involves stakeholders voting for delegates who validate transactions and create blocks on their behalf, improving scalability and governance.

These consensus mechanisms are crucial for maintaining the blockchain's decentralized nature while ensuring that all participants agree on the validity of transactions.

Blockchain technology offers a high level of transparency and immutability. All transactions recorded on the blockchain are publicly accessible and can be viewed by anyone participating in the network. Once a transaction is added to the blockchain, it becomes part of an immutable record, meaning it cannot be altered or deleted. This permanence creates a reliable and auditable history of all transactions. The transparent nature of the blockchain fosters trust among participants, as each transaction's authenticity can be verified by the entire network, reinforcing the security and reliability of the system.

Blockchain technology is central to processing peer-to-peer transactions in cryptocurrencies. It eliminates the need for intermediaries such as banks by allowing transactions to be verified and recorded directly on a decentralized ledger. Transactions are grouped into blocks and added to the blockchain through consensus mechanisms, which ensure the integrity and efficiency of the transaction process. This decentralized approach not only speeds up transactions but also reduces costs associated with traditional financial systems.

One of the primary benefits of blockchain is its enhanced security. By distributing copies of the ledger across a network of computers, the blockchain eliminates single points of failure, which significantly reduces the risk of fraud and hacking. To alter transaction records, an attacker would need to compromise a majority of the network, making such attacks economically impractical. Additionally, the concept of trustlessness is inherent in blockchain technology. Participants can engage in transactions and interact with the system without needing to trust any central authority. Instead, transactions are validated through cryptographic proof and consensus mechanisms, ensuring that all parties can rely on the system's security and accuracy without needing to trust a central institution.

Blockchain's utility extends beyond currency transactions to support decentralized applications (DApps). Platforms like Ethereum provide a foundation for creating DApps, which can execute smart contracts and manage decentralized autonomous organizations (DAOs). These applications run on the blockchain, leveraging its security and transparency to offer a wide range of services and functionalities that go beyond simple financial transactions. DApps have the potential to revolutionize various industries, including finance, supply chain management, and social media, by enabling new forms of interaction and automation.

The technology behind blockchain is continually evolving to address challenges such as scalability, interoperability, and privacy. Innovations like sidechains, sharding, and Layer 2 solutions are being developed to improve blockchain performance and efficiency. Sidechains allow for the creation of separate blockchains that can interact with the main blockchain, enhancing scalability. Sharding divides the blockchain into smaller pieces to handle more transactions simultaneously. Layer 2 solutions, such as the Lightning Network for Bitcoin, operate on top of the main blockchain to facilitate faster and cheaper transactions. These advancements aim to balance the need for scalability with the core principles of decentralization.

As blockchain technology and cryptocurrencies gain prominence, governments and regulatory bodies are grappling with how to regulate these innovations effectively. Regulatory considerations involve balancing the need to protect financial stability, ensure consumer protection, and maintain legal compliance with the desire to foster innovation. Different jurisdictions are exploring various approaches to regulation, which may include measures to combat money laundering, ensure data privacy, and address taxation issues. The evolving regulatory landscape will play a crucial role in shaping the future development and adoption of blockchain technology and cryptocurrencies.

A blockchain operates as a type of database that shares similarities with traditional spreadsheets or databases, but it differs significantly in how data is structured and accessed. While a conventional database stores information in tables and rows, a blockchain organizes data into blocks that are linked together in a chain [120].

In a blockchain, data is entered and stored through scripts, which perform tasks similar to those in a traditional database. However, the key feature of a blockchain is its distributed nature. Multiple copies of the blockchain are maintained across various machines or nodes, and all these copies must be identical for the data to be considered valid. This distribution ensures that no single point of failure can compromise the integrity of the blockchain [120].

For example, the Bitcoin blockchain records transaction information in blocks that can hold up to 4 megabytes of data. When a block reaches its capacity, it is sealed and a cryptographic hash is generated. This hash, known as the block header hash, is a hexadecimal number created through an encryption algorithm. This hash is then included in the header of the next block, linking it to the previous one and forming a continuous chain of blocks.

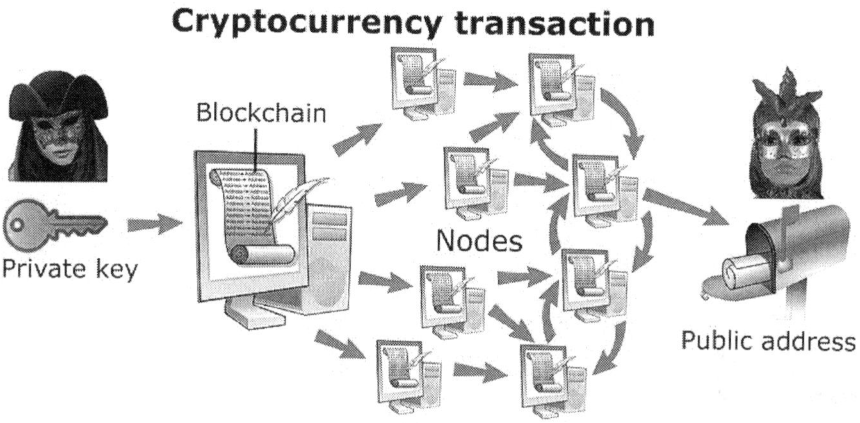

Figure 4: Simplified figurative process of a Cryptocurrency transaction: The sender uses his/her private key to note a transaction from him/her in the blockchain; The blockchain is updated across the nodes of the network; The recipient gets the transaction at his/her public address. Mikael Häggström, CC0, via Wikimedia Commons.

The transaction process on a blockchain can vary depending on the specific network. In Bitcoin's case, when you initiate a transaction using your cryptocurrency wallet, the transaction is first sent to a memory pool. Here, it is held and queued until a miner selects it. Miners then work to include this transaction in a new block, which, once filled, is closed and the mining process begins [120].

Miners compete to solve a cryptographic puzzle by varying a field called the nonce in the block header. The nonce is a value that miners adjust incrementally in their attempts to generate a hash that meets the difficulty target set by the network. The process of finding this valid hash is known as "proof-of-work" and requires substantial computational power and energy. Once a miner finds a valid hash, the block is added to the blockchain, and the miner is rewarded.

However, a block is not considered fully confirmed until it has been followed by five additional blocks. This process, known as confirmation, typically takes about one hour in Bitcoin's network due to the average time of around 10 minutes per block [120].

Other blockchains, such as Ethereum, use different processes. Ethereum, for instance, selects validators from users who have staked ether to confirm blocks. This method is generally faster and less energy-intensive compared to Bitcoin's proof-of-work system [120].

Blockchain technology, initially popularized by cryptocurrencies like Bitcoin, has expanded far beyond financial transactions. Today, it is utilized across various industries to enhance data integrity, transparency, and security [120].

Blockchain in Food Industry: In the food industry, companies like Walmart and Pfizer have adopted blockchain technology to improve supply chain transparency and traceability. IBM's Food Trust blockchain, for example, tracks the journey of food products from their origin to their final destination. This system addresses significant issues such as foodborne illnesses caused by pathogens like E. coli and salmonella. Previously, identifying the source of contamination could take weeks. With blockchain, every step a food product takes is recorded, enabling quicker identification and resolution of problems, thereby potentially saving lives and enhancing food safety.

Banking and Finance: The financial sector stands to gain immensely from blockchain technology. Traditional banking processes involve delays, as transactions are typically processed during business hours and can take several days to clear. Blockchain offers a solution by enabling transactions to be processed almost instantly, regardless of the time or day. This capability is due to the blockchain's decentralized nature, which operates continuously without interruptions. Banks integrating blockchain could see faster processing of transactions, reduced costs associated with cross-institutional fund transfers, and a more efficient settlement and clearing process for stock trades.

Currency: Blockchain is fundamental to the operation of cryptocurrencies like Bitcoin, providing a decentralized platform for currency transactions. This technology facilitates easier cross-border transactions by bypassing traditional currency exchange systems and infrastructure. Users from anywhere in the world can engage in transactions without the limitations imposed by geographical and financial barriers.

Healthcare: In healthcare, blockchain can secure patient records by providing a tamper-proof system for storing medical information. Once a medical record is created and validated, it is recorded on the blockchain, ensuring that it cannot be altered. This method offers patients confidence in the accuracy of their records and provides controlled access through encryption, thereby protecting privacy while maintaining data integrity.

Property Records: Blockchain also holds promise for revolutionizing property record management. The current process of recording property deeds is cumbersome and prone to errors, involving manual entries and physical paperwork. By recording property ownership on a blockchain, the process could become more streamlined, accurate, and less susceptible to human error. This system could be particularly beneficial in regions with unstable governance or limited infrastructure, where blockchain could offer a reliable method for documenting and verifying property ownership.

Smart Contracts: Smart contracts are programmable agreements embedded within the blockchain that execute automatically when predefined conditions are met. These contracts facilitate and enforce transactions without intermediaries, enhancing efficiency and reducing the potential for disputes. Smart contracts are used across various applications, from financial transactions to supply chain management.

Supply Chains: Similar to its application in the food industry, blockchain can track and verify the origins of materials in supply chains. This technology ensures the authenticity of products and labels, such as "Organic" or "Fair Trade." Companies can use blockchain to record every step of a product's journey, enhancing transparency and trust in the supply chain.

Voting: Blockchain technology also has potential applications in voting systems. It offers a way to securely and transparently record votes, making tampering nearly impossible and potentially increasing voter turnout. Trials, such as those conducted in West Virginia during the 2018 midterm elections, have demonstrated blockchain's capability to provide instant results and reduce the need for recounts.

Pros and Cons of Blockchain:

Pros:

- **Improved Accuracy:** By eliminating human involvement in verification, blockchain enhances data accuracy.
- **Cost Reductions:** It reduces costs by removing the need for third-party verification.
- **Increased Security:** Decentralization makes tampering more difficult, increasing the security of transactions.
- **Efficiency:** Transactions are conducted more securely and efficiently.
- **Transparency:** Blockchain technology is inherently transparent, providing clear records of transactions.
- **Financial Inclusion:** It offers an alternative banking system and a means to

secure personal information, especially in unstable or underdeveloped regions.

Cons:

- **Technology Costs:** Implementing blockchain technology can be expensive.
- **Transaction Speed:** Some blockchains suffer from low transaction throughput.
- **Illicit Use:** Blockchain has been associated with illegal activities on the dark web.
- **Regulatory Uncertainty:** Regulations regarding blockchain vary by jurisdiction and are still evolving.
- **Data Storage:** Blockchain's data storage capabilities can be limited compared to traditional databases.

Cryptography

Cryptography is a field of study and practice focused on securing communication and information through various techniques. It plays a critical role in ensuring the confidentiality, integrity, and authenticity of data, especially in digital and networked environments.

The term "crypto" derives from the Greek word "kryptos," meaning "hidden" or "concealed." In the context of cryptography, "crypto" reflects the core concept of secrecy and protection of information [121]. Cryptography itself translates to "secret writing," which encompasses techniques and methods used to ensure that messages or data are only accessible to those intended to read them. This practice is essential for securing communication, data, and transactions against unauthorized access and tampering.

Cryptography is fundamentally about keeping information concealed from unauthorized parties. This is achieved through various techniques that transform readable information into a format that appears as random data, known as ciphertext. Only those with the correct decryption key can revert this ciphertext to its original, readable form. The primary aim is to ensure that sensitive data, such as personal messages or financial transactions, remains confidential and protected from eavesdroppers or malicious actors.

By employing algorithms and keys, cryptography secures communications and ensures that data integrity and privacy are maintained [121].

In the realm of cryptocurrency, cryptography serves several critical functions. One of its primary uses is to secure transactions that occur on the network. When a cryptocurrency transaction is initiated, it is encrypted to ensure that only the intended recipient can access the details. The transaction is then verified and recorded on the blockchain, a decentralized ledger that maintains a secure and immutable record of all transactions. This cryptographic security ensures that transactions are protected from tampering and unauthorized access, thereby preserving the integrity of the entire cryptocurrency system.

Cryptography also plays a vital role in controlling the generation of new currency units within a cryptocurrency network. For example, in Bitcoin, the process of mining involves solving complex cryptographic puzzles. These puzzles are designed to be computationally intensive, ensuring that new blocks are added to the blockchain at a controlled rate. The process of mining not only secures the network but also regulates the issuance of new bitcoins, adhering to a predetermined supply schedule [121]. This cryptographic control mechanism helps prevent inflation and maintains the stability of the cryptocurrency's value.

Another critical application of cryptography in cryptocurrency is the verification of digital asset and token transfers. Cryptographic techniques are used to generate digital signatures that validate the authenticity of transactions. When a user initiates a transfer, they sign the transaction with their private key, creating a unique digital signature. This signature can be verified by others using the sender's public key, ensuring that the transaction was indeed authorized by the rightful owner. This verification process is crucial for preventing fraud and ensuring that assets and tokens are transferred securely and accurately.

Cryptography can be configured to provide different levels of anonymity in cryptocurrency transactions. Pseudo-anonymity, as seen in Bitcoin, ensures that transactions are not directly linked to real-world identities but are instead associated with cryptographic addresses. While this offers a degree of privacy, it does not fully conceal the transaction details from analysis. On the other hand, cryptocurrencies that focus on full anonymity, such as Monero, use advanced cryptographic techniques like ring signatures and zero-knowledge proofs to obscure transaction details completely. This level of privacy ensures that transactions cannot be traced back to individual users, enhancing confidentiality and protecting user identities [121].

Cryptography, as a field of study, encompasses several core concepts that are essential for ensuring the security and integrity of information in various digital systems. Among these fundamental principles are confidentiality, integrity, authentication, and non-repudiation. Confidentiality, the first core concept, involves encrypting data to prevent unauthorized access, ensuring that only authorized parties can decipher the information [122]. This process of encryption transforms plaintext into ciphertext using encryption algorithms and keys, safeguarding sensitive data such as financial transactions and personal information from prying eyes. Integrity, the second concept, focuses on maintaining the accuracy and consistency of data during storage or transmission [123]. Techniques like hash functions generate unique hash values for data, allowing for the detection of any alterations or tampering by comparing the original and recalculated hash values.

Authentication, the third core concept, plays a crucial role in verifying the identities of users or systems to prevent impersonation and ensure secure communications [124]. Digital signatures and certificates are commonly used in cryptography to confirm the identity of senders and maintain message integrity. Non-repudiation, the fourth concept, addresses the accountability of parties involved in transactions by preventing them from denying their actions [125]. Digital signatures provide cryptographic proof of involvement, ensuring that individuals cannot later disown their commitments. These core concepts collectively form the foundation of secure communication and data protection in digital environments.

In the realm of cryptography, various encryption techniques and algorithms are employed to implement these core concepts effectively. Commonly used encryption methods include DES, 3DES, AES, Kasumi Encryption Core, Blowfish, RC4, and X-MOD-DES [126]. These algorithms play a vital role in securing data and communications by applying cryptographic principles to ensure confidentiality, integrity, authentication, and non-repudiation. Additionally, the use of asymmetric encryption, which involves public and private key pairs, enhances security by enabling secure key exchange and digital signatures [127]. By leveraging these encryption techniques, organizations can establish robust cryptographic systems that protect sensitive information from unauthorized access and tampering.

Moreover, the evolution of cryptography has seen the integration of quantum principles into cryptographic protocols, leading to the emergence of quantum cryptography. Quantum entanglement, a core concept in quantum mechanics, has been harnessed to develop secure communication channels that leverage the unique properties of quantum states for encryption [128]. Quantum key distribution protocols utilize entangled particles to enable secure key exchange, offering a new paradigm for cryptographic systems resistant to quantum attacks. The fusion of quantum concepts with traditional cryptographic methods has paved the way for enhanced security measures in the face of advancing technologies and sophisticated cyber threats.

In the context of visual cryptography, another specialized area within cryptography, the core concepts revolve around sharing information in a visually encrypted form [129]. Visual cryptography schemes are based on the principles of diffusion and confusion, where data is divided into shares that individually reveal no information but collectively decrypt the original content. This approach is particularly useful for secure image sharing and authentication processes, ensuring that sensitive visual data remains protected from unauthorized access. By understanding and applying the core concepts of visual cryptography, practitioners can implement secure image encryption techniques that safeguard privacy and confidentiality.

Furthermore, the application of cryptography extends beyond traditional data encryption to encompass diverse fields such as blockchain technology and network security. Blockchain, at its core, relies on cryptographic mechanisms to secure transactions and data through decentralized consensus and cryptographic hashing [130]. By interconnecting data blocks using cryptographic hash functions, blockchain technology ensures the integrity and immutability of records, fostering trust in decentralized systems. Additionally, network security protocols leverage cryptographic principles to establish secure communication channels and protect data from cyber threats [131]. Concepts like symmetric and asymmetric encryption, along with hash functions, form the backbone of network security frameworks, enabling organizations to fortify their digital infrastructures against malicious activities.

Key cryptographic techniques are essential for securing data and communications. Symmetric encryption involves using a single key for both encryption and decryption, requiring confidentiality and key sharing between parties. Common symmetric encryption algorithms like AES and DES are widely used [132]. Asymmetric encryption, or public-key cryptography, uses a public key for encryption and a private key for decryption, eliminating the need for a shared secret key. Well-known asymmetric encryption methods include RSA and ECC [132].

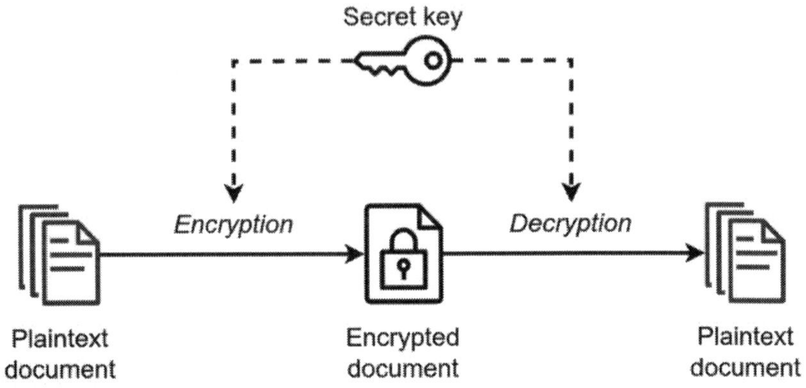

Figure 5: Simple diagram of a symmetric encryption scheme. MarcT0K (icons by JGraph), CC BY-SA 4.0, via Wikimedia Commons.

Hash functions are crucial for data integrity and security, generating unique hash values from input data. Examples like SHA-256 and MD5 are extensively used [132]. Digital signatures, combining hashing and asymmetric encryption, verify the authenticity and integrity of digital messages. By creating a digital signature with a private key and verifying it with the corresponding public key, the sender's identity is confirmed, ensuring message integrity [132].

Cryptography is the backbone of cryptocurrency systems, providing essential security and functionality to digital currencies. In the context of cryptocurrencies, cryptography ensures that transactions are secure, identities are protected, and the integrity of the entire network is maintained. Here's a detailed look at how cryptography is utilized in various aspects of cryptocurrency:

In cryptocurrencies, encryption is used to secure transactions and protect sensitive data. When a user initiates a transaction, the details are encrypted to ensure that only the intended recipient can access them. This process involves converting readable data into an unreadable format using encryption algorithms. For instance, in Bitcoin, the transaction details are encrypted using the recipient's public key. Only the recipient, who possesses the corresponding private key, can decrypt and access the transaction details. This encryption ensures that transaction information remains confidential and protected from unauthorized access during transmission.

Digital signatures are crucial for verifying the authenticity of transactions and ensuring that they are genuinely initiated by the owner of the funds. In a cryptocurrency system like Bitcoin, when a user wants to send coins, they must sign the transaction with their private key. This digital signature acts as a cryptographic proof of the sender's identity and confirms that they possess the necessary private key. The transaction, along with the digital signature, is broadcasted to the network. Other participants can then use the sender's public key to verify the signature and authenticate the transaction. This process ensures that only legitimate transactions are accepted and prevents unauthorized spending of funds.

Hash functions play a vital role in maintaining the integrity of the blockchain. When transactions are collected into blocks, each block is processed through a cryptographic hash function to generate a unique hash value. This hash value serves as a digital fingerprint of the block's contents. If even a single detail within the block changes, the hash value will be different, signalling potential tampering. Furthermore, each block includes the hash of the previous block, creating a chain of blocks (the blockchain). This linkage ensures that altering any block would require recalculating the hash values of all subsequent blocks, which is computationally impractical. Hash functions thus provide a mechanism to verify that data has not been altered and maintain the integrity of the entire blockchain.

Consensus mechanisms are cryptographic protocols used to achieve agreement among network participants on the validity of transactions and the state of the blockchain. For example, Bitcoin employs Proof of Work (PoW), where miners compete to solve complex cryptographic puzzles. The first miner to solve the puzzle gets to add the new block to the blockchain and is rewarded with newly minted bitcoins. This process involves significant computational work and ensures that only valid blocks are added to the blockchain. Other consensus mechanisms, like Proof of Stake (PoS), use different cryptographic approaches to achieve consensus. These mechanisms ensure that the blockchain remains secure and resistant to attacks by requiring network participants to perform computationally intensive tasks or demonstrate ownership of the cryptocurrency.

Cryptography also supports privacy and anonymity within cryptocurrency systems. In some cryptocurrencies like Bitcoin, while transactions are recorded on a public ledger, the identities of the parties involved are pseudonymous, represented by cryptographic addresses rather than real-world names. Advanced cryptographic techniques, such as zero-knowledge proofs and ring signatures, are used in privacy-focused cryptocurrencies like Monero to enhance anonymity. These techniques allow transactions to be verified without revealing the identities of the participants or the amounts involved. Such privacy features are crucial for users who prioritize confidentiality and want to protect their financial activities from public scrutiny.

In blockchain platforms like Ethereum, cryptography underpins the functionality of smart contracts and decentralized applications (DApps). Smart contracts are self-executing contracts with the terms directly written into code. They use cryptographic algorithms to ensure that contract conditions are met and to validate transactions automatically. This automation reduces the need for intermediaries and enhances the reliability of contractual agreements. Cryptography ensures that smart contracts are secure, tamper-proof, and executed precisely as programmed, enabling a wide range of decentralized applications beyond simple transactions.

Cryptography involves mathematical techniques designed to protect information by transforming it from a readable format to an unreadable one. This process is crucial in ensuring that cryptocurrency transactions and data remain secure from unauthorized access.

Encryption Keys and Algorithms: To encrypt data, cryptography relies on encryption keys, which are essentially algorithms or formulas that encode and decode information. These keys play a crucial role in making messages, transactions, or data values unreadable to anyone who lacks the correct key. In cryptocurrency systems, encryption ensures that only authorized users can access or interpret sensitive information [121].

In the context of Bitcoin, for example, the data from a block is processed through a cryptographic algorithm to generate a 64-digit hexadecimal number. This hexadecimal number represents a unique fingerprint of the block's contents. Regardless of the amount of data, the result is always a 64-digit string, highlighting the fixed size of the cryptographic output. This ensures that even small changes in the data produce entirely different hexadecimal numbers, which is vital for maintaining data integrity [121].

Common Encryption Algorithms: Several encryption algorithms are commonly used in cryptocurrencies to secure data. Some notable ones include [121]:

- **Advanced Encryption Standard (AES)**: A symmetric key encryption algorithm widely used for securing data.
- **Rivest-Shamir-Adelman (RSA)**: An asymmetric encryption algorithm that uses a pair of keys (public and private) for secure data transmission.
- **Elliptic Curve Cryptography (ECC)**: An asymmetric encryption method that provides high security with relatively short key lengths.

Bitcoin, in particular, utilizes elliptic curve cryptography, specifically the secp256k1 curve. This method uses the elliptic curve formula y2=x3+7y^2 = x^3 + 7y2=x3+7 to generate public and private key pairs [121]. These keys are essential for securely conducting transactions and maintaining the overall security of the Bitcoin network.

Hash Functions: Hashing is another critical cryptographic technique used in blockchain technology. Bitcoin employs the Secure Hashing Algorithm 256 (SHA-256) to encode data stored in blocks. Hash functions convert input data into a fixed-size string of characters, which is a unique representation of that data. This process is vital for several functions [121]:

- **Verifying Integrity**: Hash functions ensure that the data has not been altered during transmission or storage. Any change in the data results in a completely different hash value, making it easy to detect tampering.

- **Encrypting Transactions**: Hashing is used to encode account addresses and to maintain the structure of the blockchain by linking blocks together.

- **Mining and Validation**: In Bitcoin, hashing is central to the mining process, where miners compete to solve cryptographic puzzles and add new blocks to the blockchain.

Symmetric vs. Asymmetric Cryptography: Cryptography methods can be broadly categorized into symmetric and asymmetric types [121]:

- **Asymmetric Cryptography**: This method uses a pair of keys—public and private. The public key is shared openly, while the private key remains confidential to the owner. Data encrypted with the public key can only be decrypted using the corresponding private key. This approach ensures both encryption and authentication. In cryptocurrency, asymmetric cryptography is used to create public and private key pairs, which are fundamental for securing transactions and verifying identities.

- **Symmetric Cryptography**: This technique uses a single secret key for both encryption and decryption. The same key is used to encode the message at the source and decode it at the destination. An example of symmetric encryption is a simple substitution cipher, where letters are replaced with numbers. While symmetric cryptography is efficient and fast, it requires secure key management to prevent unauthorized access.

SHA-256 and Its Role in Cryptocurrency

SHA-256, or Secure Hash Algorithm 256-bit, is a fundamental cryptographic function used extensively in the world of cryptocurrency, particularly in Bitcoin. Developed by the United States National Security Agency (NSA) and released in 2001, SHA-256 is designed to take any input and produce a unique, fixed-length output, known as a hash. This hash is a 256-bit code represented in a 64-character hexadecimal format, consisting of numbers (0-9) and letters (A-F) [133].

The primary purpose of SHA-256 is to transform input data—such as the x and y coordinates of a public key—into a fixed-length string of characters. This process is crucial for various aspects of cryptocurrency, including generating wallet addresses and ensuring transaction security. When a public key is hashed using SHA-256, it yields a unique 256-bit hash that serves as a secure and compact representation of the original data. This hash is virtually impossible to reverse-engineer, meaning you cannot derive the original public key from the hash alone [133].

SHA-256 is considered a "trapdoor" or "deterministic" function. These terms describe functions that are easy to compute in one direction but infeasible to reverse. In practical terms, this means that while you can generate a hash from a public key or any other input, you cannot feasibly reconstruct the original input from the hash. This one-way nature is crucial for security in cryptographic applications. For instance, it is straightforward to create a public key from a private key, but reversing this process to obtain the private key from the public key is computationally impractical [133].

To illustrate the concept of irreversibility, consider the analogy of mixing paints to create a unique colour. Imagine you have a vast selection of paint colours, and you mix specific quantities of these paints to create one unique colour. If you know the exact proportions used, you can reproduce the same colour. However, if you don't have the exact formula, trying to determine the original paint mixture from the colour alone would be extremely challenging [133].

This analogy helps explain how SHA-256 works. The algorithm takes an input (like a public key), processes it through a complex mathematical formula, and produces a hash. While you can easily verify that a given hash corresponds to a particular input, reconstructing the original input from the hash is as difficult as deciphering the exact paint mixture from the resulting colour.

In Bitcoin, SHA-256 is used in several critical functions. When creating a Bitcoin wallet address, the public key is hashed using SHA-256 to produce a secure and compact address. This address is then used to receive and manage Bitcoin transactions. The security of Bitcoin transactions relies on the fact that while the address can be publicly shared and transactions can be verified, the underlying public key and the associated private key remain secure and hidden [133].

CHAPTER THREE
The Birth of Bitcoin

The Genesis of Bitcoin

The genesis of Bitcoin marks the inception of a revolutionary technology that has transformed the world of finance and beyond. Bitcoin's creation involved a combination of technological innovation, cryptographic advances, and a vision of a decentralized monetary system.

The emergence of Bitcoin as a decentralized digital currency stemmed from a period of disillusionment with traditional financial systems and centralized authorities following the 2008 global financial crisis [134]. This crisis eroded trust in conventional banking systems, paving the way for the exploration of alternative systems that could offer enhanced transparency, security, and decentralization [134]. While Bitcoin was not the first attempt at creating digital money, previous endeavours like "e-gold" and "Hashcash" failed to gain widespread adoption or address critical issues such as double-spending and centralization [134].

Bitcoin's design, introduced in 2008 by an individual or group under the pseudonym Satoshi Nakamoto, proposed a decentralized system utilizing blockchain technology to enable secure and transparent transactions without the need for a central authority [32]. The system's stability is argued to rely on a complex interplay of socioeconomic factors that are challenging to model with precision, making a convincing case for its soundness elusive [134]. Bitcoin operates on a peer-to-peer network of volunteers, distributing transactions, verifying them, and collectively maintaining a replicated ledger agreed upon by all participants [135].

The concept of a decentralized digital currency like Bitcoin has challenged the traditional financial landscape, prompting discussions on the need for a theoretical foundation and a conceptual model for its operation [136]. The technology underpinning Bitcoin, blockchain, has been instrumental in revolutionizing financial transactions by providing a publicly distributed ledger secured through cryptographic mechanisms [135]. This ledger ensures the integrity and transparency of transactions, addressing concerns related to counterfeiting and double-spending [137].

The rise of decentralized cryptocurrencies, including Bitcoin, has introduced competition into the international monetary system, leading some governments to consider the development of centralized virtual currencies known as central bank digital currencies (CBDCs) [138]. These developments highlight the evolving nature of financial systems and the impact of decentralized technologies on traditional monetary policies [138]. Additionally, the use of cryptography in cryptocurrencies like Bitcoin ensures secure and anonymous transactions, enhancing the currency's resistance to counterfeiting and fraud [137].

Bitcoin's introduction in the aftermath of the financial crisis was partly a response to concerns about government-backed fiat currencies, offering an alternative system that operates independently of central authorities [139]. The technology's decentralized nature and reliance on cryptographic principles have positioned Bitcoin as a unique financial instrument with the potential to reshape traditional economic paradigms [139]. Furthermore, the blockchain technology supporting Bitcoin has facilitated innovations in various fields, extending its applications beyond digital currency to areas like smart contracts and trusted collaborative networks [140].

The Bitcoin network officially launched on January 3, 2009, with the mining of the first block, known as the "genesis block" or "Block 0." This genesis block, mined by Satoshi Nakamoto, contained a hidden message that read, "The Times 03/Jan/2009 Chancellor on brink of second bailout for banks." This message not only served as a timestamp but also provided a commentary on the financial instability prevalent at that time [78]. The first transaction recorded in this block was the reward of 50 bitcoins, which was hardcoded into the blockchain and was unspendable due to being part of the initial block without a previous block to reference [78].

Figure 6: Logo of Bitoin. BitCoin, Public domain, via Wikimedia Commons.

The Bitcoin blockchain operates as a hashchain of blocks, where each block contains a set of transactions in a specific order and a hash of the preceding block, starting from the genesis block [141]. The process of verifying blocks in the Bitcoin network is known as mining, which involves solving complex mathematical problems and validating the block's transactions and header against the network's consensus rules [142]. The blockchain itself is a distributed append-only public ledger that records all transactions in a secure and transparent manner [143].

Nakamoto's creation of the Bitcoin blockchain in 2009 marked the beginning of a revolution in decentralized systems and cryptocurrencies [144]. The blockchain technology underlying Bitcoin has been recognized as a significant innovation, with its potential to decentralize traditionally centralized applications [145]. The blockchain's role as a distributed digital ledger that securely records transactions has been pivotal in enabling the transfer of ownership of Bitcoin and other cryptocurrencies [143].

The security and privacy aspects of blockchain technology, including those of Bitcoin, have been extensively studied [143, 144]. The blockchain's basic security properties, such as immutability and transparency, are essential for Bitcoin-like cryptocurrency systems, with additional properties desired for various blockchain applications [144]. The use of cryptographic algorithms like Secure Hash Algorithm (SHA) and RACE Integrity Primitives Evaluation Message Digest (RIPEMD) in Bitcoin ensures the integrity and security of the blockchain [146].

The Bitcoin blockchain's scalability and consensus mechanisms, such as Proof-of-Work (PoW), have been subjects of research and development to address challenges related to throughput and latency [147, 148]. Various proposals, including Bitcoin-NG, have aimed to enhance the scalability and efficiency of blockchain networks like Bitcoin [149]. The design of secure parallel-chain protocols and the adjustment of mining difficulty in Bitcoin contribute to the network's robustness and stability [150].

The launch of the Bitcoin network with the mining of the genesis block in 2009 marked a significant milestone in the history of cryptocurrencies and decentralized systems. The hidden message in the genesis block not only provided a timestamp but also reflected the financial context of the time. The blockchain technology underlying Bitcoin has since evolved to become a cornerstone of decentralized systems, offering secure and transparent transaction recording. Ongoing research continues to focus on enhancing the scalability, security, and privacy aspects of blockchain networks like Bitcoin to meet the demands of a rapidly evolving digital landscape.

Following the launch of Bitcoin, its creator, Nakamoto, remained actively involved in the project, providing software updates and engaging with early adopters through online platforms [151]. This dedication to development and communication helped establish a foundation for the cryptocurrency's growth. The first recorded Bitcoin transaction took place on May 22, 2010, when Laszlo Hanyecz exchanged 10,000 bitcoins for two pizzas, marking a significant milestone in the real-world application of Bitcoin [151].

During its initial phase, Bitcoin primarily attracted enthusiasts and experts in cryptography, with its value being relatively low and its potential not yet widely acknowledged [152]. However, as more individuals delved into the technology and its possibilities, Bitcoin's popularity surged, accompanied by a steady increase in its value. This gradual recognition of Bitcoin's capabilities and the expanding user base laid the groundwork for its eventual mainstream acceptance and adoption.

Studies have shown that early Bitcoin users encompassed a diverse range of individuals, including computer programming enthusiasts, speculative investors, libertarians, and even individuals engaged in illicit activities [153]. This varied user base highlights the multifaceted appeal of Bitcoin during its formative years. As more people explored the cryptocurrency, its user demographics evolved, reflecting shifting perceptions and applications of Bitcoin within different segments of society.

The emergence of Bitcoin as a novel financial instrument prompted extensive research into its economic, technological, and governance aspects [154]. Scholars have examined the design principles, properties, and potential applications of Bitcoin for both technical and non-technical audiences, shedding light on the risks and regulatory challenges associated with its integration into traditional financial systems [155]. This comprehensive analysis has contributed to a deeper understanding of Bitcoin's role in the evolving financial landscape.

As Bitcoin gained traction, its pricing dynamics and market behaviour attracted significant attention from researchers [156]. Studies have investigated the asset pricing properties of cryptocurrencies, analysing return statistics, market variations, and the scaling properties of price fluctuations in Bitcoin markets [157]. By exploring the statistical characteristics of cryptocurrency markets, researchers have sought to unravel the underlying mechanisms driving price movements and market trends in the realm of digital assets.

The evolution of Bitcoin from a niche interest to a global phenomenon has spurred inquiries into its societal impact and adoption patterns [158]. Researchers have explored factors influencing individuals' intentions to adopt Bitcoin, considering elements such as network effects, learning mechanisms, and social influences [159]. Understanding the drivers of Bitcoin adoption is crucial for predicting its future trajectory and assessing its role in reshaping financial behaviours and norms.

Moreover, the interplay between technological advancements and financial practices has been a focal point in studying the rise of cryptocurrencies like Bitcoin [160]. Investigations into initial coin offerings (ICOs) have highlighted the convergence of digital technologies and financialization processes, underscoring how these dynamics shape the contemporary financial landscape [161]. By elucidating the connections between technology and finance, scholars aim to elucidate the transformative potential of cryptocurrencies in redefining traditional economic paradigms.

The concept of trust has been central to the adoption and utilization of Bitcoin, with studies emphasizing the importance of trust in fostering engagement with digital currencies [162]. Research on trust design in Bitcoin ecosystems underscores the role of end-user motivations and perceptions in shaping trust dynamics within cryptocurrency networks [163]. By examining trust frameworks and user behaviours, scholars aim to enhance the understanding of trust mechanisms in decentralized financial systems.

Bitcoin's journey from an obscure digital experiment to a global phenomenon involved several key milestones. The development of the Bitcoin ecosystem, including exchanges, wallets, and merchant acceptance, played a crucial role in its growth. Over time, Bitcoin gained recognition as both a digital currency and an investment asset.

The underlying blockchain technology inspired a wave of innovation, leading to the creation of numerous other cryptocurrencies and decentralized applications. Bitcoin's success demonstrated the viability of decentralized digital currencies and paved the way for a broader exploration of blockchain technology.

Bitcoin's genesis and subsequent evolution have had profound implications for finance, technology, and society. It has challenged traditional financial systems, introduced new concepts like decentralized finance (DeFi) and smart contracts, and sparked debates about the future of money and governance.

Bitcoin's creation marked the beginning of a new era in digital currency and blockchain technology. Its impact continues to resonate, shaping the development of future technologies and influencing global financial systems. The vision articulated in Satoshi Nakamoto's white paper has become a reality, driving ongoing innovation and exploration in the world of cryptocurrencies.

Satoshi Nakamoto: The Mysterious Creator

Satoshi Nakamoto is widely recognized as the pseudonymous individual or group behind the creation of Bitcoin and the authorship of its foundational white paper. Despite the significant impact of Bitcoin on the world of finance and technology, the true identity of Satoshi Nakamoto remains shrouded in mystery, with various theories and speculations circulating about who this enigmatic figure or group might be. The name "Satoshi Nakamoto" itself carries a Japanese influence, adding to the intrigue surrounding the identity of the creator of Bitcoin [164].

The introduction of Bitcoin in 2008 through the white paper titled "Bitcoin: A Peer-to-Peer Electronic Cash System" marked a pivotal moment in the history of cryptocurrencies. This groundbreaking paper, authored by the mysterious Satoshi Nakamoto, laid the foundation for a decentralized digital currency system that operates without the need for intermediaries like banks or financial institutions [165]. The white paper outlined the innovative concept of using a peer-to-peer network to facilitate electronic transactions, revolutionizing the way people perceive and engage with traditional financial systems.

Satoshi Nakamoto's vision for Bitcoin was rooted in the principles of decentralization and trustlessness. By leveraging blockchain technology, Nakamoto introduced a novel approach to conducting secure and transparent transactions in a distributed network. The creation of Bitcoin not only introduced a new form of digital currency but also sparked a wave of interest and investment in the underlying technology of blockchain [166]. The decentralized nature of Bitcoin, as envisioned by Nakamoto, challenged conventional notions of currency and financial systems, paving the way for a paradigm shift in how value is exchanged and stored.

The significance of Satoshi Nakamoto's contribution to the world of cryptocurrencies extends beyond the creation of Bitcoin. Nakamoto's white paper served as a catalyst for the development of a vibrant ecosystem of digital assets and blockchain-based applications. The concept of a peer-to-peer electronic cash system, articulated by Nakamoto, inspired a wave of innovation in the fintech industry, leading to the emergence of diverse cryptocurrencies and decentralized platforms [167]. The legacy of Satoshi Nakamoto lies not only in the creation of Bitcoin but also in the transformative impact that this pioneering digital currency has had on the global economy and technological landscape.

The enigmatic nature of Satoshi Nakamoto's identity has fuelled speculation and intrigue within the cryptocurrency community and beyond. The decision to remain anonymous and use a pseudonym has added an aura of mystery to Nakamoto's persona, prompting countless investigations and theories about the true identity of the individual or group behind the Bitcoin creation [168]. Despite the persistent efforts to uncover the identity of Satoshi Nakamoto, the mystery endures, contributing to the enduring fascination with the origins of Bitcoin and the motivations of its elusive creator.

In the realm of digital currencies and blockchain technology, Satoshi Nakamoto occupies a legendary status as the visionary behind one of the most disruptive innovations of the 21st century. The decision to release the Bitcoin white paper under a pseudonym not only added to the mystique surrounding Nakamoto but also underscored the decentralized ethos of the cryptocurrency movement [169]. The enduring legacy of Satoshi Nakamoto's creation continues to shape the evolution of cryptocurrencies and blockchain applications, inspiring a new wave of technological advancements and financial possibilities.

As the creator of Bitcoin and the architect of its underlying principles, Satoshi Nakamoto remains a central figure in the narrative of cryptocurrency's rise to prominence. The decision to maintain anonymity and communicate solely through online channels has contributed to the enduring mystique surrounding Nakamoto's persona [170]. The impact of Nakamoto's vision extends far beyond the realm of digital currencies, influencing discussions around decentralization, trustlessness, and the future of financial systems in an increasingly interconnected world.

Satoshi Nakamoto, the pseudonymous creator of Bitcoin, began to distance themselves from the project between 2010 and 2011, eventually ceasing all public communication [166]. Despite extensive efforts to uncover Nakamoto's true identity, no definitive evidence has emerged, preserving the anonymity of the Bitcoin creator [166]. Nakamoto's withdrawal did not hinder the advancement of Bitcoin; instead, the broader community and various developers continued to progress the cryptocurrency, contributing to its widespread adoption and the emergence of numerous other cryptocurrencies and blockchain technologies [166].

Nakamoto's foundational work on Bitcoin has had a lasting impact on the financial landscape, with the decentralized nature of the cryptocurrency attracting significant interest from investors due to its innovative blockchain technology [166]. The white paper published by Nakamoto in 2008 outlined the principles of Bitcoin as a peer-to-peer electronic cash system, laying the foundation for a decentralized monetary and financial exchange system [166]. This vision resonated with many, sparking curiosity and setting the stage for the development of digital currencies and blockchain applications [166].

The development of Bitcoin under Nakamoto's guidance paved the way for the rise of financial technology (fintech) initiatives, which have transformed the financial industry [171]. Fintech, driven by digital transformation, has become a cornerstone of financial innovation, offering new avenues for conducting transactions and managing financial services [171]. The introduction of blockchain technology, as elucidated by Nakamoto, has played a crucial role in reshaping traditional financial systems and ushering in a new era of decentralized financial interactions [171].

Nakamoto's meticulous explanation of Bitcoin's operational principles and the foundational concepts of blockchain technology in the white paper set the stage for the success of the cryptocurrency and the broader acceptance of blockchain-based solutions [172]. The innovative approach to digital transactions and the secure, decentralized nature of blockchain technology have unlocked numerous possibilities beyond cryptocurrencies, including applications in supply chain management, identity verification, and smart contracts [169].

Nakamoto's influence extends beyond Bitcoin, shaping the development of decentralized finance (DeFi) and inspiring entrepreneurs to explore the potential of blockchain technology across various sectors [173]. The principles outlined in Nakamoto's white paper have acted as a catalyst for innovation, propelling research into novel applications of blockchain in areas such as energy systems, digital education, and supply chain management [170]. The immutable and transparent characteristics of blockchain have revolutionized data security and authentication systems, offering solutions to longstanding challenges in different industries [136].

Moreover, Nakamoto's vision for Bitcoin as a peer-to-peer electronic cash system has sparked discussions on the role of cryptocurrencies in the macroeconomic landscape. The disruptive potential of virtual currencies like Bitcoin has prompted debates on their viability as national currencies and their impact on traditional financial transactions. The emergence of cryptocurrencies has not only attracted investors but has also raised inquiries about their classification as digital assets and their implications for legal frameworks.

Various theories exist regarding the true identity of Satoshi Nakamoto, the anonymous individual or group behind the creation of Bitcoin and blockchain technology. Speculations include attributions to individuals like Hal Finney, Nick Szabo, and Craig Wright, as well as suggestions of collective efforts by organizations. Hal Finney, a respected cryptographer, was an early supporter of Bitcoin and received one of the first Bitcoin transactions from Nakamoto [174]. Nick Szabo, known for his work on digital currency concepts and smart contracts, has also been linked to the pseudonymous Nakamoto [175]. Conversely, Craig Wright, an Australian entrepreneur, controversially claimed to be Nakamoto, a statement met with scepticism within the cryptocurrency community [175].

Despite these conjectures, the true identity of Satoshi Nakamoto remains unknown, with no definitive evidence confirming any of the proposed theories [175]. The mysterious persona of Nakamoto has sparked ongoing debates and investigations within the cryptocurrency and blockchain communities, as researchers and enthusiasts continue to explore the origins of Bitcoin and the innovative technology it introduced [176].

The genesis of blockchain technology, credited to Satoshi Nakamoto, dates back to 2008 when Nakamoto introduced the concept in a white paper titled "Bitcoin: A Peer-to-Peer Electronic Cash System" [177]. This seminal document outlined the framework for a decentralized digital currency system based on cryptographic principles and peer-to-peer networking to facilitate secure and transparent transactions [177]. The launch of Bitcoin in 2009 marked the practical implementation of Nakamoto's vision, transforming the financial landscape and paving the way for the rise of cryptocurrencies and blockchain applications [178].

Satoshi Nakamoto's pioneering contribution with Bitcoin not only introduced a novel form of digital currency but also established the groundwork for the development of blockchain technology [179]. The innovative integration of blockchain in Bitcoin's architecture provided a secure and immutable ledger for transaction recording, addressing challenges in digital trust and decentralized systems [180]. By combining cryptographic techniques, consensus algorithms, and distributed systems, Nakamoto's creation of Bitcoin demonstrated the potential of blockchain beyond currency applications [181].

The impact of Satoshi Nakamoto's work extends beyond finance, with blockchain technology finding applications in diverse sectors such as healthcare, transportation, and supply chain management [182]. The decentralized and transparent nature of blockchain has generated interest in its capacity to revolutionize data management, security, and interoperability across industries [181]. Nakamoto's original vision for blockchain as a tool for decentralized consensus and trust has inspired innovation and research aimed at unlocking the technology's full potential.

The legacy of Satoshi Nakamoto and the emergence of blockchain technology have triggered a shift in how we perceive and engage with digital assets and information [176]. The decentralized and tamper-resistant characteristics of blockchain have challenged traditional centralized systems, offering new opportunities for secure and efficient data exchange. As researchers delve into the origins and implications of Nakamoto's contributions, the transformative influence of blockchain technology remains a focal point of academic inquiry and technological progress.

In conclusion, the mystery surrounding Satoshi Nakamoto's identity and the enduring impact of Bitcoin and blockchain technology highlight the significant influence of this anonymous innovator on the digital landscape. While Nakamoto's identity remains undisclosed, the legacy of their work continues to shape the evolution of cryptocurrencies, decentralized systems, and trustless transactions in the digital era. As researchers delve deeper into the origins and implications of Nakamoto's contributions, the importance of blockchain technology as a driver of innovation and disruption becomes increasingly evident.

How Bitcoin Works

Bitcoin is a decentralized digital currency that enables peer-to-peer transactions without the need for intermediaries such as banks or financial institutions. Unlike traditional currencies, which are issued and regulated by central authorities, Bitcoin operates on a decentralized network of computers, relying on cryptographic principles and a technology known as blockchain.

At the core of Bitcoin's operation is the blockchain, a distributed ledger that records all Bitcoin transactions. The blockchain is a continuous chain of blocks, where each block contains a list of transactions. Once a block is filled with transactions, it is cryptographically linked to the previous block, forming an immutable chain. This chain of blocks is maintained by a network of nodes, each holding a copy of the blockchain, ensuring transparency and security across the network.

The Bitcoin blockchain is a decentralized database that records all Bitcoin transactions in a secure and immutable manner. It functions through a combination of cryptographic techniques, distributed computing, and consensus mechanisms to ensure the integrity and security of the data [183].

The Bitcoin blockchain is not stored in a single location. Instead, it is distributed across a network of computers, known as nodes. Each node maintains a complete copy of the blockchain, which means that every transaction and block is replicated across the entire network. When a change is made to the blockchain—such as a new block being added—all nodes update their copies of the blockchain to reflect this change. This distributed nature ensures that the blockchain is resilient to tampering and failures, as there is no central point of control or single point of failure.

The blockchain itself is composed of a series of blocks, each of which contains several critical components. Blocks are the fundamental units of the blockchain and are designed to store data about transactions, links to previous blocks, addresses, and the code necessary to execute and validate transactions. To understand how the blockchain functions, it is crucial to understand the structure and role of these blocks [183].

When a new block is created, it contains several key pieces of information, all of which are encoded into a 256-bit number known as the block hash. This hash uniquely identifies the block and links it to the previous block in the chain. The components of a block include [183]:

- **Current Software Version**: The version of the Bitcoin client software that is used to process and validate the block.
- **Previous Block's Hash**: The hash of the block that precedes the current one,

linking the blocks together in a chain.

- **Coinbase Transaction**: The first transaction in the block, which is used to issue the reward for mining the block. This reward is in the form of newly created bitcoins and transaction fees.
- **Block Height Number**: A numerical representation of the block's position in the blockchain, indicating how far it is from the very first block (known as the genesis block).
- **Merkle Root**: A 256-bit number that represents a hash of all the transactions included in the block. This root ensures that the data within the block remains unchanged and is integral to verifying the block's content.
- **Timestamp**: The exact date and time when the block was created and added to the blockchain.
- **Target in Bits**: This represents the difficulty level of the cryptographic problem that must be solved to mine the block. It is used to control the rate at which new blocks are added to the blockchain.
- **Nonce**: A 32-bit number that miners adjust to find a valid block hash. The nonce is a critical part of the mining process and is used to produce a hash that meets the network's difficulty requirements.

Once a block is filled with transactions, it is "closed" and a unique hash is generated. This hash not only identifies the block but also includes information from previous blocks, creating a chain of blocks. The interlinking of blocks is what makes the blockchain secure and immutable. Each block's hash depends on the hash of the previous block, creating a continuous, unbreakable chain [183].

The process of adding new blocks to the blockchain is known as mining. Mining involves solving a complex mathematical problem, known as proof-of-work, which requires significant computational power. Miners compete to solve this problem, and the first miner to succeed gets to add the block to the blockchain and is rewarded with new bitcoins and transaction fees. Mining serves to validate transactions, secure the network, and regulate the creation of new bitcoins [183].

Bitcoin transactions are processed and verified through a process called mining. Mining involves solving complex mathematical problems, known as proof-of-work, which requires significant computational power. Miners compete to solve these problems, and the first miner to find a solution is rewarded with newly created bitcoins and the transaction fees associated with the transactions included in the block.

Proof-of-work serves two primary purposes: it secures the network by making it computationally impractical for any single entity to alter the blockchain, and it ensures the fair distribution of new bitcoins. The difficulty of the mathematical problems adjusts periodically to ensure that new blocks are added approximately every ten minutes, maintaining a consistent rate of block creation.

When a user initiates a Bitcoin transaction, the transaction is broadcast to the network and collected in a memory pool, where it waits to be included in a block. Each transaction contains a digital signature that verifies the sender's identity and ensures that the transaction has not been tampered with. Transactions are grouped together in a block by miners, who validate the transactions through the proof-of-work process.

Once a block is mined and added to the blockchain, the transactions within that block are considered confirmed. The confirmation process involves multiple blocks being added to the blockchain after the one containing the transaction, which increases the security and immutability of the transaction record.

To interact with the Bitcoin network, users need a Bitcoin wallet, which is a software or hardware tool that stores their private and public keys. The public key is used to receive bitcoins, while the private key is used to sign transactions and prove ownership of the bitcoins associated with the public key. The security of a Bitcoin wallet relies on the secrecy of the private key; anyone with access to the private key can control the associated bitcoins.

Bitcoin's decentralized nature means that no single entity controls the network. Instead, control is distributed across a network of nodes, each of which validates and maintains a copy of the blockchain. This decentralization enhances security by reducing the risk of a single point of failure and making it difficult for malicious actors to alter transaction records.

Bitcoin's fixed supply limit of 21 million coins is a foundational element of its design, ensuring scarcity and value preservation [184]. The process of mining, which generates new bitcoins, undergoes halving approximately every four years, reducing the rate of new coin creation and aiding in inflation control [185]. This mechanism continues until the entire 21 million bitcoins are mined, a milestone projected to be reached by around 2140 [185]. The introduction of Bitcoin halving by Nakamoto was aimed at regulating coin issuance and maintaining scarcity within the blockchain ecosystem [185].

The relationship between the hashrate and Bitcoin price has been a subject of study, with methodologies like exponential smoothing being employed to model the Bitcoin network's energy efficiency dynamics [186]. Additionally, the scalability and transaction speed of blockchain systems, including Bitcoin, have been addressed through approaches like parallel proof of work to enhance system performance [187]. The impact of halving events on the fair market value of Bitcoin has been analysed, shedding light on how this process influences the cryptocurrency's economic landscape [188].

Mining pools play a crucial role in the Bitcoin ecosystem, being significant actors in the network [189]. These pools contribute to the security, validity, and stability of the system by collectively mining blocks [190]. Furthermore, mining pools dominate the computing resources within the Bitcoin network, exerting substantial influence on network security and performance [191]. The economic implications of Bitcoin halving events have been explored, revealing their effects on the U.S. capital market and emphasizing the volatility and rapid fluctuations associated with this digital asset [192].

Bitcoin transactions are pseudonymous, meaning that while the identities of the participants are not directly revealed, their transactions are recorded on the blockchain and are publicly accessible. This transparency allows users to verify transactions and audit the network without revealing personal information.

Bitcoin faces several challenges, including scalability issues, high transaction fees during periods of high demand, and concerns about its environmental impact due to the energy-intensive nature of mining. Innovations such as the Lightning Network aim to address these challenges by enabling faster and cheaper transactions off-chain while maintaining the security of the Bitcoin network.

Bitcoin Mining

Bitcoin mining is a crucial process that underpins the operation of the Bitcoin network. It involves validating transactions, securing the blockchain, and introducing new bitcoins into circulation. This process is executed by specialized software and hardware, and it requires significant computational power. The following looks at how Bitcoin mining works [183]:

Mining is essentially the process of validating transactions and creating a new block on the Bitcoin blockchain. When transactions are conducted on the Bitcoin network, they are collected into a pool of pending transactions. Miners then select these transactions, group them into a block, and attempt to add this block to the blockchain. This process is critical for maintaining the integrity and security of the Bitcoin ledger.

At the core of mining is the concept of hashing. A hash is a fixed-length string of characters generated by a cryptographic algorithm that uniquely represents the data within a block. Miners work to find a hash that meets certain criteria defined by the Bitcoin network's difficulty target. The difficulty target is a number that dictates how hard it is to find a valid hash.

To find this hash, miners use a process called "proof-of-work." They start with the block data and a nonce—a variable number that miners change with each attempt. By modifying the nonce and hashing the block data repeatedly, miners generate different hash values. The goal is to produce a hash that is equal to or less than the network's target value. This process requires immense computational effort, as the correct nonce is not known in advance and must be discovered through trial and error.

The efficiency of mining is measured by hash rate, which is the number of hashes a miner can compute per second. High hash rates improve the likelihood of successfully finding a valid hash and earning the block reward. Miners use various types of hardware to achieve high hash rates, ranging from general-purpose computers to specialized devices known as Application-Specific Integrated Circuits (ASICs). ASICs are custom-built machines optimized specifically for mining, offering superior performance compared to general-purpose hardware.

Figure 7: Canaan AvalonMiner A10 Bitcoin Mining Machines. Canaan, CC BY-SA 4.0, via Wikimedia Commons.

Mining is a competitive process. Miners across the network are all working to solve the cryptographic puzzle and find the correct hash. The first miner to successfully find a valid hash broadcasts it to the network, and if other nodes agree that the hash is correct, the new block is added to the blockchain. This miner is then rewarded with newly minted bitcoins and transaction fees from the transactions included in the block.

Bitcoin's network adjusts the difficulty of mining approximately every two weeks, or every 2,016 blocks. This adjustment ensures that blocks are added to the blockchain roughly every 10 minutes, regardless of the total computing power of the network. If more miners join the network or if mining hardware becomes more efficient, the difficulty increases, requiring a longer string of zeroes in the hash to meet the target. Conversely, if miners leave the network or hardware becomes less efficient, the difficulty decreases.

Mining is an energy-intensive activity. The process consumes a significant amount of electricity due to the need to run mining hardware continuously at high speeds. As mining difficulty has increased over time, so has the power required to solve the cryptographic puzzles. This has led to the development of mining farms—large-scale operations with numerous mining machines working in parallel to increase hash rate and improve the chances of earning rewards.

Figure 8: Argo Blockchain Mirabel Bitcoin Mining Facility (2018). MikeBogosian, CC BY-SA 4.0, via Wikimedia Commons.

Given the competitive nature of mining and the substantial resources required, many individual miners join mining pools. A mining pool is a collective of miners who combine their computational power and share the rewards based on their contribution. This approach helps to stabilize earnings and reduces the variance associated with mining.

Figure 9: A Bitcoin mining farm. Marko Ahtisaari, CC BY 2.0, via Wikimedia Commons.

Bitcoin mining has evolved significantly since the cryptocurrency's inception, and this evolution has influenced the types of hardware and software used for mining. Initially, mining Bitcoin was feasible on personal computers due to lower network difficulty and competition. However, as Bitcoin gained popularity and more miners joined the network, the complexity of mining increased, requiring more specialized equipment [193].

When Bitcoin was first introduced in 2009, it was possible to mine using standard personal computers. At that time, the network difficulty was relatively low, and the computational power required to solve the cryptographic puzzles was within the reach of average home computers. Enthusiastic early adopters could effectively mine Bitcoin using their CPUs (central processing units), and later, GPUs (graphics processing units) as they became available. These GPUs, designed for handling parallel tasks in graphics rendering, proved to be more efficient than CPUs for mining due to their ability to process multiple computations simultaneously.

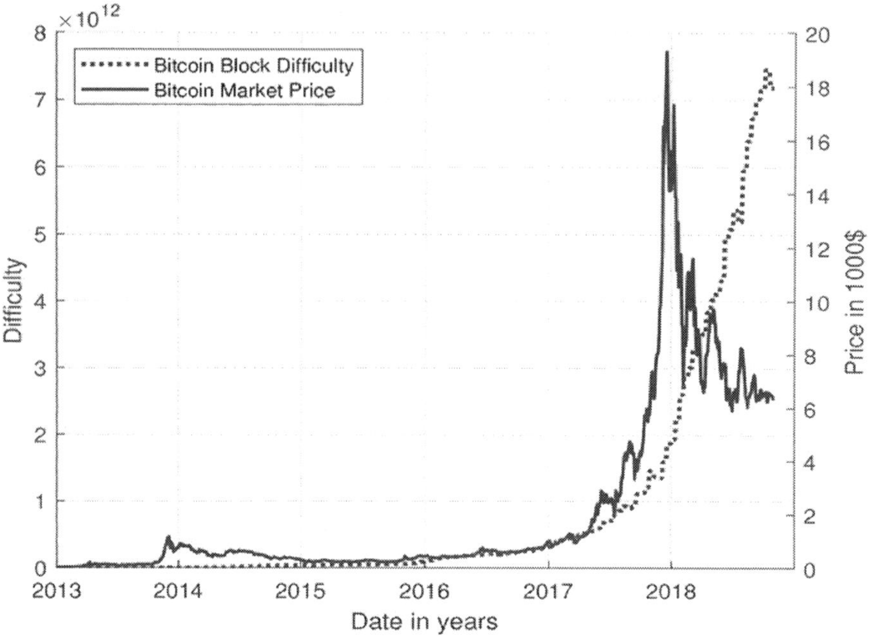

Figure 10: Development of the Bitcoin block difficulty and the market price from January 2013 until October 2018 (Blockchain Luxembourg S.A., 2018). Zade, Myklebost, Tzscheutschler and Wagner, CC BY-SA 4.0, via Wikimedia Commons.

As more individuals became interested in Bitcoin, the network's mining difficulty increased due to the growing number of participants. This increase in difficulty meant that mining on a personal computer was no longer competitive. The need for specialized hardware led to the development of Application-Specific Integrated Circuits (ASICs). ASICs are custom-built machines designed specifically for the purpose of mining cryptocurrencies. Unlike general-purpose hardware, ASICs are optimized to perform the specific calculations required for mining at much higher speeds and with greater efficiency.

The computational power required for mining has grown exponentially. As of May 15, 2024, the Bitcoin network generates approximately 600 quintillion hashes per second. This staggering number highlights the scale of competition within the network. In contrast, a typical modern personal computer, even with the latest hardware, can achieve a hashing rate of around 100 megahashes per second (100 million hashes per second). This comparison illustrates why mining on personal computers has become largely impractical for individual miners [193].

ASIC miners represent the cutting edge of mining technology. These devices can generate more than 400 trillion hashes per second, vastly outpacing the capabilities of personal computers and even GPUs. The efficiency of ASICs is a result of their specialized design, which is focused solely on performing the repetitive hashing calculations needed for mining. The significant hashing power of ASICs allows miners to compete effectively within the network and have a better chance of solving the cryptographic puzzle and earning rewards [193].

For individual miners using personal computers, the chances of successfully mining Bitcoin on their own are extremely low. The vast computational power of ASIC miners means that personal computers are no longer competitive in this arena. As a result, many individual miners have turned to mining pools, where they can combine their resources with other miners to increase their chances of solving the hash and sharing in the rewards. Mining pools distribute the work and the rewards among participants, making mining more accessible and profitable for those without access to specialized hardware [193].

The evolution of mining hardware from personal computers to ASICs reflects the broader changes in the Bitcoin mining landscape. As the network grew and the difficulty increased, the need for more efficient and powerful hardware became evident. Today, mining Bitcoin requires substantial investment in specialized equipment and infrastructure. The shift towards ASICs and mining farms demonstrates the increasing scale and professionalism of the mining industry, highlighting the challenges faced by individual miners and the growing importance of collective efforts in the mining process [193].

Options for Successful Bitcoin Mining

Bitcoin mining involves a range of hardware and software options, each with its own advantages and limitations. Here are the primary methods for successful mining [193]:

1. **Using Personal Computers and Mining Software**

Initially, Bitcoin mining was feasible with personal computers, but as the network grew, the complexity of mining increased. Today, while personal computers can still be used for mining, their efficiency is limited compared to specialized hardware. To enhance your chances of mining Bitcoin with a personal computer, you can join a mining pool. Mining pools are collaborations where multiple miners combine their computational power to increase the likelihood of solving a block. By pooling resources, miners share the rewards proportional to their contribution, making it a more practical option for individual miners.

Several software programs can facilitate mining on personal computers, such as CG-Miner and BFGMiner. These programs are compatible with Bitcoin software and provide various features for efficient mining. Popular mining pools include Foundry Digital, Antpool, F2Pool, ViaBTC, and Binance.com. Joining a mining pool allows you to leverage collective power and improve your chances of receiving Bitcoin rewards, though the rewards are divided among pool members according to their contribution.

1. **Purchasing Application Specific Integrated Circuits (ASICs)**

For those with substantial resources, investing in ASIC miners is a viable option. ASICs are specialized machines designed specifically for mining Bitcoin, offering far superior performance compared to personal computers. New ASIC miners generally cost around $10,000, though used ones may be available at lower prices. These machines can produce up to 400 trillion hashes per second, far surpassing the capabilities of personal computers, which typically generate around 100 megahashes per second (100 million).

However, owning and operating ASICs comes with significant costs beyond the initial purchase. Electricity consumption and cooling are major expenses, as ASICs require substantial power and generate a lot of heat. The competitive nature of mining means that even with ASICs, success is not guaranteed. Large mining operations, such as those run by firms like CleanSpark, which ordered 100,000 ASICs in April 2024, dominate the mining landscape. This level of investment illustrates the scale at which competitive mining operates.

Choosing the Right Mining Pool

If you decide to join a mining pool, it is crucial to research the pool's payout structure, fee policies, and overall reputation. Mining pools offer various payout schemes, such as Pay-Per-Share (PPS) or Proportional, each with different implications for how rewards are distributed. Pool fees, which typically range from 1% to 3%, can affect your overall earnings. Reading reviews and comparing different pools can help you select one that aligns with your mining strategy and maximizes your potential returns.

Here's a detailed look at some of the most popular mining pools:

Foundry Digital

Foundry Digital is a prominent mining pool known for its substantial infrastructure and influence in the cryptocurrency space. It operates under Foundry Services, a subsidiary of Digital Currency Group (DCG), which is a major player in the digital asset industry. Foundry Digital offers services that include mining pool operations, as well as hardware procurement and financial services for miners. The pool is designed to support both large-scale mining operations and smaller miners looking to leverage collective mining power. Foundry Digital is known for its transparent operations and competitive fee structures.

Antpool

Antpool, operated by Bitmain Technologies, is one of the largest and most well-known Bitcoin mining pools globally. Bitmain is a leading manufacturer of mining hardware, and Antpool benefits from the company's extensive expertise in mining technology. Antpool supports a wide range of mining algorithms and offers various payout methods, including Pay-Per-Share (PPS) and Pay-Per-Last-N-Shares (PPLNS). The pool has a reputation for reliability and provides miners with detailed statistics and analytics to track their mining performance. Antpool's significant market share and robust infrastructure make it a popular choice among miners.

F2Pool

F2Pool is another major player in the Bitcoin mining pool market and is known for its global presence. Founded in China, F2Pool has expanded its operations worldwide, making it accessible to miners in various regions. The pool supports multiple cryptocurrencies beyond Bitcoin, including Ethereum and Litecoin. F2Pool offers flexible payout options and maintains a reputation for consistent performance and reliability. It provides detailed reports and analytics to help miners optimize their operations and understand their earnings.

ViaBTC

ViaBTC is a mining pool that has gained popularity for its user-friendly interface and innovative features. Established in China, ViaBTC supports a variety of cryptocurrencies and offers several payout methods to accommodate different mining strategies. The pool is known for its transparent fee structure and user-focused approach, making it an attractive option for both novice and experienced miners. ViaBTC also provides comprehensive mining statistics and tools to help users monitor and manage their mining activities effectively.

Binance.com

Binance, one of the world's largest cryptocurrency exchanges, also operates a mining pool known as Binance Pool. Leveraging its extensive infrastructure and resources from the Binance exchange, Binance Pool provides a seamless experience for miners, including integration with Binance's trading platform. Binance Pool supports various cryptocurrencies and offers competitive fees and rewards. It is designed to cater to both individual miners and large-scale operations, providing detailed mining analytics and support. Binance Pool's integration with the Binance ecosystem offers additional advantages, such as easier conversion of mining rewards into other cryptocurrencies or fiat currencies.

Each of these mining pools—Foundry Digital, Antpool, F2Pool, ViaBTC, and Binance.com—offers unique features and benefits tailored to different types of miners. Foundry Digital is known for its extensive industry connections, Antpool for its massive infrastructure and reliable performance, F2Pool for its global reach and diverse cryptocurrency support, ViaBTC for its user-friendly design and innovative features, and Binance Pool for its integration with a major cryptocurrency exchange. Choosing the right mining pool depends on various factors, including fees, payout structures, geographical considerations, and the specific needs of the miner.

Using an ASIC for Bitcoin Mining

1. Understanding ASIC Mining

ASIC (Application-Specific Integrated Circuit) miners are specialized hardware designed specifically for the purpose of mining cryptocurrencies, particularly Bitcoin. Unlike general-purpose computers or GPUs (Graphics Processing Units), ASICs are engineered to perform a single type of task—in this case, solving the complex mathematical puzzles required for Bitcoin mining—much more efficiently. They offer high hash rates, meaning they can process vast numbers of hashes per second, which significantly increases the chances of successfully mining a block and earning rewards.

2. Choosing the Right ASIC Miner

When selecting an ASIC miner, consider factors such as hash rate, power consumption, and cost. The hash rate, measured in terahashes per second (TH/s), indicates how many hashes the machine can compute in one second. Higher hash rates typically mean better performance but come at the cost of higher power consumption. For instance, the Antminer S19 Pro offers a high hash rate but also requires substantial electricity to operate. Evaluate your budget, electricity rates, and space to determine the most suitable ASIC model for your mining operation.

3. Setting Up the Hardware

Once you have acquired an ASIC miner, the setup process involves several steps:

- **Unboxing and Assembly**: Carefully unpack the ASIC miner and assemble it according to the manufacturer's instructions. This usually involves attaching the power supply unit (PSU) and connecting the miner to a cooling system if necessary. Proper cooling is essential as ASIC miners generate a lot of heat during operation.

- **Connecting to Power and Internet**: Plug the ASIC miner into a power source and connect it to your router or modem using an Ethernet cable. Some models may support Wi-Fi, but a wired connection is generally preferred for stability and performance.

4. Configuring the Miner

To start mining, you need to configure the ASIC miner:

- **Accessing the Miner Interface**: Use a web browser to access the miner's control panel. The IP address of the miner can typically be found through your router's connected devices list or using network scanning tools.

- **Entering Pool Information**: Within the miner's interface, enter the details of your chosen mining pool. This includes the pool's URL, port number, and your worker credentials (username and password). Mining pools are groups of miners who share their computational power and rewards, which helps mitigate the variance in mining success.

- **Adjusting Settings**: Configure other settings such as the fan speed, overclocking options, and power limits if available. Some miners allow adjustments to optimize performance and energy consumption.

5. Monitoring and Maintenance

After configuration, the ASIC miner will start mining and contributing to the blockchain network. Regular monitoring and maintenance are crucial for optimal performance:

- **Monitoring Performance**: Use the miner's control panel to track its hash rate, temperature, and overall performance. Most mining software also provides real-time data and alerts for any issues.

- **Regular Maintenance**: Periodically clean the miner to remove dust and debris that can accumulate and affect cooling efficiency. Check connections and ensure that cooling systems are functioning correctly to prevent overheating.

- **Software Updates**: Keep the miner's firmware updated to ensure it operates efficiently and securely. Manufacturers often release updates to improve performance and address any vulnerabilities.

6. Evaluating Profitability

Running an ASIC miner involves several costs, primarily electricity and hardware expenses. To evaluate profitability, calculate the following:

- **Electricity Costs**: Multiply the miner's power consumption (in watts) by the cost per kilowatt-hour (kWh) of electricity in your area. This gives you the daily electricity cost.

- **Mining Rewards**: Determine the average number of bitcoins or fractions of bitcoins earned per day based on the miner's hash rate and current network difficulty. Use online mining calculators to estimate potential earnings and compare them to your electricity costs.

- **Initial Investment**: Factor in the cost of the ASIC hardware and any additional setup costs. Compare these expenses with your estimated mining rewards to gauge the return on investment (ROI).

Using a Mining Pool for Bitcoin Mining

1. Understanding Mining Pools

A mining pool is a collective of miners who combine their computational power to increase their chances of solving the complex mathematical puzzles required for Bitcoin mining. By pooling resources, members share the mining rewards based on their contributed computational effort. Mining pools address the challenge of mining difficulty and variability in reward distribution, making the process more predictable and stable compared to solo mining.

2. Choosing a Mining Pool

Selecting the right mining pool involves evaluating several key factors:

- **Reputation and Reliability**: Research pools with a strong track record for reliability and fairness. Look for pools with positive reviews from the mining community and transparent operation practices.

- **Pool Fees**: Mining pools typically charge a fee for their services, which is deducted from your share of the rewards. Fees usually range from 1% to 3% of the total earnings. Compare the fee structures of different pools to find one that aligns with your profitability goals.

- **Payment Structure**: Pools have different payment models, such as Pay-Per-Share (PPS), Pay-Per-Last-N-Shares (PPLNS), or Propotional (PROP). Each model has its own way of distributing rewards, so choose a pool with a payment method that suits your mining strategy and risk tolerance.

- **Server Location**: Opt for a pool with servers geographically close to your location to minimize latency and improve connection stability.

3. Joining a Mining Pool

Once you've selected a mining pool, follow these steps to join:

- **Register an Account**: Most mining pools require you to create an account on their website. Provide necessary information such as your email address and create a secure password.

- **Configure Mining Software**: Download and install mining software compatible with your hardware and the mining pool. Popular mining software includes CGMiner, BFGMiner, and NiceHash.

- **Enter Pool Information**: Open the mining software and enter the pool's server address, port number, and your account credentials (username and password). This information is usually provided by the mining pool when you register.

4. Configuring Your Miner

Configure your mining hardware to connect to the mining pool:

- **Access Miner's Interface**: Most ASIC miners have a web-based interface that allows you to input settings and configure connections. Access this interface using a web browser and the miner's IP address.

- **Enter Pool Details**: Input the pool's server address and port number into the miner's configuration settings. Ensure that you use the correct settings for the specific pool you've joined.

- **Set Worker Credentials**: Enter the worker credentials provided by the pool. Workers are individual mining devices or processes within the pool, and the credentials ensure that the pool can attribute your contributions correctly.

- **Optimize Settings**: Adjust settings such as fan speed, overclocking, and power limits to optimize your miner's performance. Some miners allow you to tweak these parameters to balance performance and energy consumption.

5. Monitoring and Managing Mining Activity

Once your miner is connected to the pool, continuous monitoring and management are essential:

- **Track Performance**: Use the pool's dashboard to monitor your mining performance, including hash rate, earnings, and uptime. Many pools provide real-time statistics and detailed reports on mining activity.

- **Check Payouts**: Regularly check your payout status and verify that rewards are being correctly distributed according to the pool's payment structure. Pools typically have minimum payout thresholds, and earnings are usually transferred to your wallet periodically.

- **Adjust Settings**: If you encounter issues such as reduced performance or connection problems, review and adjust your miner's settings. Ensure that your hardware is functioning correctly and that there are no network issues affecting your connection to the pool.

6. Evaluating Pool Performance

Periodically evaluate the performance of your mining pool to ensure it continues to meet your expectations:

- **Review Earnings**: Compare your earnings with other pools and analyse whether the pool's fee structure and payment model are advantageous for you.

- **Assess Pool Stability**: Ensure the pool maintains consistent uptime and does not experience frequent downtime or technical issues.
- **Consider Pool Changes**: If you find that your current pool is not meeting your needs, consider switching to another pool. Research and compare options based on fees, performance, and community feedback.

Chapter Four
Understanding Blockchain Technology

The Structure of a Blockchain

A blockchain is a decentralized, distributed ledger technology that underpins cryptocurrencies like Bitcoin. It functions as a sequential chain of blocks, each containing a set of transaction records. This structure is designed to ensure data integrity, security, and transparency in a decentralized network. Unlike traditional databases, where data is stored in tables, a blockchain organizes data into blocks, which are then linked together in a chronological order.

Components of a Block

Each block in a blockchain is composed of several key components:

- **Block Header**: This section contains metadata about the block, including:
  - **Version**: Indicates the version of the blockchain protocol used.
  - **Previous Block Hash**: The cryptographic hash of the previous block in the chain, which links the blocks together and ensures the integrity of the

blockchain.

- **Merkle Root**: A hash that represents the combined hash of all transactions within the block. It's derived from the Merkle tree, which is a data structure used to efficiently summarize and verify the integrity of large sets of data.
- **Timestamp**: Records the time when the block was created. This helps in maintaining the chronological order of the blocks.
- **Difficulty Target**: Specifies the difficulty level of the cryptographic puzzle that miners need to solve to validate the block.
- **Nonce**: A random number used in the mining process to find a hash that meets the difficulty target.

- **Transaction List**: Contains all the transactions included in the block. Each transaction records details such as the sender's and receiver's addresses, the amount transferred, and a unique transaction identifier. Transactions are verified, aggregated, and then included in the block.

Figure 11: Graphic of data fields in Bitcoin block chain. Simplified depiction: some fields are missing. Matthäus Wander, CC BY-SA 3.0, via Wikimedia Commons.

Linking Blocks

The linkage between blocks is a fundamental feature of blockchain technology. Each block contains a reference to the hash of the previous block. This creates a chain of blocks, with each block being dependent on its predecessor. The process ensures that any attempt to alter the information in a previous block would invalidate all subsequent blocks due to changes in their hashes. This immutability is a key security feature of blockchains, making tampering with past data highly impractical.

Mining and Block Creation

New blocks are created through a process called mining, which involves solving complex cryptographic puzzles. Miners compete to solve these puzzles by finding a nonce that, when hashed together with the block data, produces a hash that meets the network's difficulty target. The successful miner adds the new block to the blockchain and is rewarded with cryptocurrency. This process secures the network and ensures that blocks are added to the chain in a consistent and reliable manner.

Decentralization and Consensus

Blockchain technology relies on a decentralized network of nodes, each of which maintains a copy of the entire blockchain. Nodes collaborate to achieve consensus on the validity of new blocks and transactions. Different consensus mechanisms, such as Proof of Work (PoW) or Proof of Stake (PoS), are used to agree on which blocks are added to the blockchain. This decentralized approach eliminates the need for a central authority, reducing the risk of single points of failure and enhancing the system's resilience and security.

Security Features

The security of a blockchain is ensured through several features:

- **Cryptographic Hashing**: Each block contains a cryptographic hash of its contents. Any change in the block's data would result in a different hash, making unauthorized modifications detectable.

- **Consensus Mechanisms**: These mechanisms ensure that all nodes in the network agree on the validity of transactions and blocks. By requiring consensus, the blockchain prevents double-spending and other fraudulent activities.

- **Decentralization**: By distributing copies of the blockchain across many nodes, the network reduces the risk of data loss or tampering. Each node independently verifies the data, making it difficult for malicious actors to alter the blockchain without being detected.

Types of Blockchain Architecture

Public Blockchain

A public blockchain is an open and transparent network where anyone can participate. This means that anyone can join the network, access the blockchain data, and contribute to the validation of transactions. Public blockchains are designed to be decentralized, with no single entity having control over the network. Instead, all participants have equal access to the data and can engage in various activities such as reading, writing, and auditing the blockchain [194].

The core feature of a public blockchain is its transparency and accessibility. Since it operates on a decentralized model, no central authority manages the network, and all operations are conducted by the collective effort of its participants. This open nature ensures that the data recorded on the blockchain is immutable—once a transaction is validated and added to the blockchain, it cannot be altered or deleted. This immutability is a key aspect of public blockchains, contributing to their security and trustworthiness [194].

Advantages:

- **Decentralization and Transparency:** Public blockchains operate on a decentralized network where no single party controls the system. This promotes transparency, as all transactions and activities are visible to anyone who joins the network. The decentralized nature also encourages a broad range of participants to contribute to the network, enhancing its security and resilience.

- **Immutability:** Once data is added to a public blockchain, it is immutable. This means that it cannot be changed or tampered with. This characteristic ensures the integrity of the data and builds trust among users.

- **Rapid Transactions:** Public blockchains often support fast transactions, thanks to the collective processing power of the network participants. This can result in quicker confirmation times for transactions compared to traditional systems.

Disadvantages:

- **Cost:** Operating a public blockchain can be costly. Participants need to invest in hardware and software to run nodes, and the energy consumption for maintaining the network can be significant. These costs can be a barrier for some individuals or organizations.

- **Anonymity and Security Risks:** Since public blockchains do not require participants to provide identity verification, there is a risk of malicious actors exploiting the system. Anonymity can lead to security vulnerabilities and potential corruption if the network is targeted by attackers.

- **Processing Speed:** Public blockchains can face scalability issues, leading to slower processing speeds as the network grows. The need for consensus among a large number of nodes can slow down transaction processing times compared to centralized systems.

- **Integration Issues:** Integrating public blockchains with existing systems or applications can be challenging. The open and decentralized nature of public blockchains can create compatibility and interoperability issues with traditional systems.

Overall, public blockchains offer significant advantages in terms of decentralization, transparency, and immutability. However, they also face challenges related to cost, security, and scalability that need to be addressed as the technology evolves.

Private Blockchain

A private blockchain is a type of blockchain network where access is restricted and controlled by an authorized entity. Unlike public blockchains, where anyone can participate in the network, a private blockchain requires permission to join and interact with the system. This restriction is based on a permissioned model, meaning that only approved entities or users can access the network and its data [194].

In a private blockchain, the entity that controls the network, often called the administrator or consortium, manages all aspects of the blockchain's operation. This includes setting permissions, managing nodes, and controlling who can join the network and participate in transactions. The private blockchain operates with a higher level of confidentiality and control compared to public blockchains, as the transactions and data are only visible to those who are part of the network [194].

Advantages of Private Blockchains:

- **Controlled Access**: One of the key advantages of a private blockchain is the controlled access to the network. Participants must be invited and verified, ensuring that only authorized individuals or entities can join. This helps maintain a secure and trusted environment where transactions are known and verified by the participants.

- **Efficiency**: Private blockchains typically offer higher efficiency in terms of transaction speed and processing times. Since the network is limited to a predefined set of participants, the consensus mechanism can be optimized, reducing the time required to validate and process transactions.

- **Partially Immutable**: Although private blockchains are not as immutable as public ones, they still provide a level of data integrity and tamper resistance. The central authority or consortium overseeing the blockchain ensures that once transactions are recorded, they cannot be altered by unauthorized users.

Disadvantages of Private Blockchains:

- **Trust Issues**: A private blockchain relies heavily on the trustworthiness of the controlling entity. Since the network is permissioned and managed by a central authority or consortium, there is an inherent trust placed in this entity. This can be a drawback if the controlling entity is compromised or engages in dishonest behaviour, as the decentralized trust model of public blockchains is not present.

- **Scalability Concerns**: As the number of participants in a private blockchain increases, it can lead to scalability issues. The need to manage permissions and maintain network integrity becomes more complex with a larger number of users, which can potentially expose the network to security risks or performance bottlenecks.

- **Limited Transparency**: In a private blockchain, the visibility of data and transactions is restricted to authorized participants. While this can enhance privacy, it also limits the transparency and openness that public blockchains offer. This lack of transparency can be a disadvantage in scenarios where openness and accountability are critical.

Consortium Blockchain

A consortium blockchain represents a hybrid model between public and private blockchains. It is governed by a group of organizations or entities, rather than a single individual or entity, as in the case of private blockchains. This governance model ensures that the blockchain is permissioned, meaning that access to the network is restricted and controlled by the consortium's rules and agreements. Unlike a purely private blockchain, where control is centralized within a single organization, a consortium blockchain distributes authority and decision-making among multiple trusted parties [194].

In a consortium blockchain, participating organizations collaborate on the creation and maintenance of the blockchain, sharing the responsibility for its operation. This collaborative approach enhances the decentralization compared to a private blockchain, providing greater security and privacy for the network. The consortium establishes and enforces the rules for participation, including who can join the network and how data is accessed and managed. This structure allows for a more balanced and cooperative environment where all member organizations have an equal stake in the network's success [194].

One of the significant advantages of consortium blockchains is their ability to deliver faster transaction processing compared to public blockchains. This is because the number of participants is limited to a predefined group of organizations, reducing the complexity and overhead associated with consensus mechanisms. Additionally, consortium blockchains typically offer lower transaction costs, as the need for extensive computational resources is minimized compared to public blockchains that require high levels of mining power.

However, consortium blockchains are not without their challenges. The relationships among participating organizations can be unstable, especially if conflicts arise or if there are changes in the consortium's composition. This can affect the stability and continuity of the blockchain. Furthermore, consortium blockchains often lack a robust economic model, as they are typically not designed to handle large-scale public participation or incentivize users through tokenomics. Additionally, the flexibility of consortium blockchains may be limited due to the rigid governance structures and predefined rules set by the consortium members [194].

Overall, consortium blockchains offer a middle ground between the openness of public blockchains and the restricted nature of private blockchains, providing a controlled yet collaborative environment suitable for use cases that require a balance of privacy, security, and efficiency.

Core Components of Blockchain Architecture

Node: In blockchain architecture, a node is a critical participant in the network. Nodes are devices or systems that maintain a copy of the blockchain's distributed ledger and facilitate communication across the network. Each node stores a full or partial copy of the blockchain and contributes to the network by validating and relaying transactions and blocks. When a miner adds a new block to the blockchain, this block is broadcasted to all nodes in the network. Nodes then verify the block's validity before integrating it into their copy of the blockchain, ensuring consistency and integrity across the network [194].

Transactions: Transactions represent the core of blockchain operations. A transaction involves the transfer of assets or information between parties, often involving a contract or agreement. In the context of cryptocurrency, these assets are typically digital currencies. The blockchain network stores transaction data in a digital ledger, which is distributed across all nodes. Each transaction is recorded with a unique identifier and is linked to previous transactions to maintain an accurate and unalterable history. This decentralized storage prevents tampering and ensures transparency and traceability.

Block: A block in a blockchain functions similarly to a record in a ledger. Each block contains a collection of transactions that have been validated and grouped together. Blocks are linked to each other in a chain-like structure, with each block referencing the previous one via a cryptographic hash. This structure ensures that once a block is added to the chain, its data is secure and cannot be altered without affecting all subsequent blocks. Blocks are encrypted into a hash tree, which enhances security and integrity by creating a unique, fixed-length string of characters for each block based on its contents.

Chain: The chain is the continuous sequence of blocks linked together through their cryptographic hashes. Each block in the chain contains the hash of the previous block, forming a secure and tamper-evident chain of records. This chaining mechanism ensures that each block is firmly anchored to the previous one, creating a chronological and immutable ledger of all transactions. The integrity of the blockchain is maintained through this interconnected structure, which makes altering any single block without affecting the entire chain virtually impossible.

Miners: Miners play a crucial role in the blockchain ecosystem by validating transactions and creating new blocks. Mining involves solving complex mathematical puzzles to confirm and secure transactions, which requires significant computational power. Miners compete to solve these puzzles, and the first to succeed is rewarded with newly minted cryptocurrency and the right to add a new block to the blockchain. This process ensures that only legitimate transactions are recorded and that the blockchain remains secure and consistent.

Consensus: Consensus mechanisms are fundamental to blockchain technology, enabling a distributed network to agree on a single state of the blockchain. These mechanisms are designed to achieve agreement among nodes on the validity of transactions and the state of the ledger. Several consensus algorithms are used in blockchain systems, including [194]:

- **Proof of Work (PoW):** Requires nodes (miners) to perform computationally intensive work to validate transactions and create new blocks. The first node to solve the puzzle gets to add the block and is rewarded with cryptocurrency.
- **Proof of Stake (PoS):** Involves nodes (validators) who are chosen to create new blocks based on the amount of cryptocurrency they hold and are willing to "stake" as collateral. PoS is less energy-intensive than PoW.
- **Proof of Capacity (PoC):** Utilizes the available disk space of nodes to perform mining operations. Nodes with more storage capacity can store more potential solutions and are more likely to win the right to add new blocks.
- **Proof of Elapsed Time (PoET):** Relies on cryptographic proofs of elapsed time to reach consensus without extensive resource consumption. It ensures fairness by requiring nodes to wait for a randomly chosen period before they can propose a new block.

Blockchain Architecture Vs Database

Control: Blockchain is decentralized, meaning it lacks a central authority and has no single point of failure. Control is distributed among all network participants, who collectively maintain and validate the blockchain. In contrast, traditional databases are centralized, with a single entity or administrator having control over the database and its operations [194].

Operations: Blockchain primarily supports the insert operation, where new data is added in the form of transactions or blocks. Once data is added, it becomes a permanent part of the blockchain. Traditional databases, however, support a range of operations: Create, Read, Update, and Delete (CRUD). This flexibility allows for dynamic modifications to the data stored within a database.

Strength: Blockchain technology is robust due to its decentralized nature and cryptographic security measures. It is designed to resist tampering and ensure data integrity. Traditional databases, while generally secure, may not offer the same level of robustness against tampering, particularly if they are centralized and vulnerable to single points of failure.

Mutability: Blockchain is immutable, meaning once data is recorded in a block and added to the chain, it cannot be altered or deleted. This immutability ensures a permanent and transparent record of transactions. In contrast, databases are mutable, allowing data to be edited or deleted as needed, which can be useful for managing and correcting data but may also introduce risks of unauthorized changes.

Rights: In a blockchain, anyone with the necessary proof of work or stake can participate in writing new data to the blockchain, depending on the consensus mechanism used. This open-access nature contrasts with databases, where reading and writing permissions are controlled by a central authority or database administrator.

Speed: Blockchain transactions can be slower compared to traditional databases due to the time required for consensus mechanisms and network-wide validation. This delay ensures security and integrity but can impact performance. Databases, being centralized, can perform operations much faster, as they do not require extensive validation processes and can leverage direct access to data.

Layered Structure of Blockchain Architecture

Application Layer: The application layer is the topmost layer in blockchain architecture and is responsible for providing the end-user products and services that leverage blockchain technology. This layer hosts applications that directly interact with the blockchain network. Key components include smart contracts, decentralized applications (DApps), and user interfaces. Smart contracts are self-executing contracts with the terms of the agreement directly written into code. They automate processes and transactions without the need for intermediaries, functioning similarly to traditional contracts but in a digital and automated manner. Examples include "programs" in Solana or "chaincode" in Hyperledger [195].

Users typically interact with smart contracts through a front-end interface or API, rather than directly with the underlying code. For instance, Uniswap is a decentralized exchange that combines a user-friendly interface with smart contracts to enable seamless cryptocurrency trading. Although smart contracts are powerful, they are also potential targets for hackers due to their code's complexity. Any vulnerabilities in the code can be exploited, highlighting the importance of rigorous security audits and code reviews in this layer.

Services and Optional Components: This layer enhances the blockchain's core functionality with additional services and features that facilitate interaction, management, and governance. Services include Decentralized Autonomous Organizations (DAOs), which help manage and make decisions within decentralized networks like Arbitrum and Polygon [195]. DAOs are governed by smart contracts and provide a structured approach to decision-making and fund management.

Oracles are another critical service, bridging the gap between blockchain networks and real-world data. They provide external information, such as asset prices or weather conditions, that smart contracts need to execute accurately. Hot wallets, such as MetaMask or Kaikas, store cryptocurrencies and provide easy access for users to manage their assets. Blockchain monitors and explorers also play a vital role, allowing users to track blockchain health, detect potential issues, and ensure the network's security and efficiency [195].

Protocol (Consensus) Layer: The protocol layer establishes the rules and mechanisms for how nodes in the blockchain network achieve consensus, or agreement, on the current state of the blockchain. Consensus mechanisms are fundamental to maintaining the integrity and security of the blockchain. They include Proof of Work (PoW), where miners solve complex puzzles to validate transactions and create new blocks; Proof of Stake (PoS), which involves validators being chosen based on the amount of cryptocurrency they stake; and other consensus methods such as Proof of Capacity (PoC) and Proof of Elapsed Time (PoET) [195].

This layer also encompasses sidechains, which are separate blockchains running parallel to the main blockchain and interact with it. Sidechains help enhance the main blockchain's capabilities and scalability. Additionally, the protocol layer defines whether a blockchain is permissioned (restricted access) or permissionless (open to everyone). Propagation protocols ensure that new blocks and transactions are broadcasted and distributed efficiently across the network, while auditing mechanisms help protect against attacks and maintain consensus reliability [195].

Network Layer: The network layer facilitates the communication and interaction among nodes in the blockchain network. Nodes are responsible for discovering each other and maintaining connections to share data and transactions. The process typically starts with a node finding a bootnode, which helps it connect with other peers. Communication mechanisms and Trusted Execution Environments (TEEs) safeguard data integrity and security during transmission [195].

The network layer also includes tools like Recursive Length Prefix (RLP), used in networks like Ethereum to define how nodes locate, authenticate, and exchange information. Efficient node interaction and data propagation are critical to the network's performance and overall stability.

Data Layer: The data layer focuses on the storage, management, and encryption of blockchain data. It includes the blockchain itself—a linear sequence of blocks containing transaction data. The data layer's architecture varies among blockchains; for example, Bitcoin uses a straightforward transaction list, while Ethereum employs a more complex state trie to store contract state information.

Cryptographic primitives such as digital signatures, hash functions, and asymmetric encryption are integral to this layer, ensuring the security and confidentiality of data. Digital signatures validate transactions and prove ownership without disclosing private keys, while asymmetric encryption uses public-private key pairs to secure data. Hash functions, such as SHA-256, ensure that data remains unchanged and maintains its integrity [195].

Hardware/Infrastructure Layer: The hardware and infrastructure layer provides the physical and computational resources needed to support blockchain operations. This includes specialized mining equipment for Proof-of-Work blockchains, where miners use powerful GPUs or ASICs to solve puzzles and create new blocks. Validators in Proof-of-Stake systems also require robust infrastructure to maintain their nodes and participate in consensus [195].

Nodes come in various types: full nodes, which store the entire blockchain and participate in consensus; light nodes, which only store block summaries; and archive nodes, which retain comprehensive historical data from the genesis block. The infrastructure layer also includes virtual machines, such as the Ethereum Virtual Machine (EVM) or Avalanche Virtual Machine (AVM), which execute smart contracts and facilitate blockchain operations [195].

Overall, each layer of blockchain architecture plays a crucial role in ensuring the functionality, security, and efficiency of the blockchain network. The interplay between these layers supports a decentralized, secure, and transparent system for managing digital transactions and data.

The blockchain ecosystem is often described through a layered approach, where each layer serves distinct functions crucial for the operation and scalability of blockchain networks. Understanding the distinction between Layer 1 (L1) and Layer 2 (L2) solutions is essential for grasping how blockchains address scalability challenges and enhance performance.

Layer 1 Blockchains

Layer 1 blockchains, such as Ethereum and Bitcoin, are the foundational blockchains that operate independently and are self-sustaining. They represent the base layer of the blockchain architecture and incorporate all fundamental components, including nodes, blocks, and consensus mechanisms. L1 blockchains are typically public and permissionless, meaning that anyone can participate in the network without needing permission from a central authority. This openness and decentralization are key characteristics of L1 blockchains [195].

Despite their robustness, Layer 1 blockchains often face scalability limitations due to technical constraints. For example, Bitcoin's block size and the time between blocks restrict the number of transactions that can be processed per second. Ethereum also grapples with similar issues, which can lead to slower transaction speeds and higher fees during periods of high demand. To address these issues, some L1s have begun implementing native scaling solutions. Ethereum, for instance, is working on "sharding," a process that involves splitting the blockchain into smaller, more manageable pieces (shards) to improve throughput and reduce congestion [195].

Layer 2 Blockchains

Layer 2 solutions are designed to enhance the scalability of Layer 1 blockchains by providing higher throughput and lower transaction costs. Unlike L1 solutions, which operate as standalone blockchains, L2 solutions depend on the underlying L1 for security and fundamental operations but offer different mechanisms to increase efficiency. L2 solutions aim to address the limitations of L1s by implementing additional protocols and structures [195].

Several methods are used to achieve scaling in Layer 2 blockchains [195]:

- **State Channels**: These are private channels established between parties to conduct transactions off-chain. Only the final state of the channel is recorded on the main blockchain, which reduces the load on the primary network. An example of this is the Lightning Network for Bitcoin, which allows for rapid and low-cost transactions off the main blockchain.

- **Nested Blockchains**: These are secondary blockchains built on top of a primary blockchain. They operate with their own consensus mechanism but periodically settle final states on the Layer 1 blockchain. This method can improve scalability by offloading transaction processing from the main chain.

- **Rollups**: Rollups are solutions that bundle multiple transactions into a single batch and then submit them to the Layer 1 blockchain. This reduces the number of transactions that need to be processed directly on the main chain. Rollups can be of two types: Optimistic Rollups, which assume transactions are valid and only verify them if there is a dispute, and zk-Rollups, which use zero-knowledge proofs to validate transactions off-chain.

- **Sidechains**: These are separate blockchains that are linked to the main blockchain (Layer 1). They operate independently but are connected to the main chain through a two-way peg. Sidechains can offer specialized features and scalability improvements while maintaining a connection to the main network. Polygon is an example of a sidechain that enhances Ethereum's scalability.

In summary, Layer 1 blockchains are the core infrastructure of the blockchain network, providing fundamental operations and security. However, they often face scalability challenges that can affect performance and transaction costs. Layer 2 solutions address these limitations by offering scalable, efficient, and cost-effective methods to enhance the capabilities of Layer 1 blockchains. By understanding both layers and their respective solutions, users and developers can better appreciate how blockchain networks manage scalability and performance.

How Transactions are Processed

Blockchain transactions are processed through a series of steps that involve validating, recording, and securing the data on the blockchain. The process ensures that transactions are transparent, secure, and immutable. Here's a detailed look at how blockchain transactions are processed:

1. Transaction Creation

The process begins when a user initiates a transaction. This involves creating a digital message that details the transaction specifics, such as the amount of cryptocurrency being sent, the recipient's address, and other relevant data. The transaction request is digitally signed using the sender's private key, which ensures authenticity and integrity.

2. Broadcasting to the Network

Once a transaction is created, it is broadcasted to the blockchain network. This means the transaction data is sent to all nodes (computers) in the network. Nodes are responsible for maintaining a copy of the blockchain and verifying transactions. The transaction is then added to a pool of unconfirmed transactions, often referred to as the mempool.

3. Transaction Verification

Before a transaction can be added to the blockchain, it must be verified. Nodes in the network check the transaction against several criteria:

- **Digital Signature**: Nodes verify the digital signature to ensure the transaction was indeed signed by the holder of the private key associated with the sending address.
- **Balance Check**: Nodes check that the sender's account has sufficient funds to cover the transaction amount.
- **Double-Spending**: Nodes ensure that the same funds have not been spent in multiple transactions (i.e., preventing double-spending).

4. Transaction Selection

Miners (or validators, depending on the consensus mechanism) select transactions from the mempool to include in the next block. This selection process often involves prioritizing transactions based on the transaction fee offered by the sender. Higher fees incentivize miners to include a transaction more quickly.

5. Block Creation

Miners group selected transactions into a block. Along with transaction data, the block includes other information such as the previous block's hash, a timestamp, and a nonce (in Proof of Work systems). The nonce is a random number that miners must solve to create a valid block hash.

6. Consensus Mechanism

The block is then subjected to a consensus mechanism to validate its correctness. Different blockchains use different consensus mechanisms:

- **Proof of Work (PoW)**: Miners compete to solve a cryptographic puzzle. The first miner to solve the puzzle broadcasts the block to the network. Other nodes verify the solution, and if valid, the block is added to the blockchain.

- **Proof of Stake (PoS)**: Validators are chosen to propose and validate blocks based on the amount of cryptocurrency they hold and are willing to "stake" as collateral. The chosen validator adds the block to the blockchain.

- **Delegated Proof of Stake (DPoS)**: Token holders vote for delegates who are responsible for validating transactions and creating blocks.

7. Block Addition

Once a block is validated through the consensus mechanism, it is added to the blockchain. This involves linking it to the previous block through its hash, creating a continuous and unbroken chain of blocks. Each block contains a reference to the previous block, ensuring that any changes to earlier blocks would invalidate subsequent blocks.

8. Transaction Confirmation

After the block is added to the blockchain, all transactions within that block are considered confirmed. The confirmation process is incremental, with each new block added to the chain further confirming the transactions in the previous blocks. The more blocks added on top of a block containing a transaction, the more confirmations the transaction receives, making it increasingly secure and immutable.

9. Distribution and Updating

Once the block is added, it is distributed across the network. Each node updates its copy of the blockchain to include the new block and its transactions. This distributed nature ensures that all nodes have the same version of the blockchain and provides redundancy and security.

10. Transaction Completion

With the transaction confirmed and added to the blockchain, the transfer of assets is complete. The recipient's balance is updated, and the transaction details are now permanently recorded on the blockchain. This transparency allows anyone to view and verify the transaction history.

Consensus Mechanisms: Proof of Work vs. Proof of Stake

Consensus mechanisms are fundamental to the operation of blockchain networks, providing a method for achieving agreement among distributed nodes on the state of the blockchain. Two of the most commonly discussed consensus mechanisms are Proof of Work (PoW) and Proof of Stake (PoS). Each has its own unique characteristics, advantages, and challenges. Here's a detailed explanation of each:

Proof of Work (PoW)

Proof of Work (PoW) is one of the earliest and most widely known consensus mechanisms, prominently used by Bitcoin and several other cryptocurrencies. In PoW, miners compete to solve complex cryptographic puzzles to validate and add new transactions to the blockchain. This process involves significant computational effort and energy consumption.

Proof of Work (PoW) is the original consensus mechanism used in cryptocurrency networks, and it was first implemented by Bitcoin. It is a method designed to achieve agreement among distributed nodes in a blockchain network through a process that involves solving complex mathematical puzzles. This mechanism is fundamental to understanding how transactions are verified and blocks are added to the blockchain [196].

The concept behind Proof of Work is relatively straightforward: it requires participants, known as miners, to solve computationally intensive puzzles in order to validate transactions and add new blocks to the blockchain. These puzzles involve finding a specific hash that meets predefined criteria, a process which requires substantial processing power and time. The first miner to solve the puzzle broadcasts the solution to the network. Other nodes then verify the solution and the transactions within the new block. Once verified, the block is added to the blockchain, and the successful miner is rewarded with a predetermined amount of cryptocurrency, such as Bitcoin [196].

Proof of Work has several notable advantages, particularly for cryptocurrencies like Bitcoin. It provides a high level of security and decentralization, which are critical for maintaining the integrity of the blockchain. The competitive nature of mining ensures that no single entity can easily gain control of the network, as manipulating the blockchain would require an immense amount of computational power. As the value of a cryptocurrency increases, more miners are incentivized to participate, which enhances the network's overall security and robustness. This makes PoW a proven and effective method for maintaining a secure decentralized blockchain.

Despite its advantages, Proof of Work is not without its drawbacks. One of the primary concerns is its energy consumption. The process of solving complex puzzles requires significant computational resources, leading to high energy consumption and associated environmental impacts. This is particularly problematic for cryptocurrencies that generate a large volume of transactions, as the energy requirements can become unsustainable. For instance, networks like Ethereum, which supports smart contracts and decentralized applications, face challenges in scaling due to the limitations of PoW.

Given the energy-intensive nature of Proof of Work and its scalability issues, alternative consensus mechanisms have been developed. The most prominent of these is Proof of Stake (PoS). Unlike PoW, PoS does not require extensive computational work. Instead, it relies on validators who are chosen based on the amount of cryptocurrency they hold and are willing to "stake" as collateral. This method significantly reduces energy consumption and can improve scalability [196].

Process

1. **Puzzle Solving**: Miners use their computational power to solve a cryptographic puzzle, which involves finding a nonce (a random number) that, when hashed with the block's data, produces a hash that meets certain difficulty criteria. The difficulty of the puzzle is adjusted periodically to ensure that new blocks are added to the blockchain at a consistent rate.

2. **Block Creation**: The first miner to solve the puzzle broadcasts the newly created block to the network. Other nodes verify the solution and the block's transac-

tions to ensure they comply with network rules.

3. **Validation and Addition**: Once the block is verified by other nodes, it is added to the blockchain. The successful miner is rewarded with newly minted cryptocurrency (block reward) and transaction fees from the included transactions.

Advantages

- **Security**: PoW provides robust security due to the immense computational power required to solve the cryptographic puzzles. This makes it difficult for malicious actors to alter the blockchain.

- **Decentralization**: PoW helps maintain decentralization by allowing anyone with sufficient computational power to participate in mining and block validation.

Disadvantages

- **Energy Consumption**: PoW is energy-intensive, as it requires significant computational resources to solve puzzles. This has led to environmental concerns and high operational costs.

- **Scalability**: PoW can face scalability issues, as the process of solving puzzles and validating transactions can be slow, leading to longer transaction confirmation times and higher fees.

Proof of Stake (PoS)

Proof of Stake (PoS) is an alternative consensus mechanism designed to address some of the shortcomings of PoW. PoS relies on validators who are chosen based on the number of cryptocurrency tokens they hold and are willing to "stake" as collateral. It aims to achieve consensus with lower energy consumption and faster transaction processing.

Proof of Stake (PoS) is a consensus mechanism designed to address the limitations associated with Proof of Work (PoW), particularly in terms of scalability and energy consumption. Ethereum, a blockchain that initially used PoW, faced significant challenges as its decentralized finance (DeFi) protocols and other applications grew in popularity. This surge in activity led to high transaction fees and slower processing times. To overcome these issues, Ethereum began transitioning to a new system known as Ethereum 2.0, which utilizes PoS to improve efficiency and lower fees [196].

In a PoS system, validators play a crucial role in maintaining the blockchain. Instead of competing to solve complex mathematical puzzles as in PoW, validators in a PoS network are selected to add new transactions to the blockchain based on the amount of cryptocurrency they have staked. Staking involves committing a certain amount of the blockchain's native cryptocurrency as collateral to participate in the network's operations. The more cryptocurrency a validator stakes, and the longer they keep it staked, the higher their chances of being chosen to validate new transactions [196].

The selection process in PoS is influenced by both the quantity of cryptocurrency staked and the duration for which it has been staked. This system rewards validators who have the most "skin in the game," thereby incentivizing them to act honestly and maintain the integrity of the blockchain. Once a validator is selected, they propose a new block of transactions. Other validators then verify this block, and once a sufficient number of confirmations are made, the block is added to the blockchain.

Validators are rewarded with the blockchain's native cryptocurrency for their efforts. These rewards are distributed proportionally based on the amount of cryptocurrency each validator has staked. This incentivizes participation and helps maintain the network's security and operational efficiency.

Becoming a validator in a PoS system is not a trivial task. It requires a substantial amount of technical knowledge and a significant investment in cryptocurrency. For example, Ethereum 2.0 requires validators to stake a minimum of 32 ETH. Additionally, validators must maintain their nodes and ensure they do not validate fraudulent transactions, or they risk losing part of their staked cryptocurrency—a process known as "slashing."

For those who find the responsibilities of being a validator too demanding, there is an alternative: staking pools. In these pools, participants delegate their cryptocurrency to a pool operator who manages the validation process on their behalf. This allows individuals to earn rewards from staking without needing to manage their own validator node. Staking pools are often facilitated by exchanges and other platforms, making it accessible and straightforward for users to participate in staking and earn rewards [196].

Process

1. **Staking**: Validators lock up a certain amount of cryptocurrency (stake) as collateral. This stake represents their commitment to the network and is used to

secure the blockchain.

2. **Block Creation**: Validators are selected to create and validate new blocks based on various factors, including the amount of cryptocurrency staked and the length of time it has been staked. The selection process can vary between different PoS implementations, with some using randomization or a combination of factors.

3. **Validation and Reward**: Once a validator proposes a new block, other validators verify its transactions and ensure it complies with network rules. If the block is accepted, it is added to the blockchain, and the validator is rewarded with transaction fees or newly minted cryptocurrency.

Advantages

- **Energy Efficiency**: PoS requires significantly less energy compared to PoW, as it does not involve computationally intensive puzzle-solving. This makes it more environmentally friendly and cost-effective.

- **Scalability**: PoS can improve scalability by reducing transaction confirmation times and fees, as it does not rely on resource-intensive mining processes.

Disadvantages

- **Centralization Risk**: PoS can potentially lead to centralization, as validators with larger stakes have a higher chance of being selected to validate blocks. This could concentrate power in the hands of a few large stakeholders.

- **Security Concerns**: While PoS is generally considered secure, it can be vulnerable to attacks if a malicious actor accumulates a significant amount of stake. However, mechanisms like slashing (penalizing dishonest behavior) are often implemented to mitigate this risk.

Comparison and Use Cases

Proof of Work (PoW) is known for its high security and decentralization but struggles with energy efficiency and scalability. It is best suited for networks where security is paramount, and the energy cost can be justified, such as Bitcoin.

Proof of Stake (PoS) offers a more energy-efficient and scalable alternative to PoW. It is well-suited for networks seeking to balance security with lower operational costs and faster transaction processing. Examples of PoS implementations include Ethereum's transition to PoS and networks like Cardano and Tezos.

In summary, both Proof of Work and Proof of Stake are integral to the functioning of blockchain networks, each with its own strengths and weaknesses. PoW is celebrated for its security and decentralization, while PoS offers improvements in energy efficiency and scalability. The choice between them depends on the specific needs and goals of a blockchain network.

Energy Consumption and Economic Incentives in Proof of Work vs. Proof of Stake

Energy Consumption

One of the most significant distinctions between Proof of Work (PoW) and Proof of Stake (PoS) lies in their energy consumption. PoW, used by cryptocurrencies like Bitcoin, requires miners to solve complex mathematical puzzles to validate transactions and add new blocks to the blockchain. This process involves extensive computational effort, leading to high energy consumption. Each miner competes against others to solve the same puzzle, and the first to succeed gets to add the block to the blockchain and earn a reward. This competition among miners means that vast amounts of electrical power are expended on duplicate calculations, as each miner works independently and redundantly to solve the puzzle.

In contrast, PoS operates on a fundamentally different principle that significantly reduces energy requirements. PoS does not rely on solving mathematical puzzles. Instead, validators are chosen to create new blocks based on the amount of cryptocurrency they have staked and their staking duration. This means there is no competition among validators to solve the same puzzle. Instead, the system relies on the economic stake of validators to ensure network security. This shift from energy-intensive mining operations to staking-based validation allows PoS blockchains to function with considerably lower resource consumption, as the validation process does not require the same level of computational power.

Economic Consequences and Penalties

Both PoW and PoS mechanisms incorporate economic incentives and penalties to maintain network integrity and deter malicious behavior, but they do so in different ways.

In PoW, the economic penalty for submitting invalid information or blocks is the sunk cost of computational resources. Miners invest significant amounts of electricity, computational power, and time to solve puzzles and mine blocks. If a miner submits a block that is invalid or otherwise erroneous, the resources expended in solving the puzzle are wasted. This substantial investment in resources acts as a deterrent to malicious activity because the cost of submitting invalid blocks is high due to the energy and computational resources already consumed.

In PoS, the economic mechanism is built around the concept of staked funds. Validators in a PoS network are required to stake a certain amount of cryptocurrency as collateral. This staked amount serves as an economic incentive for validators to act in the network's best interest. If a validator attempts to validate a bad block or otherwise behaves maliciously, they risk having a portion of their staked funds "slashed." The slashing process involves forfeiting part of the staked cryptocurrency as a penalty. This penalty system creates a direct financial risk for validators, aligning their incentives with network security and integrity. The specifics of slashing, including how much of the staked funds can be forfeited, vary depending on the network's rules and protocols.

Security and Anonymity

Blockchain Security

Blockchain technology is renowned for its robust security features, which arise from its decentralized nature and cryptographic foundations. Unlike traditional centralized systems, where a single point of failure can compromise the entire system, blockchains distribute data across a network of nodes. Each node maintains a copy of the blockchain, ensuring that the system is resilient against attacks and failures. This decentralized approach significantly enhances security because there is no central authority or single point that can be targeted by malicious actors.

Key to blockchain security is the use of cryptographic techniques. Each block in the blockchain is linked to the previous block through a cryptographic hash function, creating a chain of blocks that are secure against tampering. A hash function takes an input (or 'message') and produces a fixed-size string of characters, which appears random.

Any change to the block's data will alter the hash value, making it apparent that tampering has occurred. This immutability ensures that once a block is added to the blockchain, it cannot be altered without changing all subsequent blocks, which requires consensus from the network.

Additionally, consensus mechanisms like Proof of Work (PoW) and Proof of Stake (PoS) further bolster security. In PoW, miners compete to solve complex puzzles, and the first to solve it gets to add a new block to the chain. This competition makes it computationally expensive and practically infeasible for any single entity to control the network or alter transactions. In PoS, validators are selected to create and verify blocks based on the amount of cryptocurrency they stake. This system aligns their incentives with network integrity, as they risk losing part of their staked funds if they act dishonestly.

Security Challenges in Blockchain

51% Attacks: One of the most significant security threats to blockchain networks is the 51% attack. In blockchain systems, transactions are verified and added to the blockchain by miners who solve complex mathematical puzzles. This process ensures that the blockchain remains secure and that the transactions are valid. However, if a single entity or a coalition of miners gains control of more than 50% of the network's total computational power, they can potentially undermine the blockchain's integrity. With such control, they could execute several malicious activities, including double-spending, which is the act of spending the same cryptocurrency more than once. Additionally, they could reverse recent transactions, causing a disruption in the blockchain's history and eroding trust in the network. The threat of 51% attacks is particularly concerning for smaller blockchains with less computational power, where achieving majority control might be more feasible [197].

Smart Contract Vulnerabilities: Smart contracts are a cornerstone of blockchain technology, particularly in platforms like Ethereum. These are self-executing contracts where the terms are written directly into code, allowing for automated and trustless transactions. While smart contracts offer significant benefits, including automation and reduced reliance on intermediaries, they are not without risks. Bugs or vulnerabilities in the smart contract code can lead to critical security breaches. For instance, if the code contains errors or logical flaws, it could be exploited by malicious actors to siphon off funds or manipulate the contract's execution. High-profile incidents, such as the DAO hack, have demonstrated how vulnerabilities in smart contracts can result in substantial financial losses and damage to the blockchain's reputation [197].

Privacy Concerns in Blockchain

Pseudonymity, Not Anonymity: Blockchain technology is often praised for its ability to provide privacy through pseudonymity. In a blockchain network, transactions are associated with digital addresses rather than directly linked to real-world identities. This offers a level of privacy compared to traditional financial systems. However, this pseudonymity does not equate to complete anonymity. Sophisticated analytical tools and techniques can trace and de-anonymize transactions, potentially linking them back to individuals. For instance, if a user's address is linked to their identity through external data sources or activities, their entire transaction history on the blockchain could be exposed. This challenge highlights the need for more robust privacy measures to protect users' identities [197].

Data Leakage: Blockchain's transparency, while essential for maintaining trust and preventing fraud, can also lead to unintended data leakage. Once information is recorded on a blockchain, it is immutable and visible to all participants in the network. This means that sensitive or confidential data, if not properly managed, becomes permanently accessible to anyone with access to the blockchain. For example, private business agreements or personal information, if recorded on a public blockchain, could be exposed and misused. This transparency paradox necessitates careful consideration of what data is stored on the blockchain and how privacy can be balanced with the need for openness [197].

Solutions in Development

Consensus Mechanisms: To address the risk of 51% attacks, alternative consensus mechanisms are being developed and implemented. Proof of Stake (PoS) and Delegated Proof of Stake (DPoS) are examples of these alternatives. In PoS, validators are chosen to create and validate new blocks based on the amount of cryptocurrency they hold and are willing to "stake" as collateral. This system makes it economically costly for any single entity to gain majority control, as they would need to own a significant portion of the total supply of the cryptocurrency. DPoS further refines this approach by allowing stakeholders to elect delegates who then handle block creation and validation. This not only reduces the risk of centralization but also improves scalability and efficiency [197].

Smart Contract Auditing: To mitigate vulnerabilities in smart contracts, there is a growing emphasis on rigorous auditing practices. Smart contract auditing involves a comprehensive review of the contract code by security experts to identify and rectify potential flaws before deployment. This process includes manual code reviews, automated testing, and simulations to ensure that the contract performs as intended and is resistant to attacks. By catching issues early, audits can prevent costly exploits and enhance the overall security of blockchain applications [197].

Privacy Coins: In response to privacy concerns, some blockchain projects have developed privacy-focused cryptocurrencies, known as privacy coins. Coins like Monero and Zcash incorporate advanced cryptographic techniques to enhance transaction privacy. Monero uses ring signatures and stealth addresses to obscure transaction details and improve user anonymity. Zcash, on the other hand, employs zk-SNARKs (zero-knowledge succinct non-interactive arguments of knowledge) to allow transactions to be verified without revealing any details about the sender, recipient, or transaction amount. These privacy enhancements aim to address the limitations of pseudonymity and provide users with greater control over their personal information [197].

Famous Blockchain Hacks and Their Implications

Mt. Gox: In 2014, Mt. Gox, once the largest Bitcoin exchange, faced a catastrophic security breach that led to the loss of approximately 850,000 Bitcoins, valued at around $450 million at the time. The incident was attributed to a combination of security vulnerabilities and poor management practices. This hack not only resulted in substantial financial losses for users but also raised serious concerns about the security of cryptocurrency exchanges and their ability to protect user assets. The fallout from the Mt. Gox incident highlighted the need for stronger security measures and regulatory oversight in the cryptocurrency exchange sector [197].

The DAO Hack: In 2016, a vulnerability in a smart contract on the Ethereum blockchain, known as The DAO, led to the theft of over 3.6 million Ether, worth more than $50 million at the time. The DAO was a decentralized venture capital fund built on Ethereum, and the exploit revealed critical flaws in its smart contract code. The hack prompted a controversial decision to execute a hard fork in the Ethereum blockchain to reverse the stolen funds and restore affected users. This event sparked a broader debate about the principles of blockchain immutability and the extent to which networks should intervene to correct security breaches. The DAO hack underscored the importance of smart contract security and the potential for significant consequences when vulnerabilities are exploited [197].

Blockchain Anonymity

Anonymity in blockchain systems is a nuanced concept. While blockchains offer privacy features, they do not guarantee complete anonymity. The extent of anonymity depends on the design of the blockchain and the privacy measures implemented.

Public blockchains like Bitcoin provide pseudonymity rather than true anonymity. In these networks, each participant is identified by a public key or address rather than personal information. Transactions are recorded on the blockchain and can be viewed by anyone with access to the network. While the identities behind these public keys are not explicitly known, the transaction history tied to each address is visible and permanent. This means that, with sufficient analysis, it is possible to trace transactions and potentially link them to real-world identities, especially when addresses are used in conjunction with identifiable information.

To address these privacy concerns, several blockchain projects implement additional privacy features. For example, privacy-focused cryptocurrencies like Monero and Zcash use advanced cryptographic techniques to enhance anonymity. Monero employs ring signatures and stealth addresses to obscure transaction details and enhance user privacy. Ring signatures mix a user's transaction with others, making it difficult to trace the source. Stealth addresses create unique addresses for each transaction, further obfuscating the recipient's identity. Zcash uses zk-SNARKs (zero-knowledge succinct non-interactive arguments of knowledge) to prove that transactions are valid without revealing any details about the sender, recipient, or transaction amount.

The rise of blockchain technology, cryptocurrencies, and Web3 has attracted significant attention from governments around the world. As these technologies become more integral to the global financial system, regulators are increasingly focused on how to manage and control their use, particularly with regard to anonymity and pseudonymity [198].

Government Scrutiny and Regulation

Governments have begun to scrutinize blockchain and cryptocurrency activities more closely, given their potential for both innovation and illicit use. This scrutiny has led to a growing body of regulations aimed at integrating these technologies into the traditional financial system. One of the central challenges for regulators is reconciling the inherent privacy and anonymity features of cryptocurrencies with the need for transparency and accountability. The focus has largely been on ensuring that cryptocurrencies are not used for illegal activities such as money laundering or terrorist financing [198].

Know Your Customer (KYC) and Anti-Money Laundering (AML) Regulations

A primary concern for regulators is enforcing Know Your Customer (KYC) and Anti-Money Laundering (AML) regulations. These regulations are designed to prevent illegal activities by requiring financial institutions to verify the identities of their customers and monitor transactions for suspicious activity. In the world of cryptocurrencies, this is particularly challenging due to the pseudonymous nature of many transactions. Cryptocurrencies like Bitcoin allow users to transact without revealing their real-world identities, which complicates the enforcement of KYC and AML regulations.

To address this challenge, regulators have focused on centralized exchanges (CEX), which act as intermediaries between traditional fiat currencies and cryptocurrencies. Centralized exchanges are easier to regulate because they operate under the control of specific entities that can be held accountable. These exchanges are required to implement KYC procedures and report suspicious activities, providing a level of oversight that is difficult to achieve with decentralized systems [198].

Challenges with Decentralized Exchanges (DEX)

Decentralized exchanges (DEX), on the other hand, present a significant challenge for regulation. DEXes operate without a central authority, which makes it difficult to enforce KYC and AML regulations. Users on DEXes interact directly with one another through smart contracts, bypassing traditional financial intermediaries. This decentralized nature means there is no central point of control or accountability, complicating efforts to monitor and regulate transactions [198].

Without an intermediary, regulators struggle to impose KYC checks or track transactions in a manner similar to what is done with CEXes. This lack of centralization means that DEXes can facilitate transactions in a more private and pseudonymous manner, further complicating regulatory efforts.

Implications for Privacy and Regulation

The tension between maintaining user privacy and enforcing regulatory requirements is a key issue in the ongoing development of blockchain and cryptocurrency regulations. While privacy is a core feature of many blockchain applications, governments are increasingly seeking ways to balance this with the need for financial transparency and security.

As regulators continue to develop and implement rules for the cryptocurrency space, the focus will likely remain on finding ways to incorporate effective KYC and AML measures without undermining the fundamental principles of decentralization and privacy. The evolution of regulatory frameworks will be crucial in shaping the future landscape of blockchain technology and its integration into the global financial system [198].

Chapter Five

Major Cryptocurrencies

Bitcoin has played a pivotal role in the development and popularization of cryptocurrencies, setting a precedent that has significantly shaped the industry. As the first decentralized cryptocurrency, Bitcoin introduced the concept of a peer-to-peer network where transactions could be conducted without the need for intermediaries like banks. Its innovative use of blockchain technology and the Proof of Work (PoW) consensus mechanism has inspired a wave of subsequent digital currencies. These alternative cryptocurrencies, or altcoins, often aim to build upon Bitcoin's foundational principles, offering various enhancements or specialized functionalities [199].

Over the years, Bitcoin has established itself as the de facto standard in the cryptocurrency space. It leads in terms of market capitalization, which refers to the total value of all its coins in circulation. Bitcoin's dominance is also evident in its widespread user base and overall popularity, making it a benchmark against which other cryptocurrencies are measured. Despite its leading position, Bitcoin is not the only cryptocurrency available; the rise of altcoins reflects the growing diversity within the digital currency ecosystem [199].

To understand the broader cryptocurrency landscape, it's essential to explore alternative cryptocurrencies that have emerged alongside Bitcoin. These altcoins often strive to address some of Bitcoin's limitations or to offer new features and improvements. For instance, Ethereum, one of the most notable altcoins, has introduced smart contracts and decentralized applications (dApps), which enable developers to build complex applications on its blockchain. This capability has paved the way for decentralized finance

(DeFi) systems, which seek to replicate and enhance traditional financial services in a decentralized manner [199].

Other altcoins have emerged with unique selling points, such as improved scalability or alternative consensus algorithms. For example, some cryptocurrencies are designed to handle more transactions per second than Bitcoin, which can alleviate congestion and reduce transaction fees. Additionally, while Bitcoin relies on Proof of Work (PoW) for consensus, several altcoins use different consensus mechanisms, such as Proof of Stake (PoS), which can offer greater energy efficiency and scalability [199].

Cryptocurrencies are digital or virtual currencies that use cryptographic techniques to secure transactions and control the creation of new units. They exist in the form of tokens or coins, which can be used for various purposes, from simple transactions to complex smart contracts. The term "cryptocurrency" underscores the use of cryptographic methods to ensure the security and integrity of the currency [199].

Altcoins, a term derived from "alternative coins," are cryptocurrencies that were developed as alternatives to Bitcoin. These altcoins often aim to present themselves as improved or modified versions of Bitcoin, offering new features or addressing specific issues. While they share the foundational principle of decentralization with Bitcoin, they may introduce different consensus mechanisms, enhance transaction speeds, or provide additional functionalities [199].

One of the core principles of cryptocurrencies is their commitment to decentralization. This feature means that cryptocurrencies are typically designed to operate independently of central authorities like governments or financial institutions. The decentralized nature of cryptocurrencies allows for peer-to-peer transactions, enhancing privacy and reducing the risk of government interference [199].

However, as cryptocurrencies have gained mainstream adoption, they have faced increased scrutiny from regulatory bodies. Governments around the world are exploring ways to regulate digital currencies to prevent illegal activities, ensure financial stability, and protect consumers. Despite these challenges, the foundational principle of decentralization remains a driving force behind the development and evolution of cryptocurrencies [199].

Bitcoin's pioneering role has set the stage for a diverse range of cryptocurrencies, each with its unique features and goals. While Bitcoin continues to lead the market, exploring alternative cryptocurrencies provides insight into the evolving landscape of digital finance and the potential innovations that could shape the future of blockchain technology.

When exploring the world of cryptocurrencies, you'll often encounter the term "altcoins," which stands for "alternative coins." This term broadly encompasses all cryptocurrencies other than Bitcoin. Bitcoin, launched in 2009, is considered the original cryptocurrency and has established itself as the standard against which other digital currencies are measured. In contrast, altcoins are designed to offer variations or improvements on Bitcoin's original model, utilizing different technological frameworks, consensus mechanisms, or use cases [200].

Mining-based coins are those that follow a similar process to Bitcoin for generating new units. This involves a process known as mining, where computer networks solve complex mathematical puzzles to validate and add transactions to the blockchain. The network rewards successful miners with new coins. This method is energy-intensive and has sparked significant debate over its environmental impact. Critics argue that the high energy consumption associated with mining-based coins, including Bitcoin, may outweigh their benefits, prompting a search for more energy-efficient alternatives [200].

Stablecoins are designed to address the volatility commonly associated with cryptocurrencies by pegging their value to a stable asset, typically a fiat currency like the U.S. dollar. This pegging mechanism aims to provide stability in price, making stablecoins a reliable medium of exchange and store of value. Two prominent examples are Tether (USDT) and USD Coin (USDC). These coins are especially useful in trading and financial applications where stable value is crucial, providing a bridge between the volatile world of cryptocurrencies and traditional fiat currencies [200].

Security tokens represent ownership of a real-world asset, often functioning similarly to traditional securities such as stocks or bonds but in a digital format. They can validate ownership and facilitate transactions involving assets like real estate, art, or shares in a company. The application of security tokens extends to verifying ownership and transferring rights in a secure, transparent manner, leveraging blockchain's immutable and decentralized nature. This concept allows for more efficient, automated, and accessible management of ownership rights and investments [200].

Memecoins are cryptocurrencies inspired by internet memes or popular culture phenomena. Dogecoin (DOGE) and Shiba Inu (SHIB) are notable examples. Despite their origins in humor or satire, memecoins can gain significant traction and value, often driven by social media buzz and endorsements from high-profile individuals. The value of these coins can be highly volatile and influenced by market sentiment rather than fundamental technological advancements or use cases. Memecoins highlight the unpredictable nature of the cryptocurrency market and the impact of public perception and media attention [200].

Types of Altcoins

In the cryptocurrency ecosystem, altcoins represent a broad category of digital assets beyond Bitcoin, each designed to serve different functions or address specific use cases. Understanding these distinctions can help users and investors navigate the diverse landscape of blockchain technology [199].

Cryptocurrencies

Cryptocurrencies are primarily designed to function as digital money, facilitating the transfer of value across decentralized networks. Unlike traditional currencies, which are controlled by central banks and governments, cryptocurrencies operate on a decentralized basis, leveraging blockchain technology to ensure security and transparency. Many altcoins fall into this category, aiming to provide an alternative to Bitcoin's role as a store of value and medium of exchange. These cryptocurrencies may offer enhanced features, such as faster transaction speeds or lower fees, to improve upon Bitcoin's limitations.

Tokens

Tokens, on the other hand, are blockchain-based assets that serve purposes beyond simple monetary transactions. Unlike cryptocurrencies, which operate as standalone digital currencies, tokens are often created and utilized within specific blockchain ecosystems. They can represent a stake in a project, access to a service, or even a unit of value tied to a particular asset.

Security Tokens

Security tokens are one category of blockchain-based tokens that are linked to the value of real-world assets, such as company shares or investment contracts. These tokens are often issued through Initial Coin Offerings (ICOs) and are regulated similarly to traditional securities. They offer a way to tokenize ownership stakes and provide a blockchain-based mechanism for trading and managing these assets.

Utility Tokens

Utility tokens are designed to provide access to a specific product or service within a blockchain network. For instance, tokens like Storj are used to facilitate decentralized file storage, while Namecoin provides a decentralized Domain Name System (DNS) for internet addresses. These tokens are integral to the functionality of their respective platforms, allowing users to interact with and benefit from the services offered.

Ethereum (ETH)

Ethereum, launched in 2015, is a decentralized software platform that enables the creation and execution of smart contracts and decentralized applications (dApps) without the need for intermediaries. Its native cryptocurrency, Ether (ETH), serves multiple purposes: as a medium of exchange, a payment for transaction fees and computational services within the Ethereum network, and an investment asset. Ethereum's transition to a Proof of Stake (PoS) consensus mechanism in 2022 was aimed at reducing its energy consumption, improving scalability, and enhancing network efficiency.

Tether (USDT)

Tether (USDT) is a prominent stablecoin designed to maintain a stable value by pegging its price to the U.S. dollar. Launched in 2014, Tether aims to provide a more stable digital currency that can be used for transactions and as a stable store of value within the cryptocurrency ecosystem. By holding reserves equal to the amount of USDT in circulation, Tether facilitates easier conversions between cryptocurrencies and fiat currencies while mitigating the volatility common in other digital assets.

XRP

XRP is the native cryptocurrency of the XRP Ledger, developed by Ripple in 2012. Unlike traditional consensus mechanisms such as Proof of Work or Proof of Stake, XRP employs the XRP Ledger Consensus Protocol, where transactions are verified by a network of servers and validators. This approach aims to provide faster transaction processing and lower fees compared to other cryptocurrencies. XRP has gained traction for its use in cross-border payments and financial transactions.

Binance Coin (BNB)

Initially an ERC-20 token on the Ethereum blockchain, Binance Coin (BNB) is now the native cryptocurrency of the Binance Chain. BNB is used to pay for trading fees on the Binance Exchange, offering users discounts when they use the token for transactions. Binance Coin also powers Binance's decentralized exchange and various other applications within the Binance ecosystem. Its transition to its own blockchain and adoption of a PoS consensus model highlights its evolution from a utility token to a more integrated component of the Binance network.

USD Coin (USDC)

USD Coin (USDC) is another stablecoin pegged to the U.S. dollar, launched in 2018 by the Centre Consortium, which includes Circle and Coinbase. USDC maintains its value by holding fiat reserves equal to its circulating supply, providing a regulated and stable digital asset for transactions and investments. As a regulated stablecoin, USDC benefits from transparency and compliance with U.S. financial regulations, enhancing its credibility and trustworthiness in the cryptocurrency market.

Cardano (ADA)

Cardano (ADA) is a blockchain platform developed with a research-driven approach, focusing on academic rigor and peer-reviewed research. Co-founded by Charles Hoskinson, one of Ethereum's co-founders, Cardano aims to provide a more scalable and secure blockchain ecosystem. Cardano's Ouroboros Proof of Stake (PoS) consensus mechanism is designed to enhance scalability and efficiency. The platform aspires to serve as a comprehensive financial operating system, addressing issues such as chain interoperability and legal contract tracing.

Solana (SOL)

Founded in 2017, Solana is a high-performance blockchain platform designed to support decentralized applications (dApps) and smart contracts. Known for its high transaction throughput and low fees, Solana positions itself as an "Ethereum killer" by offering faster and more cost-effective solutions for DeFi and NFT applications. The Solana blockchain's scalability and efficiency make it a competitive alternative to Ethereum, attracting significant attention and adoption in the blockchain space.

Dogecoin (DOGE)

Dogecoin (DOGE), initially created as a joke by software engineers Billy Markus and Jackson Palmer in 2013, has evolved into a widely recognized cryptocurrency. Known for its Shiba Inu mascot, Dogecoin gained popularity in 2021 due to its meme-driven culture and strong community support. Despite its origins as a novelty, Dogecoin has become accepted as a form of payment by some companies and has achieved significant market capitalization.

Shiba Inu (SHIB)

Shiba Inu (SHIB) is a memecoin inspired by Dogecoin, created with the intention of surpassing Dogecoin's success. Rising to prominence in 2021, Shiba Inu briefly exceeded Dogecoin's market capitalization, showcasing the influence of meme-driven cryptocurrencies in the market. While similar in theme to Dogecoin, Shiba Inu has carved out its niche as a memecoin with its own community and tokenomics.

TRON (TRX)

Launched in 2017 by the TRON Foundation, TRON aims to empower content creators through tokenization and decentralized applications. TRON acquired BitTorrent in 2018, integrating the file-sharing platform into its blockchain ecosystem. TRON's native token, TRX, is used for on-chain transactions and as a payment method on exchanges. Its consensus mechanism, designated proof-of-stake (DPoS), involves community voting to elect validators responsible for block creation and network maintenance.

Polygon (MATIC)

Polygon (MATIC) initially started as a layer-2 solution to address Ethereum's scalability issues but has evolved into a multi-chain ecosystem. It aims to enhance Ethereum's performance by facilitating interoperability between different blockchains. Polygon's architecture includes layers such as Ethereum, Heimdall, and Bor, which work together to improve transaction processing and scalability. Polygon supports a wide range of applications, including smart contracts, dApps, and NFTs, making it a versatile platform for developers.

Ethereum and Smart Contracts

Ethereum, introduced in 2015 by Vitalik Buterin, represents a significant advancement in blockchain technology compared to Bitcoin, offering a decentralized platform that not only supports digital currency transactions but also enables the creation and execution of smart contracts and decentralized applications (dApps) [201]. Unlike Bitcoin, which primarily serves as a decentralized digital currency, Ethereum's innovation lies in its versatility as a programmable blockchain that can accommodate a wide array of applications beyond simple monetary transfers [201].

Smart contracts are self-executing contracts with the terms of the agreement directly written into code. These contracts automatically enforce and execute the terms of an agreement when predefined conditions are met. The concept of smart contracts is integral to Ethereum's functionality, allowing developers to build and deploy complex decentralized applications. Unlike traditional contracts, which rely on intermediaries and can be subject to delays and disputes, smart contracts operate autonomously on the blockchain, ensuring transparency, efficiency, and trustlessness [202].

Smart contracts on Ethereum are written in programming languages like Solidity, which is specifically designed for this purpose. When a smart contract is deployed on the Ethereum blockchain, it is given a unique address and becomes immutable, meaning its code cannot be altered. This immutability guarantees that once the contract is live, its rules and logic remain consistent and enforceable. Transactions that trigger the contract's conditions are processed and recorded on the blockchain, ensuring all parties have access to the same information and reducing the risk of fraud.

The applications of smart contracts are vast and varied. They are used in decentralized finance (DeFi) to create financial instruments such as lending platforms, decentralized exchanges, and stablecoins. In the realm of non-fungible tokens (NFTs), smart contracts govern the creation, transfer, and trading of unique digital assets. Moreover, smart contracts are employed in supply chain management to enhance transparency and traceability, in voting systems to ensure integrity, and in various other sectors where automated, transparent, and secure execution of agreements is beneficial.

Ethereum's flexibility and support for smart contracts have been pivotal in the rise of decentralized finance (DeFi). DeFi represents a new paradigm in financial services, offering alternatives to traditional banking and financial systems through decentralized platforms and protocols. Ethereum's smart contracts enable the creation of a wide range of financial products and services, including decentralized lending, borrowing, trading, and insurance. This ecosystem operates without intermediaries, allowing for greater accessibility and innovation in financial services.

In September 2022, Ethereum underwent a significant upgrade known as "The Merge," transitioning from a Proof of Work (PoW) consensus mechanism to Proof of Stake (PoS). This shift aimed to improve the network's scalability, security, and energy efficiency. PoS replaces the resource-intensive mining process with a staking system where validators are chosen to create new blocks based on the amount of cryptocurrency they stake and their duration of staking. This transition is expected to reduce Ethereum's energy consumption significantly and enhance its capability to support a growing number of dApps and smart contracts.

Ethereum's introduction of smart contracts has revolutionized the blockchain space, providing a robust foundation for decentralized applications and innovative financial solutions. By enabling automated, transparent, and trustless execution of agreements, Ethereum has facilitated the growth of diverse applications ranging from DeFi to NFTs. Its ongoing developments and upgrades, including the transition to Proof of Stake, reflect the platform's commitment to scalability, security, and efficiency, ensuring its continued relevance and impact in the evolving landscape of blockchain technology.

Ethereum, the second-largest cryptocurrency by market capitalization, has experienced substantial growth recently. As of now, Ethereum's price stands at $1,591.12, and it boasts a market capitalization of approximately $191.3 billion [203]. This impressive valuation reflects Ethereum's growing influence and adoption within the cryptocurrency space. The ongoing Ethereum 2.0 upgrade has been pivotal in this ascent. The transition to a proof-of-stake (PoS) consensus mechanism, completed in 2022, marked a significant shift from the energy-intensive proof-of-work model. This transition aims to enhance the network's efficiency, scalability, and sustainability [203]. Currently, Ethereum is preparing for additional upgrades, including sharding—a method designed to improve transaction throughput by splitting the network into smaller, more manageable pieces. These advancements are expected to further bolster Ethereum's performance and appeal in the coming years.

Real-Life Use Cases of Ethereum

Ethereum's influence extends beyond its role as a cryptocurrency; it serves as a foundational platform for numerous real-world applications across various industries [203]:

- **Uniswap**: Uniswap is a prominent decentralized exchange (DEX) built on Ethereum. Unlike traditional exchanges, Uniswap operates without intermediaries, leveraging Ethereum's smart contract capabilities to facilitate direct trading of cryptocurrencies. This decentralized approach allows users to swap various crypto assets seamlessly, enhancing liquidity and accessibility within the crypto ecosystem.

- **Aave**: Aave is a decentralized lending platform that operates on the Ethereum network. It enables users to borrow and lend cryptocurrencies in a trustless and transparent manner. Through smart contracts, Aave eliminates the need for traditional financial intermediaries, offering a more efficient and accessible borrowing and lending experience.

- **OpenSea**: As one of the leading NFT marketplaces, OpenSea utilizes Ethereum to support the creation, buying, selling, and trading of non-fungible tokens (NFTs). Ethereum's smart contract functionality underpins OpenSea's operations, providing a secure and decentralized environment for NFT transactions and ensuring the authenticity and ownership of digital assets.

- **IBM**: IBM has incorporated Ethereum into its supply chain management solutions. The tech giant is developing a platform that enhances transparency and traceability within supply chains. By utilizing Ethereum's blockchain technology, IBM aims to provide a more secure and immutable record of transactions, improving efficiency and accountability in supply chain operations.

- **Estonia**: The Estonian government is at the forefront of blockchain adoption, using Ethereum to create a secure and tamper-proof voting system. This initiative aims to enhance the integrity and reliability of electoral processes by leveraging Ethereum's decentralized technology to safeguard against potential fraud and manipulation.

These diverse applications highlight Ethereum's versatility and its potential to drive innovation across various sectors, solidifying its position as a leading blockchain platform in the digital age.

Ripple and Cross-Border Payments

Ripple Labs, founded in 2012, has emerged as a significant player in the financial technology sector, particularly in the realm of cross-border payments. Ripple's primary objective is to enhance the efficiency and speed of international financial transactions by addressing some of the longstanding issues associated with traditional banking systems.

Ripple operates on a unique distributed ledger technology (DLT) that underpins its RippleNet network. Unlike conventional blockchain systems, RippleNet is designed to facilitate fast and secure transfers of money between financial institutions across borders. The core technology of RippleNet is the Ripple Protocol Consensus Algorithm (RPCA), which does not rely on mining but instead uses a consensus mechanism to validate transactions. This design choice enables Ripple to process transactions significantly faster than traditional systems.

Ripple's native digital asset, XRP, plays a crucial role in its ecosystem. XRP is used as a bridge currency in RippleNet's liquidity provisioning service, allowing for more efficient and cost-effective conversions between different fiat currencies. By using XRP as an intermediary, Ripple can reduce the need for pre-funded nostro accounts, which are typically required to maintain liquidity in various currencies. This approach helps financial institutions manage their liquidity more effectively and reduces the overall cost of cross-border transactions.

One of the primary advantages of Ripple's system is its speed. Traditional cross-border payments can take several days to process due to the involvement of multiple intermediaries and time zones. In contrast, RippleNet enables near-instantaneous settlement of transactions, typically within seconds. This rapid processing is particularly beneficial for businesses and individuals who need to transfer funds quickly and efficiently.

Another significant advantage is cost reduction. Ripple's technology eliminates many of the fees associated with traditional cross-border payments, such as those imposed by correspondent banks and intermediaries. By streamlining the process and using XRP for liquidity, Ripple helps lower transaction costs and provide more competitive exchange rates.

Ripple has garnered considerable attention and adoption from financial institutions worldwide. Major banks and payment service providers have integrated Ripple's technology into their systems to take advantage of its speed and cost-efficiency. The company has established partnerships with a growing number of financial institutions, further expanding its reach and influence in the cross-border payments space.

However, Ripple's journey has not been without challenges. The company has faced regulatory scrutiny, particularly from the U.S. Securities and Exchange Commission (SEC), regarding the classification of XRP as a security. These legal issues have impacted Ripple's operations and its partnerships with financial institutions. Despite these challenges, Ripple continues to innovate and work towards overcoming regulatory hurdles to solidify its position in the financial technology sector.

Looking ahead, Ripple aims to expand its network and continue enhancing its technology to address the evolving needs of the global financial system. As digital transformation accelerates in the financial industry, Ripple's focus on improving cross-border payment efficiency positions it as a key player in shaping the future of international finance.

RippleNet represents a significant departure from the traditional SWIFT network, which has long dominated international financial transactions. Unlike SWIFT, which involves multiple intermediaries and often results in lengthy transaction times and high costs, RippleNet streamlines the process by enabling direct, end-to-end transfers between banks. This reduction in intermediaries allows for near-instantaneous settlement of transactions, typically within minutes, and offers enhanced transparency throughout the process. By leveraging blockchain technology, RippleNet eliminates many of the traditional barriers and inefficiencies associated with cross-border payments [204].

Initially, RippleNet offered three distinct products: xCurrent, xRapid, and xVia. xCurrent served as a payment system tailored for banks, facilitating secure and efficient cross-border transactions. xRapid utilized XRP as a liquidity provider to enhance the speed and cost-effectiveness of currency exchanges. xVia allowed users to connect and integrate the previous two services through an application programming interface (API). In late 2019, Ripple unified these offerings under the RippleNet umbrella, focusing on expanding the use of XRP across its network [204].

A fundamental innovation of RippleNet is its use of the Interledger Protocol (ILP), a blockchain-based protocol designed for facilitating payments across different ledgers. Much like the TCP/IP protocol enables communication between different computer systems on the internet, ILP enables different financial ledgers to interact seamlessly. This interoperability reduces costs and accelerates transaction times by removing intermediaries and central control from the system. When a payment is initiated, RippleNet automatically identifies the most efficient route for transferring value, performs compliance assessments, and verifies accounts before executing the transaction [204].

During transactions, funds are securely held in escrow accounts on the participating banks' ledgers until the transaction is completed or fails based on predefined criteria. RippleNet ensures that transaction outcomes are promptly communicated to the involved banks, which then update their ledgers accordingly. This secure and transparent process enhances the reliability and efficiency of cross-border payments [204].

Ripple's journey began in early 2011 when computer engineers David Schwartz, Jed McCaleb, and Arthur Britto sought to create a more sustainable system for transferring value without relying on mining. By June 2012, they launched the XRP Ledger and subsequently founded the company OpenCoin, later renamed Ripple. The XRP Ledger, along with the Ripple Consensus Ledger and Ripple Transaction Protocol, laid the groundwork for RippleNet. Over the years, Ripple has evolved, with significant milestones including the launch of the XRPL Foundation in 2020, which aims to support the development and adoption of the XRP Ledger [204].

XRP, Ripple's native cryptocurrency, plays a crucial role in the Ripple ecosystem. It serves as a bridge currency, facilitating the exchange of various currencies with minimal transaction costs. XRP's key advantages include low transaction fees, rapid settlement times, and scalability, with the capacity to process up to 1,500 transactions per second. The token is pre-mined, meaning that most XRP tokens were created before the project's public launch. Ripple uses XRP to provide liquidity and support its network, although it has faced regulatory challenges from the U.S. Securities and Exchange Commission (SEC) regarding its classification and sale [204].

The XRP Ledger (XRPL) operates as an immutable and scalable blockchain, providing a permanent record of transactions secured by cryptographic key pairs. XRP transactions settle quickly, enabling efficient cross-border transfers and currency bridging. The XRPL is used for various applications, including its decentralized exchange (DEX), which has been operational since 2012 and allows for trading XRP and other cryptocurrencies with minimal fees. Recent developments, such as the integration of XRPL with decentralized finance (DeFi) platforms and cross-chain bridging solutions, further enhance its utility and market presence [204].

Litecoin and Faster Transactions

Litecoin, often referred to as the "silver to Bitcoin's gold," was introduced in 2011 by Charlie Lee as a decentralized digital currency aimed at providing faster and more efficient transactions compared to Bitcoin [205]. While Bitcoin was a pioneer in the cryptocurrency realm, Litecoin aimed to address some of Bitcoin's limitations, particularly in transaction speed and processing efficiency [205]. Despite sharing foundational technology and architecture with Bitcoin, Litecoin incorporates distinct features that enhance its performance [205].

The creation of Litecoin marked a significant development in the cryptocurrency landscape, offering users an alternative that mitigated some of the challenges of Bitcoin [205]. The emergence of Litecoin and other cryptocurrencies like Ethereum, Ripple, and Namecoin demonstrated the versatility and adaptability of blockchain technology, enabling the creation of diverse digital assets with unique characteristics [206]. These cryptocurrencies, including Litecoin, utilized blockchain technology to establish secure, transparent, and decentralized networks for transactions [206].

The comparison between Bitcoin and Litecoin highlights the evolution and diversification within the cryptocurrency ecosystem [205]. Litecoin's focus on improving transaction speed and efficiency showcases the iterative nature of cryptocurrency development, where new projects aim to enhance existing frameworks to offer improved functionalities [205]. The distinction between Bitcoin and Litecoin exemplifies the nuanced variations in design and objectives that characterize the multitude of cryptocurrencies available today [206].

The introduction of Litecoin and its subsequent adoption by users reflected a growing demand for digital currencies that could cater to specific user needs and preferences [205]. Litecoin's emphasis on faster transactions resonated with individuals seeking swift and cost-effective payment solutions in the digital realm [205]. This user-centric approach to cryptocurrency design contributed to Litecoin's popularity and established it as a significant player in the digital asset market [205].

Litecoin's integration of innovative features and its commitment to improving transaction speed and efficiency positioned it as a viable alternative to Bitcoin and other cryptocurrencies [205]. The success of Litecoin underscored the importance of continuous innovation and improvement in the cryptocurrency space to meet the evolving demands of users and adapt to technological advancements [205]. By focusing on enhancing transaction capabilities, Litecoin carved out a niche for itself in the competitive cryptocurrency market and demonstrated the value of targeted technological enhancements [205].

One of the primary innovations of Litecoin is its faster block generation time. Bitcoin's blockchain generates a new block approximately every 10 minutes, whereas Litecoin's blockchain produces a new block every 2.5 minutes. This reduction in block generation time significantly accelerates the rate at which transactions are confirmed and added to the blockchain. As a result, Litecoin can process transactions more quickly than Bitcoin, which is particularly beneficial for users seeking faster transaction confirmations and reduced waiting times.

The faster block generation time of Litecoin translates into increased transaction throughput. Since new blocks are added to the blockchain more frequently, Litecoin can handle a higher volume of transactions per second compared to Bitcoin. This increased capacity is crucial for maintaining network performance and ensuring that transactions are processed in a timely manner, especially during periods of high transaction demand. Litecoin's ability to manage a larger number of transactions per second makes it an attractive option for everyday transactions and microtransactions.

Another notable difference between Litecoin and Bitcoin is the hashing algorithm used in the mining process. While Bitcoin utilizes the SHA-256 hashing algorithm, Litecoin employs the Scrypt algorithm. Scrypt was designed to be more memory-intensive, which was intended to make mining more accessible to a broader range of participants and reduce the advantage of specialized hardware. By using Scrypt, Litecoin aimed to democratize the mining process and encourage greater participation in securing the network. However, as mining technology has advanced, even Scrypt-based mining has become increasingly competitive and specialized.

Litecoin also offers lower transaction fees compared to Bitcoin. The reduced fees are a result of its faster block generation time and higher transaction throughput. Lower fees make Litecoin an appealing choice for users who need to make frequent or smaller transactions, as it reduces the overall cost of using the network. The cost-effectiveness of Litecoin's transactions contributes to its utility as a practical payment method and further distinguishes it from Bitcoin.

Over the years, Litecoin has gained widespread adoption and is accepted by numerous merchants and businesses around the world. Its faster transaction times and lower fees make it a viable option for various use cases, including online payments, retail purchases, and cross-border transactions. Litecoin's reputation as a reliable and efficient cryptocurrency has led to its integration with various payment processors and financial platforms, further enhancing its accessibility and usability.

Litecoin has also been at the forefront of incorporating technological innovations. For instance, Litecoin was one of the first major cryptocurrencies to adopt the Segregated Witness (SegWit) protocol, which enhances the scalability and efficiency of the network by separating transaction data from the block. Litecoin has also been involved in experimenting with the Lightning Network, a second-layer scaling solution designed to facilitate faster and cheaper transactions by creating off-chain payment channels.

Emerging Cryptocurrencies and Altcoins

Emerging cryptocurrencies and altcoins represent the ever-expanding diversity of the crypto market, showcasing innovations and new use cases beyond the more established digital assets like Bitcoin and Ethereum.

Emerging cryptocurrencies are newly launched digital assets that have yet to establish themselves as major players in the market. They are often driven by innovative ideas, technology, or use cases that differentiate them from existing cryptocurrencies. Here are some key aspects of emerging cryptocurrencies:

- **Innovation and Technology**: Many emerging cryptocurrencies focus on solving specific problems or improving upon existing technologies. This can include faster transaction speeds, lower fees, enhanced privacy, or novel consensus mechanisms.

- **Initial Coin Offerings (ICOs) and Token Sales**: Emerging cryptocurrencies are often launched through ICOs, initial exchange offerings (IEOs), or other fundraising methods. These sales allow projects to raise capital while giving early investors an opportunity to acquire new tokens.

- **Market Volatility**: Due to their nascent stage, emerging cryptocurrencies can experience significant volatility. Their value can fluctuate widely based on market sentiment, technological developments, and adoption rates.

- **Regulatory Scrutiny**: New cryptocurrencies may face varying levels of regulatory scrutiny as they navigate legal and compliance challenges. The regulatory environment can impact their growth and acceptance.

- **Community and Development**: The success of emerging cryptocurrencies often depends on the strength of their community and development team. A strong, active community can drive adoption and support, while a skilled team can execute the project's vision effectively.

Altcoins, or alternative coins, are any cryptocurrencies other than Bitcoin. They encompass a wide range of digital assets with different features, use cases, and underlying technologies. Key characteristics of altcoins include:

- **Diverse Use Cases**: Altcoins often address specific niches or problems within the crypto ecosystem. For example, some focus on privacy (e.g., Monero), smart contracts (e.g., Ethereum), or decentralized finance (DeFi) (e.g., Aave).

- **Technology and Innovation**: Many altcoins leverage different blockchain technologies or consensus mechanisms. For instance, some use Proof of Stake (PoS) or Delegated Proof of Stake (DPoS) instead of Proof of Work (PoW).

- **Market Cap and Adoption**: Altcoins vary widely in terms of market capitalization and adoption. Some, like Ethereum and Binance Coin (BNB), have significant market caps and broad use cases, while others may be smaller and more speculative.

- **Competing with Bitcoin**: While Bitcoin remains the dominant cryptocurrency, altcoins offer alternative features or improvements. For example, Ethereum introduced smart contracts, while Litecoin focused on faster transaction times.

- **Investment Opportunities**: Altcoins can present investment opportunities for those looking to diversify their portfolios. However, they also come with risks, including higher volatility and uncertainty compared to Bitcoin.

Examples of Emerging Cryptocurrencies and Altcoins

- **Polkadot (DOT)**: Aims to enable interoperability between different blockchains, facilitating cross-chain transfers and communication.

- **Chainlink (LINK)**: Provides decentralized oracles that connect smart contracts with real-world data, enhancing their functionality.

- **Solana (SOL)**: Focuses on high-speed transactions and scalability, aiming to support a large number of transactions per second with low fees.

- **Avalanche (AVAX)**: Features a unique consensus mechanism and aims to offer high throughput and low latency for decentralized applications and custom blockchain networks.

- **Polygon (MATIC)**: Serves as a layer 2 scaling solution for Ethereum, aiming to reduce transaction fees and improve scalability.

Emerging cryptocurrencies and altcoins reflect the dynamic and innovative nature of the crypto space. They offer various solutions and improvements over existing technologies, contributing to the diversity and growth of the digital asset ecosystem.

The number of new cryptocurrencies introduced each year can vary significantly due to the rapidly evolving nature of the crypto industry. On average, hundreds of new cryptocurrencies and tokens are launched annually. This variability is influenced by several factors [207]:

- Market Trends: The emergence of new blockchain technologies, trends in decentralized finance (DeFi), non-fungible tokens (NFTs), and other innovations can lead to an influx of new projects [208].

- Initial Coin Offerings (ICOs) and Token Sales: During periods of high interest, many projects raise funds through ICOs, initial exchange offerings (IEOs), or other token sales, contributing to the creation of new cryptocurrencies [209].

- Development Platforms: Platforms like Ethereum, Binance Smart Chain, and others enable developers to create new tokens with relative ease, leading to a significant number of new projects [208].

- Market Conditions: In bullish market conditions, where cryptocurrency prices are rising and there is increased interest from investors, the number of new projects tends to increase. Conversely, during bearish periods or market downturns, the number of new launches may decrease [210].

- In 2021, for example, over 4,000 new cryptocurrencies were listed on various exchanges, reflecting a period of rapid growth and high interest in the crypto market [111]. Tracking the exact number of new cryptocurrencies introduced in any given year can be done through industry reports, cryptocurrency tracking websites, and blockchain analytics platforms [207].

- The introduction of numerous altcoins over the last decade highlights the continuous expansion of the cryptocurrency market [211]. This growth is further fuelled by the increasing importance of sentiment analysis from Twitter influencers in shaping cryptocurrency investments [209]. Additionally, the age and market capitalization of cryptocurrencies play a significant role in driving large price variations within the market [212].

- The interdependence among cryptocurrency portfolios, as evidenced by volatility spillovers, indicates the complex dynamics at play within the cryptocurrency ecosystem [213]. Furthermore, the application of machine learning in predicting cryptocurrency returns showcases the integration of cryptocurrencies within broader commodity markets [214].

The introduction of new cryptocurrencies each year is a multifaceted process influenced by market trends, fundraising mechanisms, development platforms, and overall market conditions. The cryptocurrency market's rapid evolution necessitates a deep understanding of these factors to navigate the complexities of this dynamic industry. Researchers continue to explore various aspects of cryptocurrency markets, from price prediction to market behavior, leveraging advanced methodologies such as machine learning and sentiment analysis to gain insights into this ever-changing landscape.

Tether (USDT)

Tether (USDT) is a prominent player in the cryptocurrency world, particularly within the category of stablecoins. Stablecoins are digital assets designed to maintain a stable value by pegging their worth to real-world assets, such as fiat currencies. In the case of Tether, its value is pegged directly to the U.S. dollar, meaning that one USDT is intended to always be equal to one U.S. dollar. This pegging mechanism aims to mitigate the volatility often associated with other cryptocurrencies, providing a stable store of value and making USDT a popular choice for various financial transactions [203].

Current Market Position

Tether holds a significant position in the cryptocurrency market, both in terms of its size and trading volume. As the largest stablecoin, it plays a crucial role in the crypto ecosystem. With a market capitalization of $83.22 billion as of September 27, 2023, Tether commands a substantial presence. Its trading volume is even more impressive, regularly exceeding $16.74 billion daily. This high trading volume underscores Tether's critical function as a liquidity provider and trading pair across various crypto exchanges, surpassing even many top cryptocurrencies in daily transaction activity [203].

Real-Life Use Cases of Tether (USDT)

Despite the challenges faced by the broader cryptocurrency market, including downturns like the crypto winter of 2022, Tether has proven resilient and continues to see widespread adoption. Here are several real-life use cases of Tether that highlight its versatility [203]:

- **Crypto Emporium**: Tether's stability and widespread acceptance make it a practical option for online shopping. Crypto Emporium, a digital marketplace, allows users to purchase a wide array of products—including electronics, jewelry, and luxury goods—using USDT. This integration demonstrates how stablecoins like Tether can bridge the gap between cryptocurrency and everyday consumer goods.

- **Travala.com**: For travel enthusiasts, Travala.com offers a unique use case for Tether. This travel booking platform accepts USDT for a variety of services, including flight bookings, hotel reservations, and bus tickets. By allowing transactions in Tether, Travala.com caters to the growing number of crypto users looking to leverage their digital assets for real-world travel experiences.

- **Bitrefill**: Tether is also used on Bitrefill, a platform that facilitates the topping up of mobile phone credit and the purchase of gift cards. This service makes it easy for users to use USDT to manage their mobile expenses and buy gift cards for various retailers, highlighting Tether's practicality for everyday transactions.

- **Coinsbee**: Similar to Bitrefill, Coinsbee allows users to purchase gift cards from well-known retailers using Tether. This platform provides another avenue for utilizing USDT in a practical manner, making it easier for crypto holders to convert their assets into usable retail credits.

- **Cloudbet**: Tether's application extends to the realm of online gaming and betting. Cloudbet, a platform offering sports betting and casino games, accepts USDT as a payment option. This use case underscores Tether's role in the online gaming industry, where its stability and liquidity make it an attractive choice for both players and operators.

Tether (USDT) plays a pivotal role in the cryptocurrency ecosystem by providing a stable, reliable digital asset that is widely adopted across various platforms. Its integration into everyday services and financial transactions demonstrates its versatility and utility in bridging the gap between digital currencies and real-world applications.

Binance Coin (BNB)

Binance Coin (BNB) is the native cryptocurrency of Binance, one of the largest and most influential cryptocurrency exchanges in the world. Launched in 2017, BNB initially served as a utility token for the Binance platform, offering users various benefits such as reduced trading fees. Over time, the use cases for BNB have expanded, integrating into multiple facets of the Binance ecosystem and beyond. As a utility token, BNB facilitates a range of functions including payment for transaction fees, participation in token sales, and more, making it a versatile asset within the crypto space [203].

Current Market Position of Binance Coin (BNB)

As of September 27, 2023, Binance Coin holds a significant position in the cryptocurrency market with a market capitalization of $32 billion. This impressive valuation reflects a substantial increase in value, with BNB having seen over a 1,000% rise over the past year [203]. The coin's strong market performance can be attributed to its broad utility within the Binance ecosystem and its growing adoption across various platforms. BNB's market capitalization places it among the top cryptocurrencies, highlighting its relevance and influence in the crypto world.

Real-Life Use Cases of Binance Coin (BNB)

- **Crypto.com**: BNB's utility extends beyond the Binance platform to other crypto services. On Crypto.com, a prominent cryptocurrency trading and lending platform, users can settle credit card bills using BNB. This functionality illustrates how BNB can be utilized for everyday transactions, adding practical value to the coin beyond its role in the Binance ecosystem.

- **Shopify Integration**: Shopify, a leading e-commerce platform, has embraced cryptocurrencies by integrating various payment options. One notable integration is the Binance Pay plugin, which allows businesses on Shopify to accept payments in BNB. This integration broadens the use cases for BNB, making it a viable payment option for online transactions and demonstrating its acceptance in the wider e-commerce ecosystem.

- **Binance Launchpad**: Binance Launchpad is a platform for launching new cryptocurrency projects. To participate in token sales through Binance Launchpad, users must hold and use BNB. This requirement positions BNB as a gateway to investment opportunities in emerging crypto projects, providing holders with early access to promising ventures and enhancing the coin's appeal to investors.

- **Binance NFT Marketplace**: The Binance NFT Marketplace is another area where BNB plays a crucial role. Users can utilize BNB to pay transaction fees associated with buying, selling, or trading non-fungible tokens (NFTs) on this platform. The integration of BNB in the NFT marketplace underscores its utility in various types of digital transactions and reinforces its position as a key asset within the Binance ecosystem.

In summary, Binance Coin (BNB) has evolved from a simple utility token into a multifaceted asset with a range of practical applications. Its role in reducing trading fees, facilitating payments, and enabling participation in token sales demonstrates its versatility and growing significance. With a robust market position and diverse real-life use cases, BNB continues to be a prominent player in the cryptocurrency space.

U.S. Dollar Coin (USDC)

The U.S. Dollar Coin, or USDC, is a prominent stablecoin in the cryptocurrency landscape. Like other stablecoins such as Tether (USDT), USDC is designed to maintain a value equivalent to one U.S. dollar, making it a reliable asset for minimizing volatility within the crypto market. By pegging its value to the U.S. dollar, USDC aims to provide a stable medium of exchange and store of value, distinguishing itself from more volatile cryptocurrencies [203].

Current Market Position

As of September 27, 2023, USDC is the second-largest stablecoin by market capitalization, holding a substantial $25 billion in value [203]. This positions it as a key player in the stablecoin sector, although it has faced challenges during market downturns, such as the "crypto winter" of 2022. Despite these setbacks, USDC has demonstrated resilience and recovery, reflecting its role as a critical component in the cryptocurrency ecosystem.

Real-Life Use Cases of USDC

USDC's stability and broad acceptance have led to various practical applications across different platforms and services [203]:

- **Visa and Mastercard**: Major payment networks like Visa and Mastercard have integrated cryptocurrency payments into their systems. Both allow merchants to accept payments in USDC, bridging traditional finance with the evolving world of digital currencies. This integration helps facilitate smoother transactions and greater adoption of stablecoins in everyday commerce.

- **Circle Pay**: Circle, the issuer of USDC, offers Circle Pay, a service that enables users to send and receive USDC globally at no cost. This service supports cross-border transactions, making it easier for individuals to handle digital payments without incurring traditional banking fees.

- **Coinbase Card**: For those looking to use their USDC holdings in everyday transactions, the Coinbase Card provides a practical solution. This card allows users to spend USDC at any merchant that accepts Visa payments, seamlessly converting crypto holdings into fiat currency for various purchases.

USDC's stability, combined with its growing real-world applications, underscores its importance in the cryptocurrency market. By offering a reliable and widely accepted stablecoin, USDC continues to play a crucial role in bridging the gap between traditional finance and the digital currency world.

Cardano (ADA)

Cardano (ADA) stands out in the cryptocurrency landscape for its unique approach to development and its emphasis on scientific research and peer-reviewed methodologies. Launched in 2017 by Charles Hoskinson, one of the co-founders of Ethereum, Cardano aims to provide a secure and scalable platform for developing smart contracts and decentralized applications (DApps). Its foundational goal is to create a more balanced and sustainable ecosystem for the blockchain industry by integrating academic research and a structured development process into its framework [203].

Current Market Position

As of September 27, 2023, Cardano holds a prominent position in the cryptocurrency market with a market capitalization of $8.6 billion. Although it faced significant challenges during the 2022 market downturn, Cardano has shown signs of recovery. This resilience highlights its role as a major player in the crypto space, offering investors and developers a robust platform for various blockchain applications.

Real-Life Use Cases of Cardano (ADA)

- Cardano's real-world applications underscore its versatility and potential to address significant global challenges. Here are some key use cases:

- **Identity Management**: Cardano has been utilized in identity management projects to enhance security and accessibility. A notable example is the Ethiopian government's initiative to use Cardano to create digital identities for five million students. This project aims to streamline identity verification and management, providing a secure and scalable solution for tracking educational and personal information.

- **Supply Chain Management**: In the realm of supply chain management, Cardano's Atala PRISM project demonstrates its capability to enhance transparency and traceability. This initiative uses Cardano's blockchain technology to track the supply chain of Georgian wine, ensuring that all stages of production and distribution are recorded and verified. This application of Cardano helps to improve the integrity and efficiency of supply chain operations.

- **Voting Systems**: Cardano is also being leveraged to develop secure and transparent voting systems. The Aeternity project, which operates on the Cardano blockchain, is working on a voting system intended for use in the 2023 Nigerian elections. This system aims to provide a tamper-proof method for casting and counting votes, enhancing electoral integrity and public trust in the voting process.

- **Decentralized Financial Services (DeFi)**: In the decentralized finance sector, Cardano is making strides through platforms like SundaeSwap. This DeFi platform, built on the Cardano blockchain, allows users to trade Cardano and other cryptocurrencies in a secure and decentralized manner. SundaeSwap exemplifies Cardano's commitment to expanding the capabilities of DeFi and providing users with innovative financial services.

Overall, Cardano's emphasis on scientific research and its diverse real-life use cases position it as a forward-thinking cryptocurrency with the potential to address various global issues through blockchain technology.

Dogecoin (DOGE)

Dogecoin (DOGE) stands out in the cryptocurrency world as a unique and influential memecoin. Launched in December 2013 by software engineers Billy Markus and Jackson Palmer, Dogecoin was initially conceived as a joke. It draws its inspiration from the popular "Doge" meme, which features a Shiba Inu dog along with humorous, multi-coloured text in broken English. Despite its playful beginnings, Dogecoin has evolved into a significant player in the cryptocurrency market, gaining considerable attention and value, particularly due to high-profile endorsements and viral internet culture [203].

Current Market Position

As of September 27, 2023, Dogecoin holds a market capitalization of approximately $8.56 billion, reflecting its substantial presence in the crypto space. The total supply of Dogecoin tokens exceeds 141 billion, and notably, Dogecoin does not have a fixed maximum supply [203]. This continuous issuance contributes to its inflationary nature, distinguishing it from many other cryptocurrencies that have capped supplies. Despite this, Dogecoin's popularity has remained robust, bolstered by its strong community and prominent figures endorsing it.

Real-Life Use Cases of DOGE

Dogecoin has transcended its origins as a meme to become a practical cryptocurrency with real-world applications. Here are some notable use cases [203]:

- **Tesla**: In January 2022, Tesla, the electric vehicle company led by Elon Musk, began accepting Dogecoin as a payment method. Musk's public affection for Dogecoin significantly contributed to its rise in popularity and mainstream acceptance. This move demonstrated Dogecoin's potential utility beyond mere speculation, integrating it into everyday transactions for Tesla merchandise.

- **AMC Theatres**: AMC Theatres, a leading cinema chain, announced in October 2021 that it would accept Dogecoin for online gift card purchases. This decision expanded the utility of Dogecoin, allowing fans of the cryptocurrency to use it for entertainment-related transactions and highlighting its growing acceptance in various consumer sectors.

- **AirBaltic**: In January 2022, Latvian airline AirBaltic became one of the first airlines to accept Dogecoin for flight bookings. By incorporating Dogecoin into its payment options, AirBaltic embraced the evolving financial landscape and catered to a growing demographic of crypto enthusiasts.

- **Sheetz**: In April 2022, Sheetz, a well-known convenience store chain, started accepting Dogecoin for transactions. This move was part of Sheetz's broader strategy to integrate cryptocurrencies into its payment systems, reflecting the increasing mainstream acceptance of digital currencies.

Dogecoin's transition from a novelty to a functional cryptocurrency underscores its significant impact and acceptance within the broader financial ecosystem. Its real-life use cases, driven by endorsements from influential figures and adoption by various businesses, highlight its growing relevance and potential as a digital asset.

Solana (SOL)

Solana (SOL) is a blockchain platform designed to make decentralized finance (DeFi) more accessible and scalable. Launched in March 2020 by the Solana Foundation, Solana aims to address the limitations of existing blockchain networks by significantly enhancing transaction speed and throughput. This is achieved through its innovative consensus mechanisms: Proof of History (PoH) and Proof of Stake (PoS) [203].

Current Market Position

As of September 27, 2023, Solana (SOL) stands out in the cryptocurrency market with a market capitalization of $7.96 billion, securing its position as one of the leading cryptocurrencies globally [203]. The total supply of SOL tokens is capped at 500 million, reflecting its substantial role in the ecosystem. Despite facing challenges like market volatility and technical hurdles, Solana has managed to maintain a significant presence and continues to be a prominent player in the blockchain space.

Real-Life Use Cases of Solana

Solana's real-world applications highlight its growing influence and utility within the crypto industry [203]:

- **Solana Pay:** Solana Pay is a payment processing solution designed to facilitate fast and low-cost transactions using SOL. This platform enables businesses and e-commerce platforms, such as Shopify, to accept SOL as a payment method. By integrating Solana Pay, merchants can benefit from the high-speed and low-fee transactions characteristic of the Solana network, enhancing the overall efficiency of digital payments.

- **DeFi on Solana's Fast Track:** Solana's high-performance network has attracted numerous DeFi projects, including Raydium and Serum. These platforms leverage Solana's capabilities to offer users a range of financial services. For instance, Raydium provides liquidity and automated market-making services, while Serum operates as a decentralized exchange with advanced trading features. Both platforms benefit from Solana's ability to handle high transaction volumes and deliver quick processing times, making them attractive options for users looking to lend, borrow, or trade cryptocurrencies.

Solana's focus on scalability through its unique consensus mechanisms and its practical applications in payment processing and DeFi services demonstrate its significant impact on the cryptocurrency landscape. Its ability to handle large volumes of transactions efficiently makes it a key player in the evolving world of decentralized finance [203].

TRON (TRX)

TRON is a blockchain-based platform founded by Justin Sun in 2017 with the aim of revolutionizing digital content sharing. Its mission is to create a decentralized digital world where users can share content freely without the need for intermediaries. To achieve this vision, TRON employs a Delegated Proof of Stake (DPoS) consensus mechanism. This system allows for high scalability and efficiency, as it relies on a smaller number of nodes to validate transactions, thereby speeding up the process and reducing costs compared to traditional Proof of Work (PoW) systems [203].

Current Market Position

As of September 17, 2023, TRON (TRX) stands as a significant player in the cryptocurrency landscape with a market capitalization of approximately $7.5 billion. This positions it as one of the top cryptocurrencies globally [203]. The network boasts over 98 million active accounts, reflecting its widespread adoption and utilization. TRON's robust market position is bolstered by its focus on creating a decentralized internet and its effective use of blockchain technology to facilitate this goal.

Real-Life Use Cases of TRX

TRON's utility extends beyond its technological innovations, as it has integrated into various real-life applications and partnerships [203]:

- **BitTorrent**: TRON's acquisition of BitTorrent in 2018 allowed it to leverage the popular file-sharing platform to integrate TRX tokens. BitTorrent users can now earn TRX tokens as rewards for sharing files on the network, thereby incentivizing participation and enhancing the platform's utility.

- **Samsung**: As a global leader in technology, Samsung has incorporated support for TRX tokens into its Galaxy smartphones. This integration allows users to store and manage their TRX holdings directly from their devices, reflecting Samsung's commitment to supporting emerging technologies and cryptocurrencies.

- **JustLend**: TRON's presence in the decentralized finance (DeFi) space is exemplified by JustLend, a decentralized lending platform that operates on the TRON blockchain. Users can lend and borrow assets using TRX tokens, taking advantage of the platform's decentralized nature to facilitate peer-to-peer transactions and financial services without intermediaries.

Overall, TRON's commitment to decentralization, combined with its strategic partnerships and practical applications, underscores its role as a prominent and influential cryptocurrency in the global market.

Avalanche (AVAX)

Avalanche (AVAX) is a prominent player in the cryptocurrency market, distinguished by its innovative approach to blockchain consensus. Launched by Ava Labs, Avalanche stands out due to its unique Avalanche Consensus protocol, which diverges from traditional Proof of Work (PoW) and Proof of Stake (PoS) mechanisms. Instead, Avalanche Consensus enables a more scalable and efficient validation process by allowing participants to determine the validity of transactions through a process that involves repeated random sampling of validators. This design promotes high throughput and low latency, making Avalanche a strong contender in the blockchain space [203].

As of September 17, 2023, Avalanche (AVAX) holds a market capitalization of approximately $3.19 billion, positioning it among the notable cryptocurrencies [203]. The total supply of AVAX is capped at 720 million tokens, which helps in managing inflation and sustaining value over time. Despite its relatively lower market cap compared to some of the leading cryptocurrencies, Avalanche's innovative technology and growing ecosystem contribute to its significant presence in the market.

In terms of real-world applications, Avalanche's versatility is evident through various platforms and services that utilize its native token, AVAX. Ava Labs, the organization behind Avalanche, is continuously developing a range of financial products and services, all of which can be accessed and paid for using AVAX. This integration underscores the token's utility beyond mere speculation.

Additionally, Avalanche supports decentralized finance (DeFi) applications through platforms such as Trader Joe and Pangolin. Trader Joe is a decentralized exchange (DEX) where users can trade cryptocurrencies and access liquidity using AVAX, while Pangolin offers similar services, further highlighting AVAX's role in facilitating decentralized trading and liquidity provision. These use cases illustrate how Avalanche is not only a technology provider but also a key enabler in the growing DeFi ecosystem [203].

Polkadot (DOT)

Polkadot (DOT) represents a significant advancement in blockchain technology by addressing one of the most challenging issues in the space: interoperability. Launched by Dr. Gavin Wood, one of Ethereum's co-founders, Polkadot is a Layer 1 blockchain platform designed to enable different blockchains to interconnect and communicate with one another. This concept of interoperability is crucial for creating a more cohesive blockchain ecosystem where diverse applications and systems can work together seamlessly. Polkadot achieves this through its unique open-source sharding multichain protocol, which supports multiple blockchains running in parallel, known as parachains. This parallel processing capability enhances the platform's scalability and efficiency by allowing numerous transactions to occur across various chains simultaneously [203].

As of September 27, 2023, Polkadot (DOT) holds a notable position in the cryptocurrency market with a market capitalization of approximately $4.92 billion [203]. The maximum supply of DOT is capped at 1.36 billion tokens, which helps maintain its value and manage inflation. Despite its robust market cap, Polkadot's true strength lies in its innovative approach to blockchain interoperability and scalability, making it a significant player in the evolving blockchain landscape.

In practical terms, Polkadot's architecture has led to the development of several notable projects and platforms that leverage its capabilities. One prominent example is Acala, a decentralized finance (DeFi) platform that utilizes Polkadot's infrastructure to offer a broad range of DeFi services. Acala benefits from Polkadot's scalability and interoperability to provide robust financial solutions within the DeFi space.

Another key project is Moonbeam, a smart contract platform that operates on the Polkadot network. Moonbeam enables developers to deploy Solidity smart contracts, a popular programming language for Ethereum, on the Polkadot network. This cross-compatibility allows for greater flexibility and integration within the blockchain ecosystem, with DOT being used for all transactions on the platform [203].

Additionally, Kusama serves as Polkadot's canary network, providing a testing ground for new features and upgrades before they are implemented on the main Polkadot network. This approach allows developers to experiment with and refine innovations in a real-world environment, ensuring that any new developments are thoroughly vetted and functional before their official release. Kusama's role underscores Polkadot's commitment to continuous improvement and adaptation, contributing to its overall effectiveness and relevance in the blockchain sector [203].

Polygon (MATIC)

Polygon, previously known as Matic Network, is an innovative Ethereum-based platform designed to enhance the scalability and usability of blockchain networks. Launched in 2017, Polygon operates as a Layer 2 scaling solution, addressing Ethereum's limitations with respect to transaction speed and costs [203]. Unlike Ethereum's native Proof of Work (PoW) consensus mechanism, Polygon utilizes a Proof of Stake (PoS) consensus algorithm, which contributes to its efficiency and scalability. This system enables Polygon to handle a high volume of transactions at a much lower cost than the Ethereum mainnet. The MATIC token, which is integral to the Polygon ecosystem, is used to pay for transaction fees and participate in network governance, incentivizing users to contribute computational resources to maintain and secure the network.

Current Market Position

As of September 27, 2023, Polygon (MATIC) holds a significant position in the cryptocurrency market with a market capitalization of approximately $4.76 billion [203]. The token has a circulating supply of around 9.32 billion MATIC, reflecting its broad adoption and utilization. Polygon's market presence is bolstered by its ability to offer faster and more cost-effective transactions compared to Ethereum, which has driven its integration into various platforms and applications.

Real-Life Use Cases of MATIC

Polygon's utility extends beyond mere transaction processing, influencing several sectors through its innovative technology [203].

- **Caste Certificates:** In a notable application of blockchain technology, the Indian government has partnered with Polygon to issue verifiable caste certificates. This initiative, announced in 2023, aims to leverage Polygon's blockchain for secure and tamper-proof documentation, illustrating the platform's potential for real-world administrative solutions.

- **Coinbase's NFT Marketplace:** Coinbase, a leading cryptocurrency exchange, uses Polygon's technology to power its NFT marketplace. By integrating Polygon, Coinbase reduces high gas fees associated with Ethereum transactions, making it more cost-effective for users to buy, sell, and trade NFTs. This application highlights Polygon's role in optimizing user experiences on major crypto platforms.

- **Animoca Brands:** Polygon plays a key role in the gaming industry through its collaboration with Animoca Brands. This company uses Polygon for its Play-to-Earn (P2E) gaming experiences, enabling players to earn rewards and participate in a decentralized gaming ecosystem. By leveraging Polygon's efficient and scalable infrastructure, Animoca Brands enhances the gaming experience and ensures smoother transactions.

Polygon's Layer 2 solution, through its use of the MATIC token, addresses critical issues of scalability and transaction costs while expanding its utility across various domains. This positions Polygon as a pivotal player in the ongoing evolution of blockchain technology [203].

Terra (LUNA)

Terra (LUNA) is a notable cryptocurrency and blockchain protocol designed to maintain the stability of stablecoins while facilitating the adoption of fiat currencies in the digital space. Launched in 2018 by the Terra team, the protocol operates on a unique model that links its native LUNA token to the stability of Terra's stablecoins. The LUNA token serves multiple roles within the Terra ecosystem: it is used for collateralizing the network's stablecoins, participating in governance decisions, and ensuring the overall stability of the ecosystem. By leveraging a combination of algorithmic mechanisms and economic incentives, Terra aims to offer stable, scalable, and decentralized financial solutions [203].

Current Market Position

As of September 27, 2023, Terra (LUNA) holds a market capitalization of approximately $173 million. This positions it as a significant player in the cryptocurrency space, albeit smaller compared to some of the larger market cap cryptocurrencies. With around 385 million LUNA tokens in circulation, the coin reflects a substantial yet controlled supply, aimed at maintaining its value and utility within the Terra ecosystem [203].

Real-Life Use Cases of Terra (LUNA)

Terra's utility extends into several practical applications, demonstrating its relevance and effectiveness in real-world scenarios [203].

- **Chai:** Chai is a popular mobile payment application based in South Korea. It integrates Terra's blockchain to facilitate fast and secure money transfers. Users can leverage the LUNA token within the Chai app for various financial transactions, enhancing the accessibility and adoption of cryptocurrency in everyday payments.

- **KwonPay:** Another significant application of Terra's technology is KwonPay, a payment processor also operating in South Korea. This platform allows merchants to accept payments using LUNA, integrating it into the country's financial ecosystem. The adoption of KwonPay highlights Terra's growing influence in enabling crypto payments and expanding its use cases.

- **Mirror Protocol:** Mirror Protocol offers a unique approach by allowing users to create and trade synthetic assets that mirror the value of real-world assets such as stocks, ETFs, and commodities. This protocol utilizes the Terra blockchain to facilitate transactions, providing users with innovative ways to engage in financial markets without directly trading traditional assets.

- **Anchor Protocol:** Anchor Protocol is a decentralized lending and borrowing platform built on Terra's blockchain. It provides users with the opportunity to earn high yields by depositing LUNA tokens, demonstrating the platform's capacity to offer attractive financial products. By leveraging Terra's stablecoin infrastructure, Anchor Protocol supports secure and efficient financial transactions.

Terra (LUNA) is a versatile and influential player in the cryptocurrency space, with a range of applications that enhance its stability and usability. Its role in stabilizing stablecoins and its integration into various payment and financial platforms showcase its potential and adaptability in the evolving digital economy [203].

Chainlink (LINK)

Chainlink (LINK) is a prominent player in the cryptocurrency world, particularly known for its role in connecting smart contracts with real-world data. Launched in 2017, Chainlink was designed to address a critical limitation in blockchain technology: the need for smart contracts to interact with external data sources in a secure and reliable manner. Chainlink achieves this by providing a decentralized network of oracles—data feeds that link smart contracts to external APIs, databases, and other off-chain information [203].

Current Market Position

As of September 27, 2023, Chainlink (LINK) holds a market capitalization of approximately $4.1 billion. Its strong market position is a testament to its significant role in the blockchain ecosystem. Chainlink's value proposition lies in its ability to enhance the functionality of smart contracts by integrating real-world data, which has propelled it to become one of the top cryptocurrencies. Its widespread adoption and critical infrastructure role contribute to its solid market presence.

Real-Life Use Cases of Chainlink

Chainlink's impact extends across various domains, demonstrating its versatility and importance in the crypto space. Here are some key use cases [203]:

- **Uniswap**: Uniswap, a leading decentralized exchange (DEX), utilizes Chainlink to provide accurate price feeds and other essential data. Chainlink's oracles help ensure that Uniswap's decentralized trading operations rely on up-to-date and reliable information. Users who contribute data to Uniswap's protocol can earn rewards in LINK, highlighting the token's role in incentivizing data provision and maintaining the platform's integrity.

- **Axie Infinity**: This popular blockchain-based game, known for its play-to-earn model, integrates Chainlink to enhance its gaming experience. Specifically, Chainlink's random number generation service is used to ensure fair and unpredictable outcomes in in-game battles. Node operators who provide this service are compensated in LINK tokens, showcasing Chainlink's utility in the gaming sector.

- **SWIFT**: The Society for Worldwide Interbank Financial Telecommunication (SWIFT), a global financial messaging network, is exploring blockchain technology to innovate its payment systems. Chainlink is being utilized by SWIFT to develop new decentralized payment solutions. This involvement underscores Chainlink's role in bridging traditional financial systems with modern blockchain technology, potentially transforming cross-border transactions and banking operations.

Chainlink's ability to integrate off-chain data with on-chain smart contracts through its decentralized oracle network has established it as a crucial component in both the DeFi space and traditional financial systems. Its real-life applications demonstrate its broad utility and significant impact on various sectors [203].

Chapter Six

Cryptocurrency Wallets and Exchanges

Cryptocurrency wallets and exchanges are fundamental components of the cryptocurrency ecosystem, each serving distinct but complementary roles.

Cryptocurrency wallets are digital tools used to store, manage, and secure cryptocurrencies. They come in various forms, including software (digital) wallets, hardware wallets, and paper wallets. Here's what they do:

- **Storage of Cryptocurrencies**: Wallets hold the private keys that allow users to access and manage their cryptocurrency holdings. They can store multiple types of cryptocurrencies, depending on the wallet's compatibility.

- **Transaction Management**: Wallets enable users to send and receive cryptocurrencies. By using the private key, users can sign transactions and interact with blockchain networks.

- **Security**: Wallets provide varying levels of security to protect assets from theft or loss. For example, hardware wallets store private keys offline, reducing the risk of online hacking, while software wallets might offer encryption and multi-signature features.

- **Backup and Recovery**: Most wallets offer backup and recovery options, allowing users to restore their assets if they lose access to their wallet or device. This typically involves generating and storing a recovery seed phrase.

- **User Interface**: Wallets often come with a user-friendly interface that allows users to view their balances, transaction history, and other relevant information.

Types of Cryptocurrency Wallets

- **Software Wallets**: These are digital applications that can be installed on computers or smartphones. Examples include MetaMask and Trust Wallet. They are convenient but might be more vulnerable to cyber threats.

- **Hardware Wallets**: Physical devices that store private keys offline. Examples include Ledger Nano S and Trezor. They offer enhanced security and are less susceptible to online attacks.

- **Paper Wallets**: Physical documents that contain private keys and public addresses. They are highly secure against online threats but can be easily lost or damaged.

Figure 12: Ledger Nano S - Hard Wallet - Cold Storage for Cryptocurrency. Motokoka, CC BY-SA 4.0, via Wikimedia Commons.

Cryptocurrency exchanges are platforms where users can buy, sell, and trade cryptocurrencies. They act as intermediaries, facilitating transactions between buyers and sellers. Here's what they do:

- **Trading and Exchange**: Exchanges enable users to convert one cryptocurrency into another or exchange fiat currencies (like USD or EUR) for cryptocurrencies. They provide liquidity and price discovery for various digital assets.

- **Market Access**: Exchanges offer access to a wide range of cryptocurrencies and trading pairs, allowing users to diversify their portfolios and take advantage of market opportunities.

- **Order Execution**: Exchanges support different types of orders, such as market orders, limit orders, and stop-loss orders. These features help users execute trades based on their strategies and preferences.

- **Security Measures**: Reputable exchanges implement various security measures, including two-factor authentication (2FA), cold storage for funds, and regular security audits, to protect user assets.

- **Additional Services**: Some exchanges offer additional features such as staking, lending, futures trading, and margin trading. They may also provide educational resources and tools for market analysis.

Types of Cryptocurrency Exchanges

- **Centralized Exchanges (CEXs)**: Operated by centralized entities, these exchanges handle transactions and custody of funds. Examples include Binance, Coinbase, and Kraken. They offer high liquidity and user support but require users to trust the exchange with their funds.

- **Decentralized Exchanges (DEXs)**: Operate on a decentralized network without intermediaries. Examples include Uniswap and SushiSwap. They allow users to trade directly with each other, often with enhanced privacy, but may have lower liquidity and higher fees.

- **Hybrid Exchanges**: Combine features of both centralized and decentralized exchanges. They aim to offer the benefits of both systems, such as high liquidity and decentralized control.

Cryptocurrency wallets are essential tools for managing and securing digital assets. They store the keys that allow access to your cryptocurrency holdings and are crucial for executing transactions. The choice between a hot wallet and a cold wallet depends on your priorities regarding accessibility and security [215].

Types of Wallets: Hot vs. Cold

Hot Wallets

Hot wallets are connected to the internet, making them convenient for frequent transactions. They can be accessed via software applications on your computer or smartphone. Here are some key characteristics [215]:

- **Price**: Hot wallets are typically free to use, and some even offer additional features such as interest on stored crypto. This makes them a cost-effective choice for active traders.

- **Convenience**: These wallets are ideal for regular transactions because they are always connected to the internet. This connectivity allows users to quickly send, receive, and trade cryptocurrencies.
- **Maximum Number of Cryptocurrencies**: Hot wallets can support a wide range of cryptocurrencies, from a single asset to thousands, depending on the platform.
- **Cybersecurity**: Hot wallets offer average security. Since they are connected to the internet, they are potentially vulnerable to hacking and cyberattacks. However, they often include security features like encryption and two-factor authentication.
- **Loss Protection**: They generally offer good loss protection with backup and recovery options. Most hot wallets allow access from multiple devices, making it easier to recover funds if your device is lost or stolen.
- **Ease of Transfer to Exchanges**: Hot wallets excel in this area as they are already connected to the internet, facilitating seamless transfers and trading on exchanges.

The following looks at some of the more common hot wallets and what they offer [216]:

- **Coinbase Wallet:** This wallet is tailored specifically for users of the Coinbase exchange. As a product of one of the largest and most reputable cryptocurrency exchanges, Coinbase Wallet allows for seamless integration with the Coinbase platform. It supports a range of cryptocurrencies and provides features such as built-in exchange functionality, making it a convenient choice for those heavily invested in the Coinbase ecosystem. Users benefit from its user-friendly interface and the security measures backed by the Coinbase brand.
- **MetaMask:** MetaMask is an ecosystem-specific wallet primarily designed for Ethereum and Ethereum-based tokens (ERC-20 tokens). It operates as a browser extension and mobile application, allowing users to interact with decentral-

ized applications (dApps) directly from their browser or phone. MetaMask's support for Ethereum and its compatibility with various dApps make it a popular choice for users involved in decentralized finance (DeFi) and Ethereum-based projects. Its integration with smart contracts and other Ethereum services makes it a versatile tool for Ethereum enthusiasts.

- **Trust Wallet:** Trust Wallet is a noncustodial wallet that supports a broad range of cryptocurrencies and tokens, with compatibility spanning over 300 digital assets. Available on both web and mobile platforms, Trust Wallet offers a high degree of inclusivity and flexibility. Its noncustodial nature means that users maintain full control over their private keys, enhancing security and privacy. Trust Wallet also provides features like in-app staking and decentralized exchange access, catering to a diverse array of cryptocurrency users.
- **Exodus Wallet:** Exodus is a software wallet known for its extensive support of hundreds of cryptocurrencies. It combines a user-friendly interface with advanced features, such as integrated exchange capabilities and portfolio tracking. Exodus is available on both desktop and mobile platforms, making it accessible for users who want a comprehensive and visually appealing wallet solution. Its built-in exchange functionality allows users to trade cryptocurrencies directly within the wallet, adding convenience to its feature set.

When choosing a hot wallet, users should consider factors such as design, fees, and integration with specific crypto exchanges or ecosystems. Each wallet has unique strengths that cater to different needs, whether it's ease of use, comprehensive support for multiple cryptocurrencies, or specific features aligned with certain platforms. Conducting thorough research to understand the functionality and security measures of each wallet can help users select the best option for their cryptocurrency activities.

Cold Wallets

Cold wallets, on the other hand, are physical devices or paper forms that store cryptocurrencies offline. They offer a higher level of security due to their lack of direct internet connection. Key features include [215]:

- **Price**: Cold wallets require a purchase, with prices ranging from $50 to $250. Despite the initial investment, their enhanced security can be well worth the cost.

- **Best for**: Cold wallets are best suited for long-term storage and larger amounts of cryptocurrency that you do not need to access frequently. They are designed for security rather than convenience.

- **Maximum Number of Cryptocurrencies**: Cold wallets can store anywhere from a few to thousands of cryptocurrencies, depending on the device's capacity.

- **Cybersecurity**: Cold wallets offer excellent security since they are offline and cannot be hacked remotely. The private keys are stored in a secure environment that is not exposed to online threats.

- **Loss Protection**: While cold wallets provide robust protection against online attacks, they offer average protection against physical loss. If a cold wallet is lost or damaged, you can usually recover your funds using a recovery phrase, but you will need a new device to access them.

- **Ease of Transfer to Exchanges**: Cold wallets require an additional step to connect online, often through a USB connection, Wi-Fi, or QR code. This makes them less convenient for frequent transactions compared to hot wallets.

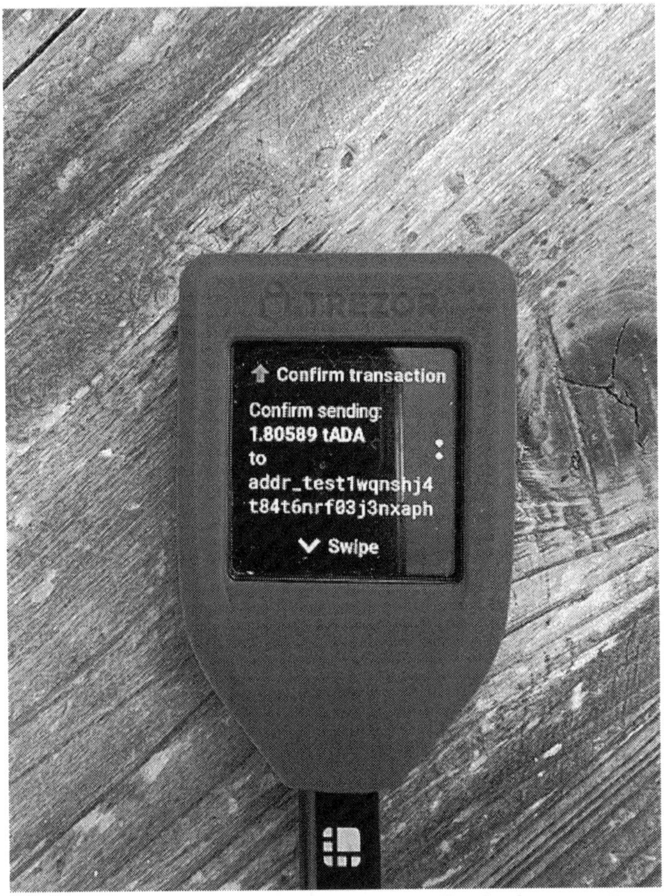

Figure 13: A Trezor model T hardware wallet displaying a Cardano Ada transaction just before manual confirmation. FlippyFlink, CC0, via Wikimedia Commons.

Paper cryptocurrency wallets offer a secure way to store digital assets offline, eliminating the risks associated with online threats such as hacking or phishing. These wallets are a form of "cold storage," meaning they are not connected to the internet, which significantly enhances their security. Here's a detailed explanation of how paper wallets work and their key features:

1. Understanding Paper Wallets

A paper wallet is essentially a physical document that contains the public and private keys for your cryptocurrency. These keys are cryptographic strings of letters and numbers that allow you to access and manage your digital assets. The public key acts like an address where others can send cryptocurrency, while the private key is used to sign transactions and access the funds. The paper wallet is designed to securely store these keys offline, protecting them from online threats.

2. Generating a Paper Wallet

To create a paper wallet, you use a secure, offline method to generate a pair of public and private keys. This can be done using various tools and services, often with specific steps to ensure security:

- **Offline Generation**: It's crucial to generate your keys on an offline computer or device to prevent exposure to potential malware or online threats. Many users download and use paper wallet generator tools that are designed to run offline.

- **Creating the Wallet**: You generate the key pair and then print or write down the public and private keys on paper. This document often includes a QR code for easy scanning of the keys.

- **Secure Printing**: The printout should be done on a secure printer, preferably not connected to the internet, to further minimize security risks.

3. Storing and Using Paper Wallets

- **Storing the Wallet**: After generating and printing the paper wallet, you should store it in a safe place, such as a safe deposit box or a secure drawer. The key is to keep it in a location that is protected from physical damage, theft, or loss.

- **Using the Wallet**: To use the paper wallet, you typically scan the QR codes with a compatible wallet application or manually enter the keys. For example, to make a transaction, you would import the private key into a software wallet or an exchange that supports paper wallet import. After the transaction, it's important to securely delete the keys from any digital device to prevent unauthorized access.

4. Advantages of Paper Wallets

- **Enhanced Security**: Paper wallets are immune to online hacking and malware since they are stored offline. This makes them a secure option for long-term storage of cryptocurrencies.

- **Cost-Effective**: Paper wallets are free to create and use, requiring only basic materials like paper and a printer.

- **Simplicity**: They offer a straightforward method for securely storing your private keys without needing additional hardware.

5. Disadvantages and Risks

- **Physical Damage or Loss**: Paper wallets are vulnerable to physical damage, such as water, fire, or general wear and tear. Losing the paper wallet means losing access to your funds, as there is no way to recover the keys.

- **Lack of Convenience**: Using paper wallets for regular transactions can be cumbersome, as it involves manually entering or scanning keys each time you need to access your funds.

- **Risk of Theft**: If the paper wallet is not stored securely, it can be stolen. Anyone with access to the private key can access the associated cryptocurrency.

6. Best Practices for Paper Wallets

- **Use a Trusted Generator**: Ensure you use a reputable and secure paper wallet generator. It's best to download the tool from an official website and verify its integrity.

- **Print Securely**: Use a secure printer and avoid connecting the device to the internet during the printing process.

- **Store Securely**: Keep the paper wallet in a safe, dry place that is protected from physical and environmental damage.

- **Backup**: Consider making multiple copies of the paper wallet and storing them in different secure locations.

Figure 14: A paper printable Bitcoin wallet with QR code consisting of one bitcoin address for receiving and the corresponding private key for spending. FlippyFlink, CC BY-SA 4.0, via Wikimedia Commons.

Paper cryptocurrency wallets are an effective method for securing digital assets offline, offering protection from online threats and hacking. However, they come with their own set of risks related to physical security and convenience. By following best practices for generating, storing, and using paper wallets, you can safeguard your cryptocurrencies and manage them securely.

Choosing the Right Wallet

The choice between hot and cold wallets involves a trade-off between security and convenience. Hot wallets are ideal for users who need easy access to their funds and conduct regular transactions, while cold wallets are suited for those who prioritize security and store their assets for the long term.

For a balanced approach, many users employ both types of wallets: keeping a smaller amount of funds in a hot wallet for daily use and a larger portion in a cold wallet for enhanced security. This strategy helps mitigate risks while maintaining accessibility to your assets.

Other Wallet Options: Custodial Wallets

Custodial wallets are another option, managed by third-party online platforms such as cryptocurrency exchanges. These wallets offer a more hands-off approach, as the platform handles the security and storage of your funds. They often provide benefits like earning interest or rewards on your holdings.

Advantages:

- **Convenience**: Easier to access and recover, as the exchange manages the wallet.
- **Features**: Some custodial wallets offer additional services, including interest payments on crypto assets.

Disadvantages:

- **Security Risks**: Custodial wallets can be attractive targets for hackers due to the large volumes of crypto they manage. They also carry the risk of platform failures or business closures, which could affect access to your funds.

In summary, choosing the right cryptocurrency wallet depends on your needs for security, convenience, and accessibility. Understanding the differences between hot and cold wallets, as well as considering custodial wallets, can help you make an informed decision for managing your digital assets.

How to Secure Your Cryptocurrency Assets

The security of your cryptocurrency assets heavily depends on how you store your private keys. Cold wallets, also known as cold storage, offer a highly secure way to protect these keys. Unlike hot wallets, which are connected to the internet and therefore vulnerable to online threats, cold wallets remain offline, significantly reducing the risk of hacking or unauthorized access [217].

Cold wallets come in various forms, such as hardware devices resembling USB drives or even more advanced models that look like smartphones. These devices store your private keys offline, meaning they are not exposed to potential online attacks. However, no storage device is completely infallible, and cold wallets are no exception. If you lose the hardware wallet or it gets damaged, you could permanently lose access to your cryptocurrencies unless you have a secure backup of your recovery seed phrase [217].

To balance security and accessibility, many users opt for a combination of cold and hot wallets. By keeping most of your funds in a cold wallet and only transferring what you need for immediate transactions to a hot wallet, you minimize your exposure to online threats. This approach ensures that only a small portion of your assets is at risk if a hot wallet is compromised.

For instance, if you are trading cryptocurrencies or need to access funds frequently, using a hot wallet for these purposes while keeping the bulk of your holdings in cold storage offers a practical balance. Once transactions are complete, you can transfer the remaining funds back to the cold wallet, maintaining the security of your long-term investments.

Most people use cryptocurrency exchanges for transactions due to their convenience. Exchanges offer custodial services, meaning they manage the storage of your private keys [217]. Reputable exchanges often have robust security measures, including institutional-level cold storage and insurance against theft. For example, platforms like Coinbase and Gemini provide enterprise-grade security and, in some cases, insurance to protect against losses due to hacks or other security breaches.

However, storing your cryptocurrency on an exchange also has its risks. If the exchange is compromised or goes out of business, your assets could be at risk. Unlike traditional bank accounts, which are insured by institutions like the FDIC, cryptocurrency holdings on exchanges generally lack such protection. While some exchanges offer insurance for certain types of losses, this coverage is often limited and does not cover all potential scenarios, such as loss due to compromised account credentials.

A prudent strategy for securing your cryptocurrency assets is to use a combination of storage methods. By maintaining a portion of your assets in cold storage for long-term security and keeping a smaller amount in a hot wallet or on an exchange for trading, you reduce the risk associated with online threats while ensuring you have accessible funds for transactions. This method also helps in managing trading balances, as you can allocate only the necessary amount to your hot wallet or exchange, protecting the rest in cold storage [217].

For long-term investments, cold storage is the ideal choice. Ensure that your cold wallet is stored in a secure, fire-proof location and that you have backup copies of your recovery seed phrase. Regularly checking on your wallet and updating backups as needed can help safeguard your assets against potential losses.

The choice between hot and cold wallets depends on your needs for accessibility and security. Cold wallets offer superior protection by keeping your private keys offline, reducing vulnerability to online threats. Combining cold and hot wallets can provide a balanced approach, protecting the majority of your assets while allowing for convenient access to funds needed for transactions. Regardless of the method you choose, it is crucial to maintain control over your private keys and implement strong security practices to safeguard your cryptocurrency investments [217].

Expect Scams in Cryptocurrency Investing

The cryptocurrency market, characterized by its wide array of digital assets and minimal regulation, has become a prime target for scammers [218]. Unlike traditional financial systems, which are more heavily regulated and monitored, the crypto world operates in a largely unregulated environment, making it an attractive space for fraudulent activities. Investors in cryptocurrencies must exercise extraordinary caution and remain vigilant against scams that exploit the complexity and novelty of digital assets. The following details the most common types of scams and how investors can protect themselves:

Common Cryptocurrency Scams

1. Giveaway Scams

One prevalent scam in the crypto space involves fraudulent giveaway schemes. Scammers promise extraordinary returns on investments through supposed "investment funds," endorsements from "experienced managers," or promotions featuring celebrities or large investment firms. In these schemes, the scammers may initially offer a small return to lure victims into investing more, only to disappear once a significant amount of money has been invested. In other cases, the scam may involve simply taking the initial payment without delivering any returns. These scams leverage the allure of high profits and the credibility of supposed endorsements to deceive investors [218].

2. Value Inflation

Value inflation scams target investors with new coins or tokens that supposedly have skyrocketing value. Scammers create the illusion of a rapidly appreciating asset, convincing investors to pour money into these tokens. However, these tokens are often worthless or designed to trap investors, making it impossible for them to cash out their investments. The value of the token may appear to increase continuously, but this is merely a façade to encourage more investment. Once investors are committed, they find that their investments cannot be redeemed or withdrawn, leading to substantial financial loss [218].

3. Romance Scams

Romance scams are a more personal type of fraud that leverages emotional connections. Scammers establish relationships with victims through dating platforms like Tinder and, after gaining their trust, introduce the topic of investment opportunities. The scammers then manipulate the victim into investing money or providing personal financial details under the guise of a romantic gesture. The emotional connection helps lower the victim's defences, making them more susceptible to fraudulent investment schemes [218].

4. Fake Cryptocurrency Exchanges or Investment Platforms

Fake cryptocurrency exchanges and investment platforms are another common scam. These platforms mimic legitimate services to trick users into entering their cryptocurrency wallet details. Unlike phishing schemes that target credit card information, these scams focus on accessing crypto wallets. Once scammers obtain the wallet details, they can steal the funds. These fraudulent platforms often appear authentic, using sophisticated tactics to replicate the look and functionality of real exchanges [218].

Protection Methods

1. Verify the Validity of Firms and Offers

To protect yourself from scams, always thoroughly verify the legitimacy of any firm, individual, or website offering investment opportunities. Scammers often create convincing facades, so it's essential to conduct in-depth research before engaging in any financial transactions. Ensure that any entity you deal with is reputable and has a proven track record [218].

2. Avoid Hasty Decisions

Fraudsters frequently employ high-pressure tactics to rush victims into making quick decisions. Avoid making hasty investments and take the time to carefully evaluate any new opportunities. Scammers use urgency to prevent you from conducting proper due diligence, so take your time to assess the legitimacy of the investment [218].

3. Ignore Unexpected Offers

Be wary of unsolicited offers or investment opportunities that come through social media, email, or instant messaging. If you did not seek out the offer yourself, it is likely a scam. Do not waste time investigating every unsolicited opportunity; instead, focus on offers that you have actively pursued or researched [218].

4. Use Anti-Phishing Protection

Implement anti-phishing protection on all your devices to guard against fraudulent websites and phishing attempts. Tools like Kaspersky Premium can help by blocking access to known fake sites and providing additional security layers. Ensure that all devices, including computers and phones, have robust protection against phishing scams.

5. Employ a Reliable VPN

While a VPN alone does not protect against phishing or fraud, it can safeguard against website spoofing and spying, especially when using public Wi-Fi networks in places like cafes, airports, or hotels. A VPN encrypts your internet connection, adding an extra layer of security when accessing cryptocurrency accounts and conducting transactions.

In the unregulated and rapidly evolving world of cryptocurrency, scams are a prevalent and serious risk. By understanding the common types of scams and implementing effective protection measures, you can reduce the likelihood of falling victim to fraud.

Always verify the authenticity of investment opportunities, avoid hasty decisions, and use security tools to safeguard your assets. Being proactive and cautious is crucial in navigating the complex landscape of cryptocurrency investing [218].

Protect your computer and phone

Protecting your computer and phone is crucial for safeguarding your cryptocurrency and tokens from theft and other cyber threats. Cybercriminals can employ various tactics to gain unauthorized access to your digital assets, and understanding these methods helps in implementing effective countermeasures [218].

Types of Threats

Criminals can exploit vulnerabilities in your devices to compromise your cryptocurrency holdings in several ways [218]:

1. **Intercepting Wallet Passwords**: Attackers can install malware that records keystrokes or captures data entered into websites. By hijacking your session, they can gain access to your cryptocurrency exchange accounts. Once they have your login credentials, they can steal your assets directly.

2. **Address Substitution**: A common tactic involves malware that modifies the recipient address in your clipboard. When you copy and paste a wallet address for a transaction, the malware changes it to one controlled by the attacker. This deception often goes unnoticed due to the long and complex nature of cryptocurrency addresses, resulting in your funds being sent to the wrong wallet.

3. **Cryptojacking**: This involves secretly installing mining software on your computer that uses your system's resources to mine cryptocurrency for the attacker. This "cryptojacking" can occur without your knowledge and can slow down your device significantly. Monero is a popular target for such attacks due to its mining algorithm's low resource requirements.

4. **Mining Application Exploits**: If you use a mining application to generate cryptocurrency, attackers might alter the application to divert your earnings to their own wallets. This can occur through malicious updates or trojanized

versions of legitimate mining software.

5. **Fake or Trojanized Cryptocurrency Apps**: Scammers can create fraudulent apps that look like legitimate cryptocurrency wallets or trading platforms. Once installed, these apps can steal your private keys or login credentials, resulting in the loss of your digital assets. An example includes fake games that promise cryptocurrency rewards but are designed to steal your funds.

Protection Methods

To defend against these threats, consider the following strategies [218]:

1. **Use Comprehensive Cybersecurity Solutions**: Employ a robust cybersecurity program that includes features like application behavior monitoring, high malware detection rates, protection against keyloggers, and secure password entry. Tools like Kaspersky Premium offer extensive protection, including safeguards against remote access, browser security, and automatic updates for software vulnerabilities.

2. **Adhere to Strict Device Hygiene**: Only download apps from trusted sources, such as official app stores, and avoid using unknown or cracked software, as these are common vectors for malware. Regularly update your software to patch vulnerabilities and prevent exploitation.

3. **Restrict Device Access**: Limit the use of your cryptocurrency transaction devices to authorized individuals only. Use strong passwords and set your devices to lock automatically after a period of inactivity. Implement full disk encryption, such as Bitlocker, to protect your data from unauthorized access.

By adopting these protective measures, you can significantly reduce the risk of losing your cryptocurrency assets to cyber threats. Ensuring that your devices are secure and that you follow best practices for digital safety will help keep your investments safe.

Create Multiple Cryptoasset Repositories

To manage and safeguard significant amounts of cryptocurrency, it's crucial to establish multiple repositories for your assets. Storing large sums exclusively in "hot" wallets—online vaults or devices connected to the internet—provides convenient access but substantially increases the risk of theft and hacking. As a best practice, investors should only keep a small portion of their assets in hot wallets for operational needs, while transferring the majority to a "cold" wallet, which is entirely offline. Cold wallets, often resembling USB sticks, offer a more secure way to store crypto assets because they are not connected to the internet, reducing exposure to cyber threats [218].

Ways to Protect Assets in a Cold Wallet

1. **Select a Secure Model**: Choose a reputable and secure cold wallet model. It's important to research and review the security features of different models. Search for information on potential vulnerabilities and security assessments. Some cold wallet models may have known weaknesses, so it's crucial to select one that has been thoroughly vetted and tested for security [218].

2. **Purchase from Trusted Sources**: Buy cold wallets only from authorized and trusted sellers. Scammers have been known to create counterfeit wallets that appear to be from well-known brands and sell them through online auctions or message boards. Ensure that you are buying from a legitimate source to avoid falling victim to these schemes [218].

3. **Use a Safe Computer for Transactions**: Conduct all wallet transactions on a personal computer that you know is secure. Avoid using public or shared devices to handle your cryptocurrency, as they may be compromised or insecure [218].

4. **Store the Wallet Safely**: Protect the physical cold wallet itself. Losing it is equivalent to losing access to your funds. Consider secure storage options such as a safe deposit box or a home safe. Take into account risks like theft, accidental loss, fire, or natural disasters. Ensuring the safety of the physical device is as crucial as protecting the digital security [218].

5. **Create a Strong, Unique Password**: Secure your cold wallet with a strong, unique password. This password should be difficult to guess and should not be easily forgotten. Avoid sharing it with anyone, and make sure it is not stored

in a manner that could be easily accessed by unauthorized individuals. Use a password manager if needed to keep track of complex passwords securely [218].

By implementing these strategies, you can significantly enhance the security of your cryptocurrency assets and mitigate risks associated with online theft and loss.

Take Care of Passwords and Keys

The protection of passwords and seed phrases is crucial in safeguarding cryptocurrency holdings, as losing or having these credentials stolen can result in irreversible loss of assets. To prevent such scenarios, it's essential to adopt rigorous practices for creating and managing passwords and keys [218].

Protection Methods:

1. **Use Long and Unique Passwords:** To enhance security, employ long, complex, and unique passwords for every account and service you use. Refrain from using easily guessable or common passwords, as these are more susceptible to brute force attacks. Storing these passwords in an encrypted password manager offers a convenient and secure way to manage multiple credentials. Password managers like those included in Kaspersky Premium can synchronize passwords across all your devices while keeping them encrypted [218].

2. **Two-Factor Authentication (2FA):** Enable two-factor authentication wherever possible to add an additional layer of security. Prefer hardware-based 2FA methods, such as a USB key or a dedicated mobile app, over SMS-based authentication, which is vulnerable to interception. Hardware keys and authentication apps provide a more secure way of confirming your identity and preventing unauthorized access [218].

3. **Regularly Check for Exposed Credentials:** Regular monitoring of your credentials is essential to identify any potential compromises. Tools like Kaspersky Premium's Password Check can alert you if your passwords have been leaked in a data breach or if they are weak. This service uses the SHA-256 cryptographic hashing algorithm to check for compromises without sending your passwords over the internet [218].

4. **Data Leak Checking:** Utilize services that scan the internet and dark web for

leaked personal data. Kaspersky Premium's Data Leak Checker can inform you if your passwords or sensitive information, such as crypto wallet credentials, are exposed in public breaches. This proactive approach helps mitigate the risk of identity theft and unauthorized access [218].

5. **Secure Storage of Sensitive Documents:** Use tools like Kaspersky's Identity Protection Wallet to securely store sensitive documents, including passport details and crypto wallet seed phrases. This encrypted cloud storage ensures that your information is protected from unauthorized access and synchronized across your devices [218].

6. **Encrypt Sensitive Data:** Convert sensitive data, such as cryptocurrency credentials, into an unreadable format with encryption tools like Kaspersky's Secret Vault. This local storage solution ensures that your data is encrypted on your device's hard drive, not in the cloud, reducing the risk of online attacks [218].

Here are examples of other tools and practices for securing passwords, using two-factor authentication (2FA), and protecting sensitive data:

1. Use Long and Unique Passwords:

Password Managers:

- **LastPass:** Offers a secure and encrypted way to store and manage your passwords. It includes features for password generation and synchronization across devices.

- **1Password:** Provides encrypted password storage and the ability to create and manage strong, unique passwords. It also integrates with multiple devices.

- **Bitwarden:** An open-source password manager that securely stores passwords and syncs them across devices. It includes features for password generation and two-factor authentication support.

2. Two-Factor Authentication (2FA):

Hardware-Based 2FA:

- **YubiKey:** A hardware security key that supports various authentication methods, including U2F (Universal 2nd Factor) and FIDO2. It provides robust security against phishing and account takeovers.

- **Thetis FIDO U2F Security Key:** Another hardware option that supports U2F and can be used for secure login to various accounts.

Mobile Apps:

- **Google Authenticator:** A widely used mobile app that generates time-based one-time passwords (TOTPs) for two-factor authentication.
- **Authy:** A mobile app that provides 2FA codes and includes cloud backup and multi-device support.
- **Microsoft Authenticator:** Offers both TOTP and push-based 2FA, with features for cloud backup and device recovery.

3. Regularly Check for Exposed Credentials:

Credential Monitoring Tools:

- **Have I Been Pwned:** A service that allows you to check if your email addresses or passwords have been involved in known data breaches.
- **Pwned Passwords:** A tool by Have I Been Pwned that lets you check if your passwords have been exposed in breaches.
- **Firefox Monitor:** A service that checks if your email addresses are involved in data breaches and alerts you if your information has been exposed.

4. Data Leak Checking:

Data Breach Notification Services:

- **BreachAlarm:** Monitors for data breaches and alerts you if your email addresses or other personal information is exposed.
- **Identity Guard:** Offers data breach monitoring and alerts you to potential leaks of your personal information.
- **SpyCloud:** Provides dark web monitoring and data breach detection services to alert you if your credentials are compromised.

5. Secure Storage of Sensitive Documents:

Encrypted Cloud Storage:

- **NordLocker:** A tool that provides secure cloud storage with encryption for sensitive documents and files.

- **Tresorit:** Offers end-to-end encrypted cloud storage for files, including sensitive documents like passport details and crypto wallet information.

- **Boxcryptor:** Encrypts files stored in cloud services like Dropbox, Google Drive, and OneDrive, ensuring that your sensitive data is protected.

6. Encrypt Sensitive Data:

Encryption Tools:

- **VeraCrypt:** An open-source disk encryption tool that can create encrypted volumes to securely store sensitive data on your local drive.

- **BitLocker:** A built-in encryption tool for Windows that provides full disk encryption to protect sensitive data on your hard drive.

- **AxCrypt:** Offers file encryption with AES-256 encryption, allowing you to secure individual files and folders on your device.

Choosing and Using a Cryptocurrency Exchange

Cryptocurrency exchanges facilitate the trading of cryptocurrencies by allowing users to buy, sell, and exchange digital assets. These exchanges function similarly to traditional financial exchanges but are tailored for the unique needs of digital currencies.

The cryptocurrency market has surged to a valuation exceeding one trillion dollars, driven by a growing interest in digital currencies and decentralized finance (DeFi). This explosion in value and interest has led to the emergence of hundreds, if not thousands, of new virtual currencies. As a result, crypto investors are increasingly seeking platforms that allow them to trade these digital assets efficiently and securely. Cryptocurrency exchanges, akin to traditional stock and commodity exchanges, serve as the platforms where participants can trade various cryptocurrencies [219-221].

Functioning of Cryptocurrency Exchanges

Cryptocurrency exchanges facilitate the buying, selling, and exchanging of digital assets, similar to how stock exchanges operate with stocks and commodities. These platforms can be accessed via mobile apps or desktop applications, much like e-brokerages, and provide users with a range of trading tools. The exchanges support various types of trading activities, including margin trading, futures, and options trading.

The operational model of cryptocurrency exchanges involves matching buyers and sellers. Traders can place either market or limit orders. A market order executes the trade immediately at the best available price, while a limit order sets a specific price at which the trade should be executed, contingent upon market conditions [219-221].

Types of Exchanges

1. Centralized Exchanges (CEXs): Centralized exchanges, such as Binance and Coinbase, are the most common platforms. Users create accounts, deposit funds, and execute trades through the exchange's interface. These exchanges handle the custody of assets and match buy and sell orders through an internal order book. They charge fees based on transaction volume and trading type. Centralized exchanges are subject to regulatory oversight and generally offer a user-friendly experience.

2. Decentralized Exchanges (DEXs): Decentralized exchanges, like Uniswap and PancakeSwap, operate without a central authority. They use smart contracts to facilitate direct peer-to-peer trading from users' wallets. DEXs rely on liquidity pools to enable trading, and users interact directly with these pools without a middleman. This model enhances privacy but can be less intuitive for beginners.

3. Hybrid Exchanges: Hybrid exchanges blend features of both centralized and decentralized models. They aim to offer the liquidity and ease of use found in centralized exchanges while incorporating decentralized settlement features.

Trading on Cryptocurrency Exchanges

When trading on a cryptocurrency exchange, users must first register and complete a Know-Your-Customer (KYC) process to verify their identity. After successful verification, users can deposit funds into their accounts through various methods, including bank transfers, credit or debit cards, and even gift cards. Once funds are deposited, users can trade cryptocurrencies such as Bitcoin (BTC), Ethereum (ETH), or other digital assets.

For example, if an investor wants to buy $10,000 worth of Bitcoin, they would follow these steps: select a reliable exchange, register and open an account, deposit funds, choose Bitcoin as the asset to buy, specify the amount, and then complete the transaction. Afterward, the transaction status can be verified in the user's account.

Order Types and Execution

Cryptocurrency exchanges support different order types [219-221]:

- **Market Orders:** These orders execute at the best available price in the market. They are ideal for immediate trades but do not guarantee a specific price.

- **Limit Orders:** These orders are executed only when the cryptocurrency reaches a specified price. They ensure a desired price but may not be executed immediately if there is no matching buy or sell order.

Pros and Cons of Cryptocurrency Exchanges

Pros:

- **Ease of Use:** Cryptocurrency exchanges simplify the process of buying and selling digital assets, making it accessible to a broad audience.

- **Legitimate Trades:** They offer a platform for conducting legitimate transactions, often with regulatory oversight.

- **Tax Reporting:** Many exchanges provide tax forms that assist users in calculating their crypto taxes.

Cons:

- **Security Risks:** Exchanges are vulnerable to hacks and cyber theft, potentially leading to loss of funds.

- **Bankruptcy Risks:** If an exchange goes bankrupt, users may lose access to their funds.

- **Lack of Private Key Control:** Users typically do not hold the private keys to their assets on exchanges, which can compromise security.

Cryptocurrency exchanges play a crucial role in the digital asset market by providing platforms for trading and managing cryptocurrencies. Understanding their operations, types, and associated risks is essential for anyone involved in cryptocurrency trading.

Centralized, Decentralized and Hybrid Exchanges

1. Centralized Exchanges (CEXs)

Centralized exchanges operate as intermediaries between buyers and sellers of cryptocurrencies. Users create accounts on these platforms, deposit their funds, and execute trades through the exchange's interface. Prominent examples include Binance, Coinbase, and Kraken [219-221].

Function and Process: Centralized exchanges function similarly to traditional stock exchanges. Users register an account and complete identity verification processes (KYC). After verification, they deposit funds, which can be either cryptocurrency or fiat currency, into their exchange wallet. Trades are executed through the platform's order book, where buy and sell orders are matched by the exchange's matching engine. Once trades are completed, users can withdraw their funds to personal wallets or bank accounts.

Centralized exchanges are governed by a single authority, which oversees all transactions and account activities. This centralized control allows for efficient management of trades and generally provides higher liquidity, meaning users can buy and sell assets quickly.

Pros:

- **Liquidity:** Centralized exchanges typically offer high liquidity, which facilitates faster transactions and better market depth.
- **Fund Recovery:** If issues arise, it is generally possible to recover funds due to the central authority overseeing the transactions.
- **Transaction Speed:** These exchanges can handle a high volume of transactions quickly due to their centralized infrastructure.

Cons:

- **Security Risks:** Centralized exchanges are susceptible to hacking, as they store a large amount of user data and funds on centralized servers.
- **Manipulation Risks:** There have been instances of trading volume manipulation and other forms of misconduct in the past.

2. Decentralized Exchanges (DEXs)

Decentralized exchanges operate without a central authority, allowing for peer-to-peer trading directly from users' wallets. Examples include Uniswap, SushiSwap, and PancakeSwap [219-221].

Function and Process: DEXs rely on distributed ledger technology and smart contracts to facilitate trades. Users connect their cryptocurrency wallets to the DEX, where transactions are executed directly from their wallets. Trades are handled through smart contracts on the blockchain, which automate the trading process without the need for an intermediary. Liquidity pools are used to support trading pairs; users who provide liquidity to these pools earn a share of the trading fees.

Decentralized exchanges prioritize user control over their funds and often do not require personal identification information, offering greater privacy.

Pros:

- **Full Custody:** Users retain control of their private keys and digital assets, minimizing the risk of theft from hacks.
- **Increased Privacy:** DEXs typically require less personal information, enhancing user privacy.
- **Reduced Cyber Attack Risk:** Distributed hosting lowers the risk of large-scale cyber attacks.

Cons:

- **Liquidity Issues:** Some DEXs struggle with lower liquidity, which can impact the ease and speed of trades.
- **Less Recourse:** Users may have fewer options for recourse if they fall victim to fraud or other issues compared to using centralized exchanges.

3. Hybrid Exchanges

Hybrid exchanges are designed to combine the features of both centralized and decentralized exchanges, aiming to offer a balanced approach to trading.

Function and Process: Hybrid exchanges integrate the high liquidity and user-friendly features of centralized exchanges with the privacy and security aspects of decentralized exchanges. They may offer centralized trading features while using decentralized settlement processes, or vice versa. Examples include Deversifi and Nash [219-221].

Pros:

- **Best of Both Worlds:** Hybrid exchanges provide the advantages of both CEXs and DEXs, offering higher liquidity and enhanced privacy.
- **Privacy and Convenience:** They strike a balance between user privacy and trading convenience.

Cons:

- **New Concept:** Hybrid exchanges are relatively new and may not yet have the volume or infrastructure of established CEXs or DEXs.
- **Volume Limitations:** They may still struggle with liquidity and trading volume compared to more established exchanges.

How Centralized Exchanges Operate

Order Matching: Centralized exchanges use an order book to list buy and sell orders. The exchange's matching engine processes these orders, matching buyers with sellers and executing trades accordingly. This system ensures that transactions are conducted efficiently and at competitive prices.

Custody and Security: Centralized exchanges manage the security and storage of users' funds. They employ various security measures, including encryption, two-factor authentication (2FA), and cold storage for the majority of assets to safeguard against hacks and breaches.

Fees: Centralized exchanges charge fees for trading and withdrawing funds. Trading fees are often a percentage of the transaction amount or a fixed fee, while withdrawal fees can vary based on the method used to move funds from the exchange to a personal wallet or bank account.

How Decentralized Exchanges Operate

Smart Contracts: Decentralized exchanges use smart contracts to automate trading processes and enforce rules without a central authority. These smart contracts ensure that transactions are executed transparently and trustlessly, with users retaining control of their funds throughout the process.

Liquidity Pools: Liquidity pools are used to facilitate trading on DEXs. Users provide cryptocurrency to these pools, which enables trading pairs on the platform. In return, liquidity providers earn a share of the transaction fees generated by the trades.

Fees: Fees on DEXs include transaction fees paid to liquidity providers and network fees for executing smart contracts on the blockchain. These fees support the decentralized infrastructure and incentivize liquidity provision.

Centralized exchanges offer ease of use and high liquidity, while decentralized exchanges provide privacy and security. Hybrid exchanges aim to combine the best features of both models. Understanding the operation and characteristics of these exchanges helps users make informed decisions about where and how to trade cryptocurrencies [219-221].

Fees in Cryptocurrency Exchanges

Deposit and Withdrawal Fees

When using cryptocurrency exchanges, both depositing and withdrawing funds usually incur fees, which can vary based on the payment method selected. Payment methods such as credit and debit cards typically attract higher fees due to the higher risk of chargebacks associated with these transactions. Chargebacks occur when a transaction is reversed, and the funds are returned to the cardholder, which can lead to potential disputes and financial losses for the exchange. To mitigate this risk, exchanges often impose higher fees on card transactions compared to other payment methods [219-221].

In contrast, methods like bank drafts or wire transfers generally involve lower fees because they have a lower chargeback risk. Bank drafts and wire transfers are direct transfers from one bank account to another and do not have the same reversal capabilities as credit card payments. As a result, exchanges can afford to charge lower fees for these methods.

Currency Conversion Fees

Another aspect of exchange fees involves currency conversion. If an exchange operates in a currency different from the one a user is depositing, a currency conversion fee will apply. For example, if a user deposits Canadian dollars (CAD) into an exchange that only accepts U.S. dollars (USD), the exchange or the bank will convert the CAD into USD, typically at an additional fee. To avoid these fees, it is advantageous to use an exchange that accepts your local currency directly, which reduces or eliminates the need for currency conversion [219-221].

Transaction Fees

All cryptocurrency exchanges impose transaction fees on buy and sell orders executed on their platforms. These fees can vary depending on the exchange and the volume of transactions. Generally, the fee rate decreases as the trading volume increases, incentivizing higher trading activity on the platform. For instance, an exchange might charge a 0.1% fee for each completed transaction, though this rate can differ based on the exchange's policies and competitive landscape [219-221].

How Exchanges Make Money

Commission Fees

The primary revenue model for centralized exchanges is through commissions on trades executed on their platforms. For each trade, the exchange charges a commission fee, which is often a small percentage of the transaction amount. This fee can be as low as 0.1%, but it can vary based on factors such as trading volume and the exchange's pricing structure [219-221].

Listing Fees and Initial Exchange Offerings (IEOs)

In addition to trading commissions, exchanges may generate revenue by charging listing fees for new cryptocurrencies. When a new coin or token is listed on an exchange, the project behind it often pays a fee to the exchange. This practice is common among newer exchanges that may struggle with liquidity and seek additional revenue streams. Similarly, exchanges may facilitate Initial Exchange Offerings (IEOs), where new tokens are sold to investors through the exchange, and a portion of the funds raised is retained as a fee by the exchange [219-221].

Native Exchange Tokens

Some well-established exchanges issue their own native tokens, which offer various benefits to holders. These tokens can be used to pay for trading fees at a discounted rate, participate in special promotions, or gain access to exclusive features on the exchange. By incentivizing the use of their native tokens, exchanges foster a proprietary ecosystem and create additional revenue streams. The issuance of these tokens also helps exchanges differentiate themselves in a competitive market [219-221].

Cryptocurrency exchanges employ a variety of fee structures and revenue models to sustain their operations. Understanding the different types of fees, including deposit, withdrawal, transaction, and currency conversion fees, as well as how exchanges monetize through commissions, listing fees, and native tokens, can help users make informed decisions about their trading activities.

Things to Check Before Selecting a Crypto Exchange

Choosing a cryptocurrency exchange is a crucial decision for anyone looking to trade or invest in digital assets. Given the complexities and potential risks involved, it is essential to carefully evaluate several factors before committing to an exchange.

Firstly, registration and regulation are important indicators of an exchange's legitimacy. Ensure that the exchange is registered as a securities broker or with relevant financial authorities in its operating country. For instance, choosing an exchange incorporated or registered in India may offer some additional regulatory oversight, which can be beneficial if any issues arise. An exchange's regulatory status can provide a level of security and assurance that it operates within legal frameworks [220].

Next, transparency about fund management is crucial. The exchange should clearly communicate how it handles and secures user funds. An exchange that manipulates or commingles funds can pose significant risks, as illustrated by the downfall of FTX, which involved risky lending practices that jeopardized users' assets. Ensuring that the exchange maintains clear, ethical practices in managing user funds can help mitigate potential losses [220].

Social media presence is another factor to consider. A reputable exchange should have a legitimate and active presence on social media platforms like LinkedIn, Twitter, or Facebook. This presence can serve as a form of accountability and provide additional channels for users to seek information and support.

The customer support system of an exchange is also critical. Before making a decision, test the exchange's customer support by contacting them through available channels, such as toll-free numbers or chat systems. Effective and responsive customer support can be invaluable in resolving issues quickly and efficiently.

Additionally, it's important to locate and verify the exchange's wallet reserves. A trustworthy exchange should disclose information about its cryptocurrency reserves. If an exchange is unwilling to provide such details, it could be a sign of potential financial instability or illegitimacy [220].

Difference Between Cryptocurrency Exchanges and Cryptocurrency Wallets

Understanding the distinction between cryptocurrency exchanges and wallets is essential for effective management of your digital assets [220].

Cryptocurrency exchanges are platforms that facilitate the trading of digital assets. They allow users to buy, sell, and trade cryptocurrencies, often including features for converting fiat currency into crypto. Exchanges may or may not use private keys for transactions, depending on whether they offer custodial services. They are designed for trading purposes rather than long-term storage.

In contrast, cryptocurrency wallets are tools used specifically for storing, sending, and receiving digital currencies. Wallets use private keys to ensure security and allow users to retain control over their assets. Unlike exchanges, wallets do not facilitate trading but are essential for securely managing cryptocurrencies. Wallets can be either online (hot wallets) or offline (cold wallets), depending on their level of security and accessibility.

Selecting the Proper Exchange for Your Investing Needs

When choosing a cryptocurrency exchange, thorough research is paramount. Investigate the exchange's reputation, historical performance, and any issues related to its security. Understanding the background of the exchange's founders and its approach to customer support can provide valuable insights into its reliability [220].

High security is a non-negotiable feature. Given the lack of comprehensive regulation in the crypto space, exchanges must implement robust security measures, including encryption, two-factor authentication, and regular security audits.

Examine the trading pairs and fee structures offered by the exchange. Different exchanges provide varying options for trading pairs and may have different fee structures. Select an exchange that aligns with your investment needs and offers competitive fees for the types of trades you plan to execute.

Lastly, consider the withdrawal and deposit options available on the exchange. A good exchange should offer multiple methods for funding your account and withdrawing funds, including bank transfers, credit and debit cards, and peer-to-peer options. Having convenient and flexible payment options can enhance your overall trading experience [220].

Understanding Trading Pairs and Liquidity

Cryptocurrency exchange trading pairs refer to the combinations of two different cryptocurrencies or a cryptocurrency and a fiat currency that can be traded against each other on an exchange. These pairs define how one asset can be exchanged for another and play a crucial role in determining the trading strategy and liquidity available to traders.

Crypto trading pairs are crucial components of cryptocurrency exchanges such as Coinbase, Binance, and KuCoin. They enable users to trade one cryptocurrency directly for another without the need to first convert either into fiat currency. This functionality is fundamental to the efficiency and flexibility of trading in the cryptocurrency market [222].

For instance, Bitcoin (BTC) is the leading cryptocurrency by market capitalization, while Tether (USDT) is a prominent stablecoin pegged to the U.S. dollar. On exchanges, these are often represented as trading pairs like BTC/USDT or BTC-USDT, depending on the platform. These pairs allow traders to swap Bitcoin for Tether or vice versa, facilitating transactions between different cryptocurrencies [222].

Trading pairs provide a means to compare the values of different cryptocurrencies relative to each other. For example, a pair like BTC/ETH allows traders to see how much Bitcoin is worth in terms of Ethereum. Similarly, pairs such as ETH/BCH illustrate the relative value of Ethereum compared to Bitcoin Cash. This comparative functionality helps traders understand the worth of various assets and make informed trading decisions based on their existing holdings. Exchanges typically offer a range of pairings, allowing users to trade cryptocurrencies they already own, such as BTC, with any pair that includes Bitcoin [222].

Among cryptocurrency pairs, BTC and ETH are the most versatile and commonly offered across exchanges. Many platforms also provide pairs involving cryptocurrencies and fiat currencies like the U.S. dollar (USD), though this is not universal. These pairs facilitate the valuation of assets without relying on fiat money, which is essential for the liquidity and functioning of the crypto economy [222].

To illustrate the importance of trading pairs, consider a real-world analogy involving foreign exchange. An American traveler planning a trip to France would need to understand the exchange rate between the euro and the U.S. dollar to budget effectively. On May 12, 2022, the EUR/USD trading pair might have shown that 1 euro was equivalent to approximately $1.04. This understanding helps the traveller manage expenses and make informed financial decisions during their trip [222].

In the cryptocurrency world, trading pairs serve a similar purpose by enabling users to exchange one cryptocurrency for another directly. This avoids the need for intermediate conversions and associated fees. For example, if a trader wishes to exchange Dogecoin (DOGE) for Shiba Inu coins (SHIB) but the exchange does not offer a direct DOGE/SHIB pair, they might use an indirect route. They could first trade DOGE for USDT using the DOGE/USDT pair and then trade USDT for SHIB using the SHIB/USDT pair. While this method works, it involves multiple trades and incurs additional fees. A direct DOGE/SHIB pair would simplify the process and reduce the trading costs [222].

This concept can be further connected to global travel. If a traveller moving from the U.S. to France and then to England could use the EUR/GBP trading pair, they would save on fees by avoiding the need to convert euros back to U.S. dollars before exchanging them for British pounds. This approach minimizes the number of transactions and associated fees, mirroring how direct trading pairs streamline cryptocurrency exchanges and reduce costs [222].

In a trading pair, the first cryptocurrency listed is called the base currency, while the second currency is the quote currency. For example, in the trading pair BTC/USD, Bitcoin (BTC) is the base currency, and the U.S. Dollar (USD) is the quote currency. This means that the price of Bitcoin is expressed in terms of USD. Traders use this pairing to trade Bitcoin for USD and vice versa.

Types of Trading Pairs

- **Cryptocurrency to Cryptocurrency (Crypto-Crypto)**: These pairs involve two different cryptocurrencies. For instance, BTC/ETH is a trading pair where Bitcoin (BTC) is traded for Ethereum (ETH) or vice versa. Crypto-crypto pairs are common on exchanges and provide liquidity for traders looking to exchange one digital asset for another without needing to convert to fiat currency first.

- **Cryptocurrency to Fiat (Crypto-Fiat)**: These pairs involve trading a cryptocurrency for a fiat currency, such as BTC/USD or ETH/EUR. This type of pairing is essential for users who want to cash out their cryptocurrencies or buy crypto using traditional money. Fiat pairs are crucial for the entry and exit points into the cryptocurrency market.

- **Stablecoin Pairs**: These involve trading a cryptocurrency against a stablecoin, such as BTC/USDT (Tether) or ETH/USDC (USD Coin). Stablecoins are designed to maintain a stable value by being pegged to a fiat currency, providing a way to hedge against volatility and simplify transactions.

Importance of Trading Pairs

- **Liquidity and Market Depth**: The availability of trading pairs impacts the liquidity and market depth of an exchange. High liquidity in a trading pair means that there are ample buyers and sellers, leading to narrower spreads and more stable prices. Exchanges with a wide range of trading pairs tend to attract more traders and provide better liquidity.
- **Trading Strategies**: Different trading pairs offer various opportunities for profit and risk management. Traders may use certain pairs to exploit market inefficiencies, diversify their portfolios, or hedge against potential losses. For instance, trading in pairs that include stablecoins can help manage volatility, while crypto-crypto pairs can provide exposure to emerging digital assets.
- **Price Discovery**: Trading pairs are integral to the price discovery process in the cryptocurrency market. The prices of cryptocurrencies are determined based on the supply and demand within each trading pair. By observing the price movements and trading volumes across different pairs, traders can gauge the relative value of assets and make informed trading decisions.
- **Accessibility and Convenience**: The range of available trading pairs can affect how easily users can trade between different cryptocurrencies and fiat currencies. Exchanges with a broad selection of pairs enable traders to access a wider range of assets and execute trades more efficiently.

Cryptocurrency exchange trading pairs are fundamental to the functioning of crypto markets. They define the possible transactions between different cryptocurrencies or between cryptocurrencies and fiat currencies. Understanding the types of trading pairs and their significance helps traders navigate the market effectively, manage their investment strategies, and optimize their trading opportunities.

In cryptocurrency trading, the concept of a base currency is crucial for understanding how trading pairs work and for effectively managing trades [223]. A base currency is essentially the reference currency against which other currencies are measured. In trading pairs, the base currency is the first currency listed, and its value is used to determine the exchange rate with the second currency in the pair, known as the quote currency.

For example, in the trading pair BTC/USDT, Bitcoin (BTC) is the base currency, and Tether (USDT) is the quote currency. This means that the value of Bitcoin is expressed in terms of Tether. If the BTC/USDT pair is quoted as 30,000, it indicates that one Bitcoin is equivalent to 30,000 Tether. Understanding which currency is the base currency helps traders determine the value of the asset they are interested in and make informed decisions based on the relative strength or weakness of the base currency [223].

The importance of base currencies extends beyond just understanding trading pairs. For traders, especially those new to the crypto market, recognizing base currencies is essential for executing trades efficiently. Most exchanges list trading pairs with popular cryptocurrencies like Bitcoin (BTC) or Ethereum (ETH) as base currencies because they are widely recognized and have high liquidity. This means that if a trader wants to buy or sell a lesser-known cryptocurrency, they might need to use a more established base currency to facilitate the trade [223].

For instance, if a trader wants to purchase a smaller or newer crypto asset that is not directly paired with their desired base currency, they might need to convert their holdings into a more commonly used base currency first. If the exchange only offers trading pairs like BTC/NEWCOIN or ETH/NEWCOIN, then the trader will need to use BTC or ETH as the base currency to trade for NEWCOIN [223].

In addition to popular cryptocurrencies, many exchanges offer stablecoin trading pairs. Stablecoins are digital assets pegged to traditional fiat currencies like the USD, and they provide stability in trading. For example, a trading pair like BTC/USDT allows users to trade Bitcoin against a stablecoin that maintains a value close to USD. This helps in reducing volatility and making transactions more predictable.

Understanding base currencies is essential for navigating cryptocurrency exchanges, executing trades, and effectively managing a trading portfolio. It helps traders to align their strategies with the trading pairs available on their chosen platforms and to make more informed trading decisions based on the relative values of different cryptocurrencies [223].

Understanding how to read cryptocurrency trading pairs is crucial for navigating crypto markets effectively. Trading pairs are represented with two currencies separated by a slash, such as BTC/USDT or ETH/BTC, and each part of the pair provides specific information about how the currencies relate to each other [222, 223].

Base Currency: In a crypto trading pair, the first currency listed is the base currency. This currency is the reference point for the trading pair, meaning it is the one being valued or measured. For example, in the trading pair BTC/USDT, Bitcoin (BTC) is the base currency. This is akin to how the euro (EUR) is the base currency in the EUR/USD currency pair. The base currency is the one that is compared against the second currency in the pair, known as the quote currency. Therefore, the value of the base currency is expressed in terms of the quote currency. In practical terms, if you see BTC/USDT, it tells you how much one Bitcoin is worth in terms of Tether (USDT), which serves as a stablecoin pegged to the US dollar.

Quote Currency: The second part of a trading pair, following the slash, is the quote currency. The quote currency is used to express the value of the base currency. It represents the amount of the quote currency required to purchase one unit of the base currency. For instance, in the pair BTC/USDT, USDT is the quote currency, and it tells you how many USDT are needed to buy one Bitcoin. Similarly, in the EUR/USD pair, the USD is the quote currency, and it indicates how many US dollars are needed to purchase one euro.

Interpreting the Pair: The combination of base and quote currencies in a pair provides the exchange rate or price of one currency in terms of another. This relationship helps traders understand how much of the quote currency they need to exchange to obtain a single unit of the base currency. For instance, if ETH/BTC is quoted at 0.0695, this means that 1 Ether (ETH) is equivalent to 0.0695 Bitcoin (BTC). Essentially, this tells a trader how much Bitcoin they would need to exchange to get one Ether.

In practical trading scenarios, reading these pairs helps traders make informed decisions based on their trading goals and market conditions. If a trader wants to buy Ether using Bitcoin, they would look at the ETH/BTC trading pair to understand how much Bitcoin is required to purchase one Ether. Conversely, if they want to sell Ether for Bitcoin, the same pair tells them the amount of Bitcoin they will receive for their Ether [223].

Trading crypto pairs with stablecoins is a prevalent practice on many cryptocurrency exchanges and plays a crucial role in the digital asset market. Stablecoins, such as Tether

(USDT), USD Coin (USDC), and Binance USD (BUSD), are digital assets designed to maintain a stable value by being pegged to fiat currencies like the U.S. dollar. This stability makes them an essential component in crypto trading pairs for several reasons.

Role of Stablecoins in Crypto Trading Pairs

Stablecoins are commonly used in trading pairs because they provide a stable reference point for valuing other cryptocurrencies. For instance, trading pairs like BTC/USDT or ETH/BUSD involve a major cryptocurrency paired with a stablecoin. This setup offers several advantages [222]:

- **Stability and Liquidity:** Stablecoins are designed to maintain a stable value, usually pegged at 1:1 with a fiat currency such as the U.S. dollar. This stability makes them an ideal reference currency for trading pairs, as they reduce volatility and provide a consistent measure for valuing other cryptocurrencies. Major stablecoins like USDT, USDC, and BUSD are highly liquid, meaning they are widely traded and accepted, which enhances their utility in trading pairs.

- **Ease of Calculation:** From an investor's perspective, using stablecoins simplifies the process of calculating and understanding the value of cryptocurrencies in terms of fiat currency. Since stablecoins are pegged to the U.S. dollar, traders can easily gauge the value of their holdings or trades in USD, making it straightforward to assess gains, losses, or market conditions.

- **Abundance of Pairing Options:** Exchanges like Binance and KuCoin offer a wide range of trading pairs involving stablecoins, providing traders with numerous options to trade various cryptocurrencies. For example, BTC/USDT, ETH/BUSD, and ADA/USDC are common pairs that allow traders to exchange Bitcoin, Ethereum, and Cardano for stablecoins, or vice versa. This abundance of pairs enhances liquidity and trading opportunities, facilitating easier access to buying and selling different cryptocurrencies.

Examples and Practical Use

Consider a trading pair like BTC/USDT. In this pair, Bitcoin (BTC) is the base currency, and Tether (USDT) is the quote currency. When trading BTC/USDT, the price of Bitcoin is expressed in terms of USDT, allowing traders to understand how much Bitcoin costs relative to a stable reference currency. Similarly, with a pair like ETH/BUSD,

Ethereum (ETH) is compared against Binance USD (BUSD), providing a stable measure of Ethereum's value [222].

Stablecoin pairs are also beneficial for executing trades in volatile markets. For example, if a trader wants to avoid the volatility of Bitcoin by temporarily converting their holdings to a more stable asset, they can trade BTC for USDT. This allows them to sidestep market fluctuations while retaining a stable value that can be easily converted back to other cryptocurrencies or fiat currency when desired.

Choosing cryptocurrency pairs for an arbitrage trading strategy involves a nuanced understanding of market dynamics and the correlations between different cryptocurrencies across various exchanges. Arbitrage trading capitalizes on price discrepancies for the same asset or trading pair between different markets or exchanges. The goal is to buy low on one platform and sell high on another, thereby making a profit from the price differential [223].

Arbitrage trading is a strategy designed to exploit price differences of the same or similar financial instruments across different markets or exchanges to generate a profit. This approach leverages the principle of buying low in one market and selling high in another, capitalizing on price discrepancies to secure what is often referred to as a "risk-free profit." Despite the term "risk-free," this strategy does involve operational risks and transaction costs that traders must consider.

Arbitrage trading hinges on the concept of exploiting price discrepancies for the same asset or related assets in distinct markets. When an asset is priced differently in two or more markets, traders can purchase it at a lower price in one market and sell it at a higher price in another. This differential allows traders to lock in a profit from the variance. Although this strategy is termed "risk-free," it is not entirely devoid of risk; it may involve operational challenges, market fluctuations, and transaction costs that can impact profitability.

Types of Arbitrage:

- **Spatial Arbitrage:** Spatial arbitrage involves buying an asset in one geographic location or on one exchange where the asset is undervalued and selling it in another location or on a different exchange where it is priced higher. For instance, if Bitcoin is trading at a lower price on one exchange compared to another, traders can purchase Bitcoin on the cheaper exchange and sell it on the more expensive one, capitalizing on the price differential.

- **Temporal Arbitrage:** This type of arbitrage exploits price differences over time. Traders may purchase an asset when its price is low and hold it until the price increases, subsequently selling it for a profit. Temporal arbitrage relies heavily on timing and the ability to predict market movements, making it more speculative.

- **Statistical Arbitrage:** Statistical arbitrage employs mathematical models and statistical techniques to identify and exploit pricing inefficiencies across various assets or markets. This form of arbitrage often involves high-frequency trading and complex algorithms to analyse and act on market data, aiming to profit from minor price discrepancies that occur with high frequency.

- **Triangular Arbitrage:** Triangular arbitrage involves converting one currency into another through a series of three trades to exploit discrepancies in exchange rates. For example, a trader might convert USD to EUR, then EUR to GBP, and finally GBP back to USD. By doing so, they can profit from the differences in exchange rates between the currencies.

How It Works:

- **Identify Price Discrepancies:** The initial step in arbitrage trading is to identify price discrepancies for the same asset across different markets or exchanges. This is typically achieved using various tools and platforms that monitor and provide real-time price data.

- **Execute Trades:** Once a discrepancy is identified, the trader needs to execute trades swiftly. This involves buying the asset in the market where it is undervalued and selling it in the market where it is overvalued. Rapid execution is crucial to ensure that the price difference remains valid and profitable.

- **Profit Realization:** The profit from arbitrage trading is realized from the price difference, after accounting for any transaction costs, fees, or spreads incurred during the buying and selling process. Efficient management of these costs is essential to ensure that the arbitrage opportunity remains profitable.

In the cryptocurrency markets, arbitrage opportunities are prevalent due to the fragmented nature of the market, where prices can vary across different exchanges. For instance, Bitcoin might be priced lower on one exchange compared to another. Traders can exploit these differences by buying Bitcoin at the lower price and selling it where the price is higher, thereby earning a profit from the price discrepancy.

Risks and Considerations:

- **Transaction Costs:** Transaction fees, withdrawal fees, and spreads can diminish the profits from arbitrage trading. Traders need to factor these costs into their strategy to ensure that the arbitrage remains profitable.

- **Execution Speed:** Arbitrage opportunities can be short-lived, and swift execution is crucial. Delays in executing trades can result in the price discrepancy closing before the trade is completed, reducing or eliminating potential profits.

- **Market Liquidity:** Adequate liquidity is necessary to execute trades without significantly impacting the asset's price. Low liquidity in one market can lead to slippage, where the actual trading price deviates from the expected price, thereby reducing potential profits.

- **Regulatory and Exchange Risks:** Different exchanges and jurisdictions have varying regulations and risks. Traders need to be aware of the regulatory environment and potential issues with the exchanges they use, including compliance and operational risks.

Arbitrage trading is a sophisticated strategy that involves exploiting price differences across markets to secure profits. While it offers opportunities for profit, it requires careful consideration of transaction costs, execution speed, liquidity, and regulatory factors.

The complexity of selecting the right cryptocurrency pairs for arbitrage lies in the varying degrees of correlation between different cryptocurrencies. Correlation measures how closely the price movements of two assets are related. For example, Bitcoin (BTC) often serves as a benchmark for the entire cryptocurrency market due to its high liquidity and wide integration across exchanges. Because of this, BTC is frequently used in arbitrage strategies. However, the correlation between BTC and other cryptocurrencies can fluctuate based on market conditions and trading volumes [223].

In practice, the effectiveness of an arbitrage strategy is influenced by the liquidity of the trading pairs. Liquidity refers to how easily an asset can be bought or sold without affecting its price significantly. Cryptocurrencies with high trading volumes and widespread usage generally exhibit higher liquidity, making it easier to execute trades without impacting the market price. Conversely, trading pairs with limited trading volume or those involving less popular cryptocurrencies often suffer from lower liquidity. This illiquidity creates opportunities for arbitrage as price discrepancies between different exchanges become more pronounced [223].

When using trading pairs with limited trading volume or trading on less widely used exchanges, the market can experience price discrepancies that are more pronounced due to the lack of liquidity. For example, if a lesser-known cryptocurrency is traded on only a few exchanges, and there is a significant difference in its price between these exchanges, an arbitrage opportunity may arise. Traders can exploit this discrepancy by buying the cryptocurrency at a lower price on one exchange and selling it at a higher price on another, thus making a profit [223].

However, implementing an arbitrage trading strategy requires a sophisticated approach and a thorough understanding of market mechanisms. It involves monitoring multiple exchanges, calculating potential profits after considering transaction fees, and executing trades quickly to capitalize on fleeting opportunities. This complexity, combined with the need for precise timing and execution, makes arbitrage trading more suitable for experienced traders rather than novices [223].

Chapter Seven
Investing in Cryptocurrencies

The Basics of Cryptocurrency Investment

Investing in cryptocurrency involves purchasing digital assets with the aim of generating a profit over time. The basics of cryptocurrency investment encompass understanding what cryptocurrencies are, the different types available, the investment strategies, and the associated risks.

Investing in cryptocurrency requires careful consideration and a thorough understanding of the risks and opportunities involved. Due to its inherent volatility and the evolving regulatory landscape, prospective investors should approach cryptocurrency investments with a well-informed strategy and clear intentions. Here's a detailed examination of key factors to consider before investing in cryptocurrency [224]:

- **Volatility and Risk Management:** Cryptocurrencies are known for their extreme price volatility. Prices can experience significant swings within short periods, influenced by market sentiment, news, regulatory changes, and macroeconomic factors. For investors who are risk-averse or uncomfortable with high levels of uncertainty, this volatility can be daunting. It's crucial to assess your own risk tolerance before diving into the crypto market. High volatility means that while there are opportunities for substantial gains, there is also a heightened risk of significant losses. Investors should be prepared for the possibility of sharp price movements and only invest funds they can afford to lose without impacting their financial stability.

- **Regulatory Environment:** The regulatory framework for cryptocurrencies is still developing and varies significantly from one jurisdiction to another. In some regions, cryptocurrencies are well-regulated, providing some degree of investor protection, while in others, the regulatory stance may be unclear or still evolving. The lack of a uniform regulatory approach can lead to uncertainties and potential risks related to legal compliance and the security of your investments. Before investing, it's essential to understand the regulatory environment in your country and any potential changes that might affect the cryptocurrency market.

- **Due Diligence and Avoiding Scams:** Given that anyone can create a cryptocurrency, there are numerous scams and fraudulent projects in the space. Conducting thorough due diligence is crucial to avoid falling victim to scams. Research the credibility of the cryptocurrency, its development team, the technology behind it, and its use case. Verify if the cryptocurrency has a legitimate whitepaper, a clear development roadmap, and an active community. Look for reviews and feedback from reputable sources and avoid investing in projects with limited information or those that promise guaranteed returns.

- **Investment Motivation and Strategy:** It's important to clarify your reasons for investing in cryptocurrency. Are you driven by the desire to follow a market trend, or do you have a well-defined investment strategy? Cryptocurrency investment should not be approached with the expectation of quick and easy profits. Instead, it's advisable to have a clear investment thesis and strategy that aligns with your financial goals. Understand the underlying technology and the potential long-term value proposition of the cryptocurrency you are considering. Make sure your investment aligns with your overall portfolio strategy and risk management approach.

- **Long-Term Perspective:** Cryptocurrencies can experience dramatic price fluctuations, making it easy for emotions to influence investment decisions. Investors may be tempted to buy impulsively during a price surge out of fear of missing out or to sell hastily during a downturn due to panic. However, such emotional reactions often lead to poor investment outcomes. Adopting a long-term perspective can help mitigate the impact of short-term volatility. Focus on the fundamental value and potential long-term prospects of the cryptocurrency rather than getting swayed by daily price movements. A well-thought-out investment strategy should incorporate the possibility of price swings and emphasize patience and discipline.

- **Diversification and Risk Management:** Investing solely in cryptocurrency exposes you to significant risk. Diversification is a key principle of risk management and involves spreading your investments across different asset classes to reduce the impact of volatility in any single investment. Consider balancing your cryptocurrency investments with other asset classes such as stocks, bonds, or real estate to manage risk effectively. Additionally, setting aside a portion of your portfolio specifically for high-risk assets like cryptocurrencies can help maintain overall financial stability.

- **Emotional Control:** Lastly, maintaining emotional control is vital when investing in highly volatile assets like cryptocurrencies. It's easy to become emotionally involved, especially when faced with rapid price changes. Developing a clear investment plan, setting specific goals, and sticking to your strategy can help mitigate the influence of emotions on your investment decisions. Regularly reviewing your portfolio and making adjustments based on your long-term objectives rather than short-term market fluctuations can lead to more disciplined and successful investing.

Deciding whether cryptocurrency is a good investment involves evaluating multiple factors, including your risk tolerance, investment horizon, portfolio diversification, and overall financial goals. Here's an in-depth look at the considerations involved in determining if cryptocurrency is a suitable investment for you:

Cryptocurrency can be a compelling investment opportunity, but its suitability depends on various individual factors. The high volatility of cryptocurrencies means that their values can fluctuate dramatically in a short period. For instance, the price of Bitcoin or Ethereum may surge or plummet within days, driven by market sentiment, technological developments, or regulatory news. This volatility can lead to substantial gains but also significant losses. Therefore, it's crucial to assess your own tolerance for both financial risk and psychological stress before investing in cryptocurrencies [224].

Your investment horizon—the period you plan to hold an investment before needing to access the funds—also plays a significant role. Cryptocurrencies might experience short-term volatility, but if you can maintain a long-term perspective, you may be able to ride out the fluctuations. Additionally, having a diversified investment portfolio can help mitigate some of the risks associated with cryptocurrency investments. Diversification involves spreading investments across various asset classes, which can reduce the impact of poor performance in any single investment.

When considering how much to invest in cryptocurrency, many financial experts recommend allocating no more than 1% to 5% of your net worth to this asset class [224]. This guideline aims to limit your exposure to the high risks associated with cryptocurrencies while allowing for potential growth. The key principle here is never to invest more than you can afford to lose. While a small allocation to cryptocurrencies can potentially enhance the risk-adjusted returns of a diversified portfolio, the exact amount should align with your overall investment strategy and risk tolerance.

Within the cryptocurrency space, diversification is also essential. Just as you diversify across different asset classes, diversifying among various cryptocurrencies can help manage risk [224]. Some cryptocurrencies, like Bitcoin and Ethereum, are considered to have more stable long-term potential compared to smaller, more speculative coins. Larger cryptocurrencies are generally more established and less prone to extreme price manipulations. However, even leading cryptocurrencies can experience significant price swings. Therefore, it's wise to carefully select which cryptocurrencies to include in your portfolio and to monitor their performance regularly.

Pros of Investing in Cryptocurrency

- **Diversification Benefits**: Historically, cryptocurrencies have exhibited low correlation with traditional asset classes like stocks and bonds. This characteristic allows for potential diversification benefits within a portfolio. Although correlations have increased in recent times, adding a small allocation of cryptocurrencies might still improve the risk-adjusted return profile of a diversified portfolio.

- **Comparisons to Traditional Assets**: Some experts compare certain cryptocurrencies, particularly Bitcoin, to traditional assets like gold. Both are considered to be durable and scarce, with their value not controlled by any central authority. This comparison is based on the idea that cryptocurrencies, like gold, are finite and can act as a hedge against inflation or economic instability.

- **Decentralization and Transparency**: Cryptocurrencies operate on decentralized and transparent distributed ledger technology (blockchains). This structure enhances network security and reduces the risk of centralized control or manipulation. The inherent transparency of blockchain technology can provide a high level of integrity and security to transactions.

Cons of Investing in Cryptocurrency

- **High Volatility**: The cryptocurrency market is notorious for its high volatility. Predicting price movements can be challenging, and the reasons behind significant price swings are not always clear. This unpredictability can lead to substantial financial losses if not managed properly.

- **Security Risks**: Although blockchain technology itself is highly secure, individual investors can be susceptible to hacking and cyber threats. The risks inherent in online activity extend to cryptocurrency investments, making it crucial to implement strong security measures such as secure wallets and two-factor authentication.

- **Lack of Regulation and Legal Protections**: Cryptocurrencies are not yet subject to comprehensive government regulation in many jurisdictions. Unlike traditional investments, such as stocks, which are protected by regulatory frameworks and legal recourse, cryptocurrency transactions may lack such protections. This absence of regulation can expose investors to additional risks and uncertainties.

Whether cryptocurrency is a good investment largely depends on your personal financial situation, risk tolerance, and investment goals. While it offers potential for high returns and diversification benefits, it also comes with substantial risks and uncertainties. It is essential to carefully consider these factors, conduct thorough research, and consult with financial advisors if needed before making investment decisions in the cryptocurrency space [224].

As a principle investment strategy [225]:

1. Understand What You're Investing In

Before investing in any cryptocurrency, it's vital to thoroughly understand the asset you're considering. Unlike traditional investments like stocks, which are backed by company fundamentals, cryptocurrencies often lack intrinsic value derived from physical assets or cash flows. For instance, Bitcoin operates without backing from tangible assets or earnings. Instead, its value is driven by market sentiment and the belief that others will pay more for it in the future.

Researching each cryptocurrency's technology, use case, and team behind it is essential. Popular cryptocurrencies like Ethereum, Dogecoin, Cardano, and Solana each have unique features and applications. Ethereum, for example, supports smart contracts and decentralized applications, while Dogecoin started as a meme but has gained traction as a means of digital transactions. Understanding the potential upsides and risks associated with these assets will help you make informed decisions and avoid investments based solely on hype or speculative trends.

2. Remember, the Past Is Past

A common mistake among new investors is assuming that past performance guarantees future results. Just because Bitcoin or another cryptocurrency experienced significant gains in the past does not mean it will continue to do so at the same rate. Historical performance can provide context, but it should not be the sole basis for investment decisions.

When evaluating a cryptocurrency, focus on its future potential rather than past achievements. Consider factors such as its technology, adoption rate, market trends, and any developments that could impact its value. Future returns depend on various variables, including market dynamics, regulatory changes, and technological advancements, rather than merely extrapolating past growth.

3. Watch That Volatility

Cryptocurrencies are known for their extreme volatility, which can result in rapid and significant price changes. This volatility can present both opportunities and risks. For seasoned traders who understand market trends and have the ability to execute trades quickly, volatility can be an advantage. However, for new investors, the erratic nature of cryptocurrency prices can be overwhelming and lead to poor decision-making.

Inexperienced investors might fall prey to emotional responses, such as buying during price surges out of fear of missing out (FOMO) or selling during downturns due to panic. To manage this risk, it's crucial to have a well-thought-out trading strategy and avoid making impulsive decisions based on short-term market movements.

4. Manage Your Risk

Effective risk management is crucial when investing in volatile assets like cryptocurrencies. Developing a clear strategy for managing risk helps protect your investment from significant losses. For long-term investors, a buy-and-hold strategy might be suitable, where they commit to holding their assets regardless of price fluctuations, believing in the long-term potential of their investments.

Short-term traders, on the other hand, may need to establish specific exit points or stop-loss levels to limit losses. For example, setting a rule to sell if the price drops by 10% can prevent a small loss from turning into a substantial one. Additionally, starting with a portion of your investment capital and keeping some funds in reserve allows you to manage unforeseen market movements without depleting your trading resources.

5. Don't Invest More Than You Can Afford to Lose

One of the fundamental principles of investing is to only use funds that you can afford to lose, especially in high-risk areas like cryptocurrency. This means avoiding investing money that is earmarked for essential purposes or future needs, such as a down payment on a house or retirement savings. Instead, allocate a portion of your discretionary funds—money that won't impact your financial stability if lost.

Investing in high-risk assets like cryptocurrencies should be done with caution and as part of a broader investment strategy. If you seek a more secure and guaranteed return, consider options like paying off high-interest debt, which offers a guaranteed return equivalent to the interest rate on the debt.

Additional Considerations

In addition to the above steps, ensure that you choose reputable exchanges and brokers with robust security measures. Despite owning cryptocurrency legally, the responsibility for securing it often falls on the platform where it is held. For added security, consider using hardware wallets or other secure storage methods to protect your assets from potential cyber threats [225].

Making the Investment

For beginners wondering how to start, follow these five steps [224]:

Step 1: Choose What Cryptocurrency to Invest In

Choosing the right cryptocurrency to invest in requires careful evaluation and understanding of each asset's unique characteristics. Just as you would assess the financial health and potential risks of a company before buying its stock, you need to analyse the fundamentals of various cryptocurrencies. Each cryptocurrency operates on different underlying technologies, has different use cases, and may be subject to various levels of market adoption and regulatory scrutiny.

Given the relatively young and rapidly evolving nature of the cryptocurrency market, it's crucial to avoid falling victim to fraud, such as pump-and-dump schemes, where the price of a cryptocurrency is artificially inflated to attract investors, only to be sold off by the perpetrators, causing the price to crash. To minimize the risk of such scams, be cautious of smaller or newer cryptocurrencies that are heavily promoted on social media. These assets might not have established track records or reliable development teams. It's advisable to focus on cryptocurrencies with a solid foundation, transparent development teams, and proven use cases.

The cryptocurrency industry is still largely unregulated, which makes it challenging to completely avoid fraud and cybersecurity risks. For example, the collapse of FTX in 2022, a platform once considered reputable, highlighted the vulnerabilities in the crypto industry. The founder, Sam Bankman-Fried, was convicted of fraud and money laundering, underscoring the need for diligent vetting of platforms and projects. Always conduct thorough research and rely on reputable sources before making any investment decisions.

Step 2: Select a Cryptocurrency Exchange

To buy cryptocurrency, you must use an exchange or investment platform. Selecting a suitable exchange is a critical step in the investment process. Key factors to consider include security, transaction fees, trading volume, minimum investment requirements, and the range of cryptocurrencies offered.

Security should be a top priority when choosing an exchange. Look for platforms with robust security measures, such as two-factor authentication, cold storage for assets, and a history of protecting user funds. Fees can vary significantly between exchanges, including transaction fees, withdrawal fees, and deposit fees, so it's important to understand the cost structure and how it might impact your investment.

Trading volume is another crucial factor, as higher volume generally indicates better liquidity, which can help ensure that your trades are executed at fair prices. Additionally, check the minimum investment requirements, as some exchanges might have minimum amounts for deposits or trades. Finally, ensure that the exchange supports the cryptocurrencies you wish to invest in, as not all platforms offer the same range of digital assets.

Step 3: Consider Storage and Digital Wallet Options

Cryptocurrencies are purely digital assets, which means you need a secure way to store them. There are two primary types of digital wallets: hot wallets and cold wallets.

·Hot wallets are connected to the internet, making them convenient for frequent transactions and easy access. Examples include web wallets and mobile wallets provided by exchanges. While they offer ease of use, they are more vulnerable to online threats, such as hacking and phishing attacks.

Cold wallets, on the other hand, are offline storage devices, like hardware wallets, that provide enhanced security by keeping your private keys away from online risks. Hardware wallets, resembling USB drives, are considered one of the safest methods for storing cryptocurrencies, as they are not connected to the internet and are less susceptible to cyber threats. Depending on your investment strategy and security preferences, you might choose to store your assets in a hot wallet for regular transactions or a cold wallet for long-term holdings.

Step 4: Decide How Much to Invest

Determining how much to invest in cryptocurrency involves evaluating your budget, risk tolerance, and overall investment strategy. Consider factors such as your financial goals, the amount of disposable income available, and the specific risks associated with cryptocurrencies.

Cryptocurrency investments often come with high volatility, so it's crucial to invest only what you can afford to lose. Many experts recommend allocating a small portion of your overall investment portfolio to cryptocurrencies, typically no more than 2-5%. This approach helps to manage risk while still allowing you to benefit from potential upside.

Most exchanges allow you to invest in cryptocurrencies on a dollar basis rather than requiring you to buy whole coins. This flexibility enables you to invest smaller amounts in high-value cryptocurrencies like Bitcoin. Focus on your total investment amount and ensure it aligns with your financial situation and risk tolerance.

Step 5: Manage Your Investments

Effective management of cryptocurrency investments is essential to achieving your financial goals. Cryptocurrencies can be used for transactions or held as long-term investments, depending on your strategy.

If your goal is to use cryptocurrency for transactions, ensure that your chosen wallet or exchange supports your spending needs and offers secure transaction capabilities. For long-term investments, regularly review your holdings and stay informed about market trends, technological developments, and regulatory changes that could impact the value of your assets.

Monitoring your investments and adjusting your strategy as needed will help you stay aligned with your financial objectives. Whether you're holding for the long term or actively trading, maintaining a disciplined approach and staying updated on market conditions will contribute to more informed decision-making and effective investment management.

Other Ways to Invest in Cryptocurrency

While directly investing in cryptocurrencies such as Bitcoin or Ethereum remains popular, several alternative investment vehicles offer exposure to the crypto market, each with its unique characteristics and risk profiles. These alternatives provide various ways to engage with the cryptocurrency sector without directly purchasing digital assets. Here's a detailed look at some of these methods [219, 224, 225]:

Crypto Futures

Crypto futures are contracts that allow investors to speculate on the future price of cryptocurrencies like Bitcoin. Futures contracts obligate the buyer to purchase, or the seller to sell, an asset at a predetermined price on a specified date. This method provides an opportunity to profit from price movements in the crypto market. Futures contracts often involve the use of leverage, which means you can control a larger position with a relatively small amount of capital. While this can amplify potential returns, it also increases the risk of significant losses, especially in a market as volatile as cryptocurrency. The high leverage and rapid price fluctuations inherent in futures trading make it a high-risk option, suitable primarily for experienced investors who can manage the complexities and risks involved.

Bitcoin ETFs

In January 2024, the Securities and Exchange Commission (SEC) approved several exchange-traded funds (ETFs) that invest directly in Bitcoin. Spot Bitcoin ETFs allow investors to gain exposure to Bitcoin's price movements without needing to buy and store the cryptocurrency themselves. These ETFs are traded on traditional stock exchanges and can be purchased through most online brokers that offer stocks and bonds. Bitcoin ETFs provide a more accessible and regulated way to invest in Bitcoin, potentially appealing to those who prefer not to deal with the complexities of managing digital wallets and private keys. Investing in a Bitcoin ETF can simplify the process of gaining exposure to cryptocurrency while also potentially offering more security and regulatory oversight compared to holding Bitcoin directly.

Crypto Exchange or Broker Stocks

Investing in stocks of companies involved in the cryptocurrency industry is another way to gain exposure to the sector. Companies like Coinbase, a major cryptocurrency exchange, or brokers like Robinhood, which facilitate cryptocurrency trading, offer opportunities for indirect investment in the crypto market. These companies typically generate significant revenue from crypto trading and related services, meaning their stock prices can be influenced by the overall performance of the cryptocurrency market. By investing in such companies, you can potentially benefit from the growth of the crypto sector while avoiding the direct risks associated with holding cryptocurrencies. However, it's important to consider that these companies also operate in broader financial markets, so their performance might not perfectly correlate with the price movements of individual cryptocurrencies.

Blockchain ETFs

Blockchain ETFs invest in companies that are involved in developing or utilizing blockchain technology, which underpins cryptocurrencies. These funds offer exposure to a range of businesses that benefit from the growth of blockchain technology but may not be directly involved in cryptocurrency trading. Blockchain ETFs typically include stocks of companies in various sectors, such as technology, finance, and supply chain management, which leverage blockchain for different applications. Investing in a blockchain ETF allows you to participate in the broader adoption of blockchain technology and gain exposure to companies that may experience growth due to this trend. However, since these companies often engage in a variety of activities beyond cryptocurrency, the investment's exposure to the direct movements of digital currencies might be diluted. This approach provides a more diversified exposure to the blockchain ecosystem but might not capture the full volatility and potential upside associated with direct cryptocurrency investments.

Each of these investment methods offers different levels of risk and exposure to the cryptocurrency market. Crypto futures provide a high-risk, high-reward opportunity for speculating on price movements with leverage. Bitcoin ETFs offer a regulated, user-friendly way to invest directly in Bitcoin. Investing in crypto exchange or broker stocks allows indirect exposure to the cryptocurrency market through companies that facilitate trading and related services. Blockchain ETFs provide a broader investment in companies utilizing blockchain technology but may dilute direct cryptocurrency exposure. Understanding the specific characteristics, risks, and potential returns of each method is crucial for aligning your investment strategy with your financial goals and risk tolerance [219, 224, 225].

Investment Strategies

Cryptocurrency investment strategies are approaches and methods used to manage and grow investments in the cryptocurrency market. Given the volatile and evolving nature of cryptocurrencies, these strategies can vary widely, depending on an investor's goals, risk tolerance, and time horizon. Here's a detailed overview of several common cryptocurrency investment strategies:

1. Long-Term Holding (HODLing)

Long-term holding, often referred to as HODLing (a misspelling of "holding" that has become popular in the crypto community), is a strategy where investors purchase cryptocurrencies and hold onto them for an extended period, regardless of short-term market fluctuations. The idea is to benefit from long-term price appreciation as the market matures and adoption grows. This strategy is based on the belief that the value of the cryptocurrency will increase significantly over time. It requires patience and a strong conviction in the chosen asset's long-term potential. Investors who use this strategy often avoid frequent trading and try to ride out the volatility.

Long-term holding, often referred to as HODLing in the cryptocurrency world, is a strategy where investors purchase digital assets and retain them for extended periods, typically years, irrespective of short-term market fluctuations [226]. The term "HODL" originated from a misspelling of "holding" in a 2013 Bitcoin forum post and has since become a rallying cry within the cryptocurrency community. This investment approach is grounded in its simplicity and the belief in the potential for substantial long-term gains [226]. Advocates of HODLing have faith that despite the inherent volatility of the cryptocurrency market, the value of their chosen digital assets will appreciate significantly over time, driven by increased adoption and integration into various sectors [226].

One of the key advantages of HODLing is its low requirement for active management [226]. Investors following this strategy refrain from frequent trading in response to market ups and downs, opting instead to hold onto their assets through market fluctuations with the aim of benefiting from overall market growth. This passive approach can be particularly beneficial during periods of high volatility, allowing investors to sidestep the stress and potential losses associated with trying to time the market [226]. However, HODLing demands patience and a strong belief in the long-term potential of cryptocurrencies, as the market can undergo significant price swings and periods of stagnation [226].

The success of the HODLing strategy hinges on the careful selection of cryptocurrencies with solid fundamentals and promising futures [226]. Investors need to conduct thorough research to ensure that their chosen digital assets align with their long-term investment goals. While HODLing mirrors the traditional "buy and hold" philosophy prevalent in traditional markets, it appeals to individuals more interested in long-term gains than short-term profits [226]. Periodic reassessment of investment choices is crucial for HODLers to confirm that their initial reasons for investing remain valid as the cryptocurrency market evolves [226].

In essence, HODLing embodies a strategic approach to cryptocurrency investment that emphasizes resilience against short-term market fluctuations in favor of long-term growth potential. By maintaining a steadfast belief in the future value appreciation of selected digital assets, HODLers aim to capitalize on the broader adoption and integration of cryptocurrencies into various sectors over time. This strategy's passive nature, coupled with the need for thorough research and periodic review of investment choices, underscores its appeal to investors seeking substantial returns over extended periods while mitigating the stress associated with short-term market volatility.

2. Dollar-Cost Averaging (DCA)

Dollar-Cost Averaging is a strategy where investors regularly invest a fixed amount of money into a cryptocurrency, regardless of its price at the time of purchase. This method spreads out the investment over time, potentially reducing the impact of volatility and lowering the average cost per unit. DCA helps investors avoid trying to time the market and can reduce the risk of making large investments at peak prices. It’s a disciplined approach that can be particularly useful in a highly volatile market like cryptocurrency.

Dollar-Cost Averaging (DCA) is an investment strategy that involves consistently investing a fixed amount of money into a specific asset, such as a cryptocurrency, regardless of its current price. By adhering to this systematic investment plan, investors have the potential to decrease their average cost per unit over time [227].

The fundamental principle of DCA lies in its simplicity and consistency, contrasting with the challenging and unpredictable nature of trying to time the market. Investors utilizing DCA commit to investing a predetermined sum of money at regular intervals, whether weekly, monthly, or quarterly, ensuring purchases are made across various market conditions, from peaks to troughs. Consequently, the average cost of the cryptocurrency acquired through DCA tends to be more balanced and less influenced by short-term price fluctuations [227].

One of the key advantages of DCA is its ability to help investors steer clear of the pitfalls of market timing, which can be particularly arduous in highly volatile markets like cryptocurrencies. By spreading out investments over time, DCA diminishes the risk of making substantial investments at peak prices and subsequently facing significant losses if the market undergoes a downturn. Moreover, DCA fosters disciplined investing behavior by encouraging consistent contributions regardless of market fluctuations, thereby instilling a habit of regular investment and steering clear of emotional decision-making driven by market hype or panic [227].

Another notable benefit of DCA is its capacity to reduce the impact of volatility, especially in markets known for erratic price movements like cryptocurrencies. Through regular investments, some purchases are made at lower prices while others are made at higher prices, leading to an averaging effect that can help smooth out the overall investment cost and potentially offer a more stable return over the long term [227].

While DCA is a valuable strategy for many investors, especially those new to cryptocurrency or those with limited time to actively manage their investments, it does come with limitations. DCA does not guarantee profits or shield against losses, and it may not be the most efficient approach in a consistently rising market where investing a lump sum upfront could potentially yield better returns. Nonetheless, for individuals seeking a structured and less stressful method to establish a position in a volatile market, DCA provides a reliable and disciplined investment approach [227].

3. Swing Trading

Swing Trading involves taking advantage of short- to medium-term price movements. Traders using this strategy buy cryptocurrencies at lower prices and sell them when prices rise, aiming to capitalize on price swings. Swing trading requires technical analysis to identify trends and entry and exit points. This strategy demands more time and attention compared to long-term holding, as traders need to monitor market conditions and be ready to act quickly.

Swing trading is an investment strategy that aims to profit from short- to medium-term price fluctuations in financial markets, including cryptocurrencies, rather than relying on long-term asset appreciation [228]. This approach involves strategically buying low and selling high or vice versa within a condensed timeframe to capitalize on market price oscillations [228]. The core principle of swing trading revolves around identifying and leveraging price movements that occur over days, weeks, or even months [228]. Swing traders strategically enter positions when they perceive an asset to be undervalued or on the brink of a price surge and exit these positions once the asset hits a target price or shows signs of reversing direction [228].

A key component of swing trading is the reliance on technical analysis to inform trading decisions [228]. Traders utilize various tools such as moving averages, Relative Strength Index (RSI), and Bollinger Bands to analyse historical price data and identify potential trends or patterns that can guide their trading strategies [228]. By leveraging these technical indicators, swing traders can make informed choices about when to enter or exit trades based on prevailing market conditions [228]. For instance, a swing trader might identify a stock or cryptocurrency that has recently experienced a price dip and exhibits indications of an impending rebound, prompting them to buy in anticipation of a price upswing [228].

Unlike long-term investment strategies that may necessitate minimal monitoring once positions are established, swing trading demands a higher level of vigilance and engagement [228]. Traders engaging in swing trading must stay abreast of market news, economic developments, and other factors that could influence asset prices [228]. This active involvement often entails continuous monitoring of charts, price movements, and news feeds to pinpoint optimal moments for executing trades [228]. Given the fast-paced nature of swing trading, practitioners must be prepared to make swift decisions and seize emerging opportunities promptly to maximize gains [228].

Risk management is a critical aspect of swing trading, given the inherent potential for losses resulting from short-term market movements [228]. To mitigate these risks, swing traders frequently employ stop-loss orders to curtail potential losses and take-profit orders to lock in gains once predefined targets are achieved [228]. Effective risk management practices are essential for safeguarding capital and ensuring sustained success in swing trading endeavours [228].

While swing trading presents lucrative prospects for profit due to its focus on short-term market dynamics, it demands a substantial commitment of time and effort from traders [228]. Successful swing traders must possess adept analytical skills to interpret market data, remain informed about evolving market trends, and actively manage their positions [228]. Moreover, the inherent volatility of the cryptocurrency market adds an additional layer of complexity to swing trading, as prices can fluctuate rapidly and unpredictably, presenting both challenges and opportunities for traders [228].

Swing trading represents a strategic approach to capitalizing on short- to medium-term price fluctuations in financial markets, including cryptocurrencies [228]. By leveraging technical analysis, actively managing risk, and staying attuned to market developments, swing traders aim to profit from the oscillations in asset prices within a condensed timeframe [228]. While demanding a higher level of engagement compared to long-term investment strategies, swing trading offers the potential for substantial gains for traders who possess the requisite skills and dedication to navigate the dynamic landscape of short-term market movements [228].

4. Day Trading

Day Trading is a strategy where investors buy and sell cryptocurrencies within the same trading day to profit from short-term price movements. Day traders make multiple trades throughout the day, relying on technical analysis, charts, and market news to make decisions. This strategy can be highly profitable but also involves significant risk due to the high volatility and fast-paced nature of the cryptocurrency market. Day trading requires considerable time, expertise, and discipline.

Day trading is a trading strategy that involves the buying and selling of financial assets, such as cryptocurrencies, within the same trading day, focusing on exploiting short-term price fluctuations [229]. This strategy requires rapid execution and constant monitoring of the markets, with day traders typically opening and closing positions within a few hours or even minutes [229]. To identify trading opportunities, day traders heavily rely on technical analysis, which involves examining price charts, patterns, and various technical indicators like moving averages, Relative Strength Index (RSI), and Bollinger Bands [229]. Technical analysis plays a central role in day trading as it helps traders make informed decisions about entry and exit points based on historical price data and current market trends [229].

In addition to technical analysis, day traders must stay informed about market news and events that can influence cryptocurrency prices, such as regulatory announcements or technological advancements [229]. Being vigilant about market news allows day traders to react promptly to news-driven price movements and adjust their trading strategies accordingly [229]. The high volatility of the cryptocurrency market presents both opportunities and risks for day traders, as while there is potential for substantial profits due to frequent price swings, rapid price changes can also lead to significant losses [229]. Effective risk management through tools like stop-loss orders is crucial for day traders to protect their capital and maintain profitability over time [229].

Day trading not only requires technical skills but also a disciplined and strategic approach, with traders needing to develop clear trading plans outlining entry and exit criteria, risk management strategies, and profit targets [229]. Emotional control is also essential in day trading to avoid impulsive decisions driven by stress or emotions, as the fast-paced nature of day trading can be intense [229]. Successful day traders need to remain focused, adhere to their strategies, and avoid letting emotions dictate their trading actions [229]. Moreover, day trading demands a significant time commitment, with traders needing to monitor the markets continuously during trading hours to identify opportunities and execute trades promptly [229].

Day trading is a strategy focused on making multiple trades within a single day to profit from short-term price movements in the cryptocurrency market, relying on technical analysis, market news, and rapid decision-making [229]. While offering the potential for substantial returns, day trading also involves significant risk, requires considerable time and expertise, and demands strict discipline and effective risk management [229]. Traders engaging in day trading must navigate the high volatility of the cryptocurrency market, stay informed about market developments, and maintain a disciplined and strategic approach to maximize their chances of success [229].

5. Arbitrage

Arbitrage involves exploiting price differences of the same cryptocurrency across different exchanges. For example, if Bitcoin is priced lower on one exchange compared to another, an arbitrageur might buy it on the cheaper exchange and sell it on the more expensive one to make a profit. Arbitrage opportunities arise due to discrepancies in supply and demand across exchanges. This strategy requires quick execution and can be limited by transaction fees, liquidity, and exchange constraints.

Arbitrage is a trading strategy commonly utilized in various financial markets, including the cryptocurrency market, that involves exploiting price differences of the same asset across different exchanges to make a profit [230]. The core concept behind arbitrage is that prices should ideally be the same across all markets once transaction costs are considered, but in reality, variations occur due to differences in liquidity, trading volumes, and market conditions [230]. For example, if Bitcoin is priced at $30,000 on one exchange and $30,200 on another, an arbitrageur can buy on the lower-priced exchange and sell on the higher-priced one to gain from the $200 difference [230].

To successfully implement an arbitrage strategy in the cryptocurrency market, traders must act swiftly to capitalize on these price differentials before they normalize [230]. Cryptocurrency markets are highly dynamic, and price gaps can be short-lived, necessitating real-time monitoring of prices across multiple exchanges and the ability to execute trades promptly [230]. Automated high-frequency trading tools and algorithms are commonly employed to streamline this process, enabling traders to exploit small and fleeting price differences efficiently [230].

However, several factors can constrain arbitrage opportunities in the cryptocurrency market. Transaction fees play a significant role, as they can eat into potential profits from arbitrage trades [230]. These fees encompass trading commissions, withdrawal charges, and deposit fees, all of which must be factored in to determine the net gain from arbitrage [230]. For arbitrage to be profitable, the price differential between exchanges must be substantial enough to cover these costs and still yield a profit [230].

Moreover, liquidity is a critical consideration in arbitrage trading. Liquidity refers to how easily an asset can be bought or sold without impacting its price significantly [230]. Limited liquidity on an exchange can impede the execution of large trades without affecting market prices, thereby limiting the effectiveness of arbitrage, especially for cryptocurrencies with lower trading volumes or on exchanges with restricted liquidity [230]. Exchange constraints, such as varying withdrawal and deposit processing times, as well as trading volume restrictions and account verification requirements, can also impact the speed and feasibility of executing arbitrage trades [230].

In addition to practical considerations, regulatory and security aspects must be taken into account when engaging in arbitrage in the cryptocurrency market [230]. Exchanges operate under different regulatory frameworks, and compliance with local regulations can influence trading activities [230]. Security concerns, such as the risk of hacking or fraud on exchanges, can jeopardize the safety of funds, underscoring the importance of using reputable and secure platforms for arbitrage activities [230].

Arbitrage in the cryptocurrency market offers opportunities to profit from price differentials across exchanges, but it requires quick decision-making, cost management, and an understanding of liquidity and exchange constraints [230]. Traders must navigate these challenges while also addressing regulatory compliance and security considerations to effectively leverage arbitrage as a trading strategy in the dynamic and evolving cryptocurrency landscape.

6. Staking

Staking involves participating in a cryptocurrency's network by holding and locking up a certain amount of its tokens in a wallet to support network operations, such as transaction processing and security. In return, stakers earn rewards, often in the form of additional tokens. This strategy is common in Proof of Stake (PoS) and other consensus mechanisms that rely on staking. It provides a way to earn passive income while contributing to the network's functionality.

Staking in the realm of cryptocurrencies is a fundamental process that enables holders of digital assets to engage in network operations and earn rewards by locking up their tokens in a digital wallet [231]. This practice is pivotal in consensus mechanisms like Proof of Stake (PoS) and Delegated Proof of Stake (DPoS), where stakers play a crucial role in validating transactions, upholding blockchain security, and ensuring the smooth functioning of the system [231]. In PoS-based networks, staking entails committing a specific amount of cryptocurrency to the network by depositing tokens into a staking wallet, typically provided by the blockchain's protocol or an approved third-party service [231]. By staking their tokens, participants actively contribute to the network's consensus mechanism, which is responsible for verifying new transactions and blocks [231].

The process of staking offers several key advantages, one of which is the opportunity for cryptocurrency holders to earn passive income by supporting the network [231]. In exchange for locking up their tokens and aiding in network operations, stakers receive rewards, usually in the form of additional tokens, based on the amount staked and the duration of the staking period [231]. This reward system incentivizes participants to contribute to network security and operations, with higher stakes potentially leading to increased rewards, reflecting the level of contribution to the network [231].

Moreover, staking plays a vital role in upholding the security and integrity of blockchain networks by creating a financial incentive for honest behaviour [231]. Participants are required to lock up their tokens, establishing a deterrent against malicious actions or attempts to compromise the network, as such actions could result in stakers losing their staked tokens [231]. This mechanism ensures that participants have a vested interest in maintaining the stability and security of the network, contributing to its overall robustness [231].

Compared to traditional mining processes like Proof of Work (PoW), staking offers advantages such as requiring less technical expertise and lower energy consumption [231]. While PoW systems rely on computational power to solve complex mathematical problems, PoS and similar mechanisms utilize staked tokens as collateral for transaction validation, making staking a more environmentally friendly and accessible option for many investors [231]. This shift towards staking aligns with growing concerns about the environmental impact of energy-intensive mining processes, positioning staking as a more sustainable alternative [231].

However, engaging in staking is not without risks, with one significant concern being the potential for "staking slashing," where participants may lose a portion of their staked tokens as a penalty for dishonest behaviour or network disruptions [231]. Additionally, staked tokens are not readily accessible, requiring participants to commit their assets for a specified period, which could pose challenges if urgent access to funds is needed or if market conditions fluctuate rapidly [231]. This illiquidity aspect underscores the importance of careful consideration before entering into staking arrangements [231].

The staking process can vary across different cryptocurrencies and their underlying protocols, with some networks mandating participants to operate and maintain their validator nodes, while others permit staking through pooled services or delegator systems [231]. Pooled staking involves consolidating tokens from multiple participants to enhance the likelihood of being selected to validate transactions, with rewards distributed proportionally among all contributors [231]. This diversity in staking mechanisms offers flexibility to participants based on their preferences and technical capabilities [231].

Staking stands as a popular strategy for earning passive income while actively supporting the functionality and security of cryptocurrency networks [231]. It presents an avenue for cryptocurrency holders to engage in network operations and receive rewards for their contributions, albeit with associated risks that necessitate careful evaluation [231]. By aligning financial incentives with network integrity, staking plays a pivotal role in the sustainable growth and operation of blockchain ecosystems, offering a more accessible and environmentally friendly alternative to traditional mining processes [231].

7. Yield Farming and Liquidity Mining

Yield Farming and Liquidity Mining are strategies where investors provide liquidity to decentralized finance (DeFi) protocols in exchange for rewards. Yield farming involves lending or staking cryptocurrencies to earn interest or rewards, while liquidity mining involves providing liquidity to decentralized exchanges (DEXs) and earning fees or tokens in return. These strategies can offer high returns but come with risks related to smart contract vulnerabilities, impermanent loss, and market volatility.

Yield Farming and Liquidity Mining are investment strategies within the decentralized finance (DeFi) ecosystem that allow investors to earn rewards by providing liquidity to various DeFi protocols. Yield Farming involves earning interest or rewards through lending or staking, while Liquidity Mining entails providing liquidity to decentralized exchanges (DEXs) and earning fees [232]. In Yield Farming, investors deposit their assets into lending platforms or yield farming protocols to receive interest payments or additional tokens as rewards, often denominated in the protocol's native token or other cryptocurrencies [232]. On the other hand, Liquidity Mining involves depositing cryptocurrencies into a liquidity pool on a DEX to facilitate trading and earning a share of transaction fees along with governance tokens or other rewards [232].

The mechanisms of Yield Farming and Liquidity Mining differ. Yield Farming involves activities like depositing stablecoins into lending protocols or staking tokens in liquidity pools on DEXs to maximize returns based on yield rates or reward incentives [232]. In contrast, Liquidity Mining specifically focuses on providing liquidity to DEXs, where liquidity providers earn a portion of transaction fees generated within the pool, along with additional rewards like governance tokens [232]. Both strategies offer opportunities for generating returns but also come with risks related to smart contract vulnerabilities, impermanent loss, and market volatility, necessitating careful analysis and risk management [232].

Smart contract vulnerabilities pose a significant risk in both Yield Farming and Liquidity Mining, as these protocols rely on complex code to manage transactions and distribute rewards. Bugs or exploits in smart contracts can lead to the loss of funds, highlighting the importance of thorough security audits and due diligence before participating in these strategies [232]. Market volatility is another risk factor to consider, as the fluctuation in asset values can impact overall returns, making it crucial for investors to monitor and assess the liquidity and trading volumes of the assets involved [232].

Moreover, changes in protocols and updates can influence reward structures and yield rates, introducing an element of uncertainty for participants in Yield Farming and Liquidity Mining [232]. These strategies require investors to have a deep understanding of the protocols they engage with, stay informed about developments in the DeFi space, and carefully evaluate the associated risks to make informed decisions [232]. Despite the potential for high returns, it is essential for investors to conduct thorough research, review security audits, and assess liquidity factors to mitigate risks effectively [232].

Yield Farming and Liquidity Mining present opportunities for investors to earn rewards by contributing assets to DeFi protocols, with each strategy offering distinct mechanisms and risk profiles. While Yield Farming focuses on generating interest or rewards through lending or staking, Liquidity Mining involves providing liquidity to DEXs and earning fees along with additional incentives [232]. However, both strategies require careful consideration of smart contract vulnerabilities, impermanent loss, and market volatility, emphasizing the importance of due diligence and risk management in participating in these investment strategies within the DeFi ecosystem.

8. ICOs and Token Sales

Initial Coin Offerings (ICOs) and Token Sales are fundraising methods used by cryptocurrency projects to raise capital. Investors purchase tokens during these events, often at a discount, with the expectation that the tokens will increase in value once the project is fully launched. Investing in ICOs and token sales can be highly speculative, as many projects are in their early stages and carry significant risk. Due diligence is essential to assess the project's potential and avoid scams.

Initial Coin Offerings (ICOs) and Token Sales are fundraising mechanisms utilized by cryptocurrency projects to secure capital for their development and launch phases. These methods enable investors to acquire project-specific tokens, often at a discounted rate, with the expectation that the token value will appreciate once the project becomes operational [233]. ICOs involve crowdfunding where new cryptocurrency or blockchain projects issue tokens to investors in exchange for established cryptocurrencies like Bitcoin or Ethereum. Typically, ICOs occur before the project is fully operational, allowing investors to purchase tokens at a reduced price in anticipation of future value appreciation [234].

While ICOs and token sales offer avenues for early investors to potentially benefit from emerging projects, they also pose significant risks that necessitate careful evaluation. Many ICO projects are in early stages without a proven track record or fully developed technology, exposing investors to potential scams and fraudulent activities due to the lack of regulatory oversight in many jurisdictions [233]. Therefore, thorough due diligence is crucial before engaging in ICOs, involving scrutiny of the project's whitepaper, team credibility assessment, and evaluation of the project's feasibility [235].

Token Sales encompass various formats, including Pre-Sales, Private Sales, and Public Sales. Pre-Sales involve early token sales before the public offering, often providing tokens at lower prices to attract initial investors and raise initial funds [236]. Private Sales, similar to Pre-Sales, target a select group of investors under specific terms and conditions, offering additional incentives to attract significant investments [237]. Public Sales represent the final stage where tokens are offered to the general public, typically through ICOs or other platforms, with prices reflecting increased risk and speculation [238].

Participating in token sales presents an appealing opportunity to invest in emerging cryptocurrency projects, although the speculative nature of these investments entails high risks. Projects conducting token sales are often in developmental stages, with no guarantee of success or fulfillment of promises, compounded by evolving regulatory landscapes that may introduce legal and financial uncertainties for investors [239]. Due diligence is paramount for investors considering ICOs and token sales, involving reviewing whitepapers, assessing team credibility, understanding the technology, and evaluating community support to gauge project legitimacy and potential [240].

ICOs and token sales offer avenues for investors to engage with and potentially benefit from emerging cryptocurrency projects. However, these fundraising methods come with substantial risks that necessitate thorough due diligence to assess project legitimacy and potential before investment. Investors must carefully evaluate projects, teams, technologies, and community support to make informed decisions regarding participation in ICOs and token sales [241].

9. Diversification

Diversification involves spreading investments across multiple cryptocurrencies to reduce risk. By investing in a range of assets, investors aim to mitigate the impact of poor performance in any single cryptocurrency. Diversification can help balance risk and reward, especially in a volatile market. Investors may choose to diversify across various types of cryptocurrencies, including established coins, altcoins, and tokens associated with different use cases and technologies.

Diversification in cryptocurrency investment is a strategic approach aimed at spreading risk by distributing capital across a range of assets, including various cryptocurrencies. This strategy is rooted in the concept that different cryptocurrencies may react differently to market dynamics, technological advancements, and regulatory changes, thereby reducing the overall risk exposure of an investment portfolio [242]. By diversifying across multiple cryptocurrencies, investors can potentially mitigate severe losses that may arise from the poor performance of a single asset. For instance, if one cryptocurrency experiences a significant decline due to market fluctuations or technical issues, other cryptocurrencies in the portfolio may remain stable or appreciate, helping to offset losses and stabilize the overall investment value [243].

One key aspect of diversification in cryptocurrency investment involves considering asset variety. Investors can achieve diversification by investing in a mix of cryptocurrencies, including established ones like Bitcoin and Ethereum, which are perceived to have lower volatility compared to newer or smaller coins. Additionally, including alternative cryptocurrencies (altcoins) that serve different purposes and utilize distinct technologies, such as those related to decentralized finance (DeFi) or non-fungible tokens (NFTs), can further enhance diversification [244]. This approach ensures exposure to a spectrum of crypto assets with varying risk profiles and growth potentials.

Moreover, diversification can extend to technological and use case diversity within a cryptocurrency portfolio. By investing in cryptocurrencies that support different technologies and applications, such as privacy-focused coins like Monero, smart contract platforms like Ethereum, or blockchain scalability solutions like Solana, investors can tap into diverse segments of the crypto market. Each type of cryptocurrency offers unique features and advancements, providing investors with exposure to various facets of the evolving crypto landscape [245].

Furthermore, geographical and platform diversity play a role in enhancing diversification in cryptocurrency investment. Including assets from different geographical markets and platforms that cater to specific user bases can help reduce the impact of localized market issues or platform-specific challenges. This approach broadens the scope of the investment portfolio and minimizes the concentration of risk associated with particular regions or platforms [246].

The benefits of diversification in cryptocurrency investing are multifaceted. Firstly, diversification aids in risk reduction by spreading investments across multiple assets, thereby mitigating the adverse effects of events that impact individual cryptocurrencies. For example, if one coin faces regulatory hurdles or technical setbacks, other assets in the portfolio can potentially perform well, offsetting losses and maintaining portfolio stability [247]. Additionally, diversification offers the potential for increased returns by enabling investors to capitalize on various growth opportunities within the crypto market. While some assets may experience rapid appreciation, others may provide steady growth, leading to a balanced portfolio that can enhance overall returns [248].

Moreover, diversification assists in managing volatility, a characteristic synonymous with cryptocurrency markets. By diversifying across assets with different levels of price fluctuation, investors can effectively navigate market volatility and create a more stable investment experience. This approach reduces the likelihood of extreme losses during turbulent market conditions, enhancing the resilience of the investment portfolio [249].

However, it is crucial to note that diversification does not eliminate all risks associated with cryptocurrency investing. Investors must exercise caution in selecting the cryptocurrencies for their portfolios and stay abreast of market trends, technological developments, and regulatory changes to make informed decisions. Over-diversification can also pose challenges in portfolio management and may dilute potential gains if selected assets underperform.

Diversification in cryptocurrency investment is a fundamental strategy that offers investors the opportunity to spread risk, balance reward, and potentially enhance returns by allocating capital across a variety of crypto assets. By diversifying across different types of cryptocurrencies, technologies, geographical markets, and platforms, investors can build resilient portfolios that are better equipped to withstand market fluctuations and uncertainties. While diversification is not a foolproof strategy, when implemented thoughtfully and in conjunction with thorough research and monitoring, it can be a valuable tool for managing risk and optimizing investment outcomes in the dynamic world of cryptocurrency.

10. Hedging

Hedging is a strategy used to offset potential losses in one investment by taking an opposing position in another. For instance, if an investor holds a significant amount of Bitcoin, they might use derivatives or other financial instruments to hedge against potential price declines. Hedging can help protect against adverse price movements but often involves additional costs and complexities.

Hedging is a financial strategy designed to reduce the risk of adverse price movements in an investment by taking an opposing position in a related asset. This approach aims to offset potential losses in one investment with gains from another, thereby protecting the investor's overall portfolio from significant declines in value. Hedging is commonly used to manage risk in volatile markets, including cryptocurrency investments [250].

For example, consider an investor who holds a substantial amount of Bitcoin. If they are concerned about potential declines in Bitcoin's price, they might employ hedging strategies to mitigate this risk. One common method is through the use of derivatives, such as futures contracts, options, or swaps.

Derivatives are financial instruments whose value is derived from the performance of an underlying asset, in this case, Bitcoin. By using Bitcoin futures contracts, an investor can agree to sell Bitcoin at a predetermined price in the future. If Bitcoin's price falls, the investor can still sell at the higher contract price, thus reducing the impact of the price drop on their overall holdings. Similarly, Bitcoin options allow investors to buy or sell Bitcoin at specific prices within a set timeframe, providing a way to benefit from or protect against price changes.

Hedging involves various financial instruments and strategies that can be tailored to an investor's specific needs and risk tolerance. Some common hedging techniques include:

- **Futures Contracts**: These are agreements to buy or sell an asset at a predetermined price on a specific date. By entering into a futures contract to sell Bitcoin, an investor can lock in a selling price, thus protecting against a potential decline in Bitcoin's market price.

- **Options Contracts**: Options give investors the right, but not the obligation, to buy or sell an asset at a specified price before or at the contract's expiration date. For example, a put option allows an investor to sell Bitcoin at a certain price, offering protection if the market price falls below this level.

- **Swaps**: Swaps are agreements to exchange cash flows or other financial instruments between parties. Cryptocurrency swaps might involve exchanging Bitcoin for another asset or cryptocurrency, potentially offsetting losses if Bitcoin's value decreases.

Benefits of Hedging include:

- **Risk Reduction**: Hedging can effectively reduce the risk of significant losses from adverse price movements. By having a counterbalancing position, investors can protect their investments from severe downturns in the market.

- **Predictable Returns**: With effective hedging, investors can achieve more stable returns. Hedging helps to smooth out the volatility of the investment portfolio, allowing for more predictable financial outcomes.

- **Improved Investment Confidence**: Knowing that potential risks are mitigated can boost an investor's confidence. This enables them to make investment decisions with a clearer understanding of their risk exposure.

However, hedging has its drawbacks:

- **Costs**: Hedging strategies often involve costs, such as premiums for options or margins for futures contracts. These costs can add up and potentially reduce overall profitability.
- **Complexity**: Implementing effective hedging strategies requires a thorough understanding of financial instruments and market conditions. The complexity of managing multiple positions and instruments can be challenging, especially for less experienced investors.
- **Potential for Reduced Gains**: While hedging can protect against losses, it may also limit potential gains. If the market moves favourably, the gains might be offset by the cost of the hedging positions, resulting in lower overall returns compared to an unhedged investment.

Hedging is a valuable strategy for managing risk in investments, including cryptocurrencies. By taking opposing positions or using financial instruments like derivatives, investors can protect themselves from adverse price movements and reduce overall risk. However, the associated costs and complexities must be carefully considered, and the effectiveness of hedging depends on the investor's ability to manage these factors and implement appropriate strategies.

Cryptocurrency investment strategies vary widely, each with its own set of risks and potential rewards. The choice of strategy depends on an investor's goals, risk tolerance, time horizon, and expertise. Whether opting for long-term holding, active trading, or alternative methods such as staking and yield farming, it's crucial to thoroughly research and understand each approach to make informed investment decisions. Diversification and risk management are key components of a well-rounded investment strategy in the highly volatile cryptocurrency market.

Technical Analysis vs. Fundamental Analysis

In the world of cryptocurrency investing, two primary methods for evaluating and making decisions about assets are technical analysis and fundamental analysis. Both approaches offer different perspectives on how to assess cryptocurrencies and their potential for investment, and each has its own set of tools, techniques, and objectives.

Technical Analysis

Technical analysis focuses on evaluating a cryptocurrency based on its price movements and trading volume. This method uses historical data, typically presented in charts, to identify patterns and trends that might indicate future price movements. The core premise of technical analysis is that all relevant information, including fundamental factors, is already reflected in the price of the cryptocurrency.

Key aspects of technical analysis include:

- **Price Charts**: Technical analysts use various types of charts, such as line charts, bar charts, and candlestick charts, to visualize price movements over different time periods. Candlestick charts, in particular, are popular for their ability to show open, high, low, and close prices in a single visualization, providing insights into market sentiment and trends.

- **Indicators and Oscillators**: Analysts employ technical indicators and oscillators to gauge market conditions. Common indicators include Moving Averages (MA), Relative Strength Index (RSI), and Bollinger Bands. These tools help traders identify potential entry and exit points, market trends, and overbought or oversold conditions.

- **Chart Patterns**: Technical analysis often involves recognizing patterns in price charts, such as head and shoulders, double tops, and triangles. These patterns are believed to signal potential future price movements based on historical behaviour.

- **Volume Analysis**: Trading volume, or the amount of a cryptocurrency traded within a specific period, is another crucial aspect. Changes in volume can indicate the strength of a price movement, with high volume suggesting strong interest and potentially validating price trends.

- **Trend Analysis**: Identifying and following trends is central to technical analysis. Analysts look for trends, whether upward, downward, or sideways, and use tools like trendlines and channels to make predictions about future price movements.

Technical analysis is advantageous for short-term trading and offers insights based on market behaviour and price action. However, it does not consider underlying factors that might influence the long-term value of a cryptocurrency. As such, it is often used in conjunction with other methods to form a comprehensive investment strategy.

Technical analysis is a critical tool for traders seeking to interpret market dynamics and forecast the price trajectories of cryptocurrencies. This method involves examining historical price data and trading volumes to discern patterns and trends that could indicate future price movements. The origins of technical analysis can be traced back to Charles Dow, whose pioneering Dow Theory laid the groundwork for what has evolved into a sophisticated array of analytical techniques used today [251]. At its core, technical analysis operates on the premise that market prices inherently reflect all available information, implying that the current price of an asset encapsulates its intrinsic value.

Dow Theory, established over a century ago by Charles Dow, remains a foundational concept in technical analysis and market trend analysis. It provides a framework for understanding and predicting market movements by identifying and interpreting trends. Dow Theory originated with the creation of the Dow Jones Industrial Average (DJIA) and the Dow Jones Railroad Average (DJRA), which have evolved to include broader market indices [252].

In 1896, Dow introduced the Dow Jones Industrial Average, which initially comprised 12 industrial companies. Dow calculated the average by summing the closing prices of these companies and dividing by 12. This index aimed to provide a snapshot of the overall health of the industrial sector. As larger corporations emerged, Dow adjusted his approach, increasing the number of companies in the index to 20 in 1916 [252]. Simultaneously, he created the Dow Jones Railroad Average to track the performance of railroad stocks, reflecting their critical role in the economy. Over time, as transportation evolved, the DJRA transitioned into the Dow Jones Transportation Average (DJTA) in 1970, incorporating airline and trucking stocks instead of railroads [252].

Dow Theory asserts that for a market trend to be considered valid, both the industrial and transportation indices must move in tandem. Dow observed that industrial output and transportation activity are closely linked—when industrial production rises, transportation activity also increases, and vice versa. This principle remains relevant today, as the DJIA and DJTA must confirm each other's signals to validate a new market trend. For example, if the DJIA shows an upward trend while the DJTA does not, the trend's validity is questioned, as both indices should ideally reflect the same directional movement.

The principles of Dow Theory provide a structured approach to analysing market trends [252]:

1. **Price Reflects All Information**: According to Dow Theory, market prices reflect all available information about an asset. This includes factors such as the asset's financial health, market conditions, and external influences. Therefore, the current price is considered a comprehensive representation of an asset's value.

2. **Types of Market Trends**: Dow Theory categorizes market trends into three main types: primary, secondary, and minor. Primary trends, which can be bullish (upward) or bearish (downward), represent the long-term direction of the market. Secondary trends are shorter-term movements that counter the primary trend, such as corrections in bull markets or rallies in bear markets. Minor trends are brief fluctuations within the secondary trends.

3. **Phases of Primary Trends**: Primary trends are divided into three phases. In a bull market, these are the accumulation phase (where informed investors begin buying), the public participation phase (where broader market participation increases), and the excess phase (characterized by speculative buying). In a bear market, the phases are distribution (where selling occurs as insiders exit), public participation (where more investors become pessimistic and sell), and panic (characterized by widespread selling).

4. **Correlation of Market Indices**: Dow Theory emphasizes that signals from different market indices should align to confirm a new trend. If one index signals a downtrend while another signals an uptrend, a new trend is not considered confirmed. Confirmation occurs when multiple indices reflect the same directional movement, whether up or down.

5. **Volume Correlation with Trends**: According to Dow Theory, market volume should correspond with price trends. In a bull market, volume typically increases, supporting the trend. In a bear market, volume generally decreases. A drop in volume during a bull market may signal a potential trend reversal, indicating

a shift toward bearish conditions.

6. **Persistence of Trends**: Dow Theory posits that market trends persist until a clear reversal occurs. This means that trends continue despite daily price fluctuations, and a trend is only considered over when there is a definite and sustained reversal in direction.

By understanding and applying these principles, traders and analysts can gain insights into market movements and make informed decisions. Although Dow Theory has evolved with modern financial markets, its core principles continue to offer valuable guidance for analysing and interpreting market trends [252].

In practice, technical analysts heavily rely on charting tools and patterns to identify potential buying and selling points. Among the essential elements of technical analysis are the recognition of bullish and bearish trends. Bullish trends suggest upward price movements, while bearish trends indicate downward movements, both driven by market sentiment. One of the most popular charting tools is the candlestick chart, which provides a visual representation of price fluctuations within specific time frames. This charting method helps traders spot trends and potential reversals by showcasing the open, high, low, and close prices in a single chart. Each candlestick reveals market sentiment and potential future price actions based on its colour and shape [251].

Support and resistance levels are also pivotal in technical analysis. Support refers to a price level where buying interest is strong enough to prevent further declines, while resistance is a level where selling pressure may halt price increases. Trendlines are used to mark these levels and help traders identify strategic entry and exit points. Prices often struggle to breach these levels without substantial market momentum, making them crucial for formulating trading strategies [251].

Moving averages are another key tool in technical analysis. They help smooth out price fluctuations over time, highlighting underlying trends and reducing noise. Traders often observe the interaction between short-term and long-term moving averages, such as the 50-day and 200-day moving averages. Significant market signals like the "death cross" (when a short-term average crosses below a long-term average) and the "golden cross" (when a short-term average crosses above a long-term average) can indicate potential market downturns or upswings, respectively.

Despite its effectiveness, technical analysis is not infallible and is best utilized in conjunction with other methods, such as fundamental analysis. Technical analysis excels in short-term trading scenarios and helps traders make decisions based on market behaviour and price action. However, it does not account for the underlying factors that might influence a cryptocurrency's long-term value. By mastering these analytical techniques, traders can enhance their ability to make strategic decisions in the fast-paced and often unpredictable cryptocurrency market [251].

Applying Technical Analysis

Applying technical analysis to cryptocurrency trading involves meticulously examining market data to forecast future price movements and make informed trading decisions. This approach has been adapted from traditional financial markets and tailored to fit the unique characteristics of cryptocurrencies. The essence of technical analysis lies in identifying patterns and signals from historical trading activity that can guide future price action [251].

Traders start by utilizing various charting tools, with candlestick charts being among the most valuable. These charts offer a detailed view of price movements within specified timeframes, with each candlestick representing the open, high, low, and close prices. The visual representation helps traders gauge market sentiment and predict future trends based on the patterns formed.

Trendlines are used to establish support and resistance levels, which are crucial for determining potential barriers to price movement. Support levels indicate where buying interest is strong, while resistance levels signify where selling pressure may arise. These levels guide traders in formulating strategies, such as buying near support and selling near resistance, to align with prevailing trends.

Moving averages, such as the 200-day moving average, offer a smoothed perspective of price trends. These averages help identify key support and resistance levels during uptrends and downtrends. The crossing of moving averages can signal significant market shifts, with traders watching for these interactions to make timely decisions [251].

Interpreting Trading Charts

Interpreting trading charts is a fundamental aspect of technical analysis, enabling traders to make strategic decisions in the cryptocurrency market. The process involves analysing statistical trends from historical trading data to identify market trends and predict future price movements. Candlestick charts play a crucial role in this interpretation by providing a detailed depiction of price action within specific timeframes. The colour and shape of the candlesticks reveal whether the price movement was positive or negative and the extent of that movement, offering insights into market sentiment [251].

Support and resistance levels, identified through trendlines, are significant in chart interpretation. These levels indicate where buying or selling interest may prevent price movements beyond these points. Traders often strategize around these levels to capitalize on market trends, buying at support and selling at resistance.

Moving averages provide a smoothed view of price trends, helping traders identify support and resistance levels during different market conditions. The crossing of moving averages can signal major market changes, guiding trading decisions [251].

While technical analysis offers valuable insights, it should be approached cautiously and used alongside other methods, including fundamental analysis. By mastering chart interpretation and incorporating various analytical techniques, traders can enhance their ability to anticipate market movements and execute trades that align with their investment strategies [251].

Identifying Trends

In the world of financial markets, including cryptocurrency trading, trends are fundamental to understanding market movements. Markets typically exhibit three primary types of trends: uptrends, downtrends, and consolidation trends. Recognizing these trends is crucial for traders seeking to make informed decisions and develop effective trading strategies [252].

Upward Trends: An uptrend is characterized by a series of higher highs and higher lows. This pattern indicates that the market is moving upward, with each successive peak being higher than the previous one, and each trough being higher than the previous trough. To identify an uptrend on a chart, traders often draw an uptrend line, which is a diagonal line connecting the lows of the price movements. This line acts as a visual representation of the underlying trend and helps traders to determine potential support levels. In addition to trend lines, moving averages can be used to identify uptrends. For example, a common method involves observing if the current price is consistently above a moving average, such as the 50-day or 200-day moving average. If the price remains above this average, it suggests an uptrend.

Downward Trends: Conversely, a downtrend is marked by lower highs and lower lows, indicating a market in decline. In a downtrend, each subsequent peak is lower than the previous peak, and each trough is lower than the preceding trough. To visualize this trend, traders draw a downtrend line above the price action, connecting the highs. This line helps highlight the resistance level and the general direction of the market's decline.

Similar to uptrends, moving averages can also be utilized to confirm a downtrend. If the price is consistently below a moving average, it indicates that the market is in a downtrend.

Consolidation Trends: During an uptrend or downtrend, the market may enter a phase of consolidation, where the price moves sideways within a narrow range. This period of lateral movement indicates that the market is not establishing a clear upward or downward direction, resulting in a relatively stable price range. Consolidation trends are often referred to as sideways markets and can be less dynamic compared to trending markets. These periods are characterized by horizontal trend lines that define the upper and lower boundaries of the trading range. Traders use different strategies in consolidation phases, such as range trading, where they buy at the support level and sell at the resistance level. Understanding consolidation trends is essential for adapting trading strategies to these less volatile periods.

Identifying and understanding these trends—upward, downward, and consolidation—allows traders to make more informed decisions. By recognizing the type of trend and utilizing tools like trend lines and moving averages, traders can develop strategies that align with the market's current phase. This insight is crucial for optimizing trading decisions and managing risk effectively in the dynamic cryptocurrency market.

Technical Indicators for Crypto Analysis

Candlestick Charts: Candlestick charts, a significant innovation in the field of technical analysis, have their origins in Japan dating back to the 1700s. Initially used by rice merchants to track and analyse the prices of rice, these charts were popularized in the West by Steven Nison through his seminal book, *Japanese Candlestick Charting Techniques.* Candlestick charts provide a visually engaging way to display price movements and are now a staple in trading platforms across various financial markets, including cryptocurrencies [252].

Each candlestick on the chart represents a specific time interval, which can vary from as short as one minute to as long as one month, depending on the trader's preference. The candlestick consists of two main components: the body and the wicks (or shadows). The body of the candlestick is the area between the opening and closing prices of a cryptocurrency within the selected time frame. It provides a visual representation of the price range where most trading activity occurred. The colour of the body helps to identify the direction of the price movement—typically, a green or white body indicates a bullish candlestick, where the closing price is higher than the opening price, while a red or black body represents a bearish candlestick, where the closing price is lower than the opening price [252].

The wicks, or shadows, extend from the body and indicate the highest and lowest prices reached during the time interval. The top wick shows the peak price, while the bottom wick reveals the lowest price. These wicks provide additional context about the price volatility within the time period, showing how far prices have moved above and below the opening and closing levels.

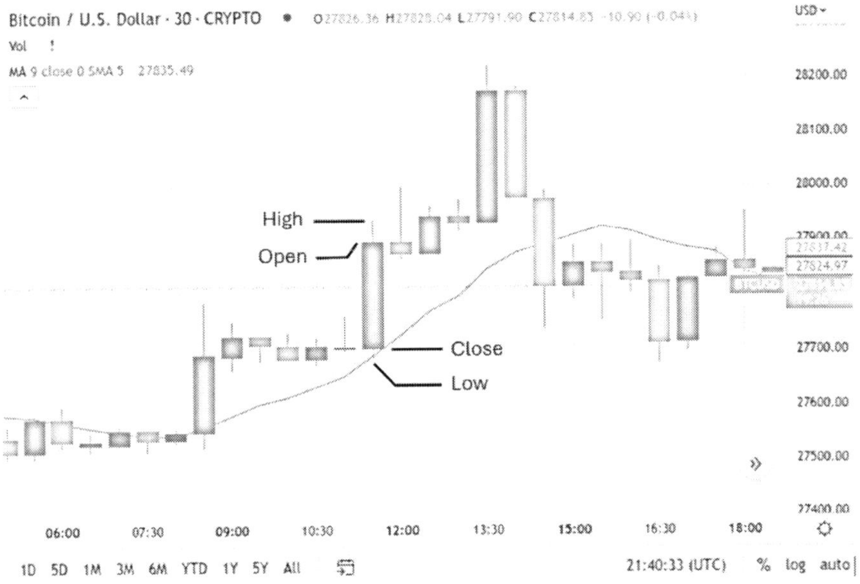

Figure 15: Example Candlestick Chart.

Candlestick charts are especially popular among cryptocurrency traders due to their ability to convey a lot of information in a compact and visual format. Traders use these charts to identify patterns and trends that can signal potential market movements. For short-term traders, candlestick charts with intervals ranging from one minute to several hours are crucial for making quick decisions. In contrast, long-term traders might focus on daily, weekly, or monthly charts to analyse broader market trends [252].

Interpreting candlestick patterns involves recognizing specific formations that can suggest future price actions. For example, a series of candlesticks might form a recognizable pattern such as a "doji," which indicates market indecision, or a "hammer," which can signal a potential reversal in trend. These patterns, when combined with other technical indicators, can help traders make informed decisions about buying or selling cryptocurrencies [252].

Overall, candlestick charts are a powerful tool for analysing cryptocurrency markets. They provide a clear and detailed view of price movements and trends, helping traders to make more informed decisions based on historical price action and potential future outcomes.

Simple/Smoothed Moving Averages (SMA): The Simple Moving Average (SMA) is one of the fundamental tools in technical analysis, used to smooth out price data over a specified period. This smoothing helps traders identify the underlying trend of a cryptocurrency by averaging out short-term price fluctuations. For instance, the SMA can be calculated over various time frames, such as 50-day, 100-day, or 200-day periods. These averages are plotted on charts to provide insight into the trend direction [253].

When the current price of a cryptocurrency is above its SMA, it often signals an uptrend, suggesting that prices are generally rising. Conversely, if the current price falls below the SMA, it indicates a downtrend, suggesting that prices are declining. A common trading signal is the crossover of short-term moving averages with long-term ones. For example, when the 50-day SMA crosses above the 200-day SMA, it's known as a "golden cross" and is typically seen as a bullish signal indicating potential for a price increase. On the other hand, a "death cross," where a short-term SMA crosses below a long-term SMA, is generally interpreted as a bearish signal suggesting a potential decline in prices. The SMAs are usually displayed on the chart alongside candlesticks, providing a clear visual representation of trends [253].

Moving Average Convergence/Divergence (MACD): The MACD indicator is a versatile tool used to gauge the strength and direction of a trend. It consists of three components: the MACD line, the Signal Line, and the Histogram. The MACD line is the difference between the 12-day and 26-day EMAs (Exponential Moving Averages), while the Signal Line is a 9-day EMA of the MACD line. The Histogram represents the difference between the MACD line and the Signal Line [253].

A key function of the MACD is to identify potential buy or sell signals. When the MACD line crosses above the Signal Line, it is referred to as a bullish crossover, suggesting a potential buying opportunity. Conversely, when the MACD line crosses below the Signal Line, it's termed a bearish crossover, indicating a possible selling point. The MACD also provides insights into momentum and trend strength. Traders often look at the direction and magnitude of the Histogram to assess whether a trend is strengthening or weakening. The MACD appears in a separate pane below the price chart, making it easier to visualize these trends and crossovers [253].

Relative Strength Index (RSI): The Relative Strength Index (RSI) is a momentum oscillator that measures the speed and change of price movements. Calculated over a default period of 14 days, the RSI ranges from 0 to 100 and is used to evaluate whether a cryptocurrency is overbought or oversold. Typically, an RSI reading above 70 suggests that the asset may be overbought, indicating a potential price correction or reversal. Conversely, an RSI reading below 30 indicates that the asset may be oversold, suggesting a possible upward reversal or buying opportunity [253].

The RSI is often plotted on a scale with two horizontal lines: 70 and 30, marking the overbought and oversold conditions, respectively. Traders use these levels to make decisions about potential entry and exit points. For example, a drop below the 30 mark might signal a buying opportunity, while a rise above 70 could signal a potential selling point. The RSI helps measure market sentiment and can be particularly useful for identifying potential reversals in volatile markets [253].

Each of these technical indicators—SMA, MACD, and RSI—provides unique insights into market trends and potential trading opportunities. The SMA helps identify general trend direction, the MACD assists in spotting momentum shifts, and the RSI gauges market sentiment. While these tools are powerful for making informed trading decisions, it's crucial for traders to use them in conjunction with other methods and strategies. Continuous learning and adaptation are essential in the dynamic world of cryptocurrency trading to enhance trading accuracy and profitability [253].

Bollinger Bands: Bollinger Bands are a widely used technical analysis tool developed by John Bollinger to measure volatility and identify potential trading opportunities. These bands consist of three key components: a middle band, which is typically a Simple Moving Average (SMA), and two outer bands that are set at a specific number of standard deviations above and below the middle band. The outer bands adjust dynamically with market volatility, expanding when volatility increases and contracting when it decreases [252].

The middle band, or the moving average, serves as a baseline to gauge the average price level of an asset over a specific period. The outer bands are calculated based on the standard deviation of the asset's price from the moving average. Commonly, the bands are set at ±2 standard deviations, which encompasses approximately 95% of price action under normal conditions. When the price moves close to or hits the upper band, it is considered overbought, suggesting a potential for a price pullback. Conversely, when the price approaches the lower band, it is considered oversold, indicating a possible price rebound [252].

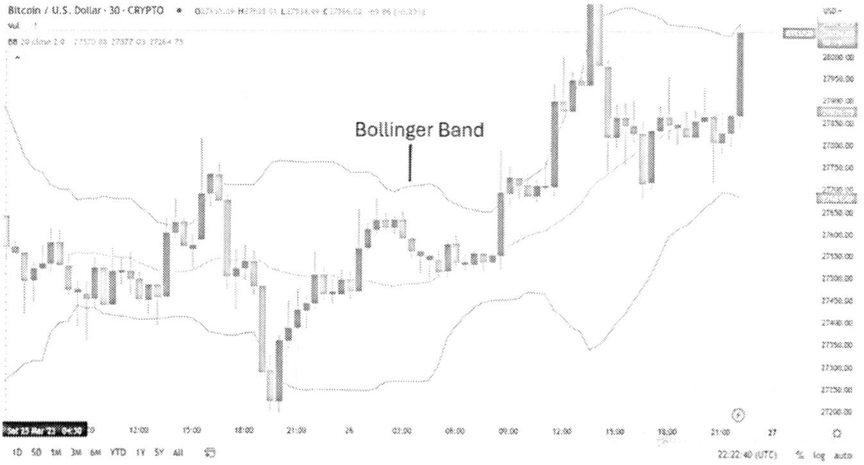

Figure 16: Bollinger Band example.

The interpretation of Bollinger Bands can vary depending on market conditions. In a bullish trend, traders often look for price breakouts above the upper band as a signal to continue trading in the direction of the trend. Similarly, in a bearish trend, price movements that break below the lower band might signal an opportunity to short sell. The bands help traders identify potential overbought or oversold conditions, allowing them to make decisions based on the likelihood of price reversions to the mean.

A fundamental concept behind Bollinger Bands is the assumption that prices will tend to revert to the mean over time. Periods of high volatility, characterized by wider bands, are typically followed by periods of lower volatility, where the bands contract. This cyclical behaviour provides traders with insights into potential market reversals or continuations based on historical price patterns and volatility metrics [252].

Overall, Bollinger Bands are a versatile tool for assessing market conditions and making informed trading decisions. By analysing the interactions between price and the bands, traders can develop strategies that capitalize on price movements and volatility trends. However, like all technical indicators, Bollinger Bands should be used in conjunction with other tools and analysis methods to enhance trading accuracy and manage risk effectively.

Where to Find Crypto Charts

TradingView: TradingView is one of the most popular platforms for accessing live trading charts for cryptocurrencies. It offers a wide range of charting tools and technical indicators that cater to both novice and experienced traders. The platform provides real-time data, allowing users to analyse price movements, trends, and market conditions. TradingView offers both a free version, which includes basic charting tools, and a premium version with advanced features, including more indicators and enhanced charting capabilities. The platform's user-friendly interface and extensive community support make it a go-to resource for many in the crypto space [252].

Coinigy: Coinigy is another robust platform that offers comprehensive charting tools and market data. It is a cloud-based service that integrates data from various cryptocurrency exchanges, providing users with a unified view of the market. Coinigy's features include advanced charting tools, real-time data, and market sentiment analysis, which can help investors understand and react to market conditions. Coinigy offers a free plan with limited features, as well as several paid options that provide more advanced tools and capabilities [252].

Cryptowatch: Owned by the Kraken exchange, Cryptowatch is a well-regarded charting and trading terminal. It allows users to analyse market movements and execute trades across major cryptocurrency exchanges. The platform is known for its real-time data and comprehensive charting features, making it a valuable tool for both analysis and trading. Cryptowatch is free to use, and its integration with Kraken's trading platform provides a seamless experience for users looking to both analyse and trade cryptocurrencies [252].

The charts generally show [252]:

Price: The price of a cryptocurrency is a fundamental parameter displayed on charts. It represents the current value of the cryptocurrency and is crucial for assessing its performance. Traders use price data to track trends, identify patterns, and make predictions about future movements. By comparing current prices with historical data (daily, weekly, monthly, or yearly), investors can gain insights into the cryptocurrency's performance over time and determine the optimal entry and exit points for their trades.

Market Cap: Market capitalization (market cap) is another critical metric displayed on crypto charts. It is calculated by multiplying the current price of a cryptocurrency by its total circulating supply. Market cap provides an indication of the cryptocurrency's overall value and is often used to compare it with other cryptocurrencies. Analyzing market cap trends over different time periods helps investors understand the cryptocurrency's growth and market position relative to its peers.

Trading Volume: Trading volume represents the total number of coins or tokens traded within a specific time period. High trading volume often indicates strong market interest and liquidity, meaning more investors are buying and selling the cryptocurrency. Monitoring trading volume helps traders gauge market activity and identify trends. For instance, an increase in trading volume during an uptrend might suggest sustained interest, while a decrease could signal a potential reversal or consolidation.

Hashrate: Hashrate measures the computational power used to mine or validate transactions for a cryptocurrency. It is typically expressed in hashes per second (hash/second). A higher hashrate indicates a more secure and robust network, as it signifies that more miners are participating in the network, making it more difficult for any single entity to manipulate or attack it. Tracking hashrate helps investors understand the health and security of a cryptocurrency's network, which can impact its long-term viability.

Circulation Supply: Circulation supply refers to the number of coins or tokens that are actively available and traded in the market. It differs from the total supply, which includes all coins that have ever been created. A high circulation supply with low demand can lead to a decrease in price, while a lower supply with high demand might drive prices up. Understanding circulation supply helps investors assess the potential for price fluctuations and the overall market dynamics of a cryptocurrency.

In summary, utilizing crypto charts effectively involves knowing where to find reliable charting tools and understanding the key metrics displayed on these charts. By analysing price, market cap, trading volume, hashrate, and circulation supply, investors can gain valuable insights into cryptocurrency performance and make informed trading decisions.

Fundamental Analysis

Fundamental analysis, on the other hand, focuses on evaluating the intrinsic value of a cryptocurrency by examining underlying factors that might influence its long-term potential. This method assesses the fundamental aspects of a cryptocurrency and its associated technology, team, use case, and market conditions.

Key components of fundamental analysis include:

- **Technology and Use Case**: Fundamental analysts investigate the technology behind a cryptocurrency, including its blockchain infrastructure, consensus mechanism, and scalability. They also assess the cryptocurrency's use case and the problem it aims to solve, which can influence its long-term adoption and value.

- **Team and Development**: The credibility and expertise of the development team are crucial factors. Analysts evaluate the team's experience, past successes, and their ability to execute the project's vision. The presence of reputable advisors and partnerships can also enhance the credibility of the cryptocurrency.

- **Market Demand and Adoption**: Fundamental analysis considers the potential demand for the cryptocurrency and its adoption within the market. Analysts look at factors such as user growth, partnerships with businesses, and the overall interest in the cryptocurrency's technology and applications.

- **Regulatory Environment**: The regulatory landscape can significantly impact a cryptocurrency's future. Analysts assess current and potential regulations that might affect the cryptocurrency's legality, compliance, and market access.

- **Tokenomics**: This refers to the economic model of the cryptocurrency, including its supply and distribution mechanisms, inflation rates, and incentives for holders and validators. Understanding tokenomics helps analysts gauge the potential for future value appreciation and inflation.

Fundamental analysis is beneficial for long-term investing as it provides a deeper understanding of the intrinsic value of a cryptocurrency. It helps investors assess whether a cryptocurrency is undervalued or overvalued based on its potential and the market environment. However, it can be time-consuming and requires a thorough understanding of the project's technology and market dynamics.

Technical analysis and fundamental analysis are complementary approaches used in cryptocurrency investing. Technical analysis focuses on price movements and market trends, providing insights for short-term trading and timing decisions. Fundamental analysis, on the other hand, evaluates the intrinsic value and long-term potential of a cryptocurrency based on its technology, team, market demand, and regulatory factors. Combining both methods can offer a more comprehensive view, helping investors make informed decisions based on both market behaviour and underlying factors.

Fundamental Analysis Before Crypto

The roots of fundamental analysis can be traced back to the early 20th century, particularly to the work of Benjamin Graham and David Dodd with the publication of "Security Analysis" in 1934 [254]. This piece of literature emerged in response to the 1929 stock market crash, aiming to equip investors with a structured approach to evaluating the intrinsic value of stocks. Graham and Dodd advocated for a meticulous examination of financial statements, focusing on metrics like earnings, revenue, and overall company health to identify undervalued stocks. Their methodology emphasized the significance of thorough financial analysis and long-term investment potential over speculative trading, marking a departure from relying solely on market trends and technical indicators.

Graham and Dodd's approach to fundamental analysis highlighted the importance of conducting a detailed assessment of a company's fundamentals to determine its true worth. By focusing on the intrinsic value of stocks, investors following their methodology sought to identify assets that appeared undervalued based on rigorous analysis rather than market sentiment. This methodical evaluation of stocks based on their fundamental quality and perceived intrinsic value was a key tenet of Graham and Dodd's investment philosophy.

Fundamental analysis, originally applied to stocks, has evolved to encompass various asset classes, including cryptocurrencies. The inherent volatility and speculative nature of the crypto market make fundamental analysis particularly relevant. While traditional methods of fundamental analysis like discounted cash flow (DCF) and price-to-earnings (P/E) ratios are less applicable to crypto assets due to their unique characteristics, the core principles of assessing value and risk remain useful.

In the early days of cryptocurrency, fundamental analysis focused largely on evaluating Bitcoin and pioneering altcoins through their technology, whitepapers, and regulatory environment. This included examining the technical feasibility and innovation of the underlying blockchain technology, as well as the credibility of the development teams and the clarity of project goals.

As the crypto space has evolved, fundamental analysis has adapted to include a broader range of factors. Today's methods encompass evaluating the expertise of project teams, analysing tokenomics (the economic model of a cryptocurrency), assessing strategic partnerships, and examining the utility and adoption of crypto-assets. Network metrics such as transaction volumes and security audit statuses also play a crucial role in assessing the value and potential of crypto projects. These modern tools help investors gauge the long-term viability and growth prospects of crypto assets, moving beyond the early focus on technological innovation and regulatory considerations.

The unique nature of blockchain technology and its departure from traditional financial systems (TradFi) necessitates a tailored approach to fundamental analysis. While traditional valuation metrics may not directly apply, the principles of assessing an asset's potential, understanding its market position, and evaluating the strength of its technological and financial foundations remain central to making informed investment decisions in the crypto space.

Development Team

When evaluating a cryptocurrency project, the development team is a crucial factor to consider. The quality and credibility of the team behind a project can significantly influence its success and potential for growth. The parameters for assessing a crypto project's team are straightforward but essential for making informed investment decisions [255].

First, examine the educational backgrounds of the team members. Reputable educational credentials from recognized institutions can be indicative of a team's expertise and knowledge in relevant fields such as computer science, finance, or engineering. Advanced degrees or specialized certifications in blockchain technology, cryptography, or software development can further enhance a team's credibility.

Next, consider the team's past work experiences. Relevant experience in the cryptocurrency space or in similar technology sectors provides insight into their ability to navigate the complexities of blockchain development and market dynamics. Team members with a track record of working on successful crypto projects, contributing to notable technological advancements, or holding influential positions in reputable companies bring valuable expertise to the table.

Previous successes with other ventures are another important factor. A history of launching and managing successful projects, particularly in the blockchain or technology sectors, demonstrates a team's capability to execute their vision effectively. It's beneficial to investigate whether the team has been involved in projects that achieved significant milestones or garnered positive industry recognition [255].

Additionally, the experience of the team members working together on previous projects can be a positive sign. Teams that have collaborated successfully in the past are often more cohesive and efficient. Shared experience on prior projects can lead to better communication, streamlined workflows, and a deeper understanding of each other's strengths and weaknesses, contributing to the overall success of the current project.

A team's educational background, relevant work experience, previous successes, and prior collaboration are key indicators of a project's potential. A team with a strong track record in the industry and a proven ability to deliver successful outcomes can be a clear sign of a promising crypto project. Investors should carefully assess these factors to gauge the team's capability and confidence in the project's future success.

Technology and Blockchain in Crypto Analysis

Blockchain technology forms the backbone of cryptocurrencies, much like power lines and power stations provide the essential infrastructure for delivering electricity. At its core, blockchain technology serves as the underlying framework that supports various crypto-assets, such as Bitcoin (BTC), Ethereum (ETH), and Polygon (MATIC). The blockchain functions as a decentralized ledger that records and verifies transactions across a network of computers, ensuring transparency and security in the process [255].

A robust blockchain infrastructure is crucial for the functionality and performance of a cryptocurrency. It affects several key aspects, including scalability, security, transaction fees, and transparency. Scalability refers to a blockchain's ability to handle a growing number of transactions per second (TPS) as more users join the network. For instance, Bitcoin's blockchain, known for its proof-of-work (PoW) consensus mechanism, has faced criticism due to its energy consumption. However, this same mechanism provides a high level of security by making it difficult for malicious actors to alter transaction records. Despite concerns about environmental impact, efforts are underway to make Bitcoin mining more sustainable, with approximately 50% of BTC mining now utilizing renewable energy sources [255].

In contrast, Ethereum's blockchain offers a different set of features. Beyond transaction security, Ethereum introduces the concept of smart contracts—self-executing contracts with the terms of the agreement directly written into code. This innovation facilitates decentralized applications (dApps) and the creation of various crypto-assets on the Ethereum network. Users need Ether (ETH) to pay for transaction fees and computational costs on Ethereum's Virtual Machine (EVM). This functionality enhances the blockchain's utility by enabling complex operations and interactions within a decentralized environment [255].

Scalability, security, and efficiency are intertwined with the blockchain's impact on a cryptocurrency's utility and, consequently, its market value. A blockchain that can process a high volume of transactions efficiently while maintaining strong security protocols can significantly enhance the value proposition of its associated crypto-assets. As blockchain technology evolves, these factors continue to influence both the practical applications of cryptocurrencies and their price movements in the market.

Token Utility and Use Cases in Crypto Analysis

Token utility and use cases are crucial factors to consider when analysing digital assets. These aspects determine how a token integrates into its ecosystem and provides value to its users. The evolution of the cryptocurrency market, especially post the 2017 ICO bubble, has underscored the importance of these elements. Investors need to critically evaluate a token's practical applications and its role within its respective blockchain network to avoid falling for superficial or speculative promises.

Ethereum (ETH), one of the pioneering blockchain platforms, is renowned for its smart contract capabilities. Ethereum's primary utility lies in enabling decentralized applications (dApps) and non-fungible tokens (NFTs) through its smart contract infrastructure. Ether, the native cryptocurrency of Ethereum, is required to pay for transaction fees and computational services on the Ethereum Virtual Machine (EVM). This necessity for Ether to facilitate operations within the Ethereum ecosystem creates inherent demand for the token, influencing its value. Ethereum's utility extends beyond mere transactions; it forms the backbone for numerous innovative applications, reinforcing its position as a critical player in the blockchain space.

Solana (SOL), on the other hand, addresses a specific need for high-speed transactions. Solana was designed to offer a blockchain platform capable of processing a large volume of transactions quickly and at low costs, making it suitable for microtransactions and decentralized applications that require rapid execution. However, Solana's focus on speed may come at the expense of the highest levels of security compared to other blockchains. The trade-off between transaction speed and security is a notable consideration for potential investors and users, impacting the token's long-term viability and attractiveness.

Avalanche (AVAX) presents another example of a blockchain with a strong focus on scalability and security. Avalanche is engineered to handle high-throughput transactions while maintaining robust security measures, positioning itself as a significant player in the space of smart contracts and decentralized finance (DeFi). AVAX, the native token of the Avalanche network, is used to pay for transaction fees and participate in network governance. The effective token utility within the Avalanche ecosystem enhances its potential for sustained demand and value appreciation.

In essence, the practical purpose and utility of a crypto-asset play a significant role in its potential success. Tokens with clear, practical applications are more likely to gain traction and drive demand over time. Evaluating a token's utility involves understanding its role within its blockchain, the problems it aims to solve, and its overall impact on the network. This leads to the next critical factor in cryptocurrency analysis: tokenomics and distribution plans, which further detail how tokens are allocated, distributed, and utilized within their ecosystems.

Tokenomics and Distribution

Tokenomics, a blend of "token" and "economics," refers to the study and design of a cryptocurrency's economic model and its underlying principles. Distribution, on the other hand, pertains to how a cryptocurrency's tokens are allocated and released into the market. Both aspects are critical in determining a digital asset's value and viability in the crypto market [255].

Bitcoin (BTC) serves as a prime example of effective tokenomics. Bitcoin's tokenomics is built around a deflationary model designed to create scarcity and drive demand. Bitcoin's total supply is capped at 21 million coins, creating an inherent limit to its availability. To reinforce this scarcity, Bitcoin employs a halving mechanism, which reduces the reward that miners receive for adding new blocks to the blockchain by 50% approximately every four years. This predictable reduction in new supply introduces an organic scarcity into the market, contributing to Bitcoin's value over time. The finite supply combined with regular halving events ensures that Bitcoin becomes increasingly scarce as more coins are mined, which can drive up demand and potentially increase its value [255].

Ethereum (ETH), in contrast, does not have a fixed supply like Bitcoin. Instead, Ethereum employs a more flexible approach to manage its token supply. Ethereum's issuance rate was historically uncapped, but recent updates, particularly EIP-1559 implemented in 2021, introduced a fee-burning mechanism that reduces the total supply of Ether over time. Under this update, a portion of the transaction fees paid in Ether is burned, effectively removing it from circulation. This mechanism helps counteract inflation and introduces a deflationary element to Ether's economics. Additionally, Ethereum allows mining nodes to charge higher fees during periods of network congestion, which can drive up the cost of transactions and subsequently impact Ether's price [255].

When evaluating new token launches, understanding the tokenomics and distribution plan is crucial. A well-structured distribution plan can mitigate risks associated with large-scale sell-offs and ensure a balanced allocation of tokens. Investors should consider the following questions [255]:

1. **How are the tokens allocated?** Understanding the breakdown of token distribution helps assess if the allocation is fair and whether there is a risk of disproportionate influence by the development team.

2. **What fraction goes to the team and operational costs?** Analysing how much of the token supply is allocated to the team and operational expenses helps evaluate the risk of potential conflicts of interest or the likelihood of team members selling large amounts of tokens.

3. **Are the team's tokens vested?** Token vesting schedules can provide insights into whether the team has a vested interest in the long-term success of the project. Vesting periods ensure that team members are incentivized to work towards the project's growth rather than making quick profits.

4. **Is there a network tax for transactions?** Evaluating transaction fees and their allocation helps determine the economic impact on users and the sustainability of the network.

5. **What is the size and plan for network fees?** Understanding the fee structure provides insights into the cost of using the network and its impact on token utility and adoption.

6. **What is the distribution plan and timeline for all its supply allocations?** A clear distribution plan and timeline help ensure transparency and manage market expectations regarding the release of tokens.

A balanced tokenomics and distribution plan fosters trust and can drive the value of a cryptocurrency. For example, Bitcoin's scarcity and Ethereum's innovative fee-burning mechanism contribute to their respective market positions. Similarly, a well-considered distribution plan and controlled token release can enhance scarcity and support price appreciation, benefiting both the project and its investors.

Partnerships, Adoption, and Ecosystem in Crypto Analysis

Partnerships, adoption, and ecosystem are crucial factors in evaluating the potential and success of a cryptocurrency project. They provide insights into the project's credibility, growth potential, and its ability to achieve its goals within the competitive crypto market [255].

Partnerships serve as a significant indicator of a crypto project's viability and future direction. Strategic alliances with reputable companies and organizations reflect a project's ability to integrate with established technologies and platforms. For instance, Solana (SOL) demonstrated its strategic vision by forming partnerships with notable tech entities such as Serum (SRM) and Chainlink (LINK) during its early development. These alliances were intended to enhance Solana's decentralized finance (DeFi) capabilities and incorporate decentralized oracle solutions, thereby strengthening its smart contract ecosystem. Such partnerships can provide additional functionality and interoperability, enhancing the project's overall value proposition and signalling its long-term commitment to innovation [255].

Adoption is another critical metric for assessing a cryptocurrency's success. It measures the extent to which the cryptocurrency is being used in real-world applications and by various stakeholders. High adoption rates typically indicate a healthy and growing user base, which can drive demand and increase the cryptocurrency's market value. Projects with robust adoption often have strong use cases and practical applications, which contribute to their sustainability and relevance in the market. For instance, a cryptocurrency that is widely accepted for payments or integrated into popular platforms is likely to experience greater demand and usage, reflecting its successful integration into the broader ecosystem [255].

Ecosystem refers to the broader network of projects, applications, and services that interact with and support the cryptocurrency. A well-developed ecosystem enhances the utility and value of the cryptocurrency by fostering innovation and expanding its use cases. This includes the availability of decentralized applications (dApps), integration with other blockchain networks, and the support of a vibrant developer community. A project with a thriving ecosystem is often better positioned for growth and can attract more users and developers, contributing to its long-term success. For example, Ethereum (ETH) benefits from a robust ecosystem of dApps, smart contracts, and decentralized finance (DeFi) solutions, which reinforce its position as a leading blockchain platform [255].

Assessing a cryptocurrency's partnerships, adoption, and ecosystem provides valuable insights into its potential for success. Strong partnerships with reputable entities, high adoption rates, and a well-developed ecosystem can significantly enhance a project's credibility and market value, making these factors essential considerations for investors and analysts.

Whitepapers and Documentation

Whitepapers and technical documentation play a crucial role in evaluating cryptocurrency projects. They serve as the blueprint of a token's utility and are essential for understanding the project's credibility, technology, and governance structure [255].

Whitepapers provide a comprehensive overview of a cryptocurrency project, including its purpose, technology, and use cases. They typically include detailed sections on the project's mission, problem statements, proposed solutions, and the technical approach used to implement these solutions. The whitepaper also outlines the token's utility, how it fits within the ecosystem, and the overall value proposition of the project. Analysing a whitepaper helps investors gauge whether the project addresses a real-world problem and how effectively it employs blockchain technology to solve that problem. This alignment with practical needs and technological innovation is key to assessing the project's potential for success.

Technical documentation complements the whitepaper by offering in-depth details about the project's technology and development processes. This includes information about the blockchain's architecture, protocols, consensus mechanisms, and any unique technological innovations. It provides insight into how the project plans to implement its proposed solutions and the technical feasibility of its approach. For instance, it might explain how the blockchain network will handle scalability, security, and transaction processing. Understanding these technical aspects is crucial for evaluating the project's ability to deliver on its promises and manage its technological requirements.

Together, these documents help investors understand and evaluate a crypto asset's value proposition. They should reveal whether the project has a solid foundation and practical applications. As Warren Buffett famously advised, "Never invest in a business you cannot understand" [255]. Applying this principle to crypto investments means ensuring that the whitepapers and technical documents provide a clear, understandable explanation of the project's goals, technology, and implementation strategies. Without this clarity, investing in the project would be speculative and risky, lacking a grounded understanding of its potential and challenges.

Code Audit and Security

A comprehensive code audit is essential for assessing the security of a crypto-asset's smart contracts and underlying technology. This process involves a detailed review conducted by reputable third-party auditing firms to identify and address potential vulnerabilities or weaknesses in the code. The audit aims to uncover any coding flaws that could lead to exploits, hacks, or other security breaches. High-quality audit reports provide transparency by documenting identified issues and the measures taken to resolve them, which helps in building trust with users and investors.

For instance, a crypto-asset that has undergone rigorous audits from well-regarded firms such as CertiK or Trail of Bits is generally considered more reliable. Successful audits and the resolution of critical issues demonstrate the project's commitment to maintaining a secure and trustworthy platform. On the other hand, projects with no audit reports, audits from questionable firms, or unresolved critical vulnerabilities should be approached with caution. Such red flags suggest that the project may not prioritize security, potentially putting users' assets at risk.

In addition to formal audits, ongoing security practices like bug bounty programs play a crucial role in maintaining a crypto project's integrity. Bug bounty programs invite independent security researchers and ethical hackers to identify and report vulnerabilities in exchange for rewards. This proactive approach helps in discovering issues that might not be caught during initial audits. Projects with established bug bounty programs and active vulnerability assessments, such as Ethereum (ETH) and Cardano (ADA), demonstrate a robust commitment to ongoing security and responsible disclosure.

Overall, rigorous code audits, regular security assessments, and bug bounty initiatives are critical components in evaluating the reliability and safety of cryptocurrency projects. These practices ensure that the project's technology is resilient against potential threats, fostering confidence among users and investors.

Regulatory Compliance

Regulatory compliance is a crucial factor in determining the long-term value and viability of a cryptocurrency. Adherence to legal and regulatory standards ensures that a crypto project operates within the boundaries set by authorities, reducing the risk of legal troubles and potential shutdowns. Several cryptocurrency platforms and token-based projects have failed or faced significant setbacks due to regulatory challenges, highlighting the importance of this aspect [255].

When evaluating a crypto asset, investors should thoroughly assess whether the project complies with the relevant regulations in all the jurisdictions it targets. This includes understanding the legal requirements for operating in specific markets, such as anti-money laundering (AML) laws, know-your-customer (KYC) regulations, and securities regulations. Compliance with these standards helps mitigate legal risks and demonstrates a project's commitment to operating within the law.

Furthermore, following industry best practices and regulatory guidelines not only fosters trust among investors but also enhances the project's credibility. A crypto project that proactively adheres to these standards is better positioned to avoid regulatory pitfalls and legal disputes. Conversely, signs of non-compliance, such as unresolved legal issues or regulatory investigations, are significant red flags. These issues can pose substantial risks, potentially leading to financial penalties, forced closures, or damage to the project's reputation.

Regulatory compliance is a vital consideration for assessing the stability and future potential of a cryptocurrency. A project's ability to navigate the complex legal landscape and adhere to relevant regulations can significantly influence its long-term success and market value. Investors should prioritize compliance when evaluating crypto assets to ensure they are not exposed to unnecessary legal risks and to support projects that demonstrate a commitment to operating within established legal frameworks.

Financial Evaluation: Market Cap, Liquidity, and Volume

Market capitalization, or market cap, is a fundamental metric used to gauge the overall value of a cryptocurrency. It is calculated by multiplying the current price of a crypto asset by its total circulating supply. For instance, if a cryptocurrency is priced at $10 and there are 1 million tokens in circulation, its market cap would be $10 million. Market cap provides a snapshot of the asset's value relative to other cryptocurrencies and can indicate its market presence and recognition [255].

A high market cap typically signifies that a cryptocurrency is well-established and widely recognized. Such assets often have a significant following and are considered relatively stable investments. Conversely, a low market cap may suggest that a cryptocurrency is either new, less well-known, or undervalued. While a low market cap can present high-risk, high-reward opportunities, it may also indicate greater volatility and less liquidity. Investors should be cautious and perform thorough fundamental analysis before investing in low market cap assets, as they can be prone to higher fluctuations and risks [255].

To assess market cap accurately, it is advisable to use on-chain crypto asset indexing platforms rather than relying solely on exchanges, as the latter may not always reflect the most current or accurate data. Websites like Coingecko are popular resources for tracking and comparing market caps of various cryptocurrencies. Most investors monitor these metrics to get a clearer picture of an asset's position in the market.

Liquidity refers to how easily a cryptocurrency can be bought or sold in the market without causing significant price changes. High liquidity means there is a substantial number of buyers and sellers, which helps ensure that transactions occur at stable prices. In a highly liquid market, the price of an asset remains relatively constant despite large trades, indicating a balanced supply and demand [255].

Liquidity is influenced by factors such as the number of active market participants and the depth of the order book on exchanges. A deep order book means that there are large quantities of buy and sell orders at various price levels, contributing to smoother trading and less price impact from individual transactions. High liquidity is desirable as it provides more flexibility and reduces the risk of slippage, where the execution price deviates from the expected price.

Trading volume represents the total number of units of a cryptocurrency traded over a specific period. It is a crucial indicator in both technical and fundamental analysis. Volume can reveal the strength of a price movement—high volume often correlates with strong buying or selling interest, signalling potential market trends or reversals.

A surge in volume can indicate increased demand or interest in a cryptocurrency, which may drive up its price. Conversely, a decline in volume might suggest weakening interest or potential price consolidation. Monitoring volume trends helps investors gauge market sentiment and the likelihood of sustained price movements [255].

Financial evaluation of a cryptocurrency involves understanding its market cap to assess its relative value, its liquidity to determine how easily it can be traded, and its volume to gauge market interest and potential price trends. Each of these metrics provides valuable insights into a cryptocurrency's market dynamics and investment potential.

Crypto Indicators for Fundamental Analysis

Network Value to Transactions Ratio (NVT): Traditional fundamental analysis tools like the price-to-earnings (P/E) ratio, which assess a company's earnings relative to its stock price, are not applicable to cryptocurrencies. This is because cryptocurrencies do not generate earnings in the conventional sense. Instead, analysts use alternative quantitative tools to evaluate crypto projects. One such tool is the Network Value to Transactions Ratio (NVT), which provides insights into a cryptocurrency's valuation by examining its network activity [255].

The NVT ratio is a measure of the relationship between a cryptocurrency's market capitalization and its transaction volume. It offers a way to evaluate the health and valuation of a token's network based on its on-chain activity. The NVT ratio is calculated using the formula:

NVT = Market Cap / Daily Transaction Volume.

How NVT is Calculated:

To calculate NVT, you first need to obtain the relevant data:

- **Market Capitalization**: This is the total value of the cryptocurrency, calculated by multiplying its current price by the total circulating supply.

- **Daily Transaction Volume**: This refers to the total value of transactions conducted on the network over a 24-hour period. This data can be retrieved from blockchain explorers, which provide detailed on-chain statistics. For Bitcoin, Blockchain Explorer is a reliable source; for Ethereum and Ethereum-based tokens, Etherscan is used; and for Binance Smart Chain tokens, BSCScan is the recommended tool.

By dividing the market cap by the daily transaction volume, you derive the NVT ratio.

Interpreting NVT:

A high NVT ratio suggests that the market capitalization of a cryptocurrency is significantly higher than its daily transaction volume. This scenario often indicates that the cryptocurrency may be overvalued. An overvaluation could imply that the market price is detached from the actual utility and transaction activity of the asset, leading to potential corrections in the future.

Conversely, a low NVT ratio implies that the cryptocurrency's market capitalization is relatively low compared to its transaction volume. This could indicate that the asset is undervalued and might be a better investment opportunity if the low valuation aligns with solid fundamental metrics and a promising outlook.

The NVT ratio acts as a reality check on a cryptocurrency's market price, providing insights into whether the asset's current valuation aligns with its actual transaction activity. An inflated NVT ratio signals that the current market price might not accurately reflect the underlying value and that a price correction could be on the horizon. Conversely, a low NVT ratio could suggest potential undervaluation, presenting a possible buying opportunity if other fundamental factors are favourable.

Market Value to Realised Value Ratio (MVRV): The Market Value to Realised Value Ratio (MVRV) is a critical metric used to assess the valuation of a cryptocurrency by comparing its market value to its realised value. This ratio helps investors gauge whether a crypto-asset is overvalued or undervalued relative to its historical purchase prices [255].

How MVRV is Calculated:

To calculate the MVRV ratio, you divide a cryptocurrency's market capitalization by its realised capitalization. Here's a breakdown of the components involved:

- **Market Capitalization (Market Cap):** This is calculated by multiplying the current price of the cryptocurrency by its total circulating supply. It represents the total market value of the asset at present.

- **Realised Capitalization (Realised Cap):** This metric provides an alternative measure of a cryptocurrency's value by considering the price at which each unit of the asset was last moved or transacted. Instead of using the current price, realised cap takes into account the actual price paid for the asset when it was last transferred between wallets. This helps to account for the value of the asset in its various holding wallets, providing a more nuanced view of its valuation.

The realised cap is calculated by summing the value of each token at the price it was last moved, rather than its current price. This approach acknowledges that tokens held in inactive wallets were acquired at past prices and thus reflects the value based on historical acquisition costs.

Interpreting MVRV:

- **MVRV Above 1:** When the MVRV ratio is significantly above 1, it indicates that the market value of the cryptocurrency is higher than its realised value. This suggests that the asset may be overvalued, as the current market price exceeds the average price at which investors purchased the asset. An MVRV above 1 can signal that many investors are currently holding gains and might be inclined to sell, leading to potential price corrections.

- **MVRV Below 1:** Conversely, when the MVRV ratio is below 1, it suggests that the market value is lower than the realised value. This situation indicates that the asset is undervalued compared to the average price at which investors acquired it. A low MVRV ratio may present an opportunity for investors to buy, as it implies that the current market price is below the historical average purchase price, suggesting potential for price appreciation.

The MVRV ratio is a valuable tool for assessing the relative valuation of a cryptocurrency. By comparing the market value to the realised value, it provides insights into whether an asset is trading at a premium or a discount compared to its historical acquisition prices. A high MVRV ratio may indicate overvaluation, while a low ratio suggests potential undervaluation. Understanding the MVRV can help investors make informed decisions by offering a perspective on whether the asset's current price reflects its true value based on historical trading activity.

Portfolio Diversification

Diversification is a fundamental investment strategy designed to spread risk by allocating capital across a variety of assets. In the context of cryptocurrency investing, diversification involves holding a range of different cryptocurrencies to mitigate the potential negative impact of poor performance in any single asset. This strategy is based on the principle that different cryptocurrencies may respond differently to market events, technological developments, and regulatory changes, reducing the overall risk of the investment portfolio.

A well-balanced crypto portfolio is one that strategically diversifies investments across various types of cryptocurrencies, each with its distinct use cases and risk profiles. This approach helps mitigate risk by not putting all investments into a single asset class, especially given the inherent volatility of the cryptocurrency market [256].

To achieve balance, an investor should allocate funds across different categories of cryptocurrencies. This typically includes major established coins like Bitcoin (BTC) and Ethereum (ETH), known for their relatively lower volatility compared to newer or smaller coins. These major cryptocurrencies often serve as the foundation of a balanced portfolio due to their widespread adoption and stability. Alongside these, an investor might include altcoins that offer different functionalities and technologies, such as those related to decentralized finance (DeFi), non-fungible tokens (NFTs), or smart contract platforms. Each of these categories can provide exposure to different market segments and potential growth opportunities.

In addition to diversifying among various cryptocurrencies, maintaining a balance between the crypto portfolio and the overall investment portfolio is crucial. Cryptocurrency investments are known for their high risk, which means they should constitute only a small fraction of an investor's total portfolio. One commonly recommended guideline is to allocate between 5% and 10% of the overall investment portfolio to cryptocurrencies [256]. This ensures that while the potential for high returns is present, the overall risk remains manageable.

Rebalancing is a key aspect of managing a well-balanced crypto portfolio. As the value of cryptocurrency investments fluctuates, the proportion of crypto assets relative to other investments can shift. For instance, if the value of cryptocurrency holdings increases significantly, it might cause the crypto portion of the portfolio to exceed the desired allocation. To maintain balance and manage risk, it may be necessary to sell a portion of the cryptocurrency holdings to rebalance the portfolio. Conversely, if the cryptocurrency market experiences a downturn, having a lower proportion of crypto assets can help protect the overall portfolio from excessive losses [256].

The core idea behind diversification is that it helps balance risk and reward. By spreading investments across multiple cryptocurrencies, investors can decrease the likelihood of experiencing severe losses from the underperformance of a single asset. For example, if one cryptocurrency suffers a significant decline in value due to a market downturn or technical issue, the other cryptocurrencies in the portfolio may remain stable or even appreciate, offsetting the losses and helping to stabilize the overall value of the investment.

Diversification in Cryptocurrency Investment involves several approaches:

- **Asset Variety**: Investors may choose to diversify by investing in various types of cryptocurrencies. This can include established coins like Bitcoin (BTC) and Ethereum (ETH), which are considered to have relatively lower volatility compared to newer or smaller coins. In addition to major cryptocurrencies, investors might include altcoins (alternative cryptocurrencies) that offer different use cases and technologies. For instance, they may invest in coins related to decentralized finance (DeFi), non-fungible tokens (NFTs), or smart contract platforms.

- **Technological and Use Case Diversity**: Diversification can also involve investing in cryptocurrencies that support different technologies and applications. For example, one might invest in cryptocurrencies focused on privacy (such as Monero), smart contracts (such as Ethereum), or blockchain scalability solutions (such as Solana). Each type of cryptocurrency may serve a distinct purpose and have unique technological advancements, thereby providing exposure to various segments of the crypto market.

- **Geographical and Platform Diversity**: Investing across different geographical markets and platforms can further enhance diversification. Some cryptocurrencies are designed for specific regions or have unique platform features that cater to different user bases. By including assets from various geographical and technological niches, investors can reduce the impact of localized market issues or platform-specific challenges.

Benefits of Diversification in cryptocurrency investing include:

- **Risk Reduction**: By holding a mix of assets, investors can mitigate the impact of adverse events affecting any single cryptocurrency. For instance, if a particular coin faces regulatory challenges or technological issues, other assets in the portfolio may perform well, balancing out the potential negative effects.

- **Potential for Increased Returns**: Diversification allows investors to capitalize on different growth opportunities within the cryptocurrency market. While some assets may experience rapid appreciation, others may provide steady growth, creating a balanced portfolio that can potentially enhance overall returns.

- **Volatility Management**: Cryptocurrency markets are known for their high volatility. Diversification can help manage this volatility by spreading investments across assets with varying levels of price fluctuation. This can lead to a more stable investment experience, reducing the likelihood of extreme losses during market turbulence.

However, diversification does not eliminate all risks. Investors must carefully select the cryptocurrencies they include in their portfolios and stay informed about market trends, technological advancements, and regulatory developments. Over-diversification can also lead to complexities in managing the portfolio and may dilute potential gains if the chosen assets underperform.

Asset Variety in Cryptocurrency Investment

Diversification is a fundamental strategy in investment that aims to spread risk and enhance the potential for returns. In the realm of cryptocurrency, investors can achieve diversification by incorporating a variety of digital assets into their portfolios. This approach helps mitigate the risks associated with the inherent volatility and unpredictability of the cryptocurrency market.

Established Cryptocurrencies: At the core of a diversified cryptocurrency portfolio are well-established coins such as Bitcoin (BTC) and Ethereum (ETH). These cryptocurrencies are considered relatively stable compared to newer or smaller digital assets. Bitcoin, as the first and most widely recognized cryptocurrency, serves as a benchmark in the market. Its broad acceptance and extensive adoption contribute to its relatively lower volatility. Ethereum, known for its smart contract functionality, also enjoys significant stability due to its widespread use and strong developer community. Investing in these major cryptocurrencies provides a foundation of stability in a portfolio, as they are less susceptible to the extreme fluctuations often seen with newer projects.

Alternative Cryptocurrencies (Altcoins): In addition to major coins, diversifying with alternative cryptocurrencies (altcoins) can introduce exposure to different technologies and use cases. Altcoins represent a wide range of digital assets that offer unique features or innovations beyond what Bitcoin and Ethereum provide. For instance, some altcoins are specifically designed for decentralized finance (DeFi) applications, which aim to recreate traditional financial systems like lending and borrowing on the blockchain. DeFi-related tokens, such as Uniswap (UNI) or Aave (AAVE), cater to these emerging financial services and present opportunities for growth as the DeFi sector expands.

Non-Fungible Tokens (NFTs): Another area of diversification within the cryptocurrency space is non-fungible tokens (NFTs). NFTs are unique digital assets that represent ownership of distinct items, such as digital art, collectibles, or virtual real estate. The NFT market has gained substantial attention for its potential to transform how digital content is owned and traded. Investing in NFTs can offer exposure to a niche market with its own dynamics and opportunities, separate from traditional cryptocurrencies.

Smart Contract Platforms: Smart contract platforms, such as Cardano (ADA) and Polkadot (DOT), represent another category of diversification. These platforms support the creation and execution of smart contracts, which are self-executing agreements with the terms directly written into code. They aim to enhance blockchain functionality by providing robust environments for building decentralized applications (dApps). Investing in these platforms allows exposure to innovations in blockchain technology and the development of decentralized ecosystems.

Diversifying a cryptocurrency portfolio involves incorporating a mix of established coins, altcoins, NFTs, and smart contract platforms. By doing so, investors can balance the risks associated with the volatility of individual assets and capitalize on various technological advancements and use cases. This strategy helps to mitigate potential losses from any single asset while providing opportunities to benefit from different segments of the cryptocurrency market.

Technological and Use Case Diversity

Technological and use case diversity in cryptocurrency investments involves strategically selecting cryptocurrencies that are built on different technological frameworks and serve various applications. This approach allows investors to spread their risk across different segments of the crypto market and take advantage of the unique advancements and opportunities each type of cryptocurrency offers.

Cryptocurrency investments have gained significant traction in recent years, with investors increasingly looking to strategically diversify their portfolios across different types of cryptocurrencies to mitigate risk and capitalize on the unique opportunities presented by various technological frameworks and applications [257]. Research indicates that by selecting cryptocurrencies built on different technological foundations and serving diverse purposes, investors can effectively spread their risk across various segments of the crypto market, enhancing their ability to benefit from the advancements and opportunities each type of cryptocurrency offers [258].

Studies have shown that the diversification benefits of cryptocurrencies, particularly Bitcoin, tend to be stable and can increase significantly during turbulent periods, highlighting the potential for risk mitigation and improved portfolio performance through strategic selection and allocation of crypto assets [259]. By investing in cryptocurrencies from different communities, investors can achieve better risk diversification, further underlining the importance of considering technological and use case diversity in cryptocurrency investments to optimize portfolio outcomes [258].

Moreover, the rise of Initial Coin Offerings (ICOs) has provided investors with alternative investment opportunities characterized by high returns, technological innovation, lower transaction costs, and increased transparency, making them an attractive option for diversifying investment portfolios [260]. Additionally, Decentralized Finance (DeFi) platforms, powered by blockchain technology and smart contracts, offer innovative financial services that enhance inclusivity and efficiency, further emphasizing the potential benefits of incorporating diverse cryptocurrency assets into investment strategies [261].

Cryptocurrencies that focus on privacy, such as Monero (XMR), are designed to offer enhanced anonymity and transaction confidentiality. Monero utilizes advanced cryptographic techniques to obscure transaction details, making it a preferred choice for users who prioritize privacy. Investing in privacy-focused cryptocurrencies can be beneficial for those who believe in the growing need for privacy solutions and want to hedge against regulatory scrutiny that could impact other types of digital assets.

On the other hand, smart contract platforms like Ethereum (ETH) represent a different technological niche. Ethereum is renowned for its ability to execute decentralized applications (dApps) and smart contracts, which are self-executing agreements with the terms of the contract directly written into code. By investing in Ethereum, investors gain exposure to a wide range of applications, from decentralized finance (DeFi) to non-fungible tokens (NFTs). Ethereum's role in powering these innovations highlights its significance in the crypto ecosystem and its potential for long-term growth.

Another critical area of technological diversity is blockchain scalability solutions, exemplified by cryptocurrencies like Solana (SOL). Solana is designed to address the scalability issues that affect many blockchain networks, offering high transaction speeds and low fees. This scalability is achieved through a combination of innovative consensus mechanisms and network optimizations. Investing in scalability solutions can provide exposure to technologies that are aimed at enhancing the overall efficiency and performance of blockchain networks, making them suitable for high-throughput applications.

By incorporating cryptocurrencies that focus on different technologies and use cases, investors can create a portfolio that benefits from various market segments. This diversification strategy not only spreads risk but also positions investors to capitalize on emerging trends and innovations within the crypto space. Each cryptocurrency serves a unique purpose and contributes to the broader blockchain ecosystem, offering a balanced exposure to different aspects of the industry.

Geographical and Platform Diversity

Geographical and platform diversity in cryptocurrency investments involves spreading investments across different regions and technological platforms to enhance risk management and capitalize on various market opportunities. This approach helps investors mitigate the impact of localized market fluctuations and platform-specific challenges by creating a more balanced and resilient portfolio.

Geographical Diversity: Investing in cryptocurrencies from different geographical regions allows investors to tap into diverse economic environments and regulatory landscapes. Cryptocurrencies often have regional focuses, addressing specific needs or opportunities within particular countries or continents. For instance, some digital assets are designed to cater to emerging markets where traditional financial systems are less developed. These cryptocurrencies might offer solutions like remittances or financial inclusion to underserved populations.

By including assets from various regions, investors can reduce the impact of region-specific economic downturns or regulatory changes. For example, a cryptocurrency that is popular in a country with strict regulatory policies may experience more volatility if those regulations become more stringent. Conversely, cryptocurrencies that perform well in more stable or burgeoning markets can offset losses from other regions. This geographical diversification helps balance the overall risk and can potentially lead to higher returns by capturing growth in different parts of the world.

Platform Diversity: Platform diversity refers to investing in cryptocurrencies that operate on various blockchain platforms or have unique technological features. Different platforms have distinct advantages and use cases, influencing the performance and adoption of their native cryptocurrencies. For example, Ethereum (ETH) is known for its robust smart contract capabilities and decentralized applications (dApps), while Binance Smart Chain (BSC) offers lower transaction fees and faster processing times.

Investing across multiple blockchain platforms allows investors to benefit from different technological innovations and network efficiencies. Some platforms may excel in transaction speed, while others might offer advanced smart contract functionalities or improved scalability. By diversifying across these platforms, investors can capture the strengths of each and reduce the risk associated with platform-specific issues.

Moreover, platform diversity helps hedge against potential challenges such as network congestion, security vulnerabilities, or changes in platform governance. For instance, if one platform experiences technical difficulties or regulatory hurdles, investments in other platforms can help stabilize the overall portfolio. Additionally, emerging platforms with novel technologies or business models can offer high-growth potential, further enhancing the diversification strategy.

Incorporating geographical and platform diversity into a cryptocurrency investment strategy provides a broader exposure to different market dynamics and technological innovations. This approach mitigates localized risks and leverages various strengths, ultimately leading to a more balanced and resilient investment portfolio.

Risks and Rewards

Cryptocurrencies are known for their price volatility, distinguishing them from traditional assets like stocks and bonds [1]. Unlike the relatively stable price movements observed in traditional markets, cryptocurrencies can undergo significant price swings within short timeframes due to various factors such as market sentiment, news events, and regulatory announcements [1]. Positive news stories about major cryptocurrencies can lead to price surges, while negative news or regulatory crackdowns can trigger sharp declines [1].

This volatility in the cryptocurrency market can result in substantial gains or losses, emphasizing the importance of timing and market conditions for investors [1]. While high volatility can offer opportunities for significant profits, it also amplifies the risk of substantial losses [1]. Investors entering the crypto market must be prepared for rapid and unpredictable price movements, necessitating a thorough assessment of their risk tolerance and investment horizon [1].

Cryptocurrencies operate in a regulatory environment that is multifaceted and constantly evolving, with different countries adopting diverse approaches to overseeing digital assets [262]. The regulatory landscape for cryptocurrencies can vary significantly, ranging from supportive frameworks to stringent restrictions or even outright bans [262]. Changes in regulations can have a profound impact on the value, legality, and usability of cryptocurrencies, making it crucial for investors to stay informed about regulatory developments and understand their potential implications [262].

Stricter regulations or bans on cryptocurrency trading in major markets have been shown to lead to sharp declines in the value of cryptocurrencies [262]. Conversely, favourable regulatory developments or institutional adoption can boost market confidence and prices [262]. Understanding the legal status of cryptocurrencies in one's jurisdiction and being aware of potential future regulatory changes that could affect investments is essential for managing regulatory risks [262].

Regulatory risks associated with cryptocurrencies stem from the possibility of governments and regulators introducing new laws and regulations that may directly impact cryptocurrency transactions [263]. These regulatory changes can create uncertainties and gaps in the regulatory framework, posing challenges for market participants [263]. The introduction of regulations in cryptocurrency markets can have significant implications for investments, necessitating a quantification of the risks and their impact on cryptocurrency investments [264].

While some countries have initiated regulatory efforts over cryptocurrencies to control risks, there remains a lack of clear understanding regarding regulatory risks in integrating cryptocurrency ecosystems with existing financial systems and economies [265]. This highlights the ongoing need for comprehensive research and analysis to address regulatory complexities and gaps in the cryptocurrency space [265]. Studies have emphasized the importance of studying market-specific regulatory risks and their influence on cryptocurrency prices [239].

The integration of cryptocurrencies into financial systems faces significant barriers to adoption, including regulatory ambiguity, security concerns, and the volatility of cryptocurrencies [266]. These challenges underscore the importance of addressing regulatory uncertainties and enhancing risk management practices to facilitate the mainstream adoption of cryptocurrencies [266]. Additionally, the regulatory challenges associated with integrating cryptocurrencies include compliance burdens related to anti-money laundering (AML) and know-your-customer (KYC) regulations [266].

Cryptocurrency investments are vulnerable to a range of security threats. Hacks, phishing attacks, and fraud are common risks in the crypto space. Security breaches at exchanges, where cryptocurrencies are traded or stored, can result in the loss of assets. Similarly, phishing attacks targeting investors' private keys or login credentials can lead to unauthorized access to funds [267].

To mitigate these security risks, it is essential to use reputable and secure exchanges and wallets. Employing strong security practices, such as using hardware wallets for storage, regularly updating software, and practicing good online hygiene, can help protect assets. Additionally, safeguarding private keys and employing two-factor authentication can further enhance security and reduce the risk of theft or loss.

Liquidity refers to the ease with which an asset can be bought or sold without significantly affecting its price. Cryptocurrencies with low trading volumes or those listed on fewer exchanges may face liquidity issues. This can make it challenging for investors to enter or exit positions at desired prices without causing substantial price impacts.

Low liquidity can lead to wider bid-ask spreads, higher transaction costs, and difficulties in executing trades efficiently. Investors should consider the liquidity of a cryptocurrency before investing, as it can affect their ability to manage positions and execute trades smoothly. Monitoring trading volumes and market depth can provide insights into a cryptocurrency's liquidity and help investors make informed decisions.

The success of a cryptocurrency investment largely depends on the viability of the underlying project. A thorough assessment of the project's team, technology, use case, and market potential is essential. Understanding the project's objectives, technological innovations, and real-world applications can help investors gauge its long-term prospects.

Evaluating the project's team, including their experience and past successes, provides insights into their ability to execute and deliver on their promises. Additionally, examining the technology behind the cryptocurrency, its adoption rate, and its competitive positioning in the market can inform investment decisions. Investing in well-researched and viable projects can increase the likelihood of positive outcomes and reduce the risk of investing in failing or fraudulent projects.

Cryptocurrency investments offer several potential rewards, making them an attractive option for investors who are willing to accept the inherent risks. These rewards can vary depending on the specific cryptocurrency, market conditions, and investment strategy. Here are some of the potential rewards of investing in cryptocurrencies:

1. High Returns on Investment

One of the most notable potential rewards of cryptocurrency investments is the opportunity for substantial financial gains. Cryptocurrencies like Bitcoin (BTC) and Ethereum (ETH) have experienced significant price increases over the years, leading to substantial returns for early investors. The high volatility in the crypto market can lead to dramatic price swings, presenting opportunities for large gains if timed correctly.

For instance, early investors in Bitcoin witnessed its price rise from a few dollars to over $60,000 at its peak. Similarly, other cryptocurrencies have delivered impressive returns, making crypto investments potentially lucrative for those who can navigate the market effectively.

2. Diversification Benefits

Cryptocurrencies can provide diversification benefits to an investment portfolio. By including digital assets alongside traditional investments such as stocks and bonds, investors can spread their risk across different asset classes. Cryptocurrencies often have low correlation with traditional financial markets, meaning their performance may not directly correlate with stock market trends or economic conditions. This diversification can help reduce overall portfolio risk and potentially enhance returns.

3. Access to Innovative Technologies

Investing in cryptocurrencies often means gaining exposure to cutting-edge technologies and innovations. Many cryptocurrencies are built on blockchain technology, which has the potential to revolutionize various industries, including finance, supply chain management, and healthcare. By investing in cryptocurrencies, investors support and benefit from technological advancements and disruptive innovations.

For example, Ethereum's smart contract functionality enables the development of decentralized applications (dApps) and decentralized finance (DeFi) projects, creating new opportunities for financial transactions and applications. Investing in such projects allows investors to participate in and benefit from technological progress and its real-world applications.

4. Early Adoption Advantage

Investors who enter the cryptocurrency market early may benefit from early adoption advantages. Being an early investor in a promising project can lead to significant rewards if the project achieves widespread adoption and success. Early adopters often have the chance to acquire tokens at lower prices before they gain mainstream attention and experience substantial growth.

For instance, early supporters of projects like Chainlink (LINK) or Polkadot (DOT) have seen significant returns as these projects gained traction and expanded their use cases. Early investment in emerging technologies and platforms can lead to substantial rewards as these projects mature and gain market recognition.

5. Potential for Passive Income

Certain cryptocurrencies offer opportunities for passive income through mechanisms such as staking, yield farming, and liquidity provision. For example, with Proof of Stake (PoS) cryptocurrencies, investors can earn rewards by staking their tokens to support network operations and validate transactions. Similarly, decentralized finance (DeFi) platforms offer yield farming opportunities where users can earn interest or rewards by providing liquidity to decentralized exchanges or lending platforms.

These passive income opportunities can provide additional revenue streams and enhance overall returns for cryptocurrency investors.

6. Decentralization and Financial Inclusion

Investing in cryptocurrencies can also contribute to broader goals of decentralization and financial inclusion. Many cryptocurrencies aim to provide financial services to underserved populations and create more equitable financial systems. By supporting projects that focus on decentralization and inclusion, investors can contribute to positive social and economic changes while potentially benefiting from the growth of these initiatives.

7. Potential for Portfolio Growth

Given the rapid development and expansion of the cryptocurrency market, there are opportunities for portfolio growth. As the market matures and new innovations emerge, the potential for profitable investments and growth within the sector increases. Investing in a diverse range of cryptocurrencies and staying informed about market trends can help investors capitalize on emerging opportunities and drive portfolio growth.

Chapter Eight

Legal and Regulatory Environment

Global Regulatory Landscape

The global regulatory landscape for cryptocurrencies is complex and rapidly evolving. It varies significantly from one country to another and involves multiple regulatory domains, including financial regulation, anti-money laundering (AML), consumer protection, and taxation. Here's an in-depth look at the global regulatory landscape for cryptocurrencies:

1. Regulatory Fragmentation

Cryptocurrency regulations differ widely across countries, reflecting varying levels of acceptance, regulatory approaches, and legal frameworks. Some countries have embraced cryptocurrencies and blockchain technology, establishing clear regulatory guidelines, while others have imposed strict restrictions or outright bans.

- **United States:** In the U.S., cryptocurrency regulation is fragmented across federal and state levels. The Securities and Exchange Commission (SEC) regulates digital assets that are classified as securities, while the Commodity Futures Trading Commission (CFTC) oversees futures and derivatives trading. Additionally, the Financial Crimes Enforcement Network (FinCEN) enforces AML regulations, and the Internal Revenue Service (IRS) addresses taxation issues related to cryptocurrency transactions.

- **European Union:** The European Union (EU) is working towards a unified regulatory framework with the proposed Markets in Crypto-Assets (MiCA) regulation. MiCA aims to provide a comprehensive regulatory structure for digital assets, including consumer protection, market integrity, and anti-money laundering measures. Member states may still have their own national regulations, but MiCA seeks to harmonize rules across the EU.

- **China:** China has taken a restrictive approach towards cryptocurrencies, particularly regarding trading and initial coin offerings (ICOs). The Chinese government has implemented bans on crypto exchanges and mining activities, citing concerns over financial stability, capital outflows, and energy consumption. However, China is actively developing its own central bank digital currency (CBDC), the digital yuan.

- **Japan:** Japan has adopted a relatively progressive stance on cryptocurrency regulation. The Financial Services Agency (FSA) regulates cryptocurrency exchanges, requiring them to register and comply with AML and consumer protection standards. Japan also recognizes cryptocurrencies as legal property, subject to taxation.

2. Anti-Money Laundering (AML) and Know Your Customer (KYC) Requirements

AML and KYC regulations are crucial aspects of cryptocurrency regulation aimed at preventing illicit activities, such as money laundering and terrorist financing. Many countries require cryptocurrency exchanges and service providers to implement KYC procedures, which involve verifying the identity of their customers.

- **Financial Action Task Force (FATF):** The FATF, an international body that sets standards for AML and counter-terrorism financing (CTF), has issued guidelines for the cryptocurrency industry. These guidelines emphasize the need for crypto service providers to implement robust AML and CTF measures, including customer due diligence, transaction monitoring, and reporting suspicious activities.

- **United Kingdom:** The UK's Financial Conduct Authority (FCA) enforces AML regulations for cryptocurrency exchanges and wallet providers. These entities must register with the FCA and adhere to AML and KYC requirements, including reporting suspicious transactions.

3. Consumer Protection and Market Integrity

Consumer protection is a significant concern in the cryptocurrency space due to the high risk of fraud, market manipulation, and volatile price swings. Regulatory authorities aim to safeguard investors and ensure market integrity through various measures.

- **Securities and Exchange Commission (SEC):** In jurisdictions like the U.S., regulatory bodies like the SEC focus on protecting investors by regulating digital assets classified as securities. They enforce rules related to disclosures, investor protections, and fraud prevention.

- **European Securities and Markets Authority (ESMA):** ESMA provides guidelines on investor protection and market integrity for cryptocurrencies and related financial products. It aims to address risks associated with market manipulation, misleading advertising, and inadequate disclosures.

4. Taxation

Taxation of cryptocurrency transactions is another critical aspect of regulation. Different countries have varying approaches to taxing digital assets, including capital gains tax, income tax, and VAT.

- **United States:** The IRS treats cryptocurrencies as property for tax purposes, meaning that capital gains tax applies to profits from trading or selling digital assets. Additionally, crypto transactions must be reported, and failure to do so can lead to penalties.

- **Australia:** The Australian Taxation Office (ATO) requires individuals and businesses to report cryptocurrency transactions as part of their income tax returns. Cryptocurrency is treated as property, subject to capital gains tax.

5. Central Bank Digital Currencies (CBDCs)

Several countries are exploring or developing CBDCs, which are digital versions of their national currencies. CBDCs aim to combine the benefits of cryptocurrencies with the stability of traditional fiat currencies.

- **China:** China is leading in CBDC development with its digital yuan, which is being tested in various pilot programs. The digital yuan aims to enhance payment efficiency, reduce transaction costs, and provide greater control over monetary policy.

- **European Central Bank (ECB):** The ECB is exploring the concept of a digital euro, which would complement physical cash and support the digital economy. The ECB is evaluating the potential benefits and risks associated with a digital euro.

6. Future Developments

The regulatory landscape for cryptocurrencies is likely to continue evolving as technology advances and market dynamics change. Regulators are working to address emerging issues such as decentralized finance (DeFi), stablecoins, and cross-border transactions.

- **Global Coordination:** Efforts are being made to achieve greater global coordination in cryptocurrency regulation. Organizations like the International Monetary Fund (IMF) and the Bank for International Settlements (BIS) are exploring frameworks for international cooperation and regulatory consistency.

- **Innovation and Regulation Balance:** Regulators face the challenge of balancing innovation with risk management. Striking the right balance is essential to foster innovation while ensuring financial stability, consumer protection, and compliance with legal standards.

The global regulatory landscape for cryptocurrencies is diverse and rapidly changing. It involves a range of considerations, including anti-money laundering and consumer protection, taxation, and the development of central bank digital currencies. Investors must stay informed about regulatory developments and adapt to evolving legal and regulatory frameworks to manage risks and capitalize on opportunities in the cryptocurrency market.

In the United States, the regulatory landscape for cryptocurrencies remains fragmented and evolving. U.S. regulatory bodies have not yet developed a unified framework specifically for cryptoassets. Instead, they apply existing financial regulations to cryptocurrencies on a case-by-case basis. This often leads to the categorization of cryptoassets as either securities or commodities, depending on their specific functions and usage [268].

The Securities and Exchange Commission (SEC) evaluates cryptocurrencies based on whether they meet the criteria of a "security" or "investment contract," using the Howey Test as a key tool. This test assesses whether an asset is an investment contract by determining if there is an expectation of profits derived from the efforts of others. If a cryptocurrency is considered to provide such an investment opportunity, it falls under the SEC's jurisdiction and must comply with securities laws. The SEC has actively enforced this stance, evident in its lawsuit against Ripple Labs in December 2020. The SEC alleged that Ripple raised over $1.3 billion through unregistered securities offerings with XRP sales, which Ripple argued were not securities but a cryptocurrency. This case highlights the SEC's rigorous approach to applying traditional securities laws to digital assets [268].

Conversely, the Commodity Futures Trading Commission (CFTC) regulates cryptocurrencies viewed as "commodities." The CFTC's oversight focuses on futures, swaps, and derivative contracts related to digital assets, ensuring market integrity and protecting investors. The CFTC's involvement is illustrated by its 2015 action against Coinflip, the operator of the Derivabit platform, for trading Bitcoin options and futures without proper registration. This action reinforced the CFTC's classification of Bitcoin and similar digital currencies as commodities. Further, in October 2020, the CFTC took legal action against BitMEX for operating an unregistered trading platform and failing to implement necessary anti-money laundering measures. These actions reflect the CFTC's commitment to regulating commodity-linked cryptocurrency markets and ensuring compliance with established financial regulations [268].

The regulatory actions of the SEC and CFTC underscore the ongoing debate and ambiguity regarding the classification of cryptocurrencies. This lack of clear regulatory guidelines has led to a complex environment where cryptocurrencies may be treated differently based on their characteristics and use cases. The need for more defined regulations is evident, as it would provide clearer guidelines for distinguishing between various types of cryptocurrencies and their corresponding regulatory obligations.

The European Union (EU) has approached cryptocurrency regulation by integrating cryptoassets into existing financial regulatory frameworks. Initially, the EU's strategy involved applying directives and regulations like the Markets in Financial Instruments Directive (MiFID) to cryptoassets deemed financial instruments. The revised Anti-Money Laundering Directive (AMLD) introduced anti-money laundering and counter-terrorist financing regimes for cryptoasset providers, including custodial wallet and exchange service providers. However, the regulatory landscape remained fragmented due to varying interpretations by individual Member States, leading to legal uncertainties and gaps in consumer protection [268].

To address these challenges, the EU enacted the Markets in Crypto-Assets (MiCA) regulation in May 2023. MiCA provides a harmonized regulatory framework for cryptoasset markets across the EU, covering assets not already regulated under existing financial services legislation. It classifies cryptoassets into three categories: asset-reference tokens, e-money tokens, and other crypto-assets such as utility tokens. MiCA mandates that cryptoasset issuers and cryptoasset service providers (CASPs) obtain authorizations from national competent authorities (NCAs). It encompasses activities related to the issuance, public offering, and trading of cryptoassets. Additionally, the EU's Transfer of Funds Regulation (TFR), published in June 2023, introduces new rules for information accompanying cryptoasset transfers, enhancing transparency and compliance [268].

The MiCA regulation represents a significant shift towards a more tailored and unified regulatory approach, aiming to address the gaps left by previous frameworks. This move reflects the EU's commitment to creating a cohesive regulatory environment for cryptoassets, balancing innovation with market stability and investor protection [268].

The United Kingdom has integrated cryptocurrency regulation within its existing legal frameworks. In 2018, the Cryptoassets Taskforce (CATF), comprising the Financial Conduct Authority (FCA), the Bank of England (BoE), and Her Majesty's Treasury (HMT), was established to address the opportunities and risks presented by cryptocurrencies. The CATF's recommendations led to a cautious yet inclusive regulatory approach [268].

In February 2023, HMT released a consultation paper on the future financial services regulatory regime for cryptoassets, outlining plans to incorporate cryptoasset regulation into the existing Financial Services and Markets Act (FSMA). The government's approach emphasizes "technology agnostic" principles and aims to apply "same risks, same regulatory outcomes" to cryptoassets and traditional financial markets [268]. This avoids creating an uneven playing field between crypto companies and traditional institutions. The FSMA 2023 and related amendments now explicitly accommodate cryptoassets within the FSMA framework, including the Regulated Activities Order (RAO) and the Financial Promotion Order (FPO). These changes ensure that cryptoassets falling under specific categories, such as security tokens, are regulated accordingly [268].

The UK's regulatory approach is characterized by a phased integration of cryptoassets into the financial system. Phase 1 focuses on fiat-backed stablecoins, requiring issuers and custodians to seek FCA authorization and adhere to Payment Services Regulations (PSRs). Phase 2 will extend regulation to other cryptoasset categories, including issuance, lending, and trading activities. This gradual approach aims to balance innovation with regulatory oversight, ensuring consumer protection and market stability while adapting existing frameworks to the unique aspects of cryptoassets [268].

China has adopted a stringent and evolving stance on cryptocurrency regulation, characterized by a series of restrictive measures. In 2013, the People's Bank of China (PBC), along with other departments, issued a notice declaring that Bitcoin did not have the legal status of a currency and prohibiting financial institutions from engaging in Bitcoin-related transactions. This move aimed to protect the yuan's status and curb money laundering risks [268].

The rise of Initial Coin Offerings (ICOs) as a fundraising method prompted further regulatory action. In 2017, the PBC and several other departments banned ICOs, labeling them as unauthorized fundraising tools that could involve financial fraud and illegal securities issuance. This prohibition was intended to protect investors from speculative and risky ventures [268].

In 2021, the Chinese government issued a comprehensive notice reinforcing its ban on cryptocurrency trading and mining. The notice reiterated that cryptocurrencies were not recognized as legal tender and aimed to further crack down on speculative trading and illegal mining activities [268]. These measures reflect China's strict and progressively clear stance on cryptocurrencies, emphasizing control over financial risks and maintaining regulatory authority over digital assets.

India's regulatory approach to cryptocurrencies has been marked by periods of skepticism, ambiguity, and gradual acceptance. In 2013, the Reserve Bank of India (RBI) issued a cautionary note about the risks of cryptocurrencies, highlighting concerns about volatility and potential illicit use. This initial stance left the market in a state of uncertainty, with no formal regulatory framework in place [268].

In April 2018, the RBI directed financial institutions to cease dealing with entities involved in cryptocurrency transactions, effectively cutting off banking services to the crypto sector. This action created significant challenges for the industry. However, in March 2020, the Supreme Court of India overturned the RBI's ban, deeming it disproportionate. This decision marked a potential shift towards a more supportive regulatory environment for cryptocurrencies [268].

Despite the Supreme Court's ruling, India continues to experience regulatory inconsistency, with various bodies offering conflicting views on cryptocurrencies. This lack of clear and cohesive regulation has impacted the stability and growth of the crypto sector in India, highlighting the need for a balanced and comprehensive regulatory framework to address the evolving dynamics of the cryptocurrency market [268].

In Canada, cryptocurrency is not recognized as legal tender, but the country has taken a proactive stance in regulating the crypto space, setting itself apart from many other jurisdictions. Canada was a pioneer in embracing cryptocurrencies within its financial ecosystem, notably becoming the first country to approve a Bitcoin exchange-traded fund (ETF). This landmark move occurred with several Bitcoin ETFs being launched and traded on the Toronto Stock Exchange, providing Canadian investors with a regulated and accessible way to invest in Bitcoin through traditional financial markets [269].

In terms of regulatory oversight for crypto trading platforms, Canada requires such entities to adhere to regulations set forth by the Canadian Securities Administrators (CSA) and the Investment Industry Regulatory Organization of Canada (IIROC). Crypto trading platforms and dealers operating in the country must register with provincial regulators, which ensures that they comply with existing securities laws and provides a framework for investor protection. This approach aims to integrate cryptocurrency trading into the existing regulatory infrastructure, enhancing oversight and accountability [269].

Moreover, Canada classifies all crypto investment firms as money service businesses (MSBs). This classification mandates that these firms register with the Financial Transactions and Reports Analysis Centre of Canada (FINTRAC). This registration is crucial for combating money laundering and terrorist financing, as it subjects crypto businesses to anti-money laundering (AML) and know-your-customer (KYC) requirements. By categorizing crypto firms as MSBs, Canada aligns them with traditional financial institutions in terms of regulatory expectations and compliance [269].

From a taxation perspective, Canada treats cryptocurrency similarly to other commodities. This means that transactions involving cryptocurrencies are subject to taxation in a manner akin to the taxation of commodities. This approach reflects Canada's view of cryptocurrencies as assets rather than currencies, impacting how gains and losses from crypto transactions are reported and taxed. Overall, Canada's regulatory framework for cryptocurrencies emphasizes integration into existing financial systems, investor protection, and compliance with anti-money laundering standards, positioning it as a leader in the proactive regulation of digital assets [269].

In Australia, cryptocurrencies are classified as legal property rather than currency, which means they are subject to capital gains tax (CGT). This taxation approach treats cryptocurrencies similarly to other forms of property, requiring individuals and businesses to pay tax on any capital gains realized from the sale or exchange of digital assets. This aligns with Australia's broader strategy of integrating cryptocurrency into existing financial frameworks while ensuring compliance with tax regulations [269].

Crypto exchanges and related platforms can operate in Australia as long as they comply with regulatory requirements set by the Australian Transaction Reports and Analysis Centre (AUSTRAC). These platforms must register with AUSTRAC and adhere to anti-money laundering (AML) and counter-terrorism financing (CTF) obligations. This regulatory oversight ensures that crypto trading activities are monitored for potential illicit activities and helps maintain the integrity of the financial system [269].

In 2019, the Australian Securities and Investments Commission (ASIC) took steps to regulate initial coin offerings (ICOs), which are fundraising mechanisms for new cryptocurrencies. ASIC introduced requirements to provide greater transparency and protect investors. Additionally, ASIC imposed a ban on exchanges offering privacy coins—cryptocurrencies designed to enhance user anonymity—due to concerns over their potential use in illicit activities. This move reflects the broader regulatory trend towards increased scrutiny of privacy-enhancing technologies in the crypto space [269].

By 2021, Australia began considering more comprehensive regulatory measures for cryptocurrencies, including the creation of a licensing framework and the potential introduction of a central bank digital currency (CBDC). The aim was to create a more structured and regulated environment for the burgeoning crypto industry. In October 2023, the Australian Treasury announced plans to introduce a new regulatory framework, with a draft expected to be released in 2024. This framework would include a 12-month transition period for businesses to comply, marking a significant step towards formalizing and enhancing cryptocurrency regulation in the country [269].

In Singapore, cryptocurrencies are classified as property rather than legal tender. This classification aligns with the country's approach to integrating digital assets into existing legal and financial systems without designating them as official currency. The Monetary Authority of Singapore (MAS) is responsible for licensing and regulating crypto exchanges under the Payment Services Act (PSA). This framework provides a structured approach to overseeing the operations of cryptocurrency platforms, ensuring they meet regulatory standards.

In 2022, MAS issued guidance to digital payment token (DPT) providers, advising them against aggressive public advertising. This caution reflects the regulatory body's efforts to mitigate risks associated with the promotion of cryptocurrency services and prevent potential consumer harm [269].

In August 2023, MAS introduced a regulatory framework for stablecoins, which are cryptocurrencies pegged to stable assets like fiat currencies. Under this framework, stablecoin issuers must meet specific criteria and receive approval from MAS to use the designation "MAS-regulated stablecoin." This regulation aims to enhance the credibility and stability of stablecoins in the market, distinguishing them from non-regulated alternatives [269].

Singapore is noted for its favourable tax regime regarding cryptocurrencies. Long-term capital gains from crypto investments are not taxed, making it an attractive environment for investors. However, companies that frequently engage in cryptocurrency transactions are subject to income tax on their gains, ensuring that businesses are taxed appropriately based on their operational activities [269].

In South Korea, cryptocurrency exchanges and virtual asset service providers are required to register with the Korea Financial Intelligence Unit (KFIU), which operates under the Financial Services Commission (FSC). This registration is part of a broader effort to regulate the crypto industry and ensure that service providers adhere to legal and financial standards [269].

In 2021, South Korea enacted a ban on privacy coins, following a trend seen in other jurisdictions concerned about the use of anonymity-enhancing technologies in illicit activities. This ban aligns with South Korea's cautious approach to regulating cryptocurrencies and reflects its commitment to preventing potential misuse of digital assets [269].

The regulatory landscape in South Korea saw a significant update in 2023 with the implementation of the Act on the Protection of Virtual Asset Users. This act designates the Financial Services Commission as the primary regulator for virtual assets and outlines legal and illegal uses of cryptocurrencies. The legislation also includes provisions for user protection, requiring issuers and service providers to follow specific practices to safeguard users. This comprehensive regulatory framework aims to provide clarity and stability in the virtual asset market, enhancing both investor confidence and market integrity [269].

Tax Implications of Cryptocurrency Transactions

Cryptocurrency transactions have significant tax implications that vary depending on the jurisdiction and the nature of the transaction. In many countries, cryptocurrencies are treated as property or assets rather than currency, which affects how they are taxed. Understanding these implications is crucial for individuals and businesses involved in cryptocurrency activities to ensure compliance with tax regulations and avoid potential legal issues.

Capital Gains Tax

In most jurisdictions, cryptocurrencies are subject to capital gains tax (CGT). This tax applies to the profit made from the sale or exchange of cryptocurrency. For instance, if an individual purchases Bitcoin at $10,000 and later sells it for $15,000, the $5,000 profit is considered a capital gain and is subject to tax. The rate at which these gains are taxed can vary based on how long the asset was held and the taxpayer's income level. Short-term gains, typically from assets held for less than a year, are often taxed at a higher rate than long-term gains, which benefit from more favourable tax rates in many countries.

Income Tax

When cryptocurrencies are earned as income—such as through mining, staking, or as payment for goods and services—they are generally subject to income tax. The value of the cryptocurrency at the time it is received is used to determine the income amount, which is then taxed according to the individual's or business's income tax bracket. For example, if a person receives 1 Bitcoin worth $20,000 as payment for consulting services, this amount is treated as taxable income and must be reported as such.

Transaction Fees and Deductions

Transaction fees incurred during cryptocurrency trades or transactions are also relevant from a tax perspective. In many jurisdictions, these fees can be deducted from capital gains, thereby reducing the taxable amount. For example, if an individual pays $100 in fees to sell cryptocurrency that results in a $5,000 gain, the taxable gain may be adjusted to $4,900. Proper documentation of these fees is essential for accurate tax reporting.

Record Keeping and Reporting

Accurate record keeping is important for tax compliance. Tax authorities require detailed records of all cryptocurrency transactions, including dates, amounts, transaction types, and involved parties. This is necessary for calculating capital gains, reporting income, and claiming deductions. Many tax authorities, such as the Internal Revenue Service (IRS) in the United States and the Australian Taxation Office (ATO), have issued guidelines for documenting cryptocurrency transactions, and failure to maintain thorough records can lead to complications and potential penalties.

Tax Treatment of Different Types of Transactions

Different types of cryptocurrency transactions may have varying tax treatments. For instance, cryptocurrency trading between different coins or tokens is generally treated as a taxable event, where the gains or losses from the trade must be reported. Similarly, using cryptocurrency to purchase goods or services is also considered a taxable event, where the fair market value of the cryptocurrency at the time of the transaction must be reported as either income or a capital gain or loss, depending on the context.

Global Tax Regulations

The tax treatment of cryptocurrency transactions can vary significantly by country. Some countries have clear regulations and guidelines, while others are still developing their approach. For instance, in countries like the United States and Australia, cryptocurrencies are generally treated as property, with specific rules for capital gains and income tax. In contrast, other jurisdictions may have different tax rates, reporting requirements, or may not yet have comprehensive regulations in place. It is essential for individuals and businesses engaged in cryptocurrency transactions to be aware of and comply with the specific tax regulations in their country or any country where they have tax obligations.

Emerging Trends and Changes

As the cryptocurrency market evolves, so too do tax regulations. Governments around the world are continuously updating their tax policies to address new developments in the crypto space. Emerging trends, such as the increasing use of decentralized finance (DeFi) platforms and the introduction of central bank digital currencies (CBDCs), may influence future tax regulations and reporting requirements. Staying informed about these changes and seeking professional tax advice is important for managing cryptocurrency tax obligations effectively.

In summary, the tax implications of cryptocurrency transactions encompass capital gains tax, income tax, transaction fees, and record-keeping requirements. The treatment of these transactions varies by jurisdiction, and staying compliant with local regulations is essential for avoiding legal issues and optimizing tax liabilities.

Tax Implications of Cryptocurrency Transactions in the United States

In the United States, the tax implications of cryptocurrency transactions are governed by the Internal Revenue Service (IRS), which treats cryptocurrencies as property rather than currency. This classification has significant ramifications for how various types of cryptocurrency transactions are taxed. Understanding these implications is crucial for both individuals and businesses involved in the cryptocurrency market to ensure compliance with federal tax laws and avoid potential penalties.

- **Capital Gains Tax:** In the U.S., cryptocurrencies are subject to capital gains tax, which applies to profits made from selling or exchanging crypto assets. When an individual sells cryptocurrency for more than its purchase price, the profit—known as a capital gain—is taxable. For example, if an individual buys Bitcoin at $10,000 and later sells it for $15,000, the $5,000 profit is considered a capital gain and must be reported on their tax return. The IRS distinguishes between short-term and long-term capital gains, with short-term gains (from assets held for one year or less) taxed at ordinary income tax rates, while long-term gains (from assets held for more than one year) benefit from reduced tax rates.

- **Income Tax:** Cryptocurrency received as income is subject to income tax. This includes cryptocurrencies earned through activities such as mining, staking, or receiving payment for services. The fair market value of the cryptocurrency at the time it is received determines the amount of income to report. For instance, if someone mines 1 Bitcoin, which is valued at $20,000 at the time of receipt, this amount is treated as taxable income. The income must be reported on the individual's tax return, and it is taxed at the applicable income tax rate based on the total taxable income of the individual or business.

- **Transaction Fees and Deductions:** Transaction fees incurred during cryptocurrency trades are deductible from capital gains. If an individual sells cryptocurrency and pays a fee to a broker or exchange, this fee can be subtracted from the capital gain to determine the net taxable amount. For example, if an individual sells cryptocurrency for a $5,000 gain and incurs a $100 transaction fee, the taxable gain would be adjusted to $4,900. Proper documentation of these fees is essential for accurate tax reporting.

- **Record Keeping and Reporting:** Maintaining detailed records of all cryptocurrency transactions is crucial for tax compliance. The IRS requires individuals to report every transaction involving cryptocurrencies, including purchases, sales, exchanges, and the use of crypto for payments. Detailed records should include the date of the transaction, the amount and type of cryptocurrency, the fair market value at the time of the transaction, and the transaction fees paid. This information is necessary for accurately calculating capital gains, reporting income, and ensuring proper tax treatment.

- **Tax Treatment of Different Types of Transactions:** Different types of cryptocurrency transactions are subject to various tax treatments. For instance, trading one cryptocurrency for another is considered a taxable event, where any gain or loss from the trade must be reported. Similarly, using cryptocurrency to purchase goods or services is also treated as a taxable event. The fair market value of the cryptocurrency at the time of the purchase must be reported as either income or a capital gain or loss, depending on the context.

- **Tax Reporting Forms:** The IRS requires the use of specific forms for reporting cryptocurrency transactions. Individuals typically use Form 1040 and attach Schedule D and Form 8949 to report capital gains and losses. Form 8949 is used to detail each transaction, including the date acquired, date sold, proceeds, and cost basis. For income from cryptocurrency, Form 1040 is used to report the income amount. Businesses involved in cryptocurrency transactions may need to use additional forms, such as Form 1120 for corporations.

- **Emerging Trends and Updates:** Tax regulations concerning cryptocurrencies are evolving as the market develops and new technologies emerge. The IRS has issued guidelines and notices to clarify tax treatment, but ongoing developments in the cryptocurrency space—such as the growth of decentralized finance (DeFi) platforms and the introduction of central bank digital currencies (CBDCs)—may influence future tax policies. Taxpayers should stay informed about these changes and consider consulting with tax professionals to navigate complex scenarios and ensure compliance with the latest regulations.

- **Penalties and Enforcement:** Failure to properly report cryptocurrency transactions can lead to penalties and enforcement actions by the IRS. Inaccurate reporting, underreporting income, or failing to disclose transactions can result in fines, interest charges, and potential legal consequences. The IRS has increasingly focused on cryptocurrency transactions, including issuing warning letters and conducting audits to ensure compliance.

According to the Internal Revenue Service (IRS), most cryptocurrencies are classified as convertible virtual currencies. This designation means they function as a medium of exchange, a store of value, a unit of account, and can be substituted for real money. As a result, any profits or income derived from cryptocurrency transactions are subject to taxation. However, understanding when and how cryptocurrency is taxed involves navigating various tax scenarios and regulations. Here's a detailed look at the tax implications and key considerations [270]:

In the U.S., the IRS treats cryptocurrencies as property rather than currency, which significantly impacts how they are taxed. Cryptocurrency transactions trigger taxable events based on changes in market value or the nature of the transaction. Here are the primary scenarios that lead to tax obligations [270]:

- **Sale of Cryptocurrency**: When you sell a cryptocurrency for more than its purchase price, the profit realized is subject to capital gains tax. For instance, if you buy 1 Bitcoin (BTC) at $6,000 and later sell it for $8,000, the $2,000 gain is taxable. The rate at which this gain is taxed depends on how long you held the asset. Short-term capital gains (from assets held for one year or less) are taxed at your ordinary income tax rate, ranging from 0% to 37% for the 2024 tax year. Long-term capital gains (from assets held for over a year) benefit from reduced rates of 0%, 15%, or 20%, depending on your overall income.

- **Using Cryptocurrency for Purchases**: When you use cryptocurrency to buy goods or services, you incur a taxable event. The taxable amount is the difference between the cryptocurrency's value at the time of purchase and its original purchase price. For example, if you bought Bitcoin for $5,000 and use it to buy a product worth $6,000, you must report the $1,000 gain as taxable income.

- **Receiving Cryptocurrency as Payment**: If you receive cryptocurrency as payment for goods or services, it must be reported as business income. The value of the cryptocurrency at the time of receipt is considered taxable income. This applies whether you are a business or an individual receiving crypto for freelance work or other services.

- **Mining and Staking**: Cryptocurrency earned through mining or staking is considered ordinary income and is taxed based on its fair market value at the time it is received. For instance, if you mine Bitcoin and its value is $10,000 at the time of mining, this amount is taxable as income.

Certain activities involving cryptocurrency are not considered taxable events under IRS guidelines [270]:

- **Buying Cryptocurrency with Fiat Money**: Purchasing cryptocurrency with traditional currency (like USD) does not trigger a taxable event. Taxes are not owed until the cryptocurrency is sold, exchanged, or used in a transaction that results in a gain.

- **Donating to Charity**: Donating cryptocurrency to a tax-exempt non-profit organization or charity is not taxable, provided the donation is made to an IRS-recognized charity. However, donating cryptocurrency may still impact your overall tax situation, such as potentially qualifying for a charitable deduction.

- **Gifting Cryptocurrency**: Giving cryptocurrency as a gift is not a taxable event for the giver, though the recipient may face tax implications depending on the value of the gift and any applicable gift exclusions.

- **Transferring Between Wallets**: Transferring cryptocurrency between personal wallets does not trigger a taxable event. Taxes are assessed only when the cryptocurrency is sold, used for purchases, or exchanged for another asset.

Key Takeaways

- **Capital Gains Tax**: If you profit from selling or exchanging cryptocurrency, you owe capital gains tax. The rate depends on how long you held the asset and your overall taxable income.

- **Use for Purchases**: Using cryptocurrency to buy goods or services results in a taxable gain or loss based on the difference between its purchase price and its value at the time of use.

- **Business Income**: Receiving cryptocurrency as payment or income from mining is taxable as ordinary income.

- **Tax Records**: Keeping accurate records of all cryptocurrency transactions, including purchase prices, sale values, and transaction fees, is essential for proper tax reporting and compliance.

Examples of Cryptocurrency Tax Events

Making a Purchase with Crypto: Using cryptocurrency to make a purchase introduces several tax implications. When you spend cryptocurrency, it is treated as a taxable event. Here's a detailed look at how it works [270]:

- **Transaction Details**: When you transfer cryptocurrency to pay for goods or services, you are responsible for both the sales tax and any capital gains tax on the transaction. For instance, if you buy a candy bar with Bitcoin, you'll need to calculate the sales tax based on the transaction's total value, which includes the cryptocurrency's worth at the time of purchase.

- **Capital Gains or Losses**: If the value of your cryptocurrency has increased since you acquired it, the transaction will result in a capital gain. Conversely, if the value has decreased, it will result in a capital loss. This gain or loss is determined by comparing the cryptocurrency's value at the time of purchase to its value at the time of use. Both the gain and the sales tax are reported on your tax return.

- **Record Keeping**: To accurately report your taxes, it's crucial to log the amount spent and the fair market value of the cryptocurrency at the time of the transaction. This will help you calculate the capital gains or losses and ensure that you comply with tax regulations.

Buying Cryptocurrency: When you purchase cryptocurrency, such as buying one Bitcoin (BTC) for $3,700 in early 2019, and later the value rises to $38,500, there are tax implications for both you and any sellers involved [270]:

- **Seller's Tax Obligation**: If you use Bitcoin to buy a car, the seller must report the transaction based on Bitcoin's fair market value at the time of sale. The seller also needs to calculate any capital gains or losses if they convert the Bitcoin to fiat currency or use it for another purchase.

- **Your Tax Obligation**: As the buyer, you must report the transaction as a capital gain. This is calculated based on the difference between the original purchase price of the Bitcoin and its value at the time you used it for the purchase. This gain needs to be included in your tax return, reflecting the profit made from the cryptocurrency investment.

Cashing Out Cryptocurrency: When you exchange cryptocurrency for fiat money, understanding your cost basis is crucial for tax purposes [270]:

- **Cost Basis Calculation**: The cost basis of your cryptocurrency includes the total amount spent, including any fees. To determine the taxable amount, subtract the cost basis from the cryptocurrency's fair market value at the time of the exchange.

- **Taxable Amount**: If you have a gain, the difference between the fair market value and the cost basis is considered taxable. Conversely, if you incur a loss, you report this loss to potentially offset other capital gains.

- **Recording Gains and Losses**: Similar to other assets, the taxable profits or losses from cryptocurrency transactions are categorized as capital gains or losses, requiring accurate record-keeping to report them correctly.

Cryptocurrency Mining: For individuals who mine cryptocurrency, the tax treatment is different [270]:

- **Taxable Income**: Mining rewards are considered ordinary income. The value of the cryptocurrency at the time it is mined is taxable as income.

- **Business Operations**: If mining is part of a business, the income is reported as business income. Miners can deduct related expenses, such as hardware and electricity costs, which can lower their taxable income.

Cryptocurrency Staking: Staking cryptocurrency involves locking it up as collateral to validate transactions on a blockchain [270]:

- **Income Tax**: Any rewards received from staking are taxable as ordinary income. The rewards must be reported based on their fair market value at the time they are received.

- **Capital Gains**: If you later use or convert the staked cryptocurrency, any resulting capital gains or losses must be reported. The gains or losses are calculated based on the cryptocurrency's value when you acquired it versus its value at the time of conversion or use.

Exchanging Cryptocurrencies: When exchanging one cryptocurrency for another, the IRS treats it as a taxable event [270]:

- **Taxable Event**: Exchanging one cryptocurrency for another is akin to converting one to fiat and then purchasing another. This process triggers a capital gain or loss on the cryptocurrency that was exchanged.
- **Reporting Gains or Losses**: Any gains or losses from the exchange must be reported. Many cryptocurrency exchanges provide tools to export trading data, which can be used to track and calculate taxable events for accurate reporting.

Understanding these various tax events helps ensure compliance with IRS regulations and can aid in effective tax planning for individuals involved in cryptocurrency transactions.

Tax Implications of Cryptocurrency Transactions in Australia

When Capital Gains Tax Applies

In many jurisdictions, including Australia, cryptocurrencies are treated as capital gains tax (CGT) assets. This means that if you hold a crypto asset as an investment, any disposal or exchange of that asset is considered a CGT event. These events can result in either a capital gain or a capital loss. A capital gain occurs if the value of the crypto asset has increased from its cost base, while a capital loss occurs if its value has decreased. It's important to note that net capital losses cannot be deducted from other types of income. However, you may be eligible for a CGT discount if you hold the asset for at least 12 months, which can reduce your taxable gain [271].

Working Out the Timing of the CGT Event

The timing of a CGT event is crucial for accurate reporting. A CGT event is triggered when you dispose of a crypto asset. This can occur in several ways [271]:

- Selling the asset
- Gifting the asset
- Trading or exchanging one crypto asset for another
- Converting the asset into fiat currency (like Australian dollars)

- Using the asset to purchase goods or services

Other events that may qualify as CGT events include the loss or destruction of the asset or the creation of contractual rights. The specific nature of the CGT event can affect when the event is considered to have occurred and how the capital gain or loss should be calculated.

Calculating Your CGT

To calculate your capital gains tax, follow these steps [271]:

1. **Gather Records**: Ensure you have accurate records of each crypto asset and all associated transactions. This includes purchase prices, dates, and the value of the assets at the time of each transaction.

2. **Convert Values**: Convert the value of the crypto assets into Australian dollars (AUD) for consistency in calculations.

3. **Determine Capital Gain or Loss**: For each CGT event, subtract the cost base (the original purchase price plus any associated costs) from the proceeds of the sale or the value of the asset at the time of the transaction. If this results in a positive figure, you have a capital gain. If it's negative, you have a capital loss.

4. **Apply CGT Discount**: If you held the asset for more than 12 months, you might be eligible for a CGT discount, which reduces the taxable amount of your capital gain.

Reporting CGT on Crypto Assets in Your Tax Return

When it comes to reporting CGT on your tax return [271]:

- **For Individuals**: If you are completing your tax return online with myTax, refer to the sections on capital gains or losses. For paper forms, follow the specific instructions provided for individuals.

- **For Companies, Trusts, or Funds**: Use the Capital Gains Tax Schedule and instructions relevant to these entities.

Keeping detailed records and using tools like online calculators can assist in managing and reporting your capital gains accurately. Always ensure compliance with local tax laws and consult with a tax professional if needed to navigate complex situations.

Legal Challenges and Case Studies

The cryptocurrency market, while offering significant innovation and opportunities for financial inclusion, has also experienced several high-profile incidents that highlight the risks and regulatory gaps within the industry. These incidents underscore the need for improved security measures and regulatory oversight to protect investors and maintain market integrity [268].

Mt. Gox Hack: In 2014, Mt. Gox, which was once the world's largest Bitcoin exchange, filed for bankruptcy following a major security breach. Approximately 850,000 BTC, worth around $450 million at that time, were stolen. This hack exposed severe vulnerabilities in the security protocols of cryptocurrency exchanges and highlighted the lack of regulatory oversight in the industry. In response, Japan, where Mt. Gox was based, enacted new legislation in 2017 to address these issues. The Payment Services Act (PSA) was revised to mandate stricter security measures for exchanges, including maintaining adequate reserves and undergoing annual audits. These changes aimed to enhance the safety of funds held by exchanges and improve investor protection [268].

Bitfinex Hack: The 2016 Bitfinex hack was another significant incident in the cryptocurrency space. Bitfinex, a prominent cryptocurrency exchange, suffered a breach resulting in the loss of 120,000 BTC, valued at approximately $72 million at that time. The hack brought attention to the security practices of cryptocurrency exchanges and the need for regulatory intervention. Following the breach, the Commodity Futures Trading Commission (CFTC) fined Bitfinex for operating an unregistered exchange and failing to implement adequate security measures. This incident underscored the importance of rigorous security standards and regulatory compliance in the cryptocurrency industry [268].

FTX Collapse: The collapse of FTX in November 2022 marked one of the most significant failures in cryptocurrency history. The crisis began when CoinDesk reported concerns about the financial health of Alameda Research, a trading firm closely linked to FTX. It was revealed that a large portion of Alameda's balance sheet was held in FTT, the native token of FTX. This revelation led to a loss of confidence among investors and users, triggering a liquidity crisis as many attempted to withdraw their funds simultaneously. The collapse was attributed to a lack of clear separation between exchange operations and trading activities. In response, U.S. regulatory bodies, including the Department of Justice (DOJ), the Securities and Exchange Commission (SEC), and the Bahamas' Financial Crimes Investigation Branch, launched investigations into the exchange and its executives for potential regulatory violations [268].

Terra-Luna Crash: In May 2022, the Terra (LUNA) and its stablecoin TerraUSD (UST) experienced a catastrophic collapse. UST began to lose its peg to the dollar, exacerbated by the interconnected mechanism between UST and LUNA. The collapse was triggered by a high yield of 19.5% offered by the Anchor protocol to UST depositors, leading to large withdrawals and a bank run. This resulted in UST depegging from the dollar and LUNA's price plummeting, causing a "death spiral" where LUNA's supply inflated dramatically while its price dropped to near zero. The collapse of Terra-Luna led to regulatory scrutiny of stablecoins. The UK's HM Treasury announced plans to regulate stablecoins as part of broader financial services legislation, and the Financial Conduct Authority (FCA) proposed regulations for fiat-backed stablecoins, signalling a move towards more stringent oversight [268].

Tornado Cash Sanctions: Tornado Cash (TC) operates as a decentralized smart contract on the Ethereum blockchain, designed to enhance transaction privacy by mixing cryptocurrencies to obscure their origin and destination. Despite its potential for legitimate use, TC has been criticized for facilitating money laundering by mixing the proceeds of cybercrimes. Since its inception in 2019, TC was implicated in laundering over $7 billion worth of cryptocurrency, including funds linked to North Korean hacking group Lazarus Group and other illicit activities such as the Harmony Bridge Heist and the Nomad Heist. On August 8, 2022, the U.S. Department of the Treasury's Office of Foreign Assets Control (OFAC) sanctioned Tornado Cash under Executive Order 13694, aimed at combating the use of cryptocurrencies in illegal activities. This marked a significant regulatory action against blockchain mixers and highlighted the ongoing challenge of balancing privacy with regulatory compliance [268].

These significant incidents in the cryptocurrency market illustrate the inherent risks and regulatory challenges associated with digital assets. They have triggered substantial regulatory responses and highlighted the urgent need for a more robust regulatory framework to address security, compliance, and financial stability concerns. As the cryptocurrency market continues to evolve, it is crucial for regulatory bodies to develop and implement comprehensive measures that protect investors and ensure the integrity of the financial system.

Challenges in Cryptocurrency Regulation

Regulating cryptocurrencies presents a unique set of challenges due to the distinctive attributes of blockchain technology and the evolving nature of digital assets. These challenges require careful consideration to develop effective regulatory frameworks that balance innovation with investor protection [268].

One of the fundamental challenges in cryptocurrency regulation is the balance between blockchain scalability and financial inclusion. Cryptocurrencies have the potential to enhance financial inclusion by providing alternative access to financial services for unbanked and underbanked populations. This potential has been widely discussed, highlighting how cryptocurrencies could challenge the exclusionary practices of traditional banking systems. However, despite the growing market capitalization of cryptocurrencies, their adoption remains limited compared to traditional financial markets. This discrepancy is largely due to scalability issues inherent in blockchain technology. For instance, Bitcoin and Ethereum, two of the most prominent cryptocurrencies, can handle only 7 and 20-30 transactions per second, respectively [268]. These limitations result in significant delays and higher transaction costs, which directly impact the broader adoption of cryptocurrencies. Consequently, the modest adoption rates may reduce regulatory motivation, as the perceived benefits of extensive regulatory measures might not outweigh the costs associated with implementing and enforcing them [268].

Another significant challenge is the pseudonymous nature of blockchain transactions, which complicates the regulation of cryptocurrencies, especially in combating fraudulent activities. Blockchain technology provides a high level of privacy by linking transactions to cryptographic addresses rather than personal identities. While this pseudonymity protects user privacy, it also makes it challenging for regulators to address issues such as money laundering, fraud, and other illicit activities. Regulatory bodies like the U.S. Securities and Exchange Commission (SEC) and the Commodity Futures Trading Commission (CFTC) have implemented regulations to tackle fraudulent activities in the cryptocurrency space [268]. However, the pseudonymous nature of blockchain transactions often hinders these efforts, as identifying individuals behind transactions can be extremely difficult without infringing on privacy rights. Balancing effective regulation with the need to protect user privacy remains a critical and complex issue.

The decentralized nature of blockchain technology, which underpins the innovation and security of cryptocurrencies, poses significant challenges for regulatory oversight and legal accountability. Unlike traditional financial systems that have clear hierarchies and regulated entities, blockchain networks operate without a central authority. This decentralization complicates regulatory efforts to enforce compliance and accountability. For example, in the case of the 2016 DAO hack on the Ethereum blockchain, the absence of a central authority made it difficult to address the theft of approximately 3.6 million ETH. The challenge for regulators is to devise mechanisms that can ensure legal accountability within decentralized systems while preserving the innovative and open nature of blockchain technology. Establishing such frameworks is essential for protecting participants and maintaining market integrity [268].

The cross-border nature of blockchain technology introduces challenges related to jurisdictional issues and regulatory arbitrage. Cryptocurrencies operate globally, leading to a patchwork of regulatory approaches where some countries impose stringent controls while others adopt more lenient stances. This disparity can result in regulatory arbitrage, where businesses and individuals exploit differences in regulatory environments by basing operations in jurisdictions with more favourable regulations. For instance, in response to stringent regulations in certain countries, many initial coin offerings (ICOs) have been launched in jurisdictions with more accommodating legal frameworks, such as Switzerland and Singapore. This practice can lead to a regulatory race to the bottom, where jurisdictions compete to attract crypto projects by offering less rigorous regulatory requirements. To address these challenges, international cooperation and the pursuit of harmonized regulatory standards become increasingly important. A coordinated approach can help mitigate regulatory arbitrage and ensure that cryptocurrency regulations are effective and consistent across borders [268].

In light of the challenges discussed, several key questions should guide regulatory efforts [268]:

1. **Should cryptocurrencies be regulated?** Regulators must weigh the benefits of incorporating cryptocurrencies into regulatory frameworks, such as enhancing consumer protection and promoting financial stability, against the potential drawbacks of overregulation, which could stifle innovation and limit financial inclusion. Finding the right balance is crucial to harnessing the benefits of cryptocurrencies while mitigating associated risks.

2. **Should existing frameworks be adapted or new ones developed?** Adapting existing regulatory frameworks to include cryptocurrencies may be more straightforward but could result in regulations that are not well-suited to the unique aspects of digital assets. Conversely, developing new, tailored regulations might offer a more precise approach but could be resource-intensive and

time-consuming. The choice between adapting existing frameworks or creating new ones impacts the effectiveness of regulatory efforts.

3. **Who should be the primary targets of cryptocurrency regulation?** Regulators need to determine whether to focus on the technology itself, the users, service providers, or specific activities within the cryptocurrency ecosystem. This decision is particularly significant in the decentralized crypto market, where traditional financial intermediaries are absent.

4. **What approaches should be taken for cryptocurrency regulation?** The goal of regulatory strategies should be to achieve "same risk, same regulatory outcomes," ensuring that cryptocurrencies are subject to regulatory measures proportional to their risk profiles. Regulators must develop strategies that align the regulatory framework for cryptocurrencies with their functions and risks, striving for parity in regulatory standards and oversight between digital assets and traditional financial instruments.

Addressing these questions and challenges is essential for developing a regulatory framework that effectively manages the risks associated with cryptocurrencies while fostering innovation and financial inclusion.

Future Trends in Regulation

The future trends in cryptocurrency regulation are expected to undergo significant shifts and developments in response to the evolving landscape of digital assets. One crucial aspect that is anticipated to shape the regulatory environment is the increased global cooperation and harmonization among regulatory bodies worldwide [272]. As cryptocurrencies transcend national borders, the need for standardized regulatory approaches becomes imperative to ensure consistency and clarity in the regulatory framework [272]. Collaborations between international regulatory entities such as the Financial Action Task Force (FATF) and the International Organization of Securities Commissions (IOSCO) are likely to play a pivotal role in establishing cohesive guidelines that address cross-border issues and promote regulatory harmonization [272].

Moreover, a key focus in future cryptocurrency regulations is expected to be on enhancing consumer protection measures [272]. With the expanding adoption of digital assets, regulators are anticipated to prioritize safeguarding investors from fraud, market manipulation, and other risks associated with cryptocurrency transactions [272]. This emphasis on consumer protection may lead to the implementation of stricter requirements for transparency and disclosure by cryptocurrency exchanges and initial coin offerings (ICOs) [272]. Additionally, regulatory frameworks are likely to introduce mechanisms for dispute resolution and compensation to protect users from financial losses due to security breaches or mismanagement by crypto service providers [272].

Stablecoins and central bank digital currencies (CBDCs) are poised to be focal points in future cryptocurrency regulation efforts [272]. The rise of stablecoins, designed to maintain a stable value relative to fiat currencies, presents regulatory challenges related to monetary policy, financial stability, and consumer protection [272]. Regulators are expected to impose stringent requirements on stablecoin issuers to ensure adequate reserves and transparency [272]. On the other hand, the emergence of CBDCs, digital currencies issued by central banks, will spark discussions on their role in the financial system and the necessity for new regulatory frameworks to address their impact on monetary policy, financial stability, and privacy [272].

As blockchain technology advances, regulators will need to adapt their strategies to accommodate new innovations and applications [273]. The evolution of blockchain solutions such as decentralized finance (DeFi) platforms and smart contracts presents both opportunities and regulatory challenges [273]. Future regulations are likely to focus on defining the legal status and operational standards for decentralized platforms, ensuring compliance with existing financial laws, and addressing security and enforceability concerns related to smart contracts [273]. Regulators will face the task of striking a balance between fostering innovation and protecting users while maintaining market integrity [273].

The integration of artificial intelligence (AI) and automation is expected to have a profound impact on cryptocurrency regulation [273]. AI can enhance regulatory oversight by analysing vast amounts of transaction data to detect suspicious activities, prevent fraud, and ensure compliance with regulatory requirements [273]. Automation tools, including automated reporting and compliance systems, have the potential to streamline regulatory processes and enhance efficiency [273]. However, the incorporation of AI and automation in regulatory practices raises concerns regarding data privacy, security, and the potential for algorithmic biases that regulators will need to address [273].

In the realm of taxation, the evolution of cryptocurrency transactions will necessitate ongoing developments in taxation frameworks to address the complexities of digital asset activities [272]. Future trends may involve the establishment of detailed guidelines for reporting and taxing various types of cryptocurrency transactions, including staking, yield farming, and non-fungible tokens (NFTs) [272]. Technological advancements may facilitate simplified tax reporting processes for individuals and businesses, potentially leveraging blockchain-based solutions to accurately track and report transactions [272]. Regulators will face the challenge of balancing tax compliance requirements with the promotion of innovation within the cryptocurrency space [272].

In conclusion, the future of cryptocurrency regulation is expected to witness a dynamic interplay between innovation and oversight as the digital asset ecosystem continues to evolve [272]. Regulators will need to remain adaptable and proactive in addressing emerging challenges and opportunities in the cryptocurrency landscape to ensure a robust and conducive regulatory environment for market participants and investors alike.

Chapter Nine
Real-World Applications

Cryptocurrencies, initially conceived as digital alternatives to traditional currencies, have evolved into versatile tools with a wide range of real-world applications. Here are some notable examples:

1. Digital Payments

Cryptocurrencies like Bitcoin and Ethereum are increasingly used for digital payments. They offer a decentralized alternative to traditional financial systems, enabling users to make transactions without intermediaries such as banks. For instance, businesses like Overstock, Newegg, and various online services accept Bitcoin as a payment method. These transactions can be processed faster and often with lower fees compared to traditional payment systems.

2. Cross-Border Transactions

Cryptocurrencies facilitate cross-border transactions by eliminating the need for currency conversion and reducing transaction times and costs. For example, sending Bitcoin or stablecoins like USDC internationally can be done in minutes, compared to days with traditional banking methods. This is especially useful in regions with limited access to banking services or where high remittance fees are a concern.

3. Decentralized Finance (DeFi)

DeFi represents a burgeoning sector within the cryptocurrency space that aims to recreate traditional financial services using decentralized technologies. DeFi platforms provide services such as lending, borrowing, trading, and earning interest on crypto assets without relying on traditional financial intermediaries. For instance, platforms like

Compound and Aave allow users to lend and borrow cryptocurrencies, while Uniswap enables decentralized trading of digital assets.

4. Smart Contracts

Smart contracts, primarily associated with Ethereum, are self-executing contracts with the terms of the agreement directly written into code. These contracts automatically execute and enforce terms when predefined conditions are met, reducing the need for intermediaries and minimizing the risk of fraud. Smart contracts are used in various applications, from managing supply chains to automating complex financial transactions.

5. Non-Fungible Tokens (NFTs)

NFTs are unique digital assets verified using blockchain technology. They represent ownership of a specific item or piece of content, such as artwork, music, or collectibles. Platforms like OpenSea and Rarible facilitate the creation, buying, and selling of NFTs. Artists and creators use NFTs to monetize their work directly, while collectors invest in digital art and rare collectibles.

6. Tokenization of Assets

Tokenization involves converting physical or financial assets into digital tokens on a blockchain. This process allows for fractional ownership and easier transfer of assets. Real estate, art, and other valuable assets can be tokenized to broaden investment opportunities and increase liquidity. For example, properties can be divided into digital tokens that represent shares in the property, making it accessible to a broader range of investors.

7. Supply Chain Management

Blockchain technology, the underlying technology for cryptocurrencies, enhances transparency and efficiency in supply chain management. By recording each step of the supply chain on a blockchain, companies can track the provenance of goods, verify authenticity, and reduce fraud. Walmart and IBM's Food Trust initiative is an example of how blockchain can improve food traceability and safety.

8. Digital Identity and Security

Cryptocurrencies and blockchain technology can enhance digital identity management by providing a secure and decentralized way to manage personal information. Blockchain-based digital identities can give users control over their data and reduce the risk of identity theft. Projects like SelfKey and Sovrin aim to provide decentralized identity solutions that allow individuals to verify their identity without relying on traditional institutions.

9. Charitable Donations

Cryptocurrencies are increasingly used for charitable donations due to their transparency and efficiency. Donations made with cryptocurrencies can be tracked on the blockchain, ensuring that funds are used as intended. Platforms like BitGive and Binance Charity facilitate cryptocurrency donations to various causes, improving transparency and accountability in the charitable sector.

10. Gaming and Virtual Worlds

Cryptocurrencies and blockchain technology are transforming the gaming industry by enabling players to own and trade in-game assets securely. Games like Axie Infinity and Decentraland use blockchain to create virtual worlds where players can buy, sell, and trade virtual items and land using cryptocurrencies. This creates new revenue streams for game developers and provides players with true ownership of their in-game assets.

Cryptocurrencies and blockchain technology are increasingly integrated into various sectors, offering innovative solutions that enhance efficiency, transparency, and accessibility. As the technology continues to evolve, its real-world applications are expected to expand further, impacting many aspects of our daily lives and economic systems.

Decentralized Finance (DeFi)

Decentralized Finance (DeFi) represents a revolutionary approach to financial services, leveraging public blockchains, primarily Ethereum, to offer a broad spectrum of financial activities without relying on traditional banking institutions. DeFi enables users to engage in financial transactions such as earning interest, borrowing, lending, buying insurance, trading derivatives, and exchanging assets directly through digital platforms. Unlike traditional finance, DeFi operates globally, peer-to-peer, and is open to all individuals with an internet connection, eliminating the need for intermediaries and associated paperwork [274].

Benefits of DeFi [274]:

- **Open Access:** DeFi platforms do not require users to open accounts or apply for services through traditional channels. Instead, access is granted simply by creating a digital wallet. This ease of entry reduces barriers to participation and democratizes access to financial services.

- **Pseudonymous Transactions:** Users do not need to disclose personal information, such as names or email addresses, to use DeFi services. This pseudonymity enhances privacy and reduces the risk of identity theft compared to traditional financial systems.

- **Flexibility:** DeFi allows for seamless movement of assets without the need for permission from third parties. Transfers are quick, and users can move assets globally without waiting for traditional banking processes or incurring high fees.

- **Speed and Efficiency:** Interest rates and rewards in DeFi platforms can update rapidly, sometimes every 15 seconds. This dynamic environment often leads to significantly higher returns compared to traditional financial markets, which operate with more rigid and slower systems.

- **Transparency:** DeFi platforms typically offer full transparency regarding transactions. Unlike traditional financial institutions, which may obscure details of transactions, DeFi provides a clear view of all operations on the blockchain, enhancing accountability and trust.

Downsides of DeFi [274]:

- **Fluctuating Transaction Costs:** Transaction fees on the Ethereum blockchain, which is commonly used for DeFi activities, can vary greatly. Active trading or frequent transactions may become expensive due to high gas fees, which can impact the overall profitability of DeFi activities.

- **Volatility and Risk:** The technology underlying DeFi is still relatively new, and the associated investment opportunities can be highly volatile. Users may experience significant fluctuations in the value of their assets, and the rapid evolution of technology means that platforms can be experimental and risky.

- **Record-Keeping and Regulation:** Users are responsible for maintaining their own records for tax purposes, which can be challenging given the decentralized and pseudonymous nature of DeFi transactions. Regulatory frameworks for DeFi vary by region, and users must stay informed about local regulations to ensure compliance and manage tax obligations effectively.

In essence, DeFi offers a transformative alternative to traditional financial systems, providing greater accessibility, privacy, and efficiency. However, users must navigate challenges related to transaction costs, volatility, and regulatory compliance to fully leverage the benefits of this emerging technology.

Decentralized Finance (DeFi) represents a transformative shift in the financial sector, leveraging blockchain technology to recreate and innovate financial services outside traditional banking systems. The core goals of DeFi revolve around creating a more accessible, efficient, and transparent financial ecosystem through peer-to-peer (P2P) transactions and decentralized protocols.

Goals of DeFi [275]:

- **Accessibility:** One of the primary goals of DeFi is to democratize access to financial services. Unlike traditional financial systems that often have barriers to entry based on geography or socio-economic status, DeFi platforms are available to anyone with an internet connection. This global reach means that individuals from underserved or remote areas can participate in financial activities, such as lending or trading, without being limited by geographic restrictions or financial institution requirements.

- **Low Fees and High Interest Rates:** DeFi aims to reduce the costs associated with financial transactions by eliminating intermediaries. In a traditional financial system, intermediaries like banks or brokers charge fees for their services, which can add up significantly. DeFi platforms allow users to negotiate interest rates directly with each other and to lend or borrow cryptocurrency with minimal fees. This direct interaction between parties can lead to more favourable terms and higher interest rates for both lenders and borrowers compared to traditional financial institutions.

- **Security and Transparency:** DeFi leverages blockchain technology to ensure the security and transparency of financial transactions. Transactions are recorded on a blockchain, which is an immutable ledger that cannot be altered once data is added. This immutability, coupled with the transparency of public blockchains, means that all transactions are visible and verifiable by anyone, although users' identities remain pseudonymous. The use of smart contracts—self-executing contracts with the terms directly written into code—adds an additional layer of security, automating and enforcing contract terms without human intervention.

- **Autonomy:** DeFi platforms operate independently of traditional financial institutions. This decentralization removes the need for central authorities to manage and administer financial services. By relying on decentralized protocols, DeFi reduces the costs associated with financial services and removes potential points of failure inherent in centralized systems. This autonomy allows users to have greater control over their financial activities, including the ability to access, manage, and transfer assets without intermediaries.

Examples and Uses of DeFi [275]:

- **Decentralized Exchanges (DEXs):** One of the most popular applications of DeFi is decentralized exchanges like Uniswap and PancakeSwap. These platforms facilitate the trading of cryptocurrencies directly between users without the need for a centralized exchange. By using smart contracts, DEXs allow users to swap tokens and provide liquidity, enhancing the efficiency and liquidity of cryptocurrency markets.

- **Liquidity Providers:** In DeFi, liquidity providers contribute funds to liquidity pools that facilitate trading on decentralized exchanges. These pools enable users to trade assets quickly by ensuring there is enough liquidity available. In return, liquidity providers earn fees from transactions executed within the pool, creating a source of passive income.

- **Lending and Yield Farming:** DeFi lending platforms allow users to lend their crypto assets in exchange for interest. Yield farming takes this a step further by enabling users to earn additional rewards through the provision of liquidity or by participating in various DeFi protocols. Flash loans, a feature in some DeFi platforms, allow borrowers to access funds without collateral, provided the loan is repaid within a single transaction block.

- **Gambling and Prediction Markets:** DeFi has also ventured into the gambling and prediction market sectors. Platforms like ZKasino and Azuro enable users to place bets on various events using cryptocurrencies. Prediction markets, on the other hand, allow users to speculate on the outcomes of events, from political elections to sports games, using decentralized mechanisms.

- **Non-Fungible Tokens (NFTs):** Although the NFT market has experienced fluctuations, it remains an integral part of the DeFi ecosystem. NFTs represent unique digital assets or collectibles and are often used in DeFi applications to represent ownership or access rights to digital goods, artwork, or other forms of content.

DeFi seeks to revolutionize the financial industry by making financial services more accessible, cost-effective, and transparent. Through its various applications, DeFi offers innovative solutions that challenge traditional financial systems and provide new opportunities for users around the world.

Decentralized Finance (DeFi) operates on the principle of eliminating traditional intermediaries like banks and financial institutions by leveraging blockchain technology. Unlike conventional financial systems that require users to open accounts and fill out extensive paperwork, DeFi allows for seamless interactions through decentralized applications (dApps) on blockchains, predominantly Ethereum. Here's a detailed look at how DeFi works and the various ways users engage with it:

DeFi leverages blockchain technology to create an open, transparent, and decentralized financial ecosystem. Blockchains are distributed ledgers where transactions are recorded in "blocks" and linked together to form a "chain." Each block contains a record of transactions, and once a block is verified and closed, it is encrypted and linked to the previous block. This immutability ensures that transaction records cannot be altered without changing subsequent blocks, which provides a high level of security and trust.

Users interact with DeFi through software called dApps, which are decentralized applications running on the blockchain. These dApps replace traditional financial institutions by automating financial services using smart contracts. Smart contracts are self-executing contracts with the terms of the agreement directly written into code. This eliminates the need for intermediaries, reduces costs, and speeds up transactions.

Engaging with DeFi [275]:

- **Lending and Borrowing**: In DeFi, users can lend out their cryptocurrency and earn interest or rewards. This lending process is facilitated through smart contracts that automate the interest calculation and distribution. Borrowers can obtain loans quickly, sometimes through "flash loans," which are short-term loans without the need for collateral, unlike traditional banking.

- **Trading**: DeFi platforms enable peer-to-peer trading of cryptocurrencies. Users can buy and sell digital assets directly with each other, bypassing traditional brokers or exchanges. This peer-to-peer approach often results in lower fees and faster transactions compared to traditional financial systems.

- **Saving and Yield Farming**: Users can deposit their cryptocurrencies into savings-like DeFi applications, which offer higher interest rates than traditional banks. Yield farming involves providing liquidity to DeFi platforms in exchange for rewards, typically in the form of additional cryptocurrency. This process can be highly profitable, although it may involve higher risks due to market volatility.

- **Buying Derivatives**: DeFi also supports trading derivatives, which are financial contracts whose value is derived from underlying assets. This includes options and futures contracts in the cryptocurrency market, allowing users to hedge against or speculate on price movements.

DeFi applications, or dApps, provide user interfaces for interacting with the blockchain. These applications facilitate transactions, loans, trading, and more by allowing users to select options and set terms via a graphical interface. Without such applications, users would need to operate through command-line interfaces, which are less user-friendly [275].

Digital wallets are essential for DeFi interactions. They store private keys, which act as passwords to access and manage digital assets. These wallets enable users to send and receive cryptocurrencies and interact with DeFi applications. When a transaction is made, the wallet uses the private key to sign the transaction, ensuring secure and irreversible transfers.

While DeFi provides significant benefits in terms of accessibility, security, and cost-efficiency, it does not offer full anonymity [275]. Transactions on the blockchain are traceable and can be viewed by anyone with the appropriate tools. Although the transactions do not include personal information like names or email addresses, they are still traceable through blockchain analysis. This transparency helps maintain the integrity of the financial system and can assist in regulatory and security measures.

DeFi represents a transformative approach to financial services, leveraging blockchain technology to create a more open, efficient, and user-driven financial system. By removing traditional intermediaries and using decentralized applications and smart contracts, DeFi offers a range of financial services with greater accessibility and lower costs, while maintaining a level of transparency and security [275].

Decentralised Finance and Wrapping Crypto in Australia

Lending and borrowing in decentralized finance (DeFi) in Australia introduces new opportunities and complexities compared to traditional finance. DeFi platforms often use familiar financial terms such as 'lending,' 'borrowing,' and 'interest,' but these terms may have different implications for taxation and ownership [276].

Lending and Borrowing in DeFi

In DeFi, lending involves providing cryptocurrency to a platform or individual in exchange for interest or rewards. Similarly, borrowing allows users to obtain funds without traditional paperwork or lengthy processes. However, these activities can trigger a Capital Gains Tax (CGT) event. A CGT event typically occurs when there is a change in beneficial ownership of a crypto asset. This change can happen in two main scenarios: exchanging one crypto asset for another or receiving a right to claim the same asset in the future [276].

For example, if you lend a cryptocurrency to a DeFi platform, the act of lending may result in a CGT event if it involves transferring the asset to an address you do not control. The capital proceeds are determined by the market value of the property received in exchange, which could be another crypto asset or a right to future delivery.

Example: Treatment of Crypto Asset Loan with Change of Ownership

Consider Sasha, who bought 100 Xcoin for $800 and lends 50 Xcoin, worth $500, at a 1% return rate. Sasha no longer retains beneficial ownership of the Xcoin once lent. The lending results in a CGT event because there is a change in ownership. At the time of lending, Sasha realizes a capital gain of $100 based on the difference between the original value and the current market value of the Xcoin [276].

Example: CGT Treatment When Lending to a DeFi Platform

Mika buys 100 ZYX coins for $1,000 and lends them to a DeFi platform. If the platform pools the ZYX coins with those from other lenders, and the terms are unclear about retaining ownership, a CGT event occurs when Mika initially lends the coins. At that time, Mika's right to receive the coins is valued at $900, resulting in a capital loss of $100. When Mika's loan is repaid, the market value of the coins has increased, leading to a capital gain of $100. Thus, Mika's new cost base for the ZYX coins is $1,000 [276].

Liquidity Pools and Providers

Liquidity pools are another integral aspect of DeFi. These pools aggregate crypto assets locked in a smart contract to facilitate decentralized lending and enhance trading liquidity. When you deposit assets into a liquidity pool, you receive tokens or rights representing your share of the pool. This transaction is a CGT event, with the capital proceeds being the market value of the received tokens or rights [276].

Example: Exchange of Crypto Asset Through the Liquidity Pool

Martha deposits one EH into the XA liquidity pool and receives 20 XA tokens. If the EH was acquired three years ago at $2 and the XA tokens are worth $20 at the time of the deposit, Martha realizes a capital gain of $18 on the deposit. This gain may be eligible for a CGT discount [276].

Crypto Asset DeFi Interest and Rewards

DeFi platforms often pay rewards in the form of additional crypto assets. These rewards are treated similarly to interest income for tax purposes. When you receive periodic rewards, you must report their market value at the time of receipt as assessable income [276].

Example: Crypto Asset Reward from DeFi Platform

Craig lends 100 stablecoin tokens valued at $10 each through a DeFi platform and earns a 1% return in the form of additional stablecoins. Craig must declare the market value of the new tokens as income, which, in this case, is $10 [276].

Wrapped Tokens

Wrapped tokens represent a crypto asset on a different blockchain or in a different format. For example, wrapping Bitcoin (BTC) into Wrapped Bitcoin (WBTC) allows Bitcoin's value to be used on the Ethereum blockchain. Wrapping involves sending the original asset to a smart contract, which mints an equivalent wrapped token. This process triggers a CGT event because it involves exchanging one asset for another, with capital proceeds equal to the market value of the wrapped token at the time of exchange [276].

Example: CGT Treatment When Exchanging Wrapped Tokens

Kal buys 1 BTC for $30,000 and wraps it into 1 WBTC, which is valued at $45,000. The wrapping process results in a capital gain of $15,000, reflecting the increase in value from the original BTC [276].

While DeFi offers innovative financial solutions, it also introduces complexities for tax purposes. Understanding how different DeFi activities—such as lending, borrowing, liquidity provision, and using wrapped tokens—affect CGT and income tax is crucial for compliance and effective financial management in Australia.

Decentralised Finance and Wrapping Crypto in the USA

In the United States, the tax implications of engaging with decentralized finance (DeFi) are intricate and multifaceted due to the evolving landscape of cryptocurrency regulations [277]. The Internal Revenue Service (IRS) categorizes cryptocurrency transactions as taxable events, treating them as property rather than currency, which extends to various DeFi activities [277]. This classification results in gains or losses from DeFi transactions being regarded as capital gains or losses, aligning with the tax principles applied to traditional cryptocurrencies [277].

When it comes to specific DeFi activities like lending and borrowing, the tax treatment follows the same principles as traditional cryptocurrencies [277]. For instance, lending cryptocurrency in DeFi can trigger a taxable event, with the IRS potentially viewing the lending transaction as a disposition of the asset, leading to capital gains or losses based on the asset's value change [277]. Similarly, borrowing cryptocurrency and subsequent repayments can impact tax liabilities based on the fluctuation in the borrowed assets' value [277].

Trading and swapping cryptocurrencies on DeFi platforms are also subject to taxation, with the IRS considering these transactions as taxable events [277]. Capital gains or losses need to be calculated and reported when trading or swapping one cryptocurrency for another, based on the difference between the fair market value at the time of the swap and the original purchase price [277]. This taxation principle applies to various DeFi activities, ensuring that gains or losses are accounted for in capital gains tax calculations [277].

Providing liquidity in DeFi protocols involves depositing cryptocurrency into liquidity pools, which the IRS deems as a taxable event due to the transfer of ownership [277]. The capital proceeds from depositing assets into a liquidity pool are equivalent to the market value of the rewards or liquidity provider tokens received, necessitating accurate reporting for tax purposes [277]. Subsequent withdrawals from the liquidity pool also trigger taxable events, requiring calculations of capital gains or losses based on the asset values at deposit and withdrawal times [277].

Yield farming and staking, common DeFi practices, are treated as taxable income by the IRS, with the fair market value of rewards received considered as taxable income to be reported in the year of receipt [277]. These rewards are taxed at ordinary income rates, emphasizing the importance of accurately reporting such income to ensure compliance with tax regulations [277]. Similarly, wrapped tokens, which represent original assets on different blockchains, can lead to taxable events based on capital gains or losses from the token conversion process [277].

Accurate record-keeping is paramount for managing DeFi tax obligations effectively, given the complexity of transactions and interactions involved [277]. Detailed records of all DeFi transactions, including dates, amounts, and values, are essential for precise calculation of gains, losses, and income, as required by the IRS [277]. Failure to report taxable events can result in penalties and interest, underscoring the significance of meticulous record-keeping in DeFi tax compliance [277].

Non-Fungible Tokens (NFTs)

Non-Fungible Tokens (NFTs) represent a groundbreaking way to digitize and verify ownership of unique assets using blockchain technology. These tokens encapsulate a broad range of digital and physical assets, such as art, videos, or digital content, converting them into tokenized forms that can be traded or sold. Let's delve deeper into how NFTs work and how they differ from other types of tokens like cryptocurrencies [278].

NFTs are created by converting an asset—whether it's a digital piece of art, a video, or even a digital collectible—into a unique token through a process called tokenization. This process involves generating a distinctive identification code, known as metadata, which is encrypted and stored on a blockchain. The blockchain serves as a secure, decentralized ledger that records the NFT's unique token. Although the asset itself—such as the actual image or video file—is stored elsewhere (like a server or cloud storage), the blockchain entry represents the token's ownership and provenance [278].

This tokenization process ensures that each NFT is unique and cannot be replicated, providing a secure way to track and verify ownership. The metadata associated with an NFT contains details about the asset, including its creator, ownership history, and any attributes that contribute to its value. The connection between the token and the asset is crucial, as it underpins the NFT's uniqueness and authenticity [278].

NFTs can be traded or exchanged on various online marketplaces, and their value can be determined by factors such as market demand, the reputation of the creator, and the uniqueness of the asset. For example, if you create an NFT by drawing a smiley face on a banana, photographing it, and tokenizing it on a blockchain, you are effectively assigning a unique digital identifier to that specific image. This NFT can then be bought, sold, or exchanged for money, cryptocurrencies, or other NFTs [278].

The value of an NFT is subjective and largely depends on the market's perception and the value assigned by the owners and buyers. Unlike traditional assets, NFTs derive their worth from their rarity, the significance of the asset they represent, and the demand within the marketplace. This means that while the actual image of the smiley face on the banana can be copied, the NFT represents a unique claim to the original version, embedded with verifiable ownership and authenticity [278].

To understand NFTs better, it's essential to contrast them with cryptocurrencies. Cryptocurrencies, like Bitcoin or Ethereum, are examples of fungible tokens. This means that each unit of cryptocurrency is interchangeable with another of the same type; for instance, one Bitcoin is equivalent to another Bitcoin. This fungibility is a fundamental characteristic of cryptocurrencies, making them suitable for transactions and exchanges in the financial ecosystem [278].

In contrast, NFTs are non-fungible. This means that while two NFTs from the same blockchain might look identical or have similar attributes, they are not interchangeable. Each NFT has a unique identification code and metadata that distinguish it from every other NFT. This non-fungibility is what makes NFTs ideal for representing unique digital or physical assets, as each token embodies distinct ownership and characteristics that cannot be duplicated or exchanged on a one-to-one basis [278].

NFTs leverage blockchain technology to create, store, and verify unique digital tokens representing various assets. By tokenizing assets, NFTs provide a secure and transparent way to establish ownership and provenance. Unlike cryptocurrencies, which are fungible and interchangeable, NFTs are inherently unique and irreplaceable, reflecting their distinct value in the market. This distinction underlines the transformative potential of NFTs in areas such as art, collectibles, and digital ownership, offering new opportunities for creators and collectors alike [278].

Non-Fungible Tokens (NFTs) have garnered significant attention for their role in the digital art and collectibles space, but their applications extend far beyond these realms. Some of the real-world applications of NFTs across various sectors include:

1. Digital Art and Collectibles

The most prominent application of NFTs is in the digital art world. NFTs provide a way to verify the ownership and authenticity of digital artworks, which can be easily duplicated. Artists use NFTs to sell their work directly to buyers, receiving royalties from secondary sales. This has democratized the art market and given artists more control over their work.

2. Gaming

NFTs are increasingly being integrated into video games to represent in-game assets such as skins, weapons, and characters. These NFTs can be bought, sold, and traded outside the game, allowing players to own unique items and potentially earn from their virtual possessions. Games like *Axie Infinity* and *Decentraland* use NFTs to enhance player engagement and create new revenue streams.

3. Virtual Real Estate

NFTs are used to buy, sell, and trade virtual land and property in digital worlds or metaverses. Platforms like *Decentraland* and *The Sandbox* allow users to purchase plots of virtual land as NFTs, which can be developed, rented, or sold. This virtual real estate market provides new opportunities for investment and creative expression in virtual environments.

4. Music and Entertainment

Musicians and entertainers are using NFTs to release exclusive content, collectibles, and experiences. NFTs can be used to sell concert tickets, backstage passes, or limited-edition tracks. For example, artists like Grimes and Kings of Leon have released NFT-based albums and concert experiences, offering fans unique ways to engage with their favourite artists.

5. Intellectual Property and Branding

Brands and intellectual property owners use NFTs to create unique digital merchandise and experiences. Companies can issue limited-edition NFTs tied to their products or brand milestones. For instance, major brands like Nike and Adidas have explored NFTs for limited-edition merchandise and digital collectibles, enhancing brand engagement and loyalty.

6. Identity and Certification

NFTs can be used for digital identity verification and certification. Educational institutions and professional organizations are exploring NFTs for issuing digital diplomas, certifications, and badges. These NFTs serve as tamper-proof records of achievements and qualifications, providing a secure way to verify credentials.

7. Real Estate

In the real estate sector, NFTs are being used to represent ownership of physical properties or deeds. This application can streamline property transactions by making ownership transfers more efficient and transparent. Real estate platforms are experimenting with NFTs to simplify processes such as buying, selling, and transferring property ownership.

8. Ticketing and Event Management

NFTs offer a new approach to event ticketing, providing a way to issue and verify tickets digitally. NFT-based tickets can prevent counterfeiting and enable secondary market transactions with built-in royalties for event organizers. This application enhances security and transparency in ticketing, benefiting both organizers and attendees.

9. Charity and Fundraising

NFTs are being used for charitable causes and fundraising campaigns. Organizations and individuals create and auction NFTs to raise funds for various causes, with proceeds going directly to charitable initiatives. This innovative approach to fundraising leverages the unique qualities of NFTs to attract donors and supporters.

10. Legal and Contractual Agreements

NFTs can represent legal agreements and contracts, offering a secure and immutable record of terms and conditions. Smart contracts, often associated with NFTs, can automate and enforce contractual obligations, reducing the need for intermediaries and enhancing transparency in legal agreements.

11. Metaverse Integration

In the growing field of the metaverse, NFTs play a crucial role in defining digital ownership and interaction. NFTs represent avatars, virtual goods, and experiences in these immersive digital worlds, allowing users to create and own unique virtual identities and assets.

NFTs have transcended their initial use cases in digital art and collectibles to become a versatile tool with applications across various industries. Their ability to represent unique assets and verify ownership through blockchain technology is transforming sectors such as gaming, real estate, music, and more. As the technology continues to evolve, the scope of NFT applications is likely to expand further, offering new opportunities for innovation and engagement.

How NFTs Work

NFTs, or Non-Fungible Tokens, are a significant innovation in the digital realm, enabling the creation and verification of unique digital assets through blockchain technology. The process of creating an NFT is known as minting, which involves several key steps to ensure the asset's uniqueness and authenticity [278].

Minting Process

Minting is the process by which an asset's information is converted into a digital token on a blockchain. At a high level, minting involves creating a new block in the blockchain, validating the NFT's information, and then closing the block to record the data. This process is crucial as it ensures the NFT's information is securely stored and verified [278].

The minting process often involves smart contracts, which are self-executing contracts with the terms of the agreement written into code. Smart contracts automate the creation, management, and transfer of NFTs. They define the rules for the NFT, including how ownership is assigned and how the token can be transferred or traded. When a new NFT is minted, the smart contract records the NFT's unique details and assigns it to a blockchain address. This address represents the owner of the NFT and is publicly available, ensuring transparency and traceability of ownership [278].

Each NFT created during this process is assigned a unique identifier that links it directly to a specific blockchain address. Even if multiple NFTs are minted for the same asset—such as 5,000 identical digital images—each token is distinguishable from the others due to its unique identifier. This ensures that each NFT remains a one-of-a-kind digital asset, even if the underlying asset itself is replicated.

Blockchains and NFT Variations

While Ethereum is the most widely known blockchain for NFTs, other blockchains can also create NFTs, albeit sometimes under different names. For example, on the Bitcoin blockchain, NFTs are known as Ordinals. Unlike Ethereum-based NFTs, which are created as tokens, Bitcoin Ordinals assign unique serial numbers, or identifiers, to satoshis—the smallest unit of Bitcoin. These identifiers work similarly to NFT tokens, allowing Bitcoin Ordinals to be bought, sold, and traded while preserving their uniqueness [278].

This variance in blockchain implementations highlights the versatility and adaptability of NFT technology across different blockchain platforms. Each blockchain provides its own mechanism for creating and managing NFTs, but the underlying principle of uniqueness and indivisibility remains constant.

Blockchain and Fungibility

The concept of fungibility is central to understanding the difference between cryptocurrencies and NFTs. Cryptocurrencies are fungible, meaning that each unit is interchangeable and equivalent in value to another unit of the same type. For instance, one Bitcoin is functionally the same as another Bitcoin, similar to how one dollar bill is equal to another dollar bill. This fungibility makes cryptocurrencies suitable as a medium of exchange in the digital economy [278].

In contrast, NFTs are non-fungible, meaning each token is unique and cannot be exchanged on a one-to-one basis with another NFT. NFTs serve as digital representations of distinct assets, and their uniqueness is akin to digital passports, each containing a unique, non-transferable identity. This non-fungibility allows NFTs to represent assets such as digital art, collectibles, or virtual real estate, each with its own specific attributes and value.

Furthermore, NFTs are extensible, meaning they can be combined or modified to create new, unique NFTs. This concept, often referred to as "breeding" in the cryptocurrency industry, allows for the generation of new tokens by merging or altering existing ones, expanding the possibilities for digital asset creation and innovation [278].

Benefits of NFTs

One of the most significant advantages of Non-Fungible Tokens (NFTs) is their capacity to enhance market efficiency. By tokenizing physical or digital assets, NFTs can streamline the sales process and eliminate the need for traditional intermediaries. For instance, artists and creators can directly connect with their audience and sell their work without relying on agents or galleries. This direct connection can lower transaction costs and enable creators to retain a larger portion of the sale price. The use of blockchain technology ensures that ownership and provenance are transparently recorded, reducing the risk of fraud and providing buyers with confidence in the authenticity of the asset [278].

NFTs also offer innovative solutions for investing in various asset classes. A notable example is Ernst & Young's development of an NFT solution for fine wine investors. By storing the wine in a secure environment and using NFTs to document its provenance, investors can securely track and trade ownership of their assets. Similarly, real estate can be tokenized, allowing properties to be divided into multiple sections, each represented by a unique NFT. This approach simplifies the complex and bureaucratic process of real estate transactions, enabling more efficient and transparent trading of property [278].

In the realm of business ownership, NFTs can function similarly to traditional stock certificates. Just as stock ownership is recorded in ledgers with details such as the stockholder's name and number of shares, NFTs can represent shares in a business. The key benefit of using NFTs is the integration of smart contracts, which automate the transfer of ownership upon sale. This automation streamlines the process and reduces administrative overhead compared to traditional stock trading [278].

Another significant benefit of NFTs lies in their potential for enhancing security. NFTs are based on immutable blockchain technology, which means that personal information associated with NFTs cannot be altered or accessed without the proper keys. This immutability makes NFTs a robust tool for identity security, ensuring that sensitive information remains protected from unauthorized access [278].

NFTs also democratize investing by enabling fractional ownership of physical assets. Tokenization allows multiple individuals to own a share of high-value items, such as artwork or real estate, by dividing the asset into smaller, tradable fractions. This fractionalization makes it possible for more people to invest in valuable assets that would otherwise be out of reach, thereby broadening access to investment opportunities [278].

Concerns About Non-Fungible Tokens

Despite their numerous benefits, NFTs are not without concerns. One major issue is the potential for digital piracy. While NFTs represent ownership through encrypted metadata and blockchain records, the digital asset itself—such as an image, video, or music file—can still be copied and distributed without permission. This means that while the NFT proves ownership and authenticity, the digital file can be easily duplicated. The responsibility to enforce ownership and prevent unauthorized use often falls on the NFT owner, who may need to take legal action against infringers [278].

Another challenge with NFTs is their liquidity. Unlike cryptocurrencies, which can be easily exchanged for other currencies, NFTs are often highly specific and appeal to niche markets. This specialization can make it difficult to sell an NFT if it falls out of favour or if the market demand shifts. For instance, if an NFT is tied to a particular trend or artist that becomes less popular, finding a buyer willing to pay a desirable price can be challenging [278].

Overall, while NFTs offer innovative solutions and benefits across various domains, they also come with their own set of challenges that need to be carefully considered by potential investors and creators.

Blockchain in Supply Chain Management

Blockchain technology is increasingly recognized for its potential to revolutionize global supply chains. Major industry players, such as Maersk, Amazon, Walmart, and DHL, are exploring blockchain to enhance their operational efficiency [279]. Blockchain addresses various challenges in logistics and supply chain management, including procurement, transportation management, tracking and tracing, customs collaboration, and trade finance [279].

One of the key advantages of blockchain in logistics is its ability to streamline processes by reducing the need for intermediaries and minimizing errors. Traditional systems often involve multiple documents and disparate systems, which can lead to issues such as invoice duplication, incorrect fees, and freight mode changes. Blockchain provides a single, transparent source of truth, consolidating information and facilitating better communication between supply chain partners. This transparency can significantly reduce the need for extensive documentation, offering real-time visibility into inventory levels and service requirements [279].

The use of smart contracts further enhances blockchain's value in transport and logistics. Smart contracts are self-executing agreements with terms encoded directly into the blockchain. They automate transactions and handle adjustments or penalties automatically, eliminating the need for manual dispute resolution. For example, if a shipment is delayed or its conditions are not met, a smart contract can automatically process the necessary actions [279].

A practical example of blockchain's benefits can be seen in the shipping of goods, such as a sweater from China to the UK. Traditional shipping processes involve numerous paper documents and manual data entry, increasing the risk of errors. With blockchain, the sweater can be equipped with an IoT-enabled chip that sends a digital signal when it leaves the factory. This signal is recorded on the blockchain, triggering automatic payment and customs processing. This system ensures that all data is accurate and tamper-proof, streamlining the entire shipment process [279].

Blockchain also offers significant improvements in safety within the shipping industry. Misdeclared or inaccurately identified dangerous cargo can lead to severe accidents, such as fires on container ships. Blockchain can provide transparent and accurate tracking of dangerous goods, reducing the risk of incidents caused by poor packing practices and incorrect documentation. By facilitating timely and accurate information exchange, blockchain enhances compliance and safety throughout the shipping process [279].

Blockchain technology has emerged as a transformative force in supply chain management, addressing several inefficiencies and challenges that traditional systems face. At its core, blockchain is a decentralized, distributed ledger technology that records transactions across multiple computers, ensuring that the data cannot be altered retroactively. This immutability and transparency make blockchain an ideal tool for enhancing supply chain operations.

One of the primary benefits of blockchain in supply chain management is its ability to provide end-to-end visibility. Traditional supply chains often involve multiple parties, including suppliers, manufacturers, distributors, and retailers, each maintaining their own records. This can lead to discrepancies, delays, and a lack of transparency. Blockchain enables all participants to access a single, immutable record of transactions, which helps synchronize information across the entire supply chain. This transparency allows for real-time tracking of goods, reducing delays and improving coordination.

Additionally, blockchain enhances traceability by providing a secure and transparent way to track the movement of goods from origin to destination. For instance, in industries like food and pharmaceuticals, where provenance and authenticity are crucial, blockchain can document every step of the supply chain. This ensures that products are genuine and meet safety standards. Consumers and businesses can verify the origin and handling of products, which helps build trust and reduces the risk of fraud.

Smart contracts, which are self-executing contracts with the terms directly written into code, further improve supply chain management. Smart contracts automate various processes, such as payment processing, order fulfillment, and compliance checks. For example, a smart contract could automatically release payment once goods are confirmed as delivered, based on data recorded on the blockchain. This automation reduces administrative overhead and minimizes errors.

Cryptocurrency, while often associated with digital financial transactions, also plays a significant role in supply chain management. Cryptocurrencies can streamline financial transactions and improve the efficiency of cross-border payments. Traditional payment systems, especially for international transactions, often involve multiple intermediaries, high fees, and lengthy processing times. Cryptocurrencies offer a decentralized alternative, enabling direct peer-to-peer transactions that can be completed more quickly and at a lower cost.

In supply chain management, cryptocurrencies can facilitate faster and more secure payments between parties in different countries. For example, a company importing goods from abroad can use cryptocurrency to pay suppliers directly, bypassing traditional banking systems and reducing transaction costs. This not only speeds up the payment process but also reduces the risk of currency exchange fluctuations and financial intermediaries' fees.

Moreover, integrating cryptocurrencies with blockchain technology can further enhance supply chain operations. For instance, cryptocurrency payments can be linked with blockchain-based smart contracts to automate and secure transactions. This integration ensures that payments are made only when predefined conditions are met, such as the delivery of goods or the completion of a service.

Overall, both blockchain technology and cryptocurrency offer substantial benefits to supply chain management. Blockchain provides transparency, traceability, and automation through smart contracts, while cryptocurrencies enhance the efficiency and cost-effectiveness of financial transactions. Together, these technologies can transform supply chain management by improving operational efficiency, reducing costs, and increasing trust and reliability across the supply chain.

Cryptocurrencies in E-Commerce

Cryptocurrencies have begun to make a significant impact in the e-commerce sector, offering both opportunities and challenges for online businesses and consumers alike. Their role in e-commerce is transforming traditional payment systems, providing new ways to transact, and influencing the overall dynamics of online shopping.

Cryptocurrencies offer several advantages in e-commerce, with one of the primary benefits being their ability to facilitate fast and borderless transactions. Traditional payment methods like credit cards and bank transfers can be slow and costly, especially for international transactions [280]. In contrast, cryptocurrencies enable near-instant transfers across borders without the need for intermediaries, significantly reducing transaction times and costs for both businesses and consumers [280]. This means that a customer in one country can easily make a purchase from an e-commerce store in another country, with the payment being processed almost immediately using cryptocurrencies such as Bitcoin or Ethereum [280].

Moreover, cryptocurrencies provide enhanced security features due to transactions being secured by blockchain technology, which employs cryptographic techniques to ensure data integrity and privacy [161]. This heightened security reduces the risks of fraud and chargebacks commonly associated with traditional payment systems, leading to fewer disputes and potentially lower costs related to payment processing and fraud prevention for e-commerce merchants [161]. The integration of blockchain in online e-commerce transactions offers various benefits such as faster and safer payments, digital identity verification to prevent fraud, easy tracking of purchased items, and improved transaction security through application development [78].

Another significant advantage of cryptocurrencies in e-commerce is the potential for increased financial inclusion, particularly for individuals who are unbanked or under-banked (Alsharu, 2024). In regions where traditional banking infrastructure is limited, cryptocurrencies can serve as a viable alternative, providing access to digital financial services and enabling participation in the global economy [281]. This expanded customer base allows e-commerce businesses to tap into new markets and customer segments that were previously inaccessible, driving growth and revenue opportunities [281].

The use of cryptocurrencies in e-commerce transactions is also associated with the concept of trust. Research has shown that consumer trust in crypto-payments is influenced by perceptions of information privacy and security [161]. When consumers perceive that their data is secure and their privacy is protected when using cryptocurrencies for transactions, it enhances their trust in the payment method and the overall e-commerce experience [161]. This trust factor is crucial for fostering consumer confidence and encouraging the adoption of cryptocurrencies in e-commerce settings [161].

Furthermore, the adoption of cryptocurrencies in e-commerce can lead to market disintermediation, where new forms of digital money and technologies embedded in decentralized networks reshape markets and commerce [282]. Blockchain-enabled technologies play a key role in enabling decentralized trusted peer-to-peer transaction ledger systems, which can potentially disrupt traditional market structures and lead to the development of sustainable business models [282]. By leveraging cryptocurrencies and blockchain technology, e-commerce platforms can streamline transactions, reduce reliance on intermediaries, and create more efficient and transparent market ecosystems [282].

Cryptocurrencies have gained popularity in e-commerce due to their advantages, but they also present challenges that need to be addressed. One significant concern is the price volatility associated with cryptocurrencies, which can lead to uncertainty for both merchants and customers [283]. The fluctuating values of cryptocurrencies like Bitcoin can complicate pricing strategies for merchants, as a drop in value before a transaction is completed could result in the merchant receiving less value than expected [283]. This volatility poses challenges for businesses in terms of financial planning and pricing strategies, making it essential for them to consider the risks involved in using cryptocurrencies for transactions [283].

Moreover, regulatory and legal issues add another layer of complexity to the use of cryptocurrencies in e-commerce [284]. The evolving regulatory landscape surrounding cryptocurrencies requires e-commerce businesses to navigate varying regulations and legal frameworks across different countries [284]. Compliance with regulations such as anti-money laundering (AML) and know-your-customer (KYC) requirements can be intricate and time-consuming, impacting how cryptocurrencies are utilized in transactions [284]. These legal challenges highlight the need for businesses to stay informed about the regulatory environment to ensure compliance when integrating cryptocurrencies into their e-commerce operations [284].

Additionally, the adoption of cryptocurrencies in e-commerce necessitates technological integration and infrastructure upgrades [285]. Businesses looking to accept cryptocurrencies as payment methods must implement cryptocurrency payment gateways and ensure the security of their systems to handle these transactions effectively [285]. This technological integration may come with additional costs and require specialized technical expertise, which can be a barrier for smaller e-commerce enterprises looking to embrace cryptocurrencies [285]. Therefore, businesses need to assess the technological requirements and potential costs associated with integrating cryptocurrencies into their e-commerce platforms [285].

E-commerce platforms and online retailers have increasingly adopted cryptocurrencies as a form of payment, showcasing a shift towards embracing digital currencies in the realm of online transactions. Major players like Overstock.com and Newegg have paved the way by accepting Bitcoin, integrating cryptocurrency payment gateways into their checkout processes [286]. This move not only caters to the growing popularity of cryptocurrencies but also aligns with the evolving landscape of digital transactions. Moreover, the emergence of new e-commerce platforms, such as OpenBazaar, signifies a deliberate shift towards supporting cryptocurrency transactions exclusively, bypassing traditional payment systems and leveraging blockchain technology to facilitate peer-to-peer transactions using digital currencies [286].

Enabling Cryptocurrency Payments in E-Commerce

Enabling cryptocurrency payments in e-commerce involves selecting an approach that aligns with the business's needs, technical capabilities, and customer expectations. There are three primary approaches for processing cryptocurrency payments, each with distinct advantages and considerations [287].

Approach #1: Using a Third-Party Crypto Payment Gateway

The first approach involves relying on a third-party cryptocurrency payment gateway, such as BitPay, CoinGate, or Coinbase Commerce. These services offer a comprehensive solution for accepting cryptocurrency payments and handling the associated complexities [287].

Capabilities:

- **Accepting Payments:** These gateways support various cryptocurrencies, allowing customers to pay with their preferred digital currency.
- **Automated Conversion:** The gateway can automatically convert received cryptocurrencies into a pre-agreed fiat currency or another cryptocurrency, mitigating the risk of price volatility.
- **Transaction Handling:** The gateway transfers the processed funds to the e-seller's merchant account and schedules payouts to the e-seller's bank account.

Benefits: Using a third-party gateway simplifies the process of accepting cryptocurrency payments. It avoids the need to set up an in-house crypto payment processing system, which can be complex and resource-intensive. The merchant can leverage the gateway's infrastructure and expertise without having to handle the technical details themselves.

Cautions: However, this approach involves complete dependence on an intermediary, which can introduce operational and security risks. Additional fees charged by the gateway can increase the overall cost of processing payments. Furthermore, the functionality and supported cryptocurrencies are defined by the third party, which limits the merchant's flexibility and control.

Recommendations: It is advisable to conduct a thorough analysis of available crypto payment gateway providers to select the one that offers the best transaction processing fees and aligns with the business's needs. A detailed comparison of solutions can help in choosing the optimal provider, ensuring economic feasibility and minimizing costs.

Approach #2: Embedding Crypto Payment Buttons

The second approach involves embedding cryptocurrency payment buttons directly into an e-commerce platform. This method allows for a seamless payment experience for customers, as they can complete transactions without leaving the website [287].

Capabilities:

- **One-Click Payments:** Customers can make payments with a single click, which simplifies the checkout process and enhances the user experience.

- **Direct Payments:** Payments are received directly into the merchant's cryptocurrency wallet, providing immediate access to funds.

Benefits: This approach is relatively fast and easy to implement compared to setting up a full payment gateway. It does not require direct integration with a payment processing system, making it an accessible option for many e-commerce businesses.

Cautions: Merchants need to manage their cryptocurrency wallets to receive, store, and manage crypto funds. For businesses with a large inventory, creating and managing individual payment buttons for each product can be time-consuming and labour-intensive.

Recommendations: Utilizing ready-to-use cryptocurrency APIs, such as Coinbase API, can streamline the creation of payment buttons and expedite the integration process. This approach can reduce the complexity of implementing cryptocurrency payments while maintaining a user-friendly experience.

Approach #3: Developing a Custom Crypto Payment Gateway

The third approach involves developing a custom cryptocurrency payment gateway tailored to the specific needs of the e-commerce business. This solution provides the highest level of flexibility and control over the payment processing system [287].

Capabilities:

- **Customized Functionality:** The gateway can support unique features such as recurring payments, dynamically adjusted prices in crypto, and complex business models like pay-as-you-go.

- **Comprehensive Support:** It can accommodate all required cryptocurrencies, including custom or less common digital currencies.

- **Integration:** The gateway can be integrated seamlessly with existing e-commerce systems, even those that are legacy or outdated.

Benefits: A custom solution offers the ability to tailor the payment processing system to the business's exact requirements, ensuring optimal performance and security. It eliminates the need for intermediaries, reducing potential risks and additional fees.

Cautions: Designing and implementing a custom crypto payment gateway requires significant time and resources. The e-commerce business is responsible for maintaining and supporting the system, which can be demanding and complex.

Recommendations: Businesses considering this approach should weigh the benefits of complete control and customization against the time and cost involved in development. Ensuring that the custom gateway aligns with the business's strategic goals and technical capabilities is crucial for its successful implementation.

Future Prospects

Looking ahead, the role of cryptocurrencies in e-commerce is likely to expand as technological advancements and regulatory clarity improve. Innovations such as stablecoins, which are designed to maintain a stable value relative to traditional currencies, could address some of the concerns related to price volatility. Additionally, increased adoption and acceptance of cryptocurrencies by mainstream financial institutions and regulatory bodies could further enhance their integration into the e-commerce ecosystem.

Chapter Ten
Security and Fraud Prevention

Cryptocurrency security is critical for maintaining the integrity and trustworthiness of digital assets. As the popularity of cryptocurrencies grows, so does the need for robust security measures to prevent fraud and protect assets from various threats. Key security practices and strategies for fraud prevention in the cryptocurrency space include:

1. Securing Cryptocurrency Wallets

Types of Wallets:

- **Hot Wallets:** These are connected to the internet and include web wallets, mobile wallets, and desktop wallets. While they are convenient for frequent transactions, they are more vulnerable to online threats.

- **Cold Wallets:** These are offline storage solutions such as hardware wallets and paper wallets. They offer enhanced security by keeping private keys away from the internet, reducing exposure to online attacks.

Best Practices:

- **Use Strong Passwords:** Ensure that wallet accounts and associated services use strong, unique passwords.

- **Enable Two-Factor Authentication (2FA):** Add an extra layer of security to wallet accounts by using 2FA, which requires a second verification step in addition to the password.

- **Regular Backups:** Regularly back up wallet data and store backups in secure locations. This ensures that funds can be recovered in case of hardware failure or other issues.

2. Protecting Private Keys

Private Keys:

- **Definition:** Private keys are cryptographic keys that control access to cryptocurrency holdings. They should be kept secret and secure.

Best Practices:

- **Never Share Private Keys:** Private keys should never be shared with anyone. If someone gains access to your private key, they can access your funds.

- **Store Keys Securely:** Use hardware wallets or secure offline methods to store private keys. Avoid storing them in plain text on your computer or online services.

3. Preventing Phishing Attacks

Phishing:

- **Definition:** Phishing attacks involve deceiving individuals into revealing sensitive information, such as private keys or login credentials, through fraudulent emails or websites.

Best Practices:

- **Verify URLs:** Always double-check the URL of websites where you enter sensitive information. Ensure that you are on the official site.

- **Be Wary of Links:** Avoid clicking on links in unsolicited emails or messages, as they may lead to phishing sites.

- **Use Anti-Phishing Tools:** Utilize browser extensions and anti-phishing software to help detect and block phishing attempts.

4. Safeguarding Cryptocurrency Exchanges

Exchanges:

- **Definition:** Cryptocurrency exchanges are platforms where users can buy, sell, and trade cryptocurrencies. They are common targets for hackers due to the large volumes of digital assets they handle.

Best Practices:

- **Choose Reputable Exchanges:** Use exchanges with a strong reputation for security and compliance. Research their security measures and history of breaches.
- **Enable 2FA:** Activate two-factor authentication on exchange accounts to add an extra layer of security.
- **Regular Withdrawals:** For long-term holding, consider withdrawing funds to a secure wallet rather than keeping them on the exchange.

5. Implementing Security Protocols

Security Protocols:

- **Encryption:** Ensure that communication channels and data storage are encrypted to protect against unauthorized access and data breaches.
- **Secure Software:** Keep all software, including wallets and exchanges, up to date with the latest security patches and updates.

6. Monitoring and Alerting

Monitoring:

- **Transaction Monitoring:** Regularly monitor cryptocurrency transactions for any unusual activity. Some services provide alerts for suspicious transactions or login attempts.
- **Security Alerts:** Enable security alerts from wallets and exchanges to be notified of any unusual or unauthorized activities.

7. Educating Users

User Education:

- **Awareness Training:** Educate users and stakeholders about common cryptocurrency scams, phishing attacks, and best practices for securing digital assets.
- **Stay Informed:** Keep up to date with the latest security threats and developments in the cryptocurrency space.

8. Regulatory Compliance

Compliance:

- **Follow Regulations:** Ensure compliance with regulatory requirements and industry standards for cryptocurrency security and fraud prevention.
- **Adopt Best Practices:** Follow industry best practices for data protection and cybersecurity as recommended by regulatory bodies.

Common Scams and How to Avoid Them

As the cryptocurrency market grows, so does the number of scams targeting individuals and investors. Understanding common cryptocurrency scams and knowing how to avoid them is crucial for protecting your digital assets.

Cryptocurrency scams have become increasingly sophisticated as the digital currency market grows. Just as financial criminals attempt to steal from traditional bank accounts or credit cards, crypto scammers are relentless in their efforts to access and pilfer cryptocurrency assets. To safeguard your digital investments, it is crucial to understand the types of cryptocurrency scams and adopt measures to protect yourself [288]. Cryptocurrency scams generally fall into two broad categories: those targeting access to digital wallets and authentication credentials, and those involving direct transfer of assets through various deceptive schemes [288].

1. Scams Targeting Digital Wallets and Authentication Credentials

One prevalent category of cryptocurrency scams focuses on obtaining access to a target's digital wallet or authentication credentials. Scammers use a range of tactics to achieve this goal, including phishing, social engineering, and malware attacks.

Phishing Attacks: Phishing involves tricking individuals into revealing sensitive information, such as private keys or login credentials, by masquerading as a legitimate entity. Scammers often create fake websites or send deceptive emails that appear to come from trusted cryptocurrency exchanges or wallet providers. These fraudulent communications aim to capture your credentials, which can then be used to access and drain your digital wallet.

Social Engineering: Social engineering attacks exploit human psychology to manipulate individuals into divulging personal information. Scammers may impersonate trusted contacts or authority figures, leveraging their perceived credibility to obtain private keys, security codes, or other sensitive details. For example, a scammer might pose as a customer support agent, claiming to need verification details to resolve an issue with your account.

Malware and Keyloggers: Malware and keyloggers are malicious software designed to infiltrate your devices and record keystrokes or capture screen activity. Once installed, these programs can log your private keys or other sensitive data, providing scammers with unauthorized access to your cryptocurrency holdings. Malware can be spread through infected email attachments, malicious downloads, or compromised websites.

Protective Measures: To defend against these types of scams, practice caution with any communication or website requesting sensitive information. Use reputable antivirus software to detect and remove malware, enable two-factor authentication (2FA) for added security, and avoid clicking on suspicious links or downloading unverified applications.

2. Schemes Involving Direct Transfers to Scammers

The second category of cryptocurrency scams involves schemes where scammers trick individuals into transferring their cryptocurrency directly. These schemes can take various forms, including fraudulent investment opportunities, fake business ventures, and impersonation tactics.

Fraudulent Investment Opportunities: Scammers often promote investment schemes that promise high returns with minimal risk. These schemes may involve fake Initial Coin Offerings (ICOs) or Ponzi schemes where new investors' funds are used to pay returns to earlier investors. Victims are persuaded to invest their cryptocurrency, only to find out later that the project is a scam and their funds have been stolen.

Impersonation and Social Media Scams: Impersonation scams involve fraudsters pretending to be well-known figures or trusted entities in the cryptocurrency space. They may use social media platforms to promote fake investment opportunities or solicit cryptocurrency donations for charitable causes. These scams often create a sense of urgency or exclusivity to persuade individuals to transfer their assets quickly.

Business Scams and Fake Deals: Scammers may also create fake business deals or partnerships to convince individuals to send cryptocurrency payments. These scams often involve elaborate schemes, such as fake contracts or phony online stores, designed to appear legitimate. Once the payment is made, the scammer disappears, and the victim is left with no recourse to recover their assets.

Protective Measures: To protect against these direct transfer scams, be sceptical of any investment opportunity that promises unusually high returns or demands immediate action. Conduct thorough research on any investment or business opportunity and verify the legitimacy of the entities involved. Use secure and reputable platforms for financial transactions and be wary of unsolicited requests for cryptocurrency transfers.

Cryptocurrency scams can be highly varied and sophisticated, targeting both digital wallet access and direct transfers of assets. By understanding the different types of scams and implementing preventive measures, you can reduce your risk of falling victim to these fraudulent activities. Always remain vigilant, exercise caution with your personal information, and seek out reputable sources for investment and transactional activities to safeguard your cryptocurrency assets [288].

Phishing Attacks in the Cryptocurrency Sector

Phishing attacks are a significant threat in the cryptocurrency space, primarily targeting individuals through deceptive practices designed to steal sensitive information. These scams involve tricking victims into revealing private keys or login credentials by impersonating trusted entities, such as cryptocurrency exchanges or wallet providers. The ultimate goal of phishing scams is to gain unauthorized access to digital wallets, which can lead to the theft of valuable cryptocurrency assets [288, 289].

Phishing attacks typically involve scammers creating fake websites or sending fraudulent emails that mimic the appearance of legitimate cryptocurrency services. These communications are crafted to look convincing, often using familiar logos, branding, and official-looking email addresses. The scammers' objective is to deceive recipients into providing their private keys or login details. These keys are crucial because they act like passwords, granting access to the victim's cryptocurrency holdings [288, 289].

For instance, a phishing email might claim to be from a well-known cryptocurrency exchange, alerting the recipient to an urgent security issue with their account. The email will include a link to a fake website that closely resembles the genuine exchange's login page. Once the victim enters their private key or login credentials on this fake site, the scammers capture this information and use it to access and drain the victim's digital wallet [288, 289].

Within the cryptocurrency industry, phishing scams often focus on obtaining private keys from users of crypto software wallets. These keys are critical for accessing the funds stored in a digital wallet. Unlike traditional banking passwords, which are usually protected by multiple layers of security, private keys in the cryptocurrency space provide direct access to the assets stored within a wallet.

Phishing attacks targeting crypto wallets operate similarly to other phishing schemes. Scammers use deceptive emails to direct recipients to a specially created website designed to capture private key information. By convincing the user to enter their private key on the fake site, scammers gain control of the wallet and can transfer the cryptocurrency to their own accounts [288, 289].

Phishing scams are among the most common attacks on cryptocurrency users. According to reports from the FBI, phishing scams affected over 300,000 individuals in 2022 and nearly 298,000 in 2023. These attacks resulted in substantial financial losses, with victims collectively losing $52.1 million in 2022 and more than $18.7 million in 2023. The scale and financial impact of phishing demonstrate the severe threat these scams pose to cryptocurrency users [288].

To protect against phishing attacks, users should adopt several key practices. First, always verify the authenticity of communications claiming to be from cryptocurrency services. Be cautious of emails requesting sensitive information or containing links to unfamiliar websites. Instead of clicking on links in emails, directly visit the official website of your cryptocurrency service by typing the URL into your browser [288, 289].

Additionally, enable multi-factor authentication (MFA) where possible, as it provides an extra layer of security beyond just private keys. Regularly update your software and use reputable security tools to detect and block potential threats. Finally, educating yourself about common phishing tactics and remaining vigilant can help prevent falling victim to these deceptive schemes [288, 289].

Social Engineering in Cryptocurrency Scams

Social engineering attacks represent a sophisticated form of deception that exploits human psychology to manipulate individuals into disclosing personal and sensitive information. Unlike technical attacks that rely on exploiting system vulnerabilities, social engineering focuses on exploiting human trust and psychological weaknesses. In the context of cryptocurrency, these scams often aim to trick users into revealing private keys, security codes, or other critical details that can lead to unauthorized access to their digital assets [288].

Social engineering attacks thrive on the manipulation of trust and credibility. Scammers may impersonate trusted contacts or authoritative figures to gain the victim's confidence. They might pose as representatives from a government agency, a reputable business, tech support, or even a personal acquaintance. By leveraging these perceived sources of authority, scammers create a convincing facade that encourages victims to comply with their requests [288].

For instance, a common social engineering tactic involves scammers posing as customer support agents. They might contact individuals via email, phone, or social media, claiming that there is an urgent issue with the person's account. To resolve the problem, the scammer requests sensitive information such as private keys or security codes. Believing they are interacting with a legitimate support agent, the victim may inadvertently disclose critical information that enables the scammer to gain control of their cryptocurrency holdings [288].

Scammers employing social engineering tactics often invest significant time and effort to build trust with their targets. They may engage in friendly conversation, provide seemingly helpful advice, or offer fake assistance to establish rapport. By creating a sense of familiarity and reliability, scammers make their eventual requests for sensitive information appear more legitimate [288].

Once trust is established, the scammer might ask the victim to reveal private keys or transfer cryptocurrency to a digital wallet. They might frame this request as a routine security measure or an urgent necessity. For example, the scammer might claim that the victim's account is at risk of being compromised unless they provide verification details or make a payment [288].

To protect against social engineering attacks, it is crucial to remain vigilant and sceptical of unsolicited requests for sensitive information. Regardless of how convincing the impersonator may appear, users should be cautious when asked to provide private keys, security codes, or make cryptocurrency transfers. It is advisable to independently verify the identity of anyone requesting such information, particularly if the request is unexpected or seems out of character for the supposed source [288].

A good practice is to use official communication channels to verify any claims or requests. For instance, if contacted by someone claiming to be from a cryptocurrency exchange or support team, users should reach out to the company directly using contact information from their official website, rather than relying on the contact details provided by the scammer [288].

Furthermore, educating oneself about common social engineering tactics and regularly updating security protocols can help mitigate the risk of falling victim to these scams. Awareness and cautious behaviour are key to recognizing and avoiding social engineering attempts [288].

Malware and Keyloggers in Cryptocurrency Scams

Malware and keyloggers represent significant threats to the security of cryptocurrency assets. These forms of malicious software are designed to infiltrate devices, capture sensitive information, and provide unauthorized access to a victim's digital holdings. Understanding how malware and keyloggers operate, how they are spread, and how to protect against them is crucial for safeguarding your cryptocurrency.

Malware, short for "malicious software," encompasses a range of harmful programs designed to compromise the security of a computer or network. Keyloggers are a specific type of malware that focuses on recording keystrokes made by the user. When installed on a device, keyloggers track every keystroke entered, including passwords, private keys, and other sensitive data. This information is then sent back to the attacker, allowing them to gain unauthorized access to cryptocurrency wallets and other accounts.

Keyloggers can also capture screen activity, including screenshots of sensitive information displayed on the victim's device. By monitoring what the user sees and types, these malicious programs can extract private information and credentials needed to access cryptocurrency holdings.

Malware and keyloggers are commonly spread through various channels, often leveraging social engineering tactics to trick users into installing them. One common method is through infected email attachments. Scammers may send emails that appear to be from legitimate sources, containing attachments that, when opened, install malware on the victim's device. These attachments can be disguised as innocuous files such as invoices, updates, or reports.

Another method involves malicious downloads. Users may inadvertently download malware by visiting compromised websites or clicking on deceptive links. These sites often pose as legitimate services or software providers, enticing users to download what they believe to be safe applications or updates. Once installed, these applications can secretly embed malware or keyloggers into the system.

Compromised websites can also serve as vectors for malware distribution. By exploiting vulnerabilities in web browsers or other software, attackers can inject malicious code into websites. When users visit these sites, the malware is automatically downloaded and executed on their devices, often without their knowledge.

To protect against malware and keyloggers, several preventive measures can be employed. First and foremost, it is essential to maintain up-to-date antivirus and anti-malware software. These tools can detect and remove known threats, providing a crucial line of defence against malicious programs.

Avoiding suspicious email attachments and links is another important practice. Users should be wary of unsolicited emails, especially those that request personal information or prompt downloads. Verifying the authenticity of email senders and checking for unusual or unexpected attachments can help mitigate the risk of malware infections.

Downloading software and updates only from reputable sources is crucial. Users should ensure that they are obtaining applications from official websites or well-known app stores that have rigorous security measures in place.

Regularly updating operating systems and software can also reduce vulnerabilities that malware might exploit. Security patches and updates are often released to address newly discovered threats and improve system defences.

Lastly, implementing strong security practices such as multi-factor authentication (MFA) can add an extra layer of protection. Even if private keys or passwords are compromised, MFA can prevent unauthorized access to cryptocurrency accounts.

Fraudulent Investment Opportunities in Cryptocurrency

Fraudulent investment opportunities are a prevalent threat in the cryptocurrency space, often targeting individuals with promises of high returns and minimal risk. Scammers employ various tactics to lure unsuspecting investors, including fake Initial Coin Offerings (ICOs) and Ponzi schemes. Understanding these schemes and their red flags is essential to protect oneself from financial loss and potential scams.

Types of Fraudulent Investment Schemes

1. Fake Initial Coin Offerings (ICOs):

Initial Coin Offerings (ICOs) are fundraising mechanisms in the cryptocurrency world where new projects issue their tokens to investors in exchange for established cryptocurrencies like Bitcoin or Ethereum. While legitimate ICOs can provide exciting opportunities for early investment in promising projects, scammers often exploit this mechanism by creating fake ICOs. These fraudulent schemes promise high returns and use sophisticated marketing tactics to attract investors. Once the funds are collected, the scammers disappear, leaving investors with worthless tokens and no recourse for recovering their investment.

2. Ponzi Schemes:

Ponzi schemes involve using funds from new investors to pay returns to earlier investors, creating the illusion of a profitable investment. In the context of cryptocurrency, these schemes often present themselves as investment platforms or trading services offering guaranteed high returns. New investors are enticed to invest their funds with the promise of significant profits, but as the scheme continues, it relies on a constant influx of new money to sustain payouts. Eventually, the scheme collapses when it becomes impossible to recruit new investors, leading to massive financial losses for those who invested last.

Characteristics of Fraudulent Investment Opportunities

Fraudulent investment opportunities often share several characteristics that can help potential investors identify red flags:

- **Unrealistic Promises:** Scammers frequently promise guaranteed high returns with little or no risk, which should be a major warning sign. In the financial world, higher returns typically come with higher risks, and any investment promising otherwise should be approached with caution.

- **Lack of Transparency:** Legitimate investments provide clear and verifiable information about their business model, team, and financials. Fraudulent schemes often lack transparency, offering little to no information about the project's management or how the returns are generated.

- **Pressure Tactics:** Scammers may use high-pressure tactics to rush individuals into making quick decisions. They may create a sense of urgency or scarcity, such as limited-time offers or exclusive opportunities, to prevent potential investors from thoroughly researching the investment.

- **Absence of Regulatory Compliance:** Genuine investment opportunities adhere to regulatory standards and often have proper registrations or licenses. Fraudulent schemes typically bypass regulatory scrutiny, operating without proper oversight or legal compliance.

To protect yourself from fraudulent investment opportunities, it is crucial to approach all investment offers with a critical eye. Conduct thorough research into any project or platform, verify the credibility of the team, and look for reviews or feedback from other investors. Be cautious of offers that seem too good to be true and avoid investments that pressure you into making hasty decisions.

Impersonation and Social Media Scams

Impersonation and social media scams are prevalent tactics used by fraudsters in the cryptocurrency space. These scams involve fraudsters posing as well-known figures or trusted entities to deceive individuals into transferring their cryptocurrency assets. By leveraging the influence and credibility of celebrities, influential personalities, or reputable organizations, scammers aim to create a sense of legitimacy and urgency, thereby tricking people into making hasty financial decisions [288].

In impersonation scams, fraudsters often mimic the identities of prominent figures or well-known entities within the cryptocurrency industry. They may use social media platforms, such as Twitter, Instagram, or Facebook, to establish fake profiles or hijack existing ones. These fraudulent accounts are then used to promote fake investment opportunities or solicit cryptocurrency donations for purported charitable causes. For instance, a scammer might create a convincing account that appears to be run by a famous cryptocurrency advocate or a prominent business leader. They might claim to be conducting a giveaway or offering exclusive investment deals, encouraging followers to send cryptocurrency to their wallet with the promise of receiving a larger return or special benefits in the future [288].

Another common tactic involves "giveaway scams," where scammers promise to double or multiply the amount of cryptocurrency sent to them. They create fake social media posts or live streams that appear to be from legitimate accounts or well-known personalities. These posts often include urgent calls to action, such as limited-time offers or exclusive opportunities, which pressure individuals to act quickly. The allure of quick and substantial returns convinces victims to transfer their cryptocurrency, only to discover that the scammer has disappeared with their funds [288].

Impersonation scams can also extend to fraudsters posing as support or security teams from cryptocurrency exchanges or wallet providers. They may contact users via direct messages or fake support channels, claiming to need verification details or security codes to resolve issues with their accounts. By exploiting the trust people place in official support channels, these scammers manipulate victims into revealing sensitive information or transferring funds under false pretences [288].

To avoid falling victim to these scams, it is crucial to exercise caution and verify the authenticity of any communication or offer related to cryptocurrency. Always double-check the legitimacy of social media accounts, cross-reference information with official sources, and be wary of any requests for sensitive information or immediate financial actions. By staying informed and vigilant, individuals can better protect themselves from the deceptive tactics used in impersonation and social media scams [288].

New Crypto-Based Opportunities: ICOs and NFTs

The emergence of new crypto-based opportunities, such as Initial Coin Offerings (ICOs) and Non-Fungible Tokens (NFTs), has opened up innovative avenues for investment. However, these opportunities also come with significant risks, as they are often targeted by scammers looking to exploit the growing interest in digital assets. While ICOs and NFTs can offer lucrative returns, they also present potential pitfalls that investors should be aware of [288].

Initial Coin Offerings (ICOs)

Initial Coin Offerings (ICOs) are a popular fundraising method in the cryptocurrency world, where new projects issue tokens to investors in exchange for established cryptocurrencies like Bitcoin or Ethereum. ICOs are designed to raise capital for new ventures, but they can also be a breeding ground for fraud. Scammers often create fake ICOs by setting up fraudulent websites that appear legitimate. These sites may promise high returns or groundbreaking technology to lure investors. Once investors deposit their cryptocurrency into the designated wallet, the scammers can quickly abscond with the funds, leaving no trace of the investment. In some cases, even if the ICO is genuine, the project's founders may engage in deceptive practices, such as making exaggerated claims about the product's potential or failing to deliver on promises, resulting in financial losses for investors [288].

Rug Pulls

A particularly notorious scam within the ICO space is the "rug pull." This occurs when the developers of a cryptocurrency project suddenly withdraw all the funds from the liquidity pool, effectively collapsing the project overnight. After raising significant capital from investors, the scammers vanish, making themselves unreachable. Investors are left with worthless tokens and no recourse to recover their investments. Rug pulls exploit the lack of regulation and transparency in the crypto space, capitalizing on the trust investors place in seemingly promising projects. To avoid falling victim to a rug pull, it is crucial to conduct thorough research into the project's team, technology, and financial practices before investing [288].

Cloud Mining

Cloud mining offers another investment avenue within the cryptocurrency sector. It involves paying a service provider upfront to lease mining hardware or hash power, with the promise of receiving a share of the mined cryptocurrency. The appeal of cloud mining is that it allows individuals to participate in cryptocurrency mining without the need to manage hardware or technical operations. However, this model is rife with potential scams. Some cloud mining platforms are fraudulent and do not own the mining equipment they claim to have. After receiving the initial investment, these platforms fail to deliver the promised mining rewards, leaving investors with no returns. While cloud mining can be legitimate, it is essential for investors to perform comprehensive due diligence. This includes verifying the legitimacy of the platform, understanding its operational details, and checking for user reviews and independent audits [288].

While ICOs and NFTs present exciting investment opportunities, they also carry inherent risks of fraud and deception. Investors should remain vigilant and conduct thorough research to safeguard their assets against potential scams. By understanding the risks associated with these new crypto-based opportunities, individuals can make more informed decisions and protect themselves from financial loss.

Best Practices for Keeping Your Assets Safe

Detecting cryptocurrency scams involves recognizing certain red flags and understanding the characteristics of legitimate projects. By following a systematic approach to evaluate cryptocurrencies and their associated projects, you can protect yourself from falling victim to fraudulent schemes [288].

Read the White Paper: A white paper is a foundational document for any legitimate cryptocurrency project. It should offer a detailed description of the cryptocurrency's technology, purpose, and operational mechanics. A well-crafted white paper will outline the protocols, algorithms, and blockchain infrastructure in clear and precise terms, often supported by technical data and formulas. Legitimate projects invest significant effort into creating comprehensive white papers that convey the credibility and feasibility of their proposals [288].

In contrast, fraudulent projects often produce poorly written white papers with vague or contradictory information. They may lack technical details or present inflated promises without substantial backing. If a white paper reads more like a sales pitch than a technical document, or if it fails to address fundamental questions about the project's functionality and goals, it may be indicative of a scam. Additionally, verify whether the ICO or project is registered with relevant regulatory bodies, such as the Securities and Exchange Commission (SEC), as unregistered offerings are often red flags .

Identify Team Members: The transparency of a project's team is another crucial indicator of its legitimacy. Reputable cryptocurrencies will provide detailed information about their team members, including their qualifications, past experiences, and roles within the project. This information is often included in the white paper or on the project's website.

For open-source projects, while the team may not always be named, you should be able to access the code and development discussions on platforms like GitHub or GitLab. This openness helps to establish the project's credibility and allows the community to review and contribute to its development. If you cannot find any information about the team or if the white paper is filled with errors and lacks verifiable details, it is advisable to proceed with caution.

Beware of "Free" Items: Scammers frequently lure individuals with offers of free coins or promises of airdrops. These offers might seem enticing, but they often serve as traps to collect personal information or to trick you into transferring funds. Remember that reputable cryptocurrency projects do not give away free tokens or assets as part of their regular operations. Any promise of free cryptocurrency should be scrutinized carefully, as it is often a tactic used to deceive and exploit individuals [288].

Scrutinize the Marketing: Marketing tactics can be revealing of a project's legitimacy. Established cryptocurrency projects typically start with modest marketing efforts and focus on solving specific problems within the blockchain ecosystem. They provide clear, well-documented explanations of their technology and objectives, rather than relying heavily on hype or extravagant claims.

Beware of projects that emphasize sensational updates, such as claims of "millions raised" or aggressive promotions. Such tactics may be used to distract from a lack of substance or genuine technological innovation. Legitimate projects focus on advancing their technology and providing transparent updates about their development progress. They avoid overhyping their potential and instead present their goals and achievements in a professional and measured manner.

Where There Is Hype, There Is Often a Warning: A significant amount of hype and flashy marketing is often a red flag. Scammers use high-profile endorsements, flashy advertisements, and promises of extraordinary returns to attract investors. Legitimate cryptocurrency ventures generally avoid overhyping and focus on delivering genuine value and technological advancements. High-pressure tactics and urgent calls to action are typically used to rush individuals into making impulsive decisions, increasing the likelihood of falling for a scam [288].

To protect yourself from cryptocurrency scams, it is crucial to remain vigilant and adopt preventive measures. Here are some key actions you can take to avoid falling victim to these deceptive schemes:

- **Do Not Share Private Keys**: Your private keys are the most critical aspect of your cryptocurrency security. They provide access to your digital assets and wallet. No legitimate cryptocurrency transaction or service requires you to share your private keys. If someone asks for them, it's a strong indication of a scam.

- **Avoid Promises of High Returns**: Be sceptical of any opportunity that guarantees substantial returns with little or no risk. Scammers often entice victims with promises of easy money. If an investment sounds too good to be true, it probably is. Always conduct thorough research before investing in any cryptocurrency project or scheme.

- **Ignore Unsolicited Investment Managers**: If someone contacts you out of the blue, claiming they can significantly grow your money, proceed with caution. Many scammers pose as investment managers or financial advisors to gain your trust and access to your funds. Legitimate investment professionals do not solicit clients through unsolicited communication.

- **Be Wary of Celebrity Endorsements**: Scammers may impersonate celebrities or well-known figures to lend credibility to their schemes. Genuine celebrities are unlikely to reach out to you personally regarding cryptocurrency investments. If you receive such communications, it's best to disregard them.

- **Verify Online Romantic Interests**: When engaging with individuals on dating websites or apps, be cautious if they ask for money, especially if the relationship is relatively new. Scammers may exploit romantic connections to solicit funds under false pretences. Meeting in person and verifying their authenticity can help protect you from fraud.

- **Ignore Phishing Alerts**: Do not click on links or respond to messages claiming that your account is frozen or at risk. These messages often come from scammers trying to gain access to your information. Instead, contact the organization directly through official channels to verify any issues with your account.

- **Verify Official Communications**: If you receive communication claiming to be from a government agency, financial institution, or utility company, do not respond directly through the provided contact information. Instead, visit the agency's official website to find the correct contact information and verify the legitimacy of the message.

- **Avoid Cash-to-Crypto Jobs**: Be cautious of job postings that offer positions related to converting cash to cryptocurrency or mining operations, especially if they ask for upfront payments or personal information. Scammers often use these job offers to exploit unsuspecting individuals.

- **Report Blackmail Threats**: If someone threatens to release explicit material or other damaging information unless you send them cryptocurrency, this is a form of blackmail. Report such incidents to the relevant authorities and do not comply with the demands.

- **Avoid "Free" Money or Crypto**: Offers of free cryptocurrency or money should be treated with scepticism. Scammers use these tactics to lure individuals into their schemes. Always verify the legitimacy of such offers before taking any action.

How to Report Scams

If you encounter a cryptocurrency scam or believe you have been targeted, there are several organizations and resources available to assist you:

- **Federal Trade Commission (FTC)**: The FTC provides a platform for reporting fraud through their fraud report system.

- **Commodity Futures Trading Commission (CFTC)**: You can file complaints or provide tips regarding cryptocurrency scams through the CFTC's complaints and tips portal.
- **Securities and Exchange Commission (SEC)**: Report securities fraud and investment scams using the SEC's fraud reporting services.
- **FBI Internet Crime Complaint Center (IC3)**: For online fraud, including cryptocurrency scams, you can file a complaint with the IC3 for investigation.
- **Contact Your Crypto Exchange**: Reach out to your cryptocurrency exchange for any additional fraud prevention resources or assistance. Many exchanges offer support and have measures in place to help protect your assets.

By remaining cautious and using these resources, you can significantly reduce the risk of falling victim to cryptocurrency scams and better safeguard your digital assets.

The Role of Regulatory Bodies in Fraud Prevention

Regulatory bodies play a crucial role in the prevention of cryptocurrency fraud, aiming to protect investors, maintain market integrity, and foster trust in the burgeoning digital asset space. Their involvement includes setting standards, enforcing compliance, and providing resources for fraud prevention and victim support.

Setting Standards and Regulations

Regulatory bodies establish frameworks and guidelines that cryptocurrency businesses must follow to operate legally. These regulations cover various aspects of the cryptocurrency industry, including anti-money laundering (AML) requirements, know-your-customer (KYC) protocols, and securities laws. For instance, the U.S. Securities and Exchange Commission (SEC) enforces regulations that require certain cryptocurrency offerings to register as securities, ensuring that they meet specific standards and provide adequate disclosures to investors. Similarly, the Financial Action Task Force (FATF) sets international standards to combat money laundering and terrorist financing, which member countries adopt and implement to regulate cryptocurrency exchanges and wallet providers.

Enforcement and Compliance

Regulatory bodies actively monitor and enforce compliance with established regulations. They investigate suspicious activities, prosecute fraudulent schemes, and impose penalties on violators. For example, the Commodity Futures Trading Commission (CFTC) investigates fraudulent practices in the trading of cryptocurrency derivatives and takes legal action against entities that engage in manipulation or deceit. In addition, national financial regulatory authorities, such as the UK's Financial Conduct Authority (FCA), supervise cryptocurrency businesses to ensure they adhere to regulatory requirements and maintain operational transparency.

Providing Resources and Guidance

Regulatory agencies also provide valuable resources and guidance to help individuals and businesses navigate the cryptocurrency landscape safely. They offer educational materials, alerts about emerging scams, and advice on recognizing fraudulent schemes. For example, the U.S. Federal Trade Commission (FTC) publishes guidelines on how to identify and avoid cryptocurrency scams, helping consumers make informed decisions. Similarly, the European Securities and Markets Authority (ESMA) provides warnings and insights into risks associated with cryptocurrency investments, empowering investors to protect themselves from fraud.

Supporting Victims and Reporting Mechanisms

In the event of fraud, regulatory bodies offer support and channels for reporting fraudulent activities. They provide platforms where victims can file complaints and seek assistance. For instance, the FBI's Internet Crime Complaint Center (IC3) allows individuals to report online fraud, including cryptocurrency-related scams, for investigation. National consumer protection agencies, such as the Australian Competition and Consumer Commission (ACCC), also handle reports of fraud and work with other authorities to address and mitigate the impact on victims.

Promoting International Cooperation

Given the global nature of cryptocurrencies, regulatory bodies collaborate internationally to combat cross-border fraud. Organizations like the International Organization of Securities Commissions (IOSCO) and the Financial Stability Board (FSB) work together to create consistent regulatory standards and share information about emerging threats. This cooperation helps to address the challenges posed by the decentralized and borderless nature of cryptocurrency transactions and enhances the effectiveness of fraud prevention measures.

Encouraging Transparency and Innovation

Regulatory bodies also encourage transparency and innovation within the cryptocurrency industry. By fostering an environment where businesses operate with integrity and adhere to ethical standards, regulators help build trust and promote sustainable growth in the sector. For instance, regulatory sandboxes allow businesses to test new technologies and business models under regulatory supervision, providing a controlled environment to ensure that innovations are both effective and compliant with legal requirements.

Case Studies of Major Security Breaches

The rise of digital currencies and blockchain technology has been accompanied by significant advancements in financial innovation. However, one major obstacle to their mainstream adoption has been hacking. High-profile thefts from cryptocurrency exchanges and platforms have shaken investor confidence and highlighted vulnerabilities in the security of digital assets.

The Reality of Blockchain Security

While blockchain technology is often praised for its security features, it is not immune to attacks. The decentralized nature of blockchains and their reliance on cryptographic principles offer a high degree of security, but these systems are still susceptible to vulnerabilities. Over the years, several major hacks have demonstrated that blockchain projects are only partially secure, undermining the perception that they are impervious to cyber threats. For instance, in 2023 alone, over $1.7 billion in cryptocurrency was stolen, down from $3.8 billion in 2022, according to blockchain analysis firm Chainalysis. This substantial decrease reflects ongoing efforts to improve security but also underscores the persistent risk of hacking [290].

Notable Cryptocurrency Hacks

1. **Ronin Network - $625 Million:** In March 2022, the Ronin Network, which supports the popular Axie Infinity gaming platform, was the target of the largest cryptocurrency hack to date. Hackers exploited vulnerabilities in the network and stole approximately $625 million worth of Ethereum and USDC. The

attack was reportedly linked to the Lazarus Group, a North Korean state-backed hacking collective. Although Sky Mavis, the developer of Axie Infinity, managed to recover $5.7 million of the stolen funds, this incident remains the largest cryptocurrency theft in history [290].

2. **Poly Network - $611 Million:** In August 2021, a lone hacker exploited a vulnerability in the Poly Network decentralized finance platform and stole over $600 million. The hacker returned a significant portion of the stolen funds after a public appeal and the establishment of return addresses by the Poly Network. The hacker's motivation appeared to be more about challenging the network than financial gain [290].

3. **FTX - $600 Million:** November 2022 saw a major setback for the crypto industry when FTX, one of the leading cryptocurrency exchanges, declared bankruptcy. On the day of its bankruptcy filing, more than $600 million was stolen from its wallets. The exchange confirmed the hack through its Telegram channel, warning users to avoid the FTX site due to malware risks. In 2024, it was revealed that a SIM card swapping ring had gained access to an FTX employee's accounts, further complicating the situation [290].

4. **Binance BNB Bridge - $570 Million:** In October 2022, Binance, a major cryptocurrency exchange, was targeted in a high-profile attack involving the Binance Smart Chain Token Hub. Hackers exploited a vulnerability in a smart contract to create and withdraw 2 million extra Binance Coins (BNB), resulting in a loss of approximately $570 million. This incident highlighted the need for more stringent blockchain security measures [290].

5. **Coincheck - $532 Million:** The January 2018 hack of the Japanese exchange Coincheck resulted in the theft of $523 million worth of NEM coins. The vulnerability was attributed to the use of a hot wallet, which is less secure compared to offline cold storage. At the time, this breach was the largest in cryptocurrency history, surpassing even the Mt. Gox hack [290].

6. **Mt. Gox - $473 Million:** One of the earliest and most significant hacks occurred in 2011 when Mt. Gox, then the largest Bitcoin exchange, lost 25,000 bitcoins worth about $400,000. The situation worsened in 2014 when the

exchange lost approximately 650,000 bitcoins from its customers and 100,000 from its own holdings, amounting to $473 million. The initial loss was attributed to stolen coins from the exchange's hot wallet [290].

7. **Wormhole - $325 Million:** In February 2022, the decentralized finance platform Wormhole experienced a $325 million theft due to an upgrade issue. Hackers exploited a vulnerability in the project's GitHub repository, leading to the theft of funds, including $47 million in the Solana blockchain's native SOL token [290].

8. **Mixin - $200 Million:** In September 2023, the Mixin Network was compromised through its cloud service provider, resulting in the theft of about $200 million in bitcoin, ether, and tether [290].

9. **Euler Finance - $197 Million:** Euler Finance, a borrowing and lending protocol on the Ethereum blockchain, was hacked on March 13, 2023, in a flash loan attack. The attackers exploited a vulnerability to steal $197 million in various cryptocurrencies. Interestingly, the hacker began returning the funds days later, citing concerns over their safety [290].

10. **Bitmart - $196 Million:** In December 2021, Bitmart, a centralized exchange, lost $196 million due to a hack. The attack drained funds from the exchange's wallets, with significant amounts funneled through Ethereum and Binance Smart Chain [290].

These high-profile hacks underscore the vulnerabilities present in the cryptocurrency space, revealing that even with advanced technology, security challenges persist. The substantial financial losses and the impact on investor confidence highlight the ongoing need for enhanced security measures and regulatory oversight. As the cryptocurrency industry evolves, addressing these vulnerabilities will be crucial for fostering greater trust and achieving mainstream adoption [290].

Chapter Eleven
The Future of Cryptocurrency

The cryptocurrency industry has undergone remarkable growth in a relatively short period, evolving from a niche technology into a major disruptor in the financial services sector. This rapid expansion is challenging to contextualize, given the nascent nature of the technology and its evolving applications. As the industry continues to mature, it raises questions about its future trajectory and the extent of its impact on our daily lives [291].

As of now, global cryptocurrency ownership is estimated to be between 200 and 300 million people, with countries like Vietnam leading in terms of crypto adoption. Research by Allied Market Research predicts that the value of the cryptocurrency market could triple by 2030, reaching nearly $5 billion [291]. This anticipated growth is driven primarily by remittances and global payments, underscoring the increasing integration of cryptocurrencies into mainstream financial transactions. This projection serves as evidence of the cryptocurrency's potential to become a central aspect of financial interactions in the future.

Looking ahead to 2050, the vision of cryptocurrencies becoming a routine part of daily transactions raises intriguing possibilities. Questions about whether cryptocurrencies will become a universal means of payment or remain a specialized domain for tech-savvy individuals are central to the debate. The future of cryptocurrencies may involve widespread adoption, making them as accessible and understandable to the general public as traditional financial instruments [291].

The inevitability of increased regulation in the cryptocurrency space is becoming clearer. Digital assets, which have thus far operated in a relatively unregulated environment, are expected to face stricter oversight as governments and regulatory bodies respond to their growing influence. While some regulations may be perceived as stifling innovation, the need for consumer protection and industry standards is undeniable. According to Daniel Seely, a financial services lawyer specializing in cryptocurrency, various countries will adopt different approaches to regulation. Some may integrate cryptocurrencies into their economic systems as legal tender, while others might impose stringent restrictions or outright bans. The evolution of international frameworks and treaties could further harmonize regulations, akin to the unified approach seen with the euro, thereby facilitating cross-border cryptocurrency transactions and usage [291].

Non-Fungible Tokens (NFTs) are poised to be a significant component of the cryptocurrency industry's growth. Initially popularized for digital artwork, NFTs have potential applications across various sectors, including sports and entertainment. By offering unique, tradable digital assets, NFTs can enhance customer engagement and brand loyalty for companies outside the traditional crypto space.

Success in the NFT space will be measured by widespread adoption of Web3 wallets and ease of blockchain interactions. As industries such as publishing, music, film, and gaming undergo further disruption, the role of NFTs and blockchain technology in establishing true digital ownership will become increasingly prominent [291].

The future of the cryptocurrency industry holds significant promise, characterized by increased adoption, evolving regulatory frameworks, and advancements in technology. While challenges such as decentralization, scalability, and security remain, the industry's trajectory suggests a growing integration into financial systems and daily life. The development of NFTs and the broader acceptance of digital assets will shape how cryptocurrencies are used and understood, potentially transforming them into a fundamental element of the global economy by 2050.

Predictions and Trends

Bitcoin's Future: Challenges and Developments

As Bitcoin continues to capture the imagination of investors and the public, its future trajectory remains heavily influenced by ongoing blockchain developments and the resolution of key issues. While Bitcoin's price fluctuations and its role as an investment are notable, the most critical factors shaping its future are related to decentralization, scalability, and security [292].

Decentralization

Decentralization is a core principle of Bitcoin, envisioned as a system where control is distributed rather than centralized. This encompasses both the distribution of Bitcoin ownership and the decentralization of the blockchain network itself. Initially, Bitcoin was designed to be accessible and controlled by a broad public, limiting the concentration of power. However, the landscape has changed significantly as large entities and institutional investors have acquired substantial amounts of Bitcoin. This trend raises concerns that Bitcoin may become increasingly centralized, especially as the available supply decreases and more coins are held by a few significant players [292].

On the blockchain side, decentralization has been challenged by the rise of large-scale mining operations. The Bitcoin blockchain was intended to be widely distributed, but the increasing market value of Bitcoin has led to the dominance of mining farms. These farms control significant portions of the network's processing power, creating mining pools that dominate the mining landscape. As of June 2024, a small number of mining pools control a substantial majority of the Bitcoin network's hash rate. This concentration of power undermines the decentralized nature of the blockchain and raises concerns about potential control by a few large entities [292].

Scalability Challenges

Scalability remains one of Bitcoin's most pressing issues. The Bitcoin network can currently handle only six to eight transactions per second, a stark contrast to other blockchains that boast much higher transaction throughput. This limitation has led to persistent issues with high transaction fees and long confirmation times. Attempts to address these problems have included various second-layer solutions, such as the Lightning Network. This solution aims to process transactions off-chain and then settle them on the Bitcoin blockchain, theoretically enhancing scalability and reducing costs. However, these solutions often come with trade-offs, potentially compromising security and decentralization. The effectiveness and adoption of these technologies will be crucial in determining Bitcoin's ability to scale [292].

Security Issues

Security is a critical concern for Bitcoin users and investors. While the Bitcoin blockchain itself remains secure, the interfaces and systems used to access and manage Bitcoin are frequent targets for scammers and hackers. Ransomware attacks and scams have become prevalent methods for stealing cryptocurrency, targeting both individuals and businesses that handle private keys. Despite the security of the blockchain, the surrounding infrastructure—such as digital wallets and exchanges—needs to be robust to protect users' assets [292].

Regulatory Developments

The regulatory environment for Bitcoin is evolving, with significant implications for its future. The approval of Bitcoin Spot exchange-traded funds (ETFs) has broadened access to Bitcoin, potentially paving the way for similar developments with other cryptocurrencies. Recent legal rulings, such as the Securities and Exchange Commission's (SEC) case against Ripple and the regulatory stance on insider trading in crypto markets, highlight the shifting landscape of cryptocurrency regulation. These developments will likely continue to shape the industry's regulatory framework over the coming years [292].

Halvings

Bitcoin's halving events, which occur approximately every four years, play a pivotal role in its economic model. During a halving, the reward for mining new blocks is reduced by half, impacting the rate at which new Bitcoin is introduced into circulation. Historically, halvings have been followed by increases in Bitcoin's price due to the reduced supply and increased demand. The next halving is expected to occur around 2028, with the final halving projected to take place in 2140. While past trends suggest that halvings could drive up Bitcoin's price, future performance remains uncertain and dependent on various market and economic factors [292].

Emerging Trends

1. Bull Market Emerges After Approval of ETFs

The cryptocurrency market has experienced a significant bull run, particularly in Bitcoin, which saw its value surge by 150% as 2024 began. At the start of the year, Bitcoin was valued around $44,000, but by late May, its price had climbed to nearly $70,000. Experts anticipate that this bullish trend could persist through 2025, with forecasts suggesting Bitcoin might reach $77,000 by the end of 2024 and potentially $123,000 by the close of 2025. This optimism is largely attributed to two primary factors: the approval of spot Bitcoin ETFs and the upcoming halving event [293].

Spot Bitcoin ETFs, which were approved by the SEC in January 2024 after years of anticipation, have played a pivotal role in driving market demand. These ETFs allow investors to gain exposure to Bitcoin without directly holding the cryptocurrency, thus simplifying investment for those wary of navigating crypto exchanges. Prominent financial institutions like BlackRock and Fidelity have emerged as leaders in this space, holding substantial Bitcoin assets and offering these ETFs to a broader range of investors, including those managing retirement accounts [293].

Additionally, the Bitcoin halving event, which occurs approximately every four years, significantly impacts Bitcoin's supply dynamics. The most recent halving took place in April 2024, reducing the reward for mining Bitcoin by half. Historically, such events have been followed by substantial price increases, although these gains have not always been immediate. Previous halvings in 2016 and 2020 resulted in price increases of 51% and 83% respectively within six months. Analysts are forecasting a similar trend following the April 2024 halving, with expectations that Bitcoin could surpass its all-time high within the subsequent six months [293].

2. The Intersection of AI and Crypto

Artificial Intelligence (AI) is increasingly intersecting with the cryptocurrency world, leading to the emergence of AI tokens. These tokens are directly associated with AI ventures and can be utilized across various applications such as blockchain protocols, decentralized web platforms, and machine learning systems. The search interest for AI tokens has surged in 2024, reflecting growing enthusiasm for this niche sector [293].

AI tokens serve multiple functions: they can be used to pay for services, access platform data, or as rewards for platform participants. They also provide governance rights to holders, allowing them to influence platform decisions. Currently, there are nearly 90 AI tokens in circulation, with their combined market value soaring from $2.7 billion in April 2023 to over $39 billion [293].

One notable example is Fetch.ai, whose token (FET) experienced a remarkable 329% increase between mid-February and mid-March 2024. Fetch.ai, along with SingularityNET and Ocean Protocol, recently formed the "Superintelligence Alliance," aiming to advance decentralized AI. This alliance represents a significant step toward creating decentralized AI systems that counterbalance the dominance of major tech corporations [293].

3. Funding, Mergers, and Acquisitions in the Crypto Market

After a tumultuous period marked by high-profile crypto bankruptcies in 2022, investor confidence rebounded in late 2023. In the final quarter of 2023, $1.9 billion was invested in crypto-related companies, with the largest investment of $225 million directed towards Wormhole, a firm specializing in cross-chain connectivity. By February 2024, funding for blockchain startups had reached a three-month high of $485 million [293].

A notable trend is the growing prominence of Bitcoin miners. Companies involved in mining have seen their stock values outperform Bitcoin itself, with firms like Marathon Digital, CleanSpark, and Riot Platforms experiencing substantial increases in their stock prices. As the Bitcoin halving approaches, larger mining operations are expected to acquire smaller, less efficient competitors. For instance, CleanSpark's acquisition of three mining facilities in Mississippi for $19.8 million in February 2024 highlights this consolidation trend [293].

Additionally, the merger of Hut 8 Mining and US Bitcoin Corp. in November 2023 resulted in the creation of Hut 8 Corp., which now boasts a $1.14 billion market cap. Such mergers and acquisitions are reshaping the crypto mining landscape, with significant implications for the industry's future [293].

4. Increasing Regulation of Cryptocurrency and Exchanges

The regulatory environment for cryptocurrencies has become increasingly stringent following the high-profile failures of exchanges like FTX. Search interest in "crypto regulation" has surged by 104% in recent years as governments and regulatory bodies intensify their oversight of the industry. The SEC, under the leadership of Gary Gensler, has been particularly active, pushing for clearer regulations and greater compliance from crypto firms [293].

In 2023, the SEC filed lawsuits against several major crypto entities, including Coinbase and Binance, for failing to adhere to regulatory requirements. Binance was ordered to pay $4 billion in fines, reflecting the severe consequences of non-compliance. Additionally, President Biden has advocated for a 30% tax on cryptocurrency mining, further signaling the government's intent to regulate the sector more comprehensively [293].

As regulatory scrutiny increases, some crypto companies are exploring operations in other countries to mitigate the impact of U.S. regulations. For instance, Gemini and Coinbase have expanded their operations to regions like the United Arab Emirates and Bermuda, respectively, citing regulatory concerns as a key factor in their decision-making [293].

5. Crypto's Growing Climate Impact

The environmental impact of cryptocurrency mining, particularly through the Proof of Work (PoW) consensus mechanism, is a growing concern. PoW requires substantial computational power and energy, leading to significant electricity consumption and water usage. According to the Cambridge Bitcoin Electricity Consumption Index, Bitcoin mining consumes approximately 1174 TWh of electricity annually—more than the Netherlands' total electricity usage. This level of consumption translates to high carbon emissions, with 67% of the energy used in crypto mining coming from fossil fuels [293].

Efforts to address these environmental issues include Ethereum's transition to Proof of Stake (PoS) in 2022, which reduced energy consumption by 99%. However, Bitcoin is unlikely to switch to PoS, and its mining practices will continue to have a substantial environmental footprint. As the industry faces growing scrutiny over its climate impact, there will be increasing pressure to adopt more sustainable practices and technologies [293].

6. Real-World Assets Turn Digital with Blockchain Technology

The tokenization of real-world assets (RWAs) is another emerging trend in the crypto space. Tokenization involves creating digital representations of physical assets on the blockchain, which can include real estate, art, bonds, and intellectual property. This process enhances liquidity, facilitates fractional ownership, and automates asset management [293].

Financial institutions are beginning to embrace asset tokenization. BlackRock, for example, launched its first tokenized asset fund, BUIDL, in 2024, using the Ethereum blockchain. This fund, in partnership with Securitize, raised $240 million in its first week. Similarly, Citigroup is exploring the tokenization of financial assets on a private blockchain to streamline transactions and reduce processing times [293].

The market for tokenized assets, valued at $2.81 billion in 2023, is expected to grow significantly, with projections reaching $9.82 billion by 2030. Some forecasts, such as those from Boston Consulting Group, suggest that up to $16 trillion worth of RWAs could be tokenized by 2030, potentially representing 10% of global GDP [293].

7. Global Officials Explore Central Bank Digital Currency (CBDC)

Central Bank Digital Currencies (CBDCs) are being explored by banking systems worldwide as a means to create a virtual currency managed by central banks. This approach aims to combine the benefits of digital currencies with the stability of central bank oversight. Currently, 132 countries are developing or testing CBDCs, encompassing 98% of the world's GDP [293].

Countries like Jamaica, Nigeria, and the Bahamas have already fully implemented CBDCs. China is leading the largest CBDC trial with its digital yuan, which is being tested in 25 cities. By 2030, the Bank of International Settlements anticipates that 15 retail CBDCs and 9 wholesale CBDCs will be operational. The SWIFT network is also working on a CBDC platform to facilitate cross-border transactions and integration with existing banking infrastructure [293].

In contrast, U.S. officials have been hesitant to embrace CBDCs, citing concerns about privacy, financial stability, and the impact on traditional banking systems. The Federal Reserve has indicated that any decision on CBDCs would require congressional approval, reflecting ongoing debates about the potential implications of digital currencies on the financial ecosystem [293].

The Role of Cryptocurrencies in the Global Economy

Cryptocurrencies have evolved from niche digital assets into a significant component of the global economy, influencing various sectors and financial systems. Initially, cryptocurrencies like Bitcoin were primarily seen as speculative investments or alternative currencies, but their role has expanded significantly, impacting everything from investment strategies to financial transactions and beyond.

Cryptocurrencies have introduced new forms of financial innovation. The rise of digital assets has given birth to various financial products and services, including decentralized finance (DeFi) platforms, which offer traditional financial services like lending and borrowing outside conventional banking systems. These platforms leverage blockchain technology to provide transparency, reduce costs, and increase accessibility. Additionally, the emergence of Initial Coin Offerings (ICOs) and Security Token Offerings (STOs) has allowed startups and companies to raise capital in novel ways, often bypassing traditional venture capital routes.

As an investment class, cryptocurrencies have attracted both institutional and retail investors. The potential for high returns, coupled with increased mainstream adoption, has made digital assets a desirable addition to investment portfolios. For instance, Bitcoin and Ethereum have become major investment assets, with their performance often seen as a barometer for the broader cryptocurrency market. The growth of cryptocurrency-related financial products, such as Bitcoin ETFs and futures contracts, has also provided traditional investors with easier access to digital assets, further integrating them into the global financial landscape.

Cryptocurrencies are increasingly used for cross-border transactions and remittances, offering a faster, more cost-effective alternative to traditional banking systems. Digital currencies enable near-instantaneous transfers across borders without the need for intermediaries, significantly reducing transaction fees and processing times. This capability is particularly beneficial in regions with limited banking infrastructure or high remittance costs. For example, cryptocurrency-based remittance services have become popular in parts of Africa and Latin America, where traditional financial systems often impose high fees and delays.

The ability to conduct transactions in cryptocurrencies also provides an alternative for people in countries with unstable currencies or economic crises. In Venezuela and Argentina, for instance, individuals have turned to cryptocurrencies to preserve value and facilitate transactions amid hyperinflation and economic instability. This adaptability underscores the potential of digital currencies to offer financial stability and accessibility in challenging economic environments.

Central Bank Digital Currencies (CBDCs) represent a significant development in the integration of cryptocurrencies into the global economy. Unlike decentralized cryptocurrencies, CBDCs are issued and regulated by central banks, combining the benefits of digital currencies with the stability and oversight of traditional financial institutions. Many countries are exploring or actively developing CBDCs as a way to modernize their monetary systems, improve payment efficiency, and enhance financial inclusion.

CBDCs could reshape the global financial system by providing a government-backed digital alternative to private cryptocurrencies. They promise to offer faster, more secure transactions and could potentially reduce the reliance on cash. However, the implementation of CBDCs also raises concerns about privacy, cybersecurity, and the potential impact on traditional banking systems. As central banks navigate these challenges, the development and adoption of CBDCs will likely play a crucial role in shaping the future of the global financial ecosystem.

The growth of cryptocurrencies has prompted increased regulatory scrutiny as governments seek to balance innovation with risk management. Regulatory frameworks are evolving to address concerns related to market stability, consumer protection, and anti-money laundering. As regulations become more defined, they will influence the development and adoption of cryptocurrencies, impacting how they are integrated into the global economy.

Moreover, the economic implications of cryptocurrencies extend to their impact on traditional financial institutions and monetary policies. The rise of digital assets has prompted banks and financial institutions to explore blockchain technology and digital currencies as a means of enhancing their services and operational efficiency. Additionally, the decentralized nature of cryptocurrencies challenges traditional economic models, particularly in areas such as monetary policy and financial stability.

In summary, cryptocurrencies are playing an increasingly prominent role in the global economy, driving financial innovation, facilitating cross-border transactions, and prompting the development of CBDCs. As the landscape continues to evolve, the integration of digital assets into the global financial system will have far-reaching implications for investment strategies, regulatory frameworks, and economic stability.

Technological Advancements and Innovations

Cryptocurrencies, despite their revolutionary promise, have often fallen short of their potential for many users. Issues such as market volatility, regulatory uncertainty, and security concerns have overshadowed the initial excitement surrounding digital assets. Global institutions like the International Monetary Fund (IMF) and the Financial Stability Board have called for tighter regulations to address these issues and mitigate potential risks. This heightened scrutiny reflects the broader need for a more robust framework to ensure the stability and integrity of the financial system as it integrates with new technologies [294].

However, the technology underlying cryptocurrencies has advanced rapidly and may hold significant promise for the future. Innovations such as tokenization, encryption, and programmability have the potential to transform financial services by enhancing efficiency, security, and functionality. Tokenization involves representing property rights to an asset, like money, on a digital ledger. This ledger is maintained by all participants in the market, making it widely accessible, synchronized, and tamper-proof. While anonymity in transactions is not a requirement and can even undermine financial integrity, tokenization offers a way to digitally manage and transfer assets more securely and transparently [294].

Encryption is another critical technological advancement, enabling a separation between compliance checks and transactions. By ensuring that only authorized parties can access sensitive information, encryption fosters transparency while maintaining trust. This technology supports the integrity of financial transactions and helps prevent unauthorized access or tampering [294].

Programmability, which includes the use of "smart contracts," allows for the automation of financial contracts without relying on intermediaries. These smart contracts can automatically execute agreements based on predefined conditions, reducing the need for trusted third parties and streamlining transactions. This capability could greatly enhance the efficiency of financial operations and reduce the potential for disputes [294].

The private sector has been at the forefront of leveraging these technological advancements. Innovations such as the tokenization of financial assets (stocks, bonds, etc.) promise to reduce trading costs, integrate markets, and expand access to various financial products. For example, stablecoins, which are digital currencies pegged to traditional assets like the U.S. dollar, can facilitate transactions within this tokenized ecosystem, provided they comply with regulatory standards. Furthermore, banks are experimenting with tokenized checking accounts, and automation technologies are enabling developers to create sophisticated financial applications similar to smartphone apps [294].

Despite these advancements, the private sector alone may not ensure that transactions are universally safe, efficient, and interoperable. Private networks for trading assets and making payments might emerge, but they could lack standardization and investment. Open ledgers might attempt to bridge these private networks, but they may not achieve widespread adoption or profitability. The risk of using private forms of money for transactions could also pose challenges for counterparties involved [294].

Central Bank Digital Currencies (CBDCs) offer a potential solution by serving as both a monetary instrument and essential infrastructure for clearing and settling transactions. CBDCs can provide safety and liquidity in payments, while also offering a platform for interoperability among different digital money networks and assets. CBDCs could enable transactions between different types of private money, facilitate escrow and conditional payments, and support basic programming for smart contracts. This dual function of CBDCs as both a currency and a technological platform could help integrate and streamline various digital financial systems [294].

Cross-border payments, in particular, could benefit from this vision. A public platform for trading digital representations of central bank reserves across borders could simplify international transactions without requiring significant changes to existing national payment systems. This platform could manage risk-sharing, currency exchange, and liquidity more effectively, leveraging the advantages of single ledger technology and programmability to ensure smooth and secure transactions. Encryption would also play a role in managing information transfer and compliance with regulations, while maintaining anonymity in certain aspects of the transaction process [294].

Overall, while cryptocurrencies were initially driven by a desire to circumvent traditional intermediaries and public oversight, their underlying technology offers valuable insights for improving financial infrastructure. By harnessing these advancements, the public sector can enhance the efficiency, safety, and interoperability of financial systems. The ongoing exploration and development of these technologies could ultimately bridge the gap between private sector innovation and public sector regulation, contributing to a more robust and equitable digital financial ecosystem.

Chapter Twelve

Cryptocurrency Mining

Cryptocurrency mining is a fundamental process in which transactions are validated and added to a blockchain ledger—a decentralized and distributed database. This process involves solving complex mathematical problems to ensure the security and integrity of the cryptocurrency network. Here's a detailed look at how mining works:

The primary goals of cryptocurrency mining are threefold. First, it serves to verify transactions by ensuring that they adhere to network rules and standards. Second, once verified, these transactions are organized into blocks and added to the blockchain, a public ledger that records all transactions. Third, mining often generates new units of cryptocurrency, offering rewards to participants and providing an incentive for continued involvement in the mining process.

In systems using Proof of Work (PoW), miners employ computational power to tackle cryptographic puzzles. These puzzles are designed to be challenging to solve but straightforward to verify. When a miner successfully solves a puzzle, they create a new block of transactions which is then broadcast to the network. Other miners and network participants verify this block and its transactions. Once confirmed, the block is added to the blockchain, and the miner who solved the puzzle is rewarded with newly minted cryptocurrency and transaction fees from the transactions included in the block.

Alternative consensus mechanisms, such as Proof of Stake (PoS), offer a different approach. In PoS, validators, or "stakers," are selected to create new blocks based on the number of coins they hold and are willing to "stake" as collateral. This method reduces the need for extensive computational power. Other models, like Delegated Proof of Stake

(DPoS) and Proof of Authority (PoA), provide additional variations in how transactions are validated and new blocks are created.

The tools used for mining have evolved significantly. Initially, cryptocurrency mining was conducted using standard computer processors (CPUs), but this method is now largely obsolete due to its inefficiency. Graphics Processing Units (GPUs) offer better performance and are widely used for mining various cryptocurrencies. Application-Specific Integrated Circuits (ASICs) are specialized hardware designed specifically for mining, offering high efficiency and performance, though they are typically used for specific cryptocurrencies like Bitcoin. Mining rigs, which are custom-built systems combining multiple GPUs or ASICs, enhance mining capacity and efficiency.

Mining presents several challenges. The energy consumption associated with mining, especially in PoW systems, can be substantial, leading to significant electricity use and environmental concerns. The difficulty of mining puzzles adjusts over time to ensure that new blocks are added at a consistent rate, which helps maintain network stability and security but can affect mining profitability. Additionally, mining power may become concentrated in a few large operations or mining pools, potentially leading to centralization and reduced network decentralization.

To address some of these challenges, individual miners often join mining pools. By combining their computational resources, miners can increase their chances of successfully mining a block and share the rewards proportionally. This approach reduces the variance in rewards and allows for more frequent payouts, as the pool distributes rewards based on the amount of work contributed by each participant.

Mining can be economically rewarding, particularly when managed efficiently with access to low-cost electricity and advanced hardware. However, the energy consumption associated with mining has sparked discussions about its environmental impact and the need for more sustainable practices. This has led to calls for the adoption of more energy-efficient consensus mechanisms.

Cryptocurrency mining plays a crucial role in many blockchain networks by validating transactions and creating new cryptocurrency units. While it is essential for the security and operation of decentralized networks, it also poses challenges related to energy use and centralization.

A variety of cryptocurrencies can be mined, each with different algorithms, mining processes, and requirements. Here's a rundown of some of the most notable ones:

1. Bitcoin (BTC)

Algorithm: SHA-256

Description: Bitcoin is the first and most well-known cryptocurrency. It uses the SHA-256 hashing algorithm, and mining it requires substantial computational power. ASIC (Application-Specific Integrated Circuit) miners are typically used for Bitcoin mining due to their high efficiency.

2. Ethereum (ETH) ***(Note: Ethereum is transitioning from Proof of Work to Proof of Stake)***

Algorithm: Ethash

Description: Ethereum uses the Ethash algorithm, which is designed to be ASIC-resistant and more accessible to GPU (Graphics Processing Unit) miners. However, Ethereum has been transitioning to a Proof of Stake (PoS) consensus mechanism with Ethereum 2.0, which will eventually phase out mining.

3. Litecoin (LTC)

Algorithm: Scrypt

Description: Litecoin is often considered the silver to Bitcoin's gold. It uses the Scrypt algorithm, which allows for both ASIC and GPU mining. Litecoin is known for its faster block generation times compared to Bitcoin.

4. Bitcoin Cash (BCH)

Algorithm: SHA-256

Description: A fork of Bitcoin, Bitcoin Cash also uses the SHA-256 algorithm, making it compatible with Bitcoin mining hardware. It was created to address Bitcoin's scalability issues by increasing block size.

5. Monero (XMR)

Algorithm: RandomX

Description: Monero focuses on privacy and anonymity. It uses the RandomX algorithm, which is optimized for CPU mining. Monero's mining algorithm is designed to be resistant to ASICs, allowing for more decentralized mining.

6. Dash (DASH)

Algorithm: X11

Description: Dash uses the X11 algorithm, which is a combination of eleven different hashing functions. This approach provides enhanced security and is designed to be ASIC-resistant. Dash offers features like faster transactions and privacy options.

7. Zcash (ZEC)

Algorithm: Equihash

Description: Zcash is known for its privacy-focused features, using the Equihash algorithm. It allows miners to use GPUs for mining, though ASIC miners have also been developed for this cryptocurrency.

8. Ravencoin (RVN)

Algorithm: KawPow

Description: Ravencoin uses the KawPow algorithm, a modified version of ProgPoW, designed to be ASIC-resistant and favor GPU mining. It focuses on asset transfer and creation on its blockchain.

9. Grin (GRIN)

Algorithm: Cuckoo Cycle

Description: Grin is a privacy-oriented cryptocurrency that uses the Cuckoo Cycle algorithm. It is designed to be ASIC-resistant and can be mined using GPUs.

10. Horizen (ZEN)

Algorithm: Equihash

Description: Horizen, formerly known as ZenCash, uses the Equihash algorithm. It emphasizes privacy and scalability and can be mined using GPUs or specialized ASICs.

11. Firo (formerly Zcoin) (FIRO)

Algorithm: MTP (Merkle Tree Proof)

Description: Firo uses the MTP algorithm, which is designed to be ASIC-resistant and favor CPU and GPU mining. It focuses on privacy and decentralized governance.

12. Dogecoin (DOGE)

Algorithm: Scrypt

Description: Originally created as a meme coin, Dogecoin uses the Scrypt algorithm, similar to Litecoin. It can be mined with both ASICs and GPUs.

13. Siacoin (SC)

Algorithm: Blake2b

Description: Siacoin uses the Blake2b algorithm. It is a blockchain-based decentralized storage platform that allows users to rent out their unused hard drive space.

14. Bea (BEA)

Algorithm: CryptoNight

Description: Bea is a newer cryptocurrency utilizing the CryptoNight algorithm, which is optimized for CPU mining. It focuses on privacy and decentralization.

15. Vertcoin (VTC)

Algorithm: Lyra2REv3

Description: Vertcoin is designed to be ASIC-resistant and promotes decentralization. It uses the Lyra2REv3 algorithm, which is suitable for GPU mining.

These cryptocurrencies vary widely in their mining algorithms, hardware requirements, and overall goals. The choice of which cryptocurrency to mine often depends on factors such as the miner's available resources, electricity costs, and the specific goals of the mining operation.

The Economics of Mining

Cryptocurrency mining involves several costs that can significantly impact its overall profitability. These costs can be categorized into hardware expenses, energy consumption, cooling requirements, maintenance and repair needs, and transaction fees [295].

Hardware Costs: One of the major expenses in cryptocurrency mining is the cost of specialized hardware, such as Application-Specific Integrated Circuits (ASICs). ASICs are custom-built devices designed specifically for mining certain cryptocurrencies, offering high performance and efficiency. However, these devices can be expensive, and their cost can greatly influence the profitability of mining operations. Additionally, as mining technology advances, older hardware may become less efficient or obsolete, necessitating further investment in updated equipment [295].

Energy Expenses: Energy consumption is another significant cost associated with mining. Mining operations require a substantial amount of electricity to power the computing equipment, particularly in Proof of Work (PoW) systems. The energy required to run and cool the hardware can be substantial, and the cost of electricity in a particular region can greatly affect mining profitability. Regions with lower energy costs are often more attractive for mining operations, as lower electricity prices can help offset the overall expenses and enhance profitability [295].

Cooling Costs: Mining equipment generates a considerable amount of heat during operation, necessitating effective cooling solutions to prevent overheating and maintain optimal performance. Cooling costs can be considerable, especially in large-scale mining operations or in regions with higher ambient temperatures. Effective cooling solutions may include air conditioning systems, industrial fans, or specialized cooling units, all of which add to the operational expenses of a mining setup [295].

Maintenance and Repair Costs: Maintaining and repairing mining equipment is essential to ensure its continued efficiency and longevity. Over time, components may wear out or malfunction, requiring repairs or replacements. Regular maintenance, such as cleaning, monitoring performance, and replacing parts, is crucial to keeping the mining equipment in good working condition. These ongoing maintenance and repair costs can accumulate and impact the overall profitability of mining operations [295].

Transaction Fees: In addition to block rewards, miners can also earn transaction fees for processing network transactions. The level of transaction fees can vary depending on network activity and demand for transaction processing. During periods of high transaction volume, fees can increase, potentially enhancing mining profitability. Conversely, during times of lower network activity, transaction fees may decrease, which could negatively affect the profitability of mining. Thus, fluctuations in transaction fees, along with other factors, can influence the financial outcomes of mining activities [295].

As such, cryptocurrency mining involves various costs, including hardware expenses, energy consumption, cooling needs, maintenance and repairs, and transaction fees. Each of these factors plays a crucial role in determining the overall profitability of mining operations, and careful management of these costs is essential for maintaining a successful and sustainable mining venture.

Cryptocurrency mining revenue is primarily determined by the amount of cryptocurrency a miner can produce over a specific period and the current market price of that cryptocurrency. To calculate mining revenue, the total amount of cryptocurrency mined is multiplied by its market price. This calculation gives an estimate of the revenue a miner can generate from their mining activities [295].

For instance, let's consider a scenario where a miner uses specialized equipment to mine Bitcoin (BTC) and is able to produce 1 BTC every 10 days. If the market price of BTC is $50,000, the revenue from mining one BTC would be $50,000. This straightforward calculation provides a clear view of the gross revenue potential from mining activities [295].

However, several factors influence the actual revenue a miner can realize. Firstly, the market price of the cryptocurrency can fluctuate significantly. The value of BTC, for example, can rise or fall based on market conditions, affecting the revenue generated from mining. When the market price is high, the revenue increases, while a drop in price leads to reduced revenue [295].

Secondly, the difficulty of the mining process plays a crucial role in determining revenue. Mining difficulty refers to how challenging it is to solve the cryptographic puzzles required to validate transactions and add them to the blockchain. As more miners join the network and mining technology advances, the difficulty of mining typically increases. This means that mining new blocks becomes more challenging and time-consuming, which can impact the rate at which cryptocurrency is produced and, consequently, the revenue generated [295].

Thirdly, the cost of electricity is a significant factor affecting mining revenue. Mining operations consume a large amount of power, and the price of electricity can vary by region. Higher electricity costs reduce the net profit from mining, as a significant portion of revenue must be spent on powering the mining equipment [295].

Lastly, the efficiency of the mining equipment used also influences revenue. Modern mining hardware, such as ASICs, offers higher performance and efficiency compared to older technologies. As mining complexity increases, more efficient equipment becomes necessary to maintain profitability. Early Bitcoin miners, for example, could generate substantial revenue with basic hardware. However, as the mining network grew and mining difficulty escalated, the revenue per unit of computing power declined. Miners had to invest in more advanced and expensive equipment to stay competitive and continue generating significant revenue [295].

Cryptocurrency mining revenue is determined by the amount of cryptocurrency mined and its market price, but is also influenced by mining difficulty, electricity costs, and the efficiency of the mining equipment. These variables can cause substantial fluctuations in revenue, making it essential for miners to consider all factors when evaluating the profitability of their mining operations.

Bitcoin Mining Economics

Understanding the financial dynamics of Bitcoin mining requires a detailed examination of the costs and revenue involved. Let's delve into a hypothetical example using data from June 2023 to illustrate these economic considerations [296].

Cost Assumptions

The cost of electricity, which is a significant factor in mining operations, is assumed to be $0.05 per kilowatt-hour (kWh). In addition to electricity, other costs such as mining pool fees, staffing, and internet expenses are estimated to account for 20% of the electricity cost. This comprehensive view helps in calculating the overall cost of mining Bitcoin [296].

Network and ASIC Assumptions

For this example, the network hash rate is set at 375 exahashes per second (EH/s), with a Bitcoin block reward of 6.25 BTC and an average transaction fee of 0.3125 BTC. The total daily revenue from mining is approximately 6.56 BTC, and the total number of Bitcoins issued per day is 945 BTC [296].

The mining hardware used in this example is the Antminer S19 XP, which has a hash rate of 140 terahashes per second (TH/s) and consumes 3,031 watts (W) of power. This model costs $4,600 and has a lifespan of 2.5 years [296].

Calculations and Analysis

To understand the economics, several calculations are necessary [296]:

1. **Hashes Required to Mine One Bitcoin**: The calculation for the number of hashes required to mine one Bitcoin is derived from the network hash rate, the number of seconds in a day, and the daily Bitcoin production. This results in approximately 34,000 EH (exahashes) per Bitcoin.

2. **Time Taken for an ASIC Miner to Mine One Bitcoin**: Using the network hash rate and the hash rate of the ASIC miner, the time required for one ASIC miner to mine a single Bitcoin is estimated to be around 7.7 years. This calculation converts exahashes to terahashes to account for the hardware's processing power.

3. **Capital Expenses (CapEx)**: Over its lifespan, the ASIC miner is expected to mine about 0.32 BTC. With the miner costing $4,600, the effective price per Bitcoin mined using this hardware is roughly $14,300.

4. **Operational Expenses (OpEx)**:

    - **Electricity Cost**: The electricity cost to mine one Bitcoin is calculated by multiplying the time required to mine by the power consumption and electricity cost, which totals approximately $10,200.

    - **Cooling and Overheads**: Cooling and other operational overheads, which are 20% of the electricity cost, amount to about $2,000.

Combining these expenses, the total cost of producing one Bitcoin is calculated to be around $26,500. This figure includes both capital and operational costs [296].

Profitability Comparison

To evaluate profitability, compare the cost of production with the market price of Bitcoin. In this scenario, the cost of mining one Bitcoin is $26,500, while buying one on the spot market costs approximately $26,600. This indicates that mining is almost breaking even under these conditions [296].

Considerations for Miners

The key question for miners is whether the cost of production is lower than purchasing Bitcoin directly from the market. For mining to be financially viable, the cost of production must be significantly lower than the market price. Given the current assumptions, small-scale miners may struggle with profitability, especially if hash rates and electricity costs are high. Conversely, large-scale miners, with access to more efficient equipment and potentially lower energy costs, may still find mining economically feasible [296].

Bitcoin mining economics involve balancing capital expenses, operational costs, and revenue against market prices. Detailed calculations and market comparisons are crucial for assessing whether mining operations are profitable under various conditions.

Bitcoin Mining

Bitcoin mining operates through a process that combines cryptography, distributed computing, and competitive guessing, all aimed at verifying and securing transactions on the Bitcoin network. To simplify, think of it like a game where participants are trying to guess a number. Here's a detailed breakdown of how Bitcoin mining works [297]:

The Guessing Game

Imagine you invite friends to play a guessing game where they need to guess a number between 1 and 100. In this game, the objective is not to guess the exact number but to be the first to guess a number that is less than or equal to a predetermined target number you have in mind. For example, if the target number is 19, and your friends guess numbers like 21, 55, and 83, they are not successful because their guesses are all higher than 19. However, if one of them guesses 16, they win because 16 is less than 19 and thus meets the target criteria. The process here illustrates the basic principle behind Bitcoin mining, where miners make multiple attempts to solve a problem to find a solution that meets certain criteria.

The Target Hash

In Bitcoin mining, the "target hash" is a crucial concept. This target hash represents a value that miners need to meet or exceed with their computational efforts. Each block in the Bitcoin blockchain requires a valid hash value that is below a certain target set by the network's difficulty level. The network adjusts this difficulty approximately every two weeks to ensure that blocks are mined at a consistent rate, roughly every ten minutes. Just as in the guessing game where the target is a specific number, the target hash in mining is a cryptographic value that miners aim to match with their computational guesses.

The Mining Process

Bitcoin mining involves solving complex mathematical puzzles through cryptographic hashing. Miners use their computational power to generate a hash value by continuously altering a piece of data called a "nonce" in the block header. They repeatedly hash this data until they find a hash value that is below the target hash set by the network. This process requires immense computational resources because miners are essentially making rapid, successive guesses to find a valid hash. The first miner to discover a hash that meets the network's criteria is rewarded with newly minted Bitcoin and transaction fees from the transactions included in that block.

Distributed Computing

Bitcoin mining relies on a decentralized network of computers, known as nodes, to perform this hashing process. Each node works independently but follows the same protocol and rules. This decentralized approach ensures that no single entity has control over the network and helps maintain the security and integrity of the blockchain. The combined computational power of all miners contributes to the network's security by making it extremely difficult for any single participant to alter the blockchain.

Cryptographic Security

Cryptography plays a fundamental role in Bitcoin mining. The process involves hashing algorithms, such as SHA-256, which transform input data into a fixed-length hash value. The hash function is designed to be one-way, meaning it is easy to compute the hash from the input but infeasible to reverse-engineer the input from the hash. This cryptographic approach ensures that the data being processed is secure and tamper-proof, reinforcing the trustworthiness of the transactions being verified.

The Hash

At the core of Bitcoin mining lies the concept of a hash. A hash is a 64-digit hexadecimal number created by applying the SHA-256 hashing algorithm to the data contained in a block. This process involves running the block's information through the SHA-256 algorithm, which generates a unique fixed-size string of characters known as a hash. For instance, if you input data into an online SHA-256 hash generator, the output is a hash like a54f83a5db7371eeefa2287a0ede750ac623e49a8ba29f248eb785fe0a678559. The hashing process itself is extremely fast, taking less than a second to produce a hash. However, reversing this process—decrypting the hash to retrieve the original data—is computationally impractical with modern hardware, often taking centuries to accomplish [297].

Hashes are crucial in Bitcoin mining as they represent the encrypted output of the block's data. If you alter even a single character in the input data, the resulting hash will change drastically. For example, if you modify the first word of a paragraph from "At" to "Aa," the hash will be transformed from a54f83a5db7371eeefa2287a0ede750ac623e49a8ba29f248eb785fe0a678559 to fbfa33ff980d1492b3a9275a1eb945d89bd6b699ca19c3c470021b8f253654af. This illustrates how sensitive the hashing process is to any changes in the input data. In Bitcoin mining, each block contains a hash of the previous block, creating a secure and continuous chain of blocks known as the blockchain.

Target Hash

The target hash plays a central role in determining mining difficulty. It is essentially a number that miners are competing to solve. This target hash is a compact representation of the mining difficulty, generated by the Bitcoin network. For example, a block hash might appear as 0000000000000000005a849c28eb24b8a5e04fcecc1ccb3eb2998e4730a456e, while the target hash could be represented in a more compact form like 0x175c739.

The target hash is a compacted version of the difficulty target and represents a number that miners must meet or exceed with their generated hashes. In this representation, the number may look like 0...000005c73900000...0, indicating that miners need to find a hash value that is numerically less than or equal to this target. The difficulty of mining adjusts over time based on the network's computational power, ensuring that new blocks are mined at a consistent rate. Miners achieve this by repeatedly hashing different nonce values until they find one that produces a hash meeting or exceeding the target hash, which is a computationally intensive and resource-consuming task.

Mining

Bitcoin mining is a process that involves the generation of a hash using a mining program, where a key component is the nonce, or "number used once." This nonce is a value that miners append to the data they are hashing in order to find a valid hash. The process begins with the nonce set to zero, and with each attempt, the nonce is incremented by one—starting from 0, then 1, 2, 3, and so on. The goal is to find a hash value that, when combined with the nonce, meets the difficulty target set by the network [297].

When a miner performs this task, the hash they produce, combined with the nonce, must be less than or equal to the target hash specified by the Bitcoin network. If the resulting hash is greater than the target hash, the attempt is considered unsuccessful, and the miner increments the nonce to try a different hash. This process is repeated continuously until a valid hash is found. The first miner to discover a valid hash that meets the target criteria has their proposed block added to the blockchain. This miner is then rewarded with newly minted bitcoins and transaction fees from the transactions included in the block.

Once a block is added to the blockchain, it contains new transactions, and the mining process starts anew with the next block. Each block has a maximum size of about one megabyte, and once it is filled with transactions, it is closed, encrypted, and mined in the same way. The continuous mining operation is essential for maintaining the blockchain, as it ensures that transactions are validated and added to the ledger.

The Bitcoin network operates around the clock with thousands of mining devices competing to solve these cryptographic puzzles. The first miner to successfully solve the puzzle and meet the target hash gets to add the block to the chain and receive the reward. To enhance their chances, miners often form mining pools, where they combine their computational power to increase their likelihood of winning the block reward. This pooled approach allows them to share rewards proportionally to their contributed processing power, making it more feasible to compete in the highly competitive mining landscape.

The Bitcoin network's mining rate, or hash rate, reflects the combined computational power of all miners. As of July 3, 2024, the network hash rate averaged slightly more than 578 exahashes per second (EH/s), which is 578 followed by 18 zeros. Given that it takes approximately 10 minutes to mine a new block, this implies an enormous number of hash attempts are made to find the correct nonce—about 3.4×10^{23} hashes for each block. This immense computational effort underscores the significant resources required for Bitcoin mining and the high level of competition within the network [297].

Proof-of-Work

The concept of Proof-of-Work (PoW) is fundamental to Bitcoin mining and serves as both a validation mechanism and a security feature. In PoW, the term "work" refers to the computational effort required to generate a valid hash that meets the Bitcoin network's difficulty target. This hash generation process acts as proof that the miner has expended sufficient computational resources to validate the transactions included in the block. Therefore, the term "Proof-of-Work" signifies that the computational effort, or "work," proves the validity of the transactions and the miner's contribution to maintaining the blockchain [297].

While PoW is often described as a consensus mechanism, it is only one part of the broader consensus process. Consensus in the Bitcoin network is achieved when a miner successfully adds a new block to the blockchain, which is then verified by other nodes in the network. These nodes check the validity of the block by verifying the hashes and ensuring that the transactions meet the network's rules. This verification process, however, does not require substantial energy or computational power, as it is performed by each node in parallel while mining the subsequent block. As new blocks are continually added, they are confirmed through this network-wide validation, ensuring that the blockchain remains accurate and secure.

Confirmation

Once a block is mined, it is not immediately confirmed. A block is considered confirmed after it has been incorporated into the blockchain and validated through multiple subsequent blocks. Specifically, a block is typically regarded as confirmed once it has been followed by six additional blocks, making a total of six confirmations. This process is critical because it enhances the security of the blockchain. If a block's information were to be altered before reaching six confirmations, it would require an impractically large amount of computational power to redo the proof-of-work for the altered block and all subsequent blocks, making such alterations highly unlikely.

Each block in the Bitcoin blockchain contains the hash of the previous block, which creates a chain of blocks. When a new block is mined, its hash includes the hash of the previous block, linking the blocks together. This linkage is crucial because even a small change in the data of a block will cause its hash to change drastically, which would disrupt the entire chain. This characteristic of block hashing ensures that once a block is confirmed, it is extremely difficult to alter any information within it without changing all subsequent blocks.

Rewards

Miners are incentivized to participate in the Bitcoin network through block rewards and transaction fees. Initially, in 2009, the reward for mining a block was 50 bitcoins. This reward undergoes a halving event approximately every four years or every 210,000 blocks. Halving reduces the block reward by half, making mining progressively less profitable but also reducing the rate at which new bitcoins are created. As of April 2024, the block reward is 3.125 bitcoins [297].

In addition to block rewards, miners also earn transaction fees from the transactions included in the blocks they mine. These fees are paid by users to incentivize miners to include their transactions in the block. As the total supply of Bitcoin approaches its cap of 21 million—expected around 2140—the block reward will eventually phase out, leaving transaction fees as the primary incentive for miners. This fee-based system ensures that miners remain motivated to secure and validate transactions even after the block reward ends.

Difficulty

Mining difficulty measures how challenging it is to find a hash that meets the network's target. Difficulty is adjusted approximately every two weeks or every 2,016 blocks, based on the network's hash rate and the time taken to mine the previous set of blocks. If miners are solving blocks too quickly, the difficulty increases to maintain the average block time at about 10 minutes. Conversely, if mining becomes less efficient or if miners leave the network, the difficulty decreases to make mining easier.

On May 1, 2024, the mining difficulty was set at approximately 83.7 trillion. This means that the probability of generating a hash below the target hash is 1 in 83.7 trillion. To illustrate the enormity of this figure, it's about 286,000 times less likely than winning the Powerball Grand Prize with a single ticket. This high difficulty level reflects the substantial computational power required to mine Bitcoin and underscores the competitive nature of the mining process [297].

Setting Up a Bitcoin Mining Operation

Setting up a Bitcoin mining operation involves several key resources and considerations to ensure effective and profitable mining [296].

Hardware Requirements: At the core of Bitcoin mining is the specialized computer known as an Application-Specific Integrated Circuit (ASIC) miner. These devices are designed specifically for mining cryptocurrencies, and they offer significant computational power compared to general-purpose computers. For Bitcoin, ASIC miners are essential because of their ability to process billions of hashes per second. Popular models from manufacturers like Bitmain and Whatsminer can cost between $3,000 to $5,000 for the latest versions. Older, second-hand models are available at lower prices but may be less efficient. The choice of ASIC miner affects the efficiency of the operation, with newer models typically providing higher hash rates and better energy efficiency [296].

Energy Supply: Electricity is a crucial component in Bitcoin mining, as miners need to run their ASIC equipment continuously. The cost of electricity directly impacts profitability, making it essential to secure a reliable and inexpensive power source. Power costs are a significant consideration; for many miners, finding low-cost electricity is a top priority. The efficiency of mining operations often depends on the local electricity rates, which can vary widely by region. In recent years, mining operations have migrated to areas with cheaper electricity, such as parts of the United States, Canada, and Russia, due to higher electricity costs elsewhere.

Internet Connection: A stable and fast internet connection is necessary to ensure that the mining equipment remains connected to the Bitcoin network. This connectivity is crucial for both submitting mining results and receiving updates from the network. The internet connection must be reliable to prevent disruptions that could hinder mining efforts or lead to potential losses.

Cooling Infrastructure: ASIC miners generate a substantial amount of heat during operation, making cooling systems essential. Proper cooling infrastructure, whether through air conditioning or specialized cooling systems, is necessary to maintain optimal operating temperatures and prevent overheating. In home setups, this might involve using additional fans or air conditioning units, while large-scale mining farms often use more advanced cooling solutions.

Operational Management: Setting up a mining operation also involves the logistical aspects of housing the equipment and ensuring its maintenance. This includes managing the physical space where the mining occurs, whether at home or in a larger warehouse. For industrial-scale operations, this can involve multiple warehouses equipped with extensive cooling and power management systems. Additionally, staffing may be required if the operation is large-scale and requires ongoing management.

Mining Pools and Revenue: Many individual miners join mining pools to increase their chances of successfully mining a block. Pools combine the computing power of multiple miners and distribute rewards based on each participant's contribution to the mining effort. Revenue for miners includes the block reward (which halves approximately every four years) and transaction fees. As of June 2023, transaction fees have averaged about 0.31 BTC per block, representing roughly 5% of the block reward. The combined revenue from block rewards and transaction fees provides the incentive for miners to maintain their operations [296].

Setting Up an ASIC Miner

Setting up an ASIC miner involves several important steps to ensure that the equipment operates efficiently and effectively. Here's a detailed guide on the process [298]:

1. Preparation is Key

Before setting up your ASIC miner, preparation is crucial to ensure a smooth installation. Begin by assessing your environment to meet the miner's requirements. Ensure you have a stable internet connection, as continuous online connectivity is essential for mining operations. Additionally, designate a dedicated electrical circuit to handle the power demands of the miner. ASIC miners can consume substantial electricity and generate a lot of heat, so a cool and well-ventilated area is necessary to prevent overheating and ensure the equipment runs optimally. Proper preparation will help avoid potential issues related to power supply, internet connectivity, and cooling.

2. Choosing the Right Hardware

Selecting the appropriate ASIC miner is a key decision that impacts your mining efficiency and overall costs. Several manufacturers, such as Bitmain, EBANG, and INNOSILICON, offer various models with different capabilities and price points. When choosing your hardware, consider factors like hash rate, energy consumption, and cost to ensure that the miner aligns with your budget and mining goals. It is also important to purchase from reputable sources to avoid counterfeit or substandard products, which can affect performance and durability. Researching and comparing different models will help you make an informed decision based on your specific needs.

3. Setting Up the Hardware

Once you have your ASIC miner, the physical setup involves several steps:

- **Connecting to Power Supply:** Start by connecting the ASIC miner to a power supply unit (PSU). Ensure that all connections are secure to avoid any electrical issues. The miner will typically have specific power requirements, so use a PSU that matches these requirements.

- **Power Connection:** Plug the power supply into a mains outlet, which is commonly required for ASIC miners. Some models might feature a power switch, so check the manufacturer's instructions for specific details. Ensure the power source is stable to prevent disruptions in mining operations.

4. Connecting to the Internet

A stable internet connection is crucial for mining operations. Use a CAT5 or CAT6 Ethernet cable to connect your ASIC miner directly to your router or network switch. While Wi-Fi adapters can be used, a wired connection is recommended for greater stability and reliability. Ensure that the cable is securely plugged in to avoid connectivity issues.

5. Configuring the Miner

To configure your ASIC miner, follow these steps:

- **Access Router Configuration:** Log in to your router's configuration menu to locate the miner's IP address. This is usually found in the list of connected devices.

- **Miner Interface:** Enter the IP address into a web browser to access the miner's configuration interface. You will be prompted to log in using default credentials, which are typically provided in the miner's manual or setup guide.

- **Configuration Settings:** Once logged in, configure your mining pool settings and wallet address. This involves entering details such as the pool's URL and your wallet address where mined coins will be sent. Follow the instructions provided by your mining pool and the miner's manufacturer for accurate configuration.

6. Joining a Mining Pool

Mining pools are essential for increasing your chances of successfully mining blocks by combining computational power with other miners. To join a mining pool, select a reputable pool such as Slushpool, F2Pool, or BTC.com. Sign up for an account with the chosen pool and follow their specific instructions to integrate your ASIC miner. Pool membership often involves entering the pool's server address and your mining credentials into the miner's configuration settings.

7. Monitoring and Maintenance

Ongoing monitoring and maintenance are crucial for the longevity and efficiency of your ASIC miner:

- **Performance Monitoring:** Regularly check the miner's performance to ensure it is running efficiently and not overheating. Many miners come with built-in monitoring tools that provide real-time statistics on hash rate, temperature, and other performance metrics.

- **Maintenance:** Periodically clean the device to remove dust and debris, which can obstruct ventilation and impact cooling. Ensure that the cooling fans and vents are functioning properly to maintain optimal operating temperatures. Regular maintenance helps prevent hardware failures and ensures consistent mining performance.

Figure 17: Antminer ASIC Miner. Steve Rainwater from Irving, US, CC BY-SA 2.0, via Wikimedia Commons.

Mining Pools and Solo Mining

In the cryptocurrency community, solo mining and pool mining represent two distinct approaches to mining digital assets, each with its own advantages and challenges. Understanding both methods is crucial for anyone considering involvement in cryptocurrency mining [299].

Solo mining refers to the process where an individual miner conducts and executes the mining process independently. This involves setting up and running mining hardware without relying on any third-party services or mining pools. Solo miners connect their mining machines directly to the cryptocurrency network and attempt to solve cryptographic puzzles to discover new blocks. If successful, the miner receives the entire block reward and transaction fees associated with the block [299].

Historically, solo mining was more feasible due to lower network difficulty and hardware requirements. However, as the complexity of mining algorithms increased and the total network hash rate grew, solo mining became increasingly challenging. Today, the profitability of solo mining is heavily dependent on the miner's hardware power and the current network difficulty. Solo miners must possess significant computational power to compete effectively. While the potential rewards can be substantial, they are infrequent and unpredictable, leading to considerable risk [299].

The essence of solo mining lies in its independence and self-sufficiency. The process begins with selecting a cryptocurrency to mine. Miners need to invest in high-performance hardware capable of solving complex mathematical puzzles. Initially, CPUs were used for mining, but as network difficulty escalated, GPUs, FPGAs, and ASICs became more prevalent due to their superior processing capabilities.

Miners must also set up a compatible digital wallet to receive and store their mined coins. A reliable and fast internet connection is necessary to stay connected to the cryptocurrency network. The mining process itself involves running mining software that connects the hardware to the network, enabling the miner to attempt to solve cryptographic puzzles. Success in solo mining depends on the computational power of the hardware and the current network difficulty, which can vary significantly [299].

To embark on solo mining, miners require robust hardware capable of handling complex calculations. Over time, the industry has evolved from using CPUs to more advanced options such as GPUs, FPGAs, and ASICs. Each type of hardware has its advantages and is suited to different cryptocurrencies. For example, ASIC miners are particularly effective for Bitcoin mining due to their specialized design [299].

In addition to hardware, miners need a digital wallet for storing mined coins and a reliable internet connection to maintain network connectivity. The setup also involves installing and configuring mining software that is compatible with the chosen cryptocurrency. Regular maintenance and monitoring are essential to ensure the mining operation runs smoothly and remains profitable.

Pool mining is a collaborative approach where multiple miners combine their computational power to increase their chances of successfully mining a block. By pooling their resources, miners can collectively solve cryptographic puzzles faster and more efficiently than they could individually. When a pool successfully mines a block, the rewards are distributed among the participants based on their contribution to the pool's efforts.

Pool mining offers several advantages, such as a more consistent and predictable income stream. This is because rewards are shared among pool members, reducing the risk of long periods without payouts. Pool mining also allows miners to leverage collective computing power, making it possible to mine cryptocurrencies with higher network difficulties than would be feasible for individual miners.

Solo mining offers several potential benefits [299]:

- **Full Reward Ownership:** The primary advantage is that solo miners receive the entire block reward and transaction fees when they successfully mine a block. This can lead to significant earnings if the miner is fortunate enough to find a block.

- **Minimal Interference:** Solo miners are less likely to experience interruptions from pool outages or other external factors that can affect mining operations.

- **No Pool Fees:** Solo miners avoid the fees charged by mining pools, potentially increasing their overall profitability.

- **Higher Long-Term Yields:** Over time, solo miners might see higher returns compared to pool mining, especially if they can sustain their operation and consistently find blocks.

Despite its potential rewards, solo mining comes with notable drawbacks [299]:

- **High Capital Requirements:** Setting up a solo mining operation requires substantial investment in hardware and infrastructure.

- **Risk of No Reward:** The chances of not finding a block for an extended period are high, leading to potential losses of investment.

- **Limited Computational Power:** Competing with large mining pools is challenging, as individual miners may lack the computational power to solve blocks efficiently.

- **Income Variability:** Earnings from solo mining can be irregular and unpredictable, with potential for long periods of zero rewards.

Pool mining also has its advantages [299]:

- **Steady Income:** Pool mining provides a more stable and predictable income stream, as rewards are distributed regularly among members.

- **Increased Mining Efficiency:** By combining resources, mining pools can tackle more complex cryptographic puzzles and mine higher-difficulty cryptocurrencies.

- **Flexibility:** Pool mining allows miners to switch between different cryptocurrencies, optimizing their efforts based on market conditions and mining profitability.

However, pool mining has its challenges [299]:

1. **External Risks:** Pools can be vulnerable to external attacks or technical issues, which can affect the mining process and reward distribution.

2. **Pool Fees:** Most mining pools charge a fee for their services, which can reduce overall earnings.

3. **Lower Rewards:** Since rewards are shared among pool members, individual payouts are typically lower than if a miner were to succeed solo.

4. **Security Risks:** Pools store substantial amounts of cryptocurrency, making them targets for attackers.

Strategies for Successful Solo Mining

To maximize the chances of success in solo mining, several strategies can be employed [299]:

- **Optimize Hardware:** Invest in high-performance mining hardware and keep it updated to maintain competitive performance.
- **Configure Software:** Use mining software that is optimized for your hardware and the cryptocurrency you are mining. Proper configuration can enhance efficiency.
- **Stay Informed:** Keep up with advancements in mining technology and trends to ensure your setup remains competitive.

Security Measures: Implement robust security practices, including strong passwords, two-factor authentication, and secure wallet storage, to protect your assets.

Monitoring and Management: Regularly monitor your mining operation's performance and adjust based on network difficulty and market conditions. Joining mining communities can provide valuable support and insights.

Solo Mining vs. Pool Mining

Choosing between solo and pool mining depends on several factors, including financial capacity, hardware capability, and risk tolerance. Solo mining offers the potential for high rewards but comes with significant risks and requires substantial investment. Pool mining provides more consistent earnings and reduces individual risk but involves sharing rewards and fees with other miners.

Both solo and pool mining have their merits and drawbacks. Solo mining might be appealing for those with significant resources and a high risk tolerance, while pool mining is often preferred for its stability and reduced individual risk.

Analysing Capital Requirement and Profitability of Solo Mining

Solo mining involves a substantial capital investment due to the high costs associated with setting up and maintaining a mining operation. For a solo miner aiming to mine on a Bitcoin network with a high hash rate, such as 1 petahash per second (1 PH/s), the capital requirements are significant. Setting up a mining farm capable of supporting this level of hash rate typically costs around $200,000. This estimate covers the hardware, such as ASIC miners, but does not include ongoing expenses like electricity and maintenance.

Given the increasing complexity of mining networks, the initial investment is only part of the total capital requirement [299].

The difficulty of mining Bitcoin, which is proportional to the network's hash rate, has risen dramatically over time. A miner with a capacity of $200,000 would face considerable challenges in finding a block. With current difficulty levels, it is estimated that it might take around 200 days of consistent mining work to successfully find a block and earn the associated reward of 12.5 Bitcoins. Although this reward is substantial, it is important to consider that Bitcoin's network difficulty is continually increasing. As complexity grows, miners will need to scale up their operations significantly, potentially requiring capital investments running into millions of dollars to maintain competitive mining power.

The Impact of New Technologies on Solo Mining

Technological advancements are continually shaping the field of cryptocurrency mining. Innovations such as more energy-efficient mining chips and the use of renewable energy sources are becoming more prominent. The trend towards sustainability is driven by environmental concerns and regulatory pressures, leading to a shift towards greener mining practices. Additionally, gamification of mining, which integrates mining activities into play-to-earn games and other interactive platforms, aims to make the process more accessible and appealing to a broader audience.

The evolution of mining technology also includes the increasing involvement of corporate entities, as companies in the mining industry explore public offerings to raise capital for expansion. This trend points to a more structured and professional approach to mining operations, which may impact solo mining viability [299].

Solo Mining and the Evolving Cryptocurrency Landscape

As technology progresses and sustainability becomes a central focus, the future of solo mining is influenced by several factors. The development of more efficient mining hardware and the adoption of green technologies suggest that solo mining could become both profitable and environmentally responsible. However, economic factors such as electricity costs and mining rig efficiency remain crucial for determining profitability. The transition from CPUs to ASICs underscores the importance of staying updated with technological advancements to remain competitive [299].

Moreover, the broader cryptocurrency ecosystem, including regulatory environments and the availability of inexpensive electricity, will impact solo mining's feasibility. New mining algorithms and networks may offer better rewards and lower energy consumption, influencing whether solo mining remains a viable option for individual miners in the future.

Mining Algorithms other than SHA-256

Mining Algorithms Overview: Scrypt, Ethash, RandomX, X11, Equihash, Blake2b, and Lyra2REv3

1. Scrypt

Scrypt is a memory-intensive proof-of-work (PoW) algorithm initially designed to be more resistant to ASIC (Application-Specific Integrated Circuit) mining compared to traditional algorithms like SHA-256. It was developed to address the limitations of earlier mining algorithms by requiring miners to use a significant amount of memory in addition to computational power. This approach is intended to level the playing field between CPU, GPU, and ASIC miners. Scrypt is used by several cryptocurrencies, with Litecoin being the most notable. The algorithm requires miners to perform memory-hard operations, which involves using a large amount of RAM, making it more challenging for ASICs to dominate mining.

Equipment Used to Mine Scrypt

Mining Scrypt-based cryptocurrencies, such as Litecoin, requires specific types of hardware that cater to the memory-intensive nature of the Scrypt algorithm. This algorithm was designed to be more resistant to ASIC mining compared to older algorithms, which initially allowed for a broader range of mining hardware. However, as Scrypt mining evolved, specialized equipment was developed to maximize efficiency. Here's a detailed look at the equipment used for Scrypt mining:

- **ASIC Miners:** Application-Specific Integrated Circuits (ASICs) are the most efficient hardware for mining Scrypt-based cryptocurrencies. ASIC miners are custom-built machines designed specifically for the Scrypt algorithm, offering significant advantages over traditional mining hardware in terms of processing power and energy efficiency. These devices are purpose-built to solve the complex cryptographic puzzles required by Scrypt, resulting in much higher hash rates compared to CPUs or GPUs. Popular models include the Antminer

L3+, which is well-regarded for its performance and energy efficiency in Scrypt mining.

- **GPUs:** Graphics Processing Units (GPUs) were historically the most popular choice for mining Scrypt-based cryptocurrencies before the advent of ASICs. GPUs offer a good balance between computational power and energy consumption, making them suitable for a range of mining tasks. While they are not as efficient as ASIC miners in terms of hash rate, GPUs are still used by hobbyists and small-scale miners who prefer more flexibility and the ability to mine different cryptocurrencies. Popular GPU models for mining include those from the NVIDIA GeForce and AMD Radeon series, which are capable of handling the memory-intensive nature of the Scrypt algorithm.

- **CPUs:** Central Processing Units (CPUs) are generally the least effective option for mining Scrypt-based cryptocurrencies due to their limited processing power and efficiency compared to GPUs and ASICs. While CPUs were once used for Scrypt mining, their lower hash rates and higher energy consumption make them less practical for serious mining operations today. CPUs may still be used by individual miners or for educational purposes, but they are not competitive with more specialized hardware.

- **Power Supply Units (PSUs):** Regardless of the mining hardware used, a reliable and sufficient power supply unit (PSU) is essential. Mining hardware requires a significant amount of power to operate effectively, and using a high-quality PSU ensures stable and continuous operation. For ASIC miners, PSUs with high wattage and efficiency ratings are necessary to support the hardware's power requirements. It is crucial to match the PSU's specifications with the needs of the mining equipment to prevent power-related issues and ensure optimal performance.

- **Cooling Solutions:** Mining hardware generates substantial heat during operation, which necessitates effective cooling solutions to maintain performance and prevent overheating. For ASIC miners, cooling systems typically include built-in fans, but additional external cooling solutions, such as air conditioners or dedicated cooling units, may be needed to manage temperatures in larger mining setups. Proper ventilation and temperature control are critical to extend the lifespan of the equipment and maintain efficient mining operations.

- **Racks and Shelving:** In larger mining operations, organizing and securing mining equipment is important for both operational efficiency and safety. Racks and shelving systems help to arrange ASIC miners, GPUs, and other components in a way that optimizes airflow and accessibility. Proper setup and organization can also aid in easier maintenance and troubleshooting.

- **Network Infrastructure:** A stable and fast internet connection is essential for mining operations to ensure constant communication with the cryptocurrency network. Mining hardware must be connected to the internet to receive and submit data, as well as to participate in the mining process. Reliable network infrastructure helps prevent downtime and ensures that mining operations are as efficient as possible.

2. Ethash

Ethash is the mining algorithm used by Ethereum and several other cryptocurrencies. It is designed to be ASIC-resistant and memory-hard, similar to Scrypt. Ethash requires miners to use a large amount of memory to store a dataset called the DAG (Directed Acyclic Graph). This dataset grows over time, increasing the memory requirements for mining. Ethash relies on a combination of hash functions to achieve a balance between computational efficiency and resistance to ASIC mining. It uses a two-step process involving hashing and random sampling, making it suitable for GPU mining while maintaining resistance to ASIC dominance.

Mining Ethash, the algorithm used by Ethereum and several other cryptocurrencies, typically requires specific types of equipment to be effective. Here's a detailed look at the equipment generally used for mining Ethash:

- **Graphics Processing Units (GPUs):** For the majority of Ethash mining operations, Graphics Processing Units (GPUs) are the primary hardware used. GPUs are favored for their ability to handle the parallel processing required by Ethash's hashing algorithm. Unlike CPUs, which process tasks sequentially, GPUs can manage multiple calculations simultaneously, making them well-suited for mining tasks. Popular GPU models from manufacturers like NVIDIA and AMD, such as the NVIDIA GeForce RTX series or AMD Radeon RX series, are commonly used. These GPUs are selected based on their hash rate (the speed at which they can solve mining algorithms), power consumption, and overall efficiency. For optimal performance, miners often use multiple GPUs in a single mining rig to increase hash power and profitability.

- **Mining Rigs:** Mining rigs are setups that house multiple GPUs to maximize mining efficiency. These rigs are designed to hold several GPUs, along with other necessary components such as a motherboard, CPU, RAM, and storage. A typical mining rig for Ethash might include anywhere from 4 to 8 or more GPUs. The rig's frame is constructed to ensure proper ventilation and cooling for the GPUs, which generate significant heat during operation. The choice of mining rig depends on the number of GPUs and the overall configuration to ensure that it can support and power all the components effectively.

- **Power Supply Units (PSUs):** A stable and sufficient power supply is crucial for mining operations. Mining rigs with multiple GPUs require power supply units (PSUs) that can handle the high power demands of the equipment. PSUs for mining rigs are typically high-wattage units, often rated from 1000W to 1600W or more, depending on the number and type of GPUs used. It is essential to select a PSU with adequate wattage and efficiency to ensure stable power delivery and avoid potential issues like power outages or hardware damage.

- **Cooling Systems:** Due to the high level of heat generated by GPUs during mining, effective cooling is vital to maintain optimal operating temperatures and prevent hardware damage. Cooling systems for Ethash mining setups include various components such as:

    - **Fans:** Additional case fans or GPU fans help to expel hot air and maintain airflow within the mining rig.

    - **Heatsinks:** These are used to dissipate heat from the GPU and other components.

    - **Cooling Pads:** For more advanced setups, liquid cooling solutions may be employed to further enhance cooling efficiency.

    - Proper cooling not only helps in maintaining the longevity of the equipment but also improves mining performance by preventing thermal throttling.

- **Motherboards and CPUs:** The motherboard is the backbone of the mining rig, connecting all the components together. It must be compatible with the number of GPUs being used and support multiple PCIe slots for connecting them. The CPU in a mining rig does not need to be highly powerful; it primarily manages the communication between the GPUs and the rest of the system. Basic CPUs are sufficient for mining operations, as the processing power of the CPU is not the primary focus in Ethash mining.

- **Storage:** While storage requirements for mining are minimal, a solid-state drive (SSD) is often used to store the operating system and mining software. An SSD is preferred over a traditional hard drive due to its faster read/write speeds, which can improve the overall efficiency of the mining rig. Storage capacity doesn't need to be extensive; typically, a drive with a capacity of 120GB to 250GB is adequate.

- **Mining Software:** To mine Ethash effectively, miners need software that interfaces with the mining hardware and connects to mining pools. Popular Ethash mining software includes Ethminer, Claymore Miner, and PhoenixMiner. The choice of software can affect performance and compatibility, so it's important to select a reliable and well-supported option. The software is configured to optimize the mining process, manage the GPUs, and submit shares to the mining pool.

- **Network Equipment:** A stable and fast internet connection is essential for mining operations. A standard network setup with a reliable router and Ethernet connection is typically used to ensure continuous communication with the mining pool and avoid connectivity issues. While Wi-Fi can be used, a wired connection is preferred for its stability and lower latency.

3. RandomX

RandomX is a PoW algorithm designed to be both ASIC-resistant and CPU-friendly. It was introduced as a replacement for the CryptoNight algorithm used by Monero, aiming to provide a more equitable mining environment. RandomX is designed to leverage general-purpose CPUs, utilizing a large amount of random memory access and computations that are hard for ASICs to perform efficiently. The algorithm's focus on CPU mining ensures that mining remains accessible to a broader range of participants, helping to decentralize the network and mitigate the influence of specialized mining hardware.

RandomX is the proof-of-work (PoW) algorithm used by cryptocurrencies like Monero (XMR), which is designed to be CPU-friendly and resistant to ASIC (Application-Specific Integrated Circuit) mining. As a result, the equipment used for mining RandomX differs significantly from that used for algorithms like Ethash or Scrypt. Here's a detailed look at the equipment generally used for mining RandomX:

- **Central Processing Units (CPUs):** Central Processing Units (CPUs) are the primary hardware used for mining RandomX. Unlike other algorithms that are optimized for GPUs or ASICs, RandomX is designed to utilize the diverse capabilities of CPUs. This includes leveraging the large cache memory and various instruction sets found in modern CPUs. CPUs from manufacturers like Intel and AMD are commonly used for RandomX mining. Specifically, processors with multiple cores and threads, such as AMD Ryzen and Intel Core i9 series, offer enhanced performance due to their ability to handle parallel processing tasks more effectively. RandomX mining benefits from CPUs with high cache sizes and advanced instruction sets, making them well-suited for the algorithm's requirements.

- **Mining Rigs:** For RandomX mining, the term "mining rig" typically refers to a setup that consists of multiple CPUs working in tandem to increase hashing power. These rigs can range from single CPU setups to more complex configurations with multiple CPUs. A mining rig for RandomX usually includes a motherboard capable of supporting multiple CPU sockets, ample RAM, and storage for the operating system and mining software. The design of the rig focuses on maximizing CPU performance and cooling efficiency. For instance, a multi-CPU mining rig might use a high-performance motherboard designed for server or workstation use, which supports multiple CPU installations and has sufficient PCIe slots for additional hardware.

- **Cooling Systems:** CPUs generate significant heat during mining operations, and effective cooling is crucial to maintaining optimal performance and prolonging hardware lifespan. Proper cooling not only helps in achieving stable and efficient mining operations but also prevents thermal throttling, which can reduce CPU performance.

- **Power Supply Units (PSUs):** Power supply units (PSUs) in RandomX mining setups need to provide reliable and sufficient power to the CPUs and other components. Unlike GPU-based mining rigs, the power requirements for CPU mining are generally lower but still require careful consideration. A PSU with adequate wattage and efficiency ratings is essential to ensure stable power delivery and avoid potential issues. For setups with multiple CPUs, a higher wattage PSU may be necessary to support the combined power demands of all components.

- **Motherboards and RAM:** Motherboards used in RandomX mining rigs must be capable of supporting the CPUs and other components. For multi-CPU rigs, motherboards designed for server or high-performance computing environments are preferred. These motherboards often come with multiple CPU sockets, ample PCIe slots, and sufficient memory capacity. RAM is also important, as RandomX mining can benefit from larger amounts of memory. Typically, 8GB to 16GB of RAM is recommended for optimal performance, though more may be used in high-end setups.

- **Storage:** For RandomX mining, storage requirements are relatively modest. A solid-state drive (SSD) is used to store the operating system, mining software, and any necessary updates. SSDs are preferred over traditional hard drives due to their faster read/write speeds, which can contribute to the overall efficiency of the mining operation. A storage capacity of 120GB to 250GB is usually sufficient for most RandomX mining setups.

- **Mining Software:** Mining software for RandomX is essential for interfacing with the CPUs and connecting to mining pools. Popular software options include XMRig and RandomX Miner. These software programs are designed to optimize CPU performance for RandomX mining and handle the complexities of submitting shares to mining pools. The software must be configured properly to match the specific hardware setup and the mining pool's requirements.

- **Network Equipment:** A stable internet connection is crucial for RandomX mining, as it ensures continuous communication with the mining pool and prevents connectivity issues. A wired Ethernet connection is preferred over Wi-Fi for its reliability and lower latency. The network equipment typically includes a router and a network cable to connect the mining rig to the internet.

4. X11

X11 is a multi-hash mining algorithm that uses a sequence of eleven different cryptographic hash functions to process blocks. Developed by Dash, X11 was created to enhance security and reduce the risk of collisions and vulnerabilities. The use of multiple hash functions makes X11 more resistant to attacks and improves its overall security profile. X11's approach also increases the complexity of mining, making it more challenging for ASICs to dominate the network compared to algorithms using a single hash function. This multi-layered approach balances mining efficiency with robust security.

X11 is a proof-of-work (PoW) hashing algorithm used primarily by cryptocurrencies such as Dash. It is distinguished by its use of eleven sequential hashing functions, which are designed to improve security and make mining more resistant to ASIC (Application-Specific Integrated Circuit) and FPGA (Field-Programmable Gate Array) dominance. Here's a detailed look at the equipment typically used for mining X11:

- **Application-Specific Integrated Circuits (ASICs):** While X11 was originally designed to be more resistant to ASIC mining compared to other algorithms, the development of ASICs specifically for X11 has advanced significantly. Modern ASIC miners are now capable of efficiently mining X11-based cryptocurrencies. These devices are highly specialized hardware built solely for mining X11, offering superior performance and energy efficiency compared to general-purpose mining equipment. Popular ASIC miners for X11 include models from manufacturers such as Bitmain and Innosilicon. These ASICs are designed to execute the eleven hashing functions of X11 at high speeds, making them highly effective for mining X11 coins.

- **Graphics Processing Units (GPUs):** Before the advent of X11-specific ASICs, GPUs were commonly used for mining X11 cryptocurrencies. Graphics Processing Units are versatile and can handle the complex computations required by the X11 algorithm. GPUs from manufacturers like NVIDIA and AMD are used in mining rigs for X11. High-performance models, such as the NVIDIA GeForce GTX 1080 Ti or AMD Radeon RX 580, are preferred due to their ability to handle the parallel processing required by X11. Mining rigs with multiple GPUs can be set up to increase hash power and improve the likelihood of solving blocks and earning rewards.

- **Mining Rigs:** For X11 mining, a mining rig is a setup that includes multiple GPUs or ASICs working together to maximize hash power. A mining rig for X11 typically consists of the following components:
  - **Motherboard:** A motherboard that supports multiple GPU installations or an ASIC unit.
  - **Power Supply Unit (PSU):** A PSU capable of delivering sufficient power to all components in the rig. For GPU-based rigs, a high-wattage PSU is required to support the power demands of multiple GPUs.
  - **Cooling System:** Adequate cooling is crucial to prevent overheating. For GPU mining rigs, this often includes multiple fans and sometimes custom cooling solutions. For ASIC miners, built-in cooling systems are typically sufficient, but additional cooling may be added if necessary.
  - **Frame or Case:** A frame or case designed to hold the GPUs or ASICs, ensuring proper airflow and accessibility for maintenance.
- **Power Supply Units (PSUs):** Power Supply Units are critical for both GPU and ASIC mining setups. For X11 mining, PSUs must provide reliable power to support the energy demands of the mining hardware. High-wattage PSUs are required for multi-GPU rigs, while ASIC miners usually have specific PSU requirements outlined by the manufacturer. It's important to choose a PSU with a good efficiency rating and sufficient wattage to ensure stable operation and to prevent power-related issues.
- **Cooling Systems:** Effective cooling is essential for maintaining the performance and longevity of mining equipment. For GPU-based mining rigs, cooling solutions include:
  - **Air Coolers:** High-performance air coolers with large heatsinks and multiple fans.
  - **Custom Cooling Solutions:** Some miners use custom setups with liquid cooling to manage heat more effectively.
  - For ASIC miners, built-in cooling systems are typically designed to handle

the heat generated during operation. However, in environments with high temperatures or in setups with multiple ASICs, additional cooling may be necessary.

- **Network Equipment:** A stable internet connection is crucial for mining X11, as it ensures continuous communication with the mining pool and timely submission of shares. Network equipment typically includes a reliable router and a wired Ethernet connection. A direct connection is preferred over Wi-Fi to minimize latency and connectivity issues.

- **Mining Software:** Mining software for X11 is essential for managing the mining process and connecting to mining pools. Software options include programs like CGMiner and BFGMiner, which are designed to handle the specific requirements of X11 mining. The software must be configured correctly to match the hardware setup and the mining pool's parameters.

- **Storage:** Storage requirements for X11 mining are relatively modest. A solid-state drive (SSD) is commonly used to store the operating system, mining software, and any necessary updates. SSDs are preferred over traditional hard drives due to their faster read/write speeds, which can contribute to overall mining efficiency.

- **Mining Pools:** Joining a mining pool is a common practice for X11 miners, as it increases the chances of successfully solving blocks and receiving rewards. Popular X11 mining pools include Dash's official pool and other third-party options. Miners need to configure their mining software to connect to the chosen pool and follow the pool's instructions for setup.

5. Equihash

Equihash is a memory-intensive PoW algorithm designed to be ASIC-resistant and is used by cryptocurrencies like Zcash. It relies on a variant of the generalized birthday problem to create a hash function that requires significant memory and computational power to solve. The algorithm involves solving a computational problem that requires storing and processing large amounts of data, which makes it challenging for ASICs to efficiently mine Equihash-based coins. This focus on memory-hard operations helps ensure a more level playing field for GPU miners and promotes network decentralization.

Equihash is a proof-of-work (PoW) hashing algorithm known for its memory-intensive requirements, which was designed to be resistant to ASIC (Application-Specific Integrated Circuit) mining and more accessible to GPU (Graphics Processing Unit) miners. As the Equihash algorithm has been adopted by several cryptocurrencies, including Zcash and Horizen, the equipment used to mine Equihash can vary depending on the specific demands of the algorithm and the technological advancements in mining hardware. Here's a detailed overview of the equipment generally used for mining Equihash:

Graphics Processing Units (GPUs): GPUs have historically been the primary hardware used for mining Equihash due to the algorithm's memory-intensive nature. Graphics Processing Units are well-suited for Equihash mining because they can handle the parallel processing required to solve the algorithm's complex computations. High-performance GPUs from manufacturers like NVIDIA and AMD are commonly used in mining rigs for Equihash.

NVIDIA GPUs: High-end models such as the NVIDIA GeForce RTX 3090 and RTX 3080 offer substantial hash rates for Equihash mining. These GPUs are favored for their advanced architecture and large amounts of memory, which are beneficial for handling the algorithm's demands.

AMD GPUs: Models such as the AMD Radeon RX 5700 XT and RX 580 are also popular choices. These GPUs provide a good balance between performance and cost, making them suitable for both small-scale and large-scale mining operations.

Mining Rigs: Mining rigs for Equihash typically consist of multiple GPUs working together to increase hash power and improve the chances of solving blocks. A typical mining rig setup includes:

- **Motherboard**: A motherboard that supports multiple GPU installations. For Equihash mining, motherboards with multiple PCIe slots are required to accommodate several GPUs.

- **Power Supply Unit (PSU)**: A high-wattage PSU is essential to provide enough power for all GPUs and other components in the rig. Power supplies with a high efficiency rating are preferred to ensure stable operation and reduce energy consumption.

- **Cooling System**: Effective cooling is crucial to manage the heat generated by multiple GPUs. This includes high-performance fans and, in some cases, custom cooling solutions such as liquid cooling to prevent overheating and maintain optimal performance.

- **Frame or Case**: A mining frame or case designed to house the GPUs and ensure proper airflow. This setup helps to keep the GPUs cool and accessible for maintenance.

Application-Specific Integrated Circuits (ASICs):

While Equihash was initially resistant to ASIC mining due to its memory-intensive nature, advancements in ASIC technology have led to the development of specialized ASIC miners for Equihash. These devices are designed to perform the specific computations required by the Equihash algorithm with high efficiency.

Equihash ASIC Miners: Companies like Bitmain and Innosilicon have developed ASIC miners tailored for Equihash. These devices are built to handle the algorithm's memory requirements and offer high hash rates with lower power consumption compared to GPUs. The Antminer Z15 by Bitmain is an example of an ASIC miner specifically designed for Equihash-based cryptocurrencies such as Zcash.

Power Supply Units (PSUs): For ASIC miners, a power supply unit is necessary to deliver the appropriate voltage and current required for the device. ASIC miners typically have specific PSU requirements outlined by the manufacturer. It's essential to use a PSU that matches the power specifications of the ASIC miner to ensure reliable operation and prevent power-related issues.

Cooling Systems: Both GPU and ASIC mining setups require effective cooling to manage heat. For GPU mining rigs, this involves high-performance air coolers or custom liquid cooling solutions. ASIC miners often come with built-in cooling systems, but additional cooling may be necessary in environments with high ambient temperatures or when running multiple units.

Network Equipment: A stable internet connection is essential for Equihash mining to ensure continuous communication with mining pools and timely submission of shares. A reliable router and a wired Ethernet connection are preferred over Wi-Fi to reduce latency and connectivity issues.

Mining Software: Mining software is required to manage the mining process and connect to mining pools. For Equihash mining, popular software options include:

- **EWBF's Cuda Miner**: A popular mining software for NVIDIA GPUs, known for its efficiency and ease of use.

- **Claymore's ZCash/Equihash Miner**: This software is widely used for AMD

GPUs and offers support for multiple mining algorithms, including Equihash.

The software must be configured to match the hardware setup and the mining pool's parameters.

Storage: Storage requirements for Equihash mining are relatively modest. A solid-state drive (SSD) is typically used to store the operating system, mining software, and updates. SSDs are preferred for their faster read/write speeds, which can contribute to overall mining efficiency.

Mining Pools: Joining a mining pool is a common practice for Equihash miners to increase the chances of solving blocks and earning rewards. Popular Equihash mining pools include F2Pool, Slushpool, and Nanopool. Miners need to configure their mining software to connect to the chosen pool and follow the pool's setup instructions.

6. Blake2b

Blake2b is a cryptographic hash function used in several mining algorithms due to its high speed and security. It is an optimized version of the Blake hash function, designed to provide strong security with fast processing speeds. Blake2b is used in algorithms like the Blake2b variant for Decred and Siacoin. The hash function's efficiency and security make it suitable for various applications, including cryptocurrency mining, where it helps achieve fast and reliable hashing performance while maintaining robust security.

Blake2b is a cryptographic hash function used in various cryptocurrencies, known for its security and efficiency. It is commonly used in the mining algorithms of several coins, including Siacoin and Decred. Mining Blake2b involves using hardware and software that can handle the specific computational demands of this algorithm. Here's a detailed overview of the equipment generally used to mine Blake2b:

Graphics Processing Units (GPUs): Graphics Processing Units (GPUs) are the most commonly used hardware for mining cryptocurrencies that utilize the Blake2b algorithm. GPUs are well-suited for Blake2b mining due to their ability to perform parallel computations efficiently. This capability is crucial for handling the hash function's operations, which involve multiple rounds of hashing and require significant processing power.

NVIDIA GPUs: High-performance GPUs from NVIDIA, such as the GeForce RTX 3080 and RTX 3070, are popular choices for Blake2b mining. These models offer substantial processing power and memory bandwidth, which are advantageous for the hashing process. NVIDIA's CUDA architecture is particularly effective for mining applications, providing efficient handling of the Blake2b algorithm.

AMD GPUs: AMD's Radeon RX 5700 XT and RX 580 are also commonly used for Blake2b mining. These GPUs provide a good balance between cost and performance. AMD GPUs are known for their high hash rates and efficient energy consumption, making them suitable for both small and large-scale mining operations.

Application-Specific Integrated Circuits (ASICs): Unlike some other algorithms, Blake2b is not as widely supported by ASIC miners due to its less standardized nature compared to algorithms like SHA-256 or Ethash. However, the development of ASICs for Blake2b is possible and has been explored in the cryptocurrency mining industry. ASIC miners for Blake2b are designed to perform the specific computations of the algorithm with high efficiency and lower power consumption compared to GPUs.

Blake2b ASIC Miners: As of now, there are fewer ASIC miners specifically designed for Blake2b compared to other algorithms. Companies specializing in ASIC mining hardware, such as Bitmain or Innosilicon, could potentially develop specialized ASICs for Blake2b if there is sufficient demand and technological feasibility. These ASICs would offer significant performance advantages over GPUs, including higher hash rates and lower operational costs.

Mining Rigs: Mining rigs for Blake2b consist of multiple GPUs working in tandem to increase the overall hash rate. A typical mining rig setup includes:

- **Motherboard**: A motherboard capable of supporting multiple GPUs, with several PCIe slots to accommodate the necessary graphics cards.

- **Power Supply Unit (PSU)**: A high-wattage PSU is essential to power all GPUs and other components in the rig. It's crucial to select a PSU with sufficient capacity and efficiency to ensure stable operation.

- **Cooling System**: Effective cooling is necessary to manage the heat generated by multiple GPUs. This includes high-performance fans and possibly liquid cooling solutions to maintain optimal operating temperatures and prevent overheating.

- **Frame or Case**: A mining frame or case designed to house the GPUs and ensure adequate airflow. Proper ventilation is important to keep the GPUs cool and prevent dust accumulation.

Power Supply Units (PSUs): For both GPU and ASIC mining setups, a power supply unit is crucial. The PSU must meet the power requirements of the hardware to ensure stable and reliable operation. For GPUs, a PSU with a high efficiency rating and sufficient wattage is needed to support the entire mining rig. For ASIC miners, the power requirements are usually specified by the manufacturer, and it is important to use a PSU that matches these specifications.

Cooling Systems: Effective cooling systems are essential for maintaining the performance and longevity of mining equipment. GPUs and ASIC miners generate significant amounts of heat during operation, which can impact their efficiency and lifespan. Mining rigs typically use high-performance fans, and some setups may incorporate liquid cooling solutions to manage temperatures. Ensuring proper cooling helps prevent overheating and maintains stable mining performance.

Network Equipment: A stable and reliable internet connection is necessary for successful Blake2b mining. Miners should use a wired Ethernet connection rather than Wi-Fi to minimize latency and connectivity issues. A reliable router and network equipment are essential to ensure consistent communication with mining pools and timely submission of shares.

Mining Software: Mining software is required to manage the mining process and connect to mining pools. For Blake2b mining, various software options are available, including:

- **CCMiner**: A popular open-source mining software that supports multiple algorithms, including Blake2b. It is compatible with NVIDIA GPUs and provides options for optimizing mining performance.

- **Claymore's MultiMiner**: This software supports AMD GPUs and offers a range of features for mining different algorithms, including Blake2b.

Storage: Storage requirements for Blake2b mining are relatively modest. A solid-state drive (SSD) is commonly used to store the operating system, mining software, and updates. SSDs are preferred due to their faster read/write speeds, which can contribute to overall mining efficiency.

Mining Pools: Joining a mining pool is a common practice for Blake2b miners to increase their chances of solving blocks and earning rewards. Mining pools aggregate the computational power of multiple miners and distribute rewards based on contributed hash power. Popular Blake2b mining pools include those dedicated to Siacoin or Decred, where miners can join and follow the pool's setup instructions.

7. Lyra2REv3

Lyra2REv3 is a PoW algorithm used primarily by the Vertcoin cryptocurrency. It is a memory-hard algorithm designed to be ASIC-resistant and favor GPU mining. Lyra2REv3 incorporates a series of hashing functions and memory-hard techniques to ensure that mining remains accessible to a broader range of participants. The algorithm's focus on memory hardness and computational complexity aims to reduce the advantages of specialized mining hardware, promoting a more decentralized network. Lyra2REv3's design helps maintain network security while ensuring that mining remains competitive and accessible.

Lyra2REv3 is a cryptographic algorithm used in cryptocurrency mining, notably for coins like Vertcoin. It is designed to be memory-intensive and resistant to ASIC mining, which means it is often mined using GPUs. Here's a detailed explanation of the equipment generally used to mine Lyra2REv3:

Graphics Processing Units (GPUs): Graphics Processing Units (GPUs) are the primary hardware used for mining cryptocurrencies that utilize the Lyra2REv3 algorithm. GPUs are well-suited for Lyra2REv3 mining due to their ability to handle memory-intensive computations efficiently. This algorithm requires significant memory bandwidth and processing power, making GPUs the most effective hardware choice.

NVIDIA GPUs: NVIDIA's high-performance GPUs are popular choices for Lyra2REv3 mining. Models like the NVIDIA GeForce RTX 3080, RTX 3070, and RTX 3060 Ti are favoured for their superior hash rates and memory capacities. NVIDIA's architecture, particularly the Ampere and Turing series, offers excellent performance for memory-intensive algorithms, which makes them well-suited for Lyra2REv3 mining.

AMD GPUs: AMD's Radeon RX 5700 XT, RX 580, and RX 570 are also commonly used for mining Lyra2REv3. AMD GPUs are known for their high memory bandwidth and competitive hash rates, which are beneficial for algorithms like Lyra2REv3 that require significant memory resources. The Polaris and Navi architectures in these GPUs provide a good balance of cost and performance for miners.

Mining Rigs: Mining rigs for Lyra2REv3 typically consist of multiple GPUs working together to maximize hashing power. A typical mining rig setup includes:

- **Motherboard**: A motherboard with multiple PCIe slots to accommodate several GPUs. Specialized mining motherboards are designed to support multiple GPUs and ensure stable operation.

- **Power Supply Unit (PSU)**: A high-wattage PSU capable of supporting all GPUs and other components. It's important to select a PSU with sufficient capacity and efficiency to ensure reliable performance.

- **Cooling System**: Effective cooling is essential to manage the heat generated by multiple GPUs. Mining rigs often use high-performance fans or even liquid cooling systems to maintain optimal temperatures and prevent overheating.

- **Frame or Case**: A mining frame or open-air case designed to house GPUs and ensure proper airflow. Proper ventilation is crucial to keep the GPUs cool and reduce dust buildup.

Power Supply Units (PSUs): For mining Lyra2REv3, the power supply unit is critical to ensure stable and efficient operation. A PSU with high efficiency and sufficient wattage is necessary to power all GPUs and other components in the mining rig. It's important to choose a PSU that can handle the total power draw of the mining setup, taking into account the number of GPUs and their power requirements.

Cooling Systems: Mining hardware generates a significant amount of heat, especially when multiple GPUs are running simultaneously. Effective cooling systems are necessary to manage this heat and maintain performance. High-performance fans, as well as potential liquid cooling solutions, help keep the GPUs and other components within safe temperature ranges. Proper cooling not only enhances performance but also extends the lifespan of the mining equipment.

Network Equipment: A stable and reliable internet connection is essential for mining Lyra2REv3. Miners should use a wired Ethernet connection rather than Wi-Fi to ensure consistent and reliable communication with mining pools. Network equipment, such as a high-quality router, ensures that the mining rig remains connected and can submit work efficiently to the pool.

Mining Software: Mining software is required to manage the mining process and connect to mining pools. For Lyra2REv3, several software options are available:

- **CCMiner**: A popular open-source mining software that supports a variety of algorithms, including Lyra2REv3. It is compatible with NVIDIA GPUs and offers various options for performance optimization.

- **Claymore's CryptoNote CPU Miner**: This software supports AMD GPUs and is known for its user-friendly interface and efficient mining performance for Lyra2REv3.

Storage: The storage requirements for Lyra2REv3 mining are relatively modest. A solid-state drive (SSD) is commonly used to store the operating system, mining software, and necessary updates. SSDs are preferred for their faster read/write speeds, which can contribute to overall mining efficiency and reliability.

Mining Pools: Joining a mining pool is a common practice for miners of Lyra2REv3 to increase their chances of solving blocks and earning rewards. Mining pools aggregate the computational power of multiple miners and distribute rewards based on the contributed hash power. Miners should select a pool that supports Lyra2REv3 and follow the pool's setup instructions to configure their mining rig.

Each of these algorithms has been developed with specific goals in mind, such as enhancing security, increasing ASIC resistance, or optimizing for particular types of hardware. Understanding the characteristics and requirements of each algorithm can help miners choose the most suitable one for their needs and capabilities.

Building a Mining Rig

A crypto mining rig is a specialized computer system designed to mine cryptocurrencies by leveraging the computational power of graphics processing units (GPUs) or application-specific integrated circuits (ASICs). These rigs are pivotal in maintaining the blockchain networks for various cryptocurrencies, such as Bitcoin, by processing data and validating transactions. The essence of mining lies in contributing to the cryptocurrency's blockchain, earning rewards through successfully solving complex cryptographic puzzles.

The core components of a mining rig typically include GPUs or ASICs, which are essential for handling the intensive computations required for mining. GPUs, known for their parallel processing capabilities, are commonly used for mining coins that rely on algorithms requiring substantial computational power. ASICs, on the other hand, are custom-built devices optimized for specific mining algorithms, offering higher efficiency and performance for coins with well-defined algorithms [300].

The mining process involves several key steps. Initially, miners verify the authenticity of transactions, ensuring that all transactions included in a block are legitimate and conform to network rules. This step is crucial for maintaining the integrity of the blockchain. Following verification, miners prevent double-spending, a scenario where the same cryptocurrency is spent more than once. This is achieved by ensuring that each transaction is unique and recorded accurately on the blockchain [300].

The heart of the mining process is hashing, which involves applying a cryptographic algorithm to process block data. This produces a 64-digit hexadecimal number, known as a hash. Miners compete to solve these cryptographic puzzles by finding a hash that meets specific criteria set by the network. The first miner to find the correct hash adds the block to the blockchain and is rewarded with newly minted cryptocurrency and transaction fees [300].

Decentralized consensus in mining is achieved through a mechanism called Proof of Work (PoW). PoW ensures that the network agrees on the state of the blockchain and prevents fraudulent transactions. The profitability of mining is influenced by several factors, including the hashing power of the mining rig, electricity costs, and the initial investment in the mining equipment. Efficient mining operations require balancing these factors to maximize returns while managing expenses [300].

Building a cryptocurrency mining rig involves assembling various specialized components to create a system capable of efficiently mining digital assets. Each component plays a crucial role in the rig's overall performance, with specific considerations for optimizing mining efficiency and profitability.

Figure 18: Mining rig setup. Gzen92, CC BY-SA 4.0, via Wikimedia Commons.

Components for Building a Mining Rig

- **GPU (Graphics Processing Unit):** The GPU is the heart of any mining rig. It performs the bulk of the computational work necessary for mining cryptocurrencies. Typically, a mining rig is equipped with multiple GPUs—often six or more—to maximize hash rate, which directly impacts mining performance. The GPU's performance is a key determinant of the rig's efficiency and profitability. GPUs are favoured over CPUs (central processing units) due to their higher hash rates and parallel processing capabilities, which are essential for handling the complex calculations required in mining. High-performance GPUs such as the NVIDIA CMP HX series, AMD RX 6800, NVIDIA GeForce RTX 3060 Ti, and Radeon RX Vega 56/64 are commonly used in mining operations [300].

- **Motherboard:** A motherboard serves as the central hub for connecting all components in the mining rig. It must be compatible with the chosen GPUs and support multiple units simultaneously. When selecting a motherboard, it's important to choose one that can accommodate between four and eight GPUs, depending on the rig's size and complexity. Compatibility issues can arise if the motherboard does not support the required number of GPUs or if there are driver conflicts, so careful selection and compatibility checks are essential to ensure smooth operation [300].

- **CPU (Central Processing Unit):** The CPU in a mining rig handles general tasks and supports the operation of the GPU. For mining purposes, a CPU with low to moderate power output is sufficient. Processors from Intel's 8th or 9th generation are often recommended for their balance of performance and energy efficiency. The CPU's primary role in a mining rig is to manage the operating system and support the overall stability of the system [300].
- **RAM (Random Access Memory):** RAM is crucial for handling temporary data and ensuring smooth operation. The amount of RAM required can vary based on the mining rig's configuration and the specific cryptocurrency being mined. Generally, 4GB to 12GB of RAM is recommended for optimal performance. Installing RAM involves opening the side brackets of the motherboard slot, inserting the RAM module into the appropriate socket, and ensuring it is securely in place [300].
- **Power Supply Unit (PSU):** A robust and reliable power supply unit is essential for powering the entire mining rig. Given that mining rigs with multiple GPUs require substantial power, it is important to select a PSU with adequate wattage to handle the load. High-efficiency, high-wattage PSUs are necessary to ensure stable and continuous operation of the rig without power interruptions or overloads [300].
- **Mining Frame:** The mining frame provides the physical structure to house and organize all the components of the mining rig. It is designed to support multiple GPUs and other hardware while ensuring proper ventilation. The frame's design facilitates airflow to dissipate heat generated by the GPUs, which is crucial for maintaining optimal performance and preventing overheating [300].

Step-by-Step Guide to Building Your Mining Rig

Building a mining rig involves a series of steps to ensure that all components are properly assembled and configured for optimal performance. This guide will walk you through each step, from assembling the frame to setting up the GPUs with PCIe risers.

Assembling the Mining Rig Frame

The first step in building your mining rig is to assemble the mining frame. Start by choosing a suitable frame that can accommodate the number of GPUs you plan to use. Brands like Veddha, Kingwin, and Hydra offer mining frames designed to support six to eight GPUs. Ensure that the frame is robust and provides adequate space for all components, as well as proper airflow to keep the system cool [300].

Once you have the frame, secure all components in place. Start by attaching the motherboard to the frame. Make sure all screws are firmly tightened to prevent any movement or vibrations that could damage the components. Properly mounting the motherboard is crucial for maintaining stability and ensuring that all connectors are accessible [300].

Installing the Motherboard, CPU, and RAM

With the frame in place, the next step is to install the motherboard, CPU, and RAM. Begin by inserting the CPU into the corresponding socket on the motherboard. Ensure that you align the CPU correctly with the socket and gently press it into place. Once the CPU is installed, secure it with the appropriate locking mechanism [300].

Next, install the RAM modules by pushing them into the RAM slots on the motherboard. Make sure to orient the RAM correctly and press down firmly until the brackets on either side of the slot click into place. This ensures that the RAM is properly seated and will function correctly.

After installing the CPU and RAM, secure the motherboard to the mining frame. Attach the power supply unit (PSU) to the rig, positioning it in a place where it can easily connect to all components. Ensure that the PSU is securely mounted and that all cables are properly connected.

Connecting the Power Supply Unit

The power supply unit is crucial for providing power to all components in the mining rig. Ensure that the PSU you choose has sufficient PCIe connectors to support the number of GPUs you plan to use. Connect the appropriate power cables from the PSU to the motherboard and other components, such as the GPUs. Properly connecting the PSU ensures that each component receives the necessary power for optimal operation [300].

Setting Up PCIe Risers and GPUs

PCIe risers are essential for connecting GPUs to the motherboard, allowing for flexible placement and orientation of the GPUs within the mining rig. To set up PCIe risers, follow these steps [300]:

1. **Attach the PCIe Riser to the GPU:** Slip the PCIe riser onto the graphics card (GPU). The riser provides a physical connection between the GPU and the motherboard.

2. **Connect the USB Cable:** Connect one end of the USB cable to the GPU and the other end to the PCIe x1 adapter. This cable establishes a connection between the GPU and the motherboard.

3. **Connect to the Motherboard:** Insert the USB-to-PCIe x1 adapter into the corresponding slot on the motherboard. This connection allows the motherboard to communicate with the GPU through the riser.

By setting up PCIe risers correctly, you enhance connectivity between the GPUs and the motherboard, which can significantly increase the mining power and potential profitability of the rig. Additionally, PCIe risers help improve airflow around the GPUs, reducing heat buildup and maintaining the stability and performance of the mining hardware.

Configuring Your Mining Rig

Once you've assembled your mining rig, the next critical step is configuring it to ensure it operates efficiently and effectively for mining. This process involves adjusting BIOS settings, setting up the operating system, and installing the appropriate mining software. Each step is essential to optimize the performance and stability of your mining operations.

BIOS Configuration for Mining

The BIOS (Basic Input/Output System) configuration is a foundational step in optimizing your mining rig. Access the BIOS menu by pressing either the Del or F2 key during the initial startup of your computer. This menu allows you to adjust several key settings that can significantly impact mining performance.

1. **PCI-e Gen Speed:** The PCI Express (PCI-e) slots on your motherboard are used to connect GPUs. Adjusting the PCI-e Gen speed can help improve the stability and performance of the GPUs. Set the PCI-e Gen speed to a lower version, such as Gen 1 or Gen 2, if you experience instability with higher speeds.

This setting ensures that the GPUs are properly recognized and can operate without errors.

2. **Mining Mode:** Some motherboards have a specific "Mining Mode" or "Crypto Mining Mode" in the BIOS. Enabling this mode can optimize the motherboard's settings for mining operations, enhancing performance and stability. This mode may adjust various parameters, including power settings and slot configurations, to better support mining activities.

3. **Boot Priority:** Setting the boot priority determines which device the system will boot from first. Ensure that the boot priority is configured to boot from your primary storage device where the operating system is installed. This setting ensures that the rig starts up correctly and loads the operating system without issues.

4. **Primary Video Output:** In a mining rig with multiple GPUs, setting the primary video output to the integrated graphics or a specific GPU can be important. This setting ensures that the system uses the correct display output, especially if you're using a dedicated GPU for mining and not for display purposes.

After making the necessary adjustments in the BIOS, save the changes by pressing the F10 key and exit the BIOS menu by pressing the ESC key. This will ensure that all the changes are applied and the system reboots with the new settings.

Setting Up the Operating System

Once you've configured the BIOS, the next step is to set up the operating system (OS) on your mining rig. For most mining rigs, Windows or Linux-based operating systems are commonly used. Ensure that the OS is installed on your primary storage device, such as an SSD, for faster boot times and improved performance [300].

1. **Install the Operating System:** Follow the standard procedure for installing your chosen OS. For Windows, use a bootable USB drive or installation media. For Linux, you can use a similar method or create a bootable USB drive with a mining-friendly Linux distribution.

2. **Install Drivers:** After installing the OS, ensure that all necessary drivers are installed, particularly for the GPUs. Proper drivers are crucial for the GPUs to

function optimally and for the system to recognize and utilize them effectively.

Installing Mining Software

With the OS and drivers in place, you can now install mining software. Mining software is used to connect your rig to a mining pool and manage the mining process [300].

1. **Choose Mining Software:** Select mining software compatible with the cryptocurrency you intend to mine. Popular options include NiceHash, Claymore, and CGMiner, among others. The choice of software will depend on the specific algorithms used by the cryptocurrency and the hardware compatibility.

2. **Configure Mining Software:** Once installed, configure the mining software to connect to your chosen mining pool. Enter the pool's address, your wallet address, and any other necessary parameters into the software's configuration file or settings interface. This setup allows your mining rig to participate in the mining pool and contribute to solving blocks.

3. **Start Mining:** Launch the mining software and monitor its performance. Ensure that the rig is operating within safe temperature ranges and that all components are functioning correctly. Regularly check the mining software's dashboard for performance metrics and earnings.

Operating System Setup for a Mining Rig

Setting up the operating system is a crucial step in ensuring that your mining rig performs optimally. When using a Windows operating system, several key tasks must be completed to configure the system for mining. These tasks include checking GPU detection, updating drivers, adjusting power settings, and configuring virtual memory.

Checking GPU Detection

The first step in configuring a Windows-based mining rig is to ensure that all GPUs are correctly detected by the operating system. This process involves verifying that each GPU is recognized and properly functioning within the system.

1. **Open Device Manager:** Access the Device Manager by right-clicking on the Start menu and selecting "Device Manager" from the list. This utility provides an overview of all hardware components connected to your system.

2. **Check GPU Listing:** In the Device Manager, expand the "Display adapters" section to see the list of GPUs installed in your mining rig. Ensure that each

GPU appears in the list without any warning icons, such as yellow exclamation marks, which indicate issues with the hardware.

3. **Verify GPU Status:** If any GPUs are not detected or show errors, troubleshoot by checking physical connections, ensuring that power cables are properly connected, and reseating the GPUs in their slots. If necessary, refer to the GPU manufacturer's troubleshooting guide.

Updating GPU Drivers

Proper GPU drivers are essential for optimal performance and stability. Updated drivers ensure that the GPUs can operate efficiently and are fully compatible with the mining software.

1. **Download Latest Drivers:** Visit the official website of the GPU manufacturer, such as NVIDIA or AMD, and download the latest drivers for your specific GPU models.

2. **Install Drivers:** Run the downloaded driver installation files and follow the on-screen instructions to install the drivers. It is generally recommended to perform a clean installation to avoid potential conflicts with previous driver versions.

3. **Restart the System:** After installing the drivers, restart your computer to ensure that the changes take effect and that the system recognizes the new drivers.

Adjusting Power Settings

To maximize mining efficiency, you need to adjust the power settings to prevent the computer from entering sleep mode and to optimize performance.

1. **Access Power Settings:** Open the Control Panel and navigate to "System and Security," then select "Power Options."

2. **Change Plan Settings:** Click on "Change plan settings" next to the selected power plan. Then, choose "Change advanced power settings" to access detailed power management options.

3. **Set Sleep Options:** In the advanced settings menu, locate the "Sleep" section and set the "Sleep after" option to "Never" for both "On battery" and "Plugged in" modes. This prevents the computer from going into sleep mode, which can

interrupt mining operations.

4. **Adjust Performance Settings:** Also, ensure that the "Turn off the display" setting is set to a time frame that is convenient for your setup or to "Never" if you prefer to keep the display on during mining.

Configuring Virtual Memory

Proper virtual memory settings are crucial for maintaining system stability and performance during mining operations. Virtual memory acts as an extension of your system's RAM and helps manage large data workloads.

1. **Access Virtual Memory Settings:** Right-click on "This PC" or "Computer" on the desktop or in File Explorer, and select "Properties." Then, click on "Advanced system settings" and navigate to the "Advanced" tab. Under "Performance," click "Settings," and then go to the "Advanced" tab.

2. **Adjust Paging File Size:** In the "Virtual memory" section, click "Change" to access paging file settings. Uncheck the option "Automatically manage paging file size for all drives."

3. **Set Custom Size:** Select the drive where you want to set the virtual memory (usually the C: drive). Choose the "Custom size" option and set both the "Initial size" and "Maximum size" to 16384 MB (16 GB). This provides ample virtual memory to support mining activities and ensures smooth performance.

4. **Apply and Restart:** Click "Set" to apply the new settings and then "OK" to confirm. Restart your computer to ensure that the new virtual memory settings take effect.

Installing Mining Software

Installing mining software is a crucial step in the cryptocurrency mining process, as it enables your mining rig to perform the necessary computations to mine cryptocurrency and connect to a mining pool. Mining software acts as the bridge between your hardware and the blockchain network, handling tasks such as managing mining operations, communicating with the mining pool, and reporting results. Several popular mining software options include CGMiner, EasyMiner, and Kryptex, each with its own set of features and compatibility with various cryptocurrencies.

- **Choosing the Right Software:** The choice of mining software depends on the cryptocurrency you intend to mine and the hardware you are using. For instance, CGMiner is renowned for its versatility and supports various cryptocurrencies, but it is more complex to set up. EasyMiner is user-friendly and provides a graphical interface, making it a good choice for beginners. Kryptex offers a straightforward setup process and supports multiple cryptocurrencies, offering flexibility for miners. Ensure you select mining software compatible with your chosen cryptocurrency and mining rig setup.

- **Configuring the Mining Software:** After selecting and installing the mining software, the next step is configuration. This involves several key tasks:

    - **Enter Mining Pool Address:** Mining pools are groups of miners who share their processing power over a network and split the rewards proportionally. You need to enter the address of the mining pool you wish to join. This address directs your mining software to the correct pool for submitting work and receiving rewards.

    - **Input Username and Password:** Most mining pools require you to create an account, and you will need to enter your username and password associated with that account. This information authenticates your connection to the pool and ensures that your mining efforts are properly attributed to your account.

    - **Specify Cryptocurrency:** The mining software must be configured to mine the specific cryptocurrency you have chosen. This is usually done by selecting the appropriate option in the software's settings or by entering the relevant details manually.

    - **Indicate Number of GPUs:** If your mining rig has multiple GPUs, you need to specify the number of GPUs the software should utilize. Proper configuration ensures that all available hardware resources are used efficiently to maximize mining output.

- **Starting the Mining Process:** Once all settings are configured, initiate the mining process by clicking the "Start Mining" button in the software. The software will begin executing mining algorithms, connecting to the mining pool, and performing the necessary calculations to mine cryptocurrency. Regular monitoring of the software's performance is important to ensure everything is running smoothly and to address any issues that may arise.

Choosing a Cryptocurrency and Mining Pool

Selecting the right cryptocurrency to mine and joining an appropriate mining pool are essential steps in optimizing your mining operations.

- **Choosing a Cryptocurrency:** The profitability of mining varies greatly depending on the cryptocurrency you choose. Factors to consider include:
  - **Profitability:** Use profitability calculators like WhatToMine, minerstat, and 2CryptoCalc to assess which cryptocurrency offers the best returns based on your hardware setup, electricity costs, and current network conditions. These calculators provide estimates of potential earnings and help you make informed decisions about which cryptocurrency to mine.
  - **Consensus Mechanism:** Different cryptocurrencies use various consensus mechanisms, such as Proof of Work (PoW) or Proof of Stake (PoS). For mining purposes, focus on PoW-based cryptocurrencies that align with your hardware capabilities.
  - **Personal Preferences:** Consider your personal interests and the long-term viability of the cryptocurrency. Some miners prefer to support emerging projects or those with specific technological advancements.
- **Joining a Mining Pool:** Joining a mining pool can significantly increase your chances of successfully mining a block and receiving rewards, as the combined computational power of the pool enhances the probability of solving cryptographic puzzles.
  - **Set Up an Account:** Register an account with the chosen mining pool. This process typically involves providing a username, email address, and sometimes additional details like payment information.

- **Configure Mining Software:** Input the mining pool's address, your account credentials, and other required settings into your mining software. This configuration enables your mining rig to communicate with the pool and submit mining results.
- **Connect Your Wallet:** Link your cryptocurrency wallet to the mining pool. This wallet will receive the rewards earned from mining. Ensure that the wallet address is correctly entered to avoid losing any earnings.
- **Initiate Mining:** After completing the setup, start the mining process. Monitor the mining software and pool dashboard to track performance, earnings, and any potential issues.

Environmental Impact and Sustainability

Global Energy Consumption of Bitcoin Mining

According to a study published by the United Nations University and the journal Earth's Future, Bitcoin mining during the 2020–2021 period consumed an astonishing 173.42 Terawatt hours (TWh) of electricity [301]. This level of energy consumption places Bitcoin in a hypothetical ranking as the 27th largest energy-consuming country globally, surpassing the energy use of Pakistan, a nation with a population exceeding 230 million people [301]. The environmental impact is equally staggering; the carbon footprint of Bitcoin mining during this period equated to burning 84 billion pounds of coal or operating 190 natural gas-fired power plants [301]. To counteract this carbon footprint, it would be necessary to plant approximately 3.9 billion trees, covering an area comparable to the Netherlands, Switzerland, Denmark, or 7% of the Amazon rainforest [301]. This immense environmental toll highlights the significant energy demands associated with Bitcoin mining.

Water and Land Footprint

Bitcoin mining also imposes a substantial burden on water resources and land use. The global water footprint of Bitcoin mining in 2020–2021 was equivalent to filling over 660,000 Olympic-sized swimming pools, an amount that could fulfill the domestic water needs of more than 300 million people in rural sub-Saharan Africa [301]. Additionally, the land footprint of Bitcoin mining activities during this period covered an area 1.4 times the size of Los Angeles. These figures underscore the extensive environmental footprint of Bitcoin mining operations beyond just energy consumption.

Energy Source Breakdown

The energy mix for Bitcoin mining heavily relies on fossil fuels. According to the report, coal accounted for 45% of Bitcoin's energy supply, followed by natural gas at 21% [301]. Hydropower, despite its significant water and environmental impacts, was the largest renewable energy source, contributing 16% of Bitcoin's electricity demand. Nuclear energy played a substantial role as well, providing 9% of the total electricity used in Bitcoin mining. Conversely, renewable sources like solar and wind energy were minimal, accounting for only 2% and 5%, respectively [301]. This reliance on fossil fuels underscores the need for more sustainable energy practices in the cryptocurrency sector.

Geographic Distribution and Impact

China was, by far, the leading Bitcoin mining nation during this period, significantly outpacing other countries. To offset the carbon emissions from China's coal-intensive Bitcoin mining operations in 2021–2022, approximately 2 billion trees would need to be planted, covering an area equivalent to Portugal and Ireland combined or 45,000 times the size of Central Park in New York City. Other major Bitcoin mining nations included the United States, Kazakhstan, Russia, Malaysia, Canada, Germany, Iran, Ireland, and Singapore. Despite the significant share held by China, the country's dominance in Bitcoin mining declined from 73% in 2020 to 21% in 2022 due to government regulations [301]. This decline led to increased shares for the United States and Kazakhstan.

Environmental Implications and Future Outlook

The environmental impact of Bitcoin mining is profound, with 67% of the electricity used in 2020–2021 coming from fossil energy sources. The carbon emissions alone from Bitcoin mining during this period exceeded 85.89 megatonnes (Mt) of CO2 [301]. This level of greenhouse gas emissions poses a serious risk of pushing global warming beyond the Paris Agreement's goal of limiting temperature rise to below 2 degrees Celsius. The top ten Bitcoin mining nations are responsible for 92-94% of Bitcoin's global carbon, water, and land footprint [301].

To mitigate these impacts, it is crucial to explore regulatory measures and technological innovations. Urgent interventions are needed to address the environmental challenges posed by the growing cryptocurrency sector. Countries with low electricity prices, such as Kazakhstan, continue to attract Bitcoin miners due to financial incentives, despite the reliance on non-renewable energy sources. Addressing these issues requires a concerted effort to promote more sustainable practices and energy sources within the cryptocurrency industry.

Electricity is the backbone of cryptocurrency mining operations, making its availability and reliability paramount. For miners, ensuring a stable and uninterrupted power supply is crucial due to the continuous computational demands of the mining process. A key consideration is the redundancy of the electricity supply; any disruption can halt mining operations, leading to potential financial losses. Texas has become a significant hub for Bitcoin mining, attracting operations due to its relatively low energy costs. However, potential investors should be cautious of the vulnerabilities in Texas's power grid, as its reliability is a concern. Power outages or instability in the grid could severely impact mining operations, underscoring the need for backup power solutions and careful evaluation of local power infrastructure [296].

The cost of electricity directly influences the profitability of mining activities. For contemporary mining operations, electricity costs exceeding $0.05 per kilowatt-hour (kWh) can render mining unprofitable. In 2022, a surge in electricity costs across the United States led to increased operational expenses for mining companies, pushing some to the brink of financial distress or even bankruptcy [296]. This highlights the critical role of energy expenses in the overall cost structure of mining and the need for miners to secure low-cost electricity to maintain profitability. High electricity costs can significantly impact the bottom line, making it essential for miners to continually monitor and manage their energy expenses [296].

Regulatory factors present another layer of risk for cryptocurrency miners. Countries like China have previously imposed restrictions on mining due to energy consumption and environmental concerns, and other nations, including Kazakhstan and Iceland, have followed suit with measures to control the demand on their energy grids. In the United States, while some states have embraced Bitcoin mining and offered incentives, there is growing federal scrutiny. New tax reporting requirements and increased oversight by agencies like the Federal Reserve are on the horizon. This evolving regulatory landscape necessitates vigilance from miners, as changes in regulations can have significant implications for their operations and profitability [296].

The environmental impact of Bitcoin mining is a significant concern, with substantial ethical and reputational implications. The high energy consumption associated with mining operations has led to criticism regarding its carbon footprint. Reports such as those from The New York Times have highlighted the extensive power used by Bitcoin mining operations, comparing it to the annual energy consumption of entire countries like Finland. On average, mining a single Bitcoin requires around 155,000 kWh, a stark contrast to the 900 kWh consumed by the average US household per month [296].

As climate issues gain prominence, companies across industries are prioritizing carbon reduction. For example, Tesla paused its Bitcoin purchases due to environmental concerns but has indicated a willingness to resume transactions once a significant portion of Bitcoin mining uses renewable energy sources [296]. In response, some mining firms are transitioning to renewable energy sources or utilizing excess power from renewable resources. Innovations such as using flared natural gas, excess solar or wind power, and hydropower from dam overflows are being explored. However, these strategies must ensure that they do not inadvertently increase overall demand for energy [296].

Chapter Thirteen
Smart Contracts and DApps

Cryptocurrency smart contracts are self-executing contracts with the terms of the agreement directly written into code. They operate on blockchain networks, most commonly on platforms like Ethereum, which support smart contract functionality. Smart contracts automate the execution of contractual agreements when predefined conditions are met, eliminating the need for intermediaries and reducing the potential for fraud or manipulation.

Understanding Smart Contracts

Smart contracts function as programmable scripts on a blockchain that automatically enforce and execute the terms of a contract based on its coded conditions. When a smart contract is deployed on a blockchain, it is stored on a decentralized network of nodes, making it immutable and transparent. The contract's code outlines the rules and regulations of the agreement and executes automatically when those conditions are met. For instance, in a token transfer agreement, a smart contract will execute the transfer once the sender provides the necessary funds and the recipient's address is verified. This process eliminates manual intervention and ensures accuracy.

One of the most significant advantages of smart contracts is their ability to operate autonomously without human intervention. This leads to increased efficiency and speed in executing agreements. Smart contracts also provide transparency, as all transactions and contract executions are recorded on the blockchain and can be audited by anyone with access. Furthermore, they enhance security by using cryptographic algorithms to protect data, reducing the risk of tampering or fraud. Additionally, the elimination of intermediaries lowers costs associated with traditional contract enforcement and management.

Smart contracts have a wide range of applications across various sectors. In finance, they are used for decentralized finance (DeFi) platforms to automate lending, borrowing, and trading processes. In real estate, smart contracts can streamline property transactions by automatically transferring ownership upon receipt of payment. Supply chain management benefits from smart contracts by automating inventory tracking and ensuring transparency in the movement of goods. Even in the legal field, they can be utilized to create self-executing agreements and automate compliance checks.

Despite their advantages, smart contracts are not without challenges. One major concern is the complexity of coding and the potential for programming errors, which can lead to unintended consequences or vulnerabilities. The immutability of blockchain means that once a smart contract is deployed, its code cannot be altered, which can be problematic if errors are discovered. Additionally, smart contracts rely on the accuracy of the data they receive; if the input data is incorrect or manipulated, the contract's execution may be compromised. Legal and regulatory considerations also arise, as the decentralized nature of smart contracts can complicate jurisdictional issues and enforceability.

The Importance of Smart Contracts

Smart contracts play a pivotal role in the blockchain ecosystem, serving as the backbone for a broad range of decentralized applications (dApps) and financial tools. Their importance stems from their ability to automate and enforce contractual agreements in a secure and transparent manner, leveraging the immutable nature of blockchain technology. By executing contracts automatically based on pre-defined conditions, smart contracts eliminate the need for intermediaries, streamline processes, and reduce costs, making them crucial for innovation across various sectors [302].

Enabling Decentralized Applications

Smart contracts are essential for developing decentralized applications (dApps), which operate without central authority or intermediaries. These applications leverage blockchain technology to provide services and execute transactions in a decentralized and trustless environment. For example, in the decentralized finance (DeFi) sector, smart contracts enable complex financial operations such as lending, borrowing, and trading without relying on traditional financial institutions. This decentralization allows users to interact with financial services directly, enhancing accessibility and reducing costs associated with intermediaries [302].

Revolutionizing Financial Transactions

One of the most significant impacts of smart contracts is their ability to transform traditional financial systems. DeFi applications, built on smart contracts, provide users with the capability to engage in financial activities without the need for banks or other financial intermediaries. Platforms like Uniswap and Compound exemplify this transformation. Uniswap allows users to trade cryptocurrencies directly through a decentralized exchange, with smart contracts handling the exchange rates and transaction execution. Compound enables users to earn interest on their assets or obtain loans without involving a traditional bank. Similarly, USDC, a stablecoin pegged to the US dollar, uses smart contracts to maintain its value and provide a stable digital currency alternative [302].

Streamlining and Automating Processes

Smart contracts offer significant advantages by automating various processes that traditionally require manual intervention. For instance, imagine you hold Ethereum and wish to convert it to USDC. Using a decentralized exchange like Uniswap, you can perform this transaction seamlessly through a smart contract. The smart contract finds the best exchange rate, facilitates the trade, and transfers the USDC to your wallet without requiring any central authority or intermediary. This automation reduces transaction times and costs, making the process more efficient and user-friendly [302].

Enhancing Security and Transparency

Another critical benefit of smart contracts is their ability to provide enhanced security and transparency. Once a smart contract is deployed on the blockchain, its code is immutable and transparent, meaning that it cannot be altered or tampered with. This immutability ensures that the contract's terms are executed exactly as programmed, reducing the risk of fraud and ensuring reliable and predictable outcomes. Furthermore, the decentralized nature of blockchain technology means that transactions are recorded on a public ledger, providing transparency and allowing users to verify the contract's execution and results [302].

Overcoming Traditional Financial Challenges

Traditional financial systems often involve high costs and inefficiencies, such as expensive currency swaps and complex loan processes. Smart contracts address these challenges by facilitating direct and automated transactions, reducing fees, and enabling global access to financial services. For example, converting currencies through traditional financial systems can be time-consuming and costly due to exchange rate fluctuations and fees. Similarly, lending and borrowing often require extensive paperwork and intermediaries. Smart contracts simplify these processes, making financial transactions more efficient and accessible, particularly in a global context [302].

How Smart Contracts Work

Smart contracts, first proposed by computer scientist and lawyer Nick Szabo in the 1990s, are digital agreements programmed to automatically execute and enforce the terms of a contract. Szabo likened them to a vending machine, which automates the process of selling a product. Just as a vending machine accepts payment, dispenses a product, and provides change without human intervention, smart contracts automate exchanges of value or information according to predefined rules. This automation allows smart contracts to execute transactions and enforce agreements without the need for intermediaries [302].

Types of Smart Contracts

Smart contracts can be categorized into three distinct types, each serving a specific purpose within the blockchain ecosystem. These categories include smart legal contracts, decentralized autonomous organizations (DAOs), and application logic contracts (ALCs). Each type plays a unique role and operates under different principles and structures [303]:

- **Smart Legal Contracts:** Smart legal contracts are designed to mirror traditional legal contracts but are executed and enforced through blockchain technology. These contracts follow a clear "if this happens, then that will happen" logic, ensuring that terms and conditions are met automatically once predefined criteria are fulfilled. For example, a smart legal contract might automatically transfer ownership of an asset or release payment when certain conditions are satisfied, such as reaching a specific deadline or verifying a condition. The immutability and transparency of blockchain technology provide greater security and accountability compared to traditional paper-based contracts. The digital nature of these contracts also allows for the use of digital signatures, which enhance the verification process. In case of non-compliance, parties involved in smart legal contracts might face significant legal consequences, reinforcing the need for adherence to the contract's terms.

- **Decentralized Autonomous Organizations (DAOs):** Decentralized Autonomous Organizations, or DAOs, represent a unique form of smart contract where governance and decision-making are managed collectively without a central authority. A DAO operates through a set of rules and protocols encoded in a smart contract on the blockchain. Members of a DAO typically hold governance tokens that grant them voting rights, allowing them to influence decisions related to the organization's operations, funding, and other key aspects. The code embedded in the smart contract dictates how the DAO functions, including how funds are allocated and how decisions are made. An example of a DAO is VitaDAO, which uses blockchain technology to support a community focused on scientific research. DAOs offer a novel way of managing organizations through decentralized and democratic processes, eliminating the need for traditional executive roles and centralized control.

- **Application Logic Contracts (ALCs):** Application Logic Contracts (ALCs) are smart contracts designed to manage and execute application-specific logic. Unlike smart legal contracts, which are centred around human or organizational agreements, ALCs facilitate interactions between machines or between different blockchain contracts. These contracts are crucial for applications that require seamless integration and communication between various devices, such as those found in the Internet of Things (IoT). ALCs enable complex interactions and data exchanges between smart devices, applications, and other blockchain-based contracts. Their role is to automate processes and manage logic within a specific application or system, ensuring that various components work together efficiently and reliably.

Each type of smart contract serves a distinct function within the blockchain ecosystem, contributing to a wide range of applications from legal agreements and organizational governance to advanced machine interactions and system integrations [303].

Popular Platforms and Accessibility

Ethereum, the most widely used smart contract platform, supports the creation and deployment of smart contracts through its blockchain. However, Ethereum is not alone in this space; other blockchains such as EOS, Neo, Tezos, Tron, Polkadot, and Algorand also support smart contracts. These contracts can be developed and deployed by anyone with the necessary programming knowledge. The code of smart contracts is stored on the blockchain, making it publicly accessible and verifiable. This transparency ensures that anyone can inspect the contract's code to understand its logic and functionality before engaging with it [302].

Programming Languages and Transparency

Smart contracts are written in various programming languages depending on the blockchain they are deployed on. For instance, Solidity is commonly used for Ethereum smart contracts, while Web Assembly and Michelson are used in other blockchain environments. On Ethereum, each smart contract's code is permanently recorded on the blockchain. This means that anyone can view the code and the contract's current state, which helps in verifying the contract's execution and ensures that it adheres to the expected rules and logic [302].

Execution and Consensus

When a smart contract receives funds or instructions, its code is executed across all nodes in the network. Each node, or computer connected to the blockchain network, stores a copy of the smart contract and its current state. The execution of the contract's code by all nodes is necessary to reach a consensus on the outcome of the contract and the resulting flow of value. This decentralized execution ensures that smart contracts can operate securely and reliably without a central authority, even when dealing with complex transactions or unknown parties [302].

Gas Fees

On platforms like Ethereum, executing a smart contract involves paying a fee known as "gas." Gas fees are essential for maintaining the network's operation and compensating miners or validators who process and validate transactions. The amount of gas required depends on the complexity of the contract and the resources needed to execute it. These fees are paid in the platform's native cryptocurrency and are necessary for executing transactions and smart contracts on the blockchain [302].

Immutability and Security

Once deployed on a blockchain, smart contracts are generally immutable, meaning they cannot be altered by their creators or any other party. This immutability ensures that the contract's terms and conditions remain unchanged, providing a secure and reliable framework for executing transactions. However, there are some exceptions where smart contracts may be designed with upgradeable features or governance mechanisms that allow for modifications under certain conditions. Despite these exceptions, the general principle of immutability helps prevent censorship and ensures that the contract operates as originally intended [302].

In summary, smart contracts are instrumental in advancing blockchain technology by enabling the development of decentralized applications and transforming traditional financial systems. They provide automation, security, and transparency, addressing inefficiencies and barriers in traditional finance and opening up new possibilities for users worldwide.

Significance of Smart Contracts for Cryptocurrency Investors

Smart contracts hold considerable significance for cryptocurrency investors, primarily due to their transformative impact on how transactions are conducted, how assets are managed, and how investments are made in the cryptocurrency space. Key aspects of their importance include:

- **Automated and Trustless Transactions**: Smart contracts automate transactions based on pre-defined rules, eliminating the need for intermediaries. For cryptocurrency investors, this means that transactions can be executed automatically and reliably once the conditions are met. This automation reduces the risk of human error and increases trust in the transaction process, as the contract's execution is governed by code rather than subjective interpretation.

- **Enhanced Security and Transparency**: Smart contracts operate on blockchain technology, which provides transparency and immutability. Investors can verify the terms and execution of smart contracts publicly on the blockchain, ensuring that the agreements are enforced as intended. The decentralized nature of blockchains also adds a layer of security, as there is no single point of failure that could be exploited.

- **DeFi and Financial Innovation**: Smart contracts are the backbone of decentralized finance (DeFi) applications, which offer a range of financial services without traditional intermediaries. Investors can participate in various DeFi activities, such as lending, borrowing, and trading, using smart contracts. This opens up new opportunities for earning yields, managing assets, and accessing financial services in a decentralized manner.

- **Efficient and Cost-Effective Operations**: By automating processes and removing intermediaries, smart contracts can significantly reduce transaction costs and processing times. For investors, this means lower fees and faster execution of trades and transactions, improving overall efficiency and potentially increasing returns on investment.

- **Programmable Investment Strategies**: Smart contracts enable the creation of complex, programmable investment strategies. For example, investors can use smart contracts to implement automated trading strategies, set up decentralized investment funds, or create tokenized assets with specific rules for their management. This flexibility allows for more sophisticated and customized investment approaches.

- **Security and Fraud Prevention**: The use of smart contracts minimizes the risk of fraud and manipulation. The terms of the contract are encoded into the blockchain, making it difficult for malicious actors to alter or tamper with the agreement. Investors benefit from increased security and reduced likelihood of disputes or fraudulent activities.

- **Access to New Financial Instruments**: Smart contracts enable the creation and management of new financial instruments, such as tokenized assets and decentralized exchanges. Investors can access a broader range of investment opportunities, including those that may not be available through traditional financial systems. This diversification can help investors manage risk and explore new avenues for growth.

- **Tokenization and Liquidity**: Smart contracts facilitate the tokenization of real-world assets, allowing them to be represented and traded on the blockchain. This process enhances liquidity and provides investors with more opportunities to trade and invest in a variety of assets. Tokenization also enables fractional ownership, making high-value assets more accessible to a wider range of investors.

The Relationship Between Smart Contracts and dApps

Smart contracts and decentralized applications (dApps) are deeply interconnected, with smart contracts serving as the foundational technology upon which dApps are built. Understanding their relationship involves exploring how each component functions and how they work together to enable various decentralized functionalities.

Smart Contracts as the Backbone of dApps

Smart contracts are self-executing contracts with the terms of the agreement directly written into code. They are deployed on a blockchain and automatically execute predefined actions when certain conditions are met. These contracts are immutable once deployed, meaning that their code cannot be altered, and they operate without the need for a central authority. The primary function of a smart contract is to facilitate, verify, or enforce the negotiation or performance of a contract, thereby removing the need for intermediaries and reducing the risk of fraud.

Decentralized applications (dApps) utilize these smart contracts to perform various functions within their systems. Essentially, dApps are built on top of blockchain platforms that support smart contracts, such as Ethereum, Binance Smart Chain, or Solana. The smart contracts embedded within these dApps handle the underlying logic and rules that govern the application's operations. For example, in a decentralized finance (DeFi) platform, smart contracts might manage lending protocols, automate trading strategies, or facilitate the issuance of stablecoins.

How dApps Leverage Smart Contracts

Automation and Efficiency: dApps rely on smart contracts to automate processes and transactions. For instance, in a decentralized exchange (DEX) like Uniswap, smart contracts facilitate the exchange of tokens by automatically executing trades based on predefined algorithms. This automation reduces the need for manual intervention and enhances the efficiency of the application.

Transparency and Security: The code of smart contracts is stored on the blockchain, making it transparent and publicly verifiable. This transparency ensures that the rules and logic of the dApp are accessible to all users, promoting trust and security. Since the execution of smart contracts is decentralized and verified by the network, it minimizes the risk of tampering or fraudulent activities.

Decentralization: dApps are designed to operate in a decentralized manner, meaning that no single entity has control over the application. Smart contracts contribute to this decentralization by running on a distributed network of nodes. Each node maintains a copy of the smart contract and executes it according to the blockchain's consensus rules, ensuring that the dApp functions without relying on a central server or authority.

Custom Functionality: Smart contracts provide the flexibility to create custom functionalities within dApps. Developers can write specific code to define how assets are managed, how transactions are processed, or how users interact with the application. This customization allows dApps to cater to a wide range of use cases, from financial services and gaming to supply chain management and governance.

Integration Examples

Consider a decentralized lending platform built on Ethereum. The platform's smart contracts manage the borrowing and lending process, ensuring that terms are met and collateral is handled correctly. Users interact with the dApp to initiate loans or deposits, while the smart contracts execute the transactions and enforce the rules automatically.

Similarly, in a decentralized gaming platform, smart contracts might manage in-game assets, ensuring that ownership and transactions are handled transparently and securely.

Popular Decentralized Applications (DApps)

The market for decentralized applications (dApps) has witnessed explosive growth in recent years. According to recent data, the compound annual growth rate (CAGR) for the dApp market has surged to 56.1%, reflecting a robust and accelerating interest in these technologies. By 2022, the daily user base for dApps had expanded by a staggering 396%, reaching approximately 2.7 million users [304]. This remarkable growth trajectory underscores the increasing adoption and reliance on decentralized technologies across various sectors. Projections suggest that the dApp market will continue to expand significantly, with an anticipated valuation of USD 368.25 billion by 2027 [304]. This growth is driven by the increasing demand for decentralized solutions that offer enhanced security, transparency, and user control compared to traditional centralized applications.

Decentralized applications, or dApps, are computer programs that operate on blockchain technology rather than relying on a central server. Unlike traditional client-server models, where a single server or controlling entity manages the application, dApps leverage a decentralized peer-to-peer (P2P) network for their backend operations. This decentralized architecture ensures that no single entity has control over the application, making it resistant to censorship and reducing the risk of single points of failure [304].

For instance, while centralized applications like Visa can handle around 10,000 transactions per second, blockchain platforms such as Solana can process up to 50,000 transactions per second, though this number can vary [304]. This scalability allows dApp users on such platforms to benefit from faster and more efficient transactions. dApps are predominantly utilized in areas such as finance, gaming, and governance. In the financial sector, dApps include cryptocurrency wallets and decentralized finance (DeFi) platforms. In gaming, dApps facilitate decentralized gaming experiences, and in governance, dApps enable decentralized organizations to make collective decisions. Ethereum, one of the leading blockchain platforms, hosts around half of all active dApps, thanks to its robust infrastructure powered by the Ethereum Virtual Machine (EVM), which supports a wide range of decentralized applications [304].

Types of dApps

Decentralized applications can be classified into three primary types based on their structure and relationship to underlying blockchain technologies [304]:

- **Type I dApps:** Type I dApps operate as their own independent blockchains. These dApps are foundational and serve as the underlying infrastructure for other applications. A prime example of a Type I dApp is Bitcoin. Bitcoin itself is a blockchain that operates as a decentralized application, providing a platform for cryptocurrency transactions without relying on any external infrastructure.

- **Type II dApps:** Type II dApps are built on top of existing Type I dApps. They function as protocols that operate on the foundational blockchain and often introduce their own native tokens. For example, Polygon is a Type II dApp that operates on the Ethereum blockchain. It enhances Ethereum's scalability and transaction throughput by providing a layer-2 solution that improves efficiency and reduces costs for decentralized applications built on Ethereum.

- **Type III dApps:** Type III dApps are built upon Type II dApps, leveraging the infrastructure and protocols established by the Type II applications. These dApps also function as protocols with their own native tokens. An example of a Type III dApp is Decentral Games, which operates on the Polygon Network. By utilizing the underlying Type II dApp infrastructure provided by Polygon, Decentral Games can offer decentralized gaming experiences with enhanced scalability and performance.

Overall, the diverse types of dApps reflect the evolving nature of blockchain technology and its applications. As the market for decentralized applications continues to grow, these types will play crucial roles in shaping the future of digital interactions and transactions.

Decentralized applications (dApps) have opened up numerous opportunities for individuals to make money in the blockchain ecosystem. Here's a detailed look at some of the best dApps for generating profit, with a focus on Aave as a prominent example.

Aave: A Leader in DeFi Lending and Borrowing

Aave is a standout dApp in the decentralized finance (DeFi) space, offering a comprehensive platform for lending and borrowing cryptocurrencies. Unlike traditional financial systems, Aave operates on the Ethereum blockchain, allowing users to earn interest on their deposits and take out loans without needing a central authority.

One of Aave's most innovative features is its flash loans. These are uncollateralized loans that must be repaid within a single transaction block. Flash loans enable users to perform complex financial maneuvers such as arbitrage, refinancing, and other investment strategies without needing initial capital. This unique functionality opens up significant profit-making opportunities for those who can strategically use these loans to exploit market inefficiencies.

In addition to flash loans, Aave supports a diverse range of cryptocurrencies, providing flexibility and multiple avenues for earning through interest accruals. Users can deposit their assets into liquidity pools and earn interest, while borrowers can access funds by providing collateral. The platform's user-friendly interface and robust security measures make it an attractive option for both new and experienced users seeking to generate income from their crypto holdings.

Other Notable dApps for Making Money

- **Yield Farming Platforms**: Yield farming, or liquidity mining, involves providing liquidity to decentralized exchanges (DEXs) or lending protocols in exchange for rewards. Platforms like Yearn.finance and SushiSwap offer users the chance to earn returns by participating in yield farming activities.

- **Blockchain Games and NFTs**: Play-to-earn games like Axie Infinity and Decentraland allow users to earn cryptocurrencies and NFTs through gameplay. These assets can be traded or sold, potentially providing significant profits for skilled players or investors.

- **Task-Based Earning**: Some dApps offer rewards for completing tasks or participating in surveys. Apps like StormX provide users with cryptocurrency for engaging in various activities, although these typically offer smaller returns compared to other methods.

- **Decentralized Exchanges (DEXs)**: Platforms like Uniswap and PancakeSwap allow users to provide liquidity to trading pairs and earn a share of the transaction fees. Users can also engage in yield farming and staking on these exchanges.

Popular dApps

Decentralized applications (dApps) have become a significant component of the blockchain ecosystem, serving various purposes across multiple domains. From gaming and finance to social networking and governance, dApps leverage blockchain technology to offer decentralized solutions and opportunities. Here's an in-depth look at several prominent dApps, each exemplifying different use cases [304, 305]:

PancakeSwap: PancakeSwap is a leading decentralized exchange (DEX) built on the Binance Smart Chain (BSC), offering an alternative to Ethereum-based DEXs like Uniswap. Since its launch in early 2020, PancakeSwap has gained considerable traction, boasting over 2.8 million users and managing $9.9 billion in total value locked (TVL). The platform enables users to trade BEP-20 tokens, which are native to BSC, and provides reduced transaction fees and faster processing times compared to traditional exchanges.

One of PancakeSwap's key features is its versatility in earning opportunities. Users can engage in yield farming, where they stake their BEP-20 tokens to earn rewards, and participate in lotteries, which provide additional ways to win cryptocurrency. PancakeSwap also offers staking for its native token, CAKE, which grants users governance rights and the ability to influence platform decisions. The low transaction fees and broad range of functionalities make PancakeSwap a popular choice among DeFi enthusiasts.

Axie Infinity: Axie Infinity is a prominent NFT-based game that has garnered widespread attention in the gaming and blockchain communities. The game allows players to create and collect digital creatures called Axies, which can be used in battles and various in-game activities. With a peak user base of 1.5 million active players and a market cap of $0.94 billion, Axie Infinity has established itself as a major player in the metaverse and NFT gaming space.

Players in Axie Infinity can earn rewards through gameplay, which can be traded or sold in the marketplace. The game's integration of NFTs enables users to own unique assets and participate in a vibrant digital economy. Axie Infinity exemplifies how blockchain technology can be used to create immersive gaming experiences that also offer financial incentives.

Uniswap: Uniswap, launched in 2018, is one of the most widely used decentralized exchanges on the Ethereum blockchain. It operates on an automated market maker (AMM) model, allowing users to trade ERC-20 tokens directly without intermediaries.

Uniswap is known for its low transaction fees and efficient trading process, which has contributed to its popularity among cryptocurrency traders.

Uniswap's decentralized nature means users retain control over their funds and are not exposed to the risks associated with centralized exchanges. Liquidity providers on Uniswap earn a share of the transaction fees generated by the platform, offering a passive income stream. The UNI token, Uniswap's governance token, grants holders voting rights on proposals affecting the platform's future. Uniswap's user-friendly interface and robust functionality make it a leading choice for decentralized trading.

OpenSea: OpenSea is a peer-to-peer marketplace for buying, selling, and trading non-fungible tokens (NFTs). With 2.3 million active users and a valuation of $13 billion, OpenSea is a major player in the NFT space. The platform allows users to trade a wide range of digital assets, including collectibles, game items, and virtual real estate.

OpenSea operates on a decentralized model, facilitating direct transactions between buyers and sellers without intermediaries. This approach reduces transaction fees and offers greater control over the trading process. The use of blockchain technology ensures the security and transparency of transactions. Despite facing criticism for insider trading and phishing attacks, OpenSea's extensive range of NFTs and its role in the growing digital asset market solidify its position as a leading NFT marketplace.

Rarible: Rarible is another prominent NFT marketplace that allows users to buy, sell, and mint digital assets. Rarible distinguishes itself with features such as gas-free minting, multiple wallet support, and credit card payments. It supports transactions in Tezos, Flow, and Ethereum, with a fixed transaction fee of 2.5% and the ability to purchase NFTs with fiat currencies.

Rarible's user-friendly interface and diverse asset offerings attract both experienced traders and newcomers. With over 15,000 unique active users, Rarible continues to grow as a popular platform for NFT trading. Its accessibility and innovative features contribute to its appeal in the competitive NFT marketplace.

Sandbox: Sandbox is a metaverse platform that allows users to purchase, develop, and monetize virtual land within a blockchain-based digital environment. With a market cap of $1.4 billion and over 160,000 property plots, Sandbox provides a space for users to invest in and create digital assets. The platform's largest virtual land sale raised $4.3 million, highlighting its significant impact in the virtual real estate market.

Sandbox's integration of blockchain technology enables users to own and develop virtual properties, fostering a creative and interactive digital ecosystem. With 39,000 daily users and a growing community, Sandbox represents a major innovation in the metaverse and digital asset investment.

1inch: 1inch Network is a DeFi aggregator that helps users find the best prices across multiple decentralized exchanges. Launched in 2019, 1inch utilizes its aggregation protocol to route trades efficiently, leveraging platforms like Ethereum, Polygon, and BNB Chain. With approximately 23,500 daily users and a market capitalization of $334.08 million, 1inch offers a comprehensive solution for optimizing trades and accessing liquidity.

The platform's ability to aggregate liquidity from various sources ensures users receive the best possible rates, making it a valuable tool for DeFi traders and investors. 1inch's focus on efficiency and cost-effectiveness enhances the overall trading experience.

Marinade Finance: Marinade Finance is the first liquid staking protocol on the Solana blockchain, launched in August 2021. With over 450 validators and $240.96 million in total value locked, Marinade Finance offers users the ability to stake Solana (SOL) tokens and receive rewards without the traditional unstaking period. This innovative approach to staking provides liquidity and flexibility for SOL holders.

Decentraland: Decentraland is an Ethereum-based virtual world where users can create, consume, and monetize content. With a market cap of $1.31 billion and an average of 600 daily users, Decentraland enables users to purchase and develop digital real estate, participate in governance, and trade unique digital assets. The MANA token, used for transactions and governance, plays a central role in the platform's economy.

Decentraland's integration of blockchain technology creates a secure and decentralized environment for virtual experiences, making it a notable project in the metaverse space.

Balancer: Balancer is a decentralized exchange (DEX) and automated market maker (AMM) protocol that stands out in the Ethereum-based decentralized finance (DeFi) ecosystem for its flexibility and user control. It enables the creation of custom liquidity pools with varying compositions of cryptocurrencies, offering a level of customization that is not commonly found in traditional AMMs.

Central to Balancer's functionality is the Vault, a sophisticated smart contract that manages all tokens across different liquidity pools. This architecture separates the accounting of assets from the pool logic itself, which enhances transaction efficiency and reduces gas costs. The Vault's design allows for multi-hop trades, where transactions can be optimized by minimizing token transfers and thus lowering overall transaction costs.

Unlike traditional AMMs that are restricted to fixed trading pairs, Balancer allows for pools containing multiple tokens in any ratio. This flexibility increases market efficiency by accommodating niche or less commonly traded tokens, thereby enhancing overall liquidity. Additionally, Balancer's advanced algorithms find the best trading paths across its pools, optimizing pricing for users. This means reduced slippage and transaction fees, while maximizing returns on trades.

The native token of Balancer, BAL, plays a dual role in governance and incentivization. Token holders can vote on critical protocol decisions, such as changes to the platform and reward structures. BAL tokens are also distributed as rewards to liquidity providers, encouraging them to contribute to the platform and participate in its governance.

Balancer's combination of innovative features and commitment to decentralization makes it a significant player in the DeFi space. It provides a robust and flexible platform for both trading and liquidity provision, appealing to both novice and experienced users in the cryptocurrency market.

Compound: Compound is a leading decentralized finance (DeFi) protocol that enables users to lend and borrow cryptocurrencies in a decentralized manner. Built on the Ethereum blockchain, Compound offers a unique peer-to-peer lending system where users can earn interest by providing liquidity to borrowers.

The protocol operates through smart contracts, which autonomously match lenders and borrowers without the need for traditional financial intermediaries. This system ensures transparency and reduces the need for third parties, allowing users to engage in lending and borrowing with greater efficiency and lower costs.

Compound incorporates an Automated Market Maker (AMM) to facilitate the lending and borrowing process. The AMM dynamically adjusts interest rates based on the supply and demand for each asset within the Compound ecosystem. This algorithmic approach helps in matching borrowers with lenders efficiently, ensuring that interest rates reflect current market conditions.

The COMP token is central to Compound's governance model. Holders of COMP tokens have the ability to vote on important protocol decisions, such as updates to the system and treasury management. This governance structure empowers users to influence the future direction of the protocol, fostering a decentralized decision-making process.

Overall, Compound's decentralized lending and borrowing platform, combined with its use of AMM and governance through COMP tokens, positions it as a pivotal player in the DeFi landscape, offering a secure and efficient alternative to traditional financial systems.

Yearn Finance: Yearn Finance is a prominent decentralized finance (DeFi) project focused on maximizing returns for cryptocurrency holders through its yield aggregator and liquidity provision services. The platform's core products, Vaults and Earn, are designed to optimize users' investment returns by automatically reinvesting and diversifying assets across various DeFi protocols.

What sets Yearn Finance apart is its use of the YFI token, which plays a crucial role in the platform's governance and investment strategy. YFI holders have the power to vote on key decisions regarding platform changes and capital allocation. This approach ensures that the platform remains agile and responsive to market conditions, continuously seeking the best investment opportunities for its users.

Yearn Finance's Vaults allow users to deposit their assets into various investment strategies, which are managed to maximize yield. The Earn product similarly provides opportunities for users to earn interest on their holdings by leveraging different DeFi strategies. Despite recent fluctuations in YFI's market price, Yearn Finance remains a significant and innovative player in the DeFi space, known for its commitment to delivering high returns and adapting to evolving market conditions.

MakerDAO: MakerDAO is a decentralized application (dApp) on the Ethereum blockchain that offers a unique solution within the DeFi ecosystem by providing a stablecoin, DAI, which is pegged to the U.S. dollar. MakerDAO enables users to receive DAI tokens in exchange for locking up ETH as collateral, helping to maintain the stability of DAI and providing a reliable stablecoin solution.

The platform is essential for stabilizing the DeFi ecosystem, as it offers a way for traders and investors to engage in cryptocurrency transactions without the volatility typically associated with other digital assets. This stability simplifies trading and investment decisions, as users can rely on a consistent value for their transactions.

Furthermore, MakerDAO's smart contract system allows borrowers to secure loans by leveraging their crypto assets, creating a trustless and transparent system. This process removes the need for intermediaries, ensuring fairness and transparency in the borrowing process.

MakerDAO's provision of the DAI stablecoin and its ability to offer decentralized loans through collateralized assets make it a crucial component of the DeFi space. It provides stability and transparency, enhancing the ease of trading and borrowing in a decentralized environment.

KAI-CHING: KAI-CHING is an innovative decentralized application (dApp) that merges gaming with finance to create an engaging financial platform. Built on blockchain technology, KAI-CHING combines traditional financial transactions with interactive gaming elements, offering users both entertainment and investment opportunities.

The platform leverages gamified finance, transforming financial activities into enjoyable gaming experiences. This approach not only makes finance more accessible but also enhances user engagement through interactive features and reward systems. Users can earn and use tokens within the platform, participate in games, and engage in investment-like activities.

KAI-CHING's infrastructure supports a variety of financial services integrated with gaming elements. Users can participate in challenges and competitions that simulate real-world trading scenarios in a controlled, low-risk environment. This gamified approach helps users understand financial concepts, risk management, and market speculation in a fun and interactive way.

Emphasizing community and social interaction, KAI-CHING encourages users to collaborate and compete with one another. Features such as leaderboards and shared challenges foster a sense of community and allow users to connect, share strategies, and engage in friendly competition.

Overall, KAI-CHING distinguishes itself by combining gaming with financial activities, offering a novel and engaging way to interact with financial markets. Its use of blockchain technology ensures transparency and security, making it a reliable platform for both entertainment and financial activities.

Curve: Curve is a decentralized exchange (DEX) known for its specialization in stablecoin trading. Unlike other DEXs, Curve is designed to facilitate efficient and low-slippage transactions involving stablecoins. This focus on stablecoin trading helps users avoid the excessive fees and slippage often encountered when trading between stablecoins and major cryptocurrencies.

Curve's automated market maker (AMM) algorithm is tailored to manage stablecoin liquidity effectively. By optimizing the trading process for stablecoins, Curve minimizes the impact of slippage, ensuring that users can trade large amounts of stablecoins with minimal price deviations.

The platform offers low transaction fees, making it a cost-effective option for stablecoin traders. This efficiency is achieved through Curve's streamlined trading mechanism, which is both fast and economical.

The CRV token is integral to Curve's governance system. Token holders can vote on protocol decisions, including changes to fee structures and liquidity incentives. This governance model allows for community involvement in the platform's development and ensures that decisions reflect the interests of its users.

Curve's focus on efficient stablecoin trading, low transaction fees, and community governance through the CRV token positions it as a valuable and unique player in the DeFi ecosystem, providing a reliable and cost-effective platform for stablecoin transactions.

In summary, these dApps exemplify the diverse applications of blockchain technology, from decentralized trading and NFT marketplaces to metaverse platforms and DeFi solutions. Each dApp offers unique features and opportunities, reflecting the growing innovation and adoption within the blockchain ecosystem.

Future Developments in Smart Contracts

As blockchain technology evolves, the capabilities and use cases for smart contracts are likely to expand. Innovations in coding languages, interoperability between different blockchains, and improvements in security measures are expected to enhance the functionality and reliability of smart contracts. Moreover, as regulatory frameworks develop to address the unique challenges posed by smart contracts, their adoption and integration into mainstream applications are anticipated to grow. Overall, smart contracts represent a significant advancement in the way agreements are executed and enforced, with the potential to revolutionize numerous industries.

Smart contracts are on the verge of transforming various sectors by offering unprecedented levels of automation, transparency, and efficiency. Their ability to execute predefined actions automatically once certain conditions are met makes them particularly attractive to industries like finance, real estate, supply chain management, and healthcare. In finance, smart contracts can streamline complex processes such as loan approvals and insurance claims by automating decision-making based on real-time data. In real estate, they can simplify property transactions by automatically transferring ownership upon completion of agreed-upon terms. The healthcare industry could benefit from smart contracts through automated patient data management and streamlined insurance claims. As blockchain technology evolves and becomes more integrated into mainstream systems, smart contracts are expected to become a standard tool, further embedding themselves into these and other sectors [306].

The Internet of Things (IoT) represents a significant frontier for smart contracts, combining the physical and digital worlds through interconnected devices. IoT devices generate vast amounts of data, which can be leveraged by smart contracts to automate processes and transactions based on real-world information. For instance, smart contracts could be used to manage utility payments by automatically deducting charges based on data from smart meters. In supply chain management, they can automate inventory management by triggering orders when stock levels reach a certain threshold. The seamless integration of smart contracts with IoT has the potential to create more efficient and responsive systems, reducing the need for manual intervention and enhancing overall operational efficiency [306].

While smart contracts enhance security through their decentralized and immutable nature, they are not without vulnerabilities. As their usage becomes more widespread, ensuring their security will be paramount. Emerging security techniques, such as formal verification and advanced cryptographic methods, will play a crucial role in protecting smart contracts from potential exploits. Additionally, privacy-preserving technologies like zero-knowledge proofs and secure multi-party computation are expected to gain prominence. Zero-knowledge proofs allow for the verification of information without revealing the underlying data, while secure multi-party computation enables collaborative data processing without exposing individual inputs. These advancements will help address privacy concerns and bolster the overall security of smart contracts [306].

As smart contracts become more integrated into various industries, they will inevitably intersect with existing legal and regulatory frameworks. This intersection is likely to prompt significant developments in how smart contracts are regulated and recognized by law. New legislation may emerge to define the legal status of smart contracts, clarify their enforceability, and establish guidelines for their use. Legal disputes involving smart contracts could set important precedents, shaping future regulations and interpretations. The evolving regulatory landscape will need to balance innovation with consumer protection, ensuring that smart contracts are both effective and compliant with legal standards [306].

Interoperability—the ability of different blockchain platforms to interact and exchange information—is a crucial trend for the future of smart contracts. As the blockchain ecosystem grows, diverse platforms and networks will need to communicate and work together seamlessly. Interoperability could enable new types of applications, such as cross-chain financial products that leverage assets from multiple blockchains or decentralized data marketplaces that aggregate data from various sources. Achieving interoperability will require advancements in cross-chain protocols and standards, ensuring that smart contracts can operate across different blockchain environments efficiently. This will open up new possibilities for innovation and collaboration within the blockchain space, expanding the potential use cases for smart contracts [306].

Chapter Fourteen
Cryptocurrencies and Society

The Social Impact of Cryptocurrencies

Cryptocurrency development is a multifaceted process that involves the creation, maintenance, and evolution of digital currencies and their underlying technologies. At its core, cryptocurrency represents a form of digital or virtual currency that leverages cryptography to ensure security. Unlike traditional currencies, cryptocurrencies operate independently of centralized authorities such as governments or financial institutions. This independence is achieved through decentralized systems that eliminate the need for intermediaries in transactions [307].

The development of cryptocurrency involves a range of activities starting with the design and implementation of algorithms and protocols. These elements are critical for enabling the creation, transfer, and verification of digital assets. One of the fundamental technologies underlying cryptocurrencies is blockchain technology. A blockchain serves as a decentralized ledger that records all transactions in a transparent and immutable manner. This technology ensures that once a transaction is recorded, it cannot be altered or deleted, which enhances the security and reliability of the cryptocurrency [307].

A key challenge in cryptocurrency development is scalability. As cryptocurrencies gain popularity, they must be able to handle increasing transaction volumes without compromising performance. Developers work on various solutions to address scalability issues, such as optimizing consensus algorithms and implementing layer-2 solutions like state channels and sidechains. These solutions aim to increase transaction throughput and reduce latency while maintaining the security and decentralization of the network [307].

Security is another critical concern in cryptocurrency development. Cryptocurrencies are often targets for cyberattacks, including hacks and fraud. Ensuring the security of digital assets involves implementing robust cryptographic techniques, conducting regular security audits, and developing secure software protocols. Developers also focus on creating secure wallets for storing cryptocurrencies, which are essential for protecting users' assets from theft or loss [307].

Regulatory compliance is an increasingly important aspect of cryptocurrency development. As cryptocurrencies become more integrated into financial systems, they face scrutiny from regulatory bodies. Developers must navigate complex legal frameworks and ensure that their projects comply with regulations related to anti-money laundering (AML), know-your-customer (KYC) requirements, and other financial regulations. This often involves incorporating features that support regulatory compliance while balancing the need for user privacy and security [307].

Additionally, cryptocurrency development extends beyond basic currency transactions. Developers work on enhancing user interfaces to make cryptocurrencies more accessible and user-friendly. They also create applications that leverage blockchain technology for various purposes, such as decentralized finance (DeFi) platforms, non-fungible tokens (NFTs), and smart contracts. These applications demonstrate the versatility of blockchain technology and its potential to transform various industries beyond traditional financial transactions [307].

One of the most promising aspects of cryptocurrency development is its potential to enhance financial inclusion. Traditional banking systems often leave out large segments of the global population, particularly in developing regions where access to banking services is limited. Cryptocurrencies can offer an alternative means of financial participation for the unbanked and underbanked by providing accessible and affordable financial services. Understanding the social dynamics of these underserved populations helps developers create solutions that address their specific needs, such as low transaction fees and easy access via mobile devices. By doing so, cryptocurrencies can help bridge the gap between different socioeconomic groups, reduce economic disparities, and promote financial empowerment on a global scale [307].

Cryptocurrency development frequently intersects with complex regulatory frameworks. The legal status of cryptocurrencies and related technologies varies widely across jurisdictions, and navigating this regulatory landscape can be challenging. Understanding the social and political context in which cryptocurrencies operate helps developers anticipate and address regulatory challenges more effectively. This includes being aware of local regulatory requirements, working with policymakers, and ensuring that projects comply with laws related to anti-money laundering (AML), know-your-customer (KYC) regulations, and other financial regulations. Balancing compliance with innovation is crucial for fostering a healthy regulatory environment that supports technological advancement while protecting users and maintaining financial integrity [307].

The volatile nature of cryptocurrency markets presents risks to consumers, including exposure to scams, fraud, and market manipulation. By understanding the social impacts and vulnerabilities of users, developers can design platforms and protocols with built-in safeguards to enhance consumer protection. This may involve implementing features such as secure transaction protocols, user education programs, and transparent practices to prevent exploitation. Ensuring that cryptocurrency transactions are fair and transparent helps build trust among users and contributes to a more stable and reliable market environment [307].

Cryptocurrency projects often rely on strong community support and active participation for their success. Understanding the social dynamics within cryptocurrency communities—such as their values, concerns, and expectations—can help developers build platforms that resonate with users and encourage their engagement. Fostering a sense of trust, transparency, and inclusivity within these communities is essential for the long-term sustainability of a project. Engaging with community members, soliciting feedback, and addressing their needs and concerns can lead to higher adoption rates and stronger project loyalty [307].

Cryptocurrency mining and transaction verification, particularly with proof-of-work (PoW) systems, can have significant environmental impacts due to high energy consumption. Understanding the social and environmental implications of these practices is critical for developing more sustainable solutions. Developers are increasingly exploring eco-friendly consensus mechanisms, such as proof-of-stake (PoS), and optimizing energy usage to reduce the carbon footprint associated with cryptocurrency operations. By addressing environmental concerns, developers can contribute to the broader goal of creating sustainable and responsible technologies [307].

The rise of cryptocurrencies has the potential to disrupt traditional financial systems and influence global economic dynamics. This includes altering the way transactions are conducted, impacting monetary policies, and affecting international trade. Understanding the social and economic implications of these shifts helps developers anticipate and navigate the challenges and opportunities that arise. By considering the broader economic context, developers can create solutions that contribute positively to economic development, stability, and the integration of cryptocurrencies into the global financial system [307].

Economic Empowerment Through Cryptocurrency Development

Economic empowerment through cryptocurrency development is a topic of growing interest due to the potential for blockchain and cryptocurrency technologies to positively impact economic stability and efficiency [308]. Cryptocurrencies offer new means of revenue generation at individual, organizational, and national levels, stimulating crypto-token-based business models and investment opportunities [309]. The development of blockchain and cryptocurrency is seen as a way to alleviate economic strains associated with recession [310]. By expanding the influence of cryptocurrencies through adoption, countries can enhance their impact on the global economy [311].

One of the most transformative impacts of cryptocurrency development is its potential to offer economic empowerment, particularly in regions where traditional banking services are sparse or inaccessible. Cryptocurrencies operate on decentralized networks, allowing individuals to engage in financial transactions directly with one another, without the need for intermediaries such as banks or payment processors. This decentralized nature reduces transaction costs and barriers to entry, making financial services more accessible and affordable for people who previously lacked access to traditional financial systems. For example, individuals in remote or underserved areas can use cryptocurrencies to receive payments, transfer funds, or make purchases without relying on expensive and often unreliable banking infrastructure [307].

The rise of decentralized finance (DeFi) platforms represents a significant leap forward in promoting financial inclusion. Built on blockchain technology, DeFi platforms offer a broad array of financial services—including lending, borrowing, staking, and earning interest—outside the traditional banking system. This inclusivity enables individuals to participate in financial activities that were previously restricted to those with access to conventional banking services. By leveraging smart contracts and blockchain technology, DeFi platforms provide an accessible and transparent way for users to manage and grow their assets. This increased accessibility has the potential to democratize financial services, helping to bridge the gap between the financially included and excluded populations.

Economic empowerment through cryptocurrency can have a ripple effect, contributing to broader economic growth and development. By providing individuals with the tools to manage and grow their wealth, cryptocurrencies and DeFi platforms can stimulate entrepreneurial activities and innovation. Small business owners and entrepreneurs in emerging markets can access capital and financial services that were once out of reach, enabling them to start and scale their ventures. This entrepreneurial spirit can drive job creation, increase productivity, and contribute to overall economic development. Additionally, the ability to access and manage funds more efficiently can help alleviate poverty and improve living standards.

Cryptocurrencies and blockchain technology can foster entrepreneurship by lowering the barriers to starting and running a business. Traditional financial systems often require extensive documentation and credit history for securing loans or investments, which can be prohibitive for many entrepreneurs. In contrast, DeFi platforms offer alternative funding mechanisms, such as decentralized lending and crowdfunding, that enable individuals to access capital more easily. This democratization of financial services encourages innovation and allows individuals from diverse backgrounds to bring their ideas to fruition, creating new business opportunities and contributing to economic growth.

Despite their potential, cryptocurrencies and DeFi platforms face several challenges that may impede their full realization of economic empowerment. Regulatory scrutiny is one significant obstacle, as governments and financial regulators seek to establish frameworks to manage risks associated with digital assets. Ensuring compliance with regulations while fostering innovation is a delicate balance that developers and policymakers must navigate. Additionally, technological barriers such as limited internet access, digital literacy, and cybersecurity concerns can affect the adoption and effectiveness of cryptocurrency solutions. Addressing these challenges requires a collaborative effort between developers, regulators, and communities to create an environment that supports economic empowerment while mitigating risks.

In the context of microfinance, cryptocurrencies have been identified as beneficial for borrowers, microfinance institutions, and educational institutions [312]. The use of cryptocurrencies in microfinance can empower individuals and communities by providing access to financial services and fostering economic development. Additionally, managing cryptocurrencies through financial intermediaries can offer numerous benefits to global financial markets and the economy [313]. This highlights the potential for cryptocurrencies to play a significant role in shaping the future of financial systems.

The economic empowerment of women is a crucial aspect of sustainable development, with financial autonomy and increased decision-making roles being key components [314]. Women's economic empowerment can lead to improved financial inclusion, asset ownership, and wealth creation, contributing to larger economic empowerment efforts [315]. Furthermore, the role of cooperatives in empowering women in developing countries has been recognized as a key factor in promoting economic independence and self-reliance [316].

In the realm of community development, economic empowerment plays a vital role in improving economic well-being and fostering sustainable growth [317]. Empowering communities through initiatives such as the development of micro-enterprises can lead to increased economic stability and prosperity. Moreover, the success of economic empowerment initiatives can have a positive impact on living standards and overall welfare within communities [318]. By stabilizing economic conditions and empowering local businesses, communities can experience significant growth and development.

The development of cryptocurrencies presents a unique opportunity for economic empowerment at various levels, from individuals to nations. By leveraging blockchain technology and embracing the potential of cryptocurrencies, societies can foster innovation, stimulate economic growth, and empower marginalized groups such as women and underserved communities. However, it is essential to address regulatory challenges, mitigate risks, and ensure inclusive access to cryptocurrency technologies to realize their full potential in driving economic empowerment.

Cryptocurrency Development and Its Impact on Financial Freedom and Independence

Cryptocurrency development is transforming the way individuals manage and control their finances. Traditionally, financial transactions and wealth management have relied heavily on intermediaries such as banks and financial institutions. These intermediaries not only charge fees but also have the power to impose restrictions, control access, and even seize funds under certain circumstances. Cryptocurrencies, however, operate on decentralized networks that do not require intermediaries. This decentralization grants individuals greater control over their wealth, allowing them to store, manage, and transfer their assets independently. By using digital currencies, people can bypass traditional financial systems, reducing their exposure to the risks of censorship or seizure of funds by authorities or financial institutions [307].

One of the most compelling aspects of cryptocurrencies is their ability to facilitate borderless transactions. Traditional banking systems often involve complex procedures, high fees, and delays when transferring money across geographic boundaries. Cryptocurrencies offer a seamless and cost-effective alternative by allowing individuals to conduct transactions globally without the need for expensive intermediaries. This accessibility is particularly beneficial for individuals in regions with underdeveloped financial infrastructure or those who are unbanked. By providing a means to engage in financial activities without geographic limitations, cryptocurrencies contribute to financial inclusion and broaden opportunities for individuals worldwide.

The emergence of decentralized finance (DeFi) platforms represents a significant advancement in financial services. Built on blockchain technology, DeFi platforms provide a wide range of financial services, including lending, borrowing, and earning interest on digital assets. These services are accessible directly through blockchain networks, eliminating the need for traditional financial institutions. DeFi platforms leverage smart contracts to automate and enforce financial agreements, offering transparency and efficiency. This innovation further enhances financial freedom by enabling individuals to participate in financial activities that were previously restricted to those with access to conventional banks. As a result, users can manage their finances more effectively, grow their wealth, and access capital without relying on traditional financial intermediaries.

Despite the promising potential of cryptocurrencies to enhance financial freedom and independence, several challenges and limitations must be addressed. Regulatory uncertainties pose a significant obstacle, as governments and financial regulators work to establish frameworks that govern the use and exchange of digital currencies. Balancing regulatory compliance with the need for innovation remains a complex issue for developers and policymakers. Additionally, technological limitations such as scalability, security concerns, and the digital divide can impact the effectiveness and adoption of cryptocurrency solutions. For example, not all regions have reliable internet access or digital literacy, which can hinder the widespread use of cryptocurrencies.

Looking ahead, the continued development of cryptocurrencies is expected to further advance financial freedom and independence. As technological innovations and regulatory frameworks evolve, cryptocurrencies and DeFi platforms are likely to become more integrated into the global financial system. This integration could reshape the financial landscape, offering new opportunities for individuals and businesses alike. The ongoing advancement of blockchain technology, coupled with increased acceptance and adoption, will likely drive the evolution of digital currencies and their impact on financial systems [307].

Social Equality and Inclusion

The ongoing development of cryptocurrencies offers a promising pathway towards fostering social equality and inclusion by democratizing access to financial services, reducing discrimination, and empowering marginalized communities. Cryptocurrencies have the potential to empower marginalized communities by providing them with financial tools and opportunities that were previously out of reach [319]. This accessibility can significantly contribute to reducing financial discrimination by enabling peer-to-peer transactions without the need for intermediaries, thereby fostering greater economic participation and empowerment for individuals who have been historically excluded from traditional financial systems [320].

Decentralized finance (DeFi) built on blockchain and smart contract platforms like Ethereum has emerged as a key driver of financial inclusion [321]. The open, permissionless, and interoperable nature of DeFi protocols enables individuals to access a wide range of financial services without the need for traditional intermediaries, thereby democratizing financial opportunities [321]. Moreover, the interdependence between online peer-to-peer lending and cryptocurrency markets has been studied to understand its effects on financial inclusion, highlighting the potential synergies between these platforms in expanding access to financial services [322].

The impact of cryptocurrencies on global income inequality and wealth distribution has been studied, with findings indicating that cryptocurrencies, along with the gold standard, have contributed significantly to reducing global inequality [323]. By providing alternative avenues for financial transactions and wealth accumulation, cryptocurrencies have the potential to level the playing field and promote more equitable distribution of resources [323]. Furthermore, the role of cryptocurrencies in emerging markets has been investigated, highlighting their potential to improve financial inclusion and economic empowerment in developing countries [324].

The ongoing development of cryptocurrencies offers a promising pathway towards fostering social equality and inclusion by democratizing access to financial services, reducing discrimination, and empowering marginalized communities. Through innovative technologies like blockchain and DeFi, cryptocurrencies have the potential to revolutionize the financial landscape, providing individuals worldwide with opportunities for economic participation and empowerment. Clear regulatory frameworks, coupled with factors like financial literacy and ease of use, are essential in driving widespread adoption of cryptocurrencies and maximizing their impact on financial inclusion. As research in this field continues to evolve, it is crucial to leverage the transformative potential of cryptocurrencies to create a more inclusive and equitable financial system for all.

Philanthropy and Social Impact Projects: The Role of Cryptocurrency

One of the most notable social impacts of cryptocurrency development is its ability to transform philanthropy by enhancing transparency and efficiency in charitable donations. Traditional donation processes often involve multiple intermediaries, such as payment processors and charitable organizations, which can introduce inefficiencies and increase the risk of funds being misallocated or misused. Cryptocurrencies, through their underlying blockchain technology, offer a solution to these challenges by providing a secure, transparent, and direct method for transferring donations. Each transaction made with cryptocurrencies is recorded on a public ledger, which allows donors to track their contributions in real-time. This level of transparency ensures that funds are directed to their intended recipients and reduces the risk of fraud, as every transaction can be verified and audited. By streamlining the donation process, cryptocurrencies can increase donor confidence and encourage greater participation in charitable giving [307].

Cryptocurrencies also have the potential to drive social impact in regions with limited access to traditional financial services. In many parts of the world, individuals and organizations face significant barriers when trying to access conventional banking systems or secure funding for social projects. Cryptocurrencies, with their borderless and decentralized nature, can overcome these barriers by providing a direct and accessible means for funding social impact initiatives. For instance, projects focused on improving healthcare, education, or environmental conservation in underserved areas can benefit from cryptocurrency donations and investments. This direct access to funding can facilitate innovation and development in crucial sectors, helping to address local needs and promote sustainable development.

Beyond direct donations, cryptocurrencies can empower communities to create their own digital currencies, known as community tokens. These tokens can be designed to serve various purposes within a local context, such as incentivizing positive behaviours, supporting local projects, or fostering community engagement. For example, a community token could be used to reward individuals for participating in environmental conservation efforts or supporting local businesses. By leveraging blockchain technology, communities can design and manage their own economic systems, tailored to their specific needs and goals. This can enhance local economic resilience, foster a sense of community ownership, and drive grassroots innovation. However, the successful implementation of community tokens requires careful planning and management to ensure their effectiveness and sustainability.

Despite the potential benefits of cryptocurrencies in philanthropy and social impact projects, several challenges need to be addressed. Regulatory scrutiny is one such challenge, as governments and regulatory bodies continue to develop frameworks for cryptocurrency use. Ensuring compliance with legal and regulatory requirements while maintaining the decentralized and transparent nature of cryptocurrencies can be complex. Additionally, technological barriers, such as the need for internet access and digital literacy, can limit the effectiveness of cryptocurrency-based solutions in certain regions. Addressing these challenges will be crucial for fully realizing the potential of cryptocurrencies in advancing philanthropy and social impact.

Looking to the future, the continued development and adoption of cryptocurrencies hold promise for expanding their role in philanthropy and social impact projects. As technology evolves and regulatory frameworks adapt, cryptocurrencies could play an increasingly significant role in supporting charitable initiatives and community-driven projects. The potential for increased transparency, efficiency, and accessibility offers a compelling vision for the future of philanthropy and social impact, driven by the innovative capabilities of digital currencies and blockchain technology [307].

Regulatory Challenges and Social Implications in Cryptocurrency Development

One of the foremost regulatory challenges facing cryptocurrency development is the complexity and variability of regulations across different jurisdictions. Cryptocurrencies operate in a global ecosystem where regulatory frameworks differ markedly from one country to another. In some regions, regulations may be stringent, aiming to prevent illegal activities such as money laundering and fraud. In others, the regulatory environment may be more permissive, encouraging innovation and investment. This inconsistency creates a fragmented landscape where developers, investors, and users must navigate a patchwork of laws and regulations. The uncertainty surrounding regulatory requirements can create barriers to entry for new participants, hinder mainstream adoption, and impede the overall growth of the cryptocurrency sector. For example, stringent regulations or outright bans in certain jurisdictions can limit the ability of cryptocurrency projects to reach global audiences, thereby constraining their potential social impact [307].

Regulatory challenges also affect the accessibility of cryptocurrencies, which is particularly concerning for marginalized communities that already face barriers to traditional financial services. In regions with less regulatory clarity or restrictive regulations, individuals may encounter difficulties in accessing cryptocurrency exchanges, wallets, and other financial services. This lack of access can exacerbate existing economic disparities and prevent these communities from benefiting from the financial inclusion opportunities offered by cryptocurrencies. On the other hand, clear and supportive regulatory frameworks could facilitate greater access to digital currencies, potentially enabling more people to engage in the financial system, save money, and participate in economic activities. Thus, how regulators approach cryptocurrency can have significant implications for financial inclusion and economic empowerment among underserved populations.

Regulatory scrutiny can also impact the development of new technologies and business models within the cryptocurrency space. While regulations are essential for ensuring market integrity and protecting consumers, overly restrictive or unclear rules can stifle innovation by imposing high compliance costs or limiting the scope of permissible activities. For example, stringent regulations on Initial Coin Offerings (ICOs) or Decentralized Finance (DeFi) platforms may discourage startups from pursuing innovative projects or entering the market. This can lead to a slower pace of technological advancement and reduced competition, ultimately limiting the potential benefits of cryptocurrency development. On the other hand, well-designed regulations that provide clear guidelines while allowing for experimentation and growth can foster a more vibrant and innovative sector.

Despite these challenges, balanced and thoughtful regulation can have positive social implications. Effective regulatory frameworks can enhance consumer protection by establishing standards for security, transparency, and fairness. For instance, regulations that require cryptocurrency exchanges to implement robust anti-money laundering (AML) and know-your-customer (KYC) procedures can help prevent fraud and illicit activities, thereby increasing trust in the cryptocurrency ecosystem. Furthermore, clear regulations can provide legal certainty, which can attract institutional investors and mainstream adoption, ultimately contributing to the stability and legitimacy of the cryptocurrency market. By fostering an environment where innovation and consumer protection coexist, balanced regulation can support the broader social benefits of cryptocurrency development.

Navigating the regulatory landscape remains a key challenge for cryptocurrency development. Stakeholders in the cryptocurrency space, including developers, investors, and policymakers, must work collaboratively to address regulatory issues and advocate for frameworks that balance innovation with oversight. This involves engaging with regulators, participating in policy discussions, and promoting best practices that align with both market needs and societal goals. As the cryptocurrency sector continues to evolve, ongoing dialogue and adaptation will be crucial in shaping regulations that support positive social outcomes while mitigating risks.

Cultural Shifts and Global Perspectives in Cryptocurrency Development

The rise of cryptocurrencies is catalysing profound cultural shifts by challenging established concepts of money and ownership. Unlike traditional fiat currencies, which are issued and regulated by central authorities, cryptocurrencies operate on decentralized networks and are governed by algorithms and consensus mechanisms. This shift fundamentally alters how people perceive and interact with money. For many, especially in younger generations, digital currencies represent a departure from the conventional banking system, offering a new paradigm of financial autonomy and innovation. The concept of ownership is also evolving, as digital assets like cryptocurrencies and non-fungible tokens (NFTs) introduce novel ways of representing and transferring value. This cultural transformation is not just about adopting new technology but rethinking fundamental aspects of economic exchange and property rights in a digital age [307].

Younger generations are at the forefront of embracing cryptocurrencies, driven by their comfort with technology and openness to alternative financial systems. For many millennials and Gen Z individuals, digital currencies are a natural extension of their digital lives, integrating seamlessly with their online activities and social interactions. This demographic is more inclined to explore innovative financial solutions, such as decentralized finance (DeFi) platforms and digital wallets, which align with their values of convenience, transparency, and financial inclusion. As these younger individuals become the dominant economic participants, their preferences and behaviours will increasingly shape the future of financial systems, potentially accelerating the adoption of cryptocurrencies and influencing how they are integrated into mainstream economic activities.

Cryptocurrencies are breaking down traditional barriers to cross-border transactions, fostering a more global perspective on finance. By operating on decentralized networks, cryptocurrencies enable instant and cost-effective transfers across geographic boundaries, circumventing the limitations of traditional financial systems that often involve high fees and delays. This global approach to financial transactions enhances financial inclusion, particularly in developing countries where access to banking services may be limited. Individuals in these regions can now participate in the global economy, access international markets, and receive remittances more efficiently. This increased connectivity also influences regulatory discussions and economic policies as governments and institutions grapple with the implications of a borderless digital economy. The need to adapt to this new financial landscape prompts a re-evaluation of existing frameworks and the development of new regulations that address the unique challenges posed by cryptocurrencies.

As cryptocurrencies gain prominence, they are influencing regulatory discussions and economic policies on a global scale. Governments and regulatory bodies are actively engaged in assessing how to address the complexities of a digital, decentralized economy. This includes developing regulations that balance innovation with oversight, ensuring consumer protection, and addressing concerns related to security, taxation, and anti-money laundering. The rise of cryptocurrencies also prompts discussions on monetary policy, as traditional financial systems must adapt to the growing role of digital assets in economic transactions. These regulatory and policy shifts are critical in shaping how cryptocurrencies are integrated into the broader financial system and how they impact economic stability and growth.

Overall, cryptocurrency development is contributing to a broader cultural shift towards digital, decentralized, and globalized financial systems. This transformation extends beyond mere technological adoption, influencing how people perceive value, engage in financial transactions, and interact with economic systems. The growing acceptance and integration of cryptocurrencies are reshaping societal attitudes towards money and ownership, fostering greater financial inclusion, and prompting a re-evaluation of regulatory and economic policies. As these changes continue to unfold, they will have far-reaching implications for society, driving further innovation and altering the landscape of global finance.

Financial Inclusion and Cryptocurrencies

As cryptocurrencies become more mainstream, they are expected to be embraced by a wider array of individuals and businesses, fostering greater financial inclusion and empowerment [325]. This surge in adoption is likely to democratize finance, granting individuals more autonomy over their finances and diminishing their dependence on conventional financial institutions. Moreover, the enhanced accessibility facilitated by cryptocurrency development will streamline the process of buying, selling, and utilizing digital currencies, thereby revolutionizing how people engage with money, finance, and the global economy [326].

While the prospects of increased adoption and accessibility are promising, certain challenges such as regulatory ambiguity and technological hurdles could impede the progress towards broader adoption, particularly for certain demographics [327]. Overcoming these obstacles will be crucial in realizing the full potential of cryptocurrencies to reshape financial landscapes and empower individuals worldwide. The social ramifications of heightened cryptocurrency adoption and accessibility are anticipated to be profound, fundamentally altering societal perceptions and interactions with financial systems [328].

Research has shown that the adoption of cryptocurrencies is influenced by various factors such as perceived usefulness, ease of use, innovativeness, attitude, perceived risk, and output quality [10]. Understanding these determinants is essential for policymakers and industry stakeholders to navigate the evolving landscape of digital currencies effectively. Studies have also highlighted the significance of subjective norms, global attention, and behavioural biases in shaping individuals' decisions regarding cryptocurrency adoption [329]. By elucidating these factors, researchers aim to provide insights that can inform strategies to promote wider acceptance and utilization of cryptocurrencies.

Moreover, the role of trust in driving cryptocurrency adoption cannot be understated, as it plays a pivotal role in instilling confidence among users and investors [330]. Establishing trust in the security and reliability of cryptocurrency systems is paramount for fostering a conducive environment for adoption. Additionally, the integration of technology acceptance models like TAM (Technology Acceptance Model) has been instrumental in understanding consumers' intentions to adopt cryptocurrency platforms [331]. By leveraging such models, researchers can delve deeper into the intricacies of user behaviour and preferences in the realm of digital currencies.

Furthermore, the impact of cryptocurrency adoption extends beyond individual users to encompass broader economic implications, including financial innovation and regulatory frameworks [332]. Policymakers and regulators play a crucial role in shaping the trajectory of cryptocurrency adoption by establishing clear guidelines and frameworks that balance innovation with consumer protection. Studies have also underscored the transformative potential of cryptocurrencies in enhancing financial inclusion and economic empowerment, particularly in developing countries [333]. By leveraging digital currencies, individuals in underserved regions can gain access to financial services and participate more actively in the global economy.

Cryptocurrencies in Developing Economies

The rise of cryptocurrency has indeed sent ripples across the global financial landscape, challenging traditional systems and drawing significant interest from both investors and policymakers. The allure of cryptocurrencies lies in their potential to disrupt and revolutionize established financial norms, offering new ways of conducting transactions, storing value, and engaging in economic activities. While much of the attention has focused on developed regions where crypto markets are already established, the impact of cryptocurrency extends far beyond these areas, with developing countries emerging as particularly interesting and transformative arenas for digital currency adoption [334].

Despite the global cryptocurrency market being predominantly centred in developed regions like North America and East Asia, developing economies are rapidly increasing their involvement in the crypto space. A 2023 Chainalysis report reveals that 40% of the world's cryptocurrency users are now based in lower-middle-income countries (LMICs). This significant proportion highlights the accelerating interest and adoption of cryptocurrencies in these regions. The adoption is driven by a combination of factors that make cryptocurrencies particularly appealing in contexts where traditional financial systems may be lacking or inadequate [334].

Research from 2022 reveals a notable trend: cryptocurrency adoption is significantly higher in developing economies, particularly across Asia, Africa, and Latin America. This trend is evident in the substantial share of cryptocurrency users in these regions compared to developed nations. For instance, countries like Thailand, Nigeria, the Philippines, South Africa, Argentina, Indonesia, and Brazil are among the top ten countries with the highest percentage of crypto users. Thailand leads with 20% of its population involved in cryptocurrency, while Nigeria, the Philippines, and South Africa each have 19%, and Argentina follows closely with 18% [335]. Indonesia and Brazil both see 16% of their populations engaged with cryptocurrencies. This high adoption rate in low- and middle-income countries highlights a growing trend of digital currency integration in regions where traditional financial systems may be less accessible or less efficient [335].

Several factors contribute to this elevated level of cryptocurrency adoption in developing economies. One major factor is the limited access to traditional banking services. In many of these countries, large segments of the population remain unbanked or underbanked, making cryptocurrencies an appealing alternative for financial inclusion. Cryptocurrencies provide a way for individuals to participate in the global economy without needing a traditional bank account, enabling access to financial services such as savings, payments, and investments [335].

Additionally, cryptocurrencies can serve as a hedge against economic instability and inflation, which are prevalent issues in some developing countries. The ability to store and transfer value in a digital form can protect individuals from the devaluation of local currencies and provide stability in uncertain economic environments [335].

The legal recognition of Bitcoin in El Salvador and the Central African Republic represents a significant milestone in cryptocurrency adoption. In 2021, El Salvador became the first country to officially adopt Bitcoin as legal tender, with the government aiming to leverage cryptocurrencies to reduce the cost of cross-border remittances and stimulate economic growth. Similarly, the Central African Republic followed suit in

2022, recognizing Bitcoin as legal tender with similar intentions of improving economic opportunities and financial inclusion [335].

However, these pioneering moves have not been without controversy. The International Monetary Fund (IMF) has voiced concerns about the potential risks associated with cryptocurrency adoption, particularly regarding financial stability. The IMF highlights the inherent volatility of cryptocurrencies, which can lead to significant fluctuations in value. This volatility poses risks to the broader financial system and could undermine economic stability if not carefully managed [335].

In both El Salvador and the Central African Republic, the implementation of cryptocurrencies as legal tender is viewed as a bold experiment aimed at harnessing the benefits of digital currencies. While these initiatives have the potential to drive economic innovation and inclusion, they also face challenges related to the integration of cryptocurrencies into existing financial systems and the broader implications for economic stability [335].

In many developing countries, traditional banking systems are not accessible to large segments of the population. These systems often suffer from inadequate infrastructure, high costs, or stringent requirements such as minimum balances, which can exclude many individuals from participating in the financial system. Cryptocurrencies offer a viable alternative by allowing people to engage in the digital economy without needing a traditional bank account. This increased financial inclusion enables individuals to store, transfer, and access value through digital means, thus bridging the gap between the unbanked and the broader economic system [334].

In countries experiencing high levels of inflation, cryptocurrencies can act as a safeguard against currency devaluation. Inflation erodes the value of traditional currencies, diminishing individuals' savings and purchasing power. Cryptocurrencies, with their decentralized nature and limited supply (as seen with Bitcoin), provide a potential hedge against such devaluation. By holding or transacting in cryptocurrencies, individuals can protect their assets from the adverse effects of inflation, preserving their purchasing power and financial stability [334].

The remittance industry is another area where cryptocurrencies offer substantial advantages. Sending money across borders traditionally involves high fees, delays, and lack of transparency. Cryptocurrencies streamline this process by providing a cheaper, faster, and more transparent means of transferring funds. For migrant workers who send remittances back to their families, this can result in significant cost savings and faster transaction times.

The ability to send and receive money quickly and affordably can have a profound impact on the economic well-being of recipients in developing countries [334].

The increasing penetration of smartphones and internet access in developing economies further supports the growth of cryptocurrency adoption. As mobile technology becomes more widespread, individuals in these regions are gaining access to mobile-based crypto wallets and decentralized financial applications (DeFi). These technological advancements facilitate the use of cryptocurrencies by providing accessible platforms for managing digital assets, engaging in financial activities, and participating in the growing ecosystem of decentralized finance [334].

The rise of cryptocurrency in developing economies is driven by several compelling factors, including the need for financial inclusion, protection against inflation, improved remittance processes, and the growing adoption of technology. As cryptocurrencies continue to gain traction in these regions, they hold the potential to bring about significant positive changes, transforming financial systems, enhancing economic stability, and providing new opportunities for individuals who have previously been underserved by traditional financial institutions. The ongoing developments in cryptocurrency adoption in developing countries will likely play a crucial role in shaping the future of the global financial landscape [334].

Remittances play a crucial role in the economies of developing countries, often accounting for a substantial portion of their GDP. Developing nations are frequently net exporters of Labor, with millions of workers migrating to other countries in search of better employment opportunities. According to the World Bank, nearly $550 billion worth of remittances were sent to low- and middle-income countries in 2019 [335]. These financial inflows are vital for many families and communities, providing essential support for everyday needs, education, and health care [335].

El Salvador serves as a notable example of a country heavily reliant on remittances. In this Central American nation, remittances constitute as much as 20% of the national economy. The vast majority of these funds—about 95%—come from Salvadoran workers based in the United States [335]. This heavy reliance on remittances underscores their importance as a financial lifeline for many Salvadorans and highlights the potential impact of changes in the remittance process.

Traditional cross-border remittance payments can be fraught with challenges. Transactions are often slow to process, taking several days to settle, and can incur high fees from intermediaries, such as banks and money transfer operators. These fees can make sending smaller amounts economically unfeasible, particularly for low-income individuals who might need to send funds frequently or in small quantities. The inefficiencies of traditional remittance systems can reduce the overall amount of money that reaches the recipients, impacting the effectiveness of financial support [335].

In many developing countries, remittances from migrants working abroad represent a crucial economic lifeline. These remittances, which are the funds sent back by individuals to their families or friends in their countries of origin, play a significant role in the economies of these nations. According to the World Bank, remittances can account for a substantial portion of a country's Gross Domestic Product (GDP), with figures reaching up to 20% and, in some cases, as high as 40% [336]. This high percentage underscores the importance of remittances in supporting household incomes, improving living standards, and fostering economic stability in these regions.

The rise of cryptocurrency has introduced a transformative alternative to traditional remittance methods. Cryptocurrencies offer an appealing solution for people in developing countries due to their potential to bypass traditional financial intermediaries, which often come with high fees and slow transaction times. The digital nature of cryptocurrencies allows for faster and more cost-effective transfers, which can be especially beneficial in regions where traditional financial infrastructure is limited or inefficient [336].

According to the Digital 2022 Global Overview Report, a collaboration between DataReportal, We Are Social, and Hootsuite, more than 1 in 10 working-age internet users globally now owns some form of cryptocurrency [336]. This statistic highlights a significant level of adoption among internet users, with developing economies showing even higher rates of cryptocurrency ownership. The higher prevalence in these regions is often attributed to several factors, including the volatility and instability of local fiat currencies, which make cryptocurrencies an attractive alternative for preserving value and conducting transactions [336].

In developing countries where conventional currencies are prone to fluctuations in exchange rates, cryptocurrencies offer a stable store of value and a means of financial security. The ability to hold and transfer funds in cryptocurrencies can help mitigate the risks associated with currency devaluation and economic instability. This stability is particularly appealing to individuals and businesses in regions where economic conditions are less predictable and where traditional financial systems may be inadequate or unreliable [336].

The adoption of cryptocurrencies is reshaping the remittance market by providing a more efficient and cost-effective way to send money across borders. With traditional remittance services often characterized by high fees and lengthy processing times, cryptocurrencies offer a streamlined alternative that reduces transaction costs and speeds up fund transfers. This shift not only benefits recipients by ensuring they receive more of the money sent but also enhances the overall accessibility of remittance services for migrants and their families [336].

Cryptocurrencies offer a promising alternative to traditional remittance methods by providing a more efficient and cost-effective means of transferring funds across borders. Digital currencies, particularly those built on blockchain technology, enable faster transactions that can be settled within minutes, regardless of the geographical distance between sender and receiver. Moreover, cryptocurrency transactions typically incur significantly lower fees compared to traditional remittance services. This reduction in costs can make it more feasible to send smaller amounts, enhancing the utility and accessibility of remittance services for users [335].

Some companies are already exploring the use of cryptocurrencies to improve remittance services. For instance, MoneyGram, a major player in the remittance industry, has experimented with stablecoin remittances on the Stellar blockchain [335]. Stablecoins are digital assets designed to maintain a stable value by being pegged to a reserve of assets, such as a fiat currency. By utilizing stablecoins, MoneyGram aims to provide a more stable and cost-effective remittance option compared to traditional methods. The Stellar blockchain offers the advantages of fast transaction times and low fees, making it an attractive platform for cross-border payments [335].

In many developing countries, economic instability is a significant issue. Hyperinflation, rampant corruption, and persistent financial hardship have plagued these regions, often as a result of flawed traditional financial systems. The local currencies in these countries frequently suffer from unpredictable inflation and volatile exchange rates, weakening their value over time. Cryptocurrencies have emerged as a viable alternative to these weak national currencies, offering a solution that bypasses many of the traditional financial system's shortcomings. Unlike fiat currencies, cryptocurrencies are decentralized and not subject to direct control by governments or banks, making them immune to local economic policies and manipulations. This decentralization allows individuals to have greater control over their assets, free from the restrictions and potential instability associated with traditional financial systems [336].

The decentralized nature of cryptocurrencies presents a compelling advantage for users in developing countries. Traditional financial systems are often marred by inefficiencies and corruption, leading to a lack of trust among citizens. Cryptocurrencies operate on blockchain technology, which utilizes a distributed digital ledger to record every transaction. This ledger is immutable, meaning that once a transaction is recorded, it cannot be altered or deleted. This feature reduces the risk of fraud and manipulation, fostering a higher degree of trust among users. In contrast to fiat currencies, which can be subject to reversals and corrupt practices, cryptocurrencies offer a transparent and reliable alternative where transactions are permanent and verifiable [336].

Despite the growing adoption of cryptocurrencies in developing countries, several challenges and limitations persist. One significant issue is the lack of widespread acceptance and recognition. Cryptocurrencies are not universally accepted as a means of payment, and their use is often restricted to specific platforms and merchants. This limitation hinders their practicality for everyday transactions and contrasts sharply with the established and globally accepted traditional payment methods. Furthermore, the regulatory environment for cryptocurrencies remains ambiguous in many regions. Approximately 80% of the world's central banks have either not adopted digital currencies or have unclear legal frameworks that do not accommodate cryptocurrencies fully [336].

Another critical challenge is the inherent volatility of cryptocurrencies. For example, Bitcoin has a maximum supply cap of 21 million coins, which creates a finite resource with its value determined solely by market demand. This limited supply, combined with high volatility, means that the value of cryptocurrencies can fluctuate dramatically. This unpredictability poses a significant risk, particularly for individuals and businesses in developing countries that may already be dealing with financial instability. Unlike traditional fiat currencies, which are managed by central banks to ensure stability, cryptocurrencies lack mechanisms to stabilize their value, making them highly susceptible to market shocks [336].

The international financial community, including institutions like the International Monetary Fund (IMF) and the World Bank, has expressed concerns about the adoption of cryptocurrencies as official currencies [336]. For instance, the IMF has cautioned that cryptocurrencies could expose countries to severe price volatility and undermine capital controls. The World Bank has similarly criticized the use of Bitcoin as legal tender, particularly in El Salvador, and has stated that it will not collaborate with the country on its cryptocurrency plans due to concerns over financial stability [336].

Despite these concerns, the potential benefits of cryptocurrencies are recognized. The IMF has encouraged the use of blockchain technology for digital upgrades to national currencies, which could provide developing countries with the technological advantages of cryptocurrencies without the associated risks of extreme volatility. This approach offers a way to harness the benefits of blockchain technology while maintaining stability through traditional currency systems [336].

The future of cryptocurrencies in developing countries remains uncertain and contentious. While cryptocurrencies offer promising solutions to longstanding financial issues and have gained substantial traction, they also come with significant risks and limitations. The debate is likely to continue as more developing countries explore the use of cryptocurrencies. The traditional global financial system is expected to evolve by integrating the benefits of blockchain technology while still grappling with the challenges posed by cryptocurrencies as official currencies. The outcome will depend on how well these nations and the global financial community can balance the innovative potential of cryptocurrencies with the need for economic stability and regulatory clarity [336].

Ethical Considerations

Cryptocurrency has rapidly evolved from a niche digital asset into a significant component of the financial landscape, revolutionizing traditional currency and transaction methods. As cryptocurrency use has become more widespread, it has raised important ethical concerns related to privacy, anonymity, and criminal activity. These issues reflect the complex interplay between the benefits of decentralization and the potential risks associated with unregulated financial environments [337].

Privacy and anonymity are among the most valued features of cryptocurrencies. Privacy refers to the ability of users to keep their personal information confidential, while anonymity pertains to the ability to conduct transactions without disclosing one's identity. Cryptocurrencies achieve these features through sophisticated cryptographic techniques and decentralized networks, which mask users' identities and transaction details [337].

The appeal of privacy and anonymity lies in their potential to protect users from various threats, including cyberattacks and government surveillance. Individuals who prioritize privacy may be motivated to use cryptocurrencies to shield their financial activities from prying eyes. For example, some users seek to protect sensitive financial information or avoid potential repercussions from authorities. However, these features also present ethical dilemmas, as the same attributes that provide privacy can also facilitate illicit activities [337].

The anonymity provided by cryptocurrencies can inadvertently create opportunities for illegal activities such as money laundering, terrorism financing, and cybercrime. The ability to conduct transactions without revealing one's identity makes it easier for individuals to engage in these activities without detection. This raises ethical concerns about whether the benefits of privacy and anonymity outweigh the risks associated with such misuse [337].

Additionally, the lack of transparency in cryptocurrency transactions can lead to tax evasion and other unethical practices. The decentralized nature of cryptocurrencies means that transactions are not subject to the same oversight and regulatory frameworks as traditional financial systems. This opacity can create loopholes for illicit activities and undermine efforts to ensure financial integrity and compliance [337].

Addressing these ethical challenges involves implementing measures to ensure that privacy and anonymity do not come at the expense of security and accountability. Various strategies can be employed to balance these concerns [337]:

- **Privacy-Focused Cryptocurrencies**: Some cryptocurrencies, like Monero, Zcash, and Dash, are designed to offer enhanced privacy features through advanced cryptographic techniques. These privacy-focused cryptocurrencies aim to provide a higher level of anonymity while still protecting users' financial information.

- **Anonymous Wallets**: These wallets allow users to store and manage their cryptocurrencies without revealing personal information. They often utilize technologies such as Tor network routing to mask users' IP addresses and enhance anonymity.

- **Decentralized Exchanges**: Decentralized exchanges enable users to trade cryptocurrencies without relying on centralized intermediaries. This approach enhances privacy and reduces the need for personal information disclosures.

- **Coin Mixing Services**: Coin mixing services combine users' cryptocurrencies to obscure transaction trails, making it more difficult to trace individual transactions. While these services can enhance privacy, they also have the potential for misuse in illegal activities.

- **Virtual Private Networks (VPNs)**: VPNs can mask users' IP addresses and locations, providing additional layers of anonymity when using cryptocurrency services.

Ethical Issues and Regulatory Considerations

The ethical issues surrounding cryptocurrency privacy and anonymity extend beyond individual user concerns to broader regulatory and societal implications [337]:

- **Balancing Privacy and Security**: Regulators must strike a balance between protecting users' privacy and ensuring that cryptocurrencies do not facilitate illegal activities. This involves developing frameworks that safeguard privacy while preventing misuse.

- **Transparency and Accountability**: Greater transparency and accountability in cryptocurrency transactions are essential to mitigate risks associated with illegal activities. Implementing measures such as know-your-customer (KYC) and anti-money laundering (AML) policies can help address these concerns.

- **Compliance with Regulations**: Ensuring compliance with regulations can be challenging due to the decentralized nature of cryptocurrencies. Clear and enforceable regulations are necessary to uphold ethical standards and address potential risks.

- **Privacy versus Public Interest**: While privacy and anonymity are critical, they must be balanced against the public interest. Ensuring that cryptocurrencies do not undermine tax compliance or contribute to illegal activities is essential for maintaining ethical practices.

The ethical implications of privacy and anonymity in cryptocurrency transactions are complex and multifaceted. While these features offer significant benefits in terms of user privacy and security, they also present challenges related to criminal activity and regulatory compliance. Addressing these ethical issues requires a nuanced approach that balances privacy with transparency and accountability. As the cryptocurrency landscape continues to evolve, ongoing dialogue and regulatory innovation will be crucial in navigating these ethical considerations and ensuring that the technology serves the public good.

Cryptocurrency and Criminal Activity

Cryptocurrency, characterized by its decentralized and often anonymous nature, has become a significant area of concern regarding criminal activity. While it offers numerous advantages, such as financial privacy and decentralized transactions, these same features can be exploited by criminals for various illicit purposes. Understanding the connection between cryptocurrency and criminal activities is crucial for developing effective regulations and measures to mitigate misuse [337-342].

Cryptocurrencies, particularly Bitcoin, have become entangled with various forms of criminal activity. A recent academic study, titled "Sex, Drugs, and Bitcoin: How Much Illegal Activity Is Financed Through Cryptocurrencies," estimates that approximately $76 billion in illegal transactions annually are facilitated through Bitcoin, constituting about 46% of all Bitcoin transactions [343]. This statistic underscores the significant role that cryptocurrencies play in enabling illegal activities.

To provide context, the study highlights that the total market for illegal drugs in the United States is estimated to be around $100 billion annually [343]. The fact that cryptocurrencies are involved in such a substantial portion of illegal transactions suggests a profound impact on how black markets operate. Much like how online payment systems such as PayPal revolutionized traditional retail by facilitating online shopping, cryptocurrencies are transforming the black market landscape by enabling a new form of 'black market e-commerce.' This shift indicates that cryptocurrencies are not merely a tool for illicit activities but are reshaping the infrastructure of illegal trade by providing more efficient and anonymous financial mechanisms [343].

Despite the alarming figures, verifying the extent of illicit activity facilitated by cryptocurrencies is challenging due to the inherent opacity of cryptocurrency transactions. Unlike traditional financial systems, cryptocurrency transactions are recorded on a public ledger, but the identities behind these transactions are often pseudonymous. This makes it difficult to definitively trace and quantify illegal activity, leading to some scepticism about the exact figures. Nonetheless, the correlation between cryptocurrency usage and illegal activities is evident and growing, indicating a clear pattern of misuse [343].

The emergence of "shadow" cryptocurrencies, such as Dash, Monero, and ZCash, has further complicated the landscape of cryptocurrency and criminality [343]. These cryptocurrencies are designed with enhanced privacy features that make it even more challenging to trace transactions. For instance, while Bitcoin transactions are recorded on a public ledger, these privacy-focused alternatives use advanced cryptographic techniques to obscure transaction details and user identities. As a result, there has been a noted shift in the criminal use of cryptocurrencies from Bitcoin to these more opaque options. This shift indicates that as technology evolves, so do the methods employed by criminals to evade detection [343].

The increased use of shadow cryptocurrencies has been associated with a decrease in the proportion of illegal activities conducted using Bitcoin. This suggests that while Bitcoin remains a significant vehicle for illicit transactions, the development of cryptocurrencies with enhanced privacy features is contributing to a reorganization of illegal activities. Criminals are leveraging these new technologies to further obscure their activities, leading to an evolving landscape where the challenge of combating cryptocurrency-related crime becomes more complex [343].

One of the primary criminal uses of cryptocurrency is money laundering. The process of money laundering involves disguising the origins of illegally obtained funds to make them appear legitimate. Cryptocurrencies facilitate this process by allowing users to transfer funds through multiple accounts or exchanges, obfuscating the trail of the money. Techniques such as "mixing" or "tumbling" services, which blend various cryptocurrencies together, further complicate tracking efforts and conceal the original source of the funds. This misuse of cryptocurrency poses challenges for regulatory bodies and law enforcement agencies striving to combat financial crime [337].

Cryptocurrencies are also utilized in various forms of cybercrime. Ransomware attacks, where attackers encrypt a victim's data and demand payment in cryptocurrency for its release, have become increasingly common. The anonymity provided by cryptocurrencies makes it difficult for law enforcement to trace the perpetrators or recover the stolen funds. Additionally, cryptocurrencies are often used to facilitate hacking activities and the theft of personal information. The ability to conduct transactions without revealing one's identity can embolden cybercriminals, making it a significant concern in the broader context of online security [337].

The anonymity of cryptocurrency transactions poses a serious risk for terrorism financing. Terrorist organizations can exploit cryptocurrencies to raise and transfer funds without detection. The difficulty in tracing cryptocurrency transactions allows these organizations to finance their activities while avoiding traditional financial scrutiny. This use of cryptocurrency for terrorism financing highlights the need for enhanced regulatory measures to prevent the flow of funds to illicit activities and ensure that financial systems are not used to support terrorism [337].

Cryptocurrency is frequently used to transact on darknet markets, which are hidden parts of the internet accessible only through specialized software like Tor. These markets facilitate the exchange of illegal goods and services, including drugs, firearms, and stolen personal information. Cryptocurrencies provide a preferred payment method for transactions on these markets due to their pseudonymous nature. This connection between cryptocurrency and darknet markets raises concerns about the role of digital currencies in supporting illegal trade and highlights the challenges in enforcing regulations in such environments [337].

The cryptocurrency space is also rife with scams and fraudulent schemes. Fake initial coin offerings (ICOs), Ponzi schemes, and phishing attacks are common examples of how cryptocurrencies can be used to deceive investors and users. Scammers exploit the relatively unregulated nature of the cryptocurrency market to perpetrate fraud, often promising high returns or innovative projects to lure individuals into investing in non-existent or malicious schemes. These activities not only harm individuals but also damage the overall credibility of the cryptocurrency industry [337].

The association between cryptocurrency and criminal activity has led to increased scrutiny and regulatory efforts. Regulators and cryptocurrency exchanges have implemented Know Your Customer (KYC) and Anti-Money Laundering (AML) policies to reduce the risk of illegal activities. KYC procedures require users to verify their identities, making it more difficult for criminals to use cryptocurrency anonymously. AML policies aim to prevent the use of cryptocurrencies for laundering money by monitoring transactions and reporting suspicious activities [337].

Law enforcement agencies have also developed techniques for tracking and tracing cryptocurrency transactions. For instance, blockchain analysis tools are used to follow the flow of funds through the blockchain, identifying patterns and potential criminal behaviour. However, the decentralized and pseudonymous nature of cryptocurrencies presents ongoing challenges for effectively preventing and addressing all forms of illegal activity [337].

Despite the potential for criminal misuse, it is essential to recognize that cryptocurrencies also offer legitimate uses and benefits. The challenge lies in balancing the need for privacy and anonymity with the requirement for transparency and accountability. Regulatory frameworks must be carefully designed to protect user privacy while addressing the risks associated with criminal activities [337].

Ethics of Regulating Cryptocurrency

The regulation of cryptocurrency introduces a range of ethical considerations. As digital currencies become more integrated into the global financial system, ensuring that regulatory measures align with the core principles of cryptocurrency—such as decentralization, privacy, and innovation—becomes increasingly important. Here, we explore the key ethical considerations in the regulation of cryptocurrency to ensure that the regulatory framework supports responsible growth without undermining the fundamental values that make cryptocurrencies unique [337].

One of the primary ethical dilemmas in regulating cryptocurrency is balancing privacy with security. Cryptocurrencies offer users significant privacy benefits by allowing transactions to be conducted anonymously or pseudonymously. However, this privacy can also be exploited for illegal activities such as money laundering, terrorism financing, and cybercrime. Effective regulation must strike a delicate balance: it should implement measures to prevent and mitigate these risks without eroding the privacy that is fundamental to the appeal of cryptocurrencies. Regulatory policies such as Know Your Customer (KYC) and Anti-Money Laundering (AML) requirements are designed to enhance security by verifying users' identities and monitoring transactions. While these measures are crucial for preventing misuse, they must be carefully crafted to ensure that they do not infringe upon the privacy rights of legitimate users [337].

Cryptocurrency is inherently tied to innovation and competition, which are key drivers of its development and success. Regulation must be designed in a way that fosters innovation rather than stifling it. Overly restrictive or burdensome regulations can hinder the growth of new technologies and limit the competitive landscape. For example, regulations that are too stringent could create barriers to entry for startups and smaller players, consolidating power in the hands of a few large entities and reducing market competition. Ethical regulation should encourage a dynamic and competitive environment where new ideas can flourish and contribute to the overall advancement of the cryptocurrency ecosystem [337].

Protecting consumer interests is a crucial aspect of cryptocurrency regulation. With the increasing adoption of cryptocurrencies, ensuring the security of funds and preventing fraud are essential priorities. Regulatory frameworks should aim to safeguard users from fraudulent schemes, scams, and the loss of funds due to security breaches. This includes implementing standards for cryptocurrency exchanges and wallets to ensure they adhere to best practices for security and transparency. Effective consumer protection measures can build trust in the cryptocurrency market and promote its responsible use, thereby supporting its long-term growth and stability [337].

Regulation must also comply with ethical standards, respecting the fundamental principles of cryptocurrency such as decentralization and anonymity. These principles are central to the ethos of cryptocurrency, which aims to create a financial system that is less reliant on centralized control and more open and accessible. Ethical regulation should avoid measures that undermine these core values or create undue restrictions that could adversely affect the functioning of decentralized networks. Regulations should be designed with a clear understanding of the technology and its implications, ensuring that they support ethical practices without compromising the foundational principles of cryptocurrency [337].

Cryptocurrency holds significant potential for providing financial services to underserved populations in developing countries. Many individuals in these regions lack access to traditional banking services and could benefit from the financial inclusion that cryptocurrencies can offer. Ethical regulation should consider the impact on these populations and strive not to impose barriers that could limit their access to financial services. Regulations should be designed to facilitate the use of cryptocurrency in a way that supports financial inclusion and economic development, rather than hindering it. This involves creating regulatory frameworks that are adaptable to the unique needs of developing countries and that encourage the positive use of cryptocurrency for economic empowerment [337].

The ethical considerations of regulating cryptocurrency are multifaceted and require a careful balance between various competing interests. Regulation must address privacy and security concerns while fostering innovation and protecting consumer interests. It should also align with the core ethical standards of decentralization and transparency and consider the potential benefits of cryptocurrency for developing countries. By addressing these ethical concerns thoughtfully and comprehensively, regulators can create a framework that supports the responsible growth of cryptocurrency and maximizes its positive impact on the global financial system [337].

The Role of Investors in Promoting Ethical Practices

Investors have a pivotal role in shaping the ethical landscape of the cryptocurrency industry. Their choices and actions can influence market behaviours, drive demand for ethical practices, and encourage companies to adhere to higher standards of social responsibility and sustainability. As the cryptocurrency sector continues to evolve, investors can leverage their influence to promote ethical practices and support a more responsible and sustainable industry [344].

One of the most direct ways investors can promote ethical practices is by selecting and supporting companies that prioritize sustainability and social responsibility. Investors have the power to direct capital toward firms that are committed to ethical operations, such as those that emphasize environmental stewardship, fair labour practices, and community engagement. By investing in companies that integrate these values into their business models, investors can create a market demand for ethical cryptocurrency practices. This not only incentivizes other companies to adopt similar practices but also helps establish ethical benchmarks within the industry.

Investors can evaluate companies based on their environmental, social, and governance (ESG) criteria. For example, they might choose to invest in cryptocurrency projects that use renewable energy sources for mining operations, adhere to fair trade principles, or engage in charitable activities [344]. By doing so, they support businesses that align with ethical standards and contribute to positive social and environmental impacts.

Beyond selecting ethical investments, investors can advocate for greater transparency and accountability within the cryptocurrency industry. This involves supporting efforts to establish clear regulatory frameworks that protect consumers and prevent abuses. Investors can engage with regulatory bodies, participate in public consultations, and support initiatives that aim to enhance the transparency of cryptocurrency transactions and operations.

Transparency and accountability are crucial for preventing illicit activities, such as money laundering and fraud, which can undermine the integrity of the cryptocurrency market. By advocating for robust regulatory measures and best practices, investors help ensure that the industry operates with a higher level of scrutiny and oversight. This, in turn, fosters a more trustworthy and secure environment for all market participants.

The environmental impact of cryptocurrency mining is a significant concern, particularly with proof-of-work (PoW) systems that require substantial energy consumption. Investors can play a role in promoting energy efficiency and environmental sustainability by supporting projects that focus on reducing their carbon footprint. This includes investing in cryptocurrencies that utilize energy-efficient consensus mechanisms, such as proof-of-stake (PoS), or those that implement innovative solutions to mitigate their environmental impact.

Investors can also encourage companies to adopt practices that minimize energy usage and promote sustainability. This might involve supporting research and development in green technologies, such as renewable energy solutions for mining operations, or advocating for the implementation of carbon offset programs. By prioritizing investments in environmentally responsible projects, investors contribute to a more sustainable future for the cryptocurrency industry.

Active engagement in corporate governance is another way investors can influence ethical practices in the cryptocurrency sector. Investors can use their shareholder rights to demand greater accountability from companies, advocate for ethical business practices, and push for transparency in corporate reporting. This includes participating in shareholder meetings, voting on corporate policies, and holding company executives accountable for their actions.

Engaged investors can also collaborate with other stakeholders, including regulators, industry groups, and non-governmental organizations (NGOs), to address ethical issues and promote industry-wide standards. By working together, investors can help drive systemic changes that foster a more ethical and responsible cryptocurrency market.

Investors have a crucial role in promoting ethical practices within the cryptocurrency industry. Through strategic investments in companies that prioritize sustainability and social responsibility, advocating for greater transparency and accountability, and supporting best practices for environmental sustainability, investors can drive positive change. Their actions not only influence market behaviour but also contribute to the development of a more ethical and responsible cryptocurrency ecosystem. By leveraging their influence, investors can help shape a future where ethical considerations are integral to the growth and success of the cryptocurrency sector.

Chapter Fifteen

Decentralized Autonomous Organizations (DAOs)

Decentralized Autonomous Organizations (DAOs) are a novel organizational model that leverages blockchain technology to create decentralized, self-governing entities. DAOs are designed to operate without a central authority or traditional management structure, instead relying on smart contracts and community consensus to make decisions and execute functions.

Decentralization is a fundamental characteristic of DAOs, setting them apart from traditional organizational structures. Unlike conventional organizations, which are typically governed by a central authority or a board of directors, DAOs distribute decision-making power among all their members or token holders. This means that no single individual or entity has control over the entire organization. Instead, power is shared across a broad base of participants, ensuring that decisions reflect the collective will of the community. This decentralized approach enhances transparency, reduces the risk of corruption, and aligns the organization's operations more closely with the interests of its stakeholders.

Autonomy is another defining feature of DAOs. Once a DAO is established and its smart contracts are deployed on a blockchain, the organization operates independently according to the pre-defined rules encoded in these contracts. This automation means that DAOs can execute transactions, manage funds, and implement governance decisions without requiring direct human intervention. The smart contracts, which are self-executing agreements coded into the blockchain, ensure that all operations are carried out precisely as programmed. This reduces the need for intermediaries and administrative overhead, while also minimizing the potential for human error or bias in decision-making.

Governance within a DAO is achieved through a democratic and transparent voting process. Members or token holders of a DAO typically have the ability to propose and vote on various changes or initiatives. This voting power is often proportional to the number of tokens held, which means that individuals with more tokens have greater influence over the decision-making process. Proposals can range from changes in the organization's operational procedures to amendments in the rules encoded in the smart contracts. Once a proposal is approved by the voting mechanism, it is executed automatically by the smart contracts, ensuring that the organization's governance is both efficient and aligned with the collective decisions of its members.

Decentralized Autonomous Organizations leverage blockchain technology to create a decentralized, autonomous, and democratically governed entity. By distributing decision-making power, automating operations, and enabling transparent governance, DAOs offer a novel approach to managing organizations that aligns closely with the principles of decentralization and collective participation.

Cryptocurrency investors may be interested in Decentralized Autonomous Organizations (DAOs) for several compelling reasons, each tied to the evolving landscape of digital assets and decentralized governance.

DAOs represent a cutting-edge governance model that aligns well with the principles of decentralization and transparency inherent in cryptocurrency. Unlike traditional organizations, DAOs are managed through smart contracts on a blockchain, which allows for decentralized decision-making and reduces the need for intermediaries. This innovative approach offers investors a new way to participate in governance, influence decision-making processes, and engage with organizations in a more democratic manner. For investors interested in the future of decentralized systems, DAOs provide a tangible example of how blockchain technology can transform traditional organizational structures.

Investors in DAOs often have the opportunity to benefit from the potential appreciation of DAO tokens, which can increase in value based on the success and growth of the organization. Many DAOs are involved in high-growth sectors such as decentralized finance (DeFi), NFT marketplaces, and blockchain infrastructure, which can present lucrative investment opportunities. By holding and actively participating in a DAO, investors can potentially benefit from the financial success of the DAO's ventures, projects, or services, similar to how early investors in traditional startups might profit from their growth.

DAOs often support or manage cutting-edge projects in the cryptocurrency and blockchain space. Investing in a DAO can provide access to innovative projects that are at the forefront of technological development. For example, a DAO might fund new DeFi protocols, develop new blockchain applications, or support emerging NFT projects. This access allows investors to be part of groundbreaking initiatives and potentially capitalize on early-stage opportunities that could shape the future of the industry.

DAOs operate on blockchain networks, which offer enhanced transparency and immutability. All transactions and governance activities within a DAO are recorded on the blockchain, making it easy for investors to verify the organization's operations and financial activities. This transparency helps build trust and ensures that decisions are made in an open and accountable manner. For investors, this level of visibility can be reassuring, as it provides clarity on how funds are managed, how decisions are made, and how the organization operates.

One of the key attractions of DAOs for investors is the ability to actively participate in the organization's governance. Token holders typically have voting rights proportional to the number of tokens they own, allowing them to propose and vote on changes, allocate funds, and influence the direction of the organization. This level of involvement empowers investors to have a direct impact on the DAO's operations and strategies, offering a more engaged and participatory investment experience compared to traditional investment models.

Investors who value the principles of decentralization and self-sovereignty may find DAOs particularly appealing. DAOs are designed to operate without centralized control, relying instead on community consensus and automated processes. This alignment with decentralization principles resonates with many cryptocurrency investors who are passionate about disrupting traditional financial systems and promoting a more open and inclusive financial ecosystem.

Investing in DAOs can also offer diversification benefits. Since DAOs often engage in a range of activities and projects across different sectors of the cryptocurrency space, they can provide investors with exposure to various aspects of the industry. This diversification can help mitigate risks associated with investing in a single project or sector, allowing investors to spread their investments across multiple opportunities within the DAO's ecosystem.

In conclusion, DAOs offer cryptocurrency investors an innovative and transparent governance model, potential for high returns, access to cutting-edge projects, and an opportunity for active participation and influence. These features align with the broader goals of decentralization and financial empowerment, making DAOs an attractive avenue for investors seeking to engage with the future of blockchain technology and decentralized systems.

The Concept and Structure of DAOs

Decentralized Autonomous Organizations (DAOs) represent a significant evolution in organizational management, leveraging blockchain technology and smart contracts to facilitate decentralized governance and operational efficiency. Here's how DAOs function [345, 346]:

Smart Contracts: At the heart of a DAO's operations are smart contracts. These are self-executing programs encoded on a blockchain network, such as Ethereum. Smart contracts automate the enforcement of rules and processes, eliminating the need for intermediaries and manual oversight. In a DAO, smart contracts define the organizational rules, operational procedures, and decision-making processes. For example, a smart contract may dictate how proposals are submitted, how votes are counted, and how funds are allocated. When members propose changes or new initiatives, the smart contract executes transactions or makes modifications automatically based on the outcome of the vote. If a proposal is approved, the smart contract ensures that the proposed actions are implemented without further human intervention.

Tokenomics: Tokens are crucial to the functioning of a DAO, serving as both a means of governance and a measure of participation. Each DAO issues its own tokens, which members hold to participate in decision-making processes. The number of tokens a member holds often correlates with their voting power, with more tokens granting greater influence over the DAO's governance. For instance, if a member owns 200 tokens, they might have twice the voting power compared to a member with 100 tokens. This token-based system aligns the interests of participants with the DAO's success, as those with more tokens have a greater stake in the outcome of decisions. Tokens can also represent ownership or claim to a share of the DAO's assets or profits, further incentivizing members to act in the organization's best interests.

Transparency: Transparency is a fundamental feature of DAOs, facilitated by the blockchain's immutable and public ledger. All transactions and governance activities within a DAO are recorded on the blockchain, ensuring that every action is visible and verifiable by all members. This level of transparency helps to build trust and accountability within the organization, as all members can see how decisions are made, how funds are used, and how proposals are handled. This visibility also serves as a deterrent to potential malfeasance, as any attempt to manipulate or corrupt the system would be easily detectable by the community.

Decision-Making and Voting: The decision-making process in a DAO is inherently democratic and relies heavily on voting mechanisms. When a member or a group of members submits a proposal, it is put to a vote among all eligible token holders. The outcome of the vote determines whether the proposed changes or actions are implemented. Smart contracts automate the execution of these decisions based on the voting results. For instance, if a DAO votes to fund a new project, the smart contract can directly transfer the allocated funds to the project's stakeholders. This process ensures that decisions are made collectively and transparently, reflecting the will of the majority while adhering to the rules encoded in the smart contracts.

Decentralization: One of the defining features of DAOs is their lack of centralized control. Unlike traditional organizations, DAOs do not rely on a central authority or management structure. Instead, they operate based on the rules programmed into the smart contracts and the collective decisions of their members. This decentralization reduces the risk of corruption or bias, as no single individual or group has disproportionate control over the organization. Members interact with the DAO through the blockchain, and all decisions are made through a consensus-driven process, enhancing the democratic nature of the organization.

DAOs leverage smart contracts, tokenomics, transparency, and decentralized governance to create an efficient and democratic organizational model. By automating decision-making processes, providing clear voting mechanisms, and ensuring all actions are recorded on a public ledger, DAOs offer a novel approach to managing organizations that aligns with the principles of decentralization and collective participation [345, 346].

Benefits of DAOs

One of the core benefits of Decentralized Autonomous Organizations (DAOs) is their decentralized nature. Unlike traditional organizations where decision-making is concentrated in the hands of a few, such as a CEO or a board of directors, DAOs distribute authority among a broad base of participants. This decentralized approach ensures that no single individual or small group has unchecked control over the organization. Instead, decisions are made collectively by a diverse group of members, which enhances the inclusivity and fairness of the governance process. By dispersing decision-making power, DAOs aim to create a more democratic and equitable structure that reflects the collective interests and expertise of a larger group [345, 346].

DAOs foster a high level of participation among their members. In a traditional organization, voting power is often limited to a select few, but in a DAO, token holders have the ability to influence decisions through voting. This participatory model empowers individuals to have a direct say in the governance of the organization, encouraging them to engage actively and contribute their perspectives. Although individual voting power may vary depending on the number of tokens held, the ability to propose and vote on changes gives members a sense of ownership and involvement. This heightened engagement can lead to more robust decision-making and a stronger connection between members and the DAO [345, 346].

Transparency is another significant benefit of DAOs. All votes and governance activities are recorded on the blockchain and are publicly accessible. This transparency creates a system where members' actions and decisions are visible to the entire community. Knowing that their votes and proposals will be publicly viewable encourages members to act in ways that align with the best interests of the organization and its community. This openness helps build trust within the DAO and deters actions that might be harmful or self-serving, as members are motivated to maintain a positive reputation and contribute constructively to the organization's goals [345, 346].

DAOs have the potential to bring together individuals from diverse geographical locations and backgrounds, fostering a global community united by a shared vision. The digital nature of DAOs means that anyone with an internet connection can participate, regardless of their physical location. This inclusivity allows DAOs to tap into a wide range of talents, perspectives, and expertise from around the world. By leveraging the collective wisdom and skills of a global community, DAOs can pursue innovative solutions and initiatives that might not be possible within the confines of a traditional, geographically-bound organization [345, 346].

Limitations of DAOs

One of the challenges facing DAOs is the speed of decision-making. In traditional organizations, a single executive or board can quickly make decisions and implement changes. In contrast, DAOs require consensus from a broad base of participants, which can be time-consuming. The need for voting and deliberation among many members can slow down the process, particularly when considering different time zones and varying priorities among members. This slower decision-making process can be a disadvantage in situations that require rapid responses or agile adjustments [345, 346].

Another limitation is the need for comprehensive education and communication among DAO members. Unlike a traditional CEO or board, who may have a deep understanding of the organization's operations, DAO members often come from diverse backgrounds with varying levels of knowledge and expertise. Educating all participants about ongoing initiatives, proposed changes, and strategic plans can be challenging. Ensuring that members are informed and engaged requires significant effort and resources, which can be a barrier to effective governance and decision-making [345, 346].

The decentralized and participatory nature of DAOs can lead to inefficiencies. The time and effort required to educate members, communicate initiatives, and facilitate voting can result in slower implementation of changes and decisions. DAOs may become bogged down in administrative tasks and extended deliberations, which can detract from their ability to act swiftly and effectively. This inefficiency can be exacerbated by the need to coordinate among a large number of individuals, potentially leading to delays and missed opportunities [345, 346].

Security is a critical concern for DAOs, as they are vulnerable to technical and cyber risks. Implementing and maintaining secure smart contracts requires significant expertise, and any vulnerabilities can be exploited by malicious actors. Despite measures like multi-signature wallets and cold storage, DAOs can still face risks such as hacks, theft of funds, and breaches of trust. Ensuring the integrity and security of the DAO's operations and assets is essential to maintaining member confidence and the organization's overall stability [345, 346].

While DAOs offer benefits such as decentralization, increased participation, transparency, and global community engagement, they also face challenges related to decision-making speed, member education, operational efficiency, and security. Understanding these benefits and limitations is crucial for anyone considering involvement in or investment in a DAO.

Notable DAOs and Their Impact

Decentralized Autonomous Organizations (DAOs) represent a diverse range of organizational structures in the blockchain and cryptocurrency space. These entities leverage smart contracts and blockchain technology to operate without traditional hierarchical management. The eight main types of DAOs each serve distinct purposes and offer unique functionalities [347]:

1. Protocol DAOs

Protocol DAOs are designed to govern decentralized protocols, such as borrowing/lending applications, decentralized exchanges (DEXs), and other decentralized applications (dapps). These DAOs focus on managing and upgrading the protocols they govern.

Examples:

- **MakerDAO**: MakerDAO governs the Maker Protocol, which facilitates the creation and management of the DAI stablecoin. MKR token holders can vote on changes to the protocol, including adjustments to collateral requirements and interest rates. MKR also serves as a safety net; if DAI's value is not fully covered by its collateral, new MKR tokens are minted and sold to cover the shortfall.

- **Uniswap**: Uniswap is a prominent DEX governed by the Uniswap Foundation. UNI token holders participate in governance, controlling aspects like protocol upgrades and the community treasury. Proposals require a minimum number of votes to be considered, ensuring that significant changes reflect broad consensus.

- **Yearn Finance**: Yearn DAO manages the Yearn Finance ecosystem, which automates yield farming strategies. YFI token holders can vote on which strategies to fund and how to allocate resources within the DAO's vaults.

2. Grant DAOs

Grant DAOs are focused on providing funding and support for various projects and initiatives within the Web3 ecosystem. These DAOs often act as charitable or strategic funding bodies.

Examples:

- **Aave Grants DAO**: This DAO funds development projects related to the Aave protocol. It supports a variety of initiatives, including integrations and developer tools, with funding distributed quarterly.

- **MetaCartel**: MetaCartel provides financial support and operational resources to early-stage decentralized applications (dapps). It awards grants to projects that aim to advance the Web3 space, including new DAOs and community-oriented initiatives.

3. Philanthropy DAOs

Philanthropy DAOs focus on social impact and charitable activities, leveraging the decentralized nature of DAOs to organize and execute philanthropic efforts.

Examples:

- **Big Green DAO**: Linked to the Big Green charity, this DAO supports initiatives aimed at improving nutrition and mental health through food justice. It reorganizes grant-making to benefit from the agility and transparency of DAOs.

- **UkraineDAO**: Coordinated by PleasrDAO and other groups, UkraineDAO raised over $3 million in ETH to support Ukrainian soldiers and aid organizations during the conflict in Ukraine. Its rapid fundraising and deployment highlight the effectiveness of DAOs in emergency philanthropy.

4. Social DAOs

Social DAOs bring together communities of like-minded individuals, such as builders, artists, and creatives. Membership often requires owning specific tokens or NFTs, or receiving an invitation.

Examples:

- **Developer DAO**: This DAO is dedicated to web3 developers, providing a platform for collaboration and knowledge sharing. Membership requires holding a genesis NFT or being invited to join the private community.

- **Friends With Benefits**: Focused on fostering creativity and community, this DAO requires holding $FWB tokens to access events and connect with other creatives. It emphasizes exclusivity and network effects.

5. Collector DAOs

Collector DAOs pool resources to invest in high-value NFTs and collectibles. Members own shares in the collected assets proportional to their contributions.

Examples:

- **FlamingoDAO**: Known for acquiring high-profile NFTs from artists like Pak and CryptoPunk #2890, FlamingoDAO exemplifies how collective investment can provide exposure to valuable digital art.

- **ConstitutionDAO**: This DAO aimed to purchase a first-edition copy of the U.S. Constitution, raising $47 million in ETH within a week. Although they were outbid, the DAO's effort showcased the potential for collective purchasing power in high-stakes auctions.

6. Investment and Venture DAOs

Investment and Venture DAOs focus on pooling capital to invest in early-stage startups, protocols, and other investment opportunities within and beyond the Web3 space.

Examples:

- **Krause House DAO**: Aims to purchase an NBA team, involving members in decisions related to team management and operations. It represents a novel approach to sports ownership.

- **MetaCartel Ventures (MCV)**: Invests in early-stage dapps, leveraging the MetaCartel community's expertise and resources to support promising projects.

- **BessemerDAO**: Founded by Bessemer Venture Partners, this DAO discusses trends and resources in the crypto industry, offering insights and investment opportunities.

7. Media DAOs

Media DAOs disrupt traditional media by enabling content creation and distribution governed by community members. Unlike centralized media platforms, Media DAOs allow individuals to earn from their contributions.

Examples:

- **BanklessDAO**: Focuses on promoting a bankless financial system through community-driven media and education. It supports the adoption of decentralized finance (DeFi) principles.

- **Decrypt**: Empowers its community to vote on content creation, allowing users to influence the type of articles and media produced.

8. SubDAOs

SubDAOs are subsets of larger DAOs, tasked with managing specific functions such as operations, marketing, or treasury management. They streamline decision-making by delegating responsibilities.

Examples:

- **Balancer Protocol**: Implemented SubDAOs to handle different aspects of its DAO's operations, making the overall governance more efficient and focused. Each SubDAO manages particular tasks or areas, allowing for quicker execution of decisions and proposals.

These various types of DAOs illustrate the flexibility and innovative potential of decentralized governance structures, each contributing uniquely to the evolving landscape of blockchain technology and community management.

As of April 2023, the largest Decentralized Autonomous Organizations (DAOs) by governance token market capitalization represent a diverse range of sectors within the decentralized ecosystem. These include [348]:

Uniswap Foundation

Project: Uniswap

Token: UNI

Market Capitalization: $3.4 billion

Project Focus: Decentralized Exchange (DEX)

Uniswap is one of the most well-known decentralized exchanges (DEXs) operating on the Ethereum blockchain. The Uniswap Foundation manages the development and governance of Uniswap through its UNI token, which allows holders to participate in the decision-making processes of the protocol. Uniswap facilitates the trading of cryptocurrencies without the need for a central authority, using automated market makers (AMMs) to match buy and sell orders.

Lido DAO

Project: Lido

Token: LDO

Market Capitalization: $2.1 billion

Project Focus: Liquid Staking Protocol

Lido DAO governs Lido, a liquid staking solution designed to provide liquidity for staked assets. Lido allows users to stake their Ethereum and other assets while maintaining liquidity through the issuance of staked tokens (e.g., stETH). This approach enables users to earn staking rewards while still being able to utilize their staked assets in other DeFi activities, addressing the liquidity challenges associated with traditional staking.

Ape Foundation

Project: ApeCoin

Token: APE

Market Capitalization: $1.5 billion

Project Focus: NFTs, Metaverse, and Entertainment in Web3

The Ape Foundation oversees ApeCoin, which is associated with a broader DeFi protocol and community-driven projects focused on art, gaming, and entertainment. ApeCoin is used to govern and support initiatives within the ecosystem, including the Bored Ape Yacht Club (BAYC) and other NFT-related ventures. The DAO fosters community involvement in the development of web3-related entertainment projects.

Arbitrum Foundation

Project: Arbitrum

Token: ARB

Market Capitalization: $1.5 billion

Project Focus: Layer 2 Blockchain on Ethereum

Arbitrum provides a Layer 2 scaling solution for Ethereum, aimed at improving transaction speeds and reducing costs through optimistic rollups. The Arbitrum Foundation governs the Arbitrum protocol, which is designed to enhance Ethereum's scalability while maintaining its security and decentralization. The ARB token is used for governance within the Arbitrum ecosystem.

Internet Computer (Service Nervous System)

Project: Internet Computer

Token: ICP

Market Capitalization: $1.4 billion

Project Focus: Web3 Infrastructure Blockchain

The Internet Computer aims to extend the functionality of the internet by providing a decentralized platform for smart contracts and applications. Governed by the Service Nervous System, ICP is used to manage the Internet Computer blockchain, which seeks to offer scalable and efficient infrastructure for web3 applications.

Aave

Project: Aave Liquidity Protocol

Token: AAVE

Market Capitalization: $1 billion

Project Focus: Lending Protocol

Aave operates as a decentralized lending protocol, enabling users to borrow and lend various cryptocurrencies. The AAVE token is used for governance and to participate in protocol upgrades and decision-making. Aave provides a decentralized platform for earning interest on deposits and borrowing assets.

BitDAO

Project: BitDAO

Token: BIT

Market Capitalization: $1 billion

Project Focus: Web3 Project Funding

BitDAO is a decentralized autonomous organization focused on funding and supporting Web3 projects. The BIT token facilitates governance and decision-making regarding investments in new blockchain projects and innovations, fostering growth within the Web3 ecosystem.

Curve.fi DAO

Project: Curve

Token: CRV

Market Capitalization: $778 million

Project Focus: Decentralized Exchange (DEX)

Curve Finance is a decentralized exchange specialized in stablecoin trading, offering low slippage and high liquidity for stablecoin swaps. The CRV token is used for governance, allowing holders to participate in protocol decisions and earn rewards.

Synthetix

Project: Synthetix

Token: SNX

Market Capitalization: $691 million

Project Focus: Derivatives Liquidity Protocol

Synthetix operates a decentralized platform for trading synthetic assets, including derivatives and other financial instruments. The SNX token is used to back the synthetic assets and participate in the governance of the protocol.

MakerDAO

Project: Dai Stablecoin

Token: MKR

Market Capitalization: $677 million

Project Focus: Smart Contract Platform

MakerDAO governs the creation and stability of the Dai stablecoin, which is pegged to the US dollar. The MKR token is used for governance and managing the stability of Dai. MakerDAO operates a decentralized platform that allows users to create and manage stablecoins through smart contracts.

These DAOs represent a broad spectrum of activities within the cryptocurrency space, from decentralized exchanges and liquid staking to Web3 infrastructure and NFT-focused projects. Each DAO's governance and operational model reflects its unique focus and contributions to the blockchain ecosystem.

Legal and Governance Challenges

Decentralized Autonomous Organizations (DAOs) represent a novel approach to organizational management, leveraging blockchain technology and smart contracts to facilitate decision-making and operations without traditional hierarchical structures. While DAOs offer innovative solutions and efficiencies, they also face significant legal and governance challenges that need addressing for broader adoption and stability.

Legal challenges facing Decentralized Autonomous Organizations (DAOs) stem from various factors, including regulatory uncertainty, legal personhood issues, regulatory compliance complexities, and difficulties in dispute resolution. DAOs operate in a legal grey area due to the decentralized and borderless nature of their operations, which traditional legal frameworks struggle to address [349]. Regulators are still grappling with how to apply existing laws related to corporate governance, securities, and financial transactions to DAOs, leading to uncertainties that can pose risks for participants and hinder DAOs from operating seamlessly across different jurisdictions [349].

One of the primary hurdles faced by DAOs is the absence of legal personhood, unlike traditional entities like corporations that have legal status enabling them to enter contracts, own assets, and be held liable for legal obligations [349]. DAOs, being decentralized and often anonymous, lack a clear legal identity, making it challenging to enforce contracts, handle disputes, and manage liability effectively [349]. While some DAOs attempt to mitigate this challenge by registering as legal entities in specific jurisdictions, this approach may contradict the decentralized ethos that DAOs aim to uphold [349].

Regulatory compliance poses another significant challenge for DAOs, as they must navigate a complex web of regulations encompassing securities laws, anti-money laundering (AML) requirements, and know-your-customer (KYC) rules [349]. Ensuring compliance while preserving the decentralized nature of the organization is a delicate balancing act, especially considering that certain activities undertaken by DAOs could fall under securities trading or investment, potentially attracting scrutiny from financial regulators [349].

Moreover, the decentralized nature of DAOs presents obstacles in dispute resolution, as traditional legal systems are ill-equipped to handle conflicts arising from DAO operations (Beck et al., 2018). The absence of a central authority in DAOs often means that resolving disputes becomes challenging, with some DAOs implementing their dispute resolution mechanisms that may not be recognized or enforceable in conventional legal systems [349].

In light of these legal challenges, it is evident that DAOs face a complex landscape where existing legal frameworks struggle to keep pace with the innovative and decentralized nature of these organizations. As regulators continue to grapple with applying traditional laws to DAOs, participants and stakeholders must navigate a terrain fraught with uncertainties and risks, highlighting the need for tailored legal solutions that can accommodate the unique characteristics of DAOs while ensuring compliance and accountability. Addressing these legal challenges is crucial for the sustainable growth and widespread adoption of DAOs in the evolving digital economy.

Governance challenges in Decentralized Autonomous Organizations (DAOs) encompass various critical aspects that can impact their effectiveness and sustainability. One key area of concern is the decision-making processes within DAOs, where the use of governance tokens for voting can lead to complexities, especially in large DAOs with numerous token holders. Ensuring fairness, transparency, and resistance to manipulation in these voting mechanisms is crucial to prevent decision-making paralysis, particularly when proposals require a supermajority or face low voter turnout [350]. Moreover, the issue of token concentration poses a significant governance challenge, as power in DAOs often correlates with the ownership of governance tokens. This concentration of power among a select few token holders can undermine the decentralized nature of the organization, giving undue influence to early investors or founders with a disproportionate amount of tokens [351].

Security risks present another major governance challenge for DAOs, primarily due to vulnerabilities in the smart contracts that govern them. These vulnerabilities, stemming from coding errors, can be exploited to cause substantial financial losses or operational disruptions. While implementing robust security measures and conducting regular audits are essential, the open-source nature of many DAOs exposes them to potential exploitation by malicious actors [352]. Additionally, as DAOs expand and grow, the coordination of decision-making processes and operational management becomes increasingly intricate. Scaling governance mechanisms to accommodate a larger participant base while upholding efficiency and engagement poses a significant challenge that DAOs must address to maintain their functionality and effectiveness [97].

Community engagement stands out as a critical governance challenge for DAOs, as active participation from a diverse group of members is vital for their success. However, motivating token holders to engage in governance activities and contribute to the organization's objectives can be challenging. Sustaining active involvement and fostering a sense of belonging among members are crucial aspects that DAOs need to focus on to ensure their longevity and effectiveness [353].

In addressing these governance challenges, DAOs must navigate a complex landscape of risks and opportunities. Security verification of blockchain smart contracts is a key area of focus, with research highlighting the importance of ensuring the correctness and security of these contracts to mitigate vulnerabilities and potential exploits [354]. Furthermore, the design of DAOs plays a pivotal role in overcoming governance challenges, with the implementation of governance mechanisms aligned with principles such as Ostrom's common governance principles offering a framework for effective decentralized decision-making and management [355].

While DAOs offer a promising alternative to traditional organizational structures, they face a range of legal and governance challenges that need to be addressed for their widespread adoption. Navigating regulatory uncertainty, ensuring legal recognition, managing governance complexities, and safeguarding against security risks are critical for the long-term success and sustainability of DAOs. As the legal and regulatory landscape evolves, DAOs will need to adapt and innovate to overcome these challenges and realize their full potential.

Creating a Decentralized Autonomous Organization (DAO)

Creating a Decentralized Autonomous Organization (DAO) involves a multifaceted process that blends technical development, strategic planning, and governance design. This includes [356]:

1. Define the Purpose of the DAO

The first and perhaps most crucial step in creating a DAO is defining its purpose. This foundational decision shapes every other aspect of the DAO's creation and operation. The purpose of a DAO could range from managing a decentralized finance (DeFi) protocol to overseeing a community-driven project or even managing investments in emerging technologies. Clearly articulating the DAO's mission helps in designing its governance model and smart contracts to align with its goals. For instance, a DAO designed to govern a DeFi protocol will have different requirements compared to one focused on community governance or funding artistic projects.

2. Design the Governance Model

Once the purpose is established, the next step is designing the governance model, which dictates how decisions are made within the DAO. Key elements to consider include:

- **Voting Rights**: Decide whether voting power will be proportional to the number of tokens a member holds or if each member will have an equal vote. This decision affects how influence and control are distributed among members.

- **Proposals**: Determine who can make proposals and what types of decisions can be put up for a vote. Will there be a cost associated with submitting proposals, or will it be open to all members?

- **Voting Process**: Define the parameters for the voting process, including the duration of voting periods and the percentage of votes required for a proposal to pass. This ensures clarity and fairness in decision-making.

- **Token Distribution**: Plan how tokens will be initially distributed and whether new tokens will be minted over time. This distribution affects the governance structure and the initial control within the DAO.

3. Code the Smart Contracts

Coding smart contracts is the technical backbone of creating a DAO. These contracts automate the DAO's governance model, managing everything from proposal creation to voting and executing decisions. Smart contracts are typically written in Solidity, the programming language for Ethereum.

- **Implementation**: Smart contracts need to precisely implement the governance rules, including proposal submission, voting mechanisms, and decision execution.

- **Testing and Auditing**: Thoroughly test and audit the smart contracts to ensure they function correctly and are free from vulnerabilities. This step is crucial as smart contracts operate autonomously and any bugs or security flaws can have significant consequences.

4. Deploy the Smart Contracts

Once tested and audited, the next step is deploying the smart contracts on the blockchain. This process involves uploading the code to the blockchain network, which establishes the DAO and its associated tokens.

- **Gas Fees**: Deployment costs, known as gas fees, depend on the complexity of the smart contracts and the network's congestion. It's essential to account for these costs in the budgeting phase.

5. Distribute the Tokens

After deployment, distribute the DAO's tokens according to the planned distribution model. This could involve various strategies:

- **Initial Distribution**: Allocate tokens to founding members, early contributors, or through a public sale.

- **Airdrops**: Distribute tokens to existing users of a product or service to encourage engagement and participation in the DAO.

6. Start the Governance Process

With the DAO live and tokens distributed, the governance process can commence. Members can now create and vote on proposals, initiating the DAO's operations and decision-making.

Best Practices for DAO Creation

1. **Smart Contract Auditing**: Given the critical role smart contracts play, it's highly recommended to have them audited by experienced professionals. This reduces the risk of vulnerabilities and enhances the security of the DAO.

2. **Gradual Decentralization**: Many successful DAOs opt for a gradual decentralization approach. This means starting with a more centralized structure and progressively transferring control to the DAO as it matures and proves its operational stability.

3. **Incentives for Participation**: To encourage active participation in governance, implement mechanisms that reward members for their involvement in voting and proposal processes. This could include financial incentives or access to exclusive benefits.

4. **Legal Considerations**: Consult with legal experts to navigate the regulatory landscape and address potential legal risks. Understanding and complying with applicable regulations can help avoid legal issues and ensure the DAO operates within legal boundaries.

Creating a DAO requires a thoughtful approach that integrates technical development, strategic governance planning, and legal considerations. By carefully defining the purpose, designing an effective governance model, coding and deploying smart contracts, and ensuring ongoing engagement and compliance, you can build a successful and resilient DAO. As such, building a decentralized organization involves a series of strategic and technical steps, each crucial to creating a functional and impactful Decentralized Autonomous Organization (DAO). This includes [357]:

1. Define the Structure of Your Organization

Before delving into coding or technical aspects, it's essential to thoroughly define the structure and purpose of your DAO. Start by clarifying the core objectives:

- **Goal Setting**: Identify what you aim to achieve with your DAO. Are you looking to create a platform for decentralized finance (DeFi), a community-driven project, or an investment vehicle? Clear goals will shape the design and functionality of your DAO.

- **Decision-Making**: Determine what decisions the DAO will make. Will it manage investments, govern a community, or oversee a protocol? Defining decision-making processes helps in designing effective governance mechanisms.

- **Problem-Solving**: Assess whether the DAO will address a specific problem or need in the market. Understanding the problem it aims to solve will guide the development of relevant features and governance models.

- **Community Impact**: Consider how the DAO will benefit its community. Will it provide value through financial returns, community engagement, or innovation? A clear vision of the community's benefits helps in shaping a supportive and active user base.

- **Technical Resources**: Evaluate the technical and programming resources required to build and maintain the DAO. This includes coding skills, blockchain infrastructure, and development tools necessary for implementation.

- **Vision and Challenges**: Formulate a vision for your DAO and be prepared for the challenges associated with the crypto market. This includes navigating regulatory uncertainties, managing community expectations, and handling technical complexities.

2. Choose Your DAO Type

Once you've defined the structure and purpose, the next step is selecting the type of DAO that aligns with your goals. Here are some common DAO types:

- **Protocol DAOs**: These DAOs focus on managing decentralized protocols. They are prevalent in the DeFi space and include well-known examples like MakerDAO, Uniswap, and Yearn Finance. They typically manage and govern decentralized applications (dApps) or financial services.

- **Investment DAOs**: These DAOs are designed to pool funds from investors to support new projects or ventures. The collective funds are used to invest in emerging opportunities, and decisions are made through the DAO's governance process.

- **Grant DAOs**: Similar to investment DAOs, Grant DAOs support projects and ideas. However, their focus is specifically on DeFi projects and innovations. They provide funding or resources to projects that align with their goals.

- **Social DAOs**: These organizations focus on social networks and community engagement within the crypto ecosystem. An example is Blockster, which supports social media interactions and community building.

- **Collectible DAOs**: Linked with NFTs (Non-Fungible Tokens), these DAOs manage and govern digital collectibles. PleasrDAO is a notable example, focusing on NFT-related investments and community activities.

- **Entertainment DAOs**: These DAOs provide decentralized entertainment and support creative projects. They allow developers to implement decentralized entertainment ideas, with Flufworld being a prominent example.

- **Philanthropic DAOs**: Though rarer, these DAOs aim to support charitable or social causes within the Web3 ecosystem. The BigGreen DAO, for example, focuses on philanthropic efforts in the blockchain space.

3. Decide on the Token

Tokens are a fundamental aspect of a DAO and play various roles:

- **Supply and Allocation**: Plan the total supply of tokens and their distribution. Decide how many tokens will be minted, allocated, and how they will be distributed among members, investors, and stakeholders.

- **Incentives and Rewards**: Design mechanisms for rewarding participants and incentivizing engagement. Tokens can be used to distribute rewards, provide voting rights, and encourage active participation.

- **Governance**: Tokens are crucial for governance. They enable members to vote on proposals, make decisions, and influence the direction of the DAO. A well-structured token system supports effective and fair governance.

- **Community Building**: Tokens help in developing and expanding the community. They can be used for fundraising, engaging users, and building a loyal base of supporters.

4. Create Your DAO

Creating a DAO involves using various tools and platforms to set up the organization. Several popular blockchain tools can facilitate this process:

- **Aragon**: Offers a user-friendly interface for creating and managing DAOs with customizable governance features.
- **Colony**: Provides tools for decentralized project management and governance.
- **Syndicate**: Focuses on investment DAOs and collaborative investment funds.
- **OpenLaw**: Facilitates the creation of legal agreements and smart contracts for DAOs.
- **DAOstack**: Offers a suite of tools for DAO governance and decision-making.
- **Orca Protocol**: Provides infrastructure for building DAOs and managing decentralized organizations.

5. Set Up the Treasury

After creating the DAO, managing its treasury is crucial for effective financial operations:

- **Secure Funds**: Use treasury management tools to secure and manage the DAO's funds. Tools such as Gnosis Safe, Multis, and Juicebox offer secure ways to handle funds and manage financial operations.
- **Crowdfunding**: If your DAO involves crowdfunding, ensure the funds are effectively managed and allocated according to the DAO's objectives.
- **Financial Management**: Tools like Llama, Parcel, and Utopia can help in tracking expenses, managing budgets, and ensuring transparency in financial operations.

6. Build and Engage the Community

The success of a DAO heavily relies on its community. Building and maintaining an engaged, supportive, and trustworthy community is essential:

- **Engagement**: Foster an active community by encouraging participation in governance, discussions, and activities. An engaged community contributes to the DAO's growth and success.
- **Support**: Provide support and resources to community members to help them get involved and contribute effectively.
- **Trust**: Build trust through transparency, regular updates, and open communication. A trustworthy community is more likely to actively participate and support the DAO's goals.

Chapter Sixteen
Cryptocurrency Exchange-Traded Funds (ETFs)

Cryptocurrency Exchange-Traded Funds (ETFs) are investment funds traded on traditional stock exchanges that track the performance of cryptocurrencies or a basket of cryptocurrencies. They provide investors with exposure to the cryptocurrency market without requiring them to directly buy or manage digital assets. Here's a detailed overview of cryptocurrency ETFs:

Cryptocurrency ETFs are investment vehicles that allow investors to gain exposure to cryptocurrencies through a regulated financial product. Instead of buying cryptocurrencies directly, investors purchase shares in the ETF, which holds the underlying cryptocurrencies or related assets. The ETF's performance reflects the price movements of the underlying assets, such as Bitcoin, Ethereum, or a diversified portfolio of digital currencies.

Types of Cryptocurrency ETFs

Cryptocurrency Exchange-Traded Funds (ETFs) come in several types, each with its distinct structure and investment strategy.

Physical ETFs: Physical ETFs directly hold the underlying cryptocurrency in custody. For example, a Bitcoin Physical ETF acquires and stores actual Bitcoin in secure vaults. Investors in the ETF own shares that represent a proportional interest in the Bitcoin held by the fund. The value of these shares reflects the current market price of Bitcoin, making it a straightforward way for investors to gain exposure to the cryptocurrency without needing to manage or secure the digital assets themselves.

Physical ETFs provide direct exposure to the cryptocurrency market and generally aim to mirror the performance of the underlying asset. They benefit from the simplicity of tracking the spot price of the cryptocurrency, which can be advantageous for investors seeking to avoid the complexities associated with cryptocurrency storage and management.

Futures-Based ETFs: Futures-based ETFs invest in cryptocurrency futures contracts rather than the actual cryptocurrencies. A futures contract is a financial agreement to buy or sell an asset at a predetermined future date for a specified price. Futures-based ETFs aim to track the performance of these contracts, which can be based on the anticipated future price of the cryptocurrency.

The key characteristic of futures-based ETFs is that they do not hold the underlying cryptocurrency but instead hold contracts that derive their value from it. This can lead to discrepancies between the ETF's performance and the spot price of the cryptocurrency due to factors like the cost of rolling over futures contracts, market volatility, and other factors influencing the futures market. As such, these ETFs may not perfectly replicate the price movements of the underlying cryptocurrency, and they often have higher management fees.

Crypto Index ETFs: Crypto Index ETFs provide diversified exposure to a range of cryptocurrencies or related assets. Instead of focusing on a single cryptocurrency, these ETFs track a basket of digital assets or blockchain technology companies. The index might include multiple cryptocurrencies such as Bitcoin, Ethereum, and others, or it might incorporate companies involved in the blockchain space.

By holding a diversified portfolio of cryptocurrencies or blockchain-related assets, Crypto Index ETFs aim to reduce the risk associated with investing in any single digital asset. This diversification can help mitigate the impact of volatility in individual cryptocurrencies and provide a broader exposure to the overall market. Index ETFs are designed to track a specific market index or benchmark, reflecting the performance of the underlying assets included in the index.

Leveraged and Inverse ETFs: Leveraged and inverse ETFs are designed to amplify or reverse the performance of a cryptocurrency. Leveraged ETFs use financial derivatives and borrowing to provide a multiple of the return of the underlying asset. For example, a 2x leveraged Bitcoin ETF aims to provide twice the daily return of Bitcoin. These ETFs are typically used by investors seeking to capitalize on short-term price movements and are not generally recommended for long-term holding due to the risks involved.

Inverse ETFs, on the other hand, aim to profit from declines in the price of the underlying asset. They use derivatives to produce returns that are inversely correlated with the performance of the cryptocurrency. For instance, an inverse Bitcoin ETF would aim to generate positive returns when Bitcoin's price falls.

Both leveraged and inverse ETFs carry higher risks and are generally intended for experienced investors who actively manage their portfolios. The amplified returns can lead to significant gains, but they can also result in substantial losses, especially in volatile markets. The performance of these ETFs can also be affected by factors such as compounding effects and market volatility, which may cause them to deviate significantly from the expected multiple of the underlying asset's return over time.

Investors interested in Bitcoin have two primary methods for gaining exposure to the cryptocurrency: through spot Bitcoin ETFs and Bitcoin futures ETFs. Each method offers distinct ways to invest in Bitcoin, with varying implications for how the investment functions and its associated risks.

Spot Bitcoin ETFs: A spot Bitcoin ETF is designed to provide investors with direct exposure to Bitcoin by holding physical Bitcoin in reserve. Essentially, the ETF owns and stores the actual cryptocurrency, and the value of the ETF shares directly reflects the value of the Bitcoin it holds. When you invest in a spot Bitcoin ETF, you are effectively investing in the underlying Bitcoin assets without having to buy and manage the cryptocurrency yourself [358].

The value of a spot Bitcoin ETF fluctuates in line with the price of Bitcoin. If the price of Bitcoin rises, the value of the ETF shares increases correspondingly, and vice versa. This direct correlation means that the ETF serves as a straightforward vehicle for gaining exposure to Bitcoin's price movements [358].

However, there are some limitations to consider. Unlike the cryptocurrency market, which operates 24/7, traditional stock exchanges where Bitcoin ETFs are traded have set trading hours. This restriction can limit the ability to react to price changes outside of regular trading times. Additionally, investors in spot Bitcoin ETFs are subject to regulatory oversight and may encounter management fees associated with the fund's operation and storage of the physical Bitcoins [358].

Bitcoin Futures ETFs: In contrast, a Bitcoin futures ETF does not hold Bitcoin directly. Instead, it invests in Bitcoin futures contracts, which are agreements to buy or sell Bitcoin at a predetermined price on a specified future date. These contracts are traded on futures exchanges, and their value is derived from the expected future price of Bitcoin rather than the current spot price [358].

The primary advantage of a futures-based ETF is that it avoids the complexities and risks associated with the direct holding of Bitcoin, such as storage and security concerns. Investors in futures ETFs are exposed to Bitcoin's price movements through the futures contracts, which can potentially offer a more convenient and regulated way to gain exposure to Bitcoin [358].

However, futures-based ETFs have their own set of challenges. The price of futures contracts can deviate from the spot price of Bitcoin due to factors such as the cost of rolling over contracts and market conditions. For instance, futures contracts may trade at a premium or discount to the spot price, depending on the supply and demand dynamics in the futures market. Additionally, the process of "rolling" contracts—where expiring futures contracts are replaced with new ones—can lead to potential gains or losses for investors, affecting the overall performance of the ETF [358].

Key Differences and Considerations: The choice between a spot Bitcoin ETF and a futures-based Bitcoin ETF depends on various factors, including investment goals, risk tolerance, and market conditions. Spot ETFs provide a direct link to Bitcoin's price but come with trading time constraints and storage considerations. Futures ETFs, on the other hand, offer a way to gain exposure to Bitcoin through futures contracts, avoiding direct handling of the cryptocurrency but introducing potential tracking errors and complexities associated with futures trading [358].

Advantages of Cryptocurrency ETFs

Accessibility: Cryptocurrency ETFs are traded on traditional stock exchanges, which significantly enhances their accessibility. Unlike direct investments in cryptocurrencies, which require navigating cryptocurrency exchanges and managing digital wallets, ETFs can be bought and sold through conventional brokerage accounts. This accessibility is particularly beneficial for investors who are not comfortable with the complexities and security concerns associated with holding and trading cryptocurrencies directly. By using a familiar investment platform, individuals can easily gain exposure to the cryptocurrency market without needing to interact with the often unfamiliar and technical aspects of digital asset management.

Regulation: ETFs are subject to regulatory oversight from financial authorities, which adds a layer of investor protection and transparency not always present in the direct cryptocurrency market. Regulatory frameworks for ETFs ensure that these products adhere to specific standards and practices, such as regular reporting and disclosure requirements. This oversight helps in maintaining a level of trust and accountability, reducing the risk of fraud and mismanagement. The regulation also typically requires adherence to established trading practices and investor protections, which can enhance the overall safety and credibility of cryptocurrency investments through ETFs.

Convenience: Investing in cryptocurrency ETFs simplifies the process of gaining exposure to digital assets. Unlike managing individual cryptocurrency holdings, which involves securing private keys and handling wallet security, ETF investors can manage their investments through their existing brokerage accounts. This convenience eliminates the need for separate cryptocurrency wallets and reduces the complexity associated with buying, storing, and selling cryptocurrencies. By integrating cryptocurrency investments into a traditional investment portfolio, ETFs streamline the process, making it more accessible and manageable for a broader range of investors.

Diversification: Index ETFs offer the advantage of diversification by providing exposure to a basket of cryptocurrencies or related assets. This diversification helps spread risk across multiple digital assets, reducing the impact of poor performance by any single cryptocurrency on the overall investment. For instance, a Crypto Index ETF might include a range of cryptocurrencies such as Bitcoin, Ethereum, and others, as well as blockchain technology companies. This diversified approach can mitigate the volatility associated with individual cryptocurrencies and provide a more stable investment profile, making it an appealing option for investors seeking to manage risk while participating in the cryptocurrency market.

Disadvantages of Cryptocurrency ETFs

Fees: Cryptocurrency ETFs come with management fees, which can affect overall investment returns. These fees are typically expressed as an expense ratio, which represents the annual costs associated with managing the ETF relative to its total assets. While these fees cover the costs of managing and operating the fund, they can erode returns over time. For instance, an ETF with a high expense ratio may underperform compared to the direct performance of the underlying cryptocurrency due to the cost of managing the fund.

Investors need to be aware of these fees and consider them when evaluating the potential returns from investing in a cryptocurrency ETF.

Tracking Error: Futures-based and index ETFs may experience tracking errors, where the performance of the ETF deviates from the performance of the underlying cryptocurrency or index. Tracking errors can occur due to various factors, such as the costs associated with rolling over futures contracts, changes in market conditions, or differences in the management fees charged by the ETF. For example, a futures-based ETF might not perfectly track the spot price of the underlying cryptocurrency due to the costs of futures contracts and the mechanics of the futures market. Investors should be mindful of these potential discrepancies when investing in ETFs and consider how they might impact the expected performance.

Regulatory Risks: The regulatory environment for cryptocurrency ETFs is continuously evolving, and changes in regulations can affect the availability and structure of these investment products. Regulatory bodies around the world are still developing and refining their approaches to cryptocurrency and related financial products. As regulations change, they could impact the ability to launch new ETFs, modify existing ones, or affect the overall market dynamics. Investors should stay informed about regulatory developments and be prepared for potential changes that could influence their investment in cryptocurrency ETFs.

Market Risks: Despite offering a more accessible and convenient way to invest in cryptocurrencies, ETFs still carry the inherent market risks associated with the underlying digital assets. Cryptocurrencies are known for their high volatility and significant price swings, which can impact the performance of ETFs that track these assets. Market sentiment, regulatory news, and technological developments can all contribute to the volatility of cryptocurrency prices. As a result, investors in cryptocurrency ETFs remain exposed to the risks of the broader cryptocurrency market, including potential sharp declines in value and overall market instability.

Examples of Cryptocurrency ETFs

ProShares Bitcoin Strategy ETF (BITO): The ProShares Bitcoin Strategy ETF (BITO) was one of the pioneering Bitcoin futures ETFs approved in the United States. Unlike ETFs that hold actual Bitcoin, BITO invests in Bitcoin futures contracts, which are agreements to buy or sell Bitcoin at a future date for a predetermined price. By tracking these futures contracts, BITO aims to reflect the performance of Bitcoin in the futures market. The ETF does not directly hold Bitcoin but rather engages in futures contracts that are traded on regulated exchanges. This structure allows investors to gain exposure to Bitcoin's price movements without needing to own or manage the underlying cryptocurrency directly. As one of the first of its kind in the U.S., BITO has been notable for its role in expanding the range of Bitcoin investment options available to institutional and retail investors alike.

Grayscale Bitcoin Trust (GBTC): The Grayscale Bitcoin Trust (GBTC) is an investment vehicle that, while not technically an ETF, operates in a similar manner by offering exposure to Bitcoin. GBTC is a trust that holds Bitcoin and issues shares that are traded over-the-counter (OTC) in the stock market. Each share of GBTC represents a specific amount of Bitcoin, providing investors with a way to gain Bitcoin exposure through a conventional brokerage account. While it functions similarly to an ETF by allowing investors to participate in Bitcoin's price movements, GBTC is structured as a trust and not an ETF. This difference in structure can result in unique market dynamics and pricing differences compared to traditional ETFs.

Purpose Bitcoin ETF (BTCC): The Purpose Bitcoin ETF (BTCC) is a Canadian ETF that directly holds Bitcoin, distinguishing it from futures-based ETFs. By holding actual Bitcoin in custody, BTCC provides investors with direct exposure to the cryptocurrency. The ETF is designed to track the spot price of Bitcoin, meaning that its performance closely reflects the actual market value of Bitcoin. This direct holding of Bitcoin can appeal to investors who prefer not to deal with the complexities of futures contracts and want a straightforward way to invest in Bitcoin. BTCC represents a significant step in the accessibility of cryptocurrency investments, particularly for investors in Canada looking for direct exposure to Bitcoin through a regulated ETF structure.

VanEck Vectors Bitcoin Strategy ETF (XBTF): The VanEck Vectors Bitcoin Strategy ETF (XBTF) is another example of a futures-based Bitcoin ETF. Similar to the ProShares Bitcoin Strategy ETF (BITO), XBTF invests in Bitcoin futures contracts rather than holding physical Bitcoin. The aim of XBTF is to track the performance of Bitcoin in the futures market, reflecting the price movements of Bitcoin futures contracts. This ETF provides investors with a way to gain exposure to Bitcoin's price fluctuations through futures contracts. As with other futures-based ETFs, XBTF's performance may differ from the spot price of Bitcoin due to factors like the costs associated with rolling over futures contracts and market conditions.

These examples illustrate the diversity of cryptocurrency ETFs available in the market. Each type of ETF offers different methods of gaining exposure to cryptocurrencies, ranging from direct holdings of Bitcoin to investments in futures contracts. The choice between these ETFs depends on factors such as investment goals, risk tolerance, and preferences for direct versus futures-based exposure. Understanding the specific structure and focus of each ETF can help investors make informed decisions about incorporating cryptocurrency investments into their portfolios.

Cryptocurrency ETFs offer a convenient way to invest in digital assets through traditional financial markets. They come in various forms, each with its own set of features, benefits, and risks. Investors should carefully consider these factors and their investment objectives when evaluating cryptocurrency ETFs.

Buying and Selling Cryptocurrency Exchange-Traded Funds (ETFs)

Buying Cryptocurrency ETFs

1. Choose a Brokerage Account

To buy cryptocurrency ETFs, you first need a brokerage account. This account can be with a traditional brokerage firm, a digital trading platform, or an online investment service that offers access to ETFs. Ensure that the brokerage is reputable and supports the specific cryptocurrency ETFs you are interested in. You will typically need to complete an account application, provide identification, and fund your account before you can begin trading.

2. Research and Select the ETF

Before purchasing, research the available cryptocurrency ETFs to find one that aligns with your investment goals and risk tolerance. Consider factors such as the type of ETF (e.g., physical or futures-based), the underlying cryptocurrencies or assets it tracks, its performance history, expense ratios, and management fees. For instance, if you prefer direct exposure to Bitcoin, a physical Bitcoin ETF like Purpose Bitcoin ETF (BTCC) might be suitable, whereas if you are interested in exposure through futures contracts, you might consider ETFs like ProShares Bitcoin Strategy ETF (BITO).

3. Place the Order

Once you have selected an ETF, log into your brokerage account and navigate to the trading platform. Enter the ticker symbol of the ETF (e.g., BITO for ProShares Bitcoin Strategy ETF) into the search bar. Specify the number of shares you wish to purchase and choose the order type (e.g., market order, limit order). A market order will execute the purchase at the current market price, while a limit order allows you to set a specific price at which you are willing to buy. Review and confirm the order details before submitting it. The purchase will be executed during trading hours, and the shares will be added to your brokerage account.

Selling Cryptocurrency ETFs

1. Review Your Position

Before selling, review your ETF holdings to determine which ETF you want to sell and how many shares you wish to liquidate. Consider your investment objectives, the current market conditions, and any potential tax implications. If your ETF has appreciated significantly or if market conditions suggest a downturn, you may decide that it is time to sell.

2. Place the Sell Order

Log back into your brokerage account and locate the ETF you wish to sell. Enter the ticker symbol for the ETF and specify the number of shares you want to sell. Choose the type of order you wish to place: a market order to sell at the current market price or a limit order to set a specific price at which you are willing to sell. Review the order details and submit the order. Similar to buying, the transaction will be processed during trading hours, and the proceeds from the sale will be credited to your brokerage account.

3. Monitor and Manage

After selling, monitor your brokerage account to ensure that the sale has been executed as expected. Keep track of any changes in your portfolio and consider rebalancing if needed. Additionally, be aware of any tax implications resulting from the sale, as you may need to report capital gains or losses on your tax return.

Bitcoin ETF Approvals in the U.S. and Australia

Approvals in the U.S.

The journey for Bitcoin ETFs in the U.S. has been marked by significant regulatory scrutiny and milestones. In 2017, the U.S. Securities and Exchange Commission (SEC) rejected the initial petition to launch a Bitcoin spot ETF, reflecting concerns about market manipulation, liquidity, and investor protection. This decision set a precedent for rigorous evaluations of future Bitcoin ETF proposals [358].

However, progress was made with futures-based Bitcoin ETFs. The ProShares Bitcoin Strategy ETF (BITO), which began trading in October 2021, represents a major breakthrough. BITO tracks Bitcoin futures contracts traded on the Chicago Mercantile Exchange (CME), rather than holding Bitcoin directly. This structure was viewed as less risky by regulators compared to holding physical Bitcoin. The rapid success of BITO, reaching over $1 billion in assets almost immediately, demonstrated strong market interest and investor demand for regulated Bitcoin exposure [358].

In June 2023, BlackRock, a major asset management firm, submitted paperwork to the SEC for a spot Bitcoin ETF, signalling a new phase of optimism in the market. Despite the submission, the SEC had not yet approved a spot Bitcoin ETF as of that time. The anticipation around BlackRock's application reflected growing confidence that such an approval could be imminent, with expectations of approval potentially occurring later in 2023. By January 2024, this optimism materialized into reality when the SEC approved several spot Bitcoin ETFs from notable financial institutions, including BlackRock, Ark Investments, 21Shares, Fidelity, and Invesco. This marked a significant step in the regulatory acceptance of Bitcoin ETFs in the U.S., allowing for more direct investment in Bitcoin through regulated financial products [358].

Approvals in Australia

Australia's approach to cryptocurrency ETFs has been notably proactive compared to the U.S. Following the launch of BITO in the U.S., the Australian Securities and Investments Commission (ASIC) issued comprehensive guidelines for ETFs tracking digital assets like Bitcoin and Ethereum. These guidelines were designed to address concerns around market security, transparency, and accurate pricing, ensuring a safer investment environment for Australian investors [358].

On May 12, 2022, Australia made history with the launch of its first Bitcoin spot ETFs. This development was a landmark event for the Australian crypto market, providing investors with a new avenue for direct exposure to Bitcoin. The approval and launch of these ETFs demonstrated Australia's commitment to integrating cryptocurrency into traditional financial markets [358].

Additionally, prior to the Bitcoin spot ETFs, Australian investors had access to an ETF focused on crypto-related companies. The Betashares Crypto Equities ETF (ASX: CRYP), launched in November 2021, offered exposure to companies that support the cryptocurrency ecosystem. Its successful launch, marked by record inflows of A$39.7 million, indicated strong investor interest and the growing role of cryptocurrencies in the broader financial market. This ETF provided a different approach to gaining exposure to the crypto economy, focusing on equities rather than direct cryptocurrency holdings [358].

Potential Future ETF Listings and Developments

The cryptocurrency ETF market is evolving rapidly, with recent developments in the U.S. influencing trends in other regions, including Australia. The U.S. Securities and Exchange Commission (SEC) has recently approved spot Ethereum ETFs, marking a significant milestone in the acceptance of digital asset investment products. This approval paves the way for Ethereum-focused ETFs to enter the market, representing a major step towards mainstream integration of cryptocurrencies into traditional financial markets. However, while the approval signifies progress, the ETFs' S-1 filings are still pending finalization, which means these products are not yet trading [359].

In Australia, the crypto ETF landscape has been more proactive. Australian investors gained access to a spot Ethereum ETF in May 2022, with the launch of the Global X 21shares Ethereum ETF (EETH). This development allowed Australian investors to directly invest in Ethereum through a regulated financial product. Despite this advancement, the Global X 21shares Ethereum ETF has garnered less attention compared to its U.S. counterparts, partly due to the comparatively smaller scale of investment flows in the Australian market [359].

Looking ahead, the cryptocurrency ETF landscape may extend beyond Bitcoin and Ethereum. In the U.S., the Chicago Board Options Exchange (CBOE) has filed two 19b-4 forms for new ETFs focusing on Solana—specifically, the VanEck Solana Trust and the 21Shares Core Solana ETF. These filings indicate a growing interest in diversifying the range of cryptocurrencies available through ETFs. Analysts speculate that Solana (SOL) could be among the next cryptocurrencies to see the introduction of a spot ETF, reflecting a broader trend towards including a wider variety of digital assets in investment products [359].

Australia's proactive stance on cryptocurrency regulation suggests that the market there might also see increased activity. Potential future developments could include additional cryptocurrency ETF listings on the Australian Securities Exchange (ASX) and Cboe Australia. There may also be the introduction of spot ETFs for other crypto assets beyond Ethereum. Furthermore, regulatory guidelines in Australia are likely to continue evolving, with ongoing refinement to address emerging trends and ensure investor protection [359].

As new ETF offerings become available, they promise to provide more accessible investment avenues for digital assets. However, it is essential for investors to remain mindful of the inherent volatility of cryptocurrency markets. While these new products can facilitate easier entry into the crypto space, they also come with risks that require careful consideration and due diligence [359].

Alternatives to Cryptocurrency ETFs

Crypto Trusts

In the realm of crypto investment, Bitcoin investment trusts are a notable alternative to traditional cryptocurrency ETFs. Although the U.S. Securities and Exchange Commission (SEC) has been cautious about approving many crypto ETFs, investment trusts have provided a pathway for investors to gain exposure to Bitcoin and other cryptocurrencies. Bitcoin investment trusts, such as the Grayscale Bitcoin Trust (GBTC), are closed-end funds that own Bitcoin on behalf of investors. These trusts are traded on over-the-counter (OTC) markets, which means they are not listed on major exchanges like ETFs [360].

One key distinction between crypto trusts and ETFs is accessibility. Crypto trusts are typically available to institutional investors, accredited investors, or high-net-worth individuals, and are not open to the general retail public. Additionally, they often require a significant minimum investment and come with lockup periods during which investors cannot sell their shares. Despite these limitations, crypto trusts provide a mechanism for gaining exposure to Bitcoin without having to buy and store the cryptocurrency directly.

However, these vehicles often trade at a premium or discount to the actual value of the underlying Bitcoin due to their closed-end fund structure [360].

Crypto ETPs

Exchange-Traded Products (ETPs) encompass a variety of investment products, including ETFs. Within the crypto space, Crypto ETPs are specifically designed to hold debt securities issued by special purpose vehicles (SPVs) that, in turn, hold underlying crypto assets. The SPV uses these crypto assets as collateral to issue the ETPs, which are then traded on financial exchanges [360].

Crypto ETPs operate under different regulations compared to ETFs. They fall under the Securities Act of 1933, which imposes less stringent regulatory requirements than the Investment Company Act of 1940, under which ETFs are registered. Consequently, Crypto ETPs do not offer the same level of shareholder protection as ETFs. Unlike ETFs, which can create and redeem shares based on market demand, Crypto ETPs generally have a fixed number of shares. This fixed supply can lead to discrepancies between the ETP's market price and the underlying crypto value, as the share price may deviate from the actual value of the collateralized crypto assets [360].

Companies That Hold Crypto

An alternative way to gain exposure to cryptocurrencies is by investing in publicly listed companies that hold significant amounts of crypto assets on their balance sheets. For example, MicroStrategy (MSTR) is well-known for its substantial Bitcoin holdings, with approximately 214,000 Bitcoins as of May 2024. Similarly, companies like Galaxy Digital Holdings (BRPHF) and Tesla (TSLA) also hold Bitcoin. Investing in these companies provides indirect exposure to cryptocurrency markets through equity ownership. However, it's important to note that these investments come with the additional risks and volatility associated with the companies' overall business operations and market performance, not just the value of the crypto assets they hold [360].

Crypto-Related ETFs

For those seeking diversified exposure to the cryptocurrency and blockchain sectors, there are ETFs that invest in companies engaged with blockchain technology and digital assets, rather than directly holding cryptocurrencies. An example is the Amplify Transformational Data Sharing ETF (BLOK), which includes a portfolio of companies involved in the development and application of blockchain technologies. These ETFs offer a way to invest in the broader crypto ecosystem, including firms that provide infrastructure and services related to digital assets. They can serve as a less direct but potentially broader method of gaining exposure to the growth and innovation in the blockchain space, without the volatility associated with holding cryptocurrencies directly [360].

Overall, these alternatives to cryptocurrency ETFs offer various ways for investors to engage with the crypto market, each with its own set of advantages and considerations.

Chapter Seventeen

Creating a New Cryptocurrency

Creating a cryptocurrency can be driven by a variety of motivations, each unique to the creator's goals and needs [361]. Here are some common reasons include:

Business Development and Innovation: Many businesses choose to create their own cryptocurrencies to leverage blockchain technology in enhancing their operations. For example, a business might develop a cryptocurrency to streamline transactions, reduce fees, or facilitate a new form of payment within its ecosystem. This approach can also be part of a broader strategy to integrate blockchain technology into their business model. By issuing their own cryptocurrency, businesses can create a new revenue stream, incentivize customer loyalty, and introduce innovative financial products. This can be particularly advantageous for industries that are heavily reliant on transactions and digital interactions.

Direct Rewards and Incentives: Another reason for creating a cryptocurrency is to directly reward service providers or employees, bypassing traditional fiat currencies. For example, a company might issue a token that represents a share of the company's profits or access to special services. This direct approach can enhance motivation and align the interests of service providers with the success of the company. By using cryptocurrency as a reward, businesses can offer a flexible and potentially valuable form of compensation that can be traded or utilized within a broader digital economy.

Community Building: Creating a cryptocurrency can also be a powerful tool for community building. Many cryptocurrencies are developed to support niche communities or specific causes. These tokens can be used to foster engagement, fundraise for community projects, or support decentralized governance. For instance, a community-focused cryptocurrency might reward participants for contributions or participation in community-driven initiatives. This approach not only builds a sense of belonging but also facilitates financial transactions within the community without relying on traditional banking systems.

Fun and Experimentation: In addition to practical applications, some individuals or groups create cryptocurrencies purely for fun or as a form of experimentation. This could involve developing a new coin or token as a personal project, educational endeavour, or a hobby. The creation of such cryptocurrencies can be a way to learn about blockchain technology, explore innovative concepts, or simply enjoy the process of creating something new. These projects often serve as learning experiences and may not have serious commercial goals but can contribute to the broader understanding of blockchain and cryptocurrency technology.

Methods of Creation

Regardless of the motivation, there are four primary methods to create a cryptocurrency, each suitable for different purposes and levels of complexity:

1. **Creating a New Blockchain**: This method involves developing a completely new blockchain from scratch. It requires a deep understanding of blockchain technology, including consensus mechanisms, cryptographic protocols, and network architecture. This approach provides maximum flexibility and control but also demands significant technical expertise and resources.

2. **Forking an Existing Blockchain**: Another option is to fork an existing blockchain. This involves modifying the codebase of an existing cryptocurrency to create a new version with different rules or features. Forking is a popular method for launching new cryptocurrencies, as it allows developers to leverage existing technology while making customizations to meet specific needs.

3. **Issuing Tokens on an Existing Blockchain**: The most accessible method for creating a cryptocurrency is to issue tokens on an existing blockchain platform, such as Ethereum or Binance Smart Chain. These platforms provide frameworks and tools for creating and managing tokens without the need to develop a new blockchain. This method is well-suited for those who want to create a token

with specific functionalities but do not require a new blockchain infrastructure.

4. **Using Specialized Platforms**: There are various specialized platforms that offer user-friendly tools for creating cryptocurrencies. These platforms provide templates and easy-to-use interfaces that simplify the process of issuing tokens or coins. They are ideal for individuals or organizations that may lack extensive technical knowledge but still want to create and deploy a cryptocurrency.

Where to Create Your Cryptocurrency

Creating your own cryptocurrency involves leveraging blockchain technology, which provides the infrastructure necessary for digital assets. Several blockchain platforms offer the tools and frameworks to help individuals and organizations create their own coins or tokens [361]. These platforms vary in their features, consensus mechanisms, and capabilities, allowing for a diverse range of cryptocurrency projects. Here's a closer look at some popular platforms where you can create your cryptocurrency:

- **Ethereum**: Ethereum is one of the most widely used platforms for creating new cryptocurrencies, particularly tokens. It provides a robust, mature environment with extensive developer support through its Ethereum Virtual Machine (EVM). Ethereum uses smart contracts—self-executing contracts with the terms of the agreement directly written into code—to create and manage tokens. This is achieved through standards like ERC-20 for fungible tokens and ERC-721 for non-fungible tokens (NFTs). Its extensive ecosystem, including decentralized applications (dApps) and DeFi projects, makes it a popular choice for token creation.

- **Binance Smart Chain (BSC)**: BSC is known for its compatibility with Ethereum's EVM, which means that projects can easily migrate or be developed on BSC with minimal changes to their existing Ethereum-based code. It offers faster transaction times and lower fees compared to Ethereum, making it an attractive alternative for creating tokens and decentralized applications.

- **Solana**: Solana is recognized for its high performance and scalability, with a consensus mechanism that combines proof-of-stake and proof-of-history. It supports smart contracts and decentralized applications, making it suitable for creating high-speed, low-cost tokens. Solana's infrastructure is designed to handle a large volume of transactions, which can be advantageous for projects requiring fast and frequent interactions.

- **EOS**: EOS focuses on providing a scalable and user-friendly environment for decentralized applications. It uses a delegated proof-of-stake (DPoS) consensus mechanism, which offers high throughput and low latency. EOS allows for the creation of custom tokens and dApps, and it emphasizes ease of use with features like free transactions and high scalability.

- **Waves**: Waves provides a platform for creating and launching custom tokens with a focus on user-friendliness and speed. It offers a straightforward interface for token creation and management and supports a range of token standards. Waves also includes a decentralized exchange (DEX) where tokens can be traded.

- **BitShares**: BitShares offers a platform for creating custom tokens with a focus on decentralized financial services. It uses a delegated proof-of-stake (DPoS) mechanism and provides tools for launching tokens and managing decentralized exchanges. BitShares emphasizes scalability and high performance.

- **NEM**: NEM's blockchain platform provides the tools for creating and managing custom tokens through its Mosaic feature. It supports various token types and offers features such as asset transfer and decentralized voting. NEM's emphasis is on security and scalability.

- **Komodo**: Komodo allows for the creation of custom tokens and blockchains with a focus on security and interoperability. It provides a framework for creating tokens with features like atomic swaps and cross-chain functionality, making it a versatile option for developers.

- **Nxt**: Nxt is a blockchain platform that supports token creation through its Asset Exchange. It offers features for creating and managing digital assets with a focus on simplicity and security. Nxt's platform provides built-in tools for issuing tokens and integrating them into various applications.

- **TRON**: TRON is known for its high throughput and low transaction fees. It supports smart contracts and the creation of custom tokens through its TRC-20 standard. TRON's focus on entertainment and content distribution makes it a popular choice for projects in these sectors.

- **IOTA**: IOTA is designed for the Internet of Things (IoT) and uses a unique technology called the Tangle, which is a directed acyclic graph (DAG) rather than a traditional blockchain. This allows for scalable and fee-less transactions, making it suitable for IoT applications and custom tokens.

- **NEO**: NEO provides a platform for creating digital assets and smart contracts. It supports various token standards and emphasizes digital identity and regulatory compliance. NEO's focus on a smart economy and interoperability with other blockchains makes it a suitable choice for developing custom tokens.

- **Cardano**: Cardano is known for its research-driven approach and high scalability. It uses a proof-of-stake consensus mechanism and provides a platform for creating and managing custom tokens through its smart contract capabilities. Cardano's emphasis on security and sustainability makes it a promising option for new cryptocurrency projects.

- **Qtum**: Qtum combines elements of Bitcoin and Ethereum, offering a hybrid platform that supports smart contracts and custom tokens. Its design focuses on blending the security of Bitcoin's UTXO model with the flexibility of Ethereum's smart contracts, providing a versatile environment for token creation.

Each of these platforms offers unique features and benefits, and the choice of platform depends on your specific needs, such as scalability, transaction costs, and development tools. Whether you are creating a community coin, a utility token, or a more complex digital asset, these blockchain platforms provide the necessary infrastructure to bring your cryptocurrency project to life.

Creating a cryptocurrency has become increasingly accessible due to advancements in blockchain technology and the availability of various online platforms and tools. These platforms simplify the process significantly, enabling individuals and organizations to launch their own cryptocurrencies with minimal technical knowledge.

Modern cryptocurrency creation platforms have streamlined the process to the point where it can be as simple as filling out an online survey. Users are typically required to provide basic information, such as their name, the number of crypto assets they wish to create, and a few additional details about the cryptocurrency's features or purposes. This user-friendly approach makes it possible for anyone, even those with limited technical expertise, to create a cryptocurrency. The platforms handle the underlying complexities of blockchain technology, allowing users to focus on defining their cryptocurrency's unique characteristics and objectives.

One significant advantage of using established blockchain platforms is the enhanced security and integration features they offer. By creating a cryptocurrency on a well-recognized blockchain like Ethereum or Binance Smart Chain, users can leverage the security protocols and infrastructure of these established networks. This not only ensures a higher level of security for the cryptocurrency but also allows it to benefit from the existing ecosystem of tools, applications, and integrations. Established blockchains often provide robust frameworks for managing tokens, which can facilitate the development and deployment of new cryptocurrencies while reducing the risk of vulnerabilities.

Automatic generators are another option for setting up a cryptocurrency, and they can complete the process in just a few minutes. These generators provide a quick and easy way to create a token, but they come with risks. The simplicity of automatic generators can attract fraudulent operators and scams, which can compromise the integrity and security of the cryptocurrency. It is crucial for users to exercise caution and thoroughly research the reputation and reliability of any platform they use to avoid falling victim to fraud.

For those seeking complete control and flexibility, creating a cryptocurrency from scratch involves building an entirely new blockchain. This method requires significant technical expertise and effort, including designing the blockchain's architecture, implementing consensus mechanisms, and ensuring security protocols. Building a custom blockchain offers unparalleled freedom to tailor the cryptocurrency to specific needs and objectives, but it also entails a substantial investment of time and resources. This approach is generally pursued by projects with unique requirements or those aiming to innovate beyond the capabilities of existing blockchain platforms.

Owning and maintaining a cryptocurrency presents several ongoing challenges, particularly for those who have created it themselves. After launching the cryptocurrency, the creator must address various tasks, including continuous programming updates, establishing and maintaining a network of nodes, and investing in marketing efforts to promote and popularize the cryptocurrency. Successful maintenance requires not only technical skills but also strategic planning and resource allocation. The creator must ensure the cryptocurrency remains secure, functional, and relevant in a competitive and rapidly evolving market.

Choosing the Right Solution to Create Cryptocurrency and Tokens

When deciding to create a cryptocurrency or token, it's crucial to select the appropriate blockchain network and understand the differences between coins and tokens. Here's a detailed overview of how to make an informed choice [361]:

Recommended Blockchain Networks

For most users looking to create a cryptocurrency or token, leveraging established blockchain networks like Binance Smart Chain (BSC), Ethereum, or Solana is advisable. These networks offer robust frameworks and standards that simplify the creation process:

1. **Ethereum (ERC-20 Standard):** Ethereum is one of the most widely used platforms for creating tokens. The ERC-20 standard provides a common set of rules that allow developers to create interoperable tokens with ease. This standard has become the de facto norm for many tokens in the crypto space. By using Ethereum, you benefit from its extensive ecosystem, including numerous wallet providers and decentralized applications (DApps) that support ERC-20 tokens.

2. **Binance Smart Chain (BEP-20 Standard):** BSC, which utilizes the BEP-20 standard, offers similar functionalities to Ethereum but with different trade-offs. BEP-20 tokens are compatible with the Binance ecosystem, including its decentralized exchange, Binance DEX. BSC is known for its lower transaction fees and faster confirmation times compared to Ethereum, making it an attractive option for those looking to minimize costs and improve transaction efficiency.

3. **Solana:** Solana provides a high-performance blockchain with fast transaction speeds and low fees. It is an excellent choice for projects that require high scalability and speed. While not as widely adopted as Ethereum or BSC, Solana's growing ecosystem and technological advantages make it a viable option for creating new tokens.

Using Sidechains

In addition to the primary blockchains, you might consider using a sidechain to enhance your project's capabilities. A sidechain operates in tandem with a main blockchain, offering additional features while benefiting from the security and decentralization of the main chain. For example, the Polygon network, a sidechain connected to Ethereum, provides lower transaction costs and faster speeds. By leveraging a sidechain, you can customize your project's functionality while still tapping into the security and network effects of a major blockchain like Ethereum.

Using Developers for Token Creation

If you lack the technical expertise to create your own cryptocurrency or token, you can opt for professional services. Many developers and firms offer services to create tokens based on pre-defined parameters and rules. This route simplifies the process but typically involves costs. For those unfamiliar with smart contracts and blockchain technology, hiring developers can be an efficient way to launch a token with minimal hassle.

Creating Your Own Blockchain and Coin

For those with ambitious plans and the necessary resources, creating a new blockchain and cryptocurrency (coin) offers maximum flexibility and control. This process is complex and requires a team of developers and blockchain experts. Unlike tokens, which are built on existing blockchains, coins require setting up an entire blockchain network, implementing consensus mechanisms, and ensuring security. This approach involves substantial programming knowledge, financial investment, and effort to establish and maintain the network.

Token vs. Coin

Understanding the distinction between tokens and coins is crucial:

- **Coins:** A coin operates on its own blockchain. Examples include Bitcoin and Ethereum. Coins are used for various purposes, including transaction fees, governance, and as a store of value. Creating a coin involves significant technical expertise and resources, including setting up a blockchain and developing network protocols. For instance, Bitcoin Cash is a fork of Bitcoin, representing a new coin with its own blockchain.

- **Tokens:** Tokens are built on existing blockchains, such as ERC-20 tokens on Ethereum. They often serve specific functions within an ecosystem, such as facilitating transactions or representing assets. Tokens are generally easier and cheaper to create than coins because they utilize existing blockchain infrastructure. They benefit from the established user base and technical support of the underlying blockchain.

Comparative Analysis

When choosing between creating a coin or a token:

- **Coins** require building and maintaining a new blockchain, finding validators, and extensive programming knowledge. They demand more time and resources but can offer higher success potential if executed well.

- **Tokens** are simpler and less costly to create. They leverage existing blockchains, have access to established user bases, and are easier to develop using publicly available tools and open-source software. They are a practical choice for most new projects looking for efficient entry into the cryptocurrency market.

Creating the Cryptocurrency

Creating your own cryptocurrency involves several crucial steps, each requiring careful consideration and planning. Here's a detailed breakdown of the process [361]:

1. Creating a New Blockchain

The foundational step in creating your own cryptocurrency is developing a new blockchain. This process demands a solid understanding of blockchain technology and at least basic coding skills. For those proficient in decentralized technologies, this task may be relatively straightforward. However, for newcomers, the complexities involved in designing and implementing a blockchain can be significant. This step includes establishing the core infrastructure of your cryptocurrency, including its protocol and network.

2. Defining Utility and Features

Before launching your cryptocurrency, it is essential to define its utility and purpose. Cryptocurrencies can serve various roles, such as acting as a means of accessing services, representing financial assets, or functioning as a medium of exchange. Clearly outlining the features and objectives of your cryptocurrency from the beginning will help guide its development and ensure it meets its intended goals. Understanding what value your cryptocurrency will provide to users is crucial for its success.

3. Designing the Economic Model

The economic model of your cryptocurrency, often referred to as the tokenomics, is vital. This includes decisions about the total supply of coins or tokens, the method of distribution, and their valuation. A well-designed economic model will encourage users to invest and participate in your cryptocurrency. It is important to create a strategy that fosters demand and incentivizes engagement, as a poorly structured economic model can undermine your project's success.

4. Navigating Legal Considerations

Legal compliance is a critical aspect of creating a cryptocurrency. Different countries have varying regulations regarding cryptocurrencies, and some may even have outright bans. It is essential to research and understand the legal landscape relevant to your project. Consulting with legal experts to navigate these complexities can help avoid potential legal issues and ensure that your cryptocurrency adheres to all applicable regulations.

5. Strategic Planning and Idea Definition

A well-defined strategic plan is crucial for the success of your cryptocurrency. This involves understanding the ecosystem in which your cryptocurrency will operate, identifying the problems it aims to solve, and determining your target audience. Creating a compelling value proposition is key to attracting potential investors and users. The initial coin offering (ICO) or security token offering (STO) should be well-planned and communicated to build interest and secure investment.

6. Developing the Blockchain and Consensus Mechanism

If you opt to create your own blockchain, you will need to select an appropriate consensus mechanism. The consensus mechanism is the method by which transactions are validated and added to the blockchain. Popular options include Proof of Stake (PoS) and Proof of Work (PoW). PoS is favored for its lower hardware requirements and variations, while PoW, used by Bitcoin, is known for its security but is costly and energy-intensive. The choice of consensus mechanism will impact the functionality and sustainability of your blockchain.

7. Establishing Smart Contract Rules

Smart contracts are self-executing contracts with the terms of the agreement directly written into code. These contracts play a significant role in your cryptocurrency project. It is important to define clear rules for these contracts, as they will operate automatically based on predetermined conditions. Once deployed, smart contracts cannot be altered, so careful design and testing are crucial to ensure they function as intended.

8. Conducting External Audits

An external audit is a critical step to ensure the security and integrity of your blockchain and cryptocurrency. Hiring a reputable audit firm to review your code and infrastructure can identify potential vulnerabilities and help mitigate risks. This process also enhances credibility with investors and users. The cost of an audit varies based on the firm's reputation and the complexity of your project but generally ranges from $3,000 to $5,000.

9. Creating a Whitepaper

A whitepaper is a detailed document that outlines your cryptocurrency's purpose, technology, and development plan. It serves as a key tool for communicating with potential investors and stakeholders. A well-crafted whitepaper should address the problem your cryptocurrency aims to solve, the innovative solutions it offers, the project roadmap, team details, and the value proposition. Investing in professional whitepaper writing services is recommended, with costs typically ranging from $1,000 to $2,000.

10. Marketing and Community Building

Effective marketing is essential for the success of your cryptocurrency. Utilize various channels, including social media, press releases, and guest blogging, to promote your project and its unique value. Building and maintaining an active community is also crucial. Engaging with your audience and providing timely support can foster trust and loyalty. Many successful cryptocurrencies have strong, dedicated communities that contribute to their growth and success.

Costs

The costs associated with creating a cryptocurrency can vary widely depending on the complexity of the project and whether you are building a new blockchain or utilizing an existing one. On average, developing a cryptocurrency from scratch can cost around $10,000 and take 5-6 months [361]. Additional expenses include external auditing, which ranges from $3,000 to $5,000, and professional whitepaper writing services, costing between $1,000 and $2,000. These estimates do not account for other potential costs, such as marketing and community management [361].

Sample Creation Processes

Create an Ethereum Token

Creating a cryptocurrency involves several steps, each crucial to ensuring that your token functions as intended and integrates smoothly within the Ethereum blockchain. Here's a detailed guide on how to create an Ethereum-based token, including the essential coding and deployment procedures [362]:

1. Preparing to Create Your Token

The process begins with using an Ethereum wallet app, which is necessary for deploying your smart contract. Start by downloading and installing the Ethereum wallet application from a reputable source. Once installed, open the app and locate the "Deploy New Contract" button, usually found at the top right corner of the interface. This button initiates the process of creating your new token.

2. Writing the Basic Solidity Contract

Upon clicking "Deploy New Contract," you'll be prompted to enter Solidity code into a source code field. Solidity is the programming language used for writing smart contracts on the Ethereum blockchain. For a basic token, you can use the following Solidity code:

```solidity
contract MyToken {
/* This creates an array with all balances */
mapping (address => uint256) public balanceOf;
}
```

In this code, `mapping` is an associative array that links Ethereum addresses to token balances. The keyword `public` ensures that anyone can view these balances. This initial code sets up the basic structure of your token's smart contract.

3. Defining the Token Supply

To specify the initial supply of tokens, add the following line of code under the existing code in the Solidity field:

```solidity
function MyToken() {
balanceOf[msg.sender] = 21000000;
}
```

This code sets the initial token supply to 21 million, but you can adjust this number according to your needs. `msg.sender` refers to the address that deploys the contract, meaning the initial supply is assigned to this address.

4. Enabling Token Transfers

To allow for token transfers between addresses, you need to add a function that handles these transactions. Include the following code:

```solidity
/* Send coins */
function transfer(address _to, uint256 _value) {
/* Add and subtract new balances */
balanceOf[msg.sender] -= _value;
balanceOf[_to] += _value;
}
```

This function enables the transfer of tokens from one address to another. The balance of the sender is decreased by the amount transferred, and the recipient's balance is increased accordingly.

5. Handling Transfer Validations

To prevent issues such as overdrafts (where someone tries to transfer more tokens than they hold), add validation checks:

```solidity
function transfer(address _to, uint256 _value) {
/* Check if sender has balance and for overflows */
require(balanceOf[msg.sender] >= _value && balanceOf[_to] + _value >= balanceOf[_to]);

/* Add and subtract new balances */
```

```
balanceOf[msg.sender] -= _value;
balanceOf[_to] += _value;
}
```

The `require` statement ensures that the sender has sufficient balance and that the transfer does not cause any overflow errors in the recipient's balance.

6. Adding Token Metadata

To include basic information about your token, such as its name, symbol, and decimals, add the following code:

```solidity
/* Initializes contract with initial supply tokens to the creator of the contract */
function MyToken(uint256 initialSupply, string tokenName, string tokenSymbol, uint8 decimalUnits) {
balanceOf[msg.sender] = initialSupply; // Give the creator all initial tokens
name = tokenName; // Set the name for display purposes
symbol = tokenSymbol; // Set the symbol for display purposes
decimals = decimalUnits; // Amount of decimals for display purposes
}
```

This code initializes the contract with the specified token details and assigns the entire initial supply to the creator's address.

7. Creating Events for Monitoring

Events are crucial for allowing Ethereum wallets and other tools to monitor activities on the blockchain. Add the following event declaration to your contract:

```solidity
event Transfer(address indexed from, address indexed to, uint256 value);
```

In the `transfer` function, emit this event to notify listeners of the transaction:

```solidity
/* Notify anyone listening that this transfer took place */
Transfer(msg.sender, _to, _value);
```

Events help track token transfers and provide transparency for transactions.

8. Deploying the Token

Once your contract code is ready, navigate to the "Contracts" tab in your Ethereum wallet app and click "Deploy New Contract." Copy and paste your Solidity code into the appropriate field. Adjust parameters such as `_supply`, `_name`, `_symbol`, and `_decimals` as needed. After confirming your settings, enter your wallet password to deploy the contract.

9. Final Steps and Considerations

After deployment, your token will be active on the Ethereum blockchain. You can interact with it, transfer tokens, and build applications around it. Ensure to test the functionality thoroughly and consider additional features or improvements based on user feedback and evolving requirements.

In summary, creating an Ethereum-based token involves writing and deploying Solidity code that defines the token's characteristics, functionality, and metadata. By following these steps, you can successfully launch your own cryptocurrency and begin building its ecosystem.

Creating a Token Using Bitbond

Before diving into the creation of your own cryptocurrency, it's crucial to understand the fundamentals of crypto tokens and the steps involved in their creation. Tokens are digital assets that exist on blockchains and can represent ownership of real-world assets or provide utility within decentralized applications (DApps). Familiarizing yourself with these basics will help you navigate the token creation process effectively. Once you have a grasp of tokenization and decentralized finance (DeFi), you'll need to prepare the necessary components for creating your token [363].

1. Supported Wallets

The first step in creating a token is to ensure you have a compatible crypto wallet. For instance, if you're using Bitbond's Token Tool, you'll need to use a supported wallet like MetaMask, Coinbase Wallet, or WalletConnect. It's important to choose a reputable wallet, as the security of your tokens relies heavily on the wallet you use. Research the features and security measures of each wallet to ensure it meets your needs. Learn more about different crypto wallets to understand their distinctions and functionalities.

2. Ensuring Sufficient Funds

Before proceeding with token creation, make sure your wallet has adequate funds to cover network and service fees. These fees are required to process transactions and deploy smart contracts on the blockchain. The fees are typically paid in the network's native cryptocurrency. For example, if you're creating a token on the Ethereum network, you will need ether (ETH) to cover these costs. Always check the current fee rates and ensure you have enough to avoid any disruptions during the creation process.

3. Researching Blockchain Networks

Choosing the right blockchain network is essential for your token's success. Each blockchain has its own governance rules, advantages, and supported token standards. Ethereum is a popular choice due to its extensive use in DeFi applications and high transaction volume, but it also suffers from congestion and high gas fees. Other blockchains might offer lower fees or different features. Research the blockchain networks to find one that aligns with your project's needs and goals.

4. Selecting a Network and Token Standard

The choice of blockchain network will dictate the token standards you can use. Token standards define the rules and functionalities of your token. Common standards include ERC-20 for fungible tokens and ERC-721 or ERC-1155 for non-fungible tokens (NFTs) on the Ethereum network. Your token's features and use cases will influence which standard is most appropriate. Ensure that the network and token standard you select support the functionalities you envision for your token.

5. Using Token Tool for Creation

Once you have your wallet and network ready, you can use platforms like Bitbond's Token Tool to simplify the creation process. Begin by navigating to Token Tool and selecting "Create Token" from the menu. Choose the "DeFi Token" option to configure and deploy your smart contract. You will need to select the network you wish to use from the drop-down menu. Token Tool supports multiple blockchain networks and their testnets.

6. Connecting Your Wallet

Connect your wallet to Token Tool by clicking on the "Connect Wallet" button. Choose from the available wallet providers and confirm the connection in your wallet's interface. Make sure your wallet is set to the same network you selected on Token Tool. Completing the profile setup may offer you a discount code for future transactions. This connection is crucial for interacting with the blockchain and deploying your token.

7. Defining Token Properties

With Token Tool, creating your token is as straightforward as filling out a form. Define the properties of your token, including its name, symbol, initial supply, and decimal units. These properties are fundamental to how your token will be identified and used. The platform simplifies the technical aspects, allowing you to focus on configuring these attributes according to your project's needs.

8. Specifying Token Features

In the "token configuration" section, you can enable specific features for your token, such as a burn rate or minting capabilities. These features affect how your token behaves and interacts within the ecosystem. Be cautious when selecting features, as smart contracts are immutable once deployed. If you activate features like minting, they cannot be disabled later. Thoroughly review and finalize these settings to avoid the need for creating a new token due to mistakes.

9. Confirming the Transaction

After configuring your token's properties and features, review all details carefully. Click on "Create Token" to initiate the process. You will then need to confirm the transaction and pay the associated fees in your wallet. This step is crucial for deploying the smart contract to the blockchain. The transaction will be processed, and once confirmed, your token will be created and deployed.

10. Managing Your Token

Upon successful deployment, you'll receive a pop-up window with a link to the block explorer and your token's address. This address allows you to manage and interact with your token on the blockchain. Use this information to track transactions, verify token details, and perform any necessary actions related to your token.

Create a BEP-20 Token

Creating a BEP-20 token involves several key steps and requires some technical knowledge, particularly in coding and blockchain deployment. BEP-20 is a token standard on Binance Smart Chain (BSC) similar to Ethereum's ERC-20, but tailored for the BSC ecosystem. Here's a detailed explanation of the process [364]:

1. Setup MetaMask and BSC Mainnet

Before you begin, ensure that MetaMask is set up and connected to the Binance Smart Chain mainnet. MetaMask is a popular cryptocurrency wallet that supports various blockchains, including BSC. If you haven't added the BSC network to MetaMask yet, you can follow specific instructions available in guides such as the "Connecting MetaMask to BNB Smart Chain" guide. This setup is crucial as MetaMask will be used for transaction approvals and interacting with the smart contract.

2. Access Remix IDE

Remix is an integrated development environment (IDE) for developing and deploying smart contracts compatible with Ethereum Virtual Machine (EVM) networks, including BSC. Navigate to the Remix IDE website. In Remix, right-click on the [contracts] folder located in the file explorer section and select [New File] to create a new file where you will write your BEP-20 smart contract.

3. Create and Name Your Contract File

Name the new file BEP20.sol. The .sol extension indicates that this file will contain Solidity code, which is the programming language used to write Ethereum and BSC smart contracts.

4. Set the Programming Language

Ensure that the programming language is set to Solidity. You can verify this by checking the language selector icon on the right side of the Remix interface. If not set to Solidity, your smart contract code will not compile correctly.

5. Insert BEP-20 Smart Contract Code

Copy the BEP-20 smart contract code into your newly created BEP20.sol file. This code defines the functionalities of your token, such as how balances are tracked and how transfers are handled. For detailed parameters and functions, you might refer to the code available on GitHub or other reliable sources.

6. Customize Token Details

Modify the smart contract code to include details specific to your token. This includes setting the token's name (e.g., Binance Academy Coin or BAC), symbol, decimals (e.g., 18), and total supply (e.g., 100,000,000). Ensure that the total supply is adjusted to match the decimal precision you specified.

7. Compile the Smart Contract

To compile the smart contract, click the compile icon on the left side of Remix. Check the [Auto compile] and [Enable optimization] boxes, then click [Compile]. This process will convert your Solidity code into bytecode that can be deployed on the BSC network.

8. Copy ABI

After compiling, click the [ABI] button to copy the Application Binary Interface (ABI) of the contract. The ABI is essential for interacting with your smart contract through various interfaces and tools.

9. Deploy the Smart Contract

Switch to the deployment section of Remix by selecting [Injected Web3] as your environment. This setting ensures that Remix interacts with the BSC network through your MetaMask wallet. Ensure that your BEP20 contract is selected and then click [Deploy]. MetaMask will prompt you to confirm the transaction and pay the necessary gas fees.

10. Verify and Publish the Contract

Once the contract is deployed, you need to verify and publish the contract source code on BscScan. Visit BscScan, paste the contract address, select [Solidity (Single)] as the compiler type, and ensure the compiler version matches what you used in Remix. This verification helps ensure transparency and security.

11. Flatten the Contract Code

In Remix, right-click on BEP20.sol and select [Flatten]. This process combines all the code into a single file, making it easier to verify on BscScan. Grant Remix permission to flatten the code and copy the contents of BEP20_flat.sol.

12. Verify and Publish the Contract Code

Paste the flattened code into BscScan, set optimization to Yes, and click [Verify and Publish]. A successful splash screen will confirm that the contract is verified.

13. Mint Tokens

With the verified contract, you can mint tokens. Go to the contract address on BscScan, select [Write Contract], and connect your MetaMask account. In the mint section, enter the amount of tokens to mint, including the decimals, and click [Write]. Confirm the transaction in MetaMask.

14. Confirm Token Minting

Once the transaction is confirmed, the tokens will be minted and sent to the address that created the smart contract. You can now manage and interact with your BEP-20 token using the contract address.

Getting Your Cryptocurrency Listed

After creating your BEP-20 token, consider listing it on a cryptocurrency exchange like Binance. This step involves completing application forms provided by the exchange and undergoing a due diligence process. Providing liquidity and accepting exchange-specific tokens (e.g., BNB, BUSD) can also be part of the listing requirements. Regular updates on your project's progress will be necessary during the application process.

Creating a BEP-20 token involves technical steps but, with tools like Remix and guidance, it becomes manageable. Ensure thorough testing and compliance with all requirements to successfully launch and manage your token.

Valuation of Your Cryptocurrency After Creation

The valuation of a cryptocurrency post-creation is a critical stage that significantly influences its success and adoption. After developing your cryptocurrency, the challenge shifts from creation to ensuring that your digital asset gains traction and attracts investors. Here's a detailed look at how this process unfolds [361]:

1. The Importance of Community and Market Interest

The success of a cryptocurrency is not solely dependent on its technical creation; it heavily relies on its market acceptance and community support. Without a dedicated user base, even the most technically sound cryptocurrency can struggle to gain traction. Building a supportive and engaged community is crucial because it helps in generating interest, creating demand, and establishing the cryptocurrency's value. Engaging with potential users, fostering relationships, and maintaining active communication are essential to cultivate a loyal following.

2. Initial Coin Offering (ICO)

One of the primary methods for valuing and raising funds for a new cryptocurrency is through an Initial Coin Offering (ICO). An ICO is a fundraising mechanism where investors purchase tokens of the new cryptocurrency in exchange for established cryptocurrencies like Bitcoin or Ethereum, or sometimes even fiat currencies. This process allows you to generate initial capital and gauge market interest in your cryptocurrency. During an ICO, you offer a portion of the total token supply to early investors, often at a discounted rate compared to the future market price. The success of the ICO not only provides necessary funding but also acts as a barometer for the potential market value of your cryptocurrency.

3. Developing a Compelling Value Proposition

To attract investors and build a strong community, it is essential to present a compelling value proposition. This involves clearly defining the problem your cryptocurrency aims to solve, the benefits it offers, and how it stands out from existing solutions. A well-articulated value proposition will resonate with potential users and investors, helping to drive interest and support. This message should be effectively communicated through marketing materials, your whitepaper, and other promotional channels.

4. Strategic Marketing and Promotion

Effective marketing is crucial for the successful valuation of your cryptocurrency. Employing a strategic marketing plan helps in reaching a broader audience and generating buzz around your project. Utilize various marketing channels such as social media, content marketing, press releases, and community engagement to raise awareness. Participating in relevant industry events, webinars, and conferences can also enhance visibility and attract potential investors.

5. Building and Maintaining a Community

A strong and active community is integral to the long-term success of your cryptocurrency. Engaging with your community through regular updates, responding to queries, and fostering discussions can build trust and loyalty. Providing incentives for community participation, such as rewards for contributions or early access to features, can also enhance engagement. A dedicated community not only supports the cryptocurrency but also helps in spreading the word and driving further adoption.

6. Post-ICO Considerations

After a successful ICO, the focus should shift to maintaining momentum and ensuring continued growth. This involves implementing the roadmap outlined during the ICO, delivering on promises, and continuously improving the cryptocurrency based on user feedback. Regular updates on progress, new developments, and strategic partnerships can help sustain interest and attract new users. Additionally, managing the liquidity and market performance of your cryptocurrency is essential to maintain its value and support its ecosystem.

7. Long-Term Value and Sustainability

The long-term valuation of your cryptocurrency depends on its ability to deliver real value and sustain its ecosystem. This involves ongoing development, maintaining a robust infrastructure, and adapting to market changes. Ensuring the cryptocurrency's utility, security, and relevance in the evolving digital landscape is key to its sustained success. Building strategic partnerships and integrating with other platforms can also enhance its value and usability.

References

1.Valencia, F., A. Gómez-Espinosa, and B. Valdés-Aguirre, *Price Movement Prediction of Cryptocurrencies Using Sentiment Analysis and Machine Learning.* Entropy, 2019. **21**(6): p. 589.

2.Shahzad, M.F., et al., *Cryptocurrency Awareness, Acceptance, and Adoption: The Role of Trust as a Cornerstone.* Humanities and Social Sciences Communications, 2024. **11**(1).

3.Gil-Cordero, E., J.-P. Cabrera-Sánchez, and M.J. Arrás-Cortés, *Cryptocurrencies as a Financial Tool: Acceptance Factors.* Mathematics, 2020. **8**(11): p. 1974.

4.Alsini, R., et al., *Forecasting Cryptocurrency's Buy Signal With a Bagged Tree Learning Approach to Enhance Purchase Decisions.* Frontiers in Big Data, 2024. **7**.

5.Kaspersky, *What is Cryptocurrency and how does it work?* 2024.

6.Samson, T.K., C.E. Onwukwe, and A.I. Lawal, *An Examination of Cryptocurrency Volatility: Insights From Skewed Error Innovation Distributions Within GARCH Model Frameworks.* Mathematical Modelling and Engineering Problems, 2023. **10**(04): p. 1297-1306.

7.Ahmadi, H., *Is Cryptocurrency Risky as an Investment Instrument? Analysis of Return and Risk With a Comparison of Sharia Stocks.* International Journal of Islamic Business Ethics, 2023. **8**(1): p. 40.

8.Goldbarsht, D., *Adapting Confiscation and Anti-Money Laundering Laws to the Digital Economy: Exploring the Australian Interplay Between Proceeds and Technology.* Journal of Money Laundering Control, 2023. **27**(3): p. 472-488.

9.Olabanji, S.O., et al., *Leveraging FinTech Compliance to Mitigate Cryptocurrency Volatility for Secure US Employee Retirement Benefits: Bitcoin ETF Case Study.* Asian Journal of Economics Business and Accounting, 2024. **24**(4): p. 147-167.

10.Rajharia, P. and M.B. Kaushik, *Cryptocurrency Adoption and Its Implications: A Literature Review.* E3s Web of Conferences, 2023. **456**: p. 03002.

11.Holt, T.J., J.R. Lee, and E.M. Griffith, *An Assessment of Cryptomixing Services in Online Illicit Markets.* Journal of Contemporary Criminal Justice, 2023. **39**(2): p. 222-238.

12.Sami, M. and W. Abdallah, *How Does the Cryptocurrency Market Affect the Stock Market Performance in the MENA Region?* Journal of Economic and Administrative Sciences, 2020. **37**(4): p. 741-753.

13.Hassan, M.K., F.A. Hudaefi, and R.E. Caraka, *Mining Netizen's Opinion on Cryptocurrency: Sentiment Analysis of Twitter Data.* Studies in Economics and Finance, 2021. **39**(3): p. 365-385.

14.Alsmadi, A.A., A. Shuhaiber, and K.S. Al-Omoush, *Rolling the Crypto Dice: The Interplay of Legal Environments, Market Uncertainty, and Gambling Attitudes on Users' Behavioral Intentions.* Human Behavior and Emerging Technologies, 2023. **2023**: p. 1-17.

15.Inci, A.C. and R. Lagasse, *Cryptocurrencies: Applications and Investment Opportunities.* Journal of Capital Markets Studies, 2019. **3**(2): p. 98-112.

16.Varma, P., et al., *Thematic Analysis of Financial Technology (Fintech) Influence on the Banking Industry.* Risks, 2022. **10**(10): p. 186.

17.Alexiadou, M., et al., *Cryptocurrencies and Long-Range Trends.* SSRN Electronic Journal, 2023.

18.Chikobvu, D. and T. Ndlovu, *The Generalised Extreme Value Distribution Approach to Comparing the Riskiness of BitCoin/US Dollar and South African Rand/Us Dollar Returns.* Journal of Risk and Financial Management, 2023. **16**(4): p. 253.

19.Asif, Z. and S. Unar, *Cryptocurrency Market Dynamics: Trends, Volatility, and Regulatory Challenges.* 2024. **13**(1).

20.Ashurbayli, N. and A. Yusifov, *Investing in Cryptocurrency as an Alternative Way of Financial Investments.* 2023. **17**(2): p. 10-16.

21.Enayati, M., S. Arlikatti, and M.V. Ramesh, *A Qualitative Analysis of Rural Fishermen: Potential for Blockchain-Enabled Framework for Livelihood Sustainability.* Heliyon, 2024. **10**(2): p. e24358.

22.Reserve Bank of Australia, *Digital Currencies.* 2024.

23.Asokan, N., *Anonymity in a Mobile Computing Environment.* 1994.

24.Chaum, D., *Security Without Identification: Transaction Systems to Make Big Brother Obsolete.* Communications of the Acm, 1985. **28**(10): p. 1030-1044.

25.Franklin, M.K. and M. Yung, *The Blinding of Weak Signatures.* 1995: p. 67-76.

26.MacKie-Mason, J.K. and H.R. Varian, *Some FAQs About Usage-Based Pricing.* Computer Networks and Isdn Systems, 1995. **28**(1-2): p. 257-265.

27.D'Amiano, S. and G.D. Crescenzo, *Methodology for Digital Money Based on General Cryptographic Tools.* 1995: p. 156-170.

28.Chen, L., *Witness Hiding Proofs and Applications.* Daimi Report Series, 1994. **13**(477).

29.Franklin, M.K. and M.K. Reiter, *Verifiable Signature Sharing.* 1995: p. 50-63.

30.*Applied Cryptography: Protocols, Algorithms, and Source Code in C.* Computer Law & Security Review, 1994. **10**(5): p. 257.

31.Brands, S., *Restrictive Binding of Secret-Key Certificates.* 1995: p. 231-247.

32.Yu, B., *Research on the Features and Functions of Bitcoin and Digital Currencies.* Advances in Economics Management and Political Sciences, 2024. **86**(1): p. 55-60.

33.Su, Z., *Analysis of Cryptocurrency and Its Combination With Quantitative Transactions.* SHS Web of Conferences, 2024. **181**: p. 02016.

34.Avcı, İ., *Analysis of Data Security and Cyber-Attack Methods in Digital Currency.* Mühendislik Bilimleri Ve Tasarım Dergisi, 2022. **10**(3): p. 1000-1013.

35.Wronka, C., *Digital Currencies and Economic Sanctions: The Increasing Risk of Sanction Evasion.* Journal of Financial Crime, 2021. **29**(4): p. 1269-1282.

36.Ozili, P.K., *Can Central Bank Digital Currency Increase Financial Inclusion? Arguments for and Against*. 2022: p. 241-249.

37.Rhoda Adura Adeleye, N., et al., *Digital Currency Adoption in Africa: A Critical Review and Global Comparison.* World Journal of Advanced Research and Reviews, 2024. **21**(2): p. 130-139.

38.Jakšić, M., V. Todorović, and J. Matić, *The Influence of Digital Currency on the Banking Sector in Europe.* Economic Themes, 2022. **60**(4): p. 481-494.

39.Tan, Y., *Legal Governance of Digital Currencies and Regulatory Sandboxes in the Blockchain Era.* 2022.

40.Chen, H., et al., *The Role of Blockchain in Finance Beyond Cryptocurrency: Trust, Data Management, and Automation.* Ieee Access, 2024. **12**: p. 64861-64885.

41.Kajtazi, A. and A. Moro, *The Role of Bitcoin in Well Diversified Portfolios: A Comparative Global Study.* International Review of Financial Analysis, 2019. **61**: p. 143-157.

42.Hulea, M., R. Miron, and V. Muresan, *Digital Product Passport Implementation Based on Multi-Blockchain Approach With Decentralized Identifier Provider.* Applied Sciences, 2024. **14**(11): p. 4874.

43.Khan, H.H., et al., *Blockchain Technology for Agricultural Supply Chains During the COVID-19 Pandemic: Benefits and Cleaner Solutions.* Journal of Cleaner Production, 2022. **347**: p. 131268.

44.Rivera, T. and D. Foderick, *Ostrom's Razor: Using Bitcoin to Cut Fraud in Hollywood Accounting.* Journal of Risk and Financial Management, 2024. **17**(4): p. 139.

45.Vulpen, P.v., J. Siu, and S. Jansen, *Governance of Decentralized Autonomous Organizations That Produce Open Source Software.* SSRN Electronic Journal, 2022.

46.Bastard, A. and A. Chaillet, *Blockchain: No Pain, No Gain? An Examination of Blockchain Technology in the Vitivinicultural Sector.* Bio Web of Conferences, 2023. **68**: p. 03009.

47.Mihus, I., et al., *The Change of the Monetary Paradigm: Financial Security and Cryptocurrency.* Financial Internet Quarterly, 2024. **20**(2): p. 89-101.

48.Kotey, S.D., et al., *Blockchain Interoperability: The State of Heterogenous Blockchain-to-blockchain Communication.* Iet Communications, 2023. **17**(8): p. 891-914.

49.Jiao, J., et al., *Executable Operational Semantics of Solidity.* 2018.

50.Bragagnolo, S., et al., *SmartInspect: Solidity Smart Contract Inspector.* 2018.

51.Amoo, A., *Research on Automatic Commodity Trading Method Based on Smart Contract.* International Journal of Smart Business and Technology, 2018. **6**(2): p. 31-38.

52.Praitheeshan, P., et al., *Security Analysis Methods on Ethereum Smart Contract Vulnerabilities: A Survey.* 2019.

53.Zhang, P., F. Xiao, and X. Luo, *SolidityCheck : Quickly Detecting Smart Contract Problems Through Regular Expressions.* 2019.

54.Baird, K., et al., *The Economics of Smart Contracts.* 2019.

55.Wang, X., et al., *ContractGuard: Defend Ethereum Smart Contracts With Embedded Intrusion Detection.* Ieee Transactions on Services Computing, 2019: p. 1-1.

56.Malik, H.R., et al., *Performance Analysis of Blockchain Based Smart Grids With Ethereum and Hyperledger Implementations.* 2019.

57.Daluwathumullagamage, D.J. and A. Sims, *Blockchain-Enabled Corporate Governance and Regulation.* International Journal of Financial Studies, 2020. **8**(2): p. 36.

58.Leuprecht, C., C. Jenkins, and R. Hamilton, *Virtual Money Laundering: Policy Implications of the Proliferation in the Illicit Use of Cryptocurrency.* Journal of Financial Crime, 2022. **30**(4): p. 1036-1054.

59.Pawar, A., *Blockchain and Cryptocurrency: A Double-Edged Sword for Financial Inclusion and Regulation.* 2024: p. 129-134.

60.Schaupp, L.C., et al., *Regulation as a Pathway to Individual Adoption of Cryptocurrency.* Digital Policy Regulation and Governance, 2022. **24**(2): p. 199-219.

61.Wiwoho, J., et al., *Islamic Crypto Assets and Regulatory Framework: Evidence From Indonesia and Global Approaches.* International Journal of Law and Management, 2023. **66**(2): p. 155-171.

62.Fletcher, E., C. Larkin, and S. Corbet, *Countering Money Laundering and Terrorist Financing: A Case for Bitcoin Regulation.* Research in International Business and Finance, 2021. **56**: p. 101387.

63.Aydoğan, B., G. Vardar, and C. Taçoğlu, *Volatility Spillovers Among G7, E7 stock Markets and Cryptocurrencies.* Journal of Economic and Administrative Sciences, 2022. **40**(2): p. 364-387.

64.Alibašić, H., *Developing an Ethical Framework for Responsible Artificial Intelligence (AI) and Machine Learning (ML) Applications in Cryptocurrency Trading: A Consequentialism Ethics Analysis.* Fintech, 2023. **2**(3): p. 430-443.

65.Khan, R.U., K. Ullah, and M. Atiq, *Regulatory Constraints, Responsibilities and Consultation (CRC) for Legal Institutionalization of Cryptocurrencies in Pakistan.* Qualitative Research in Financial Markets, 2023. **16**(4): p. 680-708.

66.Andolfatto, D., *Assessing the Impact of Central Bank Digital Currency on Private Banks.* The Economic Journal, 2020. **131**(634): p. 525-540.

67.Ozili, P.K., *Central Bank Digital Currency Research Around the World: A Review of Literature.* Journal of Money Laundering Control, 2022. **26**(2): p. 215-226.

68.Sethaput, V. and S. Innet, *Blockchain Application for Central Bank Digital Currencies (CBDC).* Cluster Computing, 2023. **26**(4): p. 2183-2197.

69.Opare, E.A. and K. Kim, *A Compendium of Practices for Central Bank Digital Currencies for Multinational Financial Infrastructures.* Ieee Access, 2020. **8**: p. 110810-110847.

70.Jung, H. and D. Jeong, *Blockchain Implementation Method for Interoperability Between CBDCs.* Future Internet, 2021. **13**(5): p. 133.

71.Mnohoghitnei, I., C.A. Neguț, and A. Horobeț, *The Future Is Near: On the Prospects of Central Bank Digital Currency Adoption in Central and Eastern European Countries.* Kne Social Sciences, 2021.

72.Hofmann, C., et al., *Central Bank Digital Currencies (CBDCs) - Proceedings of a Colloquium.* 2023.

73.Ma, W., *An Introduction to the Impact of India's Use of Central Bank Digital Currency on the International Financial System.* Frontiers in Business Economics and Management, 2023. 7(1): p. 218-220.

74.Yang, J. and S. Luo, *A Study on the Influence Mechanism of CBDC on Monetary Policy: An Analysis Based on E-Cny.* Plos One, 2022. **17**(7): p. e0268471.

75.Smirna, T.G., et al., *Central Bank Digital Currencies Analyzed in a Banking School Versus Currency School Framework.* Proceedings of the International Conference on Business Excellence, 2023. **17**(1): p. 638-648.

76.Becerra, J.R.J., et al., *Research of the Development of Green Central Bank Digital Currency, CBDC.* Advances in Economics Management and Political Sciences, 2023. **4**(1): p. 449-458.

77.Mungoli, N., *Deciphering the Blockchain: A Comprehensive Analysis of Bitcoin's Evolution, Adoption, and Future Implications.* arXiv preprint arXiv:2304.02655, 2023.

78.Albshaier, L., S. Almarri, and M. Hafizur Rahman, *A Review of Blockchain's Role in E-Commerce Transactions: Open Challenges, and Future Research Directions.* Computers, 2024. **13**(1): p. 27.

79.Danezis, G. and S. Meiklejohn, *Centrally Banked Cryptocurrencies.* 2016.

80.Barrera, J.A., et al., *Blockchain, Information Security, Control, and Integrity: Who Is in Charge?* Plastic & Reconstructive Surgery, 2023. **152**(4): p. 751e-758e.

81.Doğan, M. and G. Övenç, *Central Bank Digital Currencies Under Blockchain Technology: Discussion of Digital Bank Runs and Design Principles.* European Journal of Science and Technology, 2021.

82.Zhou, Q., et al., *Solutions to Scalability of Blockchain: A Survey.* Ieee Access, 2020. **8**: p. 16440-16455.

83.Besançon, L., et al., *A Blockchain Ontology for DApps Development.* Ieee Access, 2022. **10**: p. 49905-49933.

84.Raikwar, M., D. Gligoroski, and K. Kralevska, *SoK of Used Cryptography in Blockchain.* Ieee Access, 2019. **7**: p. 148550-148575.

85.Guo, Y., et al., *Zk-SNARKs-Based Anonymous Payment Channel in Blockchain.* Blockchains, 2024. **2**(1): p. 20-39.

86.Khan, K.M., J. Arshad, and M.M. Khan, *Investigating Performance Constraints for Blockchain Based Secure E-Voting System.* Future Generation Computer Systems, 2020. **105**: p. 13-26.

87.Nasir, M., et al., *Scalable Blockchains — A Systematic Review.* Future Generation Computer Systems, 2022. **126**: p. 136-162.

88.Elwi, D., et al., *Cooperative Mining System to Improve Bitcoin Scalability.* Ieee Access, 2023. **11**: p. 58715-58728.

89.Aumayr, L., et al., *Demand-Aware Payment Channel Networks.* 2020.

90.Kandpal, M., et al., *Towards Data Storage, Scalability, and Availability in Blockchain Systems: A Bibliometric Analysis.* Data, 2023. **8**(10): p. 148.

91.Tang, W., et al., *Privacy-Utility Tradeoffs in Routing Cryptocurrency Over Payment Channel Networks.* Acm Sigmetrics Performance Evaluation Review, 2020. **48**(1): p. 81-82.

92.Machado, C., R.R.S.d. Santos, and C.M. Westphall, *Hop-by-Hop Accounting and Rewards for Packet dIspAtching.* 2021.

93.Bai, Q., Y. Xu, and X. Wang, *Understanding the Benefit of Being Patient in Payment Channel Networks.* 2021.

94.Rejeb, A., J.G. Keogh, and H. Treiblmaier, *Leveraging the Internet of Things and Blockchain Technology in Supply Chain Management.* Future Internet, 2019. **11**(7): p. 161.

95.Alghazwi, M., et al., *Blockchain for Genomics: A Systematic Literature Review.* 2021.

96.Jung, H.S., H. Lee, and J.H. Kim, *Unveiling Cryptocurrency Conversations: Insights From Data Mining and Unsupervised Learning Across Multiple Platforms.* Ieee Access, 2023. **11**: p. 130573-130583.

97.Saad, M., et al., *Exploring the Attack Surface of Blockchain: A Comprehensive Survey.* Ieee Communications Surveys & Tutorials, 2020. **22**(3): p. 1977-2008.

98.Ozili, P.K., *Decentralized Finance Research and Developments Around the World.* Journal of Banking and Financial Technology, 2022. **6**(2): p. 117-133.

99.Velický, M., *Renewable Energy Transition Facilitated by Bitcoin.* Acs Sustainable Chemistry & Engineering, 2023. **11**(8): p. 3160-3169.

100.Yu, C., et al., *Technology and Security Analysis of Cryptocurrency Based on Blockchain.* Complexity, 2022. **2022**: p. 1-15.

101.Mathur, S., et al., *Blockchain Technology for Advancement of Smart Cities.* 2023: p. 229-238.

102.Rogers, I., et al., *Diminishing Dreams.* M/C Journal, 2022. **25**(2).

103.Nabilou, H., *Bitcoin Governance as a Decentralized Financial Market Infrastructure.* SSRN Electronic Journal, 2020.

104.Alsalami, N. and B. Zhang, *Utilizing Public Blockchains for Censorship-Circumvention and IoT Communication.* 2019.

105.Vazirani, A.A., et al., *Blockchain Vehicles for Efficient Medical Record Management.* NPJ Digital Medicine, 2020. **3**(1).

106.Alshater, M.M., et al., *Fintech in Islamic Finance Literature: A Review.* Heliyon, 2022. **8**(9): p. e10385.

107.Chowdhury, R., et al., *An Approach to Predict and Forecast the Price of Constituents and Index of Cryptocurrency Using Machine Learning.* Physica a Statistical Mechanics and Its Applications, 2020. **551**: p. 124569.

108.Kshetri, N., *The Nature and Sources of International Variation in Formal Institutions Related to Initial Coin Offerings: Preliminary Findings and a Research Agenda.* Financial Innovation, 2023. **9**(1).

109.Taher, S.S., S.Y. Ameen, and J.A. Ahmed, *Advanced Fraud Detection in Blockchain Transactions: An Ensemble Learning and Explainable AI Approach.* Engineering Technology & Applied Science Research, 2024. **14**(1): p. 12822-12830.

110.Zhang, Z., et al., *Forecasting Cryptocurrency Price Using Convolutional Neural Networks With Weighted and Attentive Memory Channels.* Expert Systems With Applications, 2021. **183**: p. 115378.

111.Raza, S.A., et al., *Google Trends and Cryptocurrencies: A Nonparametric Causality-in-Quantiles Analysis.* International Journal of Emerging Markets, 2022. **18**(12): p. 5972-5989.

112.Kovalchuk, O., R. Shevchuk, and S. Banakh, *Cryptocurrency Crime Risks Modeling: Environment, E-Commerce, and Cybersecurity Issue.* Ieee Access, 2024. **12**: p. 50673-50688.

113.Sharma, D., D. Pant, and A. Kumar, *Cryptocurrency: An Overview of Its History, Technology and Future Prospects.* International Journal of Advanced Research in Science Communication and Technology, 2023: p. 427-430.

114.Ullah, Z., et al., *Towards Blockchain-Based Secure Storage and Trusted Data Sharing Scheme for IoT Environment.* Ieee Access, 2022. **10**: p. 36978-36994.

115.Zhukovskiy, Y.L., et al., *Fossil Energy in the Framework of Sustainable Development: Analysis of Prospects and Development of Forecast Scenarios.* Energies, 2021. **14**(17): p. 5268.

116.Sapra, N., I. Shaikh, and A. Dash, *Impact of Proof of Work (PoW)-Based Blockchain Applications on the Environment: A Systematic Review and Research Agenda.* Journal of Risk and Financial Management, 2023. **16**(4): p. 218.

117.Shah, A.F.M.S., et al., *On the Vital Aspects and Characteristics of Cryptocurrency—A Survey.* Ieee Access, 2023. **11**: p. 9451-9468.

118.Ngozi Samuel Uzougbo, N., N. Chinonso Gladys Ikegwu, and N. Adefolake Olachi Adewusi, *International Enforcement of Cryptocurrency Laws: Jurisdictional Challenges and Collaborative Solutions.* Magna Scientia Advanced Research and Reviews, 2024. **11**(1): p. 068-083.

119.Ryan, E.V., *Save the Kids: The Need for Regulation of Cryptocurrency to Protect Adolescents From Fraud.* Family Court Review, 2023. **61**(3): p. 650-664.

120.Hayes, A., *Blockchain Facts: What Is It, How It Works, and How It Can Be Used.* 2024, Investopedia.

121.Seth, S., *Explaining the Crypto in Cryptocurrency.* 2024, Investopedia.

122.Boffi, A., *Foundations of Cryptography.* 2022.

123.Dupuis, F., O. Fawzi, and R. Renner, *Entropy Accumulation.* Communications in Mathematical Physics, 2020. **379**(3): p. 867-913.

124.Cañas, G., et al., *High-Dimensional Decoy-State Quantum Key Distribution Over Multicore Telecommunication Fibers.* Physical Review A, 2017. **96**(2).

125.Olijnyk, N.V., *Examination of China's Performance and Thematic Evolution in Quantum Cryptography Research Using Quantitative and Computational Techniques.* Plos One, 2018. **13**(1): p. e0190646.

126.Andono, P.N. and D.R.I.M. Setiadi, *Improved Pixel and Bit Confusion-Diffusion Based on Mixed Chaos and Hash Operation for Image Encryption.* Ieee Access, 2022. **10**: p. 115143-115156.

127.Al-Amri, R.M., D.N. Hamood, and A.K. Farhan, *Theoretical Background of Cryptography.* 2023: p. 7-15.

128.Dür, W., R. Lamprecht, and S. Heusler, *Towards a Quantum Internet.* European Journal of Physics, 2017. **38**(4): p. 043001.

129.Kumar, N.A., et al., *Architecture of Network-on-Chip (NoC) for Secure Data Routing Using 4-H Function of Improved TACIT Security Algorithm.* Wireless Communications and Mobile Computing, 2022. **2022**: p. 1-9.

130.Raghupathy, B.K., et al., *Image Security Using Visual Cryptography.* 2022: p. 281-292.

131.Abusukhon, A., Z. Mohammad, and A. Al-Thaher, *An Authenticated, Secure, and Mutable Multiple-session-keys Protocol Based on Elliptic Curve Cryptography and Text-to-image Encryption Algorithm.* Concurrency and Computation Practice and Experience, 2021. **34**(4).

132.Mathew, S. and K.P. Jacob, *Message Integrity in the World Wide Web: Use of Nested Hash Function and a Fast Stream Cipher.* 2006.

133.Kraken, *How do cryptocurrencies use cryptography?* 2024.

134.Bonneau, J., et al., *SoK: Research Perspectives and Challenges for Bitcoin and Cryptocurrencies.* 2015.

135.Park, S., et al., *Nodes in the Bitcoin Network: Comparative Measurement Study and Survey.* Ieee Access, 2019. **7**: p. 57009-57022.

136.Rahman, A.A., *A Conceptual Model for a Decentralized Central Bank Digital Currency.* 2023.

137.Ramanathan, V., et al., *Public Health Perspectives on Cryptocurrency: The Good, the Bad and the Ugly.* Indian Journal of Community Health, 2023. **35**(3): p. 372-374.

138.Fernández, M.Á.E., et al., *Central Banks' Monetary Policy in the Face of the COVID-19 Economic Crisis: Monetary Stimulus and the Emergence of CBDCs.* Sustainability, 2021. **13**(8): p. 4242.

139.Dallyn, S., *Cryptocurrencies as Market Singularities: The Strange Case of Bitcoin.* Journal of Cultural Economy, 2017. **10**(5): p. 462-473.

140.Li, Q., et al., *DareChain: A Blockchain-Based Trusted Collaborative Network Infrastructure for Metaverse.* International Journal of Crowd Science, 2023. **7**(4): p. 168-179.

141.Vukolić, M., *The Quest for Scalable Blockchain Fabric: Proof-of-Work vs. BFT Replication.* 2016: p. 112-125.

142.Javed, H., et al., *Blockchain-Based Logging to Defeat Malicious Insiders: The Case of Remote Health Monitoring Systems.* Ieee Access, 2024. **12**: p. 12062-12079.

143.Kim, S.-K. and J.H. Huh, *A Study on the Improvement of Smart Grid Security Performance and Blockchain Smart Grid Perspective.* Energies, 2018. **11**(8): p. 1973.

144.Zhang, R., R. Xue, and L. Liu, *Security and Privacy on Blockchain.* Acm Computing Surveys, 2019. **52**(3): p. 1-34.

145.O'Dair, M. and Z. Beaven, *The Networked Record Industry: How Blockchain Technology Could Transform the Record Industry.* Strategic Change, 2017. **26**(5): p. 471-480.

146.Imran, M., et al., *Research Perspectives and Challenges of Blockchain for Data-Intensive and Resource-Constrained Devices.* Ieee Access, 2022. **10**: p. 38104-38122.

147.Deval, V., et al., *Mobile Smart Contracts: Exploring Scalability Challenges and Consensus Mechanisms.* Ieee Access, 2024. **12**: p. 34265-34288.

148.Zamani, M., M. Movahedi, and M. Raykova, *RapidChain.* 2018.

149.Yu, H., et al., *OHIE: Blockchain Scaling Made Simple.* 2020.

150.Wang, X., et al., *Securing Parallel-Chain Protocols Under Variable Mining Power.* 2021.

151.Boehm, F. and P.J. Pesch, *Bitcoin: A First Legal Analysis.* 2014: p. 43-54.

152.Böhme, R., et al., *Bitcoin: Economics, Technology, and Governance.* Journal of Economic Perspectives, 2015. **29**(2): p. 213-238.

153.Rosele, M.I., et al., *The Concept of Wealth (māl) in the Sharī'ah and Its Relation to Digital Assets.* Sage Open, 2022. **12**(2): p. 215824402211024.

154.Begušić, S., et al., *Scaling Properties of Extreme Price Fluctuations in Bitcoin Markets.* Physica a Statistical Mechanics and Its Applications, 2018. **510**: p. 400-406.

155.Yelowitz, A. and M.W. Wilson, *Characteristics of Bitcoin Users: An Analysis of Google Search Data.* Applied Economics Letters, 2015. **22**(13): p. 1030-1036.

156.Hu, A.S., C.A. Parlour, and U. Rajan, *Cryptocurrencies: Stylized Facts on a New Investible Instrument.* Financial Management, 2019. **48**(4): p. 1049-1068.

157.Hałaburda, H., et al., *The Microeconomics of Cryptocurrencies.* SSRN Electronic Journal, 2021.

158.Delgado-Segura, S., C. Tanas, and J. Herrera-Joancomartí, *Reputation and Reward: Two Sides of the Same Bitcoin.* Sensors, 2016. **16**(6): p. 776.

159.Catalini, C. and J.S. Gans, *Some Simple Economics of the Blockchain.* SSRN Electronic Journal, 2016.

160.Henriques, I. and P. Sadorsky, *Can Bitcoin Replace Gold in an Investment Portfolio?* Journal of Risk and Financial Management, 2018. **11**(3): p. 48.

161.Mashatan, A., M.S. Sangari, and M. Dehghani, *How Perceptions of Information Privacy and Security Impact Consumer Trust in Crypto-Payment: An Empirical Study.* Ieee Access, 2022. **10**: p. 69441-69454.

162.Balutel, D., et al., *Bitcoin Adoption and Beliefs in Canada.* Canadian Journal of Economics/Revue Canadienne D Économique, 2022. **55**(4): p. 1729-1761.

163.Andreianova, M., et al., *Bitcoin Usage: Study on Bitcoin Usage Around the World 2020.* The Journal of Fintech, 2021. **01**(02).

164.Rosele, M.I., et al., *The Concept of Wealth (<i>māl</I>) in the Sharīʿah and Its Relation to Digital Assets.* Sage Open, 2022. **12**(2): p. 21582440221102 4.

165.Extance, A., *The Future of Cryptocurrencies: Bitcoin and Beyond.* Nature, 2015. **526**(7571): p. 21-23.

166.Sathyanarayana, S. and S. Gargesa, *Modeling Cryptocurrency (Bitcoin) Using Vector Autoregressive (Var) Model.* Sdmimd Journal of Management, 2019. **10**(2): p. 47-64.

167.Masama, B. and J.-P. Bruwer, *The Feasibility of Blockchain Technology as a Tool for Zimbabwean Financial Inclusion: An Online Desktop Review.* International Journal of Cryptocurrency Research, 2022. **2**(2).

168.Dobson, D. and A. Fernandez, *IDSov and the Silent Data Revolution: Indigenous Peoples and the Decentralized Building Blocks of Web3.* Frontiers in Research Metrics and Analytics, 2023. **8**.

169.Keogh, J.G., et al., *Optimizing Global Food Supply Chains: The Case for Blockchain and GSI Standards.* 2020: p. 171-204.

170.Choobineh, M., et al., *Blockchain Technology in Energy Systems: A State-of-the-art Review.* Iet Blockchain, 2022. **3**(1): p. 35-59.

171.Suryono, R.R., I. Budi, and B. Purwandari, *Challenges and Trends of Financial Technology (Fintech): A Systematic Literature Review.* Information, 2020. **11**(12): p. 590.

172.Wang, Z., M. Gao, and G. Lu, *Research on Oracle Technology Based on Multi-Threshold Aggregate Signature Algorithm and Enhanced Trustworthy Oracle Reputation Mechanism.* Sensors, 2024. **24**(2): p. 502.

173.Puschmann, T. and M. Huang-Sui, *A Taxonomy for Decentralized Finance.* 2023.

174.Jabbar, R., et al., *Blockchain Technology for Intelligent Transportation Systems: A Systematic Literature Review.* Ieee Access, 2022. **10**: p. 20995-21031.

175.Alqahtani, A.M. and A. Algarni, *A Survey on Blockchain Technology Concepts, Applications and Security.* International Journal of Advanced Computer Science and Applications, 2023. **14**(2).

176.Calik, E. and M. Bendechache, *Blockchain for Organ Transplantation: A Survey.* Blockchains, 2024. **2**(2): p. 150-172.

177.Cambou, B., et al., *Securing Additive Manufacturing With Blockchains and Distributed Physically Unclonable Functions.* Cryptography, 2020. **4**(2): p. 17.

178.Yang, G., C. Li, and K.E. Marstein, *A Blockchain-based Architecture for Securing Electronic Health Record Systems.* Concurrency and Computation Practice and Experience, 2019. **33**(14).

179.Sun, J., et al., *A Blockchain-Based Framework for Electronic Medical Records Sharing With Fine-Grained Access Control.* Plos One, 2020. **15**(10): p. e0239946.

180.Mijoska, M. and B. Ristevski, *Possibilities for Applying Blockchain Technology – A Survey.* Informatica, 2021. **45**(3).

181.Malouin, M., *Organisations Autonomes Décentralisées Et Enjeux De Gouvernance : Le Cas De the DAO.* Revue Organisations & Territoires, 2023. **32**(2): p. 60-72.

182.Bleakley, C., *Next Steps.* 2020: p. 215-228.

183.Floyd, D., *How Does Bitcoin Work? Definition and How to Invest*. 2024, Inestopedia.

184.Benedetti, H. and L. Kostovetsky, *Digital Tulips? Returns to Investors in Initial Coin Offerings.* SSRN Electronic Journal, 2018.

185.Fabus, J., et al., *An Empirical Examination of Bitcoin's Halving Effects: Assessing Cryptocurrency Sustainability within the Landscape of Financial Technologies.* Journal of Risk and Financial Management, 2024. **17**(6): p. 229.

186.Fantazzini, D. and N. Kolodin, *Does the hashrate affect the bitcoin price?* Journal of Risk and Financial Management, 2020. **13**(11): p. 263.

187.Shahriar Hazari, S. and Q.H. Mahmoud, *Improving transaction speed and scalability of blockchain systems via parallel proof of work.* Future internet, 2020. **12**(8): p. 125.

188.Meynkhard, A., *Fair market value of bitcoin: Halving effect. Investment Management and Financial Innovations, 16 (4), 72–85.* 2019.

189.Tovanich, N., N. Soulié, and P. Isenberg. *Visual analytics of bitcoin mining pool evolution: on the road toward stability?* in *2021 11th IFIP International Conference on New Technologies, Mobility and Security (NTMS)*. 2021. IEEE.

190.Tovanich, N., N. Soulié, and P. Isenberg, *Visual Analytics of Bitcoin Mining Pool Evolution: On the Road Toward Stability?* 2021.

191.Wang, C., X. Chu, and Y. Qin. *Measurement and analysis of the bitcoin networks: A view from mining pools*. in *2020 6th International Conference on Big Data Computing and Communications (BIGCOM)*. 2020. IEEE.

192.El Mahdy, D., *The economic effect of Bitcoin halving events on the US capital market.* Accounting and Finance Innovations, 2021. **65**.

193.The Investopedia Team, *What is Bitcoin? How to Mine, Buy, and Use It*. 2024, Investopedia.

194.Geeks for Geeks, *Blockchain Structure*. 2022.

195.Fáwọlé, J., O. Malanii, and L. Ciattaglia, *Blockchain Architecture Layers: A Comprehensive Guide*. 2024, Hacken.

196.Coinbase, *What is "proof of work" or "proof of stake"?* 2024.

197.Ross, G., *Security and Privacy in Blockchain: Challenges and Solutions*. 2023, LinkedIn.

198.Immunebytes, *Pseudonymity and Anonymity: Be Untraceable in the Blockchain World*. 2023.

199.Hayes, A., *10 Important Cryptocurrencies Other Than Bitcoin*. 2024.

200.Stax, *The Top 20 Most Popular Cryptocurrencies*. 2024.

201.Kim, S.K., et al., *Measuring Ethereum Network Peers.* 2018.

202.Chen, T., et al., *Under-Optimized Smart Contracts Devour Your Money.* 2017.

203.Sharma, T.K., *A Complete List of Top 15 Cryptocurrencies*. 2023, Blockchain Council.

204.Cornèr, K.L., *What is Ripple: Overview, history and XRP cryptocurrency*. 2024, Cointelegraph.

205.Yi, X., et al., *BlockScope: Detecting and Investigating Propagated Vulnerabilities in Forked Blockchain Projects.* 2023.

206.Moşteanu, N.R. and T. Flocea, *Revolutionizing Foreign Exchange Market: A Critical Analysis of Blockchain's Opportunities and Challenges.* European Journal of Theoretical and Applied Sciences, 2023. **1**(5): p. 33-44.

207.Klein, T., H.P. Thu, and T. Walther, *Bitcoin Is Not the New Gold – A Comparison of Volatility, Correlation, and Portfolio Performance.* International Review of Financial Analysis, 2018. **59**: p. 105-116.

208.Lorenzo, L. and J. Arroyo, *Analysis of the Cryptocurrency Market Using Different Prototype-Based Clustering Techniques.* Financial Innovation, 2022. **8**(1).

209.Chahooki, M.A.Z., K. Jahanbin, and T. Sutikno, *Cryptocurrencies Investment Framework Using Sentiment Analysis of Twitter Influencers.* Indonesian Journal of Electrical Engineering and Computer Science, 2023. **30**(2): p. 1068.

210.Pessa, A.A.B., M. Perc, and H.V. Ribeiro, *Age and Market Capitalization Drive Large Price Variations of Cryptocurrencies.* Scientific Reports, 2023. **13**(1).

211.Fasanya, I.O., O.J. Oyewole, and T.F. Odudu, *Returns and Volatility Spillovers Among Cryptocurrency Portfolios.* International Journal of Managerial Finance, 2020. **17**(2): p. 327-341.

212.Akyıldırım, E., A. Göncü, and A. Şensoy, *Prediction of Cryptocurrency Returns Using Machine Learning.* Annals of Operations Research, 2020. **297**(1-2): p. 3-36.

213.Wanidwaranan, P. and S. Termprasertsakul, *Herd Behavior in Cryptocurrency Market: Evidence of Network Effect.* Review of Behavioral Finance, 2023. **16**(3): p. 406-423.

214.Vlahavas, G. and A. Vakali, *Dynamics Between Bitcoin Market Trends and Social Media Activity.* 2024.

215.Ramirez, D., *Crypto Hot Wallet vs. Cold Wallet: The Biggest Differences.* 2024, Nerdwallet.

216.Amure, T.O., *Hot Wallet vs. Cold Wallet: What's the Difference?* 2024, Investopedia.

217.Reiff, N., *Protect Your Bitcoins Against Theft and Hacks.* 2024, Investopedia.

218.Kaspersky Team, *Protecting crypto investments: four key steps to safety.* 2023, Kaspersky Daily.

219.The Investopedia Team, *What Is a Bitcoin Exchange? How It Works, Fees, and Example.* 2024, Investopedia.

220.Maheshwari, R., *What Are Crypto Exchanges And How Do They Work.* 2024, Forbes Advisor.

221.Wilson, J., *How Crypto Exchanges Work: The mechanisms at play.* 2022, Zerocap.

222.Antolin, M., *What Are Crypto Trading Pairs?* 2022, CoinDesk.

223.Cryptopedia Staff, *What Are Trading Pairs in Cryptocurrency?* 2022, Cryptopedia.

224.Team Stash, *How to invest in cryptocurrency: a beginner's guide.* 2024.

225.Royal, J., *How to start investing in cryptocurrency: A guide for beginners.* 2024, Bankrate.

226.Saiedi, E., A. Broström, and F. Ruiz, *Global drivers of cryptocurrency infrastructure adoption.* Small Business Economics, 2021. **57**(1): p. 353-406.

227.Lu, R., V.T. Hoang, and W.-K. Wong, *Do lump-sum investing strategies really outperform dollar-cost averaging strategies?* Studies in Economics and Finance, 2021. **38**(3): p. 675-691.

228.Asness, C.S., T.J. Moskowitz, and L.H. Pedersen, *Value and Momentum Everywhere.* The Journal of Finance, 2013. **68**(3): p. 929-985.

229.Grimes, A., *The art and science of technical analysis: market structure, price action, and trading strategies.* Vol. 544. 2012: John Wiley & Sons.

230.Fang, F., et al., *Cryptocurrency Trading: A Comprehensive Survey.* Financial Innovation, 2022. **8**(1).

231.Kaur, S., et al., *A Research Survey on Applications of Consensus Protocols in Blockchain.* Security and Communication Networks, 2021. **2021**: p. 1-22.

232.Schär, F., *Decentralized Finance: On Blockchain- And Smart Contract-Based Financial Markets.* SSRN Electronic Journal, 2020.

233.Howell, S.T., M. Niessner, and D. Yermack, *Initial Coin Offerings: Financing Growth With Cryptocurrency Token Sales.* Review of Financial Studies, 2019. **33**(9): p. 3925-3974.

234.Fenu, G., et al., *The ICO Phenomenon and Its Relationships With Ethereum Smart Contract Environment.* 2018.

235.Dejong, A., P. Roosenboom, and T.v. deKolk, *What Determines Success in Initial Coin Offerings?* SSRN Electronic Journal, 2018.

236.Wis, A., *Initial Coin Offering as a Funding Source for Projects.* Acc Journal, 2019. **25**(2): p. 90-98.

237.Vidal-Tomás, D., *Blockchain, Sport and Fan Tokens.* Journal of Economic Studies, 2023. **51**(1): p. 24-38.

238.Schellinger, B., *Optimization of Special Cryptocurrency Portfolios.* The Journal of Risk Finance, 2020. **21**(2): p. 127-157.

239.Shanaev, S., et al., *Taming the Blockchain Beast? Regulatory Implications for the Cryptocurrency Market.* Research in International Business and Finance, 2020. **51**: p. 101080.

240.Myalo, A. and Г.Н. Юрьевич, *Factors of Success of Initial Coin Offering. Empirical Evidence From 2016–2019.* Finance Theory and Practice, 2019. **23**(5): p. 30-49.

241.Kim, M.S. and J.Y. Chung, *Sustainable Growth and Token Economy Design: The Case of Steemit.* Sustainability, 2018. **11**(1): p. 167.

242.Antonakakis, N., I. Chatziantoniou, and D. Gabauer, *Cryptocurrency Market Contagion: Market Uncertainty, Market Complexity, and Dynamic Portfolios.* Journal of International Financial Markets Institutions and Money, 2019. **61**: p. 37-51.

243.Hudson, R. and A. Urquhart, *Technical Trading and Cryptocurrencies.* Annals of Operations Research, 2019. **297**(1-2): p. 191-220.

244.Letho, L., G. Chelwa, and A.L. Alhassan, *Cryptocurrencies and Portfolio Diversification in an Emerging Market.* China Finance Review International, 2022. **12**(1): p. 20-50.

245.Lamine, A., A. Jeribi, and T. Fakhfakh, *Spillovers Between Cryptocurrencies, Gold and Stock Markets: Implication for Hedging Strategies and Portfolio Diversification Under the COVID-19 Pandemic.* Journal of Economics Finance and Administrative Science, 2023. **29**(57): p. 21-41.

246.Ma, Y., et al., *Portfolio Optimization in the Era of Digital Financialization Using Cryptocurrencies.* Technological Forecasting and Social Change, 2020. **161**: p. 120265.

247.Sahu, S., et al., *Analyzing Portfolio Optimization in Cryptocurrency Markets: A Comparative Study of Short-Term Investment Strategies Using Hourly Data Approach.* Journal of Risk and Financial Management, 2024. **17**(3): p. 125.

248.Han, W., et al., *The Diversification Benefits of Cryptocurrency Factor Portfolios: Are They There?* Review of Quantitative Finance and Accounting, 2024. **63**(2): p. 469-518.

249.Clément, J. and E.S.E.F. Angaman, *A K-Means Classification and Entropy Pooling Portfolio Strategy for Small and Large Capitalization Cryptocurrencies.* Entropy, 2023. **25**(8): p. 1208.

250.Conlon, T., S. Corbet, and R. McGee, *Are Cryptocurrencies a Safe Haven for Equity Markets? An International Perspective From the COVID-19 Pandemic.* Research in International Business and Finance, 2020. **54**: p. 101248.

251.James, A., *What is technical analysis for crypto trading?* 2024, The Block.

252.Amure, T.O., *What Charts Should Crypto Investors Use?* 2024, Investopedia.

253.One Trading, *Techniques, Indicators, and Applications for Crypto Technical Analysis.* 2024, One Trading.

254.Nikolaieva, O., A. Petrova, and R. Lutsenko, *Forecasting of the Stock Rate of Leading World Companies Using Econometric Methods and DCF Analysis.* International Journal of Innovative Technologies in Economy, 2020(2(29)): p. 33-41.

255.One Trading, *Learn Crypto: Fundamental Analysis.* 2024, One Trading.

256.Daly, L., *How to Create a Well-Balanced Crypto Portfolio.* 2024, The Motley Fool.

257.Chkili, W., A.B. Rejeb, and M. Arfaoui, *Does Bitcoin Provide Hedge to Islamic Stock Markets for Pre- And During COVID-19 Outbreak? A Comparative Analysis With Gold.* Resources Policy, 2021. **74**: p. 102407.

258.Guo, L., W.K. Härdle, and Y. Tao, *A Time-Varying Network for Cryptocurrencies.* Journal of Business and Economic Statistics, 2022. **42**(2): p. 437-456.

259.Abdelkafi, I., Y. Ben Romdhane, and S. Loukil, *Has COVID-19 Changed the Correlation Between Cryptocurrencies and Stock Markets?* European Journal of Government and Economics, 2023. **12**(2): p. 139-156.

260.Wats, S., S. Singh, and S. Gupta, *The Quest for ICO: Identifying and Prioritising the Factors Influencing Initial Coin Offering Selection.* International Social Science Journal, 2023. **73**(250): p. 1035-1055.

261.Olawale Adisa, N., et al., *Decentralized Finance (DEFI) in the U. S. Economy: A Review: Assessing the Rise, Challenges, and Implications of Blockchain-Driven Financial Systems.* World Journal of Advanced Research and Reviews, 2024. **21**(1): p. 2313-2328.

262.Corbet, S., et al., *Exploring the Dynamic Relationships Between Cryptocurrencies and Other Financial Assets.* Economics Letters, 2018. **165**: p. 28-34.

263.Gapurbaeva, S., et al., *International River and Sea Transportation: Specifics of Risk Management in Cryptocurrency Transactions.* Bio Web of Conferences, 2024. **107**: p. 04006.

264.Ni, X., W.K. Härdle, and T. Xie, *A Machine Learning Based Regulatory Risk Index for Cryptocurrencies.* 2020.

265.Tang, Y., et al., *Ethics of Blockchain.* Information Technology and People, 2019. **33**(2): p. 602-632.

266.Nyika, A.M., *The Role of Cryptocurrencies in Shaping the Future of Mobile Money Services in Lusaka, Zambia.* International Journal of Finance, 2023. **8**(4): p. 19-49.

267.Alyami, M., et al., *Phishing Attacks on Cryptocurrency Investors in the Arab States of the Gulf.* Journal of Risk and Financial Management, 2023. **16**(5): p. 271.

268.Xiong, X. and J. Luo, *Global Trends in Cryptocurrency Regulation: An Overview.* arXiv preprint arXiv:2404.15895, 2024.

269.George, K., *Cryptocurrency Regulations Around the World*. 2024, Investopedia.

270.Liebkind, J., *Cryptocurrency Taxes: How They Work and What Gets Taxed*. 2024, Investopedia.

271.Australian Taxation Office. *How to work out and report CGT on crypto*. 2024 [cited 2024 23/7/2024];

272.Aryamov, A.A., et al., *Taxation of Digital Assets.* Азиатско-Тихоокеанский Регион Экономика Политика Право, 2019. **50**(1): p. 96-129.

273.Salah, K., et al., *Blockchain for AI: Review and Open Research Challenges.* Ieee Access, 2019. **7**: p. 10127-10149.

274.Coinbase, *What is DeFi?* . 2024, Coinbase.

275.Sharma, R., *What Is Decentralized Finance (DeFi) and How Does It Work?* 2024, Investopedia.

276.Australian Taxation Office, *Decentralised finance and wrapping crypto.* 2024, Australian Taxation Office.

277.Nguyen, L.-T., et al., *Metaverse Banking Service: Are We Ready to Adopt? A Deep Learning-Based Dual-Stage SEM-ANN Analysis.* Human Behavior and Emerging Technologies, 2023. **2023**: p. 1-23.

278.Sharma, R., *Non-Fungible Token (NFT): What It Means and How It Works.* 2024, Investopedia.

279.Skiba, R., *Blockchain technology as a health and safety contributor in the transport and logistics industry–human resource requirements.* 2020.

280.Foley, S., J.R. Karlsen, and T.J. Putniņš, *Sex, Drugs, and Bitcoin: How Much Illegal Activity Is Financed Through Cryptocurrencies?* Review of Financial Studies, 2019. **32**(5): p. 1798-1853.

281.Alsharu, A.I., T.F. Aldowery, and N.K. Mohammed Jawad, *Jordanian Legal Provisions for Electronic Commerce: Consumer Protection Perspectives—A Comparative Study.* Beijing Law Review, 2024. **15**(01): p. 444-456.

282.Zamani, E.D. and G.M. Giaglis, *With a Little Help From the Miners: Distributed Ledger Technology and Market Disintermediation.* Industrial Management & Data Systems, 2018. **118**(3): p. 637-652.

283.Abou Tanos, B. and G. Badr, *Price Delay and Market Efficiency of Cryptocurrencies: The Impact of Liquidity and Volatility During the COVID-19 Pandemic.* Journal of Risk and Financial Management, 2024. **17**(5): p. 193.

284.Corbet, S., et al., *The Destabilising Effects of Cryptocurrency Cybercriminality.* Economics Letters, 2020. **191**: p. 108741.

285.Livieris, I.E., et al., *An Advanced CNN-LSTM Model for Cryptocurrency Forecasting.* Electronics, 2021. **10**(3): p. 287.

286.Lahkani, M.J., et al., *Sustainable B2B E-Commerce and Blockchain-Based Supply Chain Finance.* Sustainability, 2020. **12**(10): p. 3968.

287.ScienceSoft, *Cryptocurrency Ecommerce in a Nutshell*. 2024.

288.Murphy, C., *Cryptocurrency Scams: How to Spot, Report, and Avoid Them*. 2024, Investopedia.

289.Kaspersky, *Common cryptocurrency scams and how to avoid them*. 2024, Kaspersky.

290.George, K., *The Largest Cryptocurrency Hacks So Far*. 2024, Investopedia.

291.Clere, A., *Crypto 2050: what the future holds for digital currencies*, in *FinTech Magazine*. 2023.

292.Sharma, R., *What Will Happen to Bitcoin in the Next Decade?* 2024, Investopedia.

293.Zeller, A., *Top 7 Cryptocurrency Trends (2024 & 2025)*. 2024, Exploding Topics.

294.Adrian, T. and T. Mancini-Griffoli, *Technology Behind Crypto Can Also Improve Payments, Providing a Public Good*. 2023, International Monetary Fund.

295.Ivey, A., *The economics of cryptocurrency mining: Costs, revenues and market trends*. 2023, Cointelegraph.

296.Tandan, D., *What Is Bitcoin Mining? How It Works and What It Takes to Make It Pay*. 2024, Toptal.

297.The Investopedia Team, *What Is Bitcoin Mining? How to Get Started*. 2024, Investopedia.

298.Lu, L., *How to Set Up Your First ASIC Miner: A Step-by-Step Guide*. 2023, LinkedIn.

299.Sharma, T.K., *What is Solo Mining & How It Works?* 2024, Blockchain Council.

300.Bybit Learn, *What's a Crypto Mining Rig & How Do You Build One?* 2023.

301.Chamanara, S., S.A. Ghaffarizadeh, and K. Madani, *The environmental footprint of bitcoin mining across the globe: Call for urgent action*. Earth's Future, 2023. **11**(10): p. e2023EF003871.

302.Coinbase, *What is a smart contract?* 2024, Coinbase.

303.BasuMallick, C., *What Are Smart Contracts? Types, Benefits, and Tools*. 2023, Spiceworks.

304.Pontem Network, *Market Analysis of 10 Most popular dApps*. 2024, Pontem Network.

305.Morgen, D., *Best dApps: The Top 10 dApps You Should Know About*. 2024, Changelly.

306.Mosaia, *The Future of Smart Contracts: Trends and Predictions*. 2023, LinkedIn.

307.Mckinley, J., *What Are the Social Impacts of Cryptocurrency Development in 2024?* 2024, LinkedIn.

308.Alam, M.S., et al., *Is Monetary Policy a Driver of Cryptocurrencies? Evidence From a Structural Break GARCH-MIDAS Approach.* Econometrics, 2024. **12**(1): p. 2.

309.Sham, R., et al., *Cryptocurrencies Have Arrived, but Are We Ready? Unveiling Cryptocurrency Adoption Recipes Through an SEM-fsQCA Approach.* The Bottom Line Managing Library Finances, 2023. **36**(2): p. 209-233.

310.Caton, J., *Cryptoliquidity: The Blockchain and Monetary Stability.* Journal of Entrepreneurship and Public Policy, 2019. **9**(2): p. 227-252.

311.Chen, E.R., *Determining the Economic Impact of Cryptocurrency Adoption on International Trade From a Gravity Model Framework.* 2021.

312.Souza, L.L.F.d., et al., *Cryptocurrencies for Microfinance.* Bar - Brazilian Administration Review, 2021. **18**(spe).

313.Majeed, H.L., D.J. Ali, and T.L. Mohammed, *Analyzing the Performance of Bitcoin to Gold Prices, the Telecommunications Market, the Stock Price Index, and Insurance Companies' Performance From (March 1, 2021–September 4, 2023).* Uhd Journal of Science and Technology, 2023. **7**(2): p. 16-31.

314.Strydom, K., J.O. Akande, and A.J. Asaleye, *The Quest for Female Economic Empowerment in Sub-Saharan African Countries: Implications on Gender-Based Violence.* Journal of Risk and Financial Management, 2024. **17**(2): p. 51.

315.Bello, S.M., *The Role of Waqf in Enhancing the Financial Inclusion of Women Entrepreneurs in Developing Countries.* Journal of Islamic Business and Management (Jibm), 2022. **12**(01).

316.Basnet, R.K., *Role of Cooperatives in Women Empowerment in the Nepalese Context.* Cognition, 2023. **5**(1): p. 99-105.

317.Nurul Badriyah, N., et al., *Economic Empowerment Through the Development of Food and Beverage Micro Enterprises.* Journal of Community Service and Empowerment, 2023. **4**(2): p. 308-318.

318.Yusnita, V., N. Tresiana, and I.F. Meutia, *Economic Empowerment Through Community Village.* Przegląd Politologiczny, 2023(4): p. 111-124.

319.Negi, N., *The Impact of Cryptocurrency on the Global Financial System: A Quantitative Investigation.* 2023.

320.El-Chaarani, H., et al., *Factors Affecting the Adoption Of cryptocurrencies for Financial Transactions.* Euromed Journal of Business, 2023. **19**(1): p. 46-61.

321.Schär, F., *Decentralized Finance: On Blockchain- And Smart Contract-Based Financial Markets.* 2021. **103**(2).

322.Chung, S., et al., *Interdependence Between Online Peer-to-peer Lending and Cryptocurrency Markets and Its Effects on Financial Inclusion.* Production and Operations Management, 2023. **32**(6): p. 1939-1957.

323.Othman, A.H.A., et al., *The Impact of Monetary Systems on Income Inequity and Wealth Distribution.* International Journal of Emerging Markets, 2020. **15**(6): p. 1161-1183.

324.El Hajj, M. and I. Farran, *The Role of Cryptocurrencies in Emerging Markets: Investigating the Growing Adoption of Cryptocurrencies in Developing Countries, Their Potential to Improve Financial Inclusion and Economic Empowerment.* 2024.

325.Wang, W., et al., *A Survey on Consensus Mechanisms and Mining Strategy Management in Blockchain Networks.* Ieee Access, 2019. **7**: p. 22328-22370.

326.Dabbous, A., M.M. Sayegh, and K.A. Barakat, *Understanding the Adoption Of cryptocurrencies for Financial Transactions Within a High-Risk Context.* The Journal of Risk Finance, 2022. **23**(4): p. 349-367.

327.Abbasi, G.A., et al., *The Adoption of Cryptocurrency as a Disruptive Force: Deep Learning-Based Dual Stage Structural Equation Modelling and Artificial Neural Network Analysis.* Plos One, 2021. **16**(3): p. e0247582.

328.Sajter, D., *Overseas Transaction Fees: Sending Money via Bitcoin vs. Banks.* Zagreb International Review of Economics and Business, 2022. **25**(s1): p. 65-83.

329.Namahoot, K.S. and V. Rattanawiboonsom, *Integration of TAM Model of Consumers' Intention to Adopt Cryptocurrency Platform in Thailand: The Mediating Role of Attitude and Perceived Risk.* Human Behavior and Emerging Technologies, 2022. **2022**: p. 1-12.

330.Hadan, H., et al., *Gamification and Gaming in Cryptocurrency Education: A Survey With Cryptocurrency Investors and Potential Investors.* Simulation & Gaming, 2024. **55**(2): p. 196-223.

331.Castello, A. and G. Gadzinski, *Trustless, Permissionless, Non-Custodial Stablecoins in Decentralized Autonomous Organizations (DAO).* Theoretical Economics Letters, 2022. **12**(06): p. 1559-1565.

332.Biais, B., et al., *Equilibrium Bitcoin Pricing.* SSRN Electronic Journal, 2018.

333.Hai, N.H., et al., *Factors Affecting the Adoption of Cryptocurrency.* Vnu University of Economics and Business, 2023. **3**(4).

334.Harry B, *Cryptocurrency Adoption in Developing Countries*. 2023, LinkedIn.

335.Crypto 101, *Cryptocurrency Adoption in Developing Countries*. 2023, Bitstamp Learn.

336.Calimanu, S., *The rising popularity of Cryptocurrencies in developing countries*. 2022, Research FDI.

337.Protechbro Media, *The Ethics of Cryptocurrency – Privacy, Anonymity, and Criminal Activity*. 2023, Binance.

338.Silva, E.C. and M.M.d. Silva, *Research Contributions and Challenges in DLT-based Cryptocurrency Regulation: A Systematic Mapping Study*. Journal of Banking and Financial Technology, 2022. **6**(1): p. 63-82.

339.Albrecht, C., et al., *The Use of Cryptocurrencies in the Money Laundering Process*. Journal of Money Laundering Control, 2019. **22**(2): p. 210-216.

340.Dhali, M., et al., *Cryptocurrency in the Darknet: Sustainability of the Current National Legislation*. International Journal of Law and Management, 2023. **65**(3): p. 261-282.

341.Hernández Sánchez, Á., et al., *Cryptocurrencies, Tax Ignorance and Tax Noncompliance in Direct Taxation: Spanish Empirical Evidence*. Economies, 2024. **12**(3): p. 62.

342.Ahn, C. and N. Obermeier, *Cryptocurrency and the State: Evidence From South Korea*. 2024.

343.Calhoun, G., *The Ethics Of Crypto: Good Intentions And Bad Actors*. 2022, Forbes.

344.Spydra, *The Ethics of Crypto: Balancing Innovation and Responsibility*. 2023, Medium.

345.Gorman, B., *What Is a Decentralized Autonomous Organization (DAO)?*. 2023, Avast.

346.Reiff, N., *Decentralized Autonomous Organization (DAO): Definition, Purpose, and Example*. 2024, Investopedia.

347.Hennekes, B., *The 8 Most Important Types of DAOs You Need to Know*. 2022, Alchemy.

348.Chainanalysis Team, *Introduction to Decentralized Autonomous Organizations (DAOs)*. 2023, Chainanalysis

349.Beck, R., C. Müller-Bloch, and J.L. King, *Governance in the Blockchain Economy: A Framework and Research Agenda*. Journal of the Association for Information Systems, 2018: p. 1020-1034.

350.Kannengießer, N., et al., *Trade-Offs Between Distributed Ledger Technology Characteristics*. Acm Computing Surveys, 2020. **53**(2): p. 1-37.

351.Dyball, M.C. and R. Seethamraju, *Client Use of Blockchain Technology: Exploring Its (Potential) Impact on Financial Statement Audits of Australian Accounting Firms.* Accounting Auditing & Accountability Journal, 2021. **35**(7): p. 1656-1684.

352.Liu, J. and Z. Liu, *A Survey on Security Verification of Blockchain Smart Contracts.* Ieee Access, 2019. **7**: p. 77894-77904.

353.Al-Mohammad, M.S., et al., *Factors Affecting BIM Implementation in Post-Conflict Low-Income Economies: The Case of Afghanistan.* Journal of Engineering Design and Technology, 2021. **21**(1): p. 299-318.

354.Alao, O. and P. Cuffe, *Structuring Special Purpose Vehicles for Financing Renewable Generators on a Blockchain Marketplace.* Ieee Transactions on Industry Applications, 2022. **58**(2): p. 1478-1489.

355.Sánchez-Jiménez, F., et al., *Pharmacological Potential of Biogenic Amine–polyamine Interactions Beyond Neurotransmission.* British Journal of Pharmacology, 2013. **170**(1): p. 4-16.

356.Olisakwe, K., *How to Create a Decentralized Autonomous Organization (DAO): A Primer*. 2023, LinkedIn.

357.Kanga University, *62. How to Create Your Own Decentralized Autonomous Organization (DAO)?* 2024, Kanga University.

358.Smith, B., *Bitcoin ETFs: What are they and how do they work?* 2023, Betashares.

359.McGimpsey, P., *Bitcoin ETFs In Australia: The Complete Guide*. 2024, Forbes.

360.Reiff, N., *How Do Cryptocurrency Exchange-Traded Funds (ETFs) Work?* 2024, Investopedia.

361.Kanga University, *78. How to create your own cryptocurrency?* 2024, Kanga University.

362.Anurina, O., *How to Create a Cryptocurrency: Coins vs. Tokens, Tech Matters, & Examples*. 2023, MLSDev.

363.Bitbond, *Create Your Own Token in 5 minutes: A Step-by-Step Guide*. 2024, Bitbond.

364.Binance, *How to Create Your Own Cryptocurrency?* 2021, Binance.

Index

Made in United States
Orlando, FL
04 November 2026

90201665R10295